THE FLAHERTY

THE FLAHERTY

DECADES IN THE CAUSE OF
INDEPENDENT CINEMA

Patricia R. Zimmermann and
Scott MacDonald

Indiana University Press

This book is a publication of

Indiana University Press
Office of Scholarly Publishing
Herman B Wells Library 350
1320 East 10th Street
Bloomington, Indiana 47405 USA

iupress.indiana.edu

Cataloging information is available from the Library of Congress.

ISBN 978-0-253-02624-8 (cloth)
ISBN 978-0-253-02688-0 (e-bk.)

1 2 3 4 5   22 21 20 19 18 17

I remembered that he had always said that the motion picture was still an unknown continent, that no one had yet scratched the surface of its potentialities, that even his own best-loved films were only sketches, first studies for the great films of the future that might be made by the young of the future. It seemed to me that his name and spirit can best be perpetuated—can only be perpetuated as he would wish it—by an institution whose prime purpose is to help new talent to explore further and further into the possibilities of a medium so immense and so unknown.

—Frances Hubbard Flaherty

CONTENTS

ACKNOWLEDGMENTS

Like the Flaherty Seminar itself, this book has been a collaborative process, not simply between the two authors, but between them and the many people who helped make documents and memories available.

Of course, we could not have begun this project without the assistance of the women and men who have directed Flaherty activities during the past ten years. Our sincere thanks to Margarita De La Vega Hurtado, Mary Kerr, and Anita Reher, and to program manager Sarie Horowitz. They enabled us to access the voluminous Flaherty files and to make use of the extensive archive of recorded discussions.

Dan Streible (who programmed the 2011 Flaherty) and his colleagues in and around the master's program in Moving Image Archiving and Preservation in the Department of Cinema Studies at New York University were instrumental in an effort to make the recordings of Flaherty discussions accessible. Thanks to Dan and to Julia Kim, Alice Moscoso, Yvonne Ng, Laurainne Ojo-Ohikuare, Brent W. Phillips, Erik Piil, and Kimberly Tarr for their hard work and goodwill. They have been instrumental in opening the way for scholars to work with this remarkable archive.

Ithaca College provided generous grant support for archival research, final manuscript production, photographic illustrations, and time away from teaching. Numerous summer research grants and reassigned time awards from the Office of the Provost and the Center for Faculty Excellence supplied money and time to assist in thinking through the complex history of the Robert Flaherty Film Seminar. The Roy H. Park School of Communications at Ithaca College supported Patricia Zimmermann's attendance at a multitude of Flaherty Seminars, key ethnographic participant observation. Large and small grants from the Park School's James B. Pendleton Research and Production Fund facilitated primary archival and photographic research. These grants were essential in hiring ace research assistants in New York City who mined the vast archives of International Film Seminars and the Flaherty Seminars: Joshua Deal, Erin Ferro-Murray, Steve Holmgren, and Sarie Horowitz.

Hamilton College made possible Scott MacDonald's attendance at numerous Flaherty Seminars; thanks in particular to Deans Patrick Reynolds and Margaret Gentry. The college also provided a generous subvention to assist with indexing; thanks to Deans

Samuel Pellman and Margaret Gentry. Various Hamilton colleagues assisted with the transcription of Flaherty discussions; thanks, in particular, to Benjamin Salzman for patient technical support of various kinds.

Collaborative spirit infused the research process to produce this book. An amorphous, constantly changing, ephemeral organization, the Flaherty produces conversations rather than products. As a result, historical research has extended beyond primary documents into exchanges and interviews with key participants who contributed insights into particular periods of the seminar and shared a sense of the affective surround of the experience. For their analyses and memories and time, we thank Charles Benton, Sally Berger, Linda Blackaby, Mahen Bonetti, Patti Bruck, Phred Churchill, John Columbus, Jack Coogan, Nadine Covert, Kathy Geritz, John Gianvito, Faye Ginsburg, Tony Gittens, Marlina Gonzalez-Tamrong, D. Marie Grieco, Carlos Gutiérrez, DeeDee Halleck, Ed Halter, Richard Herskowitz, Margarita De La Vega Hurtado, Bruce Jenkins, Tom Johnson, Mary Kerr, Lucy Kostelanetz, Irina Leimbacher, Juan Mandelbaum, Louis Massiah, Ann Michel, Gabriella Monroy, Alyce Myatt, Dorothy Oshlag Olson, Bill Pence, Julia Reichert, B. Ruby Rich, Jay Ruby, David Shepard, Cecile Starr, Caspar Stracke, William Sloan, Barbara Van Dyke, Phil Wilde, and Chi-hui Yang. Patti Bruck and Juan Mandelbaum shared critical internal board documents as well. Jay Ruby imparted not only his own experience of the Flaherty and its offshoot Arden House as a board member and programmer but also his analytical perspectives as an anthropologist and fellow scholar of documentary.

We thank Erik Barnouw for spurring the writing of a book on the Flaherty Seminar and Ruth Bradley for having the courage to publish a substantial early foray into Flaherty history: the quadruple issue of the journal *Wide Angle* (vol. 17, nos. 1–4, 1995), edited by Erik Barnouw and Patricia R. Zimmermann, and made available for the fortieth anniversary of the Flaherty Seminars. Barnouw argued that an organization as important—and invisible—as the Flaherty Seminars deserved a scholarly book so its history could be recovered, analyzed, taught, and argued about.

Finally, we thank the many thousands of participants in the Flaherty Seminars over the decades. Although the seminar grounds independent media arts culture in beautiful and daring films, videos, and (in recent years) installations, its argumentative, collaborative, engaged, passionate audiences sustain it.

THE FLAHERTY

THE FLAHERTY

INTRODUCTION

The Flaherty: Decades in the Cause of Independent Cinema represents an unusual collaboration between two scholars and two ways of doing history. Throughout the evolution of this project, Patricia R. Zimmermann has focused on writing the institutional history of the annual Robert Flaherty Seminar, while Scott MacDonald has explored the recordings of the discussions that have taken place at the Flaherty during the decades it has operated. The structure of this volume is a braiding together of our distinct but, we hope, synergic efforts in hopes that our strategy might evoke the energy and dynamism of the Flaherty Seminar itself.

PATRICIA R. ZIMMERMANN: IMAGINING A HISTORY OF THE FLAHERTY SEMINAR

The Robert Flaherty Film Seminar is one of the oldest, continuously functioning organizations in the world dedicated to an exploration of independent cinema. It began in 1955 on the Flaherty farm in Vermont at the height of the civil rights movement, the Cold War, the Eisenhower era, and the Red Scare as a place to think through cinema as an art form rather than as a business. Before the current concept of independent cinema existed and before the development of the nonprofit media arts sector now called public media, before the Sundance Film Festival and the Tribeca Film Festival, before the Ann Arbor Film Festival and the Toronto International Film Festival, before arts funding from entities such as the New York State Council on the Arts and the National Endowment for the Arts, before the proliferation of microcinemas and niche festivals, the Robert Flaherty Film Seminar was grappling with the aesthetics, dimensions, economics, exhibition, forms, politics, and scope of cinema produced outside the confines of the commercial studio system.

The achievement of the Robert Flaherty Film Seminar is singular and significant. For over half a century—and never missing a year despite financial and organizational challenges—the Flaherty Seminar has created an ongoing experience of cinema that is annoying, collective, exasperating, exhilarating, exploratory, immersive, interactive, and urgent. The annual seminar has screened thousands of films central to the histories of independent cinema, particularly documentary and experimental film, and has hosted hundreds of intense discussions about them. Thousands of seminarians from academia, television, public media, festivals, filmmaking, foundations, microcinemas, museums, and national art cinemas have engaged the aesthetic, intellectual, and political cauldron that is the Flaherty and, as a result of their interactions with colleagues at the seminars, have reshaped international independent cinema. (The theological implications of "seminarian" might surprise most Flaherty attendees, but the seminar has always been more like a spiritual retreat than like a conference or a film festival; usually, all but very special guests stay in rather monastic college dorm rooms.) As International Film Seminars (IFS) now proclaims on its website, the Flaherty is a "one of a kind institution that seeks to encourage filmmakers and other artists to explore the potential of the moving image"—a sentiment first nurtured by Frances Flaherty herself in the early 1950s.

The Flaherty has been criticized both outside and inside the organization for what some have seen as an elitism based in the East Coast arts and intellectual scene, for its psychic destruction of filmmakers, its clique-ish and almost cultish mentality, its obsession with Cold War politics, its fear of avant-garde film, its jargon-ridden academic discussions, its production of reverence and mysticism around the "Flaherty Way," and its white privilege. For every argument against the Flaherty, however, there are counterarguments. Indeed, the volatility and lack of resolution about what the Flaherty Seminar actually is may be the best demonstration of its continuing vibrancy as an organization and as an annual, in-depth metaexperience of cinema.

The structure of the Flaherty Seminar has changed little over six decades: each year, films are screened and discussed with the filmmakers, usually with the assistance of a moderator. Many guest filmmakers have been key figures who have defined international independent cinema; they include Moussa Sene Absa, Erik Barnouw, James Benning, Lucien Castaing-Taylor, Shirley Clarke, Edwardo Coutinho, Sergey Dvortsevoy, Robert Drew, Péter Forgács, Hollis Frampton, Su Friedrich, Richard Fung, Bahman Ghobadi, Michael Glawogger, William Greaves, Kazuo Hara, DeeDee Halleck, Joris Ivens, Ken Jacobs, Mani Kaul, Richard Leacock, Chris Marker, Louis Malle, Louis Massiah, Albert Maysles, Mira Nair, The Newsreel Collective, Marcel Ophuls, Artavazd Peleshyan, Ed Pincus, Satyajit Ray, Marlon Riggs, Marta Rodriguez, Abderrahmane Sissako, Cheick Oumar Sissoko, George Stoney, Trinh T. Minh-ha, Ulrike Ottinger Johan van der Keuken, Agnes Varda, and Peter Watkins. The Flaherty structure gives equal weight and time to the films and to discussions with their makers. Through the decades, the Flaherty's exhibition strategy has been to insist that people thinking about films and candidly discussing them in an open forum is as important as the films themselves.

For many years, information about what has taken place at the annual seminar has been passed by word of mouth, and one result has been mythic tales about vociferous, gut-wrenching debates and eye-opening discoveries of new filmmakers and cinemas. As Jack Churchill, a Boston-based filmmaker whose work was screened at the first seminar in 1955, has explained, the Flaherty's general structure and reputation for volatile discussion was evident from the outset: "For one week, we ate, slept, and dreamed film. Our day consisted of three screening periods interrupted only for meals. After screening a group of films, we would return to a wood-paneled study to discuss the works with the filmmakers responsible. As one of the filmmakers whose work was critiqued, I welcomed the feedback. Although the discussions sometimes became heated, this two-way communication between filmmaker and audience was, for me, the most important part of the learning process that took place that week." The seminars take place in an atmosphere simultaneously informal yet intensive, relaxed yet disciplined, unacademic yet searching, critical yet usually constructive. Seminarians are urged to attend all discussions and be an integral part of the group process during discussions and at other times as well. The discussions are audiotaped and the tapes become part of the seminar archives—implicitly, a resource for future scholars. In their emphasis on seeing, their vividness and impact, and their concentrated focus on film to the exclusion of all other concerns, the seminars are unique. The profound experience that participants continually report is not related simply to the films programmed at the seminar but also to the process—in a sense, the "process" of the seminar is its content. The bafflements, illuminations, abrasions, awarenesses, confrontations, and connections—what can feel like the unabating assault on one's preconceptions— during group discussions and at the many other interactions among seminarians during the seminar week create, for some, a transformative experience. It is the stuff of Flaherty legend that the first Flaherty Seminar one attends is the "best," but for those who return year after year, the discourse of the seminars is more interesting than any one seminar.

Despite its longevity and endurance; its innovations and impact on filmmakers and film culture; its influence on theoretical debates in the emerging fields of film studies and visual anthropology; and its breakthroughs in providing a platform for new ways of considering the emergence of new forms of cinema—cinéma vérité, compilation documentary, video art—the Flaherty has been curiously absent from histories of American cinema, international cinema, independent film, documentary, and experimental film. The 1995 publication of a special issue of the now-defunct *Wide Angle*, then edited by longtime Flaherty seminarian (and Flaherty programmer) Ruth Bradley, is the one substantial exception.

This special issue of *Wide Angle* (vol. 17, nos. 1–4), entitled "The Flaherty: Four Decades in the Cause of Independent Cinema," edited by Erik Barnouw and Patricia R. Zimmermann includes reminiscences of Flaherty seminarians from various eras; a range of scholarly and informal essays by Barnouw, Sally Berger, Deirdre Boyle, Faye Ginsburg, Laura U. Marks, Scott MacDonald, Michael Renov, B. Ruby Rich, Thomas Waugh, Zimmermann, and others, plus extensive photography by Bruce Harding and MacDonald's edited versions of several Flaherty discussions. Ruth Bradley's willingness to devote a year of *Wide Angle* to the Flaherty demonstrates her sense of the Flaherty's significance (and her courage as editor). Except for this single publication, however, little information and certainly no detailed history of the Flaherty has been available.

The Flaherty: Decades in the Cause of Independent Cinema is an attempt to provide a substantive and detailed (and reasonably up-to-date) chronicle of the Flaherty Seminar. The importance of institutional histories of those organizations that have energized modern film culture has grown in recent years—and the accomplishments and struggles of the Flaherty have much to teach. This book has developed over more than a decade. It has involved two parallel, implicitly collaborative efforts by two longtime Flaherty veterans. My research into Flaherty history has involved burrowing into the Flaherty microfilm collection stored at Columbia University, plunging into disorganized piles of files from the IFS office in New York, including archival evidence from seminar announcements, memos, letters between Frances and participants, minutes of meetings of the board of trustees, Frances's voluminous published and unpublished writings, and conducting interviews with key Flaherty contributors, trustees, and programmers. My collaborator, Scott MacDonald, has spent many hours working through the recordings of Flaherty discussions. (He describes his process in the second part of this introduction.)

As my research proceeded, it became clear that the history of the Flaherty included several more-or-less distinct eras. Despite its continuing evocation of the original ideas of Frances Flaherty as to the role and function of the seminar, particular periods of the Flaherty Seminar's history have been determined by a variety of cinematic, cultural, and political developments. *The Flaherty: Decades in the Cause of Independent Cinema* is organized into seven chronological sections. Each section combines my analysis of institutional and programming history with one or more key or quintessential discussions from that era. In the chapter essays, I explore Frances Flaherty's ideas on film and filmmaking and on the seminar; I analyze the different periods of the seminar as they evolved and delineate crucial historical collisions at the seminars, including the frequent, decades-long clashes between documentary and experimental film.

It is unusual in the history of cinema to have access to original archival recordings of how films were received and debated; in film history, these data are usually garnered from secondhand reports in newspapers or diaries, or, if they are recorded, lie unexamined by those who might profit from it. The edited transcripts of Flaherty discussions Scott MacDonald has chosen for this volume chronicle how people from different sectors of film culture engaged particular films, as well as cinema in general, at certain moments in time. They provide a sense of how discourse around film culture has changed across six decades—from generalized philosophical meanderings by intellectuals and practitioners trained in other fields to a highly codified academic discipline with its own theories, methodologies, and languages. From the vast repository of discussions, MacDonald chose those discussions where debates fired up and where ruptures and changes in film culture seemed to be working themselves out as a heterogeneous group of seminarians unpacked what disturbed or delighted them.

The Flaherty: Decades in the Cause of Independent Cinema is an initial mapping of the expansive territory that the Robert Flaherty Seminar has explored. We have no illusions that our volume is anything like a complete history or even a definitive one. The Flaherty is too complex, labyrinthine, and vast for two historians to do more than to insist on its importance, dig into the historical record, draw what conclusions seem reasonable, and invite further mining. We hope future scholars will use our work as a springboard into the Flaherty and into those other institutions and institutional practices, both for-profit and nonprofit, that have helped to expand our film culture and our understanding of the wide world of cinema.

SCOTT MACDONALD: THE LOGISTICS OF TRANSCRIBING AND EDITING FLAHERTY DISCUSSIONS

For many Flaherty seminarians, the discussions with filmmakers immediately after screenings are the heart of the Flaherty experience, the melodrama that energizes the seminar week and instigates the confrontations of personality and ideology that become the stuff of Flaherty legend. The discussions, which are usually moderated by the year's programmers or seminarians of their choice, generally last around an hour. During the discussions, a single maker may respond to questions and statements—when necessary, with the assistance of a translator. In recent years, several filmmakers sometimes take questions together.

At their best, the discussions elicit interesting and sometimes brilliant insights from the filmmakers, many of whom see a Flaherty invitation as an honor and have clearly readied themselves for the seminar audience. And—again, at their best—the large-group discussions are an open forum that allows attendees to declare themselves about individual works and their makers and to voice their general cinematic concerns of the moment. By and large, seminarians deal with one another with respect and good humor; and as the Flaherty week evolves, the group's interchange reflects the bonding that occurs not only during screenings and large-group discussions but also during smaller-scale interchanges at meals and between events and over drinks at the informal get-togethers that precede dinner and conclude Flaherty evenings.

At their very worst—and this happens rarely, at least in my experience—the large-group discussions function as punishment for makers whose works or whose apparent attitudes offend the shared sensibilities and ideologies of seminarians. Then, "questions" become a way of goading the "guilty" makers. The fact that some invited filmmaker guests spend only a short time at the Flaherty, while attendees are together morning, noon, and night, day after day, can exacerbate an us-versus-them atmosphere. Of course, even within the most "brutal" Flaherty interrogation, there are widely varying attitudes: as I've transcribed legendary "trashings" of makers, I've heard a good many positive comments about the works being discussed. In many cases, seminarians' anger and disapproval is felt rather than enunciated, and as a result, even listening to the tapes of a discussion doesn't necessarily provide a clear sense of the discussion's pervasive mood, a mood felt by attendees and often a subject for conversation after the large-group discussions have concluded.

During various Flaherty eras, different strategies have developed for keeping the discussions efficient and engaging. The fact that the number of attendees at recent seminars has climbed to more than 150 has made discussion a good bit more cumbersome than it was during the early years. Recent programmers have generally met with those they have chosen to be moderators in order to work against the tendency of discussions to become simple Q & As with the makers. Nevertheless, a gathering of 150 cineastes is difficult to control, and the plans of programmers often fall by the wayside, particularly when a film has moved the gathering in a profound way.

The discussions included here are, of course, only the tiniest fragment of the history of seminar interchange, but my hope is that this sampling will serve several functions. First, I have chosen discussions that seem generally representative of the seminar at various moments in its history: the discussions that characterized the seminar in the 1950s are quite different from the discussions of the 1970s or of recent years. Early on, the seminar was divided between attendees and "faculty," who spoke at greater length than the "students." In more recent years, democratic interchange has been encouraged; a young first-time attendee is as likely to speak in a discussion as a longtime Flaherty veteran or even a filmmaker guest. Moderators do prepare questions for filmmaker guests but are also charged with being sure that as many seminarians as want to speak get to speak. The recent tendency to create screenings and discussions featuring more than one filmmaker is an attempt to move discussions toward larger issues in hopes (very rarely realized in fact) that the filmmakers might engage each other in productive ways.

Second, I have included discussions with specific filmmakers whose work has seemed important within the larger history and geography of independent cinema. The discussions included reflect the commitment of Flaherty programmers to both documentary, especially experimental documentary, and what has generally been called avant-garde film (i.e., forms of personally expressive, independent film that often function as challenges to conventional documentary practice). Of course, as will be clear in the discussions, filmmakers from non-Western cultures have often understood cinema practice and history in different ways from how most Western cineastes understand them.

The Flaherty is both a series of discrete, annual events and an ongoing social organism. I have tried to be alert both to the remarkable variety in the filmmaker insights evident during particular discussions at specific seminars and to the ways in which, over long periods, the Flaherty discussions have created an ongoing metadiscourse about what reality-based cinema has been, can be, and should be. During my editing of the discussions, I've also worked to evoke the many networks of personal relationship that are evident among Flaherty veterans over the decades, as well as the ways in which successive seminars reflect the changing interests and concerns of the annual programmers.

One of the unusual dimensions of the Flaherty big-group discussions is that the experiences that individuals remember and the stories they tell about them are often not reflected in the tapes of the discussions. Both D. Marie Grieco and Jay Ruby have told me that the discussion of *David Holzman's Diary* at the 1968 seminar was rather cantankerous (Grieco: "there was a bit of fury in the discussion about the David Holzman diary film" [e-mail to author, January 2010]; Ruby: "I recall a lot of people being pissed off" [e-mail to author February 2010]; and both Grieco and Ruby, as well as others I've spoken to, have remembered Willard Van Dyke claiming that the film could destroy documentary or at least cinéma-vérité documentary).

However, as will be clear in the edited version of the *David Holzman's Diary* discussion, absolutely no anger at the film is evident on the tape (I did not eliminate angry comments in my edit); indeed, this seems to have been a particularly euphoric discussion. What this discrepancy tells us is not that Grieco, Ruby, and the others are incorrect about what happened but that an interchange among a large group of people is seen differently from various angles and from various positions in time. A tape recorder provides only one angle at a single moment, and the seemingly objective evidence of the tape recording must be tempered by a commonsense recognition that what is heard on tape may not conform to what is felt during a discussion or to what people were saying to one another beyond the reach of the tape recorder (or to what was said at other moments during a seminar but is perhaps misremembered as part of the big-group discussion).

Further, a filmmaker's response to a particular seminar experience may seem affable at the seminar but hostile later and vice versa. For example, the 1970 discussion with

Hollis Frampton, included here, seems relatively friendly; however, in a letter dated August 2, 1971, to Sally Dixon, Frampton would wonder, "does this find you returned once more from Fla(gella)herty? If so, cheer up, I understand even Sisyphus has vowed not to go next year. Honestly, I still hurt from that thing, in spots. Though I wonder how much of it was sheer horror at returning to prep-school life (complete!) which I lothed [*sic*] with a hatred that still raises my snarling muscles. . . . Lawder's inextinguishable cannabis almost made it tolerable at some moments, but this is advice that you will have too late, & anyhow he said he wdn't [*sic*] go this year either." Whether Frampton's experience was as unsatisfactory as this letter would suggest, whether he felt it incumbent as an avant-garde filmmaker to respond negatively to the kind of group experience the Flaherty Seminar provides, or whether other factors were involved is hard to say. What is obvious is that each Flaherty Seminar is a complicated and evanescent process that produces complex and continually evolving responses.

In some instances, I have worked with discussions I was present at or part of; in others, I've been entirely dependent on the tape or digital recordings. Generally, I have identified discussants simply as "F" (for Flaherty seminarian); but in some cases, when I have been absolutely clear about the identity of discussants, I have used their names in hopes that knowing who says what will add to the historical interest of the discussion. These identifications are also meant to contribute to the reader's sense of the complex experience of the seminar. At any given moment during the Flaherty week, attendees are acquainted with only some of their colleagues; however, for those attendees who return to the Flaherty year after year, particular individuals become well-known "characters" in the ongoing metadrama of the seminar discussions.

Much of my research over the years has taken the form of in-depth interviews with independent filmmakers. I have learned that in most cases, a verbatim transcript of a conversation—no matter how coherent the discussion sounded when it was occurring and no matter how precise the transcription—tends to distort the nature of the original conversation. I have transcribed the discussions very carefully but then have treated each transcription as raw material from which to fabricate a "reading" of the original discussion. Especially when attendees are identified as "F," I have played fast and loose with their comments, combining and condensing what is said, while doing my best to remain true to what has seemed to me the spirit and idea content of the discussion. When the speakers are identified, I have been as true to the particulars of their comments as clarity and fairness allow.

While most of those who find their way to this book and to these edited discussions will probably not read the volume from front to back, I have chosen and ordered the discussions so that if one does read them in the order they are presented here, the reading experience will reflect the variations in Flaherty discussions as well as continuities that develop over time.

Of course, anyone who has attended even a single Flaherty might well have chosen an entirely different set of discussions. There is certainly a wealth of material to choose from (during the 1994 Flaherty, there were twenty formal discussions; during the 1993 seminar, twenty; 1992, twenty-one . . .). Hopefully, my choices will instigate a more thorough exploration of the Flaherty archives.

Frances Flaherty circa 1968. Photo courtesy of International Film Seminars, Inc./The Flaherty, New York.

1

THE FLAHERTY WAY

The Flaherty Seminar is one of the oldest, continuously running gatherings for independent film in the world. Launched by Frances Flaherty in 1955, the seminar explored the "Flaherty Way" of making films, rejecting planning and scripts required by commercial production practices. Frances was the widow of renowned documentary filmmaker Robert Flaherty. Although Robert directed the films and occupies a central, if controversial, place in documentary film history books, it was Frances who developed the Robert Flaherty Film Seminar for community, debate, dialogue, and screenings. The seminar has provided a retreat-like, closed setting for distributors, film librarians, filmmakers, funders, programmers, and scholars for more than sixty years.

Robert Flaherty, who shot films in exotic locations such as the Canadian north and Samoa and then shared production stories to eager acolytes rather than theorizing his practice, did not conceptualize the "Flaherty Way." Instead, his widow developed the "Flaherty Way" after his death. She advocated for a poetic cinema that surrendered to the materials and the environment. In Frances's vision, the "Flaherty Way" offered a more artisanal, personal cinema than the formulaic, predictable industrial model based on imposition of commercial norms, planning, and scripts. Resolutely anti-Hollywood, the "Flaherty Way" combined the explorer's journeys into the unknown, the ethnographer's observation of cultural patterns, and the Zen mystics' openness to surroundings.

The Robert Flaherty Foundation and the Robert Flaherty Seminar emerged from Frances's contention that learning to see in deeper, more complex ways could be acquired through intensive viewing and vigorous discussion. In a 1961 letter to the Guggenheim Foundation in support of a grant application by Frances, George Amberg wrote: "It may be useful to point out that Mrs. Flaherty is not, as would be natural, so much concerned with building a monument in honor of a great filmmaker and a great man, than with promoting and supporting a vital succession, establishing a tradition, making discoveries, and encouraging new talent. Toward this end, she organized the Flaherty Foundation and initiated the Flaherty Seminars, an annual venture devoted to the scholarly and critical study of the motion picture."[1]

The Flaherty Foundation and the Flaherty Seminar are significant in film history. They show the challenges of the early foundational period in the development of the nascent nonprofit public media sector in the United States in the post–World War II period. They suggest the importance of institutional histories to delineate the infrastructure bolstering cinematic cultures beyond the commercial systems. The foundation and the seminars occupy a vital interstitial zone between emergent alternative film cultures in the 1950s: 16mm exhibition, art cinemas, educational and industrial films, film festivals, film societies, independent cinema beyond commercial studios, and university film education.

The Flaherty Foundation, formed by Frances and David Flaherty, Robert's brother, in 1951, and its outgrowth, the Flaherty Seminar, inaugurated in 1955, were initially dedicated to preserving and circulating Flaherty's films. They advocated for an artisanal, independent, poetic cinema immunized from the commercial Hollywood system. Convening a small, intimate group of distributors, editors, filmmakers, scholars, and writers on the family farm in Dummerston, Vermont, for ten days in the summer, the early years of the seminar were characterized by camaraderie, intellectual and artistic intensity, and a hope that cinema go beyond commercial filmmaking with its rules and conventions.

The early seminars focused on the works and practices of Robert Flaherty. Seminarians dived into close analysis of Flaherty films, such as *Nanook of the North* (1922) and *Louisiana Story* (1948), listened to lectures by those who worked on Flaherty films, such as Ricky Leacock and Helen van Dongen, and watched experimental and documentary films produced outside the Hollywood system.

Combining the ciné-club and film society models of postscreening discussion and more intellectual models of lectures elaborating cinematic techniques, the seminar did not operate as a film festival, with public screenings of narrative films in theaters. Instead, the Flaherty Seminar was a small gathering on the family farm, seminarians applied to attend, and many films were historical rather than current releases. The seminar advanced cinematic practice and conceptual thinking in the loosely defined nontheatrical sector. The early seminars' emphasis on critical viewing, philosophical inquiry, and probing discussion distinguished it from film festivals. Its purpose was educational. It advocated for cinema as an art. Attendees were not an audience but were called participants, implying active engagement rather than passive viewing. As David Flaherty noted in 1960 after mounting five seminars on the Flaherty farm, "Yes, we think 'participants' is a better word to use than 'students.'"[2]

The Flaherty Seminar emerged in the postwar context of the Cold War (1947–91), where the United States and the Soviet Union engaged in a tense global military and strategic conflict between competing ideologies of democracy and communism. David Flaherty's use of the word *participant* rather than *student* aligns with a Cold War ideology promulgating that the United States offered individual freedoms, in contrast to the Union of Soviet Socialist Republics (USSR), which was figured as limiting freedom of expression and participation. The Cold War spurred US military buildup, a strategy of containment against the advances of communism around the globe, and the development and expansion of the United States Information Agency, a government organization to promote American culture through public diplomacy.[3] The connection between US Cold War international strategies and practices and the Flaherty Seminar is not one of direct causation as much as it is one of a discursive historical surround that illuminates interpretation of how to position its politics and practices. The seminar occupied a complicated, somewhat foggy middle ground between the individualism promoted by US Cold War ideology and the communist collectivity of the USSR: it advanced auteurs and their individual artistic vision while it fostered an intense, yet isolated, group experience.

The Flaherty Seminar never openly aligned with entertainment and news industry unions, which had been under scrutiny and attack during the various post–World War II Red Scares. In 1947, the House Un-American Activities Committee (HUAC) attacked Hollywood—almost 100 percent unionized by the postwar period—as a bastion of un-American activities. As historian Reynold Humphries contends, the red-baiting right identified Hollywood, with many of its union members supporting the antifascists in Spain and Franklin Roosevelt's New Deal in the 1930s, as communists. The Hollywood Ten included Alvah Bessie, Herbert Biberman, Lester Cole, Edward Dmytryk, Ring Lardner Jr., John Howard Lawson, Albert Maltz, Samuel Ornits, Robert Adrian Scott, and Dalton Trumbo, all of whom refused to cooperate and denounced the hearings as violations of their civil rights.[4]

America's postwar economic success was tied to commercial narrative Hollywood films, which sold the American way of life as consumption.[5] The 1947 HUAC hearings investigated screenwriters and directors from the film industry. According to Lary May, Hollywood embodied "moral experiment, cultural mixing, a militant labor movement, and middle class activism," all attributes antithetical to the promulgation of the so-called American way of consumerist monopoly capital. The pro-HUAC entertainment industry members "sought to make Hollywood a model of an unprecedented American identity rooted in consensus and consumption."[6] With its East Coast location, the Flaherty Foundation and the Flaherty Seminar were geographically distant, operating in the milieu of independent, educational, documentary, experimental, and scientific filmmakers who were not unionized and worked outside of mass culture and Hollywood. However, the foundation and seminars were never identified with media industries, unions, or pro-communist ideologies. Instead, the Flaherty Seminar proffered a concoction of art, individualism, and some critical analysis, mostly from scholars. Whether conscious or not, these inclinations insulated the seminar from ideological attacks. For example, Erik Barnouw was a key figure in the early seminars. He had worked as a radio writer in New York for CBS and NBC. By 1957, he was elected chair of the Writers Guild of America East. In his scholarly histories of broadcasting written later in the 1966, he analyzed how the Red Scare produced caution and cowardice in television.[7]

The formation of the Flaherty Foundation and the Flaherty Seminar unfolded in the context of the Truman and Eisenhower presidencies, which intensified the Cold War through military buildup and propaganda. This postwar period witnessed the advancement of expanding consumption, an ideology of consensus, and a suburban domestic revival motored by what historian Warren Sussman dubbed "unprecedented economic growth unfolding after World War II" in the context of affluence and familialism.[8] Frances and David Flaherty channeled this larger discourse of familialism, situating the foundation and the seminar not as a union of independent filmmakers but instead as a family gathering, resonating with dominant domesticating ideologies of the period.

However, the Cold War in the 1950s was not so simply the smooth production of consensus, consumerism, familialism, and homogeneity. It was also a period of social and cultural contradictions with the rise of African American blues, the Beats, the civil rights movement, and rock 'n' roll—cultural movements that challenged conformity, familialism, and suburbia with cultural pluralism and political interventions.[9] Besides showing George Stoney's chronicle of an African American midwife in his sponsored public health film, *All My Babies*, the Flaherty seminar in the 1950s steered a less interventionist and directly confrontational course, positioning itself as an organization dedicated to retrieving cinema from commercial domains and rescuing it as an art.

This orientation toward salvaging cinema as an art form of personal expression aligned more easily with the larger Cold War artistic contexts of abstract expressionism in painting and the New Criticism in literature. As Erika Doss has argued, in the postwar period, abstract expressionism—epitomized in action painter Jackson Pollack—mobilized a concept of individual, apolitical gestural freedom that rendered it a "weapon against totalitarianism." Both the Museum of Modern Art (MoMA) and the US State Department, which sent exhibitions of this style overseas to promote freedom against the strictures of the USSR's socialist realism, heralded abstract expressionism.[10] Although Frances's writings and Flaherty seminar transcripts never mention abstract expressionism directly, their presentation of the films of Robert Flaherty resonated with similar ideologies of action-based gestures, freedom, and individualism disconnected from larger political and social issues. Even from the beginning, the Flaherty Seminar was deeply embedded with auteurism and individualism, positioning it more in alignment with Cold War ideas than with the collectivities the civil rights movement or unions. The early seminars' emphasis on the formal elements and structures of the Flaherty films also paralleled the school of literary New Criticism, with its emphasis on close reading that figured the text as an aesthetic object outside of historical, political, and social contexts.[11] This exaltation of the auteur, formalistic analysis, the individual, and self-expression would also provoke political critique of the seminar's ideological orientations during the antiwar and women's movements of the 1970s—critiques that would generate tensions and debates for decades in postscreening discussions of critical theory, gender, national identities, internationalism, and race.

The Flaherty Foundation and the Flaherty Seminar condensed a particular strain of cinematic activism in the 1950s that advocated for cinema as an art form against the formulaic structures of American studio genre films and against the propaganda, state-centric intent of John Grierson's British documentary and Pare Lorentz's American state-sponsored documentary. In a letter supporting Frances Flaherty's 1961 Guggenheim Foundation grant application to secure funding to develop the *Louisiana Story* study film with outtakes, George Amberg wrote, "They [the foundation] believe that the films he made can be used to stimulate interest in and gain support for greater freedom for the independent artist."[12] Frances viewed Robert's films as offering a path beyond industrial filmmaking's strangleholds. She contended that "they go against the current—the mighty Niagara—of commercial cinema as projected by Hollywood and projected likewise as 'documentary.'"[13]

Frances advocated intellectual engagement with cinema, one that exceeded passive consumption of studio films. However, this particular activism did not offer radical interventions into Cold War political or social structures. Instead, the Flaherty Foundation and the Flaherty Seminar's activism resided in its pedagogical intentions to reframe the Flaherty films as a springboard into thinking about cinema as exploration rather than as scripted scenarios. Instead of radical restructurings of society, the Flaherty Foundation and the subsequent seminars exposed a humanist, less confrontational politics promoting independent cinema. Both the foundation and the seminars created alliances with various arts, cinema, and government institutions connected to the burgeoning 16mm nontheatrical film exhibition movement.

Robert Flaherty died on July 23, 1951. A year later, in 1952, his widow and his brother, David, formed the Robert Flaherty Foundation.[14] The Flaherty Foundation promoted Robert's films, secured distribution rights, and advocated for an independent cinema based on individual vision. It was also formed to "encourage and support the making of film in the Flaherty tradition."[15]

Frances claimed Robert's friends encouraged her to do something with his films in order to continue his legacy of a noncommercial cinema. Although Robert produced only five films in his lifetime—*Nanook of the North* (1922), *Moana* (1926), *Man of Aran* (1934), *The Land* (1941), and *Louisiana Story* (1948)—these films gained notoriety in the international ciné-club and film society circuits as examples of a poetic art cinema and a more intellectual cinematic practice.

The Robert Flaherty Foundation grew out of Frances Flaherty's reactions to and participation in the Sixth International Edinburgh Festival in August and September 1952. At the age of sixty-seven, Frances had been invited to present excerpts from some of Robert's films with commentary as part of a section of the festival called "New Directions in Documentary." Before her presentation, she listened to Sir Compton Mackenzie discuss the achievements of silent film. An audience member queried how one could achieve a visual sensibility. According to Frances, Mackenzie replied that "it would be better if you were born with it." Frances found herself in profound disagreement with this essentialist position. She believed seeing with the camera could be learned, a position derived from observing her husband, Robert, work. She had collaborated with him on the production and marketing of virtually all his films. Robert himself did not make his first film until he was forty years old.[16]

According to Frances, these filmmakers who had known Robert felt that "such a foundation had an obligation to preserve his films and make them available for study anywhere in the world."[17] Several international committees formed. The British committee included luminaries from the British documentary movements of the 1930s, including Edgar Anstey, John Grierson, and Basil Wright. The French committee, headed by Jean Benoît-Lévy, included the Cinémathèque Française, Comité du Film Ethnographique, the Institut des Hautes Études Cinématographiques, and the Musée de l'Homme. The US organizing committee included Frances and David Flaherty, as well as Richard Griffith from MoMA.[18]

In a December 1952 mailing, announcing the inauguration of the Robert Flaherty Foundation, Frances explained her own goals: "his name and spirit can best be perpetuated—can only be perpetuated as he would wish it—by an institution whose prime purpose is to help new talent to explore further and further into the possibilities of a medium so immense and so unknown."[19]

For Frances and David, the Flaherty Foundation promoted two intertwined goals: the first was preservation of Robert Flaherty's films, scattered among many different commercial and educational distributors; the second was to support younger filmmakers to learn a different, nonstudio way to produce films. The task of securing nontheatrical rights for the Flaherty films fell to David, while public speaking and advocacy for a cinema of "nonpreconception" became Frances's mission.[20] Inspired by Zen Buddhism's ideas about being present in the moment, Frances' notion of "nonpreconception" positioned itself in opposition to commercial studio narrative films reliant on scripts, the preplanning blueprints that ceded control to producers. "Nonpreconception" recovered individual, artisanal modes powered by immersion, intuition, and mysticism. It was centered in the self, sensory perception, and poetics, rather than in the dual logics of hierarchical film production organization in the studios and structures of transparent narrative causality.

In 1953, Frances explained that "[the foundation's] other purposes include two [that] I think would be particularly close to Bob's heart, to help young filmmakers learn how to make 'films of life' and to enlarge their freedom to make their films according to their own vision."[21] However, in repeated attempts to secure tax-exempt status from the US Internal Revenue Service, this emphasis on the legacy of Robert Flaherty proved detrimental. It positioned the Robert Flaherty Foundation as a memorial promoted by family members rather than an educational organization advancing a different form of cinema for emerging makers.[22]

The Robert Flaherty Foundation held its first meeting in January 1953 at MoMA, where Flaherty's papers were housed. The MoMA connection was established through Richard Griffith, curator of the museum's film library from 1951 to 1965 and author of *Grierson on Documentary* (1947), *Documentary Films* (1952), and *The World of Robert Flaherty* (1953). For the first year, MoMA also served as the headquarters for the foundation until it moved to Brattleboro, Vermont, in 1954. MoMA received checks for the Flaherty Foundation under its tax-exempt status until 1955.[23] The foundation hoped to establish Flaherty funds across the globe to support films made in the "Flaherty tradition" (defined as independent, poetic, and more artisanal). It also wanted to create festivals of Flaherty films.[24] However, neither Frances nor David controlled rights to the films. This quest for rights would consume them for the next ten years. *Nanook* and *Man of Aran* were distributed by Contemporary Films. *The Land* and *Industrial Britain* (1931), codirected with John Grierson, were distributed by MoMA.[25] Frances wrote: "We do not own the films; therefore, to obtain ownership and control and to insure preservation of the films is our first objective and biggest problem."[26]

As the Flaherty Foundation encountered setbacks in securing the nontheatrical distribution rights and in establishing a revenue stream to support international emerging artists working in the "Flaherty tradition," it revised its utopian goals toward more pragmatic pursuits. It created the Robert Flaherty Award and developed the short-lived touring Flaherty Film Festival. Frances traveled the lecture circuit, presenting the Flaherty films and the "Flaherty Way" to film societies, museums, and universities.

The first Flaherty film festivals ran in Albuquerque and Los Alamos, New Mexico, in October 1953.[27] They did not attract large audiences.[28] Frances and David hoped the Flaherty film festivals would advertise the Flaherty Foundation and generate revenue for its operation.[29] By 1954, they had expanded the festival to include films in the "Flaherty tradition." That year, Indiana University and the University of Michigan hosted Flaherty film festivals.[30] Organized by Mary Mainwaring, a graduate student writing her dissertation on Robert Flaherty and who later attended the first seminar in 1955,[31] the Indiana University Flaherty Film Festival was a success. As a result of tie-ins with the American Society for Aesthetics and the Midwestern College Art Conference, the theaters were packed.[32]

Through the encouragement of film scholar Jack Ellis, a professor at Northwestern University immersed in the Chicago film society movement, Frances attended the American Film Assembly (AFA) in Chicago in March 1954. Ellis invited Frances to discuss the goals of the Robert Flaherty Foundation at the Film Society Caucus of the AFA. The panel included Margareta Akermark and three vocal advocates for nontheatrical cinema who also later worked with Frances to help mount the seminars: Andries Deinum, who taught cinema at the University of Southern California; Cecile Starr, 16mm film reviewer for the *Saturday Review*; and Amos Vogel, founder of Cinema 16.[33]

The Film Council of America had formed in 1951 in Evanston, Illinois, with the goal of helping producers and distributors of educational, experimental, and art film reach library and college exhibition with a central information service and previews. The nontheatrical field was disparate and disorganized, spread out among libraries, museums, community centers, and film societies. Film societies were interested in procuring 16mm prints of experimental and classic films. The AFA sought to forge unity between the largely disconnected film societies that were growing in number and spreading throughout the United States. Sixty film societies attended the first meeting. Brandon Films, Cinema 16, Contemporary Films, Kinesis, the MoMA Film Library, and the *Saturday Review*—key players in nontheatrical film—supplied mailing lists to assist the Film Council of America survey of film societies. This research discovered 257 film societies. A new organization, the American Federation of Film Societies, emerged from the initial 1954 meeting and the questionnaire results. It subsequently sponsored the second AFA in New York in 1955, the same year of the first Robert Flaherty Film Seminar.[34]

Another Flaherty Foundation revenue stream derived from Frances's lectures on the "Flaherty Way," wherein she screened Flaherty films and discussed Robert's working methods. Her invited talks from 1954 to 1956 included Bennington College, the Cleveland Museum of Art, Columbia University, George Eastman House, the London Ontario Film Society, the New School, the Toronto Film Society, and Yale University.[35] After 1956, she continued lecturing at elite universities such as Bennington College, Cornell University, Northwestern University, University of California, Los Angeles; University of Michigan, and the University of Southern California. She donated her lecture fees to support the Robert Flaherty Film Seminar.[36]

Frances Flaherty's relationship with Amos Vogel, founder and programmer of Cinema 16 in New York City, suggests the interconnections between film societies, film organizations, and the 16mm sector. Cinema 16 was the most successful of the many film societies emerging in the postwar period, according to film historian Scott MacDonald.[37] These various organizations were committed to an activist agenda for cinema separated from commercial constraints, whether artisanal experimental cinema, documentary, or educational and scientific films. They also offered an educational function: they introduced audiences to more complex ways of seeing and thinking about cinema.[38]

Collaboration between the Robert Flaherty Foundation and Cinema 16 extended beyond programming to include awards for achievement in new cinematic forms. In 1954, the Robert Flaherty Foundation, Cinema 16, and the City College of New York announced the Robert J. Flaherty Award. Of the 120 submissions,[39] three films received recognition: *All My Babies: A Midwife's Own Story* (1953) by George Stoney, *Argument in Indianapolis* (1953) by television journalists Edward R. Murrow and Fred Friendly, and *The Conquest of Everest* (1953).[40] *All My Babies* exemplified the emergence of educational films in the postwar period. Produced as a teaching tool for midwives for the Georgia Public Health Department, the fifty-seven-minute film chronicled the delivery of a child by an African American midwife. The judges for the Robert J. Flaherty Award included key figures from the nontheatrical film world of the 1950s: Bosley Crowther of the *New York Times*; David Flaherty; Richard Griffith from MoMA; Lewis Jacobs, film producer and author; and Arthur Knight of the *Saturday Review*.

In 1958, Cinema 16 screened *Man of Aran* with a talk by Frances Flaherty. Vogel coached Frances to focus on Robert's "philosophy of filmmaking, his use of actual locales and non-professionals, the growing out of the scenario from the action situation."[41] She contributed her $400 honorarium to the scholarship fund for the Robert Flaherty Film Seminar.[42] Vogel had programmed some experimental films for the second seminar in 1956.[43] The 1958 inauguration of the Experimental Production Committee, an organization to fund experimentation in film form, content, and technical areas, indicated these interlocking relationships between documentary and experimental film. The organizing group included Thorold Dickinson, chief of film services at the United Nations; Frances Flaherty; Richard Griffith; Jonas Mekas, the experimental filmmaker; and Amos Vogel.[44]

Erik Barnouw, a former radio writer, directed the Center for Mass Communication (CMC) at Columbia University. In 1957, he proposed a cocktail party to discuss the future of the Flaherty Foundation. He sought to build alliances among members of the noncommercial film culture sector who often gathered at the Coffee House Club in New York City. Robert Flaherty had frequented this club, drinking and sharing stories with acolytes. The invitation list suggests the heterogeneity of the nontheatrical film sector that congealed around the Flaherty organization. The guest list included Thorold Dickinson; Robert Gardner, ethnographic filmmaker; Richard Griffith; Dorothy Oshlag Olson, Barnouw's assistant at the CMC; Rudolph Serkin, pianist and founder of the Marlboro Chamber Music Festival in Vermont; Cecile Starr; George Stoney; and Amos Vogel.[45]

In these formative years of the 1950s, the Flaherty Foundation, Frances Flaherty herself, and later the Robert Flaherty Film Seminar worked to form important alliances with academic institutions and intellectuals as the organization sought to materialize a pedagogical activism to advance a more independent, poetic, and serious cinema. In 1959, Frances, developing a plan for her public speaking tours, wrote, "I would like to go to more universities and colleges, whether or not they have special film departments."[46] In the postwar period, art cinemas, educational and scientific filmmakers, distributors of international cinemas and documentaries, film councils, museums, university and community film societies, and university film programs, formed the core of the emerging nontheatrical film culture. It was not confined to the East and West Coasts but spanned the United States, with activities and organizations in Cleveland, Ohio, and Madison, Wisconsin.[47]

The Flaherty Foundation did not emerge in isolation as a unique invention of one individual perpetuating her husband's legacy. Instead, it developed in the context of other organizations pushing for cinema as an art form that required analysis, discussion, engagement, and organizational infrastructure. In 1952, Frances Flaherty was named honorary president of the Comité du Film Ethnographique in France. She worried that this larger organization would dwarf the Flaherty Foundation and would misclassify the Flaherty films as "anthropological." In a letter to the head of the organization, Frances wrote that the Flaherty films "were something more than anthropological, they were films rather of the spirit of man."[48]

In a 1959 American Federation of Film Societies newsletter, Paul Rotha argued ciné-club and film societies promoted what he termed the "other cinema," which possessed an open attitude to films from the present and reevaluated films from the past, situating them as a critical discourse with discussions and lectures.[49] Frances participated on panels at the American Federation of Film Societies, appearing with Amos Vogel. According to Charles R. Acland, the post–World War II film society movement, dedicated to advancing cinema as artistic expression, developed much more rapidly in the United States than university film education.[50] Acland contended that film councils and film societies differed in context and goals: the former were more community based, while the latter promoted the avant-garde.[51]

An influential figure in both the nontheatrical cinema movement and the early Flaherty seminars, Cecile Starr served as the nontheatrical film editor and reviewer for the *Saturday Review of Literature*. She edited two important books anthologizing articles on exhibiting 16mm film that brought together the community-based organizations and the more experimental societies. Her first book, *Ideas on Film: A Handbook for the 16mm Film User*, was published in 1951.[52] It featured articles about art, documentary film, international cinema, music, and nature, by cinematographer Raymond Spottiswoode, Starr, filmmaker Willard Van Dyke, and Amos Vogel. It included contacts for 16mm film libraries at universities and national distributors such as Brandon Films (New York), Contemporary Films (founded by longtime Flaherty seminar ally Leo Dratfield), Coronet Films (Chicago), Encyclopedia Britannica (Chicago), MoMA, and the National Film Board of Canada. These same names and organizations appear on invitations for the Flaherty Foundation events and rosters for the Flaherty seminars in the 1950s.

Starr's second compendium, *Film Society Primer*, was published in 1956 by the American Federation of Film Societies.[53] Twenty-two articles from organizations such as Cinema 16, the Princeton Film Forum, the Roosevelt University Film Society, the St. Paul Film Society, and the Wisconsin Film Society outlined programming strategies, membership subscriptions, projection, and audience development. The George Eastman House and the MoMA Film Library contributed articles about their collections.

Jack C. Ellis attended the early film seminars. Inspired by such events, he tried to mount one at Northwestern University where he taught. He contributed an article to the *Film Society Primer* entitled "Film Societies and the Film Council of America." He chronicled how the society emerged from the first AFA held in Chicago in April 1954. Ellis contended that Europeans possessed a deeper understanding of cinema as an art form, whereas in the United States, cinema was associated with Hollywood's "preoccupation with dazzle."[54] Frances Flaherty's advocacy for an artisanal cinema of exploration needs to be situated within the context of these larger movements advancing 16mm nontheatrical cinema in the 1950s. With its dual purpose of preserving the Flaherty films and educating the next generation to consider cinema as a complex humanist art form, the Flaherty Foundation operated within the larger context that situated 16mm nontheatrical film as a way to develop better citizens.

The boisterous, bigger-than-life legend of Robert Flaherty—explorer, filmmaker, raconteur, storyteller—often overshadows the historical significance of his wife, Frances Flaherty. She crafted the intellectual infrastructure supporting documentary and independent film at the Flaherty film seminars when few film schools existed.

Robert enjoyed notoriety both in life and in death. He was the subject of articles, *New Yorker* magazine profiles, numerous books about his films that drew upon his diaries, and radio shows. These publications fashioned a myth of the independent explorer fearlessly engaging harsh landscapes beyond urban areas and innovating a more poetic, humanist, artisanal cinema. The Robert Flaherty image countered the industrial models of production of the Hollywood studios and the nationalistic models of state-sponsored propaganda units. His was the story of a mystical artistic genius who could conjure the essence of environments and people.[55]

Frances Flaherty's role as collaborator, photographer, and promoter was often obscured. Her 1955 biography written for the Lecture Bureau in New York City, the organization that booked her university talks, identifies Frances as Robert Flaherty's "active collaborator" who accompanied him with their three young daughters on his filmmaking expeditions to the Aran Islands, India, Louisiana, and Samoa.[56] In an earlier undated, never-published draft manuscript entitled "Autobiography," probably written sometime in the 1940s after the couple procured the farm in Dummerston, Frances described how she urged her husband to write about his experiences, sometimes even starting his writing.[57] In his 1964 *Film Comment* review of Paul Rotha and Basil Wright's book on Flaherty entitled *The Innocent Eye*, George Amberg criticized this volume for omitting all references to Frances Flaherty's important work on the films. He argued her importance in the Flaherty legacy was "manifest in Frances Flaherty's lifelong collaboration with her husband."[58]

After his death in 1951, Frances's role shifted from promoter and business manager of Flaherty films and Flaherty the filmmaker to amateur theorist and revisionist historian of an elaborate, mystical theology of cinema. She advanced the "Flaherty Way," elaborating six principles: an anti-Hollywood and anti-Grierson position, cinema as an art form learned through interaction with masters, form revealing itself through process, nonpreconception, seeing as exploration, and Zen. During his life, Robert Flaherty never expressed these ideas. His published interviews and writing skewed to descriptions of his encounters with Inuit or Samoans, his diaries detailing eating, sleeping, and traveling. Frances developed the "Flaherty Way" in the larger post–World War II context of her invited public speaking. At colleges, festivals, and film societies, she was called upon to explain her husband's concepts and working methods in postscreening sessions. Her immersion in the burgeoning nontheatrical film culture of the 1950s sustained a context for more philosophical thinking about cinema. Frances actively participated in this nontheatrical film culture, promoting Robert's films and legacies for almost two decades until her death in 1972.

Anthropologist Jay Ruby researched Flaherty's papers as well as Frances's diaries. He has debunked many Flaherty myths. In a seminal article, he argued that Flaherty's shooting style, especially on *Nanook of the North*, was less individual genius and instead more of a collaboration with the Inuit. He identified and demystified five persistent "Flaherty myths" emerging in writings about Flaherty: the father of documentary film, the maverick independent film artist, the metaphor of exploration, the nonpreconceiver, and the teller of tales.[59]

Flaherty's production work spanned almost four decades from 1914 to 1951. His five feature films had large gaps of time between each production. Importantly, corporations or studios provided financing for each film. The fur company Revillon Frères funded *Nanook*. Famous Players Lasky produced *Moana*. Gainsborough Pictures, an associate company of the Gaumont British Picture Corporation, underwrote *Man of Aran*. The Agricultural Adjustment Agency of the US Department of Agriculture funded *The Land*. Standard Oil of New Jersey produced *Louisiana Story*. On *Elephant Boy* (1937), produced by Alexander Korda in London, Flaherty contributed location direction in India while Zoltan Korda did studio direction. His shorts included *The Pottery Maker* (1925), produced for the Metropolitan Museum of Art in New York; *Industrial Britain*, codirected with Arthur Elton, John Grierson, and Basil Wright, for the Empire Marketing Board Film Unit in London; and *Guernica* (1949), an unfinished film for MoMA.

Conflicts with sponsors generated continual struggle for the Flahertys, whose slow production methods of cultural immersion did not match rigorous production schedules. These experiences of dealing with sponsors whose needs diverged from filmmakers' and shooting around the globe undergirded the Flaherty seminars conceptual structures. As the seminar evolved, it transformed the locations of the Flaherty films in Canada, India, Ireland, and Samoa into a more idealized goal of internationalism. It revised the experience of struggle for autonomy from sponsors into an ethos supporting artistic independent filmmaking.

The Flahertys' union was a stormy marriage of opposites: Bob was from the Midwest, whereas Frances from the East. Bob dropped out of the Michigan School of the Mines, while Frances was educated at Bryn Mawr College and in Europe. Bob preferred learning through interaction in harsh, demanding physical environments, while Frances read philosophy. Bob loved the intensities of New York City, while Frances loved the tranquility of their Dummerston farm. Bob played the violin; Frances played the piano. They found a common interest in music.[60] They were married in November 1914 in New York City after a long courtship.[61] Frances mused: "I married my husband for several very plain and simple reasons: 1. Because an innate sense for the preservation of his own genius has saved him from all educational institutions or instruction of any kind. 2. Because that genius is for A. exploration (profession: exploration and mining) and B. music and the arts (avocations: playing the violin and portrait photography)."[62]

Despite their differences, Frances and Bob operated as a collaborative team on every film except *Nanook of the North*. In his book *Robert and Frances Flaherty*, based on Robert's and Frances's diaries from the early years of their marriage and Robert's expeditions for MacKenzie, Robert J. Christopher argued that Frances sought to be Bob's collaborator. She served as his archivist, business manager, copyeditor, general editor, librarian, publicist, and secretary. She was a partner in his enterprises.[63]

In his 1953 book, *The World of Robert Flaherty*, Richard Griffiths affirmed their collaboration. He described how Frances operated as a "Cassandra," analyzing impractical approaches, discussing the day's shooting, and photographing locations and people. While Bob operated the camera, Frances took light meter readings and shot still photos. Griffiths argued that Frances's still photographs constituted the scenario. Griffiths wrote, "How they worked together neither could exactly explain, but you could sense a bit of it if you watched a Flaherty scene being filmed, and something of it comes through in 'production shots.'"[64] In 1932, Frances published *Samoa*, a book collecting her 1925 articles and photographs for *Asia Magazine*.[65] In her 1962 Guggenheim Foundation application, Frances contended that "I collaborated with my husband in the making of *Moana, Man of Aran, Elephant Boy*, and *The Land*."[66]

Frances functioned as Bob's agent and publicist. She shrewdly ascertained he could repurpose his experiences across articles, books, and public talks. Frances pushed Robert to publish articles about his Canadian expeditions, providing outlines and prodding him to write.[67] Robert published four articles about his Hudson Bay and Ungava Peninsula explorations in *Geographical Journal* and *Geographical Review* from 1915 to 1918, before the 1922 release of *Nanook*.[68] Robert's 1924 book, *My Eskimo Friends*, described his experiences with the indigenous people of the Canadian north and featured his Inuit portraits. It identified collaboration with Frances on the title page.[69]

In 1931, Frances published an article called "How I Make My Exhibition Pictures" in *The Amateur Photographer and Cinematographer*. Frances wrote how she employed miniature cameras and different focal lengths in India during the shooting of *Elephant Boy*. Her images of the elephants accompanied the article.[70] In a 1936 article entitled "Converted to the Miniature" published in *The Miniature Camera World*, Frances wrote that on their second film expedition to Samoa, "my husband thrust a still camera into my hands and said 'You've got to take stills. I am too busy.'"[71] Her still photographer role continued through the production of all the subsequent films, where her images served as research for filmmaking, production stills, and publicity. In a 1959 letter to photographer Minor White, she explained, "My job on the films was still camera, it was entirely subsidiary to the films. Stills were a sketching device during production and afterwards served as usual for publicity."[72]

Produced by Alexander Korda, *Elephant Boy* was loosely based on Rudyard Kipling's *Jungle Book* story "Toomai of the Elephants," which is about a young mahout who witnesses the wild elephant dance in the jungle. Frances later published her own book, *Elephant Dance*, in 1937. The book chronicled her year in Mysore, India, when Bob worked on the production of the narrative film *Elephant Boy*. The Flahertys spent five months in India before any motion picture film was shot. During this time, Frances used her still camera as a sketchbook for the film and as travel documentation.

Elephant Dance followed the marketing pattern the Flahertys deployed throughout their lives of recycling diaries, photographs, stories, and writing for different constituencies. As an early exposition of Frances's thinking about cinema, the book elaborates concepts that later surface in her writing and public speaking after Robert's death. First, it emphasizes detailed empirical observation rather than a deeper historical or social understanding of India with its minute descriptions of animals, food, and locations. Second, it suggests that interaction with cultural and topographic difference can elevate one's consciousness from the mundane to the mystical. An orientalism fetishizing difference as a racialized mechanism to propel a more intense state of consciousness wound through this book.

Elephant Dance featured photographs Frances shot while Robert worked on the film and edited versions of letters Frances penned to her daughters, Barbara, Frances, and Monica. Barbara lived in India with her parents, while Frances and Monica attended boarding school in England for part of the period the Flahertys resided in India.[73] *Elephant Dance* described Frances and Bob's daily living in South India: casting for a young mahout, eating curry, enduring monsoons, looking for elephants in the jungle, and meeting the maharajah. The letters revealed more fascination with animals and landscapes than with South Indian people. Writing about her travel from Bangalore to Mysore, Frances wrote, "the country changed from the desert red, growing greener and greener and more and more jungly; palm trees, coconut, date, and toddy—seas of them now and again."[74]

The letters focused on bullocks, cobras, elephants, monkeys, scorpions, and tigers, revealing a colonialist imagination where difference propels intense imaginative experience. Describing an elephant called Irawatha, Frances wrote, "I love the big fellow. I had a ride, clambered up over his tail end and sat on a pad, hanging on for dear life on to the pad ropes.... I haven't had such a thrill."[75] Frances's letters in *Elephant Dance* show how the Flahertys' India mapped a spectacular projection of the dramatic and the exotic, supported by maharajahs and servants. Out in the jungle with mahouts who rounded up animals, Frances wrote, "Now we had in our captured tusker, of course, an extraordinary film property. And we hastened to make the most of it, while the poor creature was still rebellious and fierce."[76] Her photographs in the book divided between close-ups of different Indian people she met and medium long shots of elephants.

Many of the letters detailed the casting of the young mahout, Toomai, the elephant trainer. Flaherty's camera operator found a young boy living in the elephant stables named Sabu, whom Robert cast in the title role. Frances outlined Sabu's expression of gratitude for the role, writing he was not afraid to leave the stables and work with the Flahertys: "I am not afraid of anything in the world. I am here to serve the masters."[77]

The letters culminated in the keddah, the elephant drive in the jungle of South India in Karapur. The last half of the book focuses on the behaviors of the elephants, Flaherty, jungle camps, and the mahouts' work with the elephants. Frances explained, "Now we came to that part of our Indian experience we had been waiting for, dreaming of since we dreamed of India at all, as all people do—of that strange, exotic, perhaps terrible, always exciting place they think of as the Indian jungle."[78] The letters explained how the mahouts tracked and herded elephants in the jungle, where Bob's movie camera and Frances's still camera were camouflaged under specially constructed scaffolding. "Never a time do we start out on a jungle adventure that we are not regaled with the most awful tales of danger and ferocity of the elephant in its wild state," Frances wrote.[79] Her letters related difficult jungle treks, endless waiting in huts, and her awe of the elephants' physical presence. The letters exhibited Frances's excitement about the unknown.

Theatrical screenings presented a constant struggle for each of the major films. In the 1950s, Frances found herself immersed in a quite different world of educational and nontheatrical settings where ideas mattered more than box office. Film festivals, film societies, and universities demanded more than a screening. In advancing cinema as an art, they sought explanations and production background of Flaherty's working methods to create a less commercial, more poetic cinema. A 1954 letter to writer Malcolm Brinnin, who suggested she write Robert's biography, hinted at how Frances transformed Flaherty the adventurer into Flaherty the poet: "I know now that what I most want is a book about Bob as a poet, about his 'method' as a poet's way, his philosophy of the camera as the beginning of a tradition of poetry in the film medium."[80]

George Amberg pointed out that Robert "made no pronouncements and left no written record concerning the one thing he knew best. He worked intuitively, in the sense that no conscious rationale determined his choice of content or treatment."[81] After her husband's death, Frances used their production diaries, letters, and stories as a springboard for a cinematic theory that promoted cinema as an art form and filmmaking as a mystical encounter offering deeper knowledge of the world.

Robert Flaherty kept copious diaries of his expeditions in the Canadian north. They detail the hardships of travel, sleep, and food. His two books, *My Eskimo Friends* (1924) and *The Captain's Chair* (1938), relate stories of adventure, encounters with indigenous people, expeditions, and survival in harsh environments.[82] Flaherty told stories about the Inuit in different interviews and broadcasts, the most famous of which was *The Story of Comock the Eskimo* (1968) published as a book by Edmund Carpenter, with Flaherty's collections of Inuit drawings deposited in the Royal Ontario Museum as illustration.[83]

Frances Flaherty wrote two published texts outlining Robert Flaherty's process: a short magazine column in 1952 and a short chapbook in 1960. These writings bookended the early period of the Flaherty Foundation and seminars. These two publications were key to understanding Frances's arguments for a poetic cinema of intuition and nonpreconception. By 1955, she reasoned that due to the institution of the first Robert Flaherty

Film Seminar and numerous public speaking invitations, she would need to become "more intellectual about cinema."[84]

The first piece mentioned above was a short seminal article in Cecile Starr's *Saturday Review* column called "The Flaherty Way." Frances advanced Robert's filmmaking process, expounding on exploration, magical revelations through seeing, relying on intuition and discovery rather than scripts and preplanning, and training the eye through immersion in material. Frances offered her insights into Robert's process in mystical terminology, inferring a religious epiphany through cinema production: "I wish I could convey the deep excitement of making pictures this way—the seemingly hopeless bafflement, and then the breaking of the light, one could never tell when or how or even why—the intuitive way, taking quite a lot of faith to follow, considerable inner conviction."[85] As she received more invitations to deliver university lectures and to present the Flaherty films throughout the 1950s, she penned scripts for her public presentations. These scripts included her observations about the production of the films. Outlines rather than formal lectures, they deployed clips from the four films Frances promoted as Robert's primary oeuvre: *Louisiana Story, Man of Aran, Moana,* and *Nanook of the North.* The Robert Flaherty Foundation had procured minimal nontheatrical rights for these films. The "Flaherty Way" revolved around Frances's interpretations about how Robert entered environments, engaged people, and rendered practical creative decisions. Throughout, she emphasized the collaborations necessary between Flaherty and his subjects given extreme conditions, lack of familiarity about location, and small crews.

By 1960, Frances's lectures and scripts had progressed into more developed explications about Robert's creative process and working methods in a sixty-one-page chapbook entitled *The Odyssey of a Film-Maker.* Beta Phi Mu, the international library and information studies honor society, invited Frances to revise her lectures on the Flaherty methods. Frances wrote the book at the Flaherty farm. The book launched at a party held at the Coffee House Club, one of Robert's favorite New York City drinking haunts, on March 17, 1960.[86] *Odyssey of a Film-Maker* was reprinted in 1984 as part of the Robert Flaherty Centennial Project, with copyright held by the Robert and Frances Flaherty Study Center at Claremont College in California, where Frances had deposited many of her and Bob's papers and photographs.[87]

Frances Flaherty's loose, ill-defined positions on cinema revolved around her antagonism toward codified systems of filmmaking. She criticized Hollywood for its business practices and scripts. She fought against documentary dedicated to civic education and political purpose promoted by John Grierson, with whom Robert had worked on *Industrial Britain* in the early 1930s. Frances notoriously dubbed Grierson "a teacher and a preacher," and she worked for two decades to distance the more artisanal, poetic style of Flaherty from the more institutionally driven, outcome-directed British documentary movement of the 1930s, which she considered propaganda.[88]

Frances's positioning of the Flaherty filmmaking process as a mystical spirit of independence in opposition to Hollywood had commenced decades before the postwar nontheatrical movement. In 1926, after confronting the theatrical distribution challenges of *Nanook* and *Moana,* Frances compared the motion picture industry to the steel industry with its vast private fortunes and worldwide reach.[89] In a 1936 article for *Miniature Camera World,* she noted that since *Nanook,* "we have not used their studios, actors or even their laboratories."[90]

In 1954, she argued that the Flaherty films were misunderstood "simply because they go against the current—the mighty Niagara—of the commercial cinema as projected by Hollywood."[91] Frances assessed Hollywood as a cinema stifled by preconception of material through scenarios and shooting schedules. She called this Hollywood style "the making or creating way, with its discipline of doing" and offered instead "the discovering or releasing way, with its discipline of letting be."[92] In "The Flaherty Way," she argued the accepted way of producing a motion picture was to "first write or find a story, then to turn the story into a shooting script, and then only is one ready to begin by thinking—by writing and arranging by far as possible the story, the script."[93]

Frances viewed theatrical exhibition and Hollywood as promoting formulas constraining creativity and insight. She claimed Hollywood production systems and scenario writing operated as "a slot through which every film had to pass and to which it had to be shaped like a button to a mold."[94] By 1962, she elaborated the differences between a "Flaherty film" and Hollywood in much more lofty, ill-defined terms, contending that Hollywood films pushed audiences to identify with stars while *Nanook* motored a special spectator identification with "life itself, with that universal life of which we and these people are a part. . . . [W]e become genuine and true. They are completely themselves; we in turn become ourselves and everything that might separate us from these people falls away from us."[95] Shooting without constraints can be read two ways. While it rejected Hollywood's rationalized production methods, it constituted an expensive, romanticized, self-indulgent view of filmmaking.

After trying to promote films like *Nanook of the North* and *Moana* theatrically, Frances viewed Hollywood as a monopolist unwilling to open up to independents. As the 16mm, art cinema, and film society movements developed, Frances's antagonisms toward industrial modes of production changed into a support for an artisanal cinema derived from mystical relationships with landscapes and people. After the 1948 breakup of the Hollywood studios' vertical integration controlling production, distribution, and exhibition, art cinemas emerged in postwar America in urban centers, screening works from other countries and not just studio fare—congruent with Frances's utopian goals for cinema.[96]

Frances's advocacy for a noncommercial cinematic practice continually invoked exploration and learning to see. She leveraged the biographical fact of Robert Flaherty's early work as an explorer of the Canadian north before he became a filmmaker and transformed it into a metaphor for a style of cinema bathed in a romantic notion of the artist as a conduit for visionary revelations. The "Flaherty Way" was linked to exploration, which moved from colonialist imagination of conquering new lands to a neocolonialist strategy of exploring the unknown beyond modernity to reveal deeper meaning.

Frances frequently quoted Robert Flaherty's famous adage: "All art is a kind of exploring. To discover and reveal is the way every artist sets about his business."[97] She insisted Robert's filmmaking method was based on continual interaction with filmic material and subjects, rather than a formula. Frances described how Robert shot enormous amounts of footage, only to find the film's style and structure through screening rushes and analyzing what the camera had discovered. In her view, Robert shot first and discovered ideas later.[98] The camera possessed revelatory powers based on seeing. The movie camera propelled "a new dimension of seeing, on a new level of consciousness" through discovery.[99] Frances wrote that filming was designed "to give the camera its chance, to find, in the moment-to-moment unfolding of life, that one high moment of seeing, that moment which is both recognition and revelation. . . . Words had nothing to do with it; it went beyond words."[100] To support the "exploratory" method, she frequently quoted Robert's famous line, "I was an explorer first, and a film-maker a long way after."[101]

Inflected with Zen Buddhism, nonpreconception was a key foundation underpinning Frances Flaherty's cinematic cosmology. Frances launched this concept in the early 1950s to differentiate the Flaherty style of artisanally produced, humanist, poetic documentary from the Griersonian style of a preplanned, purposeful documentary promoting nationalist agendas. She claimed she sought a word to describe "the explorer's mind" Robert Flaherty brought to cinema. Robert frequently used the word *exploring*. After his death, Frances translated this word into "nonpreconception." Frances elaborated "preconception" in "The Flaherty Way." Any preconception—scripts, scenarios, planning—was to be eradicated. The filmmaker's mind needed to be emptied so that new, unexpected stimuli could enter: "letting all thoughts of your own go in order to let what will come in."[102] She discussed "wiping our minds clean . . . like unexposed film" in order to absorb the world.[103] Frances referred to this practice as "the creative void," the "fertile state of no mind," a state of "nonpreconception."[104] She reflected, "as I find myself called upon to distinguish our teaching from documentary, I find myself using the word 'revelation' and saying simply that the films are films of revelation."[105]

By 1957, Frances was reading Zen Buddhism. It propelled her toward linking Flaherty's endless shooting with a philosophical, spiritual system he himself never embraced. "In Zen, Robert Flaherty's approach to the motion picture medium finds its history, its traditions, its school, its practice," wrote Frances.[106] By 1962, Frances had discovered Japanese haiku. She admired its sparseness. She claimed haiku masters "were practicing pure cinema."[107]

In her writing, Frances promoted nonpreconception as the most important tenet of documentary filmmaking. Robert never spoke about this concept. Frances developed her ideas about nonpreconception from disparate sources: her memories of the production process involving long nights watching rushes; her need to provide more than anecdotes to university audiences; and her quest to differentiate documentary from its state-sponsored and educational formations.

Frances sought out intellectuals with whom she could form alliances. In the iconoclastic anthropologist Edmund Carpenter, she found a kindred spirit, someone who had worked extensively among the indigenous peoples of the Canadian north and who sought to understand how they saw the world. Throughout the 1950s, Frances and the Flaherty Foundation migrated in and out of ethnographic circles in the United States and France through organizations such as the International Congress of Ethnological and Anthropological Sciences. Ethnographers saw the postwar semiprofessionalization of 16mm film as an asset to advance research documentation. The Flaherty Foundation, the Flaherty seminars, and Frances interacted continuously with anthropologists, even though Frances fought to prevent the classification of the Flaherty films as ethnographies. Instead, she argued for their "method" and their "way" of seeing, a more mystical and poetic position than ethnographic observational techniques.

Carpenter defied traditional social scientific method. He was a maverick thinker and researcher. He published three highly influential texts contributing to the development of critical ethnography: *They Became What They Beheld* (1970), *Oh, What a Blow That Phantom Gave Me* (1973), and *Eskimo Realities* (1973).[108] His writing moved beyond social scientific principles of distance and objectivity, advancing participant observation to find deeper cultural patterns. The letters between Frances and Carpenter in the late 1950s trace how Frances's statements about learning to see from the "Eskimo" were actually her rudimentary translations of Carpenter's more immersive, anthropological research in the Canadian Arctic. Carpenter initially wrote to Frances in 1958, describing a book he was developing using Flaherty's collection of Inuit carvings. He reasoned that "their primary spatial models are not visual as with Western man, but acoustic and that among them space is defined by the ear more than the eye." He explained that like Robert, he had also lived for extended periods with the Inuit.[109]

In the 1950s, Carpenter taught at the University of Toronto. He was a close friend of media theorist Marshall McLuhan. Carpenter had worked with the Flaherty collections of Inuit art, artifacts, and photographs archived at the Royal Ontario Museum as part of his ongoing research into the peoples of the Canadian north. Sir William Mackenzie had donated 360 pieces from Robert Flaherty's collection to the museum in 1914.[110] In 1959, Carpenter published a book entitled *Eskimo*, coauthored with Frederick Varley and Robert Flaherty.[111] Although the book used the word *Eskimo* in its title, Carpenter refers to his subjects as Aivilik. The book collected three sources from three different time periods to map Aivilik epistemologies, showing how three different people from three different perspectives—artist, explorer, and anthropologist—saw the same Eskimo worldview. The charcoal and pencil sketches of the Arctic landscapes and Eskimo had been rendered by Varley in 1938. The photographic images were of Eskimo carvings Robert Flaherty collected in 1910–16 and 1920–22. Carpenter wrote the text, with short sections describing Inuit ways of navigating the world: acoustic space, acuteness of observation, art, the igloo, mechanical aptitude, and orientation.

The book featured an unusual design of Varley's drawings rendered as full-page images, a visual design with large amounts of white space around images and text. Carpenter's text eschewed an academic style with footnotes and scientific distance. Instead, the text was written in a first-person point of view combining observations of Aivilik behaviors in art, building, and navigation with Aivilik stories. The book was not paginated, suggesting the Aivilik nonlinear sense of time and the expansive white spaces in the Arctic regions.

When Carpenter contacted Frances, she was drafting *The Odyssey of a Film-Maker*, expanding her scripts and talks about the Flaherty films written over eight years. Frances became enamored with one story from *Eskimo* that resonated with "nonpreconception." In a section elaborating that the Aivilik did not see distinctions between decorative and utilitarian objects, Carpenter related a story of the Aivilik carver who holds up an unworked piece of ivory and asks, "Who are you? Who hides there?" Carpenter noticed the carver did not consciously set out to render a particular animal but worked the ivory until its form was revealed: "Then he brings it out: Seal, hidden, emerges. It was always there: he didn't create it; he released it."[112] Frances also liked Carpenter's observation that the Aivilik language did not have any equivalents for the words *create* or *make*, words Frances linked to Grierson and Hollywood. Carpenter observed the carver responds to the material rather than forcing a form on it.

Contra Flaherty Seminar mythology that attributes this story to either Frances or Robert, it is important to recognize that although Frances was thinking and writing along similar lines to Carpenter, the actual story of the ivory carver and the seal derived from Carpenter's research and writing. In 1958, Frances wrote to Carpenter after reading a draft of *Eskimo*. She requested permission to incorporate this story into *The Odyssey of a Film-Maker*.[113] Carpenter agreed.[114]

In 1959, Carpenter had edited a book of poems entitled *Anerca*, the Inuit word for *soul*. The poems transcribed chants, drum songs, and incantations. Carpenter donated all book royalties to the newly formed International Film Seminars, the organization created to mount the annual Flaherty seminar. Frances wanted to "provoke a discussion of seeing" based on Carpenter's research analyzing how the Aivilik viewed the Arctic landscape.[115]

By the late 1950s and early 1960s, Frances's advocacy for the "Flaherty Way" of nonpreconception had changed. She moved from rejecting the preplanning of Hollywood and the state agendas of Grierson toward a mystical, religious ecstasy through filmmaking. Her writing expanded the metaphor of exploring into a Zen acquisition of knowledge through letting go combined with a vague humanist universalism. Undeveloped, spiritually inflected words such as *consciousness, oneness, the participation mystique, timelessness,* and *universal* appeared in her scripts. In a 1959 lecture at the Charlotte Selver Institute in New York, Frances contended that the Flaherty films were "timeless in the sense of the Mohammedan prayer." Later, she claimed that Flaherty's filmmaking was a "quest for the spirit." In an oft-repeated passage, Frances wrote: "And all that might separate us from these people falls away from us. In spite of our differences, indeed perhaps the more BECAUSE of them, we are one with them. And this feeling of oneness can deepen and become that profound and profoundly liberating experience we call 'participation mystique.'"[116] In other talks, this "participation mystique" of connection with material and the dissolution of borders emerged as an argument that cinema could bring together different cultures around the world to foster better understanding.[117] In one script, Frances even asserted that after the devastations and separations of World War I, *Nanook of the North* offered a way to bring the people of the world together for better understanding and international relations.[118]

The closing pages of *The Odyssey of a Film-Maker* appended filmmaking to spirituality, arguing the camera could liberate the spirit to generate profound experiences. The freedom to produce film independent of nation-states or studios now amplified into a religious calling for Zen enlightenment through the camera. Frances claimed, "Robert Flaherty was a mystic of the modern age," coming to the "mystic's energy and delight" by means of his surrender to the camera itself and to the material environment.[119]

The film librarian D. Marie Grieco, who participated in the New York experimental and nontheatrical film scene of the 1960s, contributed to the promulgation of the "Flaherty Way" through her film programming for the seminar and for libraries, her International Film Seminars board contributions, her invocation of Frances's ideas of nonpreconception during seminar discussions, and her writings on Frances Flaherty. She and Frances had become friends at the seminar, where Grieco admired her clear thinking, forceful presence, and intellect. At Columbia University, Grieco taught the first nonprint course focusing on film at a library school. Librarians were central to the economic sustainability of the nontheatrical sector in the 1960s because they bought and showed films. Grieco attended her first Flaherty seminar in 1966 at the urging of another audiovisual librarian. There, she witnessed Frances's charisma in postscreening discussions.

A former trustee of the International Film Seminars who programmed the 1968, 1969, and 1984 gatherings, Grieco was a key figure in the seminars' history. She was also one of the strongest advocates for Frances's notion of nonpreconception. Grieco learned about Robert and Frances Flaherty's differing intellectual styles, arguing that Robert was a poet and Frances was the intellect. As a trustee, Grieco identified herself as the historian of International Film Seminars, garnering anecdotes from Frances and working with what Frances called her "core library," a selection of anthropological, philosophical, and spiritual books that augmented her thinking. Grieco frequently made trips to the Flaherty farm to develop a bibliography. Frances's core library was interdisciplinary. It included books on anthropology, Daoism, drugs, haiku, history, music, mysticism, sociology, and Zen, as well as writings by Carl Jung and Alan Watts.[120] Grieco was an indefatigable advocate for Frances's vision. She argued that because the seminars where named for her husband, Frances's role in the documentary and nontheatrical world was marginalized.

At the 18th Annual Robert Flaherty Film Seminar in 1972, Grieco presented a memorial tribute entitled "Frances Hubbard Flaherty: A True Seer." One of the first coherent expositions of Frances's post-Robert concepts and experiences, the pamphlet drew heavily from documents deposited in the Butler Special Collections at Columbia University. The pamphlet worked with Frances's core library, analyzing what had been underlined. Grieco noted that the quotations Frances pulled from the books fell into three areas: the creative process, the educational process as an exploratory way, and responsibility to society[121]

Grieco identified Frances's quest for a seminar that expanded beyond the Flaherty films into a more educational mission to nurture the spirit. At the time of her death, Frances was involved in plans for the Robert and Frances Flaherty Study Center at the School of Theology at Claremont College, through her relationship with faculty member Jack Coogan. Grieco concluded her monograph with one of Frances's favorite quotes from French philosopher and Jesuit priest Teilhard de Chardin, a quote Frances paraphrased at many seminars to underscore the spiritual quest of the "Flaherty Way": "to see more is to become more. Fuller being is closer union . . . to see or to perish is man's condition."[122] In a 1995 tribute to the Flaherty seminars, Grieco honored Frances's conceptual models that eventually morphed into programming and discussion practices.

She wrote, "During the seminar, the bafflements, illuminations, abrasions, awarenesses, confrontations, connections . . . the continual probing of one's conceptions, misconceptions, and preconceptions—simulate the exploratory process Frances so wished to share as a way of learning to see."[123]

Inspired by Frances's intellect and by her own transformative seminar experiences, Grieco worked to revise the pervasive mythologies surrounding Robert Flaherty. She sought to prove that Frances initiated the Robert Flaherty Seminar. Grieco also promoted the idea that Frances—not Robert—constructed the "Flaherty Way."

1959 FRANCES FLAHERTY—OPENING REMARKS AT THE SEMINAR

This year, we are delighted to have guests from Canada, again from Puerto Rico, and we have another country represented this year: Korea. And of course, we're all looking forward enormously to welcoming a very special guest from India next week [Satyajit Ray]. I only want to say that I hope you'll be as happy to be members of the seminar as we are to have you.

We all have the very great privilege of having Hugh Gray with us this year. But before I ask him to open the seminar, I thought I might, just for a minute, go back to the beginnings of the seminars, and explain how they came to be. The beginning actually was my belated appreciation of the fact that the reason why my experience of working with Bob Flaherty was so profound was because of all the little things that went into the making of the films, this thing and that thing and this other thing—all things that only we who had worked very closely with Bob could possibly know, could possibly begin to understand, or could even try to explain. Bob's process of filmmaking was something that he developed, gradually, out of himself, out of the situations he found himself in; it was, so to speak, his own invention.

I remember that once Sir Carol Reed said to me, "When I look at other people's films, I can usually tell exactly how they have arrived at their effects, but when I look at your husband's films I cannot tell at all." I think he expected me then and there to explain the mystery, shot by shot. As a matter of fact, all I could do was smile because I hadn't worked this out in my own mind; at that point the films just seemed to have happened.

But after that, I thought a great deal about the process that produced the films, and I came to feel that there was something there that people who are in filmmaking would want to know, that knowing something about Bob's process might throw light on *their* filmmaking; and further, that *their* filmmaking would then in turn throw light on the experiences that *I* had had working with Bob, which I wanted to explain more deeply to myself all the time. And *that* was the beginning of the seminar.

Notes

1. George Amberg to the Guggenheim Foundation to support grant application from Frances Flaherty, 1961, The Robert J. Flaherty Papers, Butler Library, Columbia University Libraries (hereafter cited as Flaherty Papers).
2. David Flaherty to John Adair, March 22, 1960, Flaherty Papers.
3. Laura A. Belmonte, *Selling the American Way: US Propaganda and the Cold War* (Philadelphia: University of Pennsylvania Press, 2008), 3–94.
4. Barnard F. Dick, *Radical Innocence: A Critical Study of the Hollywood Ten* (Lexington: University Press of Kentucky, 1989).

5. Reynold Humphries, *Hollywood's Blacklists: A Political and Cultural History* (Edinburgh, UK: University of Edinburgh Press, 2009), 77–106.

6. Lary May, "Movie Star Politics: The Screen Actor's Guild, Cultural Conversion, and the Hollywood Red Scare," in *Recasting America: Culture and Politics in the Age of Cold War*, ed. Lary May (Chicago: University of Chicago Press, 1989), 143, 148.

7. See, for example, Erik Barnouw, *The Golden Web* (New York: Oxford University Press, 1968) and *Tube of Plenty* (New York: Oxford University Press, 1976).

8. Warren Sussman, "Did Success Spoil the United States? Dual Representations in Postwar America," in *Recasting America*, 21, 22–25.

9. See Bruce Cook, *The Beat Generation: The Tumultuous '50s Movement and Its Impact on Today* (New York: Quill Publishing, 1994); Glenn C. Altschuler, *All Shook Up: How Rock 'n' Roll Changed America* (Oxford, UK: Oxford University Press, 2004); Aldon D. Morries, *The Origins of the Civil Rights Movement: Black Communities Organizing for Change* (New York: Free Press, 1986).

10. Erika Doss, "The Art of Cultural Politics: From Regionalism to Abstract Expressionism," in *Recasting America*, 198–216; Serge Guilbaut, *How New York Stole the Idea of Modern Art: Abstract Expressionism, Freedom, and the Cold War* (Chicago: University of Chicago Press, 1983).

11. Gerald Graff, *Professing Literature* (Chicago: The University of Chicago Press, 1987).

12. George Amberg to the Guggenheim Foundation to support grant application from Frances Flaherty, 1961, Flaherty Papers.

13. Frances Flaherty to Armine Wilson, November 9, 1954, 1, Flaherty Papers.

14. David Flaherty to Henry Starr, June 3, 1961, 1, Flaherty Papers.

15. Announcement of France Flaherty Lecture at the Carnegie Museum, February 1954, 1, Flaherty Papers.

16. D. Marie Grieco, "Frances Hubbard Flaherty: A True Seer," memorial tribute to Frances Flaherty, August 29, 1972, 4–5. International Film Seminars Private Collection, International Film Seminars/The Flaherty, New York, New York (hereafter cited as IFS Collection).

17. Paul Olson, Tax Exemption Claim on behalf of the Robert Flaherty Foundation, April 15, 1956, 3, Flaherty Papers.

18. Grieco, "Frances Hubbard Flaherty: A True Seer," 6, IFS Collection.

19. Robert Flaherty Associates, Press release announcing the Robert Flaherty Foundation, December 1952, Flaherty Papers.

20. David Flaherty to Russell Lord, December 10, 1958, Flaherty Papers.

21. Frances Flaherty to Monsieur Heron of Revillon Frères, November 10, 1953, Flaherty Papers.

22. Paul Olson to the Commissioner of the Internal Revenue Service, March 15, 1956, 1; Minutes of the Directors of the Flaherty Foundation at MoMA, January 8, 1960, Flaherty Papers.

23. David Flaherty to Floria Lasky, November 31, 1955, 1, Flaherty Papers.

24. Grieco, "Frances Hubbard Flaherty: A True Seer," 6–7, Flaherty Papers.

25. Frances Flaherty to Cosette Stern, in response to a request for booking the Flaherty films, April 8, 1954, Flaherty Papers.

26. Frances Flaherty to Armine Wilson, November 9, 1954, 1, Flaherty Papers.

27. Frances Flaherty to Barbara Chapin, American Association of University Women, August 14, 1953, Flaherty Papers.

28. "New Mexico for the First Robert Flaherty Film Festival," *Albuquerque Journal*, October 25, 1953, Flaherty Papers.

29. David Flaherty to Peggy Clifford, November 24, 1953, Flaherty Papers.

30. David Flaherty to J. A. B. Gibbs, Quebec, May 17, 1954; David Flaherty to David Allen, Maryland, January 7, 1954, Flaherty Papers.

31. Mainwaring went on to serve as associate director for Encyclopedia Britannica Films, a major nontheatrical distributor.

32. "A Report on the Activities of the Robert Flaherty Foundation since July 1, 1954–March 31, 1956," 10, IFS Collection.

33. Jack Ellis to Frances Flaherty, March 25, 1954, Flaherty Papers.

34. Jack C. Ellis, "Film Societies and the Film Council of America," in *Film Society Primer*, ed. Cecile Starr (Forest Hills, NY: American Federation of Film Societies, 1956), 65–67.

35. "Report on the Activities of the Robert Flaherty Foundation, Inc., July 1, 1954–March 31, 1956, 1–3, IFS Collection.

36. "List of Lectures 1956–1958," Flaherty Papers.

37. For a thorough history of Cinema 16 and a compendium of primary documents related to its operation, see Scott MacDonald, *Cinema 16: Documents Towards a History of the Film Society* (Philadelphia: Temple University Press, 2002).

38. For an example of the diversity of programming with experimental, documentary, features, and classic art cinema in the film society sector, see Starr, *Film Society Primer*.

39. Press release from the City College of New York and Cinema 16, "Announcing the Robert J. Flaherty Award," January 23, 1954, Flaherty Papers.

40. Trained as a journalist, Stoney would later screen this same work at the Flaherty seminars in the 1950s.

41. Amos Vogel to Frances Flaherty, March 31, 1958, Flaherty Papers.

42. David Flaherty to Amos Vogel, June 2, 1955; Amos Vogel to Frances Flaherty, March 9, 1957; Frances Flaherty to Amos Vogel, November 29, 1957; Amos Vogel to Frances Flaherty, March 31, 1958; Frances Flaherty to Amos Vogel, July 16, 1958, Flaherty Papers.

43. "Works Screened at the Flaherty: 1955–1994," in "The Flaherty: Four Decades in the Cause of Independent Cinema," ed. Erik Barnouw and Patricia Zimmermann, Special Issue, *Wide Angle* 17, no.1–4 (1995): 431.

44. Memo from the organizing group for the Experimental Production Committee, May 14, 1958, Flaherty Papers.

45. Erik Barnouw to Frances Flaherty, April 2, 1957, Flaherty Papers.

46. Frances Flaherty to Colston Leigh, July 20, 1959, Flaherty Papers.

47. For example, see the range of essays from film society programmers in Starr, *Film Society Primer*.

48. Frances Flaherty to Jean Benoit Levy, June 16, 1952, Flaherty Papers.

49. Paul Rotha, "The Film Society Movement," Newsletter of the American Federation of Film Societies, March 1959, 3–4, Flaherty Papers.

50. Charles R. Acland, "Classrooms, Clubs, and Community Circuits: Cultural Authority and the Film Council Movement, 1946–1957," in *Inventing Film Studies*, ed. Lee Grieveson and Haidee Wasson (Durham, NC: Duke University Press, 2008), 149.

51. Acland, "Classrooms, Clubs, and Community Circuits," 164.

52. Cecile Starr, ed., *Ideas on Film: A Handbook for the 16mm Film User* (New York: Funk and Wagnalls, 1951).

53. Starr, *Film Society Primer*.

54. Ellis, "Film Societies and the Film Council of America," in Starr, *Film Society Primer*.

55. For example, see Richard Griffith, *The World of Robert Flaherty* (London: Victor Gollancz, 1953); Arthur Calder-Marshall, *The Innocent Eye: The Life of Robert J. Flaherty* (London: W. H. Allen, 1963); Robert Flaherty, BBC Talks, London, June 14, 1949; July 24, 1949; September 5, 1949; October 1, 1949, Flaherty Papers; Robert Lewis Taylor, "Profile on Robert Flaherty," *The New Yorker*, June 11, 1949, Flaherty Papers; Richard Barsam, *The Vision of Robert Flaherty: The Artist as Myth and Filmmaker* (Bloomington: Indiana University Press, 1988).

56. Biography of France Hubbard Flaherty for the Lecture Bureau, 1955, Flaherty Papers.

57. Frances Flaherty, "Autobiography," draft typescript, Flaherty Papers.

58. George Amberg, "The Innocent Eye," *Film Comment* 9, no. 2 (September 1964): 41.

59. Jay Ruby, "The Aggie Will Come First: The Demystification of Robert Flaherty," in *Robert Flaherty: Photographer/Filmmaker*, ed. Jo-Anne Birnie Danszker (Vancouver, BC: Vancouver Art Gallery, 1979), 66–73.

60. Biography of France Hubbard Flaherty for the Lecture Bureau, 1955, Flaherty Papers.

61. Robert J. Christopher, *Robert and Frances Flaherty: A Documentary Life* (Montreal, QC: McGill-Queen's University Press, 2005), 201.

62. Ibid., 203.

63. Ibid., 202–8.

64. Griffith, *The World of Robert Flaherty*, 50.

65. Frances Flaherty, *Samoa* (Berlin: Reimar and Hobbing, 1932).

66. Frances Flaherty, Application to the Guggenheim Foundation, 1961, 3, Flaherty Papers.

67. Christopher, *Robert and Frances Flaherty*, 207.

68. Robert Flaherty, "Reported Discovery of Large Islands in Hudson Bay," *Geographic Journal* 454 (May 1915): 440; "Mr. Flaherty's Exploration in Hudson Bay," *Geographical Journal* 56 (September 1915): 241–42; "The Belcher Islands of Hudson Bay: Their Discovery and Exploration," *Geographical Review* (June 1918): 433–58; "Two Traverses across Ungava Peninsula, Labrador," *Geographical Review* 6 (August 1918): 116–32.

69. Robert Flaherty, in collaboration with Frances Flaherty, *My Eskimo Friends* (New York: Doubleday, 1924).

70. Frances Hubbard Flaherty, "How I Make My Exhibition Pictures," *The Amateur Photographer and Cinematographer* 10 (March 1931): 46.

71. Frances Flaherty, "Converted to the Miniature," *The Miniature Camera World* (December 1936): 36.

72. Frances Flaherty to Minor White, June 4, 1959, Flaherty Papers.

73. Frances Flaherty, *Elephant Dance* (New York: Scribner, 1937).

74. Ibid., 23.

75. Ibid., 39.

76. Ibid., 91.

77. Ibid., 49.

78. Ibid., 85.

79. Ibid., 100.

80. Frances Flaherty to Malcolm Brinnin, March 26, 1954, Flaherty Papers.

81. Amberg, "The Innocent Eye," 40.

82. Robert Flaherty, *My Eskimo Friends* (New York: Doubleday, Page, 1924); Robert Flaherty, *The Captain's Chair* (New York: Scribner, 1938).

83. Comock, *The Story of Comock the Eskimo,* adapt. Robert Flaherty, ed. Edmund Carpenter (New York: Fawcett Premier Book, 1968).

84. Frances Flaherty to Jean Epstein, November 30, 1955, Flaherty Papers.

85. Frances Flaherty, "The Flaherty Way," *Saturday Review of Literature*, September 13, 1952, 52.

86. Invitation to Celebrate Publication of *The Odyssey of a Film-Maker*, March 12, 1960, Flaherty Papers.

87. Frances Hubbard Flaherty, *The Odyssey of a Film-Maker: Robert Flaherty's Story* (Urbana, IL: Beta Phi Mu, 1960).

88. Grieco, "France Hubbard Flaherty: A True Seer," 9, IFS Collection.

89. Frances Flaherty, Lecture notes on the films of Robert Flaherty, 1926, 3, Flaherty Papers.

90. Frances Flaherty, "Converted to the Miniature," 36.

91. Frances Flaherty to Armine Wilson, November 9, 1954, Flaherty Papers.

92. Frances Flaherty, "Robert Flaherty, Explorer and Filmmaker," Lecture Script, 1962, 8. Flaherty Papers.

93. Frances Flaherty, "The Flaherty Way," 52.

94. Frances Flaherty, "Lime Rock Lecture," 6, Flaherty Papers.

95. Frances Flaherty, "Robert Flaherty, Explorer and Filmmaker," Lecture Script, 1962, Flaherty Papers.

96. For a historical analysis of the rise of art cinema theaters in the 1950s, see Barbara Wilensky, *Sure Seaters: The Emergence of Art House Cinema* (Minneapolis: University of Minnesota Press, 2001). For an analysis of the different locations and practices of exhibition, including art cinemas, and their differences from commercial cinemas, see Douglas Gomery, *Shared Pleasure: A History of Movie Presentation in the United States* (Madison: University of Wisconsin Press, 1992).

97. For example, see this quote in Frances Flaherty, *The Odyssey of a Film-Maker*, 61.

98. Frances Flaherty, "Lecture Script on the Robert Flaherty Method," 1962, 6, Flaherty Papers.

99. Frances Flaherty, "Lecture on the Method of Robert Flaherty," 1962, 7, IFS Collection.

100. Ibid., 7.

101. Ibid., 1.

102. Frances Flaherty, "The Flaherty Way," 51, IFS Collection.

103. Frances Flaherty, "Lecture Script on the Robert Flaherty Method," 1962, 7, Flaherty Papers.

104. Frances Flaherty, "The Flaherty Way," 52. See also "Lecture on the Method of Robert Flaherty," 1962, 6, IFS Collection.

105. Frances Flaherty to Jean Benoit Levy, May 16, 1956, Flaherty Papers.

106. Frances Flaherty to Helen Welsh of Beta Phi Mu, March 25, 1957, Flaherty Papers.

107. Frances Flaherty, "Lecture Script on the Flaherty Method," 1962, 2, Flaherty Papers.

108. Edmund Carpenter, *They Became What They Beheld* (New York: Ballantine Books, 1970); Edmund Carpenter, *Oh, What a Blow That Phantom Gave Me* (Toronto: Bantam Books, 1972); and Edmund Carpenter, *Eskimo Realities* (New York: Holt, Rinehart, and Winston, 1973).

109. Edmund Carpenter to Frances Flaherty, May 27, 1958, Flaherty Papers.

110. Edmund Carpenter, Frederick Varley, and Robert Flaherty, *Eskimo* (Toronto: University of Toronto Press, 1959), 62.

111. Carpenter, Varley, and R. Flaherty, *Eskimo*.

112. Ibid., 32.

113. Frances Flaherty to Ted Carpenter, June 18, 1958, Flaherty Papers.

114. Ted Carpenter to Frances Flaherty, June 21, 1959; Ted Carpenter to Frances Flaherty, January 28, 1959; Frances Flaherty to Ted Carpenter, February 17, 1959, Flaherty Papers.

115. Frances Flaherty to Ted Carpenter, May 29, 1961, Flaherty Papers.

116. Frances Flaherty, "The Films of Robert Flaherty with Reference to Haiku and Zen," Lecture at the Charlotte Selver Institute, New York, 1959, 1 and 3, IFS Collection.

117. Frances Flaherty, "Robert Flaherty: Explorer and Film-Maker: The Film of Discovery and Revelation," 5, IFS Collection.

118. Frances Flaherty, "Lecture on the Method of Robert Flaherty," 5, IFS Collection.

119. Frances Flaherty, *The Odyssey of a Film-Maker*, 61.

120. Grieco, "Frances Hubbard Flaherty: A True Seer."

121. Ibid., 12.

122. Ibid., 14.

123. D. Marie Grieco, "Tribute," in Barnouw and Zimmermann, "The Flaherty," 24.

Frances Flaherty and Flaherty seminarians at the Flaherty Farm, Dummerston, VT, in the 1950s. Photo courtesy of International Film Seminars, Inc./The Flaherty, New York.

2

A SEMINAR, 1955–1959

"With a little bit of luck," wrote Cecile Starr in the *Saturday Review of Literature* in 1956, "the Flaherty Seminar in Vermont may become the basis for the most important and stimulating summertime film activity we've yet dreamed of in this country."[1] As Bill Sloan has observed, in the 1950s, the Flaherty Film Seminar was the only game in town outside of academia if you wanted to discuss cinema in a deeper, more significant way and wanted to see nontheatrical films. Sloan was the film librarian at the Museum of Modern Art (MoMA) Film Library, a former International Film Seminar trustee, and former Flaherty Seminar programmer, as well as a major advocate for documentary and experimental cinema in the nontheatrical circuits. Sloan contends that the seminar developed in the larger context of the film society movement of the 1950s. "Everyone wanted to go," he explained. "It was a goal to get to it; there was nothing else like it."[2] The Flaherty name had cachet in film circles, identified with more artistic and noncommercial practices. For Sloan and others in the East Coast nontheatrical circuits, the Flaherty offered a chance to see work beyond classic silent films and commercial releases.[3]

The Robert Flaherty Film Seminars in the 1950s offered the term *filmmaker* to suggest a more artisanal, noncommercial mode of production where one person controlled the aesthetic structure, approach, and time lines. Frances regularly used the term *filmmaker* in describing Robert Flaherty; it was a term Robert Drew, the direct cinema producer, also employed. The term suggested a difference from the division of labor of studio films, with different roles of cinematographer, director, editor, and producer.

During the 1950s, very few film festivals existed. The Venice Film Festival started in 1932 and the Cannes Film Festival in 1946. The Edinburgh International Film Festival, which featured documentary films, started in 1947, with the Berlin International Film Festival inaugurated in 1951.[4] But on the East Coast of the United States, with festivals not yet instituted, art cinemas and film societies fulfilled the role of screening documentary, experimental, and international films, as well as building audiences for exhibition practices beyond Hollywood. A more analytical film culture was also in ascendancy in the United States in the publication of specialty journals that expanded beyond journalistic reviews: *Quarterly Review of Film, Radio and Television* (1951, in Berkeley, California); *Audio Visual Communication Review* (1953, Washington DC, by the National

Education Association); and *Film Culture* (1955, New York City). Very few film schools beyond New York University (NYU); the University of Southern California (USC); and the University of California, Los Angeles (UCLA) existed.[5] As a result, the Flaherty Seminar converged the burgeoning interest in developing a more intellectual approach to cinema, the goals of the nontheatrical film societies to present cinema as art, and the need for education in cinema beyond instrumental craft training.

The first five years of the Robert Flaherty Seminar (1955–59) established its advocacy for cinema as an art form, its informal atmosphere, its mythology of promoting the "Flaherty Way," its philosophical foundations, and its retreat-like isolation. The connection with Robert Flaherty and the Flaherty family was underscored by the fact that the first four seminars (1955, 1956, 1957, 1958) took place on the Flaherty farm, with the barn serving as a projection and discussion site. Frances sponsored the seminar to "further an appreciation of her husband's work and method."[6] The seminar differed from a film festival because it gathered together film librarians, filmmakers, film society programmers, museum curators, students, and writers. By 1959, the seminar had moved to University of California, firming up its important links to academics and universities that continued throughout the decades. The seminar changed direction as it professionalized as a nonprofit.

Frances developed the idea for a seminar within the larger, more institutional context of the continuing quest of the Robert Flaherty Foundation to prove to the United States Department of Treasury that it was something more than a family memorial to the filmmaker in order to secure tax-exempt status. In his letter to the lawyers representing the foundation in its pursuit of tax-exempt status, David Flaherty asserted that the initiation of the seminars clarified the educational purpose and function of the foundation.[7] The seminar, by name and example, emphasized the educational goals of the Flaherty Foundation rather than the memorial aspect of honoring one person's legacy. In a 1955 letter written during the winter planning for the summer seminar, Frances reasoned, "this first summer we are trying out an intensive study of the films. There has been considerable dispute as to how much can be studied or imparted. We shall see what we can see."[8] The seminar was explicitly designed to emphasize sharing ideas through formal discussions, informal interactions, and lectures. Its interest in connecting master filmmakers with emerging makers was clear from the start: Frances sought to procure scholarships for students to attend.[9] Almost monk-like in her devotion to cinema, intellectual, patrician, and seventy-one years old at the time, Frances held court at the first seminar, determined to keep the Flaherty name alive and to advocate for the "Flaherty Way" of making films.

Dorothy Olson was a close friend of Frances. She attended the seminars in the 1950s. She has argued that Frances always wanted a career as a filmmaker. However, in the context of filmmaking in the 1920s and 1930s, as well as constraining gender expectations, she could not imagine doing it without her husband. The seminars provided a way to produce an intellectual experience for a younger generation, mobilizing her existing assets: the farm, the Flaherty films, the Flaherty name. Frances complained that she was intellectually isolated in Vermont, so the seminars sustained a way to foster community around ideas. Vermont was halfway between New York City and Canada, so the connection with Canadian filmmakers and the National Film Board (NFB) of Canada was a matter of geography and mutual interest, according to Olson.[10]

In a 1955 letter to Jonas Mekas, then-editor of *Film Culture*, Frances forwarded the idea of the Flaherty films promoting a pedagogical function to deepen and improve cinema. To develop cinema as an art, she argued,

> *Why don't we stop writing so much and do much ... why don't we deliberately choose one of our own and plug it for all it is worth, all of us together for once. This is exactly the sort of effort the Robert Flaherty Foundation is.... These films are life expressed in motion. When we study them we study that. They take us into new and fresh point of views; we shake off old habits. We do not learn to visualize with the top of our heads; we learn, deep down under, to see ... through the camera.[11]*

Film festivals were more accessible and open to the general public, involved choosing among screenings, and were held in major cities. In contrast, the Flaherty Seminar marshaled an opposite structure. It was intimate, with only twenty to fifty participants. It was not in an urban area but in rural Vermont, on a farm. It programmed the order in which concerts, films, and lectures would occur, organizing the experience as a mandatory collective exploration with other people engaged in cinema. As a core working principle, the Flaherty Foundation and the seminar were interested in installing a pedagogical imperative. They were designed to position the Flaherty films as a platform to learn the Flaherty process. "The Way" combined Frances's experiences on location with Bob, her experiences in the nontheatrical film culture of the 1950s, and her extensive readings in philosophy into a filmmaking catechism: independence from studio control and time lines, learning through repeated viewings of rushes or films, mystical engagement with subjects, and nonpreconception of material or ideas.

Frances possessed a dogged determination to advance cinema as an art form by bringing together master filmmakers with students to explore the possibilities of cinema. For her, the Flaherty films provided a springboard into cinema as a significant artistic enterprise and a way into a more philosophical investigation of cinema. In a typescript from 1955, Frances drafted initial ideas explaining why the film community needed the Flaherty Seminar. This document made clear that Frances saw the seminar as a way to study the Flaherty films as a touchstone for an independent, poetic cinema that was emerging in the 1950s. "His filmmaking will probably be of particular interest to independent film makers making their own films in their own way," she wrote. For Frances, the Flaherty films provided an example, a method, a Rosetta stone of how to work in cinema as an art form. She hypothesized that the films offered a clear and simple system of cinematography, editing, discipline, and philosophy of art and life. She argued that the Flaherty films supplied a self-contained rubric from which to learn the "fundamentals of cinema."[12]

The first Robert Flaherty Film Seminar was held on the Flaherty farm in Dummerston, Vermont, in 1955. Robert Flaherty was buried on the property, under a large rock bearing his name. The year before, Frances had moved the headquarters of the foundation from New York City to the farm to save money. The flyer positioned the seminar not as screenings but as a "course," an important distinction from film society and other nontheatrical screenings. The seminar ran for ten days from July 26 to August 4. The seminar was billed as "an exploration of the world of Robert Flaherty," where participants and students would watch the films, speak with people who had worked on the films, and exchange ideas about Flaherty's production methods. Collaborators such as cinematographer Richard Leacock, editor Helen van Dongen, and sound recordists Benjamin Doniger and Leonard Stark who worked on *Louisiana Story* presented special sessions. Virgil Thomas, the film's composer, offered a lecture on the music. Frances Flaherty and David Flaherty discussed the production process of other Flaherty films.

As early as the first seminar, attendance required an application and approval. The attendance fee was $75, which covered film showings, lectures, and lunch.[13] The lectures and presentations on editing, shooting, and sound delivered by the invited quests suggested the intellectual and pedagogical intentions of the seminar. This early seminar, then, did not provide a model for discussion; rather, it facilitated a structure of the master filmmaker/craftsperson from a noncommercial sector of cinema sharing knowledge and skills with a younger generation. Students at the first seminar reflected the heterogeneous sectors of the nontheatrical world of the 1950s: Charles Benton from film distributor *Encyclopedia Britannica*; Michel Brault, a French-Canadian filmmaker from the NFB; Jack Churchill, a science filmmaker; Edith Hutchinson from *Reader's Digest*; Mary Mainwaring, a graduate student from Indiana University; Lynn Robinson from the New York State Library; and Cecile Starr from *Saturday Review*.

The first seminar focused on *Louisiana Story, The Land, Moana,* and *Nanook of the North*. It also programmed films Frances and David determined evoked the Flaherty tradition of artistry, independence, and poetry. The films were not only screened, but the filmmaker was also present to discuss the film with the attendees. In most cases, the filmmaker had some connection to either the Flaherty Foundation or the East Coast nontheatrical scene. The films screened included *All My Babies* (1953) by George Stoney, which had won the Flaherty Award; *Corral* (1954) by French-Canadian filmmaker Michel Brault; *The Pirogue Maker* (1955) by Arnold Eagle, who taught film in New York City;[14] *Seifritz on Protoplasm* (1954), a scientific film by Jack Churchill who had an almost-fifty-year relationship with International Film Seminars as a trustee and ally, and *Toby and the Tall Corn* (1953) by Richard Leacock.[15]

In the 1956 "Report on the Activities of the Robert Flaherty Foundation," Frances assessed the impact and value of the first Robert Flaherty Seminar, asserting that it was geared toward young people and harbored an educational goal. "It was naturally oriented toward the future," Frances maintained.[16] However, that future was one initially plotted out and implied by Robert Flaherty himself.

The report detailed the operations of the first seminar. Richard Griffith from MoMA opened the seminar, framing this gathering as based on controversy, discussion, and inquiry—ideas rippling through the subsequent sixty years. However, records indicated that the first seminar was less participatory discussion and more of a master class based on shot-by-shot analysis of Flaherty films. A step-by-step analysis of the production process on *Louisiana Story* occupied four days. Helen van Dongen, Joris Ivens's editor who also edited *Louisiana Story*, explained the editing process over two days. Richard Leacock explained his cinematography for the film. By the second week, David Flaherty and Frances Flaherty charted the development of the Flaherty process through a chronological survey of his major films with lectures.

In this first seminar, Frances framed her pedagogy as working toward opening up the attendees and students assembled to "letting go" and "self-surrender" to the material.[17] These presenters and Flaherty insiders were called faculty. Participants were dubbed students, thus highlighting the educational function of the seminar. Frances contended that participants saw the seminar as much more than simply learning how to make films; they considered it learning about a "way of life," one fueled by camaraderie, intensity, and isolation.[18] The sessions analyzing the strategies in the Flaherty films happened during the daytime sessions, clearly bestowing prominence on the Flaherty legacy. The evenings expanded beyond the Flaherty opus. Pianist Rudolph Serkin, a neighbor, performed one evening; another evening, folk musician Richard Dyer-Bennet played. Films considered to have emanated from the "Flaherty tradition"—which could mean ethnographic, independent, or poetic—were screened.

The early seminar's amalgam of Flaherty films with other documentary and scientific films, as well as with classical and folk music sessions resonated structurally with one of the major photographic exhibitions of the 1950s: Edward Steichen's "Family of Man" exhibition at MoMA in 1955. Both shared an East Coast location, with interpersonal linkages between Flaherty Seminar participants, the Flaherty family, and MoMA. With its 503 photographs by 273 photographers ranging from professionals to amateurs in a surround style with images hanging from the ceilings and a pathway through which spectators walked, the exhibition promoted a humanist universalism about birth, life, and death. From 1955 to 1962, the United States Information Agency underwrote a tour of the exhibition to sixty-eight countries as a form of cultural diplomacy.[19]

Both the "Family of Man" exhibition and the Flaherty Seminar shared a humanist orientation with congruent ideologies and politics. Both also deployed a strategy of juxtaposition in order to spur spectator engagement and individual responses, motored more on empathy and emotion than criticality.[20] The Bauhaus-inspired structure of suspended architectural photographic panels and the juxtaposition of different kinds of images in the "Family of Man" exhibition encouraged viewers to engage in "democratic degree of freedom in relation to imagery," according to historian Fred Turner.[21] Roland Barthes, as well as subsequent critics such as Allan Sekula and Susan Sontag, criticized this apolitical, overly emotional approach as an ahistorical false universalism.[22] However, on a structural level, this idea of juxtaposition—combining Bauhaus design ideas, cinematic montage theories, and *Life* magazine photo essays—operated as an organizing conceptual model in both the "Family of Man" exhibition and the Flaherty Seminar. Both instantiated and operationalized humanism through emotion and immersion, shearing off critical, political, and social context.

In her 1956 report on the foundation, Frances describes "bull sessions" among the participants (who rented rooms at the Stone Fence Inn) as extending into the morning. Summarizing the outcome of the first seminar, Frances said, "They came to feel that we were their family and this place their home."[23] Reflecting on her experience of the first Flaherty Seminar nearly forty years later, Cecile Starr observed, "The informality, the prevailing good-will, and the natural beauty of the location, added up to an exhilarating, exhausting, unforgettable event."[24] Starr contended that seminars functioned as a key gathering for those who advocated for cinema as an art.

The Flaherty Seminar had not developed in isolation, however. The geographical location of the Flaherty farm in rural Vermont contributed to identifying the foundation more with its pedagogical than memorial functions. The idea of a retreat in a pastoral area, removed from the pressures and rhythms of daily life in cities in order to explore, foster creativity, and renew with no distractions and total concentration had been launched initially by Middlebury College in Vermont, with its renowned Breadloaf Writers Conference. Robert Frost initiated the idea of a writers' retreat in 1926. The retreat was held each summer in the Green Mountain National Forest of Vermont.[25]

In 1951, classical pianist Rudolph Serkin inaugurated the Marlboro Music Festival in Marlboro, Vermont, dedicated to developing chamber music in an intensive setting and then offering some public concerts. The model Serkin devised differed from a conservatory model of instruction: it featured master artists playing with promising young musicians.[26] Marlboro was a place where up-and-coming young virtuosos could work with established players in hopes of launching their professional careers. Both Breadloaf and Marlboro fostered creativity in a retreat-like setting with established master artists. These gatherings suggest a regional artistic context spurring the emergence of the Flaherty Seminar.

The Marlboro School of Music and Festival showed films every Sunday night in an effort to stimulate creativity through interdisciplinary links. People involved in the early seminars also had connections to the Marlboro Festival. After the first seminar, Frances asked Cinema 16 programmer Amos Vogel if he would select short experimental and first films for the 1956 Marlboro School of Music and Festival. In 1958, David Flaherty asked Vogel to program some shorts for Marlboro again.[27] Dorothy Oshlag,[28] a neighbor of Frances, was involved with the Marlboro Festival in the 1950s. As a key figure in the history of the seminar, she programmed several seminars and served as president of International Film Seminars in 1971–73.

During the 1950s, nonprofits needed a charter in Vermont. With few lawyers in the state, Paul Olson served as one of the first trustees of the Marlboro Festival. He later worked with the Flaherty Seminar throughout the 1950s to argue for tax-exempt status. Dorothy met Paul through the Flaherty Seminars, and they married in 1963.

With the success of the inaugural seminar, Frances and David spent the fall and winter of 1955–56 working to mount the second seminar. Frances was even more determined to advance Robert Flaherty's way of making and thinking about films. She wanted to involve younger people in the seminars. A special scholarship was offered to members of the American Federation of Film Societies (AFFS). In contrast to the policy of not announcing the program in advance that evolved in later decades of the seminar as an extension of the ideas of nonpreconception, the second seminar announced its program to the readers of the AFFS newsletter: Richard Griffith from MoMA; Amos Vogel with a program of films from Cinema 16; and Fred Zinnemann, feature film director of *From Here to Eternity* (1953). The seminar would feature screenings and presentations on *The Land, Louisiana Story, Man of Aran, Moana,* and *Nanook*. Charles Benton from *Encyclopedia Britannica* encouraged Frances to involve more professors from academic institutions to expand the reach and impact of the seminar. Prompted by Benton, David Flaherty invited Jack Ellis to attend the second seminar as Northwestern University's observer.[29] Frances explained to ethnographer Jean Benoît-Lévy that "our seminars, I believe, are the only ones where students can get this unadulterated approach to the technique and discipline of film as a new art."[30]

The second seminar replicated some of the programming of the first seminar. The five central films of the Flaherty opus were screened and analyzed. The days were dedicated to intensive study of the Flaherty films by seminarians. Again, the seminar participants included a mix of distributors, filmmakers, librarians, museum curators, students, and writers. Evening presentations and screenings in the barn were open to the public and required reservations. They presented a heterogeneous mix of approaches to cinema, institutions, and styles. Albert Wasserman presented his Flaherty Award film on mental health, *Out of Darkness* (1956). Jack Churchill reprised his scientific film *Seifritz on Protoplasm*. Classical pianist Rudolph Serkin and folksinger Richard Dyer-Bennet returned on separate evenings. Suzanne Bloch presented a program of medieval, Elizabethan, and Renaissance music for lute, recorders, and virginal. Robert Northshield screened his CBS film, *The Way of the Navajo* (1954). Robert Gardner, the director of the film study center at Harvard and an ethnographic filmmaker, screened John Marshall's *The Hunters* (1957), a film about the South African Bushmen. He also showed unedited rushes. Amos Vogel programmed a selection of experimental films from Cinema 16.[31]

During the day, Frances and David ensured that the Flaherty films received top billing and consideration. As one of the faculty for the second seminar, Richard Griffiths lectured on Eisenstein and showed footage from his unfinished film, *¡Que viva México!* (1930). Arnold Eagle returned, whereas Leacock, Thomson, and Van Dongen did not.[32] The seminar's participants expanded to include Luis Maisonet, Raúl Muñoz, and Angel Rivera from the Puerto Rican Community Education Film Unit. Other participants represented a variety of cinema sectors ranging from CBS, the Methodist Film Commission, the NFB, IBM, the Toronto Film Society, and several colleges and universities, including Harvard University, New York University, Northwestern University, and Radford College.[33] Dorothy Oshlag described her role at the second seminar as "handmaiden to Frances." She observed that Frances could be a "thundercloud if she didn't like something."[34]

Held at the Flaherty farm, the 1957 seminar constituted a turning point in the institutional history of the seminar. The publicity for the third seminar emphasized bringing younger filmmakers together to explore "the nature of film and to take a searching look at its future." For financial reasons, it was shorter than the first two seminars, running for only a week. Again, the Flaherty films would be intensely studied, as well as films "in the spirit of exploration which the Flaherty films represent." An advisory committee, formed to assist the programmer, featured prominent professors who taught film at major universities, belying the notion that the early seminars served filmmakers exclusively. These professors included Erik Barnouw, Columbia University; Jack C. Ellis, Northwestern University; Charles Siepmann, New York University; and George Stoney, The City College of New York.[35] Advancing the educational scope and intention of the seminar, CBS Public Affairs underwrote a scholarship at the urging of Al Wasserman, who had participated in the 1956 seminar.[36]

Cecile Starr has written that at age seventy-three, Frances felt the seminar required a director other than herself to execute planning, organizing, and programming. Frances attended a November 1956 meeting where Hans Richter, Starr, and Fred Zinnemann determined that the seminars should continue, but ascertained it needed additional assistance and expertise. The group selected Andries Deinum. He was a West Coast film scholar and professor whom Frances and Starr had met at the 1953 American Film Assembly in Chicago. Deinum had been fired from USC for his past affiliations with the Communist Party. The group explicitly did not want to connect the Robert Flaherty Foundation with any political cause related to Deinum's dismissal.[37] Deinum's salary was underwritten by Alfred Starr (Cecile's uncle), Zinnemann, and others.

The program for the 1957 seminar repeated the format of the first two years. It showcased the Flaherty films but also significantly expanded beyond them with ethnographic films, state-sponsored documentary, independent documentary, and international art films. John Marshall's *The Hunters* returned. *New Earth* (1933) by left-wing documentarian Joris Ivens; *Night Mail* (1936) by Basil Wright, produced as part of the General Post Office Film Unit under John Grierson; and *The Plow that Broke the Plains* (1936) by Pare Lorentz, produced for the Farm Security Administration were screened. *Pather Panchali* (1955) by Bengali filmmaker Satyajit Ray[38] was also shown.

According to Cecile Starr, the third seminar shifted in other ways. Almost forty seminarians representing Canada, Japan, Puerto Rico, and the United States attended—an expansion from the smaller groups of earlier years.[39] The spirit of camaraderie, goodwill, and intimacy devolved into what she termed "politics, opportunism, and contention." With a larger group, cliques formed among guests and students. The longtime animosities and rivalries between Frances Flaherty and film editor Helen van Dongen burst into the open over discussions of *The Land*.[40]

The 1958 seminar on the Flaherty farm revised the seminar's structure yet again. The Robert Flaherty Foundation offered six one-day weekend conferences from May through July on the Flaherty films, ideas, and practices, aimed at students and teachers "concerned with the vast potential of film."[41] David Flaherty and Frances Flaherty moderated the sessions. The seminar itself returned to a ten-day event. Hugh Gray, a scholar from the Department of Theater Arts at the UCLA, led the seminar discussions, moving the seminar even more toward a more traditional academic model of lectures and guided discussion. In a letter to longtime Flaherty ally Arnold Eagle, Frances reasoned that with Gray's role as discussion leader, "the atmosphere once more will be relaxed and friendly, in marked contrast to last year, when the only guiding idea, so far as I can see, was to stir up antagonisms and animosities where none existed before. Almost all of whom we have since talked with have the same feelings about it."[42] Gray would work with an advisory committee comprised of stalwarts from the previous year such as Barnouw, Ellis, Siepmann, and Stoney. Richard Griffith and Hans Richter joined the committee. The seminar fee increased from $75 to $100, with an additional charge of $60 to cover lodging and food.[43] Frances continued to lecture across the country, donating all of her speaking fees into the scholarship fund for the seminar.

David Flaherty sought to maintain the intimacy of the seminar, capping it at forty participants.[44]

The Flaherty films still occupied a central position at the 1958 seminar, with screenings of *Louisiana Story*, *Man of Aran*, *Moana*, and *Nanook of the North*. *All My Babies* and *The Hunters* returned. However, the thrust of the programming veered toward a more international perspective. Films were screened from Canada and Puerto Rico. Jean Renoir's *The River* (1951) and Jean Rouch's *Les maîtres fous* (1955) represented France. *Overture* (1958) was produced by the United Nations Film Unit.

But one filmmaker arrived from India whose presence at the seminar rippled out to the burgeoning independent film movements, the nontheatrical film community, and the seminar itself: Satyajit Ray. The United States Information Service (USIS) provided a special grant to bring Ray to the 1958 seminar. The seminars screened the first two films of his trilogy, *Aparajito* and *Pather Panchali* (1956) in advance of their theatrical release in the United States. *Pather Panchali* earned accolades on the international film festival circuit, with the grand prize at the 1956 Cannes Film Festival, recognition at the Edinburgh International Film Festival, the top award at the 1957 San Francisco International Film Festival, and first prize at the 1958 Stratford International Film Festival in Ontario.

Ray epitomized the kind of independent cinema championed by Frances. He worked outside commercial Indian cinema and operated within a poetic realist narrative style featuring everyday people.[45] Barnouw attended this seminar. For him, Ray "epitomized what many in the group were reaching for—work done not in an industry process but rather in an artisan tradition, by artists in control of what they were doing." Ray worked beyond the established hierarchies of Indian cinema. He was a "filmmaker," a term Barnouw noted was regularly used to imply an independent rebelliousness from the industrial system and the burdens of fund-raising and distribution.[46] Ray's participation in the seminar represented a pivotal moment, expanding the seminar beyond its exclusive focus on the Flaherty films and US-produced films toward an engagement with international cinema advancing similar aims of independence, noncommercial formulas, and poetics. After the seminar, the October issue of the America Federation of Film Societies newsletter published an article honoring Ray, noting that *Pather Panchali* was "praised for its poetic quality and its deep feeling for the dignity of man." The article noted Ray had attended the fourth annual Robert Flaherty Film Seminar on the Flaherty farm. "De Sica, Flaherty, Pudovkin, Renoir and Ford have all profoundly influenced me," Ray explained in the article.[47]

By 1959, the Flaherty Seminar continued to recalibrate its familialism into a more institutional and national organization. It took a major step toward professionalizing as an educational institution: the University Extension of UCLA served as host for the fifth seminar. Under its auspices, the seminar convened at the University of California, Santa Barbara, campus. An internal International Film Seminars document from the early 1960s contended that the seminars had achieved "a prestige which resulted in several universities and other organizations offering to serve as hosts to subsequent Robert Flaherty Film Seminars."[48]

The brochure for the 1959 seminar amplified the educational goals of the seminar beyond the Flaherty films. It emphasized the seminar served as "an exploration and study of films made in the Flaherty spirit," an expansion and revision from prior semi-nars that focused on analysis of the Flaherty films as a core privileged activity. By 1959, the seminar identified itself as "unique in scope and method." It sought to understand the "power of the camera to enlarge for man a vision and understanding of his environment and world," and to unleash the potential of filmmaking and television.

The seminar developed and solidified its pedagogical method. It was structured with three major open sessions a day. Small discussion meetings probed particular topics such as editing, educational films, music, narrative, nonactors, nonpreconceptions, sound, sponsorship and economics of film, and staging versus life caught unawares. The 1959 seminar brochure reiterated the notion of "study" and the commitment to "interna-tionalism." It would screen selected works from what it termed "important" American, Asian, and European filmmakers, with a focus on ethnographic filmmaking. French ethnographic filmmaker Jean Rouch was announced as the featured guest, echoing the position of Ray from the year before with the showcasing of a major international art filmmaker with a body of work.[49] However, Rouch did not attend the seminar. Instead, his wife presented the films.[50]

The staff for the 1959 seminar underscored the university linkages that the Flaherty Seminar sought to enhance and strengthen. Six of the eleven staff members were academics—Jack Ellis from Northwestern University; R. Philip Chamberlin, Hugh Gray, Evelyn Hooker, and Hans Meyerhoff from UCLA; and Edmund J. King from the University of London and Harvard University. Experimental filmmaker Shirley Clarke served on the staff, as did Jack Churchill and Frances Flaherty.

The administrative work and Flaherty family arguments leading up to the 1959 semi-nar reveal how the Flaherty Seminar operated at the junction of the development of postwar international art cinema in festivals and art houses, the exciting noncommercial domains of film societies, the expanding world of nontheatrical distribution, and the newly emerging notion of university film education. For example, in a letter to Edna Giesen, Frances Flaherty outlined some ideas that Flaherty allies had proffered for expanding nontheatrical distribution. Charles Benton of *Encyclopedia Britannica* pushed for films for secondary schools, while Erik Barnouw wanted to see more films available for universities. Learning that Jean Rouch was invited to the 1959 seminar, Amos Vogel asked Frances if the Flaherty Foundation could present him and his work at Cinema 16, so that both organizations could benefit from the publicity.[51]

By 1959, the Robert Flaherty Foundation shifted away from its goals of procuring non-theatrical distribution rights to the films and presenting touring Flaherty festivals. Frances continued to do presentations on the "Flaherty Way" with the films and pour her honoraria into seminar scholarships. The foundation's primary activity now centered on the execution and programming of the annual seminar. The idea that the seminar would always be look-ing toward the future and to the next generation intensified. According to film historian and longtime Flaherty participant and board member Erik Barnouw, from the beginning, the seminar was "meant to spur—empower—young cineastes of independent mind."[52]

However, the linkages to a larger, more established academic institution such as UCLA generated anxiety among the East Coast Flaherty insiders. The transition from a family-run operation promoting the "Flaherty Way" to a collaboration with an academic institution implied less control and less intimacy. It also threatened less focus on Flaherty himself. The first four seminars took place at the Flaherty farm—an informal retreat in a rural setting and a noninstitutional setting identified with Frances and Robert. The fifth seminar marked the institutionalization of the seminar. It solidified its academic partnerships. In a long letter to Frances and David, Arnold Eagle contended that the partnership with UCLA would be beneficial to the foundation, which he assessed as filling a need in film education in the United States. However, he worried that institutional partnerships would mean a larger seminar and less involvement from Frances and David. He argued: "I don't think the seminar can be too big and still remain effective. . . . It is the personal touch that you two provide that gives it the intimate and warm feeling that one gets when attending the seminar."[53]

Throughout the decades of the seminar, these academic connections operated in intensely contradictory ways. On the one hand, the Flaherty Seminar in the early years needed the legitimation and prestige of elite academic institutions that were also involved in the nontheatrical film society organizations. On the other hand, trustees of the seminar feared these larger institutions would threaten the intimacies and intensities of the meetings. They worried academics would rationalize the looser, more intuitive "Flaherty Way." In a letter to Arnold Eagle regarding the 1959 UCLA seminar, David Flaherty cautioned, "the more of the old guard, the faithful, we can muster out there, the better it will be."[54]

Although in later years the seminar interpreted nonpreconception not as a pedagogy but as a programming practice where a film schedule was not provided and films were not announced, the 1959 seminar evidenced a different strategy. The publicity for this seminar listed the films that would be shown and, most significantly, listed their prior festival awards. The films represented the most international scope of any seminar to date: a film from Pakistani filmmaker A. J. Kardar, *Day Shall Dawn* (1959); three films from Indian narrative filmmaker Satyajit Ray—*Pather Panchali, Aparajito,* and *World of Apu* (1959); and three films from French ethnographic filmmaker Jean Rouch—*Les fils de l'eau* (1953), *Les Maîtres Fous,* and *Moi, un noir* (1958). The four major Flaherty films, by now an ensconced tradition, were *Louisiana Story, Man of Aran, Moana,* and *Nanook of the North.* The seminar rescreened works from previous seminars, which underscored its educational intentions rather than curatorial interventions, such as John Marshall's *The Hunters.* The Robert Flaherty Award films were also featured: Churchill's *Seifritz on Protoplasm* and Stoney's *All My Babies.*[55]

This tactic of naming the films suggested three historical movements. First, it clearly represented a natural evolution from the earlier seminars on the farm that explicitly focused on the Flaherty films and the "Flaherty Way," as extrapolated by Frances. Second, it emphasized selections from the international art cinema festival circuit, a justification for intensive study and probing discussion. Third, the educational mission of the seminar to engage the next generation of filmmakers through immersive study of aesthetics, economic strategies, and production was paramount. In contrast to protocols of later seminars, films were rescreened for further study.

In 1960, the Robert Flaherty Foundation dissolved. The 1960 seminar was the last one convened under the auspices of the foundation. Its almost-decade-long quest for tax-exempt status proved unsuccessful. A new nonprofit educational corporation, International Film Seminars, Inc. (IFS), was created in hopes of attracting tax-exempt gifts. The Flaherty name was removed.

According to Dorothy Oshlag Olson, Erik Barnouw conjured the name International Film Seminars. Three converging ideas propelled him: the fact that the majority of the Flaherty films were produced outside of the United States; Frances's international orientation generated from her personal connections to film groups and filmmakers in Canada, England, France, India, Pakistan, Puerto Rico, and Scotland; and the presence of Satyajit Ray at the seminar.[56] At the time, Barnouw supervised a group of Columbia University courses on film, radio, and television. Paul Olson drew up the incorporation papers. He traveled to Washington, DC, with Barnouw and Frances to offer arguments to the US Department of the Treasury. With the arguments provided by Barnouw and the legal skills of Olson, the Treasury finally granted tax-exempt status. IFS operated quite differently from the Robert Flaherty Foundation. It functioned much more professionally with a board. It was less tied to the Flaherty family. Moreover, it was housed at Columbia University in the Center for Mass Communication, administered by Barnouw and Dorothy Oshlag. Barnouw served as the first president, a term spanning eight years.

Flaherty stalwarts Jack Churchill and Shirley Clarke served as trustees with Frances and David. David worked to build an advisory board with people from different sectors of the nontheatrical world, including Leo Dratfield from Contemporary Films, Jack Ellis from Northwestern University, and filmmaker Hans Richter.[57] Under the new administrative structure of IFS, the Flaherty Seminar's purpose clarified and sharpened. As an educational organization, it furthered the study of film as an art. It explored how film could communicate human values. It sought to gather together people from different countries. It created a space to convene emerging and established practitioners working in all aspects of the nontheatrical cinema field—academics; filmmakers; film society programmers; intellectuals; museum curators; musicians; nontheatrical film distributors; scientific, ethnographic, and educational film producers; and writers—to discuss the future of cinema.[58]

1958 ROBERT GARDNER WITH JOHN MARSHALL—ON *THE HUNTERS* (1957)

> *Robert Gardner*: About three years ago, I was a graduate student in anthropology at Harvard, and John was an undergraduate student. We met and talked about film and about what he and his family were doing in Africa. By that time, they had spent two or three years in Africa among the Bushmen, doing ethnographic and cinematic work. I had come from Seattle where I had done a little film, where I'd also taught the history of art, and somehow, all these things converged to make sense out of a proposal, and I don't know who made it, that the Peabody Museum go earnestly into the matter of using photography and film. It seemed like a good idea; enough people had talked about it and enough people agreed that it was, and so, with the backing of the museum, we were able to set up a room about fifty-feet square, divided according to our needs. One part of the room is a space for storing film. I was telling

Mrs. Flaherty that we have long lists of films we'd like to store there, but no money to buy them, so there is still room if anybody wants to give us some film.

We have editing facilities at the museum, of course, and all of the usual apparatus for seeing films and putting them together. No Moviola yet, but I've gotten so used to working without one, and I think John has, too, that I don't miss it. We're in the process of installing a sound facility; it's going to be awfully good because it's a Selson interlock system—I'm sure some of you know what I mean—what's called a sound-chain, a way to put many sounds together in synchrony. This usually can only be achieved by going to New York or to Hollywood, so having it right under our thumbs is going to be very good; we're going to be able to do things with sound that as a rule are impossible to do. The cost is usually so high that people do as much as they possibly can beforehand, then race through narration sessions and through the mixing sessions, working much more quickly than they might like.

What we hope will happen eventually is that we'll be successful enough with the film the Marshalls brought back and presented to the museum, to be able to interest agencies of one kind or another—educational institutions, government organizations, private foundations—to support the same sort of project in other parts of the world. Right now, we are two people working on half a million feet of film; it feels a bit like trying to bail out the Pacific Ocean. It's a tremendous job to just see all the material, and to think about pulling twenty-five films together out of this material is, to say at least, boldly optimistic. But I think we'll do it, if we can get the money we need and if we can keep our health.

Since money is so hard to get, and since brains seem to cost a lot less than films, we also *think* at the museum, or at least we think we think. We think about what film has to offer anthropology. Or we can put it the other way: what does anthropology have to offer film? It would also be nice to have some people helping us, not just mechanically or financially, but conceptually, to arrive at—if I may put it in one word—a *style* that makes sense from the point of view of film and anthropology. Toward that end, I've persuaded my department at Harvard to offer a course which will be, I think, the first course ever given at Harvard on film. It will be a seminar primarily for graduate students in anthropology.

Well, I thought I would throw out a couple of ideas that I hope John won't take too much exception to—I've written these thoughts down without consulting him. I'm going to read two sentences and then develop their implications a little bit. The first sentence: "Vision, the act of seeing, is an inventive process." Sounds pretty banal, but perhaps it's good to get it said right away. The second: "Filming, the act of recording optical phenomenon, insofar as it is used as a means of giving expression to vision, is a creative process." Now, what I'm interested in is the implications of these two statements for anthropology and for the idea of using film in anthropology.

I think one implication is that anthropology is not a science in the natural sciences sense—maybe it's a social science. It's not a science because it has no means for measuring the variables of its subject matter. We don't have cloud chambers, we don't have temperature gauges, we don't have completely accurate scales; we don't have *any* of the instruments that provide the kinds of measurements that anybody can make on phenomena and everyone can agree on. We do have IBM machines, but we don't really put people through them, just pieces of paper. Really, all we have as anthropologists is our sense organs, which we know are fallible.

As one of the humanities, anthropology's chief concern is with relations between people, and its best means of discerning these relations is by way of sensitive observation, through informed feelings. Some anthropologists prefer to investigate the relations between different forms of basketry in South America, but I think that most anthropologists would agree that it is the relations between people that are the main concern of anthropology, and as I say, we have no way of understanding these relations except through observation.

At the same time, simply observing human relations, seeing or feeling them, doesn't add to any corpus of knowledge about these relations until we can *convey* our observations, our feelings. And our principle mode of conveying such things up until today has been through writing. All anthropologists write and they write a lot. But it's conceivable that amongst the possible choices, the possible ways in which feelings and observations can be expressed, film—particularly when film is a creative process—can, like our eyes, serve as a way of making evaluations. What I'm saying here I think is that every time we look at something, we are evaluating. If anthropology uses film, the possibility exists for having a new kind of moral science, a branch of learning solely concerned with the evaluation of human experience.

F *(Flaherty seminarian)*: I'm not sure I follow. Do you mean that the idea of a moral science necessarily follows from the idea that film is an interpretive medium?

Gardner: I'm saying that a moral science of anthropology is more feasible using film because film makes a more palpable evaluation of human experience than most anthropologists' writing can.

The other thing that I wanted to take up is something a little bit more concrete, what I call *style*, for want of a better word: that is, the particular form in which an anthropological film emerges. I've set one criterion for judging whether a factor is important or unimportant: whether it enhances or clarifies the meaning of whatever image or sequence is being used. Let's say an evaluation has been made about something and that a person making a film wants to convey this evaluation. I'm interested in finding out what stylistic factors are necessary to make this meaning most clear—or, let's say, least cloudy. One is composition: that is, how we frame what we see. Another is steadiness: the steadiness of the image, whether a tripod is used or not. Focus is another factor; we can use focus to clarify. Sometimes we can use *distortion* to clarify—of course, distortion can also be used to muddle things up, as a way of escaping meaning or of substituting an irrelevant meaning. Still another factor is what kind of film stock are you going to use: are you going to use fast film or slow film? Choosing slow film probably means that you're going to use color: *why* are you going to use color? What's important about color? If it enhances meaning, maybe it's important. And how are we to think about sound? I'm thinking about such things as sync; is it important to use sync? Is it important to go to all the trouble of setting up a very awkward and cumbersome technical arrangement in order to get the words or the breath or whatever it is at the same time that the picture is being taken? Sound also involves the spoken word and I hope John will talk about that. Basically, how free are we as anthropologists to use imagination in putting films together?

Another factor is training: how much training is necessary for making anthropological films? I'm taking for granted that technical training is available; of course, somebody who doesn't know how to use the camera, no matter if he has the best intentions, shouldn't begin. But I mean training in the field: in John's and my case, in Africa. How much training should we have in the language that's being spoken? How much training in the discipline of anthropology itself? How much psychological training should the filmmaker have? Should he be analyzed?—I'm not being facetious here; I think a lot of films collapse because of the naïve psychology of the person making them.

I'd like to ask John, since I've sprung all this on him, whether he wants to say anything.

F: I'm not quite sure just how much interpretive leeway you feel an anthropologist has, not necessarily in film as a means of conveying some aspect of this work, but in any form of communications.

Gardner: That's an impossible question to answer. I think every anthropologist would agree that honesty is essential. In other words, you can at least create this threshold: if he is honest, he is perfectly free to interpret as he will. This, of course, includes both honesty to himself as well as honesty to his data. Perhaps, if you disagree with his interpretation, you might say that he didn't gather the right data or that his data is dishonest. There's a lot of subjectivity here.

F: You're allowing a great deal of subjectivity, providing the man has his credentials, that he is in fact an anthropologist.

Gardner: An anthropologist is a professional observer; he's equipped to a certain extent to look for certain things and he will find them more quickly than a nonanthropologist. But if he lacks sensitivity, if he lacks discernment, if he lacks sympathy, it doesn't make any difference how much training he's had.

John?

John Marshall: I'd like to say a little bit about the difference between the kind of imaging that goes on when one reads and when one watches a film, and why film is the thing to help anthropologists make a contribution to understanding their subject. There are obviously things you can do with writing that you can't do with film; but what you can do with film that you can't do with writing?

There are a number of anthropological books where you don't feel anything at all; you read about the structure of a society or a people and you get the impression of somebody setting up little paper dolls here and little paper dolls there and rustling them together and taking them apart—you don't get any sense of real life. There are also anthropological books that are honest and quite beautifully written. When one reads these books, one can imagine, one can see, and feel; one can get a sense of the vital importance of such a thing as social structure, which is life itself. In this kind of work, you do actually create images when you read the words; they're little doors that lead to images.

Having said that, I think there's still a difference and a very important one between what happens when you image from this reading and the kind of thing you see on the screen during a film. This difference has to do with all kinds of traditions in language and certain linguistic limitations on words themselves: that is, associations that a culture will have with words. When you read something about an unfamiliar culture, even something that makes a vital impression, you're inevitably using old ideas; these old ideas have to be latent in you in order for your reading to mean something. Words evoke images based on what you've already internalized. But when you see something about an unfamiliar culture on the screen, it's always new, because the person you're seeing is right there; you're forced to take into account something totally different, totally outside yourself.

I think this makes the whole idea of anthropological film valid.

Hugh Gray: Any other questions?

F: Just a quick one: are these two films we're going to see both done by your group?

Gardner: No, these are two films that were given to the museum, and there are two reasons for showing them: one reason is that everyone who has not seen *Song of Ceylon* [1934] should see it, particularly when you're attending a film seminar, but they represent two quite divergent styles in what's called anthropological film. *Song of Ceylon* is done with great imagination, with great sensitivity, with great liberality as far as the reality of a culture is concerned. The other film was done by someone who's got one interest only and that is in illustrating what the diet of a particular group of people is. The two films represent very distinct options. [The incomplete record of the films shown at the 1958 seminar does not make possible an identification of the film shown with *Song of Ceylon*.]

Notes

1. Quoted in Cecile Starr, "Recollections of Frances Flaherty and the Early Flaherty Seminars," in "The Flaherty: Four Decades in the Cause of Independent Cinema," ed. Erik Barnouw and Patricia Zimmermann, *Wide Angle* 17, Special Issue (1995): 170 (hereafter cited as "The Flaherty").
2. Bill Sloan, phone interview by Patricia R. Zimmermann, July 28, 2009.
3. Bill Sloan, phone interview.
4. Lee Grieveson and Haidee Wasson, eds., *Inventing Film Studies* (Durham, NC: Duke University Press, 2008), 408–9.
5. Ibid.
6. Internal Revenue Service Tax Exemption Petition from the Robert Flaherty Foundation, 1956, The Robert J. Flaherty Papers, Butler Library, Columbia University Libraries (hereafter cited as Flaherty Papers).
7. David Flaherty to Floria Lasky of Fitelson and Mayers, New York City, September 19, 1955, Flaherty Papers.
8. Frances Flaherty to Virginia Sears, February 26, 1955. See also David Flaherty to Jean Epstein, January 6, 1955, Flaherty Papers.
9. Frances Flaherty to Natalie Chapin, February 5, 1955, Flaherty Papers.
10. Dorothy Olson, phone interview by Patricia R. Zimmermann, September 25, 2009.
11. Frances Flaherty to Jonas Mekas, October 5, 1955, International Film Seminars Private Collection, International Film Seminars/The Flaherty, New York (hereafter cited as IFS Collection).
12. Frances Flaherty, draft of ideas for development of Flaherty Seminar, ca. 1955, IFS Collection.
13. Robert Flaherty Foundation, flyer inviting advanced students and workers in films to participate in an exploration of the world of Robert Flaherty, 1955, IFS Collection.
14. Eagle had worked with the radical and communist-oriented Workers Film and Photo League in the 1930s, had shot still photos for Roosevelt's Works Progress Administration, and ended up as a cameraman on *Louisiana Story* in the late 1940s.
15. "Works Screened at the Flaherty: 1955–1994," in "The Flaherty," 24.
16. "A Report on the Activities of the Robert Flaherty Foundation, Inc., July 1, 1954–March 31, 1956," IFS Collection.
17. Ibid., 4.

18. Ibid., 5.
19. Eric J. Sandeen, *Picturing an Exhibition: The Family of Man and 1950s America* (Albuquerque; University of New Mexico Press, 1995), 95–103.
20. Fred Turner, *The Democratic Surround: Multimedia and American Liberalism from World War II to the Psychedelic Sixties* (Chicago: University of Chicago Press, 2013), 205–9.
21. Ibid., 183.
22. Roland Barthes, "La Grande Famille des Hommes," in *Mythologies* (Paris: Editions du Seuil, 1957), 173–76; Allan Sekula, "The Traffic in Photographs," *Art Journal* (Spring 1981): 15–21; Susan Sontag, "Happenings: An Art of Radical Juxtaposition," in *Against Interpretation and Other Essays* (New York: Delta Books 1981), 263–74.
23. "A Report on the Activities of the Robert Flaherty Foundation, Inc., July 1, 1954–March 31, 1956," 5.
24. Starr, "Recollections of Frances Flaherty and the Early Flaherty Seminars," in "The Flaherty," 170.
25. For an anecdotal history, see Theodore Morrison, *Breadloaf Writers' Conference: The First Thirty Years 1926–1955* (Middlebury, VT: Middlebury College Press, 1976).
26. For an institutional history from the point of view of musicians, see Diana Burgwyn, *Marlboro Music: A Fifty Year Portrait, 1951–2000* (Marlboro, VT: Marlboro Music Festival, 2001). For a history from the point of view of its founding artistic director, see Rudolph Serkin, *Marlboro Music: The First 25 Years 1951–1975* (Marlboro, VT: Marlboro School and Music Festival, 1976).
27. Frances Flaherty to Amos Vogel, August 29, 1955; David Flaherty to Amos Vogel, May 17, 1958, Flaherty Papers.
28. Dorothy Oshlag was a print journalist with *Architectural Forum* and *Time*; she eventually worked with Erik Barnouw at the Center for Mass Communication at Columbia University. Oshlag had met Frances Flaherty at a New York Film Council lunch in the mid-1950s.
29. Frances Flaherty and Charles Benton exchanged a series of letters regarding increasing outreach to academics at universities between 1955 and 1956. See also Frances Flaherty to Francis Butler, March 28, 1958; "Special Scholarship," *American Federation of Film Societies Newsletter* (Spring 1955), 3; David Flaherty to Jack Ellis, June 11, 1956, Flaherty Papers.
30. Frances Flaherty to Jean Benoît-Lévy, May 16, 1956, 2, Flaherty Papers.
31. "Invitation to Robert Flaherty Foundation Events in Connection with Its Second Annual Seminar," 1956, IFS Collection.
32. Starr, "Recollections of Frances Flaherty and the Early Flaherty Seminars," in "The Flaherty," 170.
33. "A Partial List of Participants in the Robert Flaherty Film Seminar," 1962, 109, IFS Collection.
34. Dorothy Olson, phone interview by Patricia R. Zimmermann, September 18, 2009.
35. "Announcement of the Third Annual Robert Flaherty Film Seminar, 1957," IFS Collection.
36. Frances Flaherty to Al Wasserman, June 5, 1957, Flaherty Papers.
37. Cecile Starr, "Informal Report on Meetings with Frances Flaherty," November 10–11, 1956, Flaherty Papers.
38. Ray attended the seminar the following year.
39. David Flaherty to Arnold Eagle, August 7, 1957; David Flaherty to Amos Vogel, October 1, 1957, Flaherty Papers.
40. Starr, "Recollections of Frances Flaherty and the Early Flaherty Seminars," in "The Flaherty," 171.
41. "Announcement of Week-End Conferences, 1958 at the Flaherty Foundation in Dummerston, Near Brattleboro, Vermont," Archives of the International Film Seminars, New York.

42. Frances Flaherty to Arnold Eagle, February 27, 1958, Flaherty Papers.
43. "Announcement for the Fourth Annual Robert Flaherty Seminar, August 18–28, 1958," IFS Collection.
44. David Flaherty to Arnold Eagle, June 12, 1958, Flaherty Papers.
45. "Special Announcement," Robert Flaherty Foundation, 1958, IFS Collection.
46. Erik Barnouw, "Dummerston Days," in "The Flaherty," 173.
47. "AFFS Honors Satyajit Ray," *American Federation of Film Societies Newsletter*, October 1958, 6, Flaherty Papers.
48. "The Robert Flaherty Film Seminars-Background Information," 1963, 1, IFS Collection.
49. "Announcement for the Fifth Annual Robert Flaherty Film Seminars," 1959, 1, IFS Collection.
50. David Flaherty to Empire Films, July 31, 1959, Flaherty Papers.
51. Frances Flaherty to Edna Giesen, May 1, 1959; Amos Vogel to Frances Flaherty, May 13, 1959, Flaherty Papers.
52. Erik Barnouw and Patricia R. Zimmermann, "Prologue," in "The Flaherty," 1.
53. Arnold Eagle to Frances Flaherty and David Flaherty, July 11, 1959, 2, Flaherty Papers.
54. David Flaherty to Arnold Eagle, June 3, 1959, Flaherty Papers.
55. "Announcement for the Fifth Annual Robert Flaherty Film Seminars," 1959, 2, IFS Collection.
56. Dorothy Olson, phone interview by Patricia R. Zimmermann, September 25, 2009.
57. David Flaherty to Arnold Eagle, November 9, 1960, Flaherty Papers.
58. "Draft Proposal to the Louis W. and Maud Hill Foundation," May 26, 1961, Flaherty Papers.

The 1969 Flaherty Seminar at Hotchkiss in Lakeville, CT. Photo courtesy of International Film Seminars/Inc./The Flaherty, New York.

3

AN ORGANIZATION, 1960–1969

By 1960, the family-run Flaherty Foundation had transformed into a nonprofit organization, International Film Seminars (IFS). The Flaherty Seminar's administration moved from a family-run project located on the Flaherty farm in Vermont to the Center for Mass Communication (CMC) at Columbia University in New York City, a significant shift from the idyllic, isolated setting in the rural Northeast to the epicenter of US intellectual life in an embassy, major global media, museum entrepôt. Across the decades the Flaherty Seminar straddled these contradictory locations: the administrative and operational nerve center would remain in New York City, while the seminar itself would be held outside of New York in a more pastoral, retreat-like setting, an evocation of the Flaherty farm seminar experience in Dummerston, Vermont.

In the first twenty years, the seminar gathered together people who might never have met in their regular work lives: distributors, film academics, journalists, librarians, programmers, and students. Filmmakers from various university specialty film units documenting agriculture, education, and health also attended. This heterogeneity of participants generated intensity and interdisciplinarity. Many felt they were carving out a new territory for considering a more artistic and intellectual cinema than John Grierson's conceptualization of documentary as a driver of national citizenship and identity. Frances Flaherty disdained Grierson. She contended he imposed a state ideology onto subject matter and a specific form of instrumental spectatorship onto spectators. Although these participants represented a large, diverse swathe of the 1960s media ecology, they were homogeneous in other ways. A majority of the participants and all the seminar programmers hailed from the east coast corridor that stretched from New York City to Boston to Philadelphia to Vermont to Montreal and Toronto—in other words, artistic, business, intellectual, and media hubs. Most participants were white and male. Many women attendees were wives of participants.

The seminar seeded a significant shift in language defining independent film. The history of the Flaherty Seminar provides an instructive reminder that independent film is not a static category but an endlessly changing and shape-shifting constellation of aesthetic approaches, distribution strategies, exhibition sites, histories, ideologies, institutions, organizations, people, practices, and sectors. As Erik Barnouw observed,

"Over the decades Flaherty became a venue where new working alliances took shape and genres caught fire. These confrontations, dedicated to Robert Flaherty, seemed to chronicle the story of independent filmmaking since his time."[1] The seminar both reflected and contributed to the history of independent film. In the 1950s, artisanal, individual, and poetic vision demarcated independent film at the Flaherty, a distinctly anti-Hollywood position. In the 1960s, prompted by direct cinema pioneer Robert Drew and other American direct cinema practitioners like Ricky Leacock and D. A. Pennebaker, the term *filmmaker* emerged. It suggested new lighter-weight cameras and sound recorders as well as small crews, which not only liberated the camera to move but also disposed of the division of labor of Hollywood and the networks, thus offering more creative control.

"The Flaherty Seminar had a cachet in the 1960s," mused Bill Sloan, the longtime and extremely influential film librarian at the Museum of Modern Art (MoMA). In 1958, Sloan had been instrumental in establishing the New York Public Library's film library. He explained the importance of the Flaherty Seminar during this period: "There was nothing else like it; festivals had not come in yet. It was well known in documentary and film society circles. People wanted to go; it was a goal, to get to attend it."[2] According to Sloan, almost all film exhibitions outside of the film society movement were commercial or focused on the history of silent film. Richard Griffith, the head of film at MoMA, knew Frances; he was a key figure at the early seminars. The Flaherty provided a place to view difficult-to-access documentary, experimental, and international cinema. It was a rare chance to meet the filmmakers themselves. Sloan attended his first seminar in 1964. "Nothing has its intensity," Sloan recalled.[3]

The period from 1960 to 1969 can best be described as the "Erik Barnouw and direct cinema meets poetic realism" years. Barnouw was now a historian of mass communication, and one of the first scholars to research and write about documentary. He had worked to establish IFS as a nonprofit organization disconnected from the Flaherty name, moving its headquarters to CMC at Columbia University in New York City. CMC served as a funnel for government media contracts and print publications. Barnouw was a professor of mass communications there and head of the center. He served as the first president of IFS from 1960 to 1968—seminal years that refined how the seminar was produced, what was programmed, and who participated. Barnouw worked to internationalize the seminar to align it with its new organizational identity. He shaped both the internal operations and public presentation of the seminar as "an annual opportunity for young filmmakers to exchange ideas in an informal, concentrated session, under the stimulus of leading film artists and their work." For Barnouw, the seminars operated similarly to writers' conferences as retreats to embolden and inspire the next generation.[4]

In 1964, Barbara Van Dyke became the first executive director of IFS, a position she commanded for seventeen years.[5] She was married to Willard Van Dyke, director of the film department at MoMA and a well-known documentary filmmaker. She was also an employee of CMC. Beginning in 1960 when CMC achieved nonprofit status, attorney Paul Olson served as clerk. He donated his time as IFS clerk for nearly fifty years. He eventually married Dorothy Oshlag, who later served as president and a seminar programmer.

In the 1930s, Barnouw was a gifted script writer for CBS and NBC radio. In the 1940s, he had established a reputation in media circles as president of the Radio Writers Guild. During World War II, Barnouw was in charge of the Armed Forces Radio Service Educational Division. By 1957, he assumed the chair of the Writers Guild of America. He was an extraordinarily prolific media historian, producing the landmark three-volume *History of American Broadcasting* (1966).[6] Barnouw's early scholarship focused on radio and television, shifting to film later. His book, *The Sponsor: Notes on a Modern Potentate* (1978), developed from presentations he delivered at the Flaherty Seminar in the 1950s.[7]

Dorothy Oshlag Olson has observed that Barnouw relished the experience of the Flaherty Seminar where he could learn about emerging film movements and new ideas. He also loved teaching and exploring media with students. In the Flaherty Seminar, he found a place that combined these two passions: it facilitated engagement with emerging scholars and makers and sparked ideas.[8] His CMC offered IFS desk space, a neutral zone that positioned the Flaherty as an organization rather than as a family tribute, and visibility in the New York art and media scenes. Like many who found themselves intoxicated by the sense of community and exploration of the Flaherty, Barnouw would have a lifelong involvement on the board of trustees, as a programmer, and later as a scholarly chronicler of the seminar's history.

Olson worked for Erik Barnouw at the CMC for seventeen years and with the Flaherty for six decades. Olson had attended Oberlin College, where she majored in philosophy. Graduating in the pit of the Great Depression, she worked as a journalist for a local newspaper. Eventually, in 1940, she landed a job at *Architectural Forum*, at the time owned by Time Inc. As men were drafted into the US war effort in Europe and the Pacific, opportunities for women opened up. A few years later, Olson moved to the Time Inc. corporate offices in New York City. In 1945, Time Inc. sought a foothold in foreign markets; they sent Olson to Europe to investigate printing facilities. She stayed four years. When she returned to the United States, she landed a job at CMC working with Barnouw. Together, they produced films for the US Department of Health on venereal disease and other public health topics.[9]

Olson had participated in the early seminars at the farm. Robert Flaherty loved the intensity of New York City, while Frances sought out the quiet and repose of the farm in Dummerston. According to Olson, despite Frances's quest for solitude, she felt isolated there. After Robert's death, she wanted to surround herself with interesting intellectuals, artists, and ideas. Olson contended that Frances always wanted to be a more central part of film culture but was always positioned as second fiddle to Robert. She claimed Frances was the intellectual and marketing power behind the films. The establishment of the seminars gave her authorship, prestige, recognition, and space. Frances was an intimidating, strong presence. Frances and Dorothy became close friends.[10] At the 1956 seminar, Olson served as a sort of handmaiden to Frances, who, she observed, could be "a thundercloud if she didn't like something."[11]

Olson participated in the New York Film Council, where she had initially met Frances. Many of the people who participated in the Film Council ended up attending the Flaherty Seminar. At the monthly council meetings, films were screened with their makers present for discussion, paralleling the Flaherty model. The seminar in the 1950s relied on word of mouth—the council functioned as a clearing house for information on the nontheatrical sector and generated news about the Flaherty.

One of the first IFS annual meetings took place not in New York City, but at the Flaherty farm in Vermont. Erik Barnouw presided. Trustees were veterans of the Flaherty Seminars on the family farm in the 1950s: David Flaherty, Frances Flaherty, film scholar Arthur Knight, Dorothy Oshlag, and Cecile Starr.[12] In late 1960, Frances decided to turn over to IFS the controlling interest in *Nanook of the North*. IFS would accrue 51 percent of the royalties in hopes that these funds, although never a large amount, might help to fund the seminar in some small way. Frances would retain the remaining 49 percent.[13]

The new nonprofit organization also instituted an impressive advisory board. In the words of David Flaherty, the board's membership was crafted "to give the organization a truly international character." The advisory board members included former seminarians and colleagues whom Frances and David had met through the noncommercial media circuits and gatherings in the 1950s: film director Thorold Dickinson (Great Britain), filmmaker A. J. Kardar (Pakistan), feature narrative film director Satyajit Ray (India), ethnographic filmmaker Jean Rouch (France), and documentary filmmaker Henri Storck (Belgium).[14] Dickinson was also one of the first professors of film in the United Kingdom. From 1956 to 1960, he served as chief of film services at the United Nations, an organization whose mission resonated with Frances's goals of humanism and internationalism through cinema. Storck not only codirected *Misère au Borinage* (1933) with radical Dutch filmmaker Joris Ivens but had also cofounded the Cinémathèque Royale de Belgique.

The transition from family legacy project to nonprofit institution generated debate in Flaherty seminar circles. This pattern of rancorous boards would surface across the decades as those connected with Frances and the seminars butted heads with the larger noncommercial media worlds of distributors, exhibitors, museums, and universities. Throughout the 1950s, various academics such as Jack Ellis from Northwestern University and Robert Steele from Boston University tried to collaborate with Frances to augment the visibility and prestige of the seminar. Their dedication to the exploration of documentary, their interest in advocating for the noncommercial cinema sectors, and their passion for the seminar experience energized their contributions.

Enthused by the seminar and the idea of creating dialogues between emerging and established filmmakers, Steele set up a Flaherty working group in Boston called the Boston Committee of Friends of Flaherty. Steele possessed a big vision: he wanted to keep David Flaherty working full time to advance the Flaherty seminar, coordinate the new literature published on Flaherty and his films, create a study center at the Flaherty farm, establish an endowment, and preserve the Flaherty films.[15]

However, the group's explicit interest in connecting the Flaherty to university film education precipitated Frances's concern and ire. In an angry letter to Frances in 1961, Steele observed: "You speak of your regret we couldn't have all continued to work together. We will continue working together, I hope, but we just can't do what we envisioned. It seemed you pulled a rug from beneath us which sent us reeling and set up conditions which make it impossible for us to continue the launching of an education program as we all thought was needed and desired."[16]

Frances often lashed out at people who tried to either redirect the Flaherty Seminar or who offered a different point of view on Robert Flaherty. For example, she criticized virtually every book written about Robert Flaherty. She marked up the page proofs on Richard Griffith's book on Flaherty called *The World of Robert Flaherty* (1953). Frances was doctrinaire about how to advance the Flaherty legacy, controlling it like a corporate brand where it could only be represented by her, a family member, or a person who knew or worked directly with Robert. She insisted all lectures about him include screening his films.

In a 1959 letter to Elisabeth Loosley, in response to a request for a two-thousand-word article about the "Flaherty Way," Frances explained that she preferred lecturing and showing the films rather than writing, which did not fully capture the mysteries of the Flaherty experience:

> The Foundation and the seminars center around a way of filmmaking that Robert Flaherty developed. That "way" is my lecture and the film excerpts accompanying it, which help toward an understanding.... Let me simply say this much: the "way" is applicable to one kind of film, and that is the film of real life, in which people are not acting but being themselves ... in one case it is an intellectual experience, in the other an experience much deeper. The motion picture is capable of giving us this deeper experience, this is its claim to being an art. This is its claim also to a special power as an education tool.[17]

As the decade progressed, Frances became more and more estranged from the seminar, feeling it had moved beyond the Flaherty films and their poetic realist style. As the decade ended, she only appeared at the seminar when a Flaherty film was screened.

The 1960 seminar returned to Vermont, but the seminar had outgrown the Flaherty farm. As David Flaherty explained to Arnold Eagle: "The response this year has been so amazing that we decided the other day that our barn simply wasn't big enough to accommodate all the good students who want to come, so we're hiring a hall big enough to take a hundred or more, the Dummerston Grange, only a mile from our place."[18]

Erik Barnouw programmed the 1960 seminar. This seminar significantly altered the form and scope of the event, suggesting a new direction shifting away from the Flaherty Foundation. The 1959 seminar screened nineteen films. The 1960 seminar showed more than forty, expanding the number of shorts. Barnouw made a significant intervention into the direction of the seminar, offering a heterogeneous mix of community education films, documentary, educational films, experimental works, narrative, and sponsored films. Works represented Canada, France, Italy, Pakistan, Russia, and the United States. Four Flaherty films were screened: *Louisiana Story, Man of Aran, Moana,* and *Nanook of the North.* Nikos Cominos's *The Louisiana Story Study Film* (1962) was shown in its early version at this seminar, a project of Frances and David to utilize the outtakes from the film to explain Robert Flaherty's creative process. Richard Leacock showed recent work. He had been Flaherty's cameraman on *Louisiana Story* and a very close friend of the Flaherty family.

This seminar traveled beyond the Flaherty canon.[19] Barnouw's choices extended the notion of a seminar by juxtaposing works from different sectors of the noncommercial and commercial media sectors. Jack Churchill screened classroom films produced under the auspices of Educational Service Inc. A selection of films made for the United Nations was shown. Recent works from the National Film Board (NFB) of Canada appeared, including *Universe* (1960) by Tom Dale. *La pyramide humaine* (1960), an ethnofiction shot in Ivory Coast; *Les maîtres fous* (1954), about the Hauka people from Niger in Ghana; and *Moi, un noir* (1958), shot in Ivory Coast, were screened. French ethnographer Jean Rouch, a key figure in the cinéma vérité style of handheld camera of provocation and collaboration with subjects, directed these films. Rouch was unable to attend.

Belgium filmmaker Henri Storck screened *Symphonie paysanne* (1942–44), a project that featured five films—one for each season plus a film about folk rituals—shot during the war chronicling the life of Belgium peasants. Storck became interested in cinema after seeing *Moana* at a cinematheque in Brussels in 1930. He shared Flaherty's humanist and poetic vision.[20] At this seminar, the poetic realist narrative works of Robert Bresson (*Pickpocket* [1953]), Jean Renoir (*Rules of the Game* [1939], *Le déjeuner sur l'herbe* [1959], and *Le testament du Docteur Cordelier* [1959]), and British screenwriter Gavin Lambert's[21] *Another Sky* (1954)—a film about a women's sexual awakening in Morocco—were juxtaposed with Al Wasserman's[22] CBS-sponsored documentaries *Hoffa and the Teamsters* (1959) and *Out of Darkness* (1956)—the latter about mental illness.

This program also solidified the seminar's ongoing relationship with the NFB and its filmmakers.[23] Experimental filmmaking was again represented in the abstract animation films of Robert Breer and the works of Hilary Harris, the experimental and documentary filmmaker and sculptor. However, it was not a central thrust of the programming arc. Experimental film functioned as examples of the poetic impulse, which could invigorate educational/scientific films and long-form documentary.

The first offshore Flaherty occurred in 1961 in Puerto Rico, programmed by Dorothy Oshlag. Barnouw was in India on a Fulbright Award to research Indian cinema. Oshlag brought projectors into the village. Films were projected at night, with participants sitting on logs. The Puerto Rican films from the Division of Community Education grew out of a United States Information Agency (USIA)–backed project to promote filmmaking in South America. The American administrator sent to run the project ended up staying in Puerto Rico. Money was left in the budget, and so the group reached out to the Flaherty in hopes of mounting a seminar there. Willard Van Dyke had established connections with this group through his government contacts with the USIA.[24] This seminar continued the programming structure of the 1960 seminar, with a mix of genres and nations.

Satyajit Ray's *Pather Panchali* (India) was screened outdoors. Frances brought her own 35mm print of the film without subtitles. Unspooling in a dining room of a small hotel perched high in the mountains of the island, *Pather Panchali* captivated attendees and became one of the legendary screenings in the history of the seminar. Dorothy Oshlag Olson described how "at night the sliding glass doors could be opened: the jungle soundtrack of tree frogs and night animals wove itself into the film. It was magical. At the end, the entire group was completely silent. Tears were seen."[25]

The Puerto Rican filmmaker Amilcar Tirado's *Una voz en la montaña* (1952), *El puente* (1954), *El santero* (1956), and *El contemplado* (1957), documentaries about everyday people in Puerto Rico, were screened. Works produced in the Division of

Community Education of Puerto Rico, headed by Tirado, inaugurated a movement to feature the works of one master filmmaker at the seminar. Canadian Claude Jutra's *La lutte* (1961) and Shirley Clarke's *The Connection* (1962) were shown. Three Flaherty films were screened. Sponsored films included works by Flaherty regular Jack Churchill. Kent MacKenzie's *The Exiles* (1961), an independently produced narrative about Native Americans in Los Angeles, continued the emphasis on poetic realism. Hilary Harris showed *Picketing the Polaris Sub Base* (1960) and *San Francisco to Moscow Peace March* (1960). Willard Van Dyke had been an early participant in the Flaherty Foundation efforts. A filmmaker, museum official, photographer, and programmer, Willard Van Dyke showed *Mayo florido* (1954), an experimental film shot in Puerto Rico. This was to be the start of Van Dyke's long association with the seminar.[26]

From 1960 to 1968, seminar programmers exposed deep links with the Flaherty Foundation in the 1950s, engagement with the developing noncommercial sector, and involvement with the operation of IFS. As filmmakers, librarians, professors, and television producers, they hailed from varied parts of film culture. None programmed or curated public exhibitions as their exclusive full-time job, although some were involved in film exhibition as an offshoot emanating from their librarian roles. All had previously attended seminars. Most spent time at seminars on the Flaherty farm and knew the Flaherty family. They saw themselves as intellectuals engaged in figuring out this complicated new world of independent film, in all of its myriad styles and across all of its venues in distribution and exhibition. As a group, the majority resided in the East Coast.

In 1962, George Amberg put together a program at the University of Minnesota. He was a filmmaker who taught in New York City. In 1963, Erik Barnouw and Hugh Gray programmed a seminar at the Experiment in International Living in Vermont. A professor of film at University of California, Los Angeles (UCLA), the English-born Gray wrote public information notices for the British during the war. He later moved to writing screenplays for Hollywood. In alignment with the poetic realist thrust of the seminars during this period, Gray later translated André Bazin's important two-volume compendium of essays, *What Is Cinema?* (1968), into English.

Jane Beveridge, wife of filmmaker James Beveridge, programmed the 1964 seminar held at Arden House, a move Barnouw facilitated. Near Newburgh in upstate New York, Arden House had been originally owned by railroad magnate Edward Harriman. Isolated, the house sat on top of a hill and featured a large music room suitable for screenings. The seminar remained at Arden House—a shorter trip upstate from New York City than Vermont—until 1968. In 1965 and 1967, Edith Zornow[27] mounted the seminar. Sumner Glimcher worked with Barnouw and Olson at CMC as a filmmaker and distributor. He programmed the 1966 seminar. An early advocate for film in public and university libraries, D. Marie Grieco programmed the 1968 seminar.

As indicated by this list of programmers, a very heterogeneous group of Flaherty insiders—academics, filmmakers, librarians, and TV producers—constructed the Flaherty experience as a distinctive seminar, an immersion into the developing, labyrinthine, and often-confusing independent filmmaking sector. Taken as a group, their programs were significantly denser and longer than the programs on the farm, showing many more films from a much more diverse set of sectors—documentary, educational films, ethnographic film, experimental works, government films, sponsored films, and television shows. The model expanded from the Flaherty films toward a much more diverse and heterogeneous set of films that charted the different nooks and crannies of the independent film sector.

Although documentary remained the dominant modality and several Flaherty films were always screened in a reverential homage, experimental and narrative films started to appear. The narratives represented examples of poetic realism, focusing on complex characters and attention to cinematic form. Examples include *Shadows* (1959) by John Cassavetes at the 1962 seminar and *Tokyo Story* (1953) by Yasujiro Ozu at the 1964 seminar. Never a majority, experimental films sustained a provocation to consider poetic form, rather than realist content, a sort of training ground for the eye to see differently: *Seaward the Great Ships* (1961) by Hilary Harris in 1962, *Thanatopsis* (1962) by Ed Emshwiller in 1964, *Delta, Phase I* (1962) by Bert Haanstra in 1965, *Entr'acte* (1924) by René Clair in 1965, *Raga* (1958) by Jordan Belson in 1965, *Summit* (1963) by Stan Vanderbeek in 1966, *Castro Street* (1966) by Bruce Baillie in 1967, *Duo Concertantes* (1964) by Larry Jordan in 1967, and *Songs* (1964) by Stan Brakhage in 1967. Russian constructivists peppered the seminar as well, with *Kino Pravda* (1922–23) by Dziga Vertov in 1962. As a group, these works extended the "Flaherty Way" advocated by Frances, operating within a formalist, lyrical, and mystical aesthetic that was not confrontational to spectators.

During this period, the seminars provided an aesthetic and intellectual map of the international terrain of renewed emphasis on realism reaching from documentary to narrative. The ingredients for this style included actual places, close observation, a focus on real people and not actors, and positioning the camera into relationships with subjects. They eschewed voice-over, exploited the possibilities of the newer lightweight image and sound recording technologies, and looked for content of nonelites.

The seminars created a weave between the poetic realism in the narrative films of Michelangelo Antonioni, Roberto Rossellini, John Cassavetes, and the realist reenactments of Peter Watkins in *Culloden* (1964). They also combined the new ways of doing ethnography promoted by John Marshall and Jean Rouch that emphasized deeply considered participant observation with the poetic traditions of the British documentary movement in the 1930s and 1940s that focused on everyday people. For example, Basil Wright's *Night Mail* (1936) and Humphrey Jennings' *Fires Were Started* (1943) were programmed in the 1962 seminar.

All of these cinematic movements provided a powerful historical and international context for the most distinguishing feature of the seminar during this period: cinéma vérité and direct cinema documentary. In 1963, a presentation entitled "Poetry Vérité vs Cinéma Vérité," illustrated with clips from the two different styles, indicated that the shift away from the camera on a tripod to the handheld camera provoked some controversy even as it opened up and redefined independent filmmaking. The central theme of these years revolved around the new form of documentary called direct cinema in the United States and cinéma vérité in Canada and France that relied on the new lightweight cameras and sound: this was a cinema of astute observation, the everyday, mobility, proximity, and the unexpected. But it was not a cinema with any simple borders, definitions, or forms. Instead, as the Flaherty programs of this period mapped this film movement, cinéma vérité/direct cinema encompassed a wide range of practices ranging from ethnofiction, a focus on the everyday, reenactment, and shooting close to subjects not usually seen in network films. Robert Drew, producer of *Primary* (1960), had attended the 1958 seminar following his Nieman Fellowship at Harvard University where he was developing a form of what he has called "candid filmmaking that did not yet exist, one that would require special talents."[28] It was there that he saw work by Ricky Leacock, Flaherty's cameraman, and invited him to join his team. Also in the late 1950s, cinematographer D. A. Pennebaker, who later joined the team that shot *Primary* and became a direct cinema director in his own right, showed some of his early short films at the Flaherty farm, where he met critic Gideon Bachman.[29] The seminar gathered together those exploring ways of working with new technologies and new ideas about interacting with subjects. At the Flaherty Seminars, they found common ground and each other.

As the decade progressed, the seminar presented virtually every important film and filmmaker in the history of this style of documentary, demonstrating that the movement not only spanned countries but also many different forms and institutional sectors. Important historical figures such as James Blue, Michel Brault, Joyce Chopra, Shirley Clarke, Robert Drew, Robert Gardner, Craig Gilbert, Susumu Hani, Hilary Harris, David Hoffman, Leo Hurwitz, Austin Lamont, Richard Leacock, Colin Low, Albert Maysles, David Maysles, P.J. O'Connell, Alain Resnais, Jean Rouch, Johan van der Keuken, Al Wasserman, Haskell Wexler, and Frederick Wiseman showed their films.[30] With the exception of Chopra, who had codirected the landmark *Happy Mother's Day* (1963) with Leacock, and Clarke, whose film on *The Connection* (1962) challenged some of the observational tenets emerging in the US version of direct cinema, this group was decidedly male and white. These works emphasized the camera and how it interacted with and photographed people in their everyday environments; they jettisoned a central deductive expository argument and a narrator.

Despite its broad programming, the seminars in the 1960s exposed a heavy bias toward documentary—whether ethnographic, independent, network television, sponsored, or state supported. This heterogeneity of genres and styles sharpened documentary practice. However, programs suggested an interest in formal elements rather than specific geographic political contexts. Some of the trustees felt that the legacy of Flaherty must continue in works that evoked his aesthetic, independence, and style, with its emphasis on seeing and shooting rather than editing. In his 1962 internal report, "Some Notes on the Flaherty Seminars," IFS trustee Jack Churchill explained that the early seminars were "built initially around the idea of assembling as many as possible of those who had worked with Robert Flaherty to talk about the process of making a Flaherty film" to inspire filmmakers and students.[31] Ethnographic films resonated with the Flaherty oeuvre because they were films about "primitive peoples," a problematic racialized approach when considered through the lens of contemporary postcolonial theories.[32]

As the seminar's programming in the 1960s broadened beyond relationships with Robert Flaherty or tributes to him, the seminar's impact, argued Churchill, diminished. He noted that a key to the success of the Flaherty seminar was the presence of the filmmakers themselves. "This sensing process is one of the fundamental qualities of the seminar," Churchill observed. For him, Frances's commitment to enacting nonpreconception distinguished the seminar process, an emphasis on "the specific concrete instance . . . of the actual resolution of real problems . . . a tangible situation."[33] Nonpreconception seemed to invoke a kind of romanticism of engaging with a situation, an elevation of experience and seeing over concept and design. It constituted a style of making films dependent on perception and the camera rather than the logics of the editing room. In Churchill's explanation, nonpreconception depended on interaction with the empirical world through the lens of the camera—an attitude antagonistic to experimental filmmaking with its conceptual interventions into film form and spectatorship. In 1963, experimental filmmakers Ken Jacobs, Jonas Mekas, Flo Jacobs, and several companions crashed the Flaherty Seminar. Arnold Eagle, Jacobs's former teacher, was there. Eagle had called Jacobs's films "anti-art." As Jacobs remembers, "The trip with Jonas in '63 was a lark; people's disdain of us was amusing." At midnight, Jacobs and Mekas screened hand-carried copies of *Blonde Cobra* (Ken Jacobs, 1963) and *Flaming Creatures* (Jack Smith, 1963).[34]

Although the seminar seemingly excluded experimental filmmakers, its participants reflected how independent film in this period spanned multiple areas of the media landscape. Participants in these seminars reflected the heterogeneity of the growing noncommercial sector, especially in the northeast corridor between Washington, DC, and Montreal. Filmmakers—both participants and presenters—mostly hailed from metropolitan centers such as Boston, Montreal, and New York. Librarians attended, indicating the growing interest in libraries on the East Coast to purchase films for their collections. Representatives from the MoMA Circulating Library, the New York Public Library, the New York State Library in Albany, and New York University (NYU) Library attended. These important libraries were among the first organizations to buy 16mm films. Their librarians populated the seminar. As Bill Sloan recalled, the seminar was a place to see works with filmmakers, which was a thrilling experience. It also served as a marketplace to shop for works to add to library collections.[35] In addition, many of the early companies that distributed 16mm films for educational sectors sent representatives, such as Brandon Films, Contemporary Films, and *Encyclopedia Britannica*.

Bill Pence attended the 1962 and 1963 seminars as a young man in his early twenties eager to contribute to art film distribution. He claimed the intimate seminar experience proved seminal, with its emphasis on discussion and nonpreconception that had "a pull and an urgency."[36] Pence noted that these earlier seminars in the 1960s showed more films in the Flaherty tradition—anthropological and neorealist—than later seminars. Through his participation in these seminars, Pence met Richard Griffith, curator of film at MoMA, who learned of his background in bringing classic art films to college towns. Later, in 1965, Griffith connected Pence with Saul Turell, who was buying Janus Films to promote new releases of international art cinema from directors such as Ingmar Bergman and François Truffaut. By 1974, Pence inaugurated the Telluride Film Festival, modeled after the Flaherty with its conversations with filmmakers, egalitarian nature, esprit de corps, intimacy, remote location, and a strategy of not announcing the program in advance to force the audience to engage the work.[37]

During this period, the majority of attendees self-identified with the term *filmmaker*, a moniker suggesting artisanal independence. As identified on participants lists of the period, the term *film maker* (during this period, always spelled as two words) appeared to be linked to anyone doing film production and not working for the Hollywood studios. "Film maker" functioned as a cover term, a way to unify a wide-ranging, vast field that moved across different sectors of film culture. The film makers were connected with many diverse, high-profile, influential commercial, educational, and noncommercial media sectors such as the audiovisual unit of the American Friends Service Committee; the Visual Education Unit of the Boy Scouts of America; Chicago City Junior College; Dartmouth Film Society, Educational Services Inc.; George Eastman House; Harvard Medical School; Harvard School of Public Health; Henry Jaffe Enterprises; the Television, Radio and Film Commission of the Methodist Church; MoMA; Museum of Fine Arts in Boston; National Council of Churches; the NFB; National Gallery of Art; NBC; *The New Yorker*; Time Life; J. Walter Thompson advertising agency; the United Nations; the US Department of the Interior; USIA; WGBH in Boston; WNBQ in New York City; and WNDT-TV. Producers from small film production companies in Boston and New York City showed up as well. Each seminar also attracted anthropologists and ethnographic filmmakers.[38]

Although the mythology of the Flaherty Seminar hinges on the idea that the seminars have always concentrated on gathering together all the disparate filmmakers for substantive conversation about the art and technique of cinema, the records of seminar attendees and trustees present a different story. In actuality, the seminars included—and depended upon—professors like Barnouw who were affiliated with major universities. Major figures who defined the field of university-level film production and film studies education in the early 1960s as one integrating theory and practice participated: George Amberg, New York University; Henry Breitrose, Stanford University; Hugh Gray, UCLA; John Marshall, Harvard University; Robert Steele, Boston University; Sol Worth, University of Pennsylvania; and Colin Young, UCLA. Faculty, graduate students, and undergraduates from Boston University, Cornell University, Fordham University, Lawrence College, Lehigh University, Montclair State College, University of Minnesota, and University of Wisconsin also attended.

By the end of this period, Barbara Van Dyke, Willard's second wife, was installed as executive director. IFS was run by a board of trustees that included longtime Flaherty stalwarts George Amberg, Jack Churchill, Frances Flaherty, Dorothy Oshlag Olson, and Willard Van Dyke. It also had a large advisory committee. The advisory committee read as a who's who of the noncommercial independent film scene in the 1960s: Shirley Clarke, Thorold Dickinson, Leo R. Dratfield, Arnold Eagle, Hugh Gray, Richard Griffith, Arthur Knight, Siegfried Kracauer, Richard Leacock, Albert Maysles, Hans Richter, Lionel Rogosin, Cecile Starr, Robert Steele, George Stoney, and Amos Vogel, to name only a few. Educational and classic film distributors, film exhibitors, film makers, film scholars, and journalistic critics, the majority of whom lived and worked in New York City, comprised this group.[39]

From 1960 to 1967, as IFS further established itself as a nonprofit under the aegis of Columbia University, it transitioned the seminar operations from the farm in Vermont to New York City, signaling the finality of the move from family-run memorial project to national and international media arts organization. Seminar programming extended beyond the Flaherty films and Robert's collaborators. These seminars threaded together cinéma vérite, direct cinema, ethnography, industrial and educational film, Italian neo-realism, poetic realism, and various European new waves—all to explore the potentiali-ties of cinema. In 1964, Frances, who now served on the IFS board of trustees, pointed out that "the seminars are an exchange of film experience as a basis for discussing the potentialities of the medium in Robert Flaherty's exploratory spirit."[40]

The seminars branded themselves by pulling from Frances's writing on Robert Fla-herty, repeatedly using words such as *discovery, exploration, the future, intensive viewing,* and *unique* in their announcements. They repeatedly emphasized the "intimacy" of the seminar experience and the opportunities to commingle with established filmmakers. The seminar always promoted the seminars as offering emerging makers and film students unique access to engage more accomplished and established filmmakers. In addition, the announcements reiterated that filmmakers came from across the globe.[41] As journalist Harvey Fondiller mused, the Flaherty Seminar served as "fresh air for filmmakers," suggesting its location in rural areas away from cities and its propulsion toward new ways to consider cinema.[42] As the seventh Flaherty Film Seminar announce-ment proclaimed, the seminar would "bring together film makers and film students in a searching look at the art of the film and its growing world role."[43] The seminars grew to almost one hundred participants. In a review of the sixth annual seminar in 1960 in *Better Movie Making*, Lou Lachter identified the communal aspect of the seminar, noting that "this 10 day study of great films and filmers succeeds so well because of the real contri-butions made by the students, the speakers and the truly fine Flaherty tradition."[44] As Leonard Lipton observed in a 1966 *Popular Photography* article entitled "Should You Go to the Flaherty Seminar?" the seminar brought together cinematographers, distributors, editors, film librarians, filmmakers, producers, and students to argue about cinema.[45] With relatively few film schools and with film societies and museums offering classic and international art cinema programming, the seminars filled a gap in film culture. They offered a way to watch films unavailable elsewhere. They provided a place to analyze, argue and discuss the future of cinema. In a 1961 article in *Photo Methods for Industry*, Arnold Eagle advanced the Flaherty Film Seminar provided time space and time to contemplate "the 'why' of the moviemaker's art."[46]

The year 1968 was a watershed in international politics and rebellious upheavals in Paris. This volatile context pushed the Flaherty Seminar in a major new direction. It shifted the focus away from cinéma vérite and direct cinema to experimental shorts—the first seminar with the avant-garde as a major focus rather than as a sidebar to fortify and inspire documentary vision. D. Marie Grieco programmed a staggering number films—ninety-two, nearly 30 percent more than the year before.

Working at the Long Island Library, Grieco found the suburbs stifling. They lacked artistic and intellectual stimulation and a sense of community. She went into New York to see films at Cinema 16 "to keep her mind going." Considering Amos Vogel the "godfa-ther of independent cinema," she deeply admired how he possessed the ability to make connections between the arts through unexpected juxtapositions in the programming. Her friend Joan Clark, an audiovisual librarian, had initially encouraged Grieco to attend the Flaherty Seminar in 1966. At that seminar, Grieco explained she was "knocked out by Frances Flaherty" with her sharp intellect and her interdisciplinary approach to cinema. In Grieco's partisan and pro-Frances view, "Robert was the poet, Frances was the intellect." Grieco and Frances established a close friendship. Grieco traveled frequently to the Flaherty farm in Vermont, where she commenced to catalog Frances's vast core library, overflowing with many volumes on Buddhism, fine arts, poetry, and religion. The library also included books by Edmund Carpenter, the radical anthropologist of the Arctic, William James (author of *Varieties of Religious Experience*), and volumes by Alan Watts (author of *The Way of Zen* and *Nature, Man and Woman*, among many others) Grieco later wrote a chapbook on Frances's views on cinema, working through her ideas on discovery and nonpreconception that formed the intellectual and public relations backbone of the seminar for decades.[47]

The 1968 seminar was in many ways an intervention into and a reaction to a seminar programmed the previous year by New York television producer Edith Zornow. The 1967 program promoted documentary across a variety of realist forms, focusing on direct cinema, documentary reenactments, international documentaries emerging from the various European new waves, and television documentary. The films screened constituted some of the defining works in cinéma vérité and direct cinema documentary history: Peter Watkins documentary reenactment, *Culloden* (1964); Donn Alan Pennebaker's direct cinema profile of Bob Dylan, *Don't Look Back* (1967); Peter Adair's direct cinema film *Holy Ghost People* (1967); Shirley Clarke's interrogation of cinéma vérité interviews in *Portrait of Jason* (1967); Frederick Wiseman's *Titicut Follies* (1967) and Allen King's *Warrendale* (1968). Ivan Passer represented the Czech new wave with his films *Psalm* and *A Boring Afternoon*. French feminist Nelly Kaplan, with her *Abel Gance: Yesterday and Tomorrow*, and Alain Resnais, with *Toute la mémoire du monde* (1956) elaborated the French new wave impulse in documentary. Joris Ivens's *Rotterdam-Europoort* (1966) appeared, most likely as an example of his more poetic rather than political filmmaking.[48] Interestingly, no Flaherty film was screened that year—a break with the seminar tradition of homage to Flaherty films that Frances had advanced. A few experimental works by Stan Brakhage, Peter Campus, and Larry Jordan peppered the program, suggesting the utilitarian value of the avant-garde's lyrical impulses to deepen documentary camerawork.

Grieco's program veered fiercely in the opposite direction of Zornow's program. It stood as an irrefutable turning point in Flaherty Seminar history. The program featured more experimental films than any Flaherty that preceded it—a major intervention into an organization historically associated with documentary. Her program challenged the idea of the avant-garde as lyrical, by showing a mix of animation, compilation, conceptual, ironic, and technological explorations in works by filmmakers such as Scott Bartlett (*OffOn*, 1967; *Moon*, 1969); Bruce Conner (*A Movie*, 1958; *Vivian*, 1965; *Ten Second Film*,1965; *The White Rose*, 1967; *Cosmic Ray*,1962; *Report*, 1963–67; *Breakaway*,1966); James Broughton (*The Bed*, 1968), Storm de Hirsch (*Third Eye Butterfly*, 1968); Will Hindle (*Billabong*, 1968; *FFTCM*, 1967; *Chinese Firedrill*,1968; *Non Catholicam*, 1963); John and Faith Hubley (*The Cruise*, 1966; *Urbanissimo*, 1966); Derek Lamb (*Housemoving*, 1968); Norman McLaren (*Pas de deux*, 1968), and Robert Nelson (*The Grateful Dead*, 1967; *The Great Blondino*, 1967; *Oh Dem Watermelons*,1965; *The Off Handed Jape*, 1967).

Grieco showed not only the *Louisiana Story Study Film* (1962), bringing together Nick Cominos, Frances Flaherty, and Ricky Leacock, but also screened *Grass: A Nation's Battle for Life* (1925), the documentary film about the Bakhtiari migration across Iran that was inspired by *Nanook of the North*, produced by Merian C. Cooper, Marguerite Harrison, and Ernest Schoedsack.

Grieco also brought *David Holzman's Diary* (1967), Jim McBride's sly intervention into personal filmmaking and spoof of the distanced observational tenets of direct cinema, to the 1968 seminar. This interventionist direction questioning the basic tenets of cinematic form, documentary, narrative structure, and representation continued with the screening of Jean-Luc Godard's *Les carabiniers* (1963).[49] Grieco was also most likely the first Flaherty programmer to screen works produced by an African American filmmaker who was a featured guest: William Greaves with his USIA-sponsored *First Festival of Negro Arts* (1966) and his WNET-produced *Still a Brother* (1968), a film chronicling black pride.[50]

This seminar had a deep impact—it rattled preconceptions about documentary and stretched its borders and concerns. For example, visual anthropologist Jay Ruby attended his first Flaherty in 1968. He had been at UCLA, leaving in 1967 to teach at Temple University in Philadelphia. At the seminar, the experimental works of Bartlett, Conner, and Hindle excited him, demonstrating the possibilities of what one could do with cinema. He also saw *David Holzman's Diary*. As Ruby wrote, "It was a year when a group of avant-garde West Coast makers . . . challenged seminar goers to expand their horizons. The intensity of the event and the single-mindedness of the participants were very attractive to me."[51] He was intellectually energized by the ideas the seminar cracked open. "I thought it was the most exciting place to be," Ruby explained. "I thought I had seen the future."[52]

In fact, it was at this seminar that Ruby first saw Timothy Asch's work in progress about the Yanomami, *The Feast* (1970), a collaboration with anthropologist Napoleon Chagnon. The film was completed in 1970. Asch had worked with ethnographic filmmaker Robert Gardner at Harvard University. *The Feast* was made in the context of American direct cinema and the Francophone cinéma vérité of the 1960s, with their advocacy for observation and their utilization of lightweight 16mm equipment.[53] The film provoked a late-night conversation at the seminar between Asch, Ruby, and Sol Worth, who determined visual anthropology needed recognition within the field of anthropology. That evening, they decided they would ask the American Anthropological Association "for screening sessions that were considered equal to the paper presentations—an important step in the professional acceptance of ethnographic film." They also agreed to form a new society for visual anthropology, the Society for Anthropology of Visual Communication (subsequently renamed the Society for Visual Anthropology), and institute a journal, *Studies in Visual Communications*. Ruby ended up becoming a Flaherty regular, attending seminars from 1968 through 1980. He returned in the late 1980s and early 1990s. He programmed the 1978 Flaherty Seminar. For Ruby, the Flaherty served as a model for his annual conferences on visual anthropology at Temple University.[54]

Grieco's deep admiration, friendship, and work with Frances from 1966 until her death in 1972 positioned Grieco in the role of revisionist historian of the Flaherty legacy, reinserting Frances as Robert's collaborator. At the memorial honoring Frances Fla-herty at the Eighteenth Annual Robert Flaherty Film Seminar in 1972, Grieco wrote a moving tribute that argued for the complexity of Frances's intellectual contributions. She explained the operative ideas undergirding Frances's vision of the seminar's pro-cess of engagement: discovery, exploration, nonpreconception, and probing the creative process.[55] She also advanced the notion that the experience and structure of the Flaherty emanated from Frances's intellectual, musical, and spiritual ideas—a way to unleash new ways of seeing.[56]

However, Grieco's canonization of Frances's concepts and vision of the seminar did not reign undisputed. Willard Van Dyke challenged this Zen mysticism with a more aggressive politics. Frances and Willard clashed on ideological and aesthetic grounds. Flaherty Seminar participants from the 1960s and 1970s trace some of the origins of the contentious and volatile discussions at the seminar directly to Van Dyke, known in film circles for his self-aggrandizing style, short temper, and strong will.[57] Connected, high profile, and opportunistic, Willard also championed the new, more politically confron-tational forms of independent film emerging in the 1960s and 1970s.

As president of IFS, Willard also brought important relationships with the Ford and Rockefeller Foundations to the organization. According to anthropologist Jay Ruby, Van Dyke was a reformed left-winger, although never a communist. He held a strong belief, Ruby observed, that film could "change the world. . . . He saw documentary as a way to crusade for the poor, for victims. . . . He was not interested in poetry."[58] Willard conveyed an attitude of superiority, which some seminarians felt emanated from a deep insecurity about his intellectual prowess. His reputation in the world of New York film culture conveyed a certain aura of authority. He saw himself as bringing ideas about "truth and justice" to the seminar.

Once situated as president of IFS, Willard installed his wife, Barbara, as executive director, in what some former seminarians describe as the "Van Dyke" takeover.[59] With Willard, Barbara had attended her first seminar in 1964, entranced by its artistic and intellectual intensities. With its cauldron of cinéma vérité, civil rights, and direct cinema works, she contended that this particular seminar presented a "new way of recording life."[60] These ideological and epistemological tensions between lyrical artistry, poetic realism, political engagement, and a wider palette of cinematic techniques continued to surge through the subsequent decades of the seminar. These battles between Frances and Willard have often been presented in seminar mythology as a battle of different politics and oppositional strong wills. However, these tensions perhaps more pointedly underscore the challenges of transitioning from a more isolated, familial way of operat-ing toward a more institutional, public mode.

Whether one interprets this clash between Frances and Willard as different kinds of experience in cinema, personalities, politics, or sexism, or just the conflicts motored by larger historical changes in film culture, it is clear that Willard's presidency denoted the end of the Frances era of the seminar. In 1969, Willard coprogrammed the seminar with D. Marie Grieco, an aggressive intervention toward more openly political direc-tions that disrupted Frances's ideas about poetry. Significantly, this program continued D. Marie Grieco's notions of an aesthetic and conceptual avant-garde. Grieco was a strong advocate for Frances's ideas, interpreting the tenets of "nonpreconception" through experimental films engaging directly with altering perception.

With a nod to Flaherty traditions, Van Dyke and Grieco showed *Moana* and the rarely screened *Twenty Four Dollar Island*. They brought classics of Soviet cinema with *Earth* (1930) by Aleksandr Dovzhenko and *Storm over Asia* (1928) by Vsevolod I. Pudovkin. They intermingled these films with direct cinema works such as *The Bride Stripped Bare* (1967) by Tom Palazzolo, *High School* (1968) and *Law and Order* (1969) by Frederick Wiseman, and *Sean* (1969) by Ralph Arlyck. This seminar also screened films by avant-gardists Scott Bartlett, Jordan Belson, Robert Breer, Will Hindle, George Kuchar, Standish Lawder, Jonas Mekas, and John Whitney. Grieco programmed Bruce Baillie films with *Afro-Dance* (1970), and *Paul Robeson* (1970), the black culture–identified work of African American filmmaker St. Clair Bourne. Student films from the Studio Museum of Harlem also screened. Willard insisted on showing the controversial, challenging *Wavelength* (1967), the seminal work of Canadian structural filmmaker Michael Snow, which prompted Frances to remark, "I feel like a canary that has fallen over on its back with its feet up and died."[61] *Borom Sarret* (1969), Senegalese filmmaker Ousmane Sembène's first film, and works by Yugoslavian animator Nedeljko Dragic and screenwriter Boro Draskovic represented a move into more international cinemas, especially various new waves erupting in the 1960s and 1970s.

The film that marked the end of the Frances era and the beginning of the Willard era (or regime, depending on how one interprets his social justice orientation), was Dennis Hopper's *Easy Rider* (1969), an independently produced narrative film chronicling drugs, motorcycle culture, sex, and youth. Perhaps metaphorically signaling new cinematic adventures for the Flaherty Seminar to explore, Willard opened the 1969 seminar with this landmark independent narrative film. Frances stormed out of the screening. She remained absent for many days. Later that fall, when the film opened at the Brattleboro cinema in Vermont, Frances went to see the film again. She revised her position. She proclaimed, "I was wrong; that film was about something!"[62]

1963 FRANCES FLAHERTY—ON *NANOOK OF THE NORTH* (1922) AND *MOANA* (1926)

[In the following discussion I have focused primarily on *Moana*.]

> *Flaherty seminarian (F):* What was the impact of *Nanook* when it came out?
> *Frances Flaherty:* Well, that's important, you see. That's the beginning of the transition between *Nanook* and *Moana*; if *Nanook* hadn't been box office, there probably wouldn't have been any more Flaherty films. It *had* to be box office. I keep thinking about the last conversation between Bob and Nanook. The shooting was finished and Bob was waiting for the once-a-year boat that was to take him back to civilization. They were sitting on the cobbled shore of the bay. Nanook was very sad because now there'd be no more shooting for what he called "the aggie," and there were so many more wonderful hunting scenes they still could make. Bob tried to comfort him, and pointing to the pebbles on the beach, he said to Nanook, "As many white men as these pebbles on the beach will see Nanook and his family."

Bob had faith that what *he* liked, other people in the world would like. Now I'm not going into the story of what happened when he brought that film down to the Hollywood distributors. What they said is barely repeatable! *Nanook* was not taken by a Hollywood distributor but by a French distributor, Pathé, who distributed newsreels. The reason they took it I think was because Jean Revillon was a friend of the head of Pathé. Pathé wanted to cut the film up into newsreels, and Jean persuaded them to take it as a whole. And it got shown.

Two years after the film came out, Nanook and his family died of starvation, as many of the Eskimos did, and by that time, the film had gone around the world. News of Nanook's death was published as far away as Tokyo. In Malaya [i.e., on the Malay Peninsula], there was a new word for "strong man": "nanook." And ten years later, I bought an Eskimo pie in Berlin; it was called a Nanook, and Nanook's fine old face smiled up at me from the wrapper. So that was the impact of this first strange new kind of feature film, of just ordinary people doing the ordinary things they do, being themselves. Not long ago, two German directors told me that *Nanook* was still running in Germany. I said, "Have you any idea why a film as simple as this should keep going on and on?" And one of them said, "Yes, it's because we can identify with those people." And then it occurred to me that that is exactly what happens in a Hollywood film: Hollywood has stars so that we can identify with the stars. In this case, instead of the star, we're identifying with a real person. For the first time on the screen, a real person became a world character.

So of course, it was *Nanook*'s box office success that attracted the attention of Hollywood. Paramount came to Bob and said he could go anywhere in the world he wanted; he could write his own ticket. All he had to do was bring back another *Nanook*. Just at that time, we happened to meet an old friend who had been living in a village in Samoa. He told us the village was beautiful, the people were beautiful. And he said that there we could find, as much as we could find anywhere, what was left of the beautiful old Polynesian culture. He said to Bob, "Go to the village of Safune on the island of Savai, and you may be in time to catch something of that beautiful culture before it passes entirely away."

Well, a beautiful culture was one thing, but this time, we were making a film for *Hollywood*, and Bob had absolutely no illusions about what Hollywood expected of him. They wanted drama; they wanted thrills and excitement. It could be natural drama; *Nanook* had the ice and the snow and the storms. We asked ourselves as we boarded the boat for Samoa—and this time we *were* a *we*; we went as a family—what would we find in Samoa to match the drama of the dramatic north? We began thinking about all the things that we'd heard that might work into the film. Sea monsters, for instance, like tiger sharks, or a giant octopus. That seemed very exciting to us and very possible; we began conjuring up all kinds of scenes that we might make of terrible encounters with these monsters. Actually, a report came from another ship at sea that they had sighted a giant octopus with a body the size of a whale. So then we were sure that we were on the right track, and Bob lost no time. No sooner were we landed than he was off looking for a giant octopus and tiger sharks.

For weeks and weeks, he combed that island from end to end, until at last he had to give up; he had to admit they simply were not there. Then I remember the weeks and weeks, miserable weeks, that he just sat on our veranda with every thought falling away from him, learning the first hard lesson of what it takes to make a *true* film of a people that you do not know: that you cannot preconceive, and that if you do preconceive, you're lost; you're off to a false start before you begin. What you have to do is to let go, let go of every thought of your own, wipe your mind clean, fresh, innocent, newborn, become as sensitive as unexposed film in order to take up the impressions around you, and then let what will, come in. This is not easy. The philosophers have called this state the "creative void" or the "fertile state of no mind." Some of you may have come across those expressions, but what we have come to call it, in the seminar, is *nonpreconception*—the beginning of discovery.

Well, what happened in Samoa was this: all of our equipment, about sixteen tons of it, had been piled on the shore, and for insurance purposes it was all marked up with dollar signs. The Samoans drew their own conclusions: Robert Flaherty was an American millionaire; he was a great chief in his own country. So promptly, they made him a great chief of Safuni. Once that happened, the curtain went up and the drama began.

From that moment on, every single chief on the island had to drink kava with the great chief from America; all the dancers had to be brought out for him to see, all the singers had to sing for him; great feasts were made for us; and the talking chiefs had a great time preparing hours-long speeches which they would make in our honor. This went on so long that I wondered if we were ever going to get time to do any filming at all, until suddenly I realized that this, after all, was *exactly* what we'd come for: here was the old Polynesian life, a beautiful tapestry of human relations, ritual human relations, being spread out before us. *That* was what we'd come to film.

Bob gave himself up to the camera: we filmed and we filmed and we filmed. Two hundred and fifty thousand feet of film went through the camera and went into a cave underground, our darkroom, where two Samoans were there to process it. After they finished each processing job, they would come leaping and singing through the village, calling out for the whole village to hear how well they had *cooked* it. [laughter] And then they'd bring it to us.

Our projector was set up under the coconut palms, and in front of the projector there was a lovely green sward. As soon as the villagers saw the light coming from the projector, you would begin to hear the shuffle of feet because showing the rushes was the *great* event. The *whole* village would come, and then they would tell us what they thought; they'd tell us, "You know, this was funny but that was just right, but that was amusing and this was wonderful." We had told them that they mustn't come in their shirts; we wanted them in their old costumes; we wanted to bring back the spirit of old Polynesia. The chiefs sent out an edict through the whole village that now the people must no longer pay attention to the missionary. [laughter] They must go back to their old ways. And when they saw themselves on the screen like this, they were actually reduced to tears. And they would tell us about the old ways; and now they could help us make the film. The whole village was involved. So that was the way the film finally, little by little, week by week, month by month, got built up.

F: There is one point that has always remained in my mind, Frances. The film climaxes with this great ceremonial, religious moment and the great trial of tattooing. This contrasts with *Nanook* in a really interesting way: there, the antagonist, the thing you struggled with, was the weather, nature: you needed discipline to survive it. Here, in this island paradise, man *manufactured* his own discipline: tattooing. Everything that people will see now, those who have not seen *Moana*—every little section, every segment, whether it's collecting leaves or capturing the wild pig—ultimately leads to this great moment of the ceremony and of the tattooing, which gives the film a kind of emotional climax.

Flaherty: That's exactly it; that's what we found to be the real drama in Samoa—and *not* tiger sharks!

1967 FREDERICK WISEMAN—ON *TITICUT FOLLIES* (1967)

Bill Sloan: I think this is the first time anyone here has seen this film. It might be interesting for Fred to talk a bit about the background of the project, how the film was produced. In addition to being a filmmaker, Fred is also a lawyer, which may well bring up some questions about invasion of privacy and perhaps other legal issues that are involved in a film like this.

Frederick Wiseman: Just briefly about the background of the film: it took me over a year to get permission to go into Bridgewater State Hospital, a year of negotiations and a lot of maneuvering with the attorney general's office and the commissioner of corrections.

I got in because the superintendent of the prison liked the idea of a film being made there; he assumed there was nothing I would do that would hurt the place.

I wanted to start in the spring because they have this annual show each spring called "The Titicut Follies." The permission came in April of 1966, and a couple days later, I started to film. It took us about eight weeks to shoot and about nine months to edit.

I didn't say it was Bridgewater in the film because I don't think the place itself is terribly important.

F: Why did you make a film about Bridgewater?

Wiseman: What's the mountaineering phrase: "because it's there"? Because it's an interesting subject for a film!

F: How do you expect to use the film?

F: And where has it been shown?

Wiseman: It hasn't shown anywhere; it's just finished. It's going to have its first public screening at Lincoln Center.

F: But what use will you make of it in Massachusetts?

Wiseman: It'll be shown to whoever has a dollar and a half.

F: On television?

F: Do you expect theatrical release?

Wiseman: I *don't* expect theatrical release actually, but some people I've talked to think it will get into theaters. I'd be surprised.

F: Why are everyone's questions so hostile?

[Many voices talking at once]

F: It's partly the shock . . .

F: People are just interested.

F: Before we get into the issue of mental health, I want to say that I feel this is one of the most beautiful and moving films—and if I were ever going to let anybody try to make a picture about me, I'd trust you. The film is *that* honest. It's the deepest look into human beings that I've seen.

F: I don't know how many others here have worked in mental hospitals. I did for a summer, and I will say that this film is magnificent. For one thing, the experience of being there is overpowering, in ways that you can't miss with the footage—but to render it as you did into a film that is so powerful and yet possible to take and to *really* take—magnificent. And it's so true, too. Given the subject, there's a danger of becoming cruel or of becoming ridiculous—but this is so human.

F: Had you been in this hospital before you asked permission to shoot there?

Wiseman: I used to teach criminal law and I would take students down there—seven or eight years ago. Then, when I was looking around for a subject for a film, I thought this would be appropriate.

F: Being a reporter myself, I'm always concerned with the question of ethics when dealing with a situation where people have no control over their rights, over their privacy. And how far should one go for sensationalism's sake? This is my primary worry on a subject like this.

F: This *exists*, though.

F: So what?

Wiseman: Are you asking whether the film was made to exploit the sensational aspects of the place?

F: Yes.

Wiseman: The answer is no.

F: What constructive purpose does the film serve?

Wiseman: If the film doesn't make that clear, then it's a failure.

F: If the film is turned over to a distributor who decides to exploit it in a sensational way, would you stop it?

Wiseman: I don't care how the film is advertised as long as it's not cut; it has to be presented just the way it is.

F: Why?

Wiseman: Because it's *my* film.

F: This film ought to be seen by many, many people: the more people you can get to see it, the better.

F: I thought it was a magnificent film—the real high point of this seminar—but I am curious about the legal mechanics. What did you do in terms of releases?

Wiseman: I got releases from all those people who were competent to give releases and for those who weren't, from the superintendent acting in what's called in loco parentis. The privacy issue is very complicated. It involves not only the privacy of individual inmates or the possible effect on their families, but also another issue: does the state have the right of privacy to prevent people from knowing that this kind of situation exists? You can get into all kinds of very complicated questions with the privacy issue, but I think that's the least interesting aspect of the film.

F: One man mentions his address. Did you check to see if his family is still living there? They might see the film in a local movie theater.

Wiseman: The fact of the matter is that most of the inmates you see in the film are forgotten people; many of them have been at Bridgewater for forty or fifty years. For example, the guy who sang the song in front of the TV set—his name is Kippy—was picked up in 1922 on the Massachusetts vagrancy law, which at that time was very vague, a catchall. Kippy died at Bridgewater this winter, forty-five years later. Some of the guards have been there a very long time, too; they say that Kippy was a little eccentric but that there was nothing terribly unusual about him, at least for the first ten or twelve years he was there, and even up until he died.

F: How much of what you show did you know you were going to film? Did you know you wanted to film a force-feeding?

Wiseman: I knew the kinds of events that took place there and I knew that I wanted to organize the film around the variety show, because that would provide a structure, and in fact "The Titicut Follies" *was* an enormous help with structuring the film. It also represented a point of view toward the events that were taking place at Bridgewater. So I knew the kinds of thing that went on, but mostly we [Wiseman and John Marshall, who did the camerawork] were just wandering around the place. Ultimately, the guards began to tip me off about where the goodies were.

F: I think your film is a fantastic look at the human condition, but what bothered me, from a filmmaking point of view, is that I felt the guards were often playing to the camera and that we lost reality as a result. I don't know how you get around that, but it seemed blatant to me. You can say, "The man playing to the camera is *part* of the reality, but . . ."

Wiseman: I don't think they were playing to the camera to any great extent. For instance, in the scene where the guy is stomping around in his cell, and the guards are saying, "Keep the room clean, Jim"—I was able to shoot that because I'd seen exactly the same scene about four times, always on washday.

The guards are just as much inmates of the place as the prisoners; they're old friends and have an established way, their shtick, for dealing with situations. This is what they do with Jim on washday.

F: It's not their relationship with the prisoners that bothered me; it's more the relationship I felt between the guards and the camera.

F: Those guards make some very strange choices, given the fact that they're playing for the camera, but I suspect, as Fred has pointed out, that they'd be making strange choices, camera or no camera, given the world that they're functioning in.

Just a point about the responses to the camera. I was terribly aware that a lot of those people spoke up, not to the camera per se, but as part of what happens to a community when they're being filmed. Often it's a good organizing tool to go around with a film team, because filming brings excitement into situations that under normal conditions can seem like a bore.

F: I want to ask you about the scene with Malinowski being force-fed. That was a very moving sequence, and a fascinating sequence, intellectually and emotionally: I mean the intercutting between his being tube fed and being laid out for burial. That was the only time in the film when you did something like that. I like it very much, but I wonder, is it fair to have just one unique sequence like that, even if it is a virtuoso sequence?

F: If I were in a conference with my producer and we were talking about this film, my first reaction would be to say, "That sequence is a break in style; let's not use it." On the other hand, it works so beautifully and it is so apropos to that moment that I accept the break in style.

F: Well, it *did* bother *me*, and I *did* see it as a break in style.

F: During the tube feeding, the doctor has a cigarette in his mouth. Did you ask him to smoke?

Wiseman: No, but he always came through! [laughter]

F: Did you ask people to do things over again?

Wiseman: No, I tried to avoid that and just let the events happen.

F: One of the shocking things is not so much that the people working there *do* what we see, though that itself is troubling, but that they will do these things on camera! I mean, they lacked the sensitivity to realize how they would look!

Wiseman: Well, that's really the influence of Hollywood. The people at Bridgewater thought that they were the stars of the film; that, coupled with the fact that they were always involved very intensely in some kind of activity, made them sort of forget about how they might look to an audience.

F: How could that doctor not be concerned about his professional image?

Wiseman: I'm sure he didn't really think his professional image was being tarnished. He thought he was being photographed because he was doing a good job and that being filmed was very flattering.

F: I want to bring up a very different issue. Most of our questions seem to be about whether the film was real, was it ethical, was it legal, how did you get it? The other area that interests me is how the film relates to the idea of film art. Is *Titicut Follies* just a kind of newsreel with a great deal of power and feeling, or something more? I'm thinking, for instance, of Goya's etchings of war, which although they are very brutal, even shocking, are accepted as art. I'm not sure if anyone has any feelings about this, but I'm inclined to feel that maybe the film *shouldn't* be thought of as art—which is not meant to put it down.

Willard Van Dyke: It's quite obvious that this film is a consciously made work that's put together to affect an audience, and that it affected this audience tremendously. What *is* a work of art, if it's not that? I don't understand your question.

F: John Marshall's name is on the film. I assume this is the John Marshall who did *The Hunters*, and I did have the feeling that *Titicut Follies* was shot by somebody who was trained in anthropological work. Did you work the camera?

Wiseman: No, John worked the camera. John and I worked out a series of signals about what was to be shot.

F: How did you become a filmmaker? Where did you learn?

Wiseman: I learned by doing. This is my first film.

F: What I'm trying to ask is, if John Marshall shot the film, what was your part in making it; why is it *your* film?

Wiseman: I selected what was to be shot, I did the sound, and I edited the film.

F: Why do lawyers make good filmmakers? André Cayatte, who made *We Are All Murderers* [*Nous Sommes Tous des Assassins*, 1952], is a former lawyer.

Wiseman: In my case, it's a testament to the Yale Law School. When I was there, everybody was writing novels and poetry. [laughter]

Adrienne Mancia: This is the second time I've seen *Titicut Follies*, and I had a strange reaction to the film today. After listening to this discussion, I think I know why. When I first saw it, I just thought, "Gee, that's a good film." I didn't see it as related to anything else. I loved the structure of it, the use of the "Follies." The way it brings you into this black comedy is like *Cabaret* [the reference is to the 1966 Broadway production], and I loved the way it worked as human drama.

Since that first screening, people have been calling me up, asking, "Is this a mental health film? Is it meant to expose institutions?" And when I saw it today, I *didn't* like it. I felt you were exploiting the subjects. I think that my initial response— seeing it in the screening room just as a film and, shocking or shattering as it was, enjoying it—was my honest response. I think that having people trying to justify the film in this room has corrupted that original reaction.

F: I didn't see it as mental health film at all.

F: I've *made* mental health films, and I've worked in that kind of situation, and I don't think the film is exploitive at all; in many ways, it's more revealing than the films that Harvard Medical School does.

F: This isn't a sensationalistic film at all. I happen to have been to Bridgewater, though not as a patient. I think the scene that moved me the most—and I don't think any of the film was put on at all—is when Jim is being shaved and then he goes back to his cell. All that baiting of Jim—that's not acting. And I think that scene puts Jim way, way above the guards. I think it makes the film something way above a news story, way above sensationalism. I think this is a tremendous film; it reveals a great problem that people should talk about, deal with. The patients are in many ways sane and they're in there because of us. I feel those inmates have real dignity, as opposed to all the other people we see there, *real* dignity. I couldn't conceive of a better film on the subject.

F: I agree. All during the film I was thinking that in many ways this was a black-and-white *King of Hearts* [1966, Philippe de Broca], which is about the inmates of a mental institution who get let out into a town in France during World War I. The idea of the film is that the supposedly insane inmates are saner than the "sane" people around them. Here, I felt many times that the inmates were at least as sane as, or saner than, the guards.

F: I think it was very important that you accurately created a sense of this institution, and that it's very important that the film did not come between us and the patients. I *don't* think the patients come out looking sane. "Sane" is defined by society and those inmates obviously have disabilities that would not allow them to function in society as it is. And the guards, too, have disabilities that would not allow them to function in society as it is—though the guards come off worse because they don't have to be there.

But the patients came off as real people. Their *lives* were there, not just their gestures or their eccentricities and disabilities. We really got into those lives, and when the film was over, most of us felt we had to get outside because it felt as if we had been inside that place for an awfully long time.

F: It seems to me that there's a misconception that needs to be clarified. Our notion of the insane is that they are screaming and carrying on all the time. This kind of thing *does* happen from time to time, but between those episodes they can seem and act as sane as anyone else. Filmmakers will of course choose the scenes where they act strangely, rather than when they are acting in a more normal way. Many people defined as insane could hold jobs and be successful.

F: I was part of a crew shooting footage in Bridgewater for television, and we went into a room and a reporter said, "Get that guy who's making all those funny gestures!" I didn't do it; I couldn't do it. I wonder if you had reservations about things that you shot.

Wiseman: I think it would have been a mistake to solely shoot patients acting strangely, and I don't think that was done.

The whole notion of a "mental health film" bothers me because it's like the use of psychiatric language at the end of the case conference we filmed, where the psychiatrist ruffles his papers and says, "paranoid reactions, undifferentiated schizophrenic." That's just a way of dismissing the patient by classifying him. *Titicut Follies* may be good or it may be bad, but I certainly wouldn't want to classify it as a "mental health film."

1968 WILLARD VAN DYKE—OPENING REMARKS AT THE SEMINAR

Willard Van Dyke: Ladies and gentlemen, welcome to the opening session of the fourteenth annual Robert Flaherty Seminar. This is a *seminar*; it is *not* a film festival. It's a place where we gather together to look at films, to talk about films, to explore our attitudes toward films. It's *not* a place where formulas are given; it's not a place where you will find easy answers. It's a place where you have to explore. That exploration began with Robert Flaherty, but in a sense, it's been the necessary attitude of every artist who ever lived. An artist explores the reality that is in front of his canvas, in front of his lens—in front of his eyes, in front of his heart, in front of his mind. And he tries to put what he sees and understands into some kind of form. In our case, we're interested in what film artists do with reality.

We will go through a process of exploration. And if this is like any of the other Flaherty seminars, that process of exploration will reveal some surprising things, surprising in the way we see films after we've seen *these* films, surprising in the things that we discover within ourselves.

I must emphasize again that this is *not* a festival. No prizes are given, no awards, no accolades. There are no commercial interests; there are no paid officers. Nobody gets to take away a medal or a little piece of paper that says his film was a great film or even that it was shown here. All the artist knows is that the film *was* shown here and that we talked about it.

We are surprised to have to tell you that Marco Bellocchio decided that it was more important for him to stay in Venice and wreck the Venice Film Festival than to come to the Flaherty. Perhaps there is a time when things have to be wrecked; but there's also a time for affirmation. For us, the fact that we're here is evidence that we believe in affirmation. At least we believe in search, we believe in finding the reasons behind things. We're sorry Bellocchio is not with us, but we are very happy to be able to welcome a very distinguished group of guests from San Francisco, from New York, from all over the country, who will be with us for varying lengths of time during this period.

We here are not concerned with "audiovisuals"; we're not concerned with "media"; we're not concerned with "mediacy." We're not concerned with any of the labels with which we try to escape the fundamental problem: the problem of the artist who is confronting the reality of the world around him.

If some of you who will be seeing these films are teachers, you are very fortunate indeed, because you will find these films great instruments for teaching, more useful and more affecting than films made by craftsmen (and sometimes hacks) to fill empty spots in school curricula.

After this, there will be no more speeches; from now on, we will talk together. Occasionally someone will introduce films. In order to have a more relaxed atmosphere for discussion, we'll move from this building to other buildings. We'll have coffee breaks and various and sundry events that Barbara [Van Dyke] will tell you about tomorrow morning. My wife is in charge of the housekeeping specifics, and I'm in the fortunate position of having the privilege of introducing what we're about to do here.

We will see two distinct groups of films tonight. The first group will consist of three contemporary American films: *A Question to Mister Humphrey* [date unknown], *How Do You Like the Bowery?* [1960, Dan Halas, Al Raymond], and *French Lunch* [1967]. *A Question to Mister Humphrey* was made by one of our guests—there's Mr. Edwin Lynch; and *French Lunch* was made by Nell Cox who is sitting up here in front. You'll have an opportunity to discuss these films with Mr. Lynch and Miss Cox when we're over in the snack bar later on.

And now I would like to introduce Mrs. Robert Flaherty, who is sitting in the front. [applause] And Monica Flaherty, on the end in the back. [applause]

Just one more word. Many of us are filmmakers, and *every* filmmaker wishes that his films could be projected under the most perfect conditions possible. We've done the very best we can to accommodate a wide variety of films (in one case, two films being projected at the same time): films in color and black and white, 16-millimeter films and 35-millimeter films, and films in various aspect ratios. This room was designed by one of America's great architects; but this architect didn't realize that you should have more than three ports in the projection booth wall, and he didn't realize that a vertical screen such as the one behind me here is not usable for motion pictures! We've brought in a screen wide enough to accept CinemaScope. Our screen is not masked either for CinemaScope or for the other aspect ratios; unfortunately this is something we cannot do.

But after all, this is a work session, a time for planting seeds, for seeing how seeds grow, for looking at the growth of artists' cinema. All the imperfections at our screenings and the fact that while here we will sleep two in a room, and so on—these are minor inconveniences. If you can bear with them, I think you will find the films themselves well worth the experience.

Thank you. [applause]

1968 JIM MCBRIDE AND L. M. KIT CARSON—ON *DAVID HOLZMAN'S DIARY* (1967)

F: What's nice about this film is that it seems to capture the questions that face all filmmakers. Why do we make movies? What are we trying to do for ourselves? I mean, true, we're trying to improve society and help the migrant workers and all that, but why do we make *films*? And I wonder if maybe we make films for the very same reason David does: we're trying to prove we have an identity.

Jay Ruby: I don't really have a question, just a comment. I love to be conned, and you conned me like I've not been conned for a long time. Thank you! [laughter]

Jim McBride: It's a very strange thing. We showed the film at the Berlin Film Academy and the students liked it a great deal, and then when they introduced me as the filmmaker, the students got very angry. They felt they'd been taken advantage of somehow. And I suppose that's true. I didn't know how to feel about that reaction then, and I still don't. I was just talking to Robert Nelson; he saw the film in Brussels and kind of felt the same way—that he'd been tricked.

Somebody told me I should put the credits at the beginning. [laughter]

F: Did you think about not putting any credits on at all?

McBride: I didn't think of it, but the distributor did. I don't really know how I feel about it. But that's probably what they're going to do.

F: A lot of people walk away not believing the credits anyway. [laughter]

F: I still don't believe them! [laughter]

F: If you release it without the titles, you're throwing the whole thing away; the titles have got to be there.

McBride: We're trying to figure out some way of telling people that we made the film, but perhaps not on the film itself.

Sol Worth: I don't think you tricked me. I don't think so at all. I feel that you did something very strange to me, but I think it was honest as hell. It was the most moving insight into a filmmaker that I have ever seen, and I really want to say the same thing as Jay Ruby: thanks. I *sure as hell* don't feel tricked; I feel that somebody gave me a gift.

McBride: Thank you.

F: I've got to ask David [laughter], "How's Penny?" [laughter]

L. M. Kit Carson: It's funny that life follows art: she turned out to be exactly what she's like in the film. [laughter]

F: I think this is one of the most brilliant acting jobs that I've ever seen.

McBride: Me, too. [applause]

Jay Ruby: Who else in the film was acting? Was the woman in the car acting?

McBride: No, she was real. [laughter]

Ruby: And the girl across the street?

McBride: That was invented; she's a friend of mine. All the others were not really *actors* but friends who were willing to work on the film.

Ruby: What about the policeman?

McBride: A friend of mine.

Frances Flaherty: I wonder if you could tell us how much and what kind of direction you gave the actors.

McBride: Well, it's important to know that actually, three of us made the film: me and Kit and the cameraman, Mike Wadleigh. I'm not sure I can take credit for directing Kit. Practically everything that Kit says in the film as David are Kit's own words, based on ideas that I wanted him to express and things that I wanted to happen. We spent a few days together before we started shooting. We'd go over each monologue; I would tell Kit what I would like him to do, and then he would put it in his own words. Every time we would go over a monologue, it was different and Kit would bring something new to it—incredibly brilliant insights. We shot almost everything in one or two takes because Kit was so good. The two of us working together, improvising together, created what David ultimately said in the film.

I know how good Kit is because I've had the experience of making this film twice. The first time, I worked with another actor who wasn't as good. We had practically finished the film, a year before this version was made. I was working at an industrial film house at the time, and I would cut the film there in the evenings; and when I left that job, I packed everything into a cardboard box and put it in my car. I left it there for a couple of days, and when I came back to get it, everything had been stolen: all of the original, the work print, the track, everything. I had to abandon the project because I didn't have the wherewithal to do it again. Then, six or eight months later, the possibility of remaking the film arose, and we did it.

Adrienne Mancia: I think we'd all like to hear from Kit.

L. M. Kit Carson: I want to answer the question about direction, because I was more aware of Jim's direction than Jim was. I'd worked on stage for about a year and a half but stopped because that's a terrible life. I'd never worked with anyone else in film. Jim definitely directed me. I would argue with him about the character sometimes; in the middle of improvising, I might say, "David's not this stupid; I don't want him to be this stupid." And Jim would say, "No, he is *just* that stupid, and you can't say anything else." He would make me go into this room and practice; he'd tell me, "Come out when you're ready and I'll listen to it and if it's not good we'll do it again." So, no matter what he says, he *did* direct. [laughter]

Mancia: Did you really live this character?

Carson: We had four days to shoot because I was in school in Texas and was in New York City just for Easter break. I realized I was totally responsible for every second of this person, so, yeah, I did live the role, and I lived in "David's" apartment; I was sleeping with the equipment. I was exactly like David, and the deterioration he undergoes in the film was partly the physical deterioration on my part during those days. Also, I broke up with a girlfriend while I made this film.

Arnold Eagle: The camerawork is brilliant; how much of the film did Kit actually shoot?

McBride: The cameraman was Mike Wadleigh, who's great. Kit did shoot a lot of the film.

Mancia: I think that almost every shot was taken from where Kit was or where he could have placed the camera, even the young man, "Dutch," coming up to get Penny's things.

McBride: We didn't do anything that one man couldn't do, except the interview with the woman in the car. There, the microphone wasn't actually tied to the camera; Kit was holding it. But when he shot the overhead shot with the fisheye lens, he had the tape recorder hanging on his shoulder and the mic around his neck.

Donald Skoller: Not only was I completely suckered into the premise, I still can't quite believe anything that you're saying here right now. The one time I wondered about things was the moment when the girl woke up from her sleep and charged the camera. Did you want to tip us off there? In "Occurrence at Owl Creek Bridge," the Ambrose Bierce story (and film), we find out at the end that all the action was happening in that instant before the man dies. It's a surprise ending, but you could argue that Bierce tips us off when he has the man see the eye of the rifleman through the sight of the gun, which is absolutely impossible. Did you want to tip your hand at any point in the film?

McBride: No, I didn't, but I feel the same way as you do about that scene.

F: I wonder if there were things that happened spontaneously during the shooting that no one controlled but that fed back into the film?

McBride: Well, that lady in the car . . . [laughter]

Mancia: You see her in that photograph of David and then you see her in the car later . . .

McBride: The way you see it in the film was exactly how it happened. We were out on the street taking that photograph and she was standing on the balcony there, and she started talking to us.

Serendipitous things happened all the time. When we started out, I had ten pages of notes, notes to myself and to Kit about what we were going to do, what the film was going to be like; but those notes represent only about two-thirds of what's actually in the film. At this point I can't really separate what happened from what was planned. If you asked whether a particular shot was preconceived or happened accidentally or happened on the spur of the moment, I couldn't tell you. It was a very strange process.

Robert Nelson: Has the girl in the car seen the film?

McBride: No.

Nelson: Do you have a release for her?

McBride: I don't have a release.

Nelson: *Is* she a girl?

McBride: She's . . . I really can't tell you exactly. [laughter] She's a girl *now*.

Mancia: They can use their imaginations.

Carson: I'm going to answer your question about serendipity, with some examples. The soundtrack is more conscious than the image. The streets are just there and they have what they have; all you have to do is make the shots and then it's a matter of selection. While we were shooting the phone call in the telephone booth, I saw that something was happening across the street. A man was lying down and cops were around him. I shouted to Jim and he sent Mike over and got that.

The soundtrack developed differently. For instance, the United Nations vote you hear as Mike carries the camera around the little park was on the radio one night and Jim just liked it and taped it and later realized how he could use it. The Newark riots were happening at the time, and they were on the radio constantly. Those are elements of texture in the film that weren't originally planned.

McBride: The lady in the car was the most felicitous accident, but it's funny because the first time I made the film, we met a woman something like her and nothing came of it—we didn't have any film in the camera or something—and I always wanted to go back and look for her. I didn't find *her*, but I found something better. It's just that magical thing. It was the same thing with that old man on the street; I had a scene in mind of a man dying on the street, and then this happened.

Mancia: This is the kind of thing Mrs. Flaherty has spoken to us about so often: we find that magic happens because we're open to magic.

Willard Van Dyke: Jim, were you satisfied with Pepe's performance?

McBride: I was. I think the scene where he's standing in front of the mural talking to David is kind of long, but that's OK.

Carson: That scene is there because Penny was a terrible actor and we felt we had to acknowledge that in the film. [laughter]

McBride: That's why that scene is there at that point in the film, but that's not why it's included.

Alvin Fiering: It seems strange to me that there's been some negative critical reaction toward *David Holzman* because the filmmakers did just what we want filmmakers to do. When you go to a fictional film, the filmmakers always try to give you an illusion of reality. It's just that most films don't use the diary form. The film from Howard University that we saw earlier [an untitled film by Ben Land] is a more conventional film; it has actors who are trying to seem as real as they possibly can in order to convince us that they're real, and yet it doesn't have that same quality. We think to ourselves, "It's just a movie"—I find it a much less involving and satisfying experience than *David Holzman*.

Mancia: I don't think we want to get into talking about the Ben Land film when there's so much to ask about *David Holzman's Diary*.

McBride: One thing that upsets me about the discussions we've had here is that when we get onto interesting subjects that don't directly relate to the guy we're talking to, the moderator always pulls the discussion back to the specific film. It seems to me that the function of the seminar should be to talk about anything we're interested in talking about. We don't have to talk about *David Holzman's Diary* anymore.

Joan Clark: There's something very important in this film that's related to *David Holzman* and to the film from Howard, too. Your film *is* an illumination; it's an illumination of pretense. Jay says it's a put-on, but it is *not* a put-on; there *is* illumination in it, about the put-ons that Holzman has with himself. The film about his illusions is illuminating. In the Howard film and in some of the other films we've seen—let's not mention them now—we feel angry and cheated because there is this *pretense* of illumination but no real illumination. You've actually illuminated pretense itself.

McBride: I *was* serious about the film.

Sol Worth: I want to go back to what Al said. I've been thinking about my own reactions, and why one film, the Howard film, didn't affect me and this one did. *David Holzman* illuminated the world for me; how Jim did the film technically is one thing, but he communicated on a personal human level because he sees very deeply into the hang-ups and responses that I feel as a filmmaker. As far as I'm concerned, the Howard film was right on the surface; and I felt cheated because I want something deeper from a film.

Carson: Technically and personally are not two separate things, in this case especially. I think the reason *David Holzman* succeeds is because it's a collaboration; the three of us understood what we were doing and contributed together. I think this film is important because it demonstrates a good way of making films. The reason why the Howard film doesn't work is because those people were actors and could not get more deeply involved than that.

Fiering: I'm not sure that you guys who have made *David Holzman* are fully enough aware of how good it is. [laughter] When someone said, "Why is the movie so good," you started to say something about technique, but I think you could have been just as technically adept as you are and made a lousy movie—if you hadn't made the film universal, if it had just been some schmucky guy talking into his tape recorder. I think the film transcends all the technical aspects and gets down to a much more basic aspect of the human condition.

The Howard film is about the inability of a boy and a girl of different races to relate. I think it's a very nicely done film on that subject, even if it is clichéd in many ways. It's about a very meaningful subject in our society, and I was quite moved by it, but your film gets into really basic issues. Is there any meaning to life? Can we hope to know anything? There are probably a hundred questions that *David Holzman* is dealing with; it goes much deeper than can a white girl make it with a black boy.

Van Dyke: I'd just like to respond to the issue of technique. It wasn't by accident that they showed you the Angenieux lens; it wasn't by accident that they pointed out the Nagra. This film could not have been conceived or executed had not those two pieces of equipment been invented. The techniques they make possible are part and parcel of the whole approach to cinéma vérité, which was what Jim and Kit were writing a book about when they took time off to make this movie.

Mancia: Willard, I think in a way this *is* their book on cinéma vérité.

McBride: That's why we couldn't finish the book!

F: In commercial cinema, Godard is probably the only filmmaker who does not bore me, and I think the reason for this is that I'm always aware that he is making a film, that he is using the techniques and skills and his whole consciousness to compose a slice of life in relation to whatever concept of truth or reality is presented in the final product. What really fascinates me about cinema is that we are aware that someone has within his consciousness images that he can translate to film form and present to us. I'm fascinated not only by what I see, but by what I can sense of the man behind the form.

Now, I think that in the Howard film, the thing that really turns me off is that Land is not working with an authentic concept of black consciousness; he's working with an imposed concept. This is a concept that many black people accept, but in fact this preoccupation with whiteness is not a *black* concept, it's a white concept. I think that the new thing that Ron Karenga [Maulana Ndabezitha Karenga (born Ronald McKinley Everett)] is getting into involves throwing away this outer concept, this outer shell, and getting into the inner consciousness. I think Land has not faced what I call the deluded image of blackness, and as to the form of his film, I had the feeling that NET had asked him to make a film for them, and as a result, he did not seem to be working in his own way with the medium.

Theodore Wing: I'm a scholarship student here, and as you've noticed, I've not said anything, though I've noticed many things. I don't mean to insult anybody when I say this, but what I feel is that the people who can really say things that would be helpful to filmmakers are not saying them at this seminar. People who are not really working with the medium are telling us what they observe, but the real feeling and the thoughts and the technical points that should be brought out are not being conveyed and there are important things that are being missed in this discussion.

The Howard film, if you want to call it "The Howard Film," is a direct expression of Ben Land and, yes, it's true that NET asked Ben Land to produce a film, but in fact, this white girl, Sally, is Ben Land's girlfriend, and in the film you see the things that are taking place with them. It's not a cliché; this film is a direct expression of Ben Land. Now, the editor on this project went and cut it up into an unbelievable mess; it was a lousy job and the film came out kind of nasty, but if you had seen the complete production, I think you would have felt quite differently.

I don't think many of you are aware of what Ron Karenga represents to the black man. There's this big gap between the documentaries that are now coming out on NET, even *Still a Brother* [1968, William Greaves], and your comments. There are things that none of you seem to understand—maybe a few do understand, but that's not coming across. You don't seem to understand what we're trying to say as black people, as movie producers. Land's film is not an expression of the cliché of the white girl trying to make it with a black boy; it represents what Ron Karenga has been saying. But if you don't *understand* what Ron Karenga represents, what his philosophy is and what can come of a relationship between two *people*—not a *white* person and a *black* person—if you're not willing to allow this to creep into your mind, then you'll never understand this film.

We have more feeling for *David Holzman* because it's about a filmmaker, and you're all interested in filmmakers and filmmaking. But if we take *David Holzman's Diary* outside of this group here, how many people in an audience will appreciate it, people not educated to what an Éclair or a Nagra is, who don't care about the feelings and frustrations of a filmmaker? How many people could really relate to this in a theater where they're not viewing the film in a group of moviemakers? A lot of you just don't seem to get this.

Mancia: Everybody's pointing at the clock, and we're being left with a lot of questions. I'm sorry that you didn't speak up before; you had things to offer. I hope everybody who has something to contribute to the discussion will do so. We'll be talking about all these issues in future discussions.

I think Jim and Kit were a little hesitant about showing their film today; I hope they feel better about it now. [applause]

1969 MICHAEL SNOW—ON *WAVELENGTH* (1967)

Standish Lawder: Canadian Michael Snow is many things: he's a painter, a sculptor, and a musician, and I think probably all these ingredients are important to Michael Snow, the filmmaker. You made *Wavelength* about a year and a half ago?

Michael Snow: It was shot in 1966.

Lawder: And it received a few showings, some notice, and then went to an international experimental film competition in Knokke-Le-Zoute, Belgium. Every few years there's a massive competition, seven days of experimental film from all over the world—sort of the Academy Awards for experimental film—and *Wavelength* won the top prize and has since been seen by a great many people and has influenced a great many films. I teach a survey course in film history; we start off with Lumière, Méliès, and Porter, and this year I ended with *Wavelength*.

Mike, do you want to say anything about the film, or shall we just throw it open?

Snow: Throw it open, I guess.

Willard Van Dyke: Sort of half-facetiously over the years, I've been saying that every film, no matter how short, is ten minutes too long, and now at last I have seen a film that is *exactly* the right length! Couldn't be one frame shorter. I enjoyed every single frame of *Wavelength*; I think it's a great, great achievement.

Snow: Thank you.

Lawder: Tell them the story you told me—I think it provides a nice capsule definition of the film . . .

Snow: A friend of mine was teaching in a school in New Mexico, mostly Navajo kids, and he showed them a lot of films, including *Wavelength*. The kids put out a mimeographed collection of reviews, some of them really fantastic, and one of the reviews was of *Wavelength*: it was just one line, written by, I'm told, an eight- or nine-year-old, who said that the film is "Drano for the mind." [laughter]

F: The soundtrack seemed quite complex; how many tracks did you mix?

Snow: There are two tracks. Originally, I wanted to have the sine wave, the glissando, on tape, so that it could be controlled separately, but then I made the optical version you heard, which is different every time I hear it. I mean I've never heard all those typewriters and bongo drums before. [laughter]

F: That's probably the longest hearing test I've ever been subjected to!

I noticed an interesting effect; as the sound rose in frequency, the sound seemed to move around the room.

F: I can't understand why the film works so well. If I had known what it was before I came, I wouldn't have come, but it *does* work. I wonder how you knew when you started that this was going to work.

Snow: Well, I didn't, really.

F: What was your conception?

Snow: It was pretty much what you see, except that the color changes and other visual elements were improvised, bearing certain things in mind. All the kinds of film stock that we used, the various events that would occur, were organized before I shot.

F: I enjoyed the film very much and I hope you won't rebuke me for my question: it may be because I'm an academic that I ask it. The film has several levels of meaning for me and I wonder if you would care to articulate what *you* feel to be any kind of verbalizable meaning of the film? Philosophically, does it say anything about the universe, or time, or the human condition?

Snow: Hmm. I don't claim to know the answers to the questions that the film raises. I do think that it says certain things and is concerned with certain things. Of course, everyone sees things in their own way, and I guess that's partly what the film is all about. I hesitate to try and explain—obviously I'm not saying this very well—but the film is meant to put you in a situation where you're made to *experience* a consideration of the nature of reality. I think that's as much as I can say.

F: When you made the film, were you concerned about boring us—which you *didn't*; I liked it very much. I mean, did you say, "Well, let's see, I need something here because I'm afraid the viewers' attention might start falling away"?

Snow: I never thought about the film being boring; I just wanted the proper duration for the zoom. Of course, I had never seen this done before, so I didn't know whether the length I chose would be right. I do think that if the film were shorter, the zoom would be moving too fast for what happens in the film—maybe it could be longer. Of course, there's money, too—the length you saw was what I could afford to do.

Everything had to happen at a certain place in the zoom. The first thing I shot was the man dying, because he [Hollis Frampton] was only available to die, I think, on a Wednesday; so after that, I had to start earlier in the zoom and hope that his death was going to arrive at the right point.

I made an attempt to give everything you see an equal position in the little world the film creates. And I attempted to place the various events so that they would have their utmost power for what they're doing. In *Wavelength*, events of color or of light are just as important as more narrative events such as the man dying. There's inevitably a tension there because naturally, you have more identification and sympathy for when there's a person in that room—but in reality, everything that you're seeing is colored light.

F: A group of articulate and intelligent students agreed on the term *transcendental* as the most satisfying to describe the effect of the film and I wonder if that seems a fitting term to Mr. Snow?

Snow: Well . . .

Lawder: He's too modest to say it is.

Snow: I do love it! [laughter]

F: How much editing did you do afterward?

Snow: I'd hoped to do everything during the shooting, but some color things didn't work out, and a reel of other color material went missing. But other than that, there wasn't much editing.

F: The tension in the film is a mystery to me. I don't even care about *how* you did it technically. I think the film is wonderful—I couldn't take my eyes off it. So this is a very small question. You have one place where you jump back in time—was that on purpose?

Snow: It's a repeat: first you see the negative of that part, then the positive version—the only shift of that kind in the film.

F: Toward the very end, the original picture dissolves into the full-screen seascape. Did you run out of zoom at that point and have to dissolve into the seascape?

Snow: No. That was a decision that I've often worried about. It's hard to describe the decision in words, but I felt that the dissolve would relate to the things that were happening in the superimposition of the colors, that it would make some kind of reference to earlier events and fold the film back in on itself. But now it's really a moot point, whether I should have continued the zoom or made that dissolve. But sometimes I think the dissolve was a mistake.

F: I loved it. But where did you get the idea? That's a terrible question to ask anyone, I know, but this is a difficult film to talk about.

Snow: It goes back to my other work and other areas of thinking. I meant *Wavelength* to sum up and crystallize, at least for myself, certain thoughts that I've had about many things.

Lawder: One of the things that's impressive is the monumental simplicity of the concept of the forty-five-minute zoom. There's no compromise at all.

Do you buy my saying earlier that your concern with music and sculpture and painting had something to do with this film?

Snow: Oh, yeah, definitely. For years, I've been operating in each of these areas more or less separately. I worked as a professional musician and then I painted and made sculpture and films, too. I went back and forth between all these fields, sometimes thinking maybe they should all be together somehow. In a way, the color issues that used to be a painting concern have come together in *Wavelength*; and I was able to bring sound in, not as background, but to be every bit as powerful as the image.

I think of the whole soundtrack, in this case and in other films, too, as being music. For example, I find the sounds of the guy entering the room—the breaking of glass and so on—against the sine wave, beautiful in a musical sense.

F: Would it be wrong from your point of view to connect *Wavelength* with the vision of Samuel Beckett?

Snow: I don't know of a connection there.

Lawder: Yoko Ono liked the film but complained about the people. Why are there people?

Snow: [laughter] I can't imagine the film *without* the people!

Lawder: You've talked about their function as a sort of punctuation.

Snow: Yes, they're a kind of punctuation, but the things that happen with the people are events like other visual events, just of a different order. The room itself is static; it doesn't move, but in a sense, the guy dying is in a passage from complete mobility, which the people represent whether we see them inside or outside, to object-hood. I wanted the visuals to create a kind of visual scale, just as the glissando is an audio scale—it goes from the lowest note that you hear to the highest. I wanted the imagery to encompass a range of movements and kinds of movements.

F: How did you think about the space in the room? Is it a three-dimensional room or a set of two-dimensional planes?

Snow: The space is both a three-dimensional illusion and a two-dimensional fact. One of the things I find interesting is that when you arrive at the photograph at the end, you're seeing a two-dimensional plane and yet it represents something limitless: you're back on the screen, just that sheet of fabric hanging there, yet you're presented with an image of spatial infinity.

F: Michael, I'd like to hear what you think about people who *don't* get the film. I think there are many members of every audience, including this one, who dislike *Wavelength*, are very bored with it. But those who feel this way don't feel comfortable *saying* that because they don't want to criticize you; or they don't want to sound as if they're not sensitive or spiritual enough to catch on.

Snow: I don't see any reason why they shouldn't dislike it. Richard Serra took the film to Holland where it caused a riot; the audience tried to tear the screen down during the film.

Van Dyke: I'd like to know what *you* mean by "don't get it."

F: I think there's a substantial minority here, maybe it's close to a majority, who didn't like *Wavelength*.

Van Dyke: Oh, that's different from "don't get it."

F: Is there someone who would like to venture an adverse assessment of the film?

F: I found it very irritating, but I liked it very much.

F: I heard someone in an elevator telling his wife it was a "blood-curdling bore." [laughter]

F: This isn't exactly adverse. I'm subject to epileptic seizures. I was fascinated by the film, but I was also afraid that after a certain point, the sound was going to set me off.

F: I wasn't afraid, but I was wondering how long I would be able to bear the film. Would I be able to stay to the very end? I wondered if it was doing something physically destructive to my nervous system.

F: I was sitting next to her and started to play games with my ear, which gave a whole new dimension to the film.

F: Stan, I was wondering if you would like to talk about the memorable screening at the College Art Association.

Lawder: Yes, this was an after-dinner crowd at a convention in a huge room—maybe a thousand people. The entire end of the room was the screen and there was a very powerful light behind a long-throw lens. It transformed that room beautifully. For the first few minutes, the audience was fascinated, then they got very irritated and became louder and louder in their irritation—but toward the end the crowd became deathly silent, and again, fascinated.

Frances, did you want to say something?

Frances Flaherty: I'm afraid this is rather belated. My mother had a canary and it hung in a cage, unfortunately very near our piano. One day, I started to practice on the piano, and after a moment, I realized that something was happening above my head. I looked up and the poor little bird was on the bottom of the cage with his legs up in the air. I was afraid my playing had almost killed him.

I had that same feeling watching *Wavelength*. [laughter] I thought I'd end up in between the aisles with my feet sticking up! [laughter]

F: Michael, do you feel that the best situation for viewing the film is sitting in chairs in an auditorium? My question implies that I don't think so.

Snow: I do think that the traditional theater setup is right for it.

F: I prescreened the film before using it with my class and I had the most awful case of fidgets, as did a couple of students who saw it with me. So we put mattresses on the floor so that people could relax and so that people who had fidgets could enact them or have their own private dramas. I think the film worked well this way.

F: I had a psychological impression and wonder if other audiences have reported the same thing—that the theater environment merged with the space within the film, especially through the sound: I felt that I could almost swim through the sound up into the screen.

Snow: I've felt that way myself. You're seeing this room that can seem like a continuation of the screening room; the film can make you think about that.

Lawder: We have lots more films to see so why don't we have just a few more questions.

F: How did you judge when to change the kinds of sounds we were hearing?

Snow: The first section is realistic, sync sound, and you hear the traffic outside the windows while you see it. Then when the image becomes negative, which is more abstract and not the way you would generally see a room, the sound shifts from being realistic, representational, to being—this is hard to describe—abstract in one sense but actually more *real* in a concrete sense than the sound of the traffic.

F: I wonder if you've ever thought about going in the opposite direction, starting close-in and zooming out?

Snow: It's been suggested that I screen *Wavelength* that way sometime.

F: I almost had the feeling when you reached the photograph that what you were going to do was start back. I had no sense of how long I'd been watching. I knew the film was forty-five minutes long and for all I knew, we were only twenty minutes into it. [laughter]

F: The film creates a sense that you're being hypnotized. On the other hand, it's such a damned tour de force that you're always standing outside of it a little bit and marveling at what's going on. So I feel like I was pulled in two different directions, neither of which was satisfactorily resolved for me.

F: At a certain point, well into the film, I stopped thinking, and all of a sudden the girl came in, and by this time I was so hypnotized about getting to the spot where the zoom was taking us that I wanted her to get out of there! [laughter]

Snow: Everything that happens with the people is sort of announced and also echoed in one way or another. An example is when the guy comes in and dies: his coming in is announced by the breaking of glass, then it's realistic sound and he stumbles in and falls, and then there's a whole set of color events, like a ripple, a kind of visual echo.

F: I had the impression that, even though you were working within time, you managed somehow to destroy it. In a sense, you destroyed space as well; you stayed within the space-time thing, but you managed to also destroy it—do you know what I mean?

Snow: Yes.

F: The film is so rich that I keep searching for antecedents. I can think of certain premonitions in Warhol and in Godard. I wonder if you could list antecedents, influences?

Snow: A film I made in 1964, *New York Eye and Ear Control,* is one.

F: And other people's work?

Snow: No other filmmakers. I think that among painters, Vermeer is about the best artist. And I had an idea that I'd like to do something that was related to the kinds of things that his paintings do. I guess he's an influence in a way.

Notes

1. Erik Barnouw and Patricia Zimmermann, "Prologue," in "The Flaherty: Four Decades in the Cause of Independent Cinema," ed. Erik Barnouw and Patricia Zimmermann, *Wide Angle* 17, Special Issue, (1995): 1 (hereafter cited as "The Flaherty").
2. Bill Sloan, phone interview by Patricia R. Zimmermann, July 28, 2012.
3. Ibid.
4. Erik Barnouw to George Stevens, USIA, Flaherty Papers.
5. "International Film Seminars Organization," in "The Flaherty," 414.
6. See Erik Barnouw, *Media Marathon,* an autobiography of Barnouw's life in media (Durham, NC: Duke University Press, 1996).
7. "Erik Barnouw, 93, Columbia Professor and Legendary Media Historian," Columbia University press release, July 25, 2001. Retrieved July 14, 2012 (http://www.columbia .edu/cu/news/01/07/erikBarnouw.html). See also Erik Barnouw, *The Sponsor: Notes on a Modern Potentate* (Oxford: Oxford University Press, 1978).
8. Dorothy Olson, phone interview by Patricia R. Zimmermann, September 19, 2009.
9. Ibid., September 27, 2009.
10. Ibid.
11. Ibid.
12. Minutes, International Film Seminars Annual Meeting, May 29, 1961, 1, Flaherty Papers.
13. David Flaherty to John Rocray, October 18, 1961, Flaherty Papers.
14. David Flaherty to Dorothy Burritt, November 20, 1960, Flaherty Papers.
15. Robert Steele, Report of the Boston Committee of Friends of Flaherty, 1961, 1–4, Flaherty Papers.
16. Robert Steele to Frances Flaherty, April 27, 1961, Flaherty Papers.
17. Letter from Frances Flaherty to Elizabeth Loosley, January 21, 1959, Flaherty Papers.
18. David Flaherty to Arnold Eagle, August 12, 1960, Flaherty Papers.
19. "1960," in "The Flaherty," 432.
20. Biography of Henri Storck, retrieved July 14, 2012 (http://www.fondshenristorck.be).
21. As a journalist in England, Lambert advocated for the Free Cinema movement, which promoted greater realism in film. Initially trained in the United Nations film unit, Wasserman was later to become a major figure in the world of network broadcast documentary, working at CBS from 1955 to 1960, then moving to NBC where he produced the news show *White Paper.* From 1976 to 1986, he produced the influential investigative news show *60 Minutes.*
22. Christopher Lehmann-Haupt, "Al Wasserman Dies at 84; Filmmaker and Pioneer of TV Documentaries," *New York Times,* April 10, 2005. Retrieved July 14, 2012 (http://www .nytimes.com/2005/04/10/nyregion/10wasserman.html).
23. It is important to remember that the NFB in Montreal was actually in the northeast region, only a few hours north of Vermont.
24. Dorothy Olson, phone interview by Patricia R. Zimmermann, September 18, 2009.
25. "Recollections: Dorothy O. Olson," in "The Flaherty," 50.
26. "1961," in "The Flaherty," 433.
27. She was a TV producer at WNDT, which later transformed in the flagship public television station WNET.
28. "Recollections: Robert Drew," in "The Flaherty," 12.
29. "Recollections: D. A. Pennebaker," in "The Flaherty," 52.

30. "Works Screened at the Flaherty 1955–1994," in "The Flaherty," 432–38.

31. Jack Churchill, "Some Notes on the Flaherty Seminars," March 23, 1962, 1, Flaherty Papers.

32. Ibid., 4.

33. Ibid., 6.

34. "Recollections: Ken Jacobs," in "The Flaherty," 33.

35. William Sloan, phone interview by Patricia R. Zimmermann, July 28, 2009.

36. Bill Pence, phone interview by Patricia R. Zimmermann, July 30, 2009.

37. Ibid.

38. "1960 Robert Flaherty Seminar Enrollment"; "1961 Flaherty Seminar Enrollments"; "1962 Flaherty Seminar Participants List"; "1963 Flaherty Seminar Enrollment"; "Participants: Tenth Robert Flaherty Film Seminar, Brattleboro, Vermont, 1964"; "Participants: Eleventh Robert Flaherty Film Seminar, Arden House, 1965"; "Participants: Twelfth Robert Flaherty Film Seminar, Arden House, 1966"; "Participants: Robert Flaherty Film Seminar 1967," typescript, IFS Collection.

39. "Financial Statement 11 Nov 66," 1966, IFS Collection.

40. Frances Flaherty to David Stewart, October 20, 1964, Flaherty Papers.

41. Announcement flyer, Flaherty Foundation Seminar, 1960; Announcement flyer, Flaherty Foundation Seminar, 1961; Announcement flyer, The Eighth Flaherty Film Seminar, 1962; Announcement flyer, Ninth Annual Robert Flaherty Film Seminar, 1963; Announcement flyer, Tenth Annual Robert Flaherty Film Seminar, 1964; Announcement Flyer, Eleventh Annual Robert Flaherty Film Seminar, 1965; Announcement flyer, Twelfth Annual Flaherty Film Seminar, 1966; Announcement flyer, Thirteenth Annual Seminar, The West Coast Flaherty Film Seminar 1967, IFS Collection.

42. Harvey Fondiller, "Flaherty Seminar: Fresh Air for Filmmakers," *Popular Photography*, February 1964, 112–13.

43. Announcement flyer, The Seventh Flaherty Film Seminar, 1961, IFS Collection.

44. Lou Lachter, "Robert Flaherty Seminar," *Better Movie Making*, January/February 1961, 16.

45. Leonard Lipton, "Should You Go to the Flaherty Seminar?," *Popular Photography*, July 1966, 140.

46. Arnold Eagle, "Industrial Motion Pictures," *Photo Methods for Industry*, October 1961, 26.

47. D. Marie Grieco, phone interview by Patricia R. Zimmermann, October 28, 2012.

48. List of Films: 1967, "The Flaherty," 437–38.

49. For a review of the significance of the film's narrative and visual strategies, see Robert Ebert, "Les Carabiniers," *Chicago Sun Times*, October 29, 1968. Retrieved July 14, 2012 (http://rogerebert.suntimes.com/apps/pbcs.dll/article?AID=/19681029/REVIEWS /810290301/1023).

50. For a fuller discussion of the career of William Greaves, see Adam Knee and Charles Musser, "William Greaves: Documentary Filmmaking and the African American Experience," *Film Quarterly* 4, no. 3 (1992), reprinted in full on the William Greaves website. Retrieved July 1, 2012 (http://www.williamgreaves.com/filmquarterly.htm).

51. Jay Ruby, "Recollections," in "The Flaherty," 64.

52. Jay Ruby, phone interview by Patricia R. Zimmermann, September 12, 2009.

53. Jay Ruby, "Out of Synch: The Cinema of Tim Asch," *Visual Anthropology Review* 11, no. 1 (1995): 20–24.

54. Ruby, "Recollections," 64–65.

55. D. Marie Grieco, "Frances Hubbard Flaherty: A True Seer," IFS Collection, 31.

56. Jack Coogan, phone interview by Patricia R. Zimmermann, September 15, 2009.

57. Dorothy Olson, phone interview by Patricia R. Zimmermann, September 15 and 25, 2009; Jack Coogan, phone interview by Patricia R. Zimmermann, September 15, 2009.

58. Jay Ruby, phone interview by Patricia R. Zimmermann, September 21, 2009.
59. Ibid.; Dorothy Olson, phone interview by Patricia Zimmermann, September 15, 2009.
60. Barbara M. Van Dyke, "Eighteen Years of Name Tags," in "The Flaherty," 310, 311.
61. Jay Ruby, phone interview by Patricia R. Zimmermann, November 19, 2009.
62. Van Dyke, "Eighteen Years of Name Tags," in "The Flaherty," 315.

The 1976 Flaherty Seminar at Pine Manor Junior College, Chestnut Hill, MA. Photo courtesy of International Film Seminars, Inc./The Flaherty, New York.

4

POLITICS, CULTURAL AND FORMAL, 1970–1980

As a more visible and political US independent film and media sector unfolded in the 1970s, it engaged, grappled with, and was recalibrated and redefined by questions of identity. This media sector emerged in tandem with the civil rights, sexual orientation, and women's movements. These larger political confrontations in US society flooded into the seminar as a continuing series of conflagrations and disputes centering on equity, privilege, and representation. Conflicts critiqued hidden agendas and uncritical positions in considering gender, race, and sexual orientation in how guests were selected, how seminar discussions developed, and how the International Film Seminars (IFS) board and administrative structures functioned.

One interpretation of the escalating arguments about issues of representation at the seminar might posit that the seminar was simply absorbing and reflecting the debates infusing the larger public media culture in the United States. Many academic disciplines in the humanities and social sciences decentered white privilege in their methods, research practices, and theories. New voices—African American, Asian American, Latino/Latina, queer, women—gained ground and visibility in the 1970s. Another interpretation might proffer that the unexamined internal operations of the seminar itself were to blame: its structure was locked into the legacies of the Flaherty films, the mythologies of Robert Flaherty created by Frances, and privileged large media organizations such as Columbia University, the MoMA, and the National Film Board (NFB) of Canada.

In the late 1960s and early 1970s, seminar programmers often promoted open calls for films, soliciting submissions and then laboriously analyzing and reviewing which films to include in the final program. By the late 1970s, as the 16mm independent film field expanded and the number of films available exponentially increased, programmers abandoned the open call system as too unwieldly. Instead, they selected films that carved out new content, directions, formal strategies, and questions, pushing the boundaries of independent cinema. These programmers were academics, librarians, and museum curators who in their professional institutional capacities and through their locations in major cities encountered a large range of films.

In the late 1960s and 1970s, the definition of independent film migrated from the poetic and the individual to a more collective and oppositional position, marking a more critical form and interventionist politics propelled by the anti–Vietnam War, civil rights and women's movements. By the 1980s, the term *independent* became increasingly identified with emergent forms such as video. An expanding public media sector interrogated the political economies of distribution and exhibition. Screenings in media arts centers, museums, university film societies, as well as expansion in the number of university film/media degrees programs, provided many more exhibition venues than in the 1950s and 1960s where films societies functioned as one of the only places to see such works. During the 1970s and 1980s, independent distributors such as New Day Films, Third World Newsreel, and Women Make Movies developed to promote these films to burgeoning black studies, ethnic studies, film studies, and women's studies programs at universities and colleges.

The period from 1970 to 1980 demonstrated gradual—and in some ways pivotal—movement away from the intimacy of the first two periods of the seminar. With their emphasis on close readings of the Flaherty films and the commanding and patrician presence of Frances Flaherty, who promoted the poetry and spirituality latent in filmmaking, the early seminars reflected a more individualistic, somewhat cocooned orientation. During the 1970s, the seminar programming transformed. It became more international. It focused more and more on socially engaged documentary. Cinéma vérité and direct cinema—strong legacies in the seminar's history—continued to appear, especially as forms evolved. As African American, antiwar, Asian American, civil rights, Latino/Latina, and women filmmakers adopted this style, it became more complex and more self-reflexive.

More arguments about ethics, ideas, and politics erupted during this period of the seminar's history. The mystical, poetic, and visual side of filmmaking advanced by Frances Flaherty butted heads with the politically and socially engaged interests of Willard Van Dyke. Van Dyke had directed the important documentary *The City* (1939). He was more educated in the history and theories of cinema than Frances, having had a long filmmaking career with various organizations such as CBS, the Federal Farm Security Administration (where he worked with Pare Lorentz on *The River* [1938]), Ford Motor Company, MoMA, the left-leaning collective Nykino, and the Office of War Information during World War II.[1] Intellectual powerhouses such as Jay Ruby and Sol Worth from the world of academic anthropology probed the ethics and power relations of the films' relationships to their contexts, subjects, and viewers at the seminar during this period. Contentious, forceful figures such as Van Dyke transformed discussions into surgical units as they dissected the impact, meanings, and strategies of the films. Throughout this tumultuous period, Barbara Van Dyke helmed as IFS's executive director.

The presidents of IFS during this period reflected this expansion and diversity of viewpoints beyond the Flaherty films and family. They also firmly anchored the seminar in the East Coast corridor of high-profile museums and universities with national and international prestige and name recognition. Willard Van Dyke, by this time head of the influential film library at MoMA, served as president of the board of trustees from 1968 to 1971. Dorothy Oshlag Olson followed him, leading IFS from 1971 to 1973, the first woman to hold this position. Austin Lamont followed Oshlag Olson as president from 1973 to 1974. He was an educational film critic, filmmaker, and writer who had worked on health and science film projects at Harvard University. The important MoMA connection continued when film librarian William Sloan held the presidency from 1974 to 1977. Temple University anthropologist Jay Ruby was president from 1977 to 1981. This group of IFS presidents evidenced how the second decade of IFS as an organization depended on the connections, contributions, and time of administrators, librarians, scholars, and writers linked to the noncommercial sectors through established large organizations.

The programmers from this period also reflected organizational changes in direction and vision, further solidifying the linkages between IFS and prestigious East Coast corridor institutions, particularly MoMA, the NFB, Temple University, and York University in Toronto. Programmers represented people who were intimately engaged in different sectors of film culture on a full-time basis: arts administrators in prominent roles at MoMA, like Willard Van Dyke (1969, 1970) and Adrienne Mancia (1971); film librarians such as Nadine Covert (1972), D. Marie Grieco (1968), and Bill Sloan (1972, 1975); and scholars such as anthropologists Jay Ruby (1978) and John Katz (1980).[2]

As D. Marie Grieco analyzed it, the conflicts embedded in the Flaherty Seminar revolved around gender issues. In the late 1960s, documentary filmmaking, the Flaherty Seminar, and the New York independent film scene were dominated by experienced, high-profile male arts administrators, filmmakers, scholars, and writers such as Erik Barnouw, George Stoney, and Willard Van Dyke, who were situated in prestigious institutions with international recognition in New York City. On the other side were the film librarians, who were for the most part—with the exception of Bill Sloan—women. These conflicts suggested a very wide divide between men in the public eye as directors, scholars, and writers and women behind the scenes, on the ground with public libraries promoting and providing space for an independent film culture to unspool in smaller, more dispersed, community-based venues.

As US independent film practices infiltrated documentary and experimental genres, libraries' purchasing of films for their media collections provided key economic support to sustain this noncommercial sector. Before the development of media centers and before museums beyond MoMA offered screenings, film librarians were the perhaps one of the largest groups of professionals to buy and exhibit independent film in the 1960s and 1970s. At Columbia University, Grieco taught the first nonprint course ever offered at a library school.[3] Grieco introduced librarian Nadine Covert to the seminar in 1971. Covert became a decades-long Flaherty Seminar advocate, serving as programmer and trustee to the seminar.[4]

Most of the libraries buying film were located on the East Coast. These film librarians were not only buying film but also mounting public exhibition programs as part of library public outreach efforts. The New York Public Library established the first film library in 1958. Bill Sloan, who became a Flaherty regular in 1964 and later headed up the Circulating Film Library at MoMA, worked there. As a Cold War response to the launch of Sputnik by the Soviets, the US Congress passed an act that allocated money to stimulate getting 16mm educational films into the schools.[5] *Encyclopaedia Britannica* profited from this initiative and sent staff to the seminar in the 1950s.[6] The Educational Film Library Association had formed in 1943. By 1966, it began to sponsor the important American Film Festival, one of the significant places to see documentaries, experimental films, science and educational films, and shorts in the 1960s and 1970s.[7] Many librarians attended this event to hunt for films for their collections.

Other Flaherty insiders and regulars interpreted the conflict differently: a battle of wills and competing ideologies between Frances Flaherty, the founder of the seminar, and Willard Van Dyke, who started attending in the early 1960s, programmed a volatile seminar in 1969, and functioned as president of IFS from 1968 to 1971. Somewhat unschooled in cinematic language and self-taught in film culture, Frances advocated an idealized, romantic view of the filmmaking process. She saw documentary filmmaking as a mystical process of spiritual discovery. For her, documentary practice derived from how one experienced and saw the world through a camera lens.

In contrast, Willard brought decades of administrative and production experience as an arts administrator, filmmaker, photographer, and producer. He possessed vast knowledge of many sectors of the film industry, spanning the artistic, to the commercial, to the government-sponsored, to the political. Not only had he worked closely with photographers involved with Group f/64 but had also served as one of the cinematographers on Pare Lorentz's *The River* (1937). He collaborated with a variety of left-leaning film groups in the 1930s such as American Documentary Films, Frontier Films, and Nykino. Later, in the 1940s, he worked for the Federal Office of War Information in the Bureau of Overseas Motion Pictures. Through that office, he operated a liaison office to Hollywood.

With *Moana* and *Louisiana Story*, Frances and Robert Flaherty experienced production management problems with the commercial film industry and sponsors. In contrast, Willard moved easily across many different sectors of commercial film production, producing films for the Ford Motor Company, McGraw-Hill, and the US Information Service. At CBS, he was a close associate with Walter Cronkite on *The Twentieth Century* (1957–68) documentary program. In 1966, he took over as director of the film library at MoMA, one of the most authoritative film libraries in the world.[8]

If Frances's world of film revolved around the five feature-length films her husband produced with a small familial operation, Willard's sense of film production extended across a much wider swathe of forms and institutions of cinema that frequently involved larger groups of people collaborating.[9] Bill Sloan identified the "clash of personalities" between Frances and Willard in the 1960s and early 1970s: "Willard was a thorn in her side [Frances]. He wanted to open up the seminar and she wanted the seminar to revolve around Bob [Robert Flaherty]."[10]

By most accounts, the administrative, artistic, and ideological battles between Frances and Willard were pitched and heated. Both were strong-willed people holding very defined, yet opposing, views about the function and purpose of cinema. Frances was inward directed, searching for lyricism and spirituality through the participation mystique and poetic realism. Willard was more outward directed, interested in probing the relationships between film and social change. Frances resented that Willard was president of IFS, a situation that underscored the Flaherty Seminars' deepening alliances in New York City and away from rural Vermont.[11] Frances had created an intensive, special, unique gathering in Vermont that focused on Robert Flaherty as a locus for discussions and thinking about documentary. In contrast, Willard pushed the seminar into the explosive and vast independent film culture detonating in the 1960s. Frances embraced the mysteries of Zen; Willard engaged politics through cinema.[12]

During the 1970s, the seminar gradually diminished the bold experimental thrusts of the 1968 and 1969 seminars. It moved more and more into political documentary, screening many of the major works of 1970s US independent film. Programs interwove direct cinema—a seminar perennial—with more voices-from-the-margins-engaged cinema that utilized compilation footage and interviews. Structuralist works peppered the seminar in these years, with projects by Hollis Frampton (*Lemon* [1969], screened in 1970 and 1975), Ernie Gehr (*Serene Velocity*, [1970], screened in 1970), and J. J. Murphy (*Sky Blue Water Light Sign* [1972], screened in 1977), as well as experimental compilation by Bruce Conner (*Valse Triste* [1977], screened in 1977).

The programs from the 1970s suggested Willard's vision triumphed. Three intermingling patterns appeared. First, animation and experimental films were less and less salient, offered as a way to shape a heterogeneous program. They continued the legacy of the poetic aspects of documentary, especially in the works of Bruce Conner, NFB animation, and West Coast experimentalists. Second, direct cinema and observational ethnographic cinema expanded—a major strain of Flaherty offerings in the 1970s. It is important to remember that the major practitioners of direct cinema lived and worked in New York, so programmers had easy access to these directors. Third, American politically engaged documentary cinema became more and more prominent, redefining the seminar as a place where new styles and new voices converged. More African Americans, regional filmmakers, and women appeared at the seminar.

In the 1970s, most of the major American directors and cinematographers of direct cinema showed work at the Flaherty Seminar: Peter Adair, Ralph Arlyck, Les Blank, Joan Churchill, Maxi Cohen, Robert Drew, Elliot Erwitt, Craig Gilbert, Chuck Hudina, Alan King, Jeff Kreines, Danny Lyon, Albert and David Maysles, Tom Palazzolo, D. A. Pennebaker, Frederick Wiseman, and Ira Wohl. This preponderance of direct cinema practitioners exposed a regional orientation, with many of these featured filmmakers living in either New York City—where they did independent projects as well as work for various sponsors—or Boston—with ties to ethnographic film, Harvard University, and WGBH public television.

The proximity of these filmmakers to the various locations of the seminar cannot be underestimated: for an organization perennially challenged by lack of resources, drawing in filmmakers from the East Coast corridor proved very cost effective, reducing travel budgets. Most of these direct cinema filmmakers were Americans, with the exception of Nick Broomfield (United Kingdom), Louis Malle (France), Jean Rouch (France), and Michael Rubbo (Canada), all of whom presented slightly less distant observational strategies. Probably unintentionally, the programming mapped a direct cinema/cinéma vérité triangle between the East Coast, Eastern Canada, and Europe.

At the Flaherty, however, direct cinema was often programmed with ethnographic cinema, a historical legacy of the seminars going back to its origins in the 1950s where anthropological filmmakers contributed to the elaboration of a documentary practice of exploration promoted by Frances. A key Flaherty board member and participant in the 1960s, Colin Young developed the term *observational cinema* for ethnographic films that drew some of their strategies from direct cinema (immersion in events, light-weight cameras and sound) but focused on groups rather than individuals and rituals rather than the crisis structure. Throughout the 1970s, ethnographic and observational films were programmed, with presentations by important, field-changing figures such as Timothy Asch, Ted Carpenter, Napoleon Chagnon, John Marshall, and the Netsilik Eskimo Project.

Although the seminar programming in the 1970s continued to pivot around hetero-geneous film practices involving animation, documentary, experimental, and narrative genres, it is clear from seminar programs that American political documentary came to dominate programming. The other genres provided historical reminders of the neo-realist and poetic interests of past seminars. These films established new contours for independent film, now defined not only by its opposition to Hollywood and corporate sponsors but also through its explicit critique of dominant ideologies and governments. For example, Amalie R. Rothschild directed the early feminist film, *Nana, Mom and Me* (1975). She later became Willard Van Dyke's lover. She contended: "I always thought of the Flaherty Seminar as "film camp" and the 1970s were extraordinary years. Every important social issue documentary of the decade was shown and heatedly discussed."[13]

Rothschild's memory was bolstered by evidence. The list of independently produced politically engaged films screened at the seminar during this period far outnumber the direct cinema and observational films. Landmark feminist films screened included *And You Act Like One Too* (1976); *Antonia: Portrait of the Woman* (1974); *Anything You Want to Be* (1972); *Betty Tells Her Story* (1972); *David: Off and On* (1972); *Growing Up Female: As Six Become One* (1971); *It Happens to Us* (1972); *Joyce at 34* (1972); *Nana, Mom and Me* (1975); *Old-Fashioned Woman* (1974); *Union Maids* (1976); *With Babies and Banners* (1979); and *The Woman's Film* (1971). Feminist filmmakers became a major force at the seminar, with more women presenting films than in previous decades.

If the 1950s and 1960s had featured women such as Frances Flaherty and Helen van Dongen who worked with and propped up the great men of documentary behind the scenes, the 1970s seminars showcased women as filmmakers who gave voice to a myriad of women's issues such as abortion rights, feminist politics, identity, maternity, sexual-ity, and union organizing that had been silenced: Abigail Child, Liane Brandon, Joyce Chopra, Martha Coolidge, Cinda Firestone, Holly Fisher, Jill Godmilow, Lorraine Gray, Barbara Kopple, Julia Reichert, Amalie R. Rothschild, Susan Seidelman, Judy Smith, Agnes Varda, and Claudia Weill. Experimental documentarian Shirley Clarke, who had two decades of engagement with the seminar as a presenter and board member, returned in 1973 for a live video performance entitled "Videospace Troupe Presentation," that entailed audience participation in pulling a rope.

This infusion of feminist filmmakers into the formerly mostly all-male bastion of the Flaherty Seminar spurred change both at the seminar itself and in the larger media landscape. At the 1971 seminar, intense discussions percolating around the work of the women filmmakers prompted an emergency breakfast meeting. The breakfast presented a formal agenda: the importance of women's issues in documentary. The breakfast attendees included a large list of women filmmakers and programmers: Chloe Aaron, Suzanne Baumann, Kit Clarke, Nadine Covert, Deborah Dickson, Mary Feldbauer

Jansen, Tana Hobnan, Victoria Hochberg, Jeanne Mulcahy, Kristine Nordstrom, Julia Reichert, Amalie Rothschild, Janet Sternburg, and Miriam Weinstein. Many in attendance at the Flaherty Seminar breakfast joined the steering committee.[14]

As a result of this breakfast, Julia Reichert and Jim Klein ascertained the need for more substantive development of viable infrastructure to support feminist film distribution. Heated controversies had blazed through the seminar discussion after the screening of their film *Growing Up Female* at this seminar. Reichert and Klein were self-distributing the film in order to reach specific women's groups, bypassing television or theatrical exhibition. The following year, Reichert and Klein met filmmaker Liane Brandon (director of *Anything You Want to Be* and *Betty Tells Her Story*) at the seminar. They discussed the need for a way to distribute feminist films to women's political organizations. Together, they formed New Day Films, an important feminist film distribution collective, in 1972. The purpose of New Day Films was to connect the films to the women's movement.[15]

African American filmmakers, many involved with public television programs such as the influential *Black Journal* (1967–70), also presented works from an African American perspective such as *Harvest 2000 Years* (Haile Gerima, 1976), *I Am Somebody* (Madelyn Anderson, 1970), *Killer of Sheep* (Charles Burnett, 1978), *Nation of Common Sense* (St. Clair Bourne, 1975), and *Voice of La Raza* (William Greaves, 1972). These filmmakers constituted the historically significant figures of African American documentary and feature film in the 1970s. The seminars also featured work from many regional film workshops located in Appalachia, California, New York, and Puerto Rico. Later renamed Appalshop, which became one of the most important centers for regional community expression, the Appalachian Community Film Workshop screened many of their important early works, such as *Hog Killing* (1971), *Judge Wooten and Coon on a Log* (1971); and *The Millstone Sewing Center* (1972), with filmmakers Mimi Pickering, Bill Richardson, and Herb E. Smith in attendance.

Politically oppositional films in the compilation and interview genres also screened at the seminars in greater numbers than ever before, thus signaling the shift away from the neorealist and the poetic toward hard-hitting muckraking exposés and movement works: *Attica* (1974); *Free Voice of Labor: Jewish Anarchists* (1980); *Harlan County USA* (1976); *Hearts and Minds* (1974); *IF Stone's Weekly* (1973); *Men's Lives* (1974); *Millhouse: A White Comedy* (1971); *Paul Jacobs and the Nuclear Gang* (1979); *People's War* (1970); *¡Que Hacer!* (1970); and *Selling of the Pentagon* (1971). In 1973, the works of the political collective Newsreel appeared at the Flaherty Seminar, as did recovered films from the Workers Film and Photo League, presented by Tom Brandon of Brandon Films.

Despite the administrative moniker of IFS, the thrust of the seminar programming during this period revealed a majority of American filmmakers as well as a preponderance of white males. However, some international films diversified the programs, many with some connection to international political movements: Santiago Alvarez (Cuba); Joris Ivens (the Netherlands); Miguel Littin, *El chacal de Nahueltoro* (Chile,1969); Chris Marker (France); Marcel Ophuls (France); Anand Patwardhan (India); Gabriela Samper, *Los santisimos hermanos* (Columbia, 1969); Ousmane Sembène, *Tauw* (Senegal, 1970); and Agnes Varda (France). Ophuls was the featured master filmmaker at the 1972 seminar, Ivens in 1979.

Conflicts between different historical positions and professional and social alliances rippled through this period. The mix of the strong (and for some, problematic and insensitive) Willard Van Dyke (a fervent champion of independent film), with the waning influence of the Flaherty family on the seminar, indicated a tectonic change. The rise of the Van Dyke family (Barbara as executive director and Willard as president) and the influx of academics Jay Ruby and Sol Worth trained in thinking about images within more intellectual methodologies suggested not only an organizational reorientation but also a movement into larger intellectual contexts. The evolution of oppositional film practices integrated with the anti-Vietnam War, civil rights, and women's movements of the 1970s congealed.

Some Flaherty veterans involved in the seminars during this time attributed the transformation of the seminars from a small group of like-minded people gathered to explore cinema into a more contentious gathering galvanized by critiques and interventions to the feisty, intimidating Willard Van Dyke. They contended he saw the prestige of the seminar as a means through which to secure his position and standing at MoMA. Others contended that the influx of academically trained scholars from anthropology and film studies propelled the language of the seminar discussions from one of heartfelt, intuitive reaction to a more abstract, distant critique.[16] However, it is difficult to prove that any one of these factors contributed to the recalibration of the seminars' content, discussions, and esprit de corps. Instead, it is perhaps more prudent to argue that all of these factors and trends—many of them situated within the larger political and historical and political convergences of the destabilizations of the civil rights, the women's movement, and the Vietnam War—generated a discursive force field to push the seminar in new directions. This combination of academics, film professionals, and political activists shifted the seminars away from the exploratory, the humanist, and the poetic and into a more intellectual and political environ.

The legendary postscreening arguments skewering filmmakers that have fertilized the Flaherty Seminar mystique in media culture irrefutably commenced during this period. Willard, an insistent vocal presence in discussions, spearheaded many of these discomfiting altercations. However, it is not accurate to attribute this more intellectually aggressive seminar tactic to Willard Van Dyke's difficult personality alone. Anthropologists Jay Ruby and Sol Worth were key figures in the seminars in the 1970s. While Willard might have been perceived as adopting an aggressive, personal attack mode, it was Ruby and Worth who brought forward questions of image ethics and relationships between filmmakers and subjects, key operational concerns in ethnographic practice.[17] As Jay Ruby explained:

> The Flaherty Seminar is also known as a place where filmmakers are roasted and, at times, personally attacked. This reputation is partially the result of the intensity of the discussions— passions and fatigue sometimes cause people to overreact. Willard Van Dyke, Sol Worth and I guess, myself, were known to have an explosive way of critiquing a film. Sometimes the critiques appeared to the makers as personal attacks and they responded accordingly. The seminar is a place where the differences between makers, teachers, critics and scholars become intensified. Academics and other wordsmiths make a living "fighting" with words. Filmmakers do not.[18]

Some participants from the 1970s referred to Ruby, Worth, and Willard Van Dyke as the "Big Three" because they were always quick to enter into postscreening discussions. They raised issues about the latent assumptions in the films or the implications of stylistic choices. Sarah Elder was a documentary filmmaker recognized for her longtime collaborative documentary work with indigenous peoples in Alaska. She attended many seminars in the 1970s. She recalled: "I was fiercely certain that the documentary profession had to challenge its elitist legacy, that it had to include more members in the club. The club (makers, critics, programmers and even many audiences) was made up of mostly white intellectuals—and here I was, another initiate being baptized into the community of passionate brethren. It was definitely 'brethren' in those days. I so understand that I was in a culture with a collective memory of transcendent screenings, unforgettable debates, heroes, elders, clowns and aristocracy; a talented community with a deep moral code and an exquisite sense of seeing."[19]

Elder also noticed scant attention paid to what was then called "third world" filmmakers, collaborative filmmaking practices, indigenous people, or the powerless. She argued that the seminar often advanced an uncritical American/Eurocentric cult of the individual artist and a Westernized aesthetic, a contention supported by the programming records. Even with these critiques, the seminar in the 1970s functioned as a key nodal point in the development independent media culture, a place where a heterogeneous group from different parts of film culture of different ages converged around works that had limited public exhibition.

As the Van Dyke family superseded the Flaherty family—with son Murray Van Dyke often serving as seminar projectionist—the seminar programming underwent a dramatic reorientation. The 1950s and 1960s seminars established what became a longstanding formula of looking closely at the films of Robert Flaherty as a cinematic visionary, independent filmmaker outside the Hollywood studio system, pathbreaker, and role model. These seminars screened several Flaherty films and asked participants to listen carefully to those who contributed to their production process and to probe deeply. As the influence of the Flaherty family on IFS retreated in the 1970s, this structure endured but with some revamping. Now, instead of screening a panoply of Flaherty films, programmers screened only one Flaherty film. Instead of positioning Robert Flaherty as the master filmmaker, programmers invited an established master filmmaker with international recognition whose body of work served as the throughline for the seminar.

Three of the most influential and significant seminars of the 1970s (1972, 1978, and 1979) all featured eminent independent documentary filmmakers with large bodies of work who intervened into the ethics, framing, and practice of documentary. These were filmmakers of recognized identifiable international impact and significance. In 1972, programmers Nadine Covert and Bill Sloan featured French documentarian Marcel Ophuls. In 1978, Jay Ruby brought in French ethnographic filmmaker Jean Rouch. In 1979, Bill Sloan positioned Dutch radical filmmaker Joris Ivens in the role of master filmmaker.[20]

The 1972 seminar was particularly important in the seminar's history because Covert and Sloan subtly redirected the programming philosophies of the seminar. Reacting to previous years' programs where they felt the films were too similar, they launched a new strategy to mix up the programming with different formats and genres. They also programmed films not only because they were artistically or politically significant, but also for their potential to ignite discussions on topics that needed debate in the emerging, still-undeveloped independent film world. As Covert recalled, earlier seminars had focused almost exclusively on what were considered "outstanding films" of the year. While she and Sloan did not entirely dispose of this criterion, they also searched for works that would "catalyze discussion." Their strategy signified redirection toward considering the reception of the films. The Flaherty audience possessed a highly sophisticated view of cinema.[21] They reasoned that their programming needed to provide interactivity and questioning rather than awe at exceptional artistry. Covert and Sloan's thinking about how to program the seminars—an established filmmaker, a heterogeneous mix of genres and formats, and provocations of deeply engaged discussion—became a key operational tactic of seminar programming as the decades progressed.

During this period, IFS initiated two projects that garnered a high level of impact in the media landscape beyond the rather isolated seminar: the highly contested restoration of *Nanook of the North* and the Arden House Seminars for public television executives. The first provides an example of the seminars' continuing promotion of the historical legacy and significance of Robert Flaherty. The second illustrates how the seminar's unique model based on a retreat-like isolation, sophisticated film programming that challenged expectations, and vigorous discussion of ideas was exported to the television sector. If the former hinged on the archival and the historical, the latter revolved around opening up dialogues between the auteurs of independent film and the managers of television organizations to work toward engaging and remaking the future of the new public broadcasting network.

In 1960, Frances Flaherty transferred the ownership of *Nanook of the North*, previously held by Flaherty and the Revillon Furs Company, to IFS. Her hope was that the rental income would underwrite the development of seminars, a beneficent idea that never really provided the level of funding the seminar required. According to David Shepard, 51 percent of the rights went to IFS and the remaining 49 percent to the Robert and Frances Flaherty Study Center at Claremont School of Theology in California.[22] However, when IFS received the prints, Erik Barnouw discovered that they were in a "woeful condition."[23] In addition, another print was circulating, often referred to as the "narration version," a shortened print produced after World War II in 1946 with not only the poetic intertitles removed but also with outtakes from the original film inserted. Shepard contended that Flaherty himself had reedited this version. Leo Dratfield distributed the shorter version through his nontheatrical company Contemporary Films, selling hundreds of prints to educational institutions and libraries. David Shepard recounted that he recalled that Frances Flaherty "hated the narration because it did not give the viewer opportunity to explore the image."[24] IFS wanted to create a new negative to restore the film to the cinematographic beauty of the 1922 version. Shepard has also argued that Dratfield needed a restored version of the print because he was making dupe negatives from a well-used version.[25]

By the 1970s, IFS had commissioned David Shepard, by this time at the University of California, to study the problem in order to determine if filmic material in better condition might be available from other archives.[26] Shepard started to attend the Flaherty Seminar in 1965 when he was very young. There, he met regulars such as Shirley Clarke and considered Frances Flaherty one of his most influential teachers of cinema. In 1967, Shepard had lived with Frances Flaherty at the farm in Brattleboro, Vermont. He contended that Frances initiated the idea to restore *Nanook of the North*.

Shepard discovered that except for one small roll, the original negative of *Nanook* had burned in 1960. The 35mm master positive print to protect this version had been destroyed in an unfortunate fire at the NFB in 1967. Other copies—first-generation 35mm prints from 1937, master prints, nitrate dupe negatives—were damaged by decomposition, deterioration, overuse in exhibition, and scratch marks. The MoMA print, for example, was marred with scratches.[27] In the early 1970s, according to Shepard, IFS "allocated a virtually unlimited budget for the restoration of the film upon learning of this crisis situation, and the Museum of Modern Art agreed to survey every archive in the world in an attempt to located surviving prime prints."[28] Shepard argued that at the time, IFS did not have the clout to work with international archives, primarily because it operated as an entirely volunteer organization. On the other hand, Willard Van Dyke, due to his affiliation with MoMA, a member of the influential Fédération Internationale des Archives du Film (FIAF), could open doors to foreign archives that held negatives and prints of the film.

Prints of *Nanook* were located at the National Film Archive in London and the Royal Film Archive, Belgium. The original fifty-five-minute running time of the film was sourced from a 1921 review of *Nanook of the North* in the entertainment industry trade magazine *Variety*.[29] However, Shepard ascertained that the original version of the film was projected at twenty-one frames per second. To project a new print at the standardized twenty-four frames per second, shot length needed to be slightly extended through printing to maintain the pacing of the original film.[30]

The retrieved archival negative and prints of *Nanook* provided scenes and frames that could replace the damaged ones. The basic source for the restoration was the nitrate print from the National Film Archive, with the night scenes tinted blue. The old nitrate print was soaked in a bathtub filled with water for two weeks, so the emulsion would swell and fill in the scratches, and then wound loosely around a core.[31] The original intertitles were retrieved from a print in London and inserted into the film, often with printing several lengths of each title and splicing the negative together. To help reduce the abrasions to the image, the other scenes from the film were processed through wet gate printing where the liquid fills up the scratches. An assistant editor analyzed each shot on an upright Moviola editing machine, marking "with a white crayon every individual frame which still showed a blemish."[32] Frames and scenes with material from other print sources replaced damaged images. Every shot of the film was retrieved. Using the National Film Archive print as a template, the restoration entailed matching the contrast of darks and lights within scenes, pulling images from different sources, and employing optical printing.[33] Byron Laboratories in Washington, DC, performed more than fifty lab tests with different developing times, exposures, and solution temperatures to address the problem of matching contrast from so many different sources.[34] Eventually, a new, balanced fine-grain 35mm negative of *Nanook of the North* was produced in 1972 with a new soundtrack. Frances saw the restoration before dying later that year.

Willard Van Dyke was not only president of IFS as this time but was at MoMA, a convergence of institutional affiliations that facilitated a restoration project of this complex scope. Many on the board accused Willard of self-aggrandizement through appending himself not only to IFS but to the Flaherty name. By the 1970s, Willard was one of the few Flaherty "elders" who had known Robert Flaherty. However, the *Nanook* crisis, as identified by Barnouw, extended beyond the pitiful state of this film. In fact, the restoration itself provoked a crisis of nearly epic dimensions between the board and Willard Van Dyke.

As an underfunded nonprofit operating almost entirely on volunteer labor, IFS was always strapped for funds. Many board members felt that the best use of the endowment was to support the mounting of the seminar, financing guests, and underwriting scholarships for attendees. They vociferously disagreed with the deployment of endowment funds for the restoration, which they considered a vanity project propelled by Van Dyke to augment his reputation at MoMA and in the larger international film world. Many on the board were not happy with the restored version and the new score. Willard Van Dyke had decided that the original score would hurt rentals and sales. He commissioned a new contemporary music score by Peter Serkin and Toshi, which rankled many trustees as an unmitigated act of arrogance.

Some trustees asserted that in the quest for pristine *Nanook* images, those involved with the restoration had stolen material from the Flaherty farm, Frances, and from IFS itself. Those involved in the restoration countered that IFS and its trustees had also stolen material. These angry and sometimes personally brutal debates about the deployment of IFS endowments developed in a larger institutional context of internal disagreements about a range of issues: the career aspirations of various board members and IFS personnel; the direction and vision of IFS; the legacy of *Nanook of the North*; the role of the Flaherty family history; and warring factions between career filmmakers, librarians, and programmers.

Pitched antagonisms between those adhering to an idea of the poetic and the romantic in cinema and those promoting a more political vision also surfaced. In addition, the strategies for sustainability of a small nonprofit media organization never really resolved, perhaps as a result of the informal alliances and networks lacking systematic governance that kept IFS and the seminar going in the first place.[35] As a project that was not centered on producing the seminar, the *Nanook* restoration opened up a fault line in the organization. Despite the rancor, Films Inc., under the aegis of Flaherty seminar veteran Charles Benton, financially salvaged the Shepard restoration. His version assumed the position as the definitive version of *Nanook of the North*.

The second initiative that expanded beyond the confines of the actual seminar was what the Flaherty trustees referred to colloquially as the "Arden House Seminars," which were actually called the Public Television and Independent Film Seminars. They constituted a powerful collaboration between the newly formed Corporation for Public Broadcasting (CPB), IFS, and the National Endowment for the Arts (NEA). Managed by IFS executive director Barbara Van Dyke, the Arden House Seminars ran from 1971 to 1981. They commenced just one year after US Congressional approval in 1970 to form the Public Television Service. Arden House Conference Center, formerly the Harriman

Estate, was about an hour north of New York City. Columbia University owned and operated it as a conference center. It was poised atop a mountain in a woodland setting, with excellent screening facilities and elegant space for discussion gatherings. Public television executive David Stewart had attended several Flaherty Seminars in the 1960s and now served on the board of CPB. He approached the seminar about mounting a week-long intensive session based on the Flaherty Seminar model to create dialogues between independent filmmakers and public television program managers.[36]

The Arden House Seminars began during a time of fervent political debate between Democrats and Republicans about the role of public broadcasting in the United States. A 1965 Carnegie Commission Report argued that American broadcasting, with its three commercial networks nationalizing and solidifying discourse, needed to feature programs that documented and explored the diversity of American life. The Public Broadcasting Act of 1967 advocated that a public service was imperative to produce a healthy citizenry.[37] As communications scholar Robert Avery has pointed out, President Lyndon Johnson propelled this act as part of his "Great Society" initiatives.[38] A Carnegie Commission Report of 1967 demonstrated that the national networks had eroded localism. The report also defined public television as programming not supported by advertising, underscoring the idea of television functioning as a "social unifier and spiritual uplifter."[39] However, as Patricia Aufderheide has argued, despite these lofty and somewhat utopian goals, Richard Nixon launched a five-year attack against public television, contending that its public affairs programming was antiadministration and elitist. These attacks reduced foundation funding. They also framed public television as a political battleground. Nixon vetoed appropriations for CPB.[40]

In 1968, David Stewart had worked on the staff of the NEA but had committed to joining CPB. He proposed a small joint fund between CPB and NEA that would finance mutually beneficial activities. One idea revolved around creating a gathering for public television executives and program managers. In 1970, Stewart attended the Flaherty Seminar at Hotchkiss with the intention of securing advice from Barbara, Willard, and Edith Zornow, an educational television producer who was also intimately involved in the seminar as a board member and programmer. As Stewart saw it, the public television field needed what he called "something like a Flaherty" because "the Flaherty format of screenings and discussions had been perfected."[41]

Stewart knew firsthand that very few public television executives and program managers spent much time watching programs and almost never discussed them. He also knew that the American political scene was rife with controversies over questions of social change provoked by the civil rights, Vietnam War, and women's movements. He deeply understood that even affluent public television stations could not afford staff producers to create programming. After the Nixon veto, public television experienced "growing pains within the fragile noncommercial system that more than once threatened to pull it apart."[42]

Working with the Van Dykes and Zornow, Stewart developed the idea that independent filmmakers and public television executives could forge an interdependency by meeting to screen controversial material in the context of engaged discussions in a retreat-like environment modeled on the Flaherty Seminar. The Arden House Seminars were shorter than the regular Flaherty Seminar, running for five days instead of ten. The gatherings were controversial and rancorous, crammed with intense debates. As Stewart remembered, these seminars "were rarely marked by out of control laughter. It was a pretty serious crowd: earnest, determined, highly intelligent, and creative people who took their professions, and frequently themselves, quite seriously."[43]

Across the eleven years of the Arden House Seminars, a highly distinguished and professionally visible group of Flaherty board members, filmmakers, and trustees programmed: Erik Barnouw (film and media historian); James Blue (filmmaker and producer); Ed Emshwiller (filmmaker); D. A. Pennebaker (filmmaker); Jay Ruby (visual anthropologist); and Amos Vogel (film programmer).[44] Jay Ruby has observed that not only did public television program managers need to have more time to look at programs but also required consciousness-raising about the current state of documentary and experimental film. They needed to know more about the independent film milieu, a world remote from their prior executive experiences in commercial broadcasting.[45] Many films screened at the annual Flaherty Seminars migrated to the Arden House gatherings. The Arden House Seminars were more aggressive about pushing participants to see and think about cinema in new ways, given the explicit goal of creating alliances between independent producers and public television and shorter duration.

As Ruby saw it, the Arden House Seminars showed the public television executives works they would never have looked at or known existed, such as *The Battle of Chile* (1975), installations by Nam June Paik, and video art by Steina and Woody Vasulka. In Ruby's assessment, these seminars provoked "more intense discussions" than the regular Flaherty Seminars. Because of the national political struggles over the existence of public broadcasting and the very real political economy of needing to acquire outside programming from independents, the stakes were much higher. Stewart observed that "shouting matches and enraged stalkings out were not uncommon."[46] The questions circulating at Arden House were not confined to the films but also extended to the questions of how a publicly funded television system might operate. Questions raised at these gatherings included what public television was prepared to show audiences, how much it could enter into highly politicized issues, and how much political and aesthetic radicalism could the system broadcast.

As the 1980s approached and the seminar entered its fourth decade, its organization, participants, programming, and structure had changed. IFS established the Flaherty as a nonprofit organization apart from the Flaherty family, solidifying its visibility and position in New York City with the presidency of Willard Van Dyke and the executive directorship of his wife, Barbara. The list of trustees expanded from those who knew and had worked closely with Robert or Frances Flaherty or who had attended the early seminars into a diverse group of independent media partisans from academia, film distribution, the professional programming world, and public libraries. The programming expanded beyond Flaherty films, with a much more heterogeneous mix of formats and genres. Instead of focusing on the oeuvre of Flaherty, established international filmmakers were featured.

The poetic and the political camps of the Flaherty battled it out in discussions, with direct cinema programmed side by side with more political compilation films. After a large opening in the late 1960s, the poetic impulse faded as political cinema occupied more space in programming and discussions. The participants who came to the Flaherty changed as well. As visual anthropology and film studies developed in the 1970s, more academics appeared, importing a more analytical, combative, and sophisticated style of interrogating films rather than simply experiencing them. Some Flaherty veterans found their discourse unnecessarily abstract. More African American, political filmmakers, and women were featured. More guests came from outside the United States. More film distributors and programmers from the expanding activist, educational, noncommercial, and politically oppositional sectors attended. The seminar grew, moving from a small intimate group on the farm to a congregation of more than one hundred people. As the public media sector blossomed out of experimental arts and political media movements in the 1970s, the seminar transformed from a familial endeavor into a nodal point for urgent debates boiling up in the functions and practices of independent film. By the end of the period, the seminar's definition of independent film was resolutely interventionist, noncommercial, and provocative. This redefinition of the term independent film was directed toward rewiring preconceptions about distribution, exhibition, filmmaking, and social and political ideologies.

1970 HOLLIS FRAMPTON—ON *ZORNS LEMMA* (1970)

Hollis Frampton: I have no prepared statement. I will say that I finished *Zorns Lemma* at the end of March, and in the month that followed, I saw it something like twenty-five times. I have not seen it at all since May, and in a sense, this is the first time I've seen it fresh. It's like taking a vacation from your wife—probably a good idea once in a while. What I have to say about the experience of seeing it fresh is simply that I find myself, for the first time, perhaps, in the position of being my own audience and really seeing the film for the first time.

There was a certain quality, or set of qualities, that I wanted the film to have when I was making it. I wanted it to generate a kind of pressure, if possible an extreme pressure, within the viewer's sensibility and then systematically to release that pressure. When I saw the film during the days after it was completed, I was minutely familiar with every frame in it, and with every sort of molecule that it contained, and I was in such an extreme state of fatigue that instead of its generating the pressure I've mentioned, instead of the pulse driving the substance of the film through the optic nerve and into the brain, I just sat there, feeling that *Zorns Lemma* was a very leisurely, very quiet, very serene sort of film. Other people did not feel that way at the time. And now, after taking a vacation from it, I no longer feel that way myself.

I say all this to forewarn you that if you have any questions about *Zorns Lemma*, you may not get a completely uncluttered answer. I'm no longer quite as clear about my feelings about the film as I might have been in May. I do feel that *Zorns Lemma* is the fullest statement I've yet made.

Flaherty seminarian (F): What is your response to the advertisement for the film that appeared in the New York Film Festival ad, comparing it with the mathematical precision of a Lewis Carroll?

Frampton: Oh, really? I haven't seen that squib. I was up in the country when the Film Festival decided to include *Zorns Lemma*; they got hold of me via the fire chief of

Leonardsville, New York. I told them, "Go ahead! I made the film to be shown: show it."

Now, Lewis Carroll—that's quite remarkable. I happen to be very fond of Lewis Carroll. As far as the mathematics thing, of course, Zorn was a mathematician; his lemma is an axiom in set theory, which states simply that every partially ordered set contains a maximal fully ordered subset. I am not a mathematician; I'm, so to speak, a spectator of the sport of mathematics.

I've been questioned by mathematicians about *Zorns Lemma*; they say what does this have to do with mathematics? They're upset about my title. They're very concerned with the purity of their discipline, and they feel that I'm kind of dumping twenty-seven-hundred-odd pictures into one of their favorite topics in advanced mathematics. It's simply that one wants a title that will be remembered.

The film is an effort to control a very large body of material and to control it in a way that I believe it hasn't been controlled before. The film consists of a partially ordered set of all the elements in it and their combinations. It's basically a sort of house-that-Jack-built form, a very childish cumulative verse form, if you like, in one sense at least.

The question is, what is the maximal fully ordered subset within the partially ordered set? It turns out to be—it's as if I'm revealing the secrets of the Mystery Chef at home or something like that!—not the alphabet but the *pulse*, the one-second pulse of the film, which is what I believe to be the ordering principal in all film: all film goes through the projector at twenty-four frames per second and that is the maximal fully ordered subset of the partially ordered set of all films.

Does that answer your question?

F: Why were the *I*s and *U*s not included? That bothered me a lot.

Frampton: I'll tell you very simply why I did that. To begin with, there was the matter of symmetry; that is to say, the Roman alphabet is a twenty-four-letter alphabet, which has a certain internal resonance with the twenty-four-frames-per-second quality of film. There was also the reinforcing condition of the statistical sparsity of *I*s, *J*s, *U*s, and *V*s in the environment.

As to the film's bothering you, in all kindness, I have to give you the same answer that Igor Stravinsky gave a young lady who said, "Mr. Stravinsky, I like your *Firebird* and *Rite of Spring* very much, but I don't like any of your later works. Why is that?" He said, "Madam, that's a matter for your physician, not for me."

F: Why did you have a host of voices articulating the final statement? It fragmented my attention.

Frampton: Well, that's good. I used the voices, of course, to carry the one-second pulse over into the final section; at that point, it goes from the picture track, the *visual* channel, to the *audible* channel.

But also I wanted to keep that text, or that portion of the original text—it's a very beautiful Latin text which I have butchered, bowdlerized, mistranslated, bent to my own purposes, and everything else—I wanted to keep it from being merely "philosophical." You know, you have some guy with a honey baritone voice saying in Dylan Thomas-ese, "The first bodily form I judge to be light," and everybody is "Wow, philosophy!" I wanted Grosseteste's text to be *in the film*, and not seem like some old guy's piece of boring medieval light philosophy that I smarmed on top of the film as the mystical explanation of it all. I wanted it to be *not* philosophical; and also, I wanted to push it down to a level where the key words would jut out, all the stuff about the four elements and the business of counting and measure.

I chose women's voices because women are less rhetorical in their use of their voices than men.

F: In terms of communication, I don't see what advantage you got. If I invited you to dinner and I took all the steak and ice cream and the beans and everything and mixed them all up and put them in a fire hose and squirted them at you, you would say, "Why invite me to dinner and then do that?"

Frampton: I would think you had bizarre ideas of the role of a host!

I am not here, however, in the role of a host; I am here in the role of a guest, like you. We are *all* at the banquet, as it were. We are all here with our nutritive needs, our appetites, our queasinesses of stomach of the moment, and so forth. We are partaking of crumbs, if you will, at the great feast of the art of the cinema.

I'm responsible for my own films. I think filmmakers are, as any artist is, responsible in a certain sense for their whole art, their whole tradition, the entire resources of their art. But on the other hand, I cannot propose to dress the table individually for each person; I can only propose things that meet my needs and bud them off, if you will, in the belief that my needs are not so very queer, that there are others who have similar needs. I doubt that I'm utterly unique.

I think that's more honest than to say, "Well, I'm going to please all these people." I was at pains I thought to keep the flavors separated, in fact, rather than putting them all in a fire hose.

Sol Worth: I don't mean to defend your film because I don't think it needs that, but I think sometimes people forget that the notion of communication has at least two parts: there is somebody who articulates something and there is somebody who presumably is supposed to receive that articulation—and both have a responsibility. I think Hollis certainly has met *his* responsibility.

I think *Zorns Lemma* is one of the toughest films I have ever seen. I think to compare it to squirting steak out of a hose at the dinner table is grossly misleading. I would say it's as if you sat down to an exquisite meal of food that you've never eaten before, and you thought it was garbage because you were maybe used to hamburger. I think most of us have not had this experience. I haven't. I really don't know how to look at something like this yet. I think it's tough, just tough as hell.

F: I thought it was a beautiful film, but I was trying to show that he chose a different way to use words. Normally, when you hear a series of words, you hear them spoken by the same person, and I found that the choice here was very stimulating, but certainly not a conventional way to string together words for ease of communication.

Frampton: Could I enter this colloquy? I think that it was an utterly *conventional* way (in the exact sense of the word) to put words together, and I meant precisely for it to *be* conventional, rather than vernacular or fluid or linear or what have you.

I'm interested in the idea of the mental effort demanded by work. I do not apologize to you if you're tired at the end of the film; that means you've worked. No muscle can be strengthened without exercising it to the point where it aches.

You [Sol Worth] said you did not know how to look at a film like this. I made this film because *I* didn't know how to look at it myself. I think if we only make the films that we *know* how to look at, we might as well cash in our chips and go home. We're not here to do what we already know how to do. All around us, we see the fruits of doing what we already know how to do. And some of them are very strange fruits indeed.

F: But you wouldn't separate work from play, would you?

Frampton: No! Well, *work*. In America, work is by definition the thing you hate to do. In that sense, of course, I am ready to separate work from play. But I think work, in the sense that I work at making art, is the activity of human life. There are tempting aphorisms along the way. "If you play when you work, you work when you play," or some shit like that. The only durable pleasure, the only *real* pleasure in life, is work—but here, I don't mean working for hourly wages. I'm talking about when you work in connection with your whole needs as a human being. Play is certainly part of work in that sense.

F: There's a blank second between the end of each alphabet and the beginning of the next. Did you think about that when you were setting up that section of the film?

Frampton: I thought a lot about that. The blank second is there really for the same reason that the dark screen is there during the reading of the *Bay State Primer*. Of course, I had to find a way into one of the controlling axes of the material in *Zorns Lemma*, the alphabet, and the *Bay State Primer* provided that.

But I also thought about the condition of going to see a film. You walk in off the street when a film is going on and you arrive with this level of retinal saturation; you're so full of cars and people bumping into you and negotiating the popcorn booth that you're blind. Only after a while do you begin to see. I wanted *Zorns Lemma* to be visible from its proper beginning, so the screen is black during the reading of the *Bay State Primer* to empty the eye, so that when the visuals come on, you're receiving them through a completely open channel.

F: Could you talk about specific mathematical formulas that you may have used in your film?

Frampton: I was saying to someone earlier today that when I was a little boy, I learned how to count to ten and say my ABCs, and I received approval for doing that. I was so intensely gratified by that approval that I'm still doing it. [laughter]

I have made films that have used, from the point of view of artists who are sociologically intimidated by mathematics, abstruse mathematical concepts—like the Fibonacci series, for example. For mathematicians, this is baby stuff. *Zorns Lemma* is based on simple counting. You have 108 dozen slots with a certain kind of material dissolving out as another kind of material is dissolving in—but no, there's no formula.

F: So it's not like every ten sequences something happens?

Frampton: There are skips as long as ten alphabets in which no slot is replaced; and there are skips as short as one, but they average out to four-and-a-half alphabets per replacement.

There are some hidden goodies that have to do with percentages and so forth. When you're making a very long thing like this, something that's very laborious, it's got to be fun for *you*, too. So you begin to put in things that are for yourself and the people that Turgenev called "les six inconnus," the six people you don't know who may dig them up. I reasoned that if you're making a very large-scale thing with a lot of material in it, there will be five classes of deviations from the plan that will automatically creep in. First, you're going to make mistakes. Second, there are going to be omissions: you're going to leave things out that should be there. Third, there will be elements of fakery—small junctures where you'll have a minute problem that you don't know how to solve, but in terms of the overall structure, there's no point in wasting time so you fake it. There will be serious lapses of taste, which are common in long works and terrible in short ones. And finally, there will be breaches of decorum: you've established a decorum for the thing and you'll blow it. Reasoning that all these things would be in there anyway, I decided to put them in deliberately so I would know where they were. And I can describe them so that you will recognize them. There are twenty-four of each.

F: You calculated your own mistakes?

Frampton: Well, it's necessary, really, if you're trying to be *totally* responsible for something.

F: Don't you then set up new mistakes as you add the known "mistakes" into the film?

Frampton: Well, I checked the film over very thoroughly [laughter]. In fact, when they were timing the rolls in the lab, they found a shot upside down, after I'd gone over the film about ten times!

Omissions: you have a list of words and let us say you wish it to be complete and you realize that you have left out twenty-four words that you would like to have. (This makes assumptions about my choice of the words that in fact are not true: I did not determine in advance which words I wanted and then go out and get them. One time, I saw a truck with the word *quirk* going down the street; short on Qs, there I was, running madly after the truck trying to set my F-stop when it turned the corner on two wheels and was gone. So I looked up "Quirk" in the phone book, and it turned out that the Quirk Trucking Company was in Elizabeth, New Jersey, and I thought, "Oh my Christ, I can't be doing this!" But anyway, let's say there were twenty-four words that I wanted but didn't have. What I did was just type them up and superimpose them over images of New York; those are the burn-in titles: "oboe," "damn," "kelp," "ebony," and so on.

The "errors" are all black-and-white graphics shot through color filters, as though twenty-four times I had goofed and used the wrong filter. There are four each of six colors: yellow, cyan, magenta, red, green, and blue.

The images I faked are color collages where, say, I took a fragment of some chick's dress and pasted a word out of the newspaper on top of it, and so forth. I think on a second viewing these become *extremely* prominent.

The lapses of taste include the word *kennel*, which is made out of alphabet pretzels.

The breaches of decorum are black-and-white photographs that were made seven years ago when I first began to get interested in the graphic element of the word in deep space surroundings and the tension between the two kinds of space. I made a lot of 35mm black-and-white photographs. Immediately as I got into making them, I decided that I didn't like them, but then again, I *had* the negatives and they were in some sense part of the material I had gathered for the film, so I made black-and-white prints. The word *leather* is a black-and-white still photograph on which I placed a cherry tomato—a breach of decorum in the grossest sense. There are a bunch of things like that. "Wig" has a toothbrush lying on it. These lapses are there to keep the film from being tasteful.

Also, I did anticipate that I would make errors in length. I had twenty-seven hundred cuts to make, each twenty-four frames long exactly. I know where at least twenty-four of the errors are; there are twelve shots that are twenty-five frames long and twelve that are twenty-three.

These are some of the things that I did to amuse myself as I was working on this very long thing.

F: Should the receiver of *Zorns Lemma* bring some emotional capacity, or is your work not involved with emotion?

Frampton: I will quote Annette Michelson, a philosopher of art, who pointed out to somebody, in my presence, that intellect *is* one of the passions.

It's part of the madness of Western man, the detestable split man, our insane distinctions: the ivory tower and the streets, the heart and the mind, the intellect and the passions. . . . That's all bullshit.

I think we are where we are now, partly because of schizoid behavior like that. We *do* have the ivory tower and the streets, but these days, the intellectuals are in the streets and the killers are in the ivory towers. Making my films requires a certain amount of mental effort that would not be worth making were one not feeling very strongly that there is a general value for human beings in the intimations of perfection that, when it's good, art can give us. And horrors that attend *bad* art: you take a bad watercolor painter from Austria and you magnify that badness into the social scale and you get Adolf Hitler. Hitler liked Wagner; I don't care how anybody here feels about Wagner, *I* think Wagner is an absolute catastrophe. Had Adolf Hitler liked the music of Johann Sebastian Bach, Europe would be a different place today.

I think making art that is as rich as you can make it and as perfect as you can make it says something not to the point of human perfectibility but to the point of clearing our minds of rubbish, as we need constantly to do, and of getting order and internal resonance and so forth into the way we live.

I happen to believe that art is *the* typical—not the *fundamental* probably: that would be eating or having sex or breathing—but the *typical* human activity. I think that it produces the only absolutely permanent wealth the human race has. What I'm trying to say I suppose is that I don't think of art as a decorative thing, something you introduce to a rich kid to complete his finishing. I think it's an absolute necessity; it's nourishment for the affections, as food is nourishment for the body.

I used the word *passion* earlier. "Emotion" is a somewhat clinical word: "emotionally disturbed children." Every work of art is an equation for an emotion. There are works of art that are simply equations for greed—that's an emotion. And there are very complex films for very complex emotions.

F: I think most would agree there. I would like to interrupt to say how *you* have affected *me.* Your films have given me a distance from the elements within a film. I am able to journey further into the medium than has been possible for me for a long time. *Zorns Lemma* was a rush. I would like to continue to see your work.

Frampton: Thank you.

F: Would you say that there are qualities in your work that are also in the films of Michael Snow? Many of us saw *Wavelength* last year.

Frampton: The ghastly truth of the matter is that a couple of hysterical underground film critics have discerned something they believe to be a "movement." I'm not very happy about the word; in hospitals, it's usually applied to the bowels. By the time something gets big enough to be very obviously a movement, it is in fact the culture in the process of defecating.

But the truth is, of course, that Mr. Snow and Mr. Frampton and Mr. Jacobs and Mr. Sharits and Ms. Wieland and Mr. Breer are personally acquainted with each other, have been for a good many years, and are in agreement on some fundamental aesthetic principles—though I would be awfully embarrassed if you asked me to name these fundamental aesthetic principles. To put it less coyly, or in less critic-ese, we dig each other's work and we understand it.

Last spring, somebody said to me, "You know all these people; do you all get together one night a week and decide what is to be done on the aesthetic front. Do you decide, well, *this* is up Snow's alley and he should make this film; and Sharits should attack from the flank of color flicker; and Frampton could make a monotonous pulse film six hours long"? This makes art seem like the "international Jewish plot to take over the world" or something like that. And the answer is, no, we don't.

To put it as precisely as possible, I would say that each new work begins within the body of your own work and in relation to the whole body of work of film that already exists; as you continue to work, you begin to grow an aesthetic which the charitable would liken to the nimbus which surrounds the archangels, or something like that (the not so charitable would compare it to an odor that seems to follow you around). Let us say topologically that these nimbi are circles and that it's possible for a number of those circles to overlap. The Snow aesthetic and the Frampton aesthetic overlap, but there's absolutely nothing programmatic about this.

The very small, very tight space that's overlapped by all the circles is where critics gather.

F: You said that today you viewed the film as an outsider, not having seen it for a while. Did you gain any insight into the person who made it?

Frampton: Hmm. It's been a third of a year: that is, one twenty-first of my physical substance has been replaced. I work, as I think other artists work, very much at the borders of instinct, where the risk is and the fun is to be had. After the work is done, a process of rationalization usually begins: that is to say, I attempt to articulate fully in my own mind what the real qualities of the film in fact are. But this is done only with the idea of using what has been done as a springboard into the next thing. The work you've done is a place to stand; then you put your foot out and wish another stone into existence, and it can be some time before you find whether you got wet up to your waist or not.

F: Let me try to rephrase what I think was his question. Most artists who have done something as complex as *Zorns Lemma* have some fantasy of how they would like it to be looked at. Do you, and if so, what is it?

Frampton: That's a terrible question to ask anybody who makes things that are extended in time. If you ask a guy who writes books, makes film, or makes music that question, you get him on the level of his own vanity. Somebody asked James Joyce that question: "Mr. Joyce, your work is so complicated, what do you expect of your readers?" And Joyce said, "Obviously, I expect my readers to spend the balance of their lives in the study of my work!"

There are no preconditions at all. If I had to reduce another film you have seen here, *Artificial Light*, to a platitude, I would say that that film expresses, possibly pessimistically, my own notion about the problem of knowledge and the impossibility of knowing anything in one pass, so to speak, or in any finite number of passes.

Once the work is done, I've discarded it. It has got to make it on its own. I have no conditions or expectations on how my work is to be seen. I personally like to look at a film that requires concentration, on a full stomach—that is to say, when my mind is fairly relaxed so I don't have some other immediate sensory goal. I go to the bathroom beforehand. But that's all.

F: Sol Worth talked about this being one the toughest films he's ever received. What does that mean to you?

Frampton: I like the idea that it's tough. Sure. I wanted it to be a hard-nosed film.

1970 ERIK BARNOUW, PAUL RONDER, AND BARBARA VAN DYKE— ON *HIROSHIMA-NAGASAKI, AUGUST 1945* (1970)

Erik Barnouw: A little chronology. In 1968, I received a clipping from Japan which said that the film of Hiroshima and Nagasaki, taken by Japanese cameramen in 1945, had finally been returned to the Japanese government and that a showing would be held that spring. A letter was sent to Japan to try to get more information, and a professor from the University of Tokyo wrote us to say that he had learned there was two hours and forty-five minutes of film that had been shot by nine cameramen, that the original was in nitrate, but that an acetate copy had been returned to the Japanese government.

The Japanese government had dealt only with the State Department, but they guessed that the original 35mm material was in the hands of the Defense Department. We wrote a very brief letter to Clark Clifford, who had just become the secretary of defense, and sent copies to the president of Columbia University and to Secretary of State Dean Rusk, saying that we understood that film that had been withheld for a long time had been made available for a showing in Japan and that Columbia University would like to have the privilege of releasing the same material in the United States. To our surprise, two weeks later, we received a note from an assistant secretary of defense, saying that the National Archives had been directed to give us access to the material and to reproduce it for us if we wanted to have it reproduced.

We went to Washington to see exactly what this was and found two hours and forty-five minutes of film, arranged in sequences, which the army had apparently put a narration on; they called it "Effects of the Atomic Bomb." There was surprisingly little footage dealing with the effects on human beings, but we decided there was enough material to work with, and we had it reproduced. Then we spent about a year arguing about what to do with it. We didn't know whether to make a long film or a short film, et cetera, and finally decided we wanted a short film of around sixteen minutes.

During this year, we worried that other people would get hold of this material, but apparently nobody else was interested in it. It was earlier this year [1970] that we felt ready to have a public preview of our film at the Museum of Modern Art and to begin distribution. The reaction to the film was very sudden. We immediately got tremendous demand from peace groups and conservation groups, so that after only four or five months something like five hundred copies (16mm prints) have gone into distribution. *Playboy* magazine bought a print!

At first, the television networks showed no interest whatever in the material; but the morning after the United Press put out an enthusiastic story about the film, each of the networks sent a motorcycle courier who arrived before nine o'clock, demanding a preview print. In due time, CBS returned their print, and ABC returned theirs, but NBC said they'd like to hang on to theirs a little bit more; they wanted to look for a good news hook.

In contrast, Steve Scheuer, who has a local program on a UHF station in New York, immediately said, "May I have the film and use it with a discussion?"; he was the first to show the film on television in the United States. It was shown on national television in a number of other countries, including Sweden. It wasn't until many months later that a national showing came about in the United States, and only then, partly because the press, led by the *Boston Globe* and *Variety*, began to needle the networks for not being interested. Finally, NET asked for it, and contracted to use it on the twenty-fifth anniversary of the dropping of the bombs.

What happened in Japan is also of interest. The Japanese government acquired a print of the original two and three-quarter hours of footage from the United States and decided to have a showing of it on noncommercial television, but they decided to eliminate all footage showing human beings. So what the Japanese saw was a screening that included nothing but rubble. There was an outcry, and the government explained that they had done this to protect the relatives of the victims and the victims themselves. But the protest continued. Meanwhile, another print was taken into Japan by a professor but was seized by customs and confiscated.

Finally, however, the Tokyo Broadcasting System asked for television rights to our film and showed it, and they put it on television. *Hiroshima-Nagasaki* had a tremendous impact all over Japan, so much so that it was repeated a couple of weeks later. In other words, the Japanese people saw the full impact of this material through *our* film.

Willard Van Dyke: One of the things we discovered was that not only had the Japanese not seen the footage, but there was a curtain of silence around what had happened. I think part of why the film had such a tremendous effect in Japan was because people didn't talk about Hiroshima and Nagasaki, though it was known that if you were a woman from there, you were not marriageable.

Barnouw: Throughout the time we were working on it, we knew very little about how this material had originated. Barbara Van Dyke, who was associate producer, took on the task of looking for more footage because we felt there must be other material buried here and there. Donald Richie suggested we contact Akira Iwasaki who might know something about this material, so Barbara wrote to him. He didn't answer until after the film had come out and he had read the reviews of the Museum of Modern Art showing, and later saw the film. At that point, he wrote Barbara a long letter in which he revealed that *he* in fact was the man who had produced the original film and who had done the first cut.

Iwasaki said the film was begun on the initiative of the Japanese themselves. He was part of a documentary film unit that received a small grant from the Ministry of Education to go out and document what had happened at Hiroshima and Nagasaki. The cameramen went to work, but then the American occupation arrived on the scene, stopped the work, arrested one of the cameramen, and halted the project. Iwasaki said that he went around protesting this, and after a period of protest during which there was no shooting, the occupation apparently changed its mind and said the project could go on under the supervision of the Strategic Bombing Survey.

Then after a certain amount of material had been accumulated—I don't know how much—suddenly, they were told to hand over everything, outtakes and all, and this material was taken back to Washington, classified "Secret," and nothing more was heard of it.

Apparently during the intervening years, the Japanese kept asking for this material to be returned, and finally—I haven't been able to find out why—it was returned late in 1967. This material is now declassified and is apparently available from the National Archives to anybody who wants it.

Van Dyke: When Mr. Awasaki had seen our film, he said he regretted that Americans had made this film, and he wrote a long article about this for a Japanese magazine, saying that he wished that the Japanese had made this film, but that he was grateful that someone had.

Barnouw: I doubt that there was anything legal about declaring this material secret. The right to classify information is to protect military secrets, but there is no way that this film, after the war was over, could have been a military threat to the United States. It might have been a threat to congressional appropriations for H-bomb research, and probably this was the reason. If so, this was a completely improper use of the classification authority. This is also a case where something done *by somebody else* was seized and declared secret by the Defense Department. The powers of an occupying power are probably fairly unlimited, but in this case, not only did the occupation withhold this material from us and from the Japanese people but from the rest of the world also. I think this is a subject that filmmakers have a stake in and ought to be interested in.

Maybe you have questions you'd like to ask.

F: May I put in a footnote?

Barnouw: By all means.

F: In 1958, I imported from Japan a number of the shots that you've got in your picture. These shots were obtained directly from Japan, so I have a strong feeling that when the material was impounded by the occupation, the Japanese government retained at least one print. I don't remember exactly where we got it, but we needed it, we asked for it, and we got it.

Barnouw: The National Archives said that the film as a whole was not declassified until 1967, but that some feet, and they didn't specify which, had been declassified earlier and made available. This may be that material. But you said you got yours from Japan—that puzzles me.

F: I'm sure we got it from Japan because we always went to the country of origin for footage about that country.

Van Dyke: We always suspected that *somebody* at the Japanese documentary studio had it, and recently we got word from Bernard Christian, who was head of the *Newsweek* office there, that only after the original cut of the material was shown on Japanese television and after our film was shown, somebody had the courage to come up with that hidden print, which we have not yet had a chance to see. We are very anxious to see whether it is the same as our original material.

Barnouw: We're also anxious to see whether there was more material than we obtained from the Defense Department.

F: Let me add another footnote. In 1945, I worked for the intelligence services in the Pacific Ocean area, and I remember the higher-ranking officers discussing the problem of getting intelligence materials. I know that we had boxes and boxes of film taken by the Japanese and confiscated. There was much more than this footage. I never saw it, but I remember some of the guys who were working in that area coming out sick. That material must exist somewhere.

Barnouw: The Defense Department *swears*—I have a letter—that they have absolutely no other material, that they are withholding nothing. But their letter is written in such a way as to leave open the possibility that material was destroyed in 1945.

F: Another note about more material: a few years ago I read an interesting article in *Scientific American* by a scientist who had studied the effects of the bomb on people, the long-term effects. I don't know who hired him to do this; he was part of a group. He had access to all kinds of photography; he made mention of it in the article, and so I'll try to dredge it up and you can probably write to him and find out.

Van Dyke: There was also footage that was shot by the air force; through a friend, we found a color film that he had worked on as an editor. Where that negative is, who knows?

Barnouw: This was later, in 1946. That film was apparently not classified as secret; it was simply not distributed outside the army.

F: I'd like to say something about the film we've just seen. We've had a lot of talk here about films in which the soundtrack and the visual image are at odds with each other, but in this case, there is an unusually happy marriage between the soundtrack and the visual images. The soundtrack is restrained, and the narration beautifully said.

Barnouw: I think this is Paul's first narration, and it's interesting how this came about. Paul had written a script that was exactly what we felt we wanted. Paul offered to make a scratch track of the narration, just so that we could hear it and judge it more objectively, so he did. When we listened to it, and we were really listening to see whether the narration was what we wanted, our conclusion was that Ronder himself should narrate it, so that's how you [to Ronder] became a narrator, is it not?

Paul Ronder: Yes.

I'd like to also say that the woman's narration is by Kazuko Oshima who I know would love to be here to talk about the reaction to the film in Japan. Doing the narration was a very important experience for her. Her mother had always wanted to speak to the world about the bomb and now her daughter was able to.

I want to make a brief statement and then I would like to ask a question. The original material is an amazing document of people *not* dealing with their feelings, not dealing with the fundamental issues. The film that the Defense Department made is basically a kind of pseudoscientific document, full of graphs and charts and men with pointers and Geiger counters. The inhumanity of that approach is devastating. It reaches its epitome in one shot that will forever stay in my mind: you see a man standing in his garden—this is in the section on biological damage— and he's holding up a turnip or some enormous vegetable which is deformed. The narration says something like, "This is Mr. Hadashi, whose wife and children were killed by the bomb, showing you his turnip; you'll notice swelling on the left side."

Van Dyke: Paul, there's another shocking shot in that original material. In fact, we had to turn the soundtrack off when we were looking at the footage because over one of those long pan shots of total devastation, the music on the soundtrack is Bach's *Jesu, Joy of Man's Desiring*!

Ronder: What I tried to do in my narration was to retrieve the humanity in those events, by finding things that would move or disturb people, would reach down deep: I wanted images that would strike you somehow. I used some very poetic images: for example, I describe that while the people were dying, wild flowers were growing as a result of the radiation.

My question is, does this approach, this fundamentally aesthetic moral approach, increase your feeling of the horror of this event, or does it make the feeling of horror less powerful. I showed the film once to a group of fairly militant blacks who said they felt the film was almost a song to the bomb, to how big it was, to how strange and wondrous it was—there was complete silence at the center and it did strange things with the shadows. This made me wonder, when you see these shots of destruction and hear this information, what does it *do*? This ties in with our questioning during the seminar about how you change people.

F: I agree with your comment about the poetic images, and I think the juxtaposition of the footage with the comment about the flowers is just shattering. I'm sorry therefore that Oppenheimer's comments follow this.

Barnouw: Our policy decision on the film was that we would not deal with the question of whether the bomb should have been dropped, so we completely avoided getting into the political situation; we wanted the emphasis to be on the present, and it seemed to us that Oppenheimer saying that the world would never be the same and that "Now I'm become death, destroyer of worlds" was a natural transition to this idea. We wanted to end with a statement about the present power of atomic weapons, so that the final thought would not be, should they have done what they did back then, but are we crazy right now.

F: But you act as if the bomb just fell out of the sky and happened to these people.

Barnouw/Van Dyke: Well, it did.

F: Yeah, but somebody had something to do with that!

Van Dyke: There's another film, *The Decision to Drop the Bomb*, that Fred Freed did for NBC, an extraordinary document using a great deal of historic footage that does a remarkable job of tracing everything that led up to the moment when the bombs were dropped.

F: Something bothered me about the moment in the film that David brought up. Your talking about the flowering of the vegetation reminds me of Marguerite Duras's script for *Hiroshima, Mon Amour* [1959, Alain Resnais], which you may have been unconsciously recalling. As you were narrating, I kept waiting to see the vegetation. In the Resnais film, the vegetation *is* shown and it's an extraordinarily powerful moment. I don't mean this in any sense as a criticism of your film; after all, we're talking about an absolutely great director who could do whatever he wished, could fake his material. He wasn't working with documents. But the point is that in general, your film was not nearly as alive to me as the Resnais film; the faked footage in *Hiroshima, Mon Amour* is far more frightening and bothers me more deeply than the documentary footage in this film.

Barnouw: We wanted it to be a historical document that would move people deeply. We wanted it to be something that would become obligatory for high school and college courses.

F: In my view, graphic material gets abused with some regularity. Your use of the material is low key and I appreciate that.

Barnouw: When we first saw the original two and three-quarter hours, we were dismayed at how little footage there was in which there were human beings. Paul, you doubted that there *was* a film, unless we did some tricks or something. There was some discussion of whether we should try to simulate scenes, but we rejected that idea and decided instead to use some blank screen and relatively empty shots. Originally, we discarded some footage because it was uninteresting; we later retrieved it when we realized that we could do a sequence saying, "This was a prison" and a certain number of people died here; "This was a school" and so and so many people died here—just the statistics make those empty shots interesting and powerful. We tried to make a virtue of the fact that there were so many pictures in which there were no human beings.

　　I was quite surprised when we first showed the film that people saw as much horror in it as they seemed to; they saw more horror than there *is* on the screen. I think this is partly because of the way the verbal material that Kazuko speaks introduces you to the human experience without you seeing any human beings. We tried to make you imagine the event first, before we showed you any people. As a result, and I don't know that we could have expected this, when you do finally see people, all the previous experience from the words is apparently carried into the very few shots in which people appear.

　　Incidentally, the Defense Department did a marvelously complete shot list, which we got from the National Archives. It had a complete description of every shot; this was very useful because it gave us the information about what was a school and what was a prison, et cetera.

F: I share your viewpoint about the film being heightened by the lack of people; in fact, the one shot that sticks out in my mind was the long, empty pan of the destruction of the city; it jarred me when I saw this one bicycle figure going along the canal, which made me think of *Night and Fog* [1955, Alain Resnais]: the shots of the camps with no people in them heightened the effect of that film.

Barnouw: I was annoyed with that bicycle. We resisted the temptation to remove it.

F: I think this film is revolutionary. It is extremely revolting, really hard to look at, and its effect is doubled because of your use of something like classical deadpan humor. The scene of the man not moving his facial muscles, while the film is telling you that his mother died, his father died, his uncle died, his aunt died, his cousin died, his feet were cut off, his ears were cut off, and *he* died. He never changes his expression, and the quality of the narration, which is monotonous in tone, is so effective because it doesn't scream; it just says this is what happened and this is what happened and this is what happened. You can still tell that the person who is narrating the film cares about what he's saying—but that's probably privileged information because I know Paul. I think it's a remarkable, revolutionary piece.

Barnouw: One of the most touching reactions we got to the film was in a newspaper story from Hiroshima, to the effect that the television audience in Hiroshima on the night it was broadcast was 60 percent larger than normal. The newspaper story described people in the hospital there, survivors of the bomb, watching the film. Apparently, there was a lot of discussion among the hospital authorities about whether the survivors should be allowed to see the film, and they finally decided that in one particular ward, the patients would be allowed to watch the film. Most of them wanted to watch it, and apparently throughout the film, they kept saying, "Yes, that's exactly how it was."

The appreciation of the film was such that shortly after it was over, it was broadcast nationally a second time.

Ronder: I was talking about Hiroshima to a psychiatrist who said that the most amazing thing to him about Hiroshima was not only the destruction we inflicted on the Japanese but the destruction we inflicted on ourselves by dropping the bomb. I wonder how much of the paranoia we see in our foreign policy has been created by our dropping the bomb on Japan. I think a destructive act really goes both ways.

Van Dyke: The air force film that we saw was really an obscene document; the conclusion of the film was that this horrible thing won't happen to us because we'll be prepared.

Barnouw: "This is what happened to a nation that was not prepared."

Ronder: I worry about the fear our film creates. Does that fear make you better, or does it really say to you, "Wow, it's good that we have all these atomic bombs so no one bombs *us*, because I wouldn't like to look like *that*!" I don't know what the fear does, what the next step is, how you put yourself back together.

F: We've seen newsreel footage used in various ways at this seminar. We've seen *Kino Pravda* [1920s, Mikhail Kaufman, Elizaveta Svilova, Dziga Vertov], and last night we saw *People's War* [1969] from the Newsreel Group, and then this tonight. I'm very curious about what Stan Lawder thinks because he had very strong reaction to the newsreel footage that Bob Kramer brought from Vietnam.

Standish Lawder: These various uses of newsreel material have a certain generic similarity. Both *People's War* and this film show us images of things we "know a good deal about," and both reshape our sensitivity toward these events. I think what *Hiroshima-Nagasaki* is going to do, in a very indirect, subtle way, is change the public consciousness, or global consciousness, of whoever sees it. We can no longer think of the atom bomb in quite the same way we did before.

Barnouw: If it can do what you say it will, that's great!

F: To me, the film seems too general; I would have liked a film organized in a more focused way, either concentrating on causes or some other particular issue.

Barnouw: The virtue of the film from the distribution point of view is that it can be used in many different contexts: groups for the preservation of the environment are using it all over the country, and peace groups are using it with a slightly different emphasis. In a history class, it would have a still different function. We hope it acquires different meanings in different group situations; the minute you would try to make it specifically useful for any of those situations, you would limit the use of the film.

Hollis Frampton: When I knew I was going to see an atom bomb film, I assumed it would contain atrocities and so forth, and so I gritted my teeth and thought, "I'm in for it." Now the truth of the matter is that I've been "in for it" all my life in that sense—we all have. We're totally saturated with images of that kind, and just as a simple matter of adaptation, a kind of anesthesia supervenes.

Curiously, your film was *not* atrocious in the way that documentary footage of the mass burials of the emaciated bodies from the concentration camps is atrocious. But what I got out of the Japanese cameramen's footage was a sense of the utter numbing and maiming and annihilation of the spirit in those who *survived* the bomb. They can't do anything about the devastation around them, except stand there like sleepwalkers, holding the cameras—something they still remember how to do.

I don't think it's a question of low key-ness or high key-ness. It's not the imagery of atrocities and not the mere idea of butchering and maiming and destroying; it's the terrible subtraction of any possibility of action in the face of this enormity. Something in the enormity of the event kills, in the Japanese survivors and in *us*, the reason why it's *worthwhile* to be alive.

1977 BARBARA KOPPLE AND HART PERRY—ON *HARLAN COUNTY USA* (1976)

F: Were you ever in fear for your lives?

Barbara Kopple: Yes, the scabs and gun thugs told us that if we were ever caught alone, we'd be killed; and during the last couple of weeks of the strike, the violence started to intensify and we carried weapons—only at night. We didn't want to be caught with weapons during the day since that would give them an excuse to kill us. I remember one night we were shooting in the miners' homes down below where they had outdoor plumbing, and I had to go to the bathroom. We always went on the buddy system: Hart was nice enough to come with me . . .

Hart Perry: I tried to talk Barbara out of it, hoping she would wait until morning . . .

Kopple: Well, you know how those things are! [laughter]

Hart had an M1; I had a 357 Magnum—and this was just to go to the bathroom!

Also, remember that early-morning picket line that you see? It was well before dawn and the line was mostly women and the film crew. And from out of nowhere came tracer bullet shots, and we didn't know whether they were trying to kill us or just shooting over our heads. So then the strikebreakers pulled up and the head strikebreaker, as you saw, pointed his gun at Hart. I mean all he had to do was move a finger and one of us wouldn't be here anymore. I figured, stupidly, they're not going to hurt a woman as much as a man, so I stood in front of Hart, but they grabbed me, then grabbed Hart, and took each one of us individually to beat us up. I was pretty lucky because I had the recorder across my body and a long aluminum pole with a microphone on the end of it, and I started beating the guy back.

Neither of us knew where the other one was, and Hart kept rolling and I kept recording—as best we could.

Perry: Later, in a John Birch publication, one of the gun thugs described how he was beaten up by a woman sound recordist . . . [laughter]

Kopple: And given a concussion!

Perry: It was a very confusing scene and getting pistol-whipped was certainly terrifying. But we continued to film. The Éclair camera was damaged; one of the most dramatic scenes in the film is too dark as a consequence.

Since it was four thirty in the morning, Basil Collins, the head gun thug, stuck his 45 in one of the miner's stomachs and I heard a gun fall to the ground: the miner had two pistols in his back pocket. The miner stuck his other pistol in Basil's stomach, and another strikebreaker came up and cocked a pistol at the miner's head. I was around ten feet away, recording this—all you can see in the film is a little glint off Basil's gun. It was a very confusing and disturbing experience; I wasn't sure whether I should smash the guy over the head with the camera or record the event.

F: Did the police ever bother you?

Kopple: No, the first day I came into Harlan, I was introduced to the head of the state
police and had a pretty interesting interview with him. He felt that in Harlan
County, murder was just a crime of passion. The real criminals were the burglars
and the robbers.

Perry: We did get arrested for double parking—while the engine was running and
someone was in the car!—and spent most of a day in jail.

F: I understand that you spent five years of your life making the film; I wonder if you
could talk about that.

Kopple: Well, at the beginning, the idea was just a film about the Miners for Democracy.
After Joseph Yablonski was murdered, there was a siege within the United Mine
Workers with miners saying, okay, we're sick and tired of the dictatorship of W. A.
Boyle; we want a union leadership that's really going to represent us. There had never
been a real election in the UMW. Yablonski had been killed because he ran against
Tony Boyle; he was the first challenge to leadership since the time of John L. Lewis.
Now, three men, one of them [Arnold Miller] disabled with black lung, were running
against Tony Boyle. So the film began as an idea for a story about the rank-and-file
coal miners challenging the leadership.

Funding the film was difficult. We were given a loan of $9,000 at the beginning,
with the promise that that person would put up the money for the entire film. When
I got back after the first shoot, I made the mistake of showing this fine gentleman the
rushes, and he decided that a twenty-six-year-old woman couldn't possibly make a
major political film and refused further funding.

After traveling for a year in the coalfields, meeting people who were dying
with black lung and listening to old-timers talk about the thirties and burst into
original song, I felt very strongly about what I was seeing and hearing and wanted to
continue. And at that point, I learned about foundations. I discovered that
to be funded by a foundation, you had to be nonprofit and tax exempt; you had to
write proposals that explained everything, from what you were going to shoot to
exactly where you were going to distribute your film; and you had to have a board of
directors made up of the most incredible minds that you could ever want to meet:
labor historians, economists, whatever.

I figured, okay, if that's what they want, I'll try to do it. I must have applied to
hundreds of foundations, and got rejected by many of them—though I would do all
sorts of things to keep that application process going. I would go into banks and say,
"Hey, why not invest in my film on coal mining!" They'd look at me like I was crazy,
so then I'd say, "Well, can I use your Xerox machine and your stamp machine?" If
they said yes, I'd sit there and Xerox 117 proposals, collate them all over the floor of
the bank, and stamp them.

I applied to some foundations three years in a row until they finally gave me
grants. This process continued for the entire four years of making the film. I did get
some support, though when I finished the film, I was $60,000 in debt.

Perry: Barbara developed a technique. Most of the time, you get rejected by
foundations; and if you're sensitive about that, the process can be quite difficult. But,
though the rejection letters were piled high, Barbara *wasn't* sensitive: she would call
the foundation people up and ask why she was rejected. And she would find her way
to other foundations and apply to those, using the information she got.

Probably some of the grants were given just so Barbara would stop calling! [laughter]

Kopple: Some of the rejection letters were great. I got one that said that they only funded birds and trees because they don't talk back. I could do a book on my rejections.

F: Are there coal miners in your family? Where does your enormous dedication come from?

Kopple: I don't know. I guess that I chose to be an activist first and a filmmaker second. I think the sixties encouraged my sense that if you really get together, you can change things. Sometimes it takes whole lives to make change, but you *can* move forward.

My uncle [Murray Burnett] is a really good writer: he wrote the play, *Everybody Comes to Rick's* [cowritten by Joan Alison, the play was never produced], which was later the basis for *Casablanca* [1942, Michael Curtiz]. He was totally ripped off: he got $8,000 for the play, while the film has made millions. I learned something from that.

F: Barbara, how did you get permission to film in the jail, in the courtroom, and at the stockholders' meeting?

Kopple: In the courtroom I used a wireless microphone to tape what was said. When I thought that I wasn't going to be able to record where I wanted to record, I'd put the wireless mike on one of the defendants; there was usually so much commotion in the courtroom, with everybody getting up and saying things to the judge, that nobody noticed. Hart, recognizing this confusion, would open the back doors to the courtroom, push the camera two stops, and film. Later we lip-synched what we had.

We just walked right into the jail, smiled nicely at the jailer, followed the people who were going to jail—and shot.

Because I didn't think the stockholders would let either of us in, I had already miked the miner, and when they did agree to let one of us in, we thought, all right, we'll just have the camera going. I stayed outside and Hart went inside and shot. I did have a certain amount of trepidation because the microphone was on one of the defendants; I was afraid she would get sentenced and we wouldn't see the microphone for six years. [laughter] But we got both sound and image.

F: Could you talk about the editing process?

Kopple: The editing process was one of the most supportive times of the whole film. Five or six people worked on the editing, one or two of them for nine months. Nancy Baker was the primary editor; she worked incredibly hard and was entirely committed.

We edited where I live. We'd screen ten hours of rough-cut material, then sit around the table and discuss it. You couldn't just say, "Well, this doesn't work" or "This is boring" or "There's no flow"—we needed to figure the film out politically and come up with practical solutions. Some of the people who worked on the editing had never worked on a film before, but they were politically committed and wanted to learn.

Editing was a very cerebral process because there was so much stuff going into the film: there was stock footage, material on black lung, on safety, on corruption, on mining itself, on the national coal contract, *plus* the whole story of Harlan. And trying to weave the music in so that it worked was a huge job. *Harlan County* was shaped in the editing so that it develops characters and moves forward.

We got almost everything into the film that was shot for it—except for the material on strip mining, which was a whole other bag of worms: we tried to fit it in but just couldn't.

Perry: When we were shooting the film, we were working with a general structure, which was to tell the story of the Harlan strike: develop characters, create parallel action.

Kopple: Harlan was the story, but once we got to the editing, we didn't know whether the history would all come first and then the story of Harlan, or what. Also, things that you thought might work *didn't* work, and we saw that if you pulled certain things out, a whole reel would fall apart.

    One person who saw the finished film said that when he came out of the theater he had a splitting headache. My uncle asked, "Why?" and the guy said, "I got a headache just thinking about what went into the editing!"

F: In my first experience with the film, I was so overwhelmed, and in some ways threatened, by the barrage of information, that I didn't see the film I saw tonight. This is my third time. I'd like you to address the question of the person who is not from the South and is not knowledgeable about the political issues around mining. What were your expectations about that person's ability to respond to the film?

Kopple: This is going to sound terrible, but I never thought about that. When I was filming in Harlan, I didn't even care if a film about the events ever came out. I was more engaged in the struggle itself and maybe was using the filmmaking as a vehicle to help me get into and through what was happening. Sometimes you're like a dumb animal behind the camera with a tape recorder; for me, the struggle was to keep going from day to day, to stay alive, to keep raising the money—I didn't think of anything beyond that.

    I never even thought that whatever I would make would be shown anywhere. I figured, okay, my friends will see it; maybe the Whitney will show it [the Whitney Museum of American Art's New American Film and Video Series]; trade unionists and the people in Harlan will see it. But I never expected anything like what has happened with the film and am still amazed by it.

F: *Harlan County* opens a hole in my thinking about film in its relationship to other films we've seen during this week, films that are so complex that you can't get them the first time. This creates a film-experience-over-time, at least for those who feel some magic in that first experience. You find yourself coming back to the film, and your experience of it becomes deeper and deeper. This way of experiencing documentary suggests that the informational "rules" you use in designing films that are intended to be seen just once are not relevant for a film like this. I *needed* to see *Harlan County* more than once, and in the spaces between my exposures to the film, my understanding of the situation grew.

F: I want to come back to the question about whether people would know the history of coal mining. I knew hardly anything at all. And I feel I know a lot now. Much of the information is very clear, especially the dedication and commitment of the miners.

Kopple: Thank you.

F: I saw the film in Sydney with two thousand people who knew nothing about that strike, and the film had a fantastic response.

    May I ask you about your shooting ratio?

Kopple: We shot about fifty hours of film over a three-year period. Whole films could be made, on black lung or on mine safety, from the footage we didn't use.

F: I'm interested in the reactions of the strikers to the filming. Occasionally, I sense a certain embarrassment on the picket line, a hesitation to talk to the camera.

Kopple: When I first came into Harlan County, I was lucky because a lot of the people who were strike organizers had been part of the Miners for Democracy movement, and since I had been shooting that for the whole year before, I knew people.

We first got to Harlan about four thirty in the morning, and I went to see one of the organizers and asked what was happening. He said, well, just down the road and over the bridge, you'll see the people on strike and the state troopers, too. So we drove across the bridge and saw the women with switches and the state troopers with clubs; and I thought, "I can't just get out of this car and say 'Hi! I'm from New York and we're here to film your story.'"

The next day, the organizer introduced us, and at first the women didn't trust us. They gave phony names, said they were Martha Washington, Florence Nightingale, and Betsy Ross. It took a week of our being on the picket line all the time, and being in a car accident about the third day: here was our car all battered and our equipment broken, but we came to the picket line anyway. They looked at us as if we were really out of our minds, but then they just opened up to us, and from then on, we lived with the miners in their homes, and they fed us. We did everything with them from butchering hogs to starting the *Harlan Labor News*: everybody wrote articles, and people learned how to use an A. B. Dick machine. I'd bring films to show them, like *Native Land* [1942] by Leo Hurwitz. We were really engaged in that life.

I lived there for thirteen months, and after a while, people forgot we were filming. I remember Lois (the heavyset woman who pulls the gun out of her dress) saying, "Barbara, are you going to be on the picket line today?" I said, "Shh, Lois, we're *filming*; you're not supposed to say that"; and she said, "I know, but I have to write your name down—are you going to be there?" They forgot that we were filmmakers!

F: I think that the amount of time that you spent with those people really shows up in the film.

Perry: Earlier, someone talked about the length of time that it takes to make a movie. I think the time for the filming was extremely important in many ways: for establishing a relationship with the people so that they don't react negatively to the camera, for getting particular types of shots, for seeing things develop over a period of time, for being able to take the care to get a particular type of lighting, and to actually think about what you're doing, to *discover* what you're doing. So the period of time is crucial, and taking your time is also liberating: since there's no budget, no commercial producer, there's freedom in working this way.

Kopple: For me and I think probably for everyone who worked on the film, it was a great honor to be down there. These people let us become part of their struggle, and I learned so much from that. You don't make a film by yourself: it takes a lot of committed people giving their time and energy and support all the time. Similarly, running a strike means that the strikers are there every single day, even if their lives are in danger. These people aren't victims; they're courageous people who aren't afraid to fight back at a time in this country when many people *are* afraid.

I've been lucky to be able to travel around the country, and I've seen many audiences open up and start to deal with issues in their own lives. A woman in Dallas, Texas, stood up and said, "I've been a Republican all my life; I've hated unions, but after seeing this, I have to reassess where I am." A woman in San Francisco told us how she fought against the American Nazi party. A factory worker stood up and talked about the occupational health hazards in the factory where he works. The film is encouraging people to deal with real issues. That's just incredible.

F: You must've gone into that situation with some preconceptions about how miners live, work, and think, about how management works and reacts. What, if any, of *your* preconceptions had to be readjusted?

Kopple: When I'm in a situation that I'm not familiar with, I just go with whatever happens and refuse to be shocked by anything. Whatever anybody wants to lay on me, whether it be good or bad, I'll go with it just to see what that's like. I mean, we did some pretty crazy things while we were in Harlan.

What I thought, academically, about trade unions was totally different from what I felt when I saw and experienced the reality. I got much more politicized when I started to learn, from the perspective of the miners, who the enemy is, and how you fight the enemy. I learned a lot.

F: One thing that I really value in the film is that you came from New York City to Harlan where you were definitely outsiders. It seems to me that a lot of us who see the film are also outsiders, but the film provides a political context for the events we're looking at and for a lot of things about this country. It gives you a feeling for the South and for working people. I think people who are not from that experience won't think of people from the South or of working people in the same way again.

Also, we're very conscious of there being a crew and while sometimes I hate that in films, here I think it really works to bring the audience in.

Kopple: Sometimes what happens is that people find it easier to identify with the filmmakers than with the real issues and what's happening. I tried to get the feeling of the crew out of the film as much as possible: for example, by cutting out a lot of our questions. It was important to me that people were focused on the struggle that was going on down there.

Perry: Stylistically, we were trying to let the people develop as characters, so we didn't want to do formal interviews but to record nuances of behavior, scenes as they developed, magical moments when people interrelated.

F: Barbara, could you explain your role as director of the film?

Kopple: I started *Harlan County* in 1972, and during the several years of making the film, many people worked on various parts of the project. It was rough to get a single set of people to come away from their lives for such a long time. My own role included raising money, figuring out who to work with, how to shoot what we shot, to understand what was going on—everything from the leadership struggle at the UMW to what was happening to the people themselves. I was the only person who was involved with the project all the way through—though many other people came in and brought tremendous energy and support and worked very hard to make the film what it is.

Perry: Barbara had the vision for the movie. As far as the filming itself goes, Kevin Keating filmed the first part; Nancy Baker played the most important role in the editing. Barbara's direction was very clear because she had a complete understanding of what the overall project was. In a fiction film, you have a script; everything is premeditated; the film director can be an auteur. In many documentaries, you're not sure exactly what you're going to be filming the next day; you're working a bit more like a jazz musician. There *is* a focus, almost a psychological focus, a vision for what the movie is, and as professionals, you fit into that vision. It's a different sort of direction from what happens in fictional films.

F: And you were able to communicate your vision successfully to all the different people you worked with?

Kopple: Well, that was really necessary. Of course, I worked with people I have known for many years and had worked with before. Hart and I have worked on a lot of stuff together. It took unique people to be willing to come down and put themselves in that kind of situation, so these were people who didn't need us to say, "Get this shot! Do this, do that." These people were technically adept and politically committed; they could communicate with the people, which was very important; and they acted well in the face of danger.

F: You said that when you first got there, the strike was on and the troopers were out. You open the film with these lovely shots down in the mine. When did you get those and how did you go about getting permission from the company to go down there?

Kopple: That scene was shot in a different mine in Harlan County, at the Eastover Mining Company. Hart met the mine foreman while he was in a store buying baloney. We told him that we wanted to film. The guy who owned that mine was rather young and very egotistical, and we talked him into letting us film so that he could show his grandchildren what he did and how happy the miners were and how good the conditions were—that kind of thing.

The last coal mine that you see was Consolidation Coal. I went through the usual process of writing them a letter and asking permission, and of course I was turned down. But that was when the national coal contract was just about to begin, so the local union in that area were really good friends of mine—I've known them since 1972. They told the management that some students from New York had brought some filming equipment and wanted to go into the mine. So we went down and filmed.

I had spoken on the phone to the guy in charge. Phil Parmet, who was shooting, slipped a couple of times, forgetting to call me Susie—we had made up different names. Phil called me Barbara, and at the end of the day the head guy said, "Are you this Barbara Kopple that's doing that film?" He got very excited and called some thugs to come out and take the film from us, so I gave them some rolls of unexposed film and we beat it out of there. [laughter]

F: Were the strikebreakers imported from all different places?

Kopple: Some were local people, living right next door to the coal miners. Some were imported from a local prison: the company got them out. There were strikebreakers who were convicted murderers, others who were security guards. It was a very mixed group.

F: Has the situation there healed?

Kopple: Has it healed? There are still lots of things happening. The Ku Klux Klan moved into Harlan County after the strike was over, and the people who were the scabs during the strike became the Klan, along with the coal operators and state troopers. I can tell you a lot of stories about what happened to the people in the film who became leaders. The woman who stood up in the courtroom to say that this country's laws aren't made for the working people became a real leader and was working with Georgetown, one of the black communities down there, where people were getting evicted from their homes. She was put in jail for allegedly kidnapping the wife of a Klansman and taking her across the state line; and during the time she was in jail, the Klan had paramilitary rallies, and the girls in the home economics class at the high school were making gowns and hoods for the Klan members.

Anybody with progressive ideas was intimidated. If people were interracially dating, they were firebombed. The stories go on and on. A week after the film was finished, I took it to Harlan County to show it to the people there, and the Klan hung a goat with the initials KKK on its belly, right by the place where I was going to screen the film. So that was an armed screening: miners stood outside with shotguns to make sure nothing happened.

Before that event, they had called me up and were telling me what was happening, so I brought *Ku Klux Klan: The Invisible Empire* [1965, CBS Reports] and we showed that and Hurwitz's *Native Land* from house to house, all over Harlan County. When we were showing the films in Georgetown, two state troopers pulled up and asked what the films were. I said they were educational films, and they said, "We want them," and the whole black community just surrounded us and the films, guiding us inside away from the troopers.

We had planned to have a revival meeting the next day, but the Klan told the guy who ran the revival center that if the meeting was held, the place would be firebombed, so we went around to tell the people who didn't have telephones *not* to come. The fight still goes on.

F: Did you record any confrontations between strikebreaking families and union families?

Kopple: Just one, but I didn't use it because they were both drunk.

F: One of the things I'm sensing about this whole seminar is the positive energy force that can come from dedicated filmmakers.

Kopple: What's come out of films like *Union Maids* [1976, Jim Klein, Miles Mogulescu, Julia Reichert] and other films about social change is the understanding that there's a need to fund social change films. Most foundations don't. We came up with the idea that maybe *we* should start a fund that would finance only social change films, and that in fact has happened. The Film Fund will be a membership organization in which community-organizing groups all over this country will be able to vote on the board of directors and on the kinds of films they want to see made. The current board of directors—filmmakers, community people, and foundation people—had our first meeting and the selection committee is now in progress. In February-March the group is giving away $250,000 and hopefully next time it will be $500,000.

The kinds of films that the Film Fund wants to fund—well, it's open-ended: we're thinking of films on nuclear power, films on women's issues, films on occupational health hazards, anything that's progressive and moves us forward.

F: How is *Harlan County* being distributed and who is seeing it?

Kopple: The answer has a lot of different parts. Many of the trade unions are doing benefits with it. It showed at the longshoremen's convention. It's being used a lot in the minefields; the miners have their own prints. It's being used for brown lung and black lung rallies.

About a month ago, right after the Sinking Creek Festival in Tennessee, I went to Kentucky where there's another strike going on, just like the one in Harlan. The miners are fighting against the nonunion Blue Diamond Coal Company—you may remember about a year ago there was a mine explosion and twenty-six miners were killed. I showed the film down there to 350 miners and their wives in a cafeteria.

F: Harlan County is distributed by Cinema 5. I suspect this must create some problems or some restrictions in terms of getting the film into the hands of some of the people you'd like to have see it.

Kopple: I went through a long process of trying to decide whether to distribute the film myself or to have someone else distribute it. With the help of a lot of friends, we were able to raise about $170,000 to do self-distribution, but after a painful struggle, we decided against that because if the film didn't do well, I would have to pay this money back with 5½ percent interest—after two years, that might be $200,000. Plus, it would also make me into a businessperson, a kind of work which I'm not very good at and don't want to do. Theaters tend to rip off independents. If you don't immediately have more product to follow what they're showing, they'll just say, "When you want to collect, sue us."

Instead of making a financial contract with the distributor, I made a political contract with him. This enables me to have ten political benefits a year, of my choice, for which he can't charge. Groups in Appalachia get the film for nothing, and when it goes into nontheatrical distribution, community groups that can't afford the rental get it for 50 percent off; and union members get a dollar or $1.50 off the ticket if they show their union cards.

This means that I don't struggle with the distributor about how much money he's going to put into distributing the film. I figured he's a capitalist and he's going to do as much as he can to make a buck, so I told him, "It's all on you: whatever you want to do, do it; I don't care if you spend $20,000 or $200,000 to open the film. I'm not dealing with that." He gets 70 percent of everything the film makes, theatrically and nontheatrically, for fifteen years, and he also gets to recoup advertising, prints, and all the costs that distributors invent. Cabin Creek gets 30 percent, though Cabin Creek hasn't seen a penny, yet.

F: Is there a project in development now?

Kopple: Just a dream. What I'd like to do next is a fiction film about the Triangle Shirtwaist fire of 1911. Triangle was a factory where mostly women worked—young women, older women, Jewish and Italian immigrants. They went on strike for better benefits and for more workplace safety, things like that. This was also a period when women couldn't vote, so you can imagine the situation these people were in. They raised a lot of consciousness in 1909; and in 1911, there was a fire in that factory and 146 women burned to death: the safety doors were locked and there was only one fire escape, which fell. After that, major industrial reforms took place; there were marches of twenty thousand in the streets; unions united—it's a very important event in labor history.

F: Why do you want to go to the past for your next picture?

Kopple: I guess because I feel those events are very contemporary. The same kinds of things are happening now, in the South. There's a whole movement of industry to the South, where there's practically no unionization among southern textile workers, autoworkers, steelworkers. The right-to-work laws in the South allow for total exploitation of the people down there.

F: When you took *Harlan County* to the Cannes Festival, I heard it was a disaster. Was that because you got critical opposition?

Kopple: No. Cannes is a hustling buyers' market with everybody wheeling and dealing.

In Europe, as in this country, documentaries aren't considered real films, so at festivals they get put into very small screening spaces—plus the scheduling of Cannes was so crazy that people would leave half an hour early because they wanted to catch another film. There were no discussion panels; you didn't know who was seeing your film; people would be walking in and out, not knowing where they were or what they were looking at. It was just poor organization at Cannes and a playing down of documentary.

F: Are you preparing a book on the making of *Harlan County*?

Kopple: Yes, Independent Publishers of the Americas (IPFA) is a nonprofit, tax-exempt publisher that's being set up. I've decided to work with a woman from West Virginia to write the story behind the film, which will really be an analysis of the coalfields, the energy crisis, the nationalization of energy, the whole history of the UMW. The book is designed to help this publishing project get started because IPFA is going to print alternative kinds of books—books on South Africa, books that would never have a chance to be published anywhere else—and all the royalties from our book are going to go to this group.

F: Can you give us some idea of the main achievements of the historic contract the miners struck?

Kopple: Wages were increased to about $57 a day; vacations went from five to ten days; pensions were increased from $150 a month to $250 a month; they did lose the right to strike but supposedly were getting a grievance procedure.

The miners talk about whether ten days is really enough time to get all the coal dust out of your lungs.

F: Was there a great demand for the film in Hollywood after you got the Academy Award?

Kopple: No. The film had already opened in January, before the Academy Awards happened in March. The way that people really started to know about *Harlan County USA* was at the New York Film Festival—the three greatest days of my life. I remember picking up the film when it was finished, just before the festival, thinking, "I spent four years of my life on this!" Having the festival accept the film and realizing there was going to be a big audience—1,100 people for three days, including the miners' wives and the miners—I was excited but also scared. I was worried that the miners might think I exploited them. What if everybody hated it? But people said good things about the film and responded so warmly—incredible.

F: Is it still dangerous for you to travel in some of those areas—now that the film is so well known?

Kopple: Do I find it dangerous? Yeah—because the Klan is still in Harlan County. But I do think that the film has provided some real protection for the people there. Now when things start to happen, it's a lot easier to get the press in there and a lot of publicity by showing the film. I think it's possible that the film has helped to save people's lives. We did a lot of things for Bessie Lou Cornett when she was thrown in jail: telegrams came in from all over the country; the jail had never seen anything like it. [applause]

Notes

1. James L. Enyeart, *Willard Van Dyke: Changing the World through Photography and Film* (Albuquerque: University of New Mexico Press, 2008), 300–1.
2. "Robert Flaherty Seminar Programmers," in "The Flaherty: Four Decades in the Cause of Independent Cinema," ed. Erik Barnouw and Patricia Zimmermann, *Wide Angle* 17, Special Issue (1995): 415 (hereafter cited as "The Flaherty").

3. D. Marie Grieco, phone interview by Patricia R. Zimmermann, October 28, 2012.

4. Nadine Covert, phone interview by Patricia R. Zimmermann, July 28, 2009.

5. See "The Nation," *New York Times*, February 2, 1958, E2; Howard Thompson, "The 16 mm Blackboard: Non-Theatrical, Education Movies Indicated Diversity and Quality," *New York Times*, September 1, 1957, 65; "Citations Given for 16mm Film," *New York Times*, April 26, 1957, 5; Howard Thompson, "Newcomers in 16mm," *New York Times*, April 21, 1957, 97; Howard Thompson, "Newcomers to the Non Theatrical Film Scene," *New York Times,* May 3, 1957, 113.

6. Bill Sloan, phone interview by Patricia R. Zimmermann, July 28, 2009.

7. "Board of Directors," *School and Society* 57 (1943): 497; "Introducing EFLA," *Scholastic* 9, no. 49 (1946): 11; "Organized," *Education for Victory* (June 1, 1943): 2.

8. James L. Enyeart, *Willard Van Dyke*, 143–68.

9. Jay Ruby, phone interview by Patricia R. Zimmermann, September 21, 2009; Jack Coogan, phone interview by Patricia R. Zimmermann, September 15, 2009.

10. William Sloan, phone interview by Patricia R. Zimmermann, July 28, 2009.

11. Dorothy Olson, phone interview by Patricia R. Zimmermann, September 25, 2009.

12. Jack Coogan, phone interview by Patricia R. Zimmermann, September 15, 2009.

13. "Recollections: Amalie R. Rothschild," in "The Flaherty," 61.

14. Ibid.; Patricia R. Zimmermann, "Midwives, Hostesses, and Feminist Film," in "The Flaherty," 207.

15. See the New Day Films website for a thumbnail sketch of this history, retrieved March 17, 2010 (http://www.newday.com/history.html).

16. William Sloan, phone interview by Patricia R. Zimmermann, July 28, 2009; Dorothy Olson, phone interview by Patricia R. Zimmermann, July 25, 2009; Jack Coogan, phone interview by Patricia R. Zimmermann, September 15, 2009; Jay Ruby, phone interview by Patricia Zimmermann, September 21, 2009.

17. Jay Ruby, phone interview by Patricia R. Zimmermann, September 21, 2009; Nadine Covert, phone interview by Patricia R. Zimmermann, July 28, 2009.

18. "Recollections: Jay Ruby," in "The Flaherty," 63.

19. "Recollections: Sarah Elder," in "The Flaherty," 17.

20. "List of Films Screened," in "The Flaherty," 443–51.

21. Nadine Covert, phone interview by Patricia R. Zimmermann, July 28, 2009.

22. David Shepard, phone interview by Patricia R. Zimmermann, August 28, 2012.

23. David Shepard, "The Nanook Crisis (1960–1975)," in "The Flaherty," 372.

24. David Shepard, phone interview by Patricia R. Zimmermann, August 28, 2012.

25. Ibid.

26. Shepard would go on to serve as an IFS trustee for ten years in the 1970s.

27. David Shepard, phone interview by Patricia R. Zimmermann, August 28, 2012.

28. Shepard, "The Nanook Crisis (1960–1975)," in "The Flaherty," 372–74.

29. "Review: 'Nanook of the North,'" *Variety*, December 31, 1921. Retrieved July 20, 2016 (http://variety.com/1921/film/reviews/nanook-of-the-north-1200409377).

30. David Shepard, phone interview by Patricia R. Zimmermann, August 28, 2012.

31. Ibid.

32. Shepard, "The Nanook Crisis (1960–1965)," in "The Flaherty," 373.

33. Ibid.

34. Ibid., 374.

35. Nadine Covert, phone interview by Patricia R. Zimmermann, July 28, 2009; William Sloan, phone interview by Patricia R. Zimmermann, July 28, 2009; Jay Ruby, phone interview by Patricia R. Zimmermann, November 19, 2009; Dorothy Olson, phone interview by Patricia R. Zimmermann, September 18, 2009.

36. Barbara Van Dyke, "Eighteen Years of Name Tags," in "The Flaherty," 314.

37. Patricia Aufderheide, "Public Television and the Public Sphere," *Critical Studies in Mass Communication* 8 (1991): 171.

38. Robert K. Avery, "The Public Broadcasting Act of 1967: Looking Ahead by Looking Back," *Critical Studies in Mass Communication* 24, no. 1, (October 2007): 358–64.

39. Aufderheide, "Public Television and the Public Sphere," 172–73.

40. Ibid., 174.

41. David Stewart, "The Arden House Public TV Seminar and INPUT," in "The Flaherty," 420.

42. Ibid., 420.

43. Ibid., 421.

44. Ibid., 420–21.

45. Jay Ruby, phone interview by Patricia R. Zimmermann, September 21, 2009.

46. David Stewart, "The Arden House Public TV Seminar and INPUT," in "The Flaherty," 420.

The 1998 Flaherty Seminar at Wells College, Aurora, NY. Photo courtesy of International Film Seminars, Inc./The Flaherty, New York.

5

SHOCK OF THE NEW, 1981–1989

The 1980s commenced. The seminar entered its fourth decade. Its organization, participants, programming, and structure changed dramatically. During this period, the Flaherty functioned as a space outside commercial media sectors, an interstitial zone where new forms, genres, and sectors of independent cinema and video converged. At the 1980s seminars, the term *independent* became increasingly defined by its expanding heterogeneity. It operated within a diverse media exhibition ecosystem comprised of media arts centers, museums, public television, and the newly hatched festival circuit. Independent film also included more African Americans, Asian Americans, Latinos/Latinas, and women. Board arguments about diversity and seminar debates about aesthetic form, gender, identity, and race unfurled. More women programmed the annual seminar, screened their films, videos, and installations, and served on the board. More experimental work appeared at seminars, displacing the hegemony of realist documentary styles. Video was programmed, suggesting new technological formats with which to produce independent work.

The 1980s witnessed the recalibration of American independent film as a movement. The expansion of film exhibition circuits in colleges and universities, the increase in the production of feature-length documentaries and narratives, and the multiplication of university-level film and media degrees contributed to the growth of independent film. This period of the Flaherty Seminars opened up to video art, a form emerging in the late 1960s with the advent of the Portapak. It divided into two sectors: one, activist guerrilla work and the other, a more poetic experimentalism pushing the limits of technology and perception. Five seminars provoked new ways to think through the multiplicities of independent media: 1983 (Bruce Jenkins and Melinda Ward, the 1984 seminar programmed by D. Marie Grieco); 1986 (Tony Gittens and Linda Blackaby); 1987 (Richard Herskowitz); and 1989 (Pearl Bowser and Grant Munro). All became touchstones for subsequent programs, offering conceptual models, scope, and structure.

After 1989, more specialty film festivals were established across the United States and in the world, partially in response to unprecedented concentration in the media industries. They provided venues for works not screened at class A festivals with markets like the Berlin Film Festival and the Cannes Film Festival. The Flaherty Seminar served an important function in the emerging field of public media beginning to take shape after the more interventionist period of the 1960s and 1970s. It offered a place where distributors, exhibitors, filmmakers, funders, museum curators, programmers, scholars, and students could gather to argue vigorously and learn more. It create space to ponder deeply about the emerging and increasingly complex aesthetic, funding, infrastructural, and political domains defining independent media.

As International Film Seminars (IFS) established the Flaherty as a nonprofit organization distinct from the Flaherty family, it solidified its position and visibility in New York City with the presidency of Willard Van Dyke and the executive directorship of Barbara Van Dyke. In the 1980s, three women from the arts administration and library world helmed the Flaherty: Emilie de Brigard, president (1981–83); Esme I. Dick, president and executive director (1983–86); and Pearl Bowser, president (1986–89). These women brought considerable acuity, experience, and skills to their roles. Yet, the organization's gendered division of labor, commencing with Frances Flaherty supporting her husband's filmmaking through marketing, continued. Erik Barnouw and Willard Van Dyke assumed highly visible public roles, while women, such as Frances, D. Marie Grieco, Dorothy Olson, and Nadine Covert, motored behind-the-scenes operations that sustained the seminar.

Instead of focusing on the Flaherty films, established international filmmakers were featured as master filmmakers with large bodies of work legitimated as significant by programmers and scholars. Their work represented a modernist impulse to reroute cinematic approach, content, and form. However, the conceptual strategies of seminar programming during this period countered what might be interpreted as a reinvigoration of auteurism. In different configurations, seminars in the 1980s instituted a heterogeneous mix of genres that established the structural philosophy of most seminars to follow. This heterogeneity echoed poststructuralist theory emerging in many scholarly areas at the time. Film studies and visual anthropology academics also began to attend in larger numbers. For some, their style was unnecessarily dense and combative, an affront and assault on the intuitive approach advocated by Frances and then D. Marie Grieco. This meta-system of heterogeneity translated into programming much more diverse and international guests. However, the programming continued to focus on North American works, explained in part by budgetary constraints on honoraria and travel.

During the 1980s, the seminar sharpened its relationship with independent media, emerging as a distinct sector in the United States with a more developed infrastructure of nonprofit distributors, museum exhibitors, media centers, film and media studies programs at colleges and universities, and committed public and private funders. The seminar also moved to universities and retreat centers replete with cafeterias, dormitories, auditoriums equipped for film projection, and conference rooms for discussion. The public media sector had expanded and professionalized. In the early 1980s, independent film emerged as a distinct category outside the studio system, a large umbrella category spanning documentary, experimental, narrative, and hybrid forms. By 1989, the seminar's operational definition of independent film was as heterogeneous as the programming. Rather than a fixed and stable category, independent film suggested a fluid, shape-shifting practice across genres, forms, institutions, and nations.

This period marked a significant shift in who programmed the seminar. In its first three decades, an eclectic, insider East Coast coterie of academics, board members, filmmakers, Flaherty family members, friends, and librarians contributed as seminar programmers. In contrast, the programmers of the 1980s evidenced a movement toward professional programming. These programmers were more than Flaherty devotees or cohorts of East Coast film culture. Their backgrounds and institutional positions demonstrated the increasing professionalization of seminar programmers as highly educated gatekeepers and shrewd connoisseurs skilled in navigating the many layers of the independent media ecology.

During the 1980s, most Flaherty programmers were major figures in the development and programming of independent film in the United States. They helped to elaborate it as a distinct and important part of film culture. Erik Barnouw, Linda Blackaby, Tony Gittens, Richard Herskowitz, Bruce Jenkins, Julie Levinson, Deac Rossell, and Melinda Ward had received graduate training in film and media studies at major elite US universities. They possessed vast knowledge of the histories of the arts and cinema, and possessed the academic training, cultivated taste, and curatorial experience in thinking about programming across multiple forms and genres. They worked at major academic institutions and media arts centers, which afforded continual, intensive immersion throughout the year in works and the debates they ignited. The institutions they worked for defined and mapped independent media: the Boston Film and Video Association (Julie Levinson), Columbia University (Erik Barnouw), Cornell Cinema (Richard Herskowitz), the Library of Congress Motion Picture, Broadcasting and Recorded Sound Division (Erik Barnouw), Media Study Buffalo (Bruce Jenkins), the Museum of Fine Arts in Boston (Deac Rossell), the Neighborhood Film Project in Philadelphia (Linda Blackaby), the Walker Art Center (Bruce Jenkins and Melinda Ward).

In contrast to programmers from the 1950s, '60s, and '70s, these programmers had undergone training in the historical and theoretical debates undergirding cinema as an academic research discipline. They also came to seminar programming work with much deeper experience exhibiting films around the year. As professionals working for major art world, community, and university exhibition venues, they brought more on-the-ground experience in thinking through how audiences engaged with films, filmmakers, and ideas. For example, Grant Munro was a Canadian animator with the National Film Board (NFB) of Canada. D. Marie Grieco, a close friend of Frances Flaherty, was one of the first librarians to pioneer film as an important part of library collections.[1] Of the programmers from the 1980s, only Barnouw, Grieco, Lawder, and Munro were long-term Flaherty Seminar veterans, with decades of interaction and participation in the annual seminars. Barnouw and Grieco were also long-term board members.

The administration of the Flaherty Seminar through IFS remained in New York City rather than in Vermont. New York City was increasingly becoming a nexus for independent filmmaking. Lucy Kostelanetz, a filmmaker and former arts administrator for the New York State Council on the Arts (NYSCA) in the 1970s, attended the Flaherty for the first time in 1982, right after leaving her post with NYSCA. She subsequently served on the IFS board during the 1980s and the 1990s. Kostelanetz brought arts administration acumen to the board. She mobilized a mission to professionalize the seminar as an arts organization. She was interested in stabilizing the seminar administratively, financially, and logistically.

As Kostelanetz transitioned from arts administrator to filmmaker, she also experienced the power of the Flaherty to ignite community and inspiration. She wrote, "In 1982, I was fortunate enough to enter a singular 'community' of individuals who are committed to nourishing and affirming the creative work of independent media voices," a place, she pointed out, filled with a "world of people to help, support, encourage, and inspire me."[2] As a board member with responsibility for the organization as opposed to the week-long immersion experience itself, she witnessed challenges of sustainability and viability as serious budget problems continually confronted the Flaherty. For her, the organization needed to develop beyond a dedicated in-group of trustees who functioned more like passion project volunteers than as board members of a nonprofit arts organization. She discovered that private and public funders as well as individual donors did not find the seminar an attractive grantee. Its intensive, retreat-like nature and small group size lacked the large body counts and public visibility of other exhibition venues. The seminar also never assessed its own impact.[3] Federal and state grants to arts groups required organizational assessment for fiscal accountability.

Although this period featured some of the most challenging and important programming of any Flaherty, for Kostelanetz, it also festered organizational tensions. Beyond the glamour of the seminar's guests and postscreening discussions, problems lurked in the board's differing views on the future of the organization. On one side, the more intuitive, experiential Flaherty stalwarts who had experienced the familial, club-like intimacies of the seminars in the earlier decades saw professionalization as a detour from the heart and soul of the much mythologized "Flaherty experience," an insider's conversion experience that defied rational language. On the other side, the more strategic and younger board members with experience in the nonprofit public media sector determined the need for more deductive and transparent organizational strategies.

A board member, documentary filmmaker, and president in the 1980s, Juan Mandelbaum noted IFS had gathered a board of academics and filmmakers who, despite their deep affections for the Flaherty Seminar, lacked the administrative, business management, and financial experience necessary for nonprofit organizational survival. For example, only one or two board members during this time possessed financial skills. Mandelbaum contended the board confronted continual issues with various executive directors, due to the continuing economic struggles to maintain IFS, a tradition of familialism, and volatile strong personalities.[4]

The seminar now ran with many more participants. Within the larger context of the independent media sectors of festivals, funding, programming, and public television, its familialist modus operandi of committed, contentious, and passionate volunteers posed a significant destabilizing threat to its continuity and viability. Nadine Covert was a librarian and editor with long-term involvement in the Flaherty. She had programmed a seminar and served on the board. She remembered that in the 1980s, board member Pearl Bowser hired two consultants to undertake organizational analysis of the seminar. The report revealed what Covert had observed firsthand: the seminar had no historical record of what it had actually accomplished in film/media culture, no written manual on how to produce the seminar, no written policy or board procedures, and no viable infrastructure.

In a 2007 essay surveying the institutional history of the Flaherty Seminar entitled "International Film Seminars: A Work in Progress" published by the National Association of Media Arts and Culture (NAMAC), Covert explained the serious challenges the Flaherty organization confronted from the 1980s to the late 1990s as a "midlife crisis."[5] She recognized the important international documentary luminaries who had screened at the seminar: William Greaves, Barbara Kopple, Louis Malle, Chris Marker, Mira Nair, Marcel Ophuls, Lourdes Portillo, Jean Rouch, Ousmane Sembène, and Trinh T. Minh-ha. Although the artistic and intellectual intensities of the seminar had profound effects on distributors, film festivals, filmmakers, programmers, and scholars, Covert argued impact "was difficult to quantify, and funders like to see higher attendance figures."[6] She carefully and deftly distinguished the transformative impact of the seminar on participants from the continuing administrative problems that unmoored its institutional operations and structure. She underlined that IFS had been "perennially underfunded and understaffed," relying in its initial years on volunteer board members and later on a part-time staff. Part of the organizational problem radiated out from the fact that it only produced a one-week event. It lacked a more public presence and visibility throughout the year.

NYSCA was one of the first state arts agencies to fund cinema and video. It not only supported independent filmmaking but also bolstered the exhibition of independent film in museums such as the Museum of Modern Art (MoMA). Moreover, it provided grants for exhibition at colleges and universities across the state. At Colgate University, video artist John Knecht launched a decades-long public program of independent cinema supported in part by NYSCA funds. At the State University of New York at Buffalo, filmmaker Tony Conrad and experimental film scholar Bruce Jenkins established an important hub for alternative media exhibition upstate at Media Study/Buffalo, far away from New York City in northwestern New York state.

The connection between the Flaherty and NYSCA revealed complex, contentious, and significant currents. New York governor Nelson Rockefeller inaugurated NYSCA with bipartisan support with the populist goal to make the arts available to everyone, not just the elite. It functioned as a major arts funder, among the largest of any state arts funders and a leader in funding media arts. In 1981, B. Ruby Rich assumed the role of director of the film program at NYSCA. In Chicago, she had worked as a film programmer at the School of the Art Institute and also as a film critic, where her smart, searing film reviews earned her a reputation as an insightful, provocative interpreter of contemporary cinema. Rich determined NYSCA employed an overly narrow definition of media: she advanced it supported "leftovers from the 1970s from the first generation of film and independent media." She discovered that media arts organizations were small and operated with enormous amounts of nepotism. They screened feminist films, personal cinema, and shorts from the 1970s. Rich interrogated their ideologies, infrastructures, and programming, asking "Why didn't NYSCA go further, how to expand access, how to diversify who was on the panel by including more people of color, documentary makers?"[7]

Although some in the New York state media arts sectors considered her aggressive leadership an attack against the white male avant-garde, Rich rerouted funding to distribution, documentary, and smaller organizations dedicated to exhibition. She pushed for conferences such as the "Show the Right Thing Conference" in 1989, a landmark gathering to increase capacity for independent exhibition. It sought to bring people from smaller venues together to forge new alliances for independent film exhibition.[8] In the 1980s, NYSCA's film and media program facilitated a major infusion of resources to the independent media sector in the state. It provided grants for exhibition and production. It advocated works enter communities both downstate in New York City and upstate in rural areas and smaller cities. First as director of the film program and later in 1987 as director of the electronic media and film program for NYSCA, Rich galvanized multicultural programming in the New York state media arts sector.

The Flaherty Seminars had received NYSCA funding as a media arts organization housed in New York state. The grants required that the seminars be held at a venue in the state. Under Rich's leadership, NYSCA pushed the seminars to consider a larger diversity of styles and a much more multicultural mix of filmmakers. Rich had first attended the Flaherty Seminar in 1973. She observed the Flaherty was "a key meeting place in the history of documentary," but nonetheless an "exception to any other program . . . they needed to expand the universe they were speaking to."[9]

Despite rumors circulating among Flaherty veterans that Rich and NYSCA were exceptionally antagonistic to the seminar, Rich recognized the seminar's unique contribution to film culture. She contended the Flaherty was "one of the only places outside academia where you could talk about film ideas . . . for filmmakers, programmers, exhibitors, there was nowhere else to have that conversation." Rich ascertained filmmakers could screen at the Flaherty and as a result, establish a career through connections with academics, curators, distributors, opinion leaders, and programmers.[10] However, Rich, a specialist in feminist, Latin American, and queer cinema, disagreed with aficionados and trustees that the seminar was unique in film culture. She situated its historical roots within the European experimental ciné-clubs of the 1920s, which also featured post-screening filmmaker discussion. She also compared the Flaherty Seminar to the Argentine and Cuban cine club movements, far more radical and political than the Flaherty, where humanist sensibilities tended to frame social problems as individual stories.[11]

By the 1980s, many new producers offering different stories and new aesthetic forms entered the documentary and experimental media worlds. These African American, Asian American, gay and lesbian, Latino/Latina, and women makers were not affiliated with the commercial documentary, direct cinema, or white male New York avant-garde sectors that populated the Flaherty in its first twenty-five years.[12] According to Rich, the panels assembled to review NYSCA grants for exhibition thought the Flaherty "looked like a private club in terms of its programmers and programming."[13] NYSCA and its peer review panels facilitated a cultural transition in arts programming, carving out space for the emerging voices and innovative practices of the era. NYSCA pushed the Flaherty Seminar, MoMA, and the Whitney Museum to diversify their programming with these new voices.[14] The 1980s shifts in seminar programming toward collectives such as Paper Tiger Television, community media groups, experimental/documentary hybrid work, multicultural producers, and video art reflected not only the changing ecologies of public media operating beyond major institutions but also underscored NYSCA's prioritization of distribution and exhibition.

For eighteen years, Barbara Van Dyke functioned as a force field in the seminar's administration. As the wife of the verbally aggressive and volatile Willard Van Dyke, trustees also found her a controversial figure. When she stepped down from the executive director position in 1982, the seminar's operations worked differently than in the 1960s. Van Dyke transformed the seminar from an East Coast–centric Flaherty family project into a more national media arts organization with a much larger mandate to provide a place to explore independent film and media. She had also been key in spearheading the Public Television and Independent Film Seminars. Also known as the Arden House Seminars (1971–81), these seminal gatherings translated the Flaherty Seminar structure of nonpreconception, rigorous viewing, and vigorous discussion into a think tank for public television program directors to expand their vision of cinema and to help them connect with independent producers in order to procure content. Van Dyke's administrative and programming efforts for the Arden House Seminars represented one of the first moves of the seminar to bring together two different media constituencies: the independent film community and public television. Van Dyke's administration and vision of the Arden House Seminar had produced a tangible result: the creation of a space for collaboration and dialogue between two groups who might not have encountered each other at a critical juncture in public media history.

When Van Dyke resigned in 1982, Esme I. Dick assumed the executive director position, a role she held from 1982 to 1988. Dick was considered an able administrator, skilled at running meetings and managing seminar logistics. However, the executive directorship remained only a part-time job, suggesting an organization running more on the passions of its partisans than on a more sustainable model of revenue-stream generation.

In the context of the development of the nonprofit media arts field, the expansion of film and video degrees at the undergraduate and graduate level at North American universities, and increased arts funding for the public media and independent film sector, the role of the Flaherty Seminar shifted in the 1980s. As the Flaherty Seminar diversified its programming and welcomed a larger number of participants, it depended more heavily on private and public funding. These external funders signified an important change beyond the support of embassies underwriting filmmakers from outside the United States and participants with ties to the Flaherty family. These funders pressured the Flaherty to extend beyond its mostly white, mostly male, East Coast coterie and familialized operating style.

The period between 1981 through 1989 represented not only a redirection for IFS as an organization but also for the Flaherty Film Seminars as a media exhibitor and think tank. From 1973 to 1980, few experimental works were screened. Bruce Conner's films, which had appeared many times at seminars, were exceptions: they suggested intersections between documentary and experimental form. Caroline Leaf and Norman McLaren's experimental animations were also shown. This programming gap cannot be interpreted as a doctrinaire anti-avant-garde response, however. Several important Flaherty trustees from the museum and public library sectors such as D. Marie Grieco and William Sloan were strong advocates of short experimental films. This distancing of seminar programming from the experimental sector pivoted on multiple pressure points: the commanding presence of Willard Van Dyke who advocated for politically engaged documentary, the discursive powers of those who forged the field of visual anthropology such as Jay Ruby and Sol Worth, and the insulation of the seminar from larger currents of film culture due to its origins as a family-run enterprise. The seminar operated as a gathering for media insiders.

By the 1980s, both video art and video activism had dramatically expanded, especially across the State of New York, a particularly vibrant sector of emerging film and media culture with a history extending back to the early 1960s. Many media collectives, exhibitors, groups, and organizations formed between 1965 and 1980, such as the Experimental Television Center (Owego), Hallwalls (Buffalo), the Ithaca Video Project, Media Study/Buffalo, Videofreex (Lanesville), and Visual Studies Workshop (Rochester).[15]

By this period, the seminar's programming adapted to a more explicit heterogeneous style that combined the classics, documentary, experimental, feature films, and new forms, a strategy initially formulated by Nadine Covert and William Sloan in the 1970s. An artist, director of the experimental film *Necrology*, and professor, Standish Lawder programmed the 1981 seminar at the University of California, one of the few seminars to be held away from the East Coast. This seminar highlighted the West Coast independent documentary and experimental scenes. It screened feature-length films that received Academy Award nominations, such as *From Mao to Mozart* (1979) and *Eight Minutes to Midnight: A Portrait of Dr. Helen Caldicott* (1981).

The seminar continued some of programming threads from previous periods by showcasing works of Flaherty Seminar insiders, longtime participants, and trustees such as Erik Barnouw, Sumner Glimcher, and Robert Osborn's *Fable Safe* (1971); Erik Barnouw, Paul Ronder, and Barbara Van Dyke's *Hiroshima-Nagasaki August 1945* (1970); and Amalie Rothschild's *Conversations with Willard Van Dyke* (1981). It programmed historical films, focusing on *Nanook of the North* (1922) and John Huston's *Let There Be Light* (1946), a once US government–banned film about posttraumatic stress psychiatric symptoms in seventy-five veterans following World War II.[16] The 1981 seminar also featured works from the NFB, continuing the long relationship that the Flaherty Seminar had enjoyed with that state-supported organization, with *Fiddlers of James Bay* (1980) and four works by Donald Brittain,[17] including *Memorandum* (1967), *Volcano: An Inquiry into the Death of Malcolm Lowry* (1976), *Small Is Beautiful: Impressions of Fritz Schumacher* (1978), and *Paperland: The Bureaucrat Observed* (1979). Brittain's presence continued a strategy that had emerged in seminar programming in the 1970s to feature an established filmmaker with a large body of work, paralleling the earlier focus on the works of Robert Flaherty as master artist.

The program interwove two documentary traditions with long seminar trajectories: the compilation film and direct cinema. At this seminar, each style focused on the portrait. Continuing American direct cinema observational modes, this seminar screened *Can't It Be Anyone Else?* (1980) by Bill Couturié and John Korty; *From Mao to Mozart* by Murray Lerner; and *Werner Herzog in Peru* (work in progress that later became *Burden of Dreams*, 1980) by Les Blank. *From Mao to Mozart*, a film that followed violinist Isaac Stern's collaboration with the China Central Symphony Society in Beijing, was nominated for the documentary Academy Award in 1980. Lee Grant directed the narrative independent feature *Tell Me a Riddle* (1980) based on Tillie Olsen's short stories. A compilation film composed of banned footage from the bombing, *Hiroshima-Nagasaki August 1945* illustrated the power of compilation as evidentiary-based deductive argument.

Of the thirty-seven films screened, only five were directed by women. Nearly all the other filmmakers were white males. The women filmmakers included Amalie Rothschild, Mary Benjamin, Martha Sandlin, Nancy Schreiber, and Lee Grant. Rothschild, who had attended many seminars in the 1970s and eventually had an affair with Willard Van Dyke, screened her interview film, *Conversations with Willard Van Dyke*. Nancy Schreiber[18] screened *Possum Living* (1981). Mary Benjamin showed *Eight Minutes to Midnight*, a portrait film following Dr. Helen Caldicott speaking about the medical dangers posed by nuclear power. The film was nominated for an Academy Award in 1981.[19] Lee Grant[20] also screened *The Willmar 8* (1981), a direct cinema film following eight women who went on strike against a Minnesota bank over sex discrimination and unequal pay.

Martha Sandlin's *A Lady Named Baybie* (1979) was an important example of women's filmmaking. More a film made by and about women than a feminist film, the film featured Rev. Baybie Hoover and her friend Virginia Brown, two elderly blind women who sang gospel songs for money in the streets of New York. The film represented a significant moment in independent film history. In *The Christian Science Monitor*, Arthur Unger noted, "Not only is it superb TV and superb filmmaking, 'Baybie' is also probably a harbinger of the kind of independently produced nonfiction TV we will be seeing in the future."[21]

At the 1981 seminar, experimental films returned but not in large numbers. These films did not reroute the seminar from its long-form documentary programming strategy. The experimental films variegated the programming rhythm and refocused conceptual threads. Even more importantly, the experimental works functioned not as interventions into cinematic form but as a continuation of Frances Flaherty's initial goals to consider cinema as art. Most of the films were produced by West Coast–based filmmakers, a rerouting of the seminar from its East Coast orientation: *America Is Waiting* (1981) by Bruce Conner, a film evoking the traditions of compilation; *Necrology* (1971) by Standish Lawder, the seminar's programmer; and *Southern California* (1979) by Louis Hock, whose installation and multiscreen projections utilized observations of the immigrant Mexican communities where he lived. Hock was later linked to the Border Arts movement in Southern California, producing collaborative works in installation, performance art, and video. Hock's seminar appearance indicated a move from 16mm film to video, a reorientation that would accelerate during this period. Merging the poetic and the observational, Manny Kirchheimer's[22] *Stations of the Elevated* (1981) was also screened. It problematized the borders between documentary and experimental modes. Disposing of narration and refusing to be a portrait, this film's subject was the first to chronicle graffiti in New York City. Due to problems obtaining licenses for the music of Charles Mingus and Aretha Franklin sprinkled throughout the film, *Stations of the Elevated* was not theatrically released until 2014, when it was finally restored and licenses obtained.[23]

During the 1980s, the seminars included more programmers trained in critical studies at universities as well as many more women: Melinda Ward from the Walker Art Center in Minneapolis in 1983; D. Marie Grieco, the New York City–based film librarian, in 1984; Linda Blackaby, a well-respected Philadelphia community and festival programmer, in 1986; Julie Levinson, a PhD in film studies with museum programming experience and a college-level teaching background, in 1988; and Pearl Bowser, filmmaker and educator, in 1989. Combined with seminars programmed by Erik Barnouw, Richard Herskowitz, and Bruce Jenkins, this period screened more work by women than any of the seminars from the previous decades. These works spanned documentary, experimental film, feature-length narrative, and video art. Major women filmmakers—African American, Asian American, Australian, Chinese, Indian, Japanese, Latino/Latina, Vietnamese, and white American—whose work has entered the canon of independent cinema screened at these seminars: Beth B (*Letters to Dad*, 1979), Jane Campion (*Passionless Moments*, 1984), Ayoka Chenzira (*Zajota and the Boogie Spirit*, 1989), Michelle Citron (*What You Take for Granted*, 1983), Cecilia Condit (*Not a Jealous Bone*, 1987), Julie Dash (*Daughters of the Dust*, 1991), Helen De Michiel (*Change of Address*, 1982), Anne Flournoy (*Louise Smells a Rat*, 1982), Su Friedrich (*Damned If You Don't*, 1987), Tami Gold (*Prescription for Change*, 1986), Jill Godmilow (*Far from Poland*, 1984), DeeDee Halleck (*De Peliculas*, 1988), Martha Haslanger (*Revolution*, 1979–83), Joan Logue (*30 Second Spot*, 1982), Mira Nair (*India Cabaret*, 1985), Michelle Parkerson (*Gotta Make This Journey: Sweet Honey in the Rock*, 1983), Pratibha Parmar (*Sari Red*, 1988), Lourdes Portillo (*La Ofrenda: The Days of the Dead*, 1988), Joanna Priestley (*Rubber Stamp Film*, 1983), Deborah Shafer (*Witness to War: Dr. Charlie Clements*, 1985), Leslie Thornton (*There Was an Unseen Cloud Moving*, 1988), Trinh T. Minh-ha (*Reassemblage: From Firelight to the Screen*, 1982), Lise Yasui (*Family Gathering*, 1989), and Pamela Yates (*When the Mountains Tremble*, 1984).

This recalibration in seminar programming toward showing the works of more women had no simple, causal explanation. Instead, it represented a confluence of multiple historical contexts. NYSCA had been insisting the seminar be more inclusive. Programmers had studied film theory, now a key component of graduate film studies programs. The independent documentary, experimental, and narrative film scenes were more open to women than the commercial industries. University film degree programs proliferated. Grants to produce independent media increased. The seminar's programming intensified engagement with contemporary political media practices beyond direct cinema, cinéma vérité, compilation, and direct cinema documentary. The experimental arts and public media scenes in community centers, museums, public television, and universities seemed to produce more cutting-edge programs and discover more new work than the Flaherty Seminars. Unlike these larger institutions, it did not program throughout the year. Its East Coast club-like atmosphere sometimes insulated it from larger independent media. In contrast, seminar programmers seemed to absorb currents and practices emerging in other sectors of independent media. They brought these sectors into conversation, a unique approach.

During the 1980s, video art migrated into the seminar, a logical move explained by the seminar's geographic location in the State of New York and the Northeast. Video art had a rich history in the region during the 1970s with the emergence of many art and political video collectives. Many institutions across New York state supported video art: Everson Museum in Syracuse, Experimental Television Center in Owego, Media Study/ Buffalo, NYSCA, the Whitney Museum, and the many universities and colleges teaching video art courses such as Ithaca College, the School of Visual Arts in New York, State University of New York at Buffalo, and Syracuse University.

Although video (both documentary and experimental) never dominated seminar programming, its engagement with innovative visual styles and new technologies opened up the seminar beyond its vectors of compilation, direct cinema, Flaherty humanistic portrait documentary, and long-form documentary for theatrical and public television. In the realm of video documentary, the seminar featured Skip Blumberg (*First International Whistling Show,* 1978, and *JGLNG,*1976), Richard Fung (*Way to My Father's Village,* 1988), John Greyson (*The ADS Epidemic,* 1987), DeeDee Halleck (*Herb Schiller Reads the New York Times #3: A Paper Tiger Sampler,* 1981), Louis Hock (*Mexican Tapes: A Chronicle of Life Outside the Law,* 1986), Louis Massiah (*Bombing of Osage Avenue,* 1986), and Ilan Ziv (*Consuming Hunger,* 1987). Significantly, many of these makers were connected with important, emerging East Coast–based nonprofit institutions that offered video advocacy and training: Downtown Community Television (Alpert), Paper Tiger Television (Halleck), and Scribe Video Center (Massiah). Fung and Greyson worked out of Toronto. Hock was the only the West Coast video maker.

Experimental video also began to enter seminar programming during the 1980s. However, it never constituted the majority of works screened, functioning more as a way to create heterogeneity and texture in the programming. The seminar's video programming did not constitute an innovative contribution to film and media culture. Instead, it represented catching up with the multiple currents that were redefining independent media that had in many ways outpaced the seminar. Auteurist experimental video art and community-based political video had at least a decade of development in the 1970s on both the East and West Coasts.[24] During this period, major figures from the world of video art screened their work: Max Almy (*Perfect Leader,* 1983), Juan Downey (*Laughing Alligator,* 1979), Philip Mallory Jones (*Contemplation,* 1987, and *Dreamkeeper,* 1989), Joan Logue (*30 Second Spots*), Victor Masayesva (*Itam Hakim Hopiit,* 1984), Daniel Reeves (*Smothering Dreams,* 1981), Edin Velez (*Meta Mayan,* 1981), and Bill Viola (*Hatsu Yume,* 1981, and *Vegetable Memory,* 1979–80). Many had deep connections to the Northeast video art scene: Philip Mallory Jones lived in Ithaca, where he administered and curated the Ithaca Video Project; Daniel Reeves had attended Ithaca College; Velez, Logue, and Downey were based in New York; and Bill Viola had studied at Syracuse University.[25] Underscoring the technical challenges of including more video at the seminar, Ann Michel and Phil Wilde, principals of the video production company Insights International in Ithaca and New York City, were added to the projection team.

In the context of featured makers, heterogeneity of forms, and new directions provoked by more elaborate programming structures, the 1980s stood as one of the most significant in the seminar's history. This period heralded the era of the professional programmer, a movement away from independent cinema enthusiasts and the Flaherty inner circle of the earlier decades. Educated in feminist, Marxist, and structuralist-inflected film studies, these programmers brought analytical and historical depth to their research and curatorial preparations, signifying a decisive break from the notion of "good works." These programmers moved the seminar from unsystematic notions of "good work" to a more rigorous assessment of significant work. They also constructed overall programming architectures through juxtapositions, resonances, and weavings. No longer a grab bag of miscellany or acclaimed works, the programs interrogated conceptual questions such as the role of experiments in form (1983 and 1984); ethnicities, race, genre, class, and sexual orientation (1986); different temporalities and practices (1987); or race and nation (1989).

Programmers with academic film studies training who worked full time at prominent institutions in noncommercial media centers dominated during this period. While the history of the seminar revealed a constant influx of scholars from a variety of fields despite the fervent imaginaries of Flaherty veterans who idealized the role of filmmakers and practitioners, it was only in the 1980s, with the establishment of film studies as a doctoral-level discipline in the 1970s, that programmers' professional backgrounds changed. Trained in academic film history and theory, they were affiliated with the public media sectors of festivals, libraries, and museums. With the exception of Melinda Ward from Minneapolis, all the programmers resided in the East Coast corridor spanning Boston, lower Canada, and New York. Erik Barnouw, the broadcast and documentary historian, programmed the 1982 seminar. Deac Rossell, a scholar of early cinema and a well-respected curator from Boston, programmed the 1985 seminar. Linda Blackaby, director of the Neighborhood Film/Video Project (of International House), Philadelphia, and Tony Gittens, an African American television producer and film festival programmer from Washington, DC, programmed the 1986 seminar. A film studies scholar who also worked in museums and independent media centers in Boston, Julie Levinson programmed the 1988 seminar.

Each seminar imported something new to the Flaherty experience. Barnouw introduced video art with Daniel Reeves and Edin Velez. Rossell explored the initial surge of the theatrical feature-length documentary with *Living at Risk: The Story of Nicaraguan Family* (1984); *Maids and Madams: Apartheid Begins in the Home* (1987); *When the Mountain Tremble* (1984); and *Witness to War* (1985). Blackaby and Gittens mixed together animation, documentary, experimental, and fictional work through resonances. They instituted a shift to more international dialogue with works from and about Argentina, Canada, Central America, China, Hopi, India, Japan, Nicaragua, the Philippines, South Africa, and the United States. Their seminar showcased Henry Hampton's *Eyes on the Prize* (1987–90), a public television chronicle of the civil rights movement, indicating a mix of different institutional contexts for independent media from museums, to theaters, to public television. A first for the seminar, Levinson created a program where almost half the filmmakers were women— Camille Billips, Cecelia Condit, Kate Davis, Jennifer Fox, Sharon Greytak, Sachiko Hamada, Mira Hamermesh, Margot Starr Kernan, Sherry Milner, Joanna Priestley, Leslie Thornton, and Lise Yasui. Her seminar featured Australian cinéma vérité maker Dennis O'Rourke as featured maestro with his films *Yap: How*

Did You Know We'd Like TV? (1980) and *Cannibal Tours* (1988). She screened films from the UK's Sankofa Film Collective. Levinson mixed video art, classics, direct cinema, experimental film, and video art. She initiated a dialogue on race in independent film with artists such as Camille Billips, Juan Downey, Richard Fung, Sankofa Film Collective, Lise Yasui, Edin Velez, and Billy Woodberry.

These seminar debates about aesthetic form, gender, internationalism, and race aligned the Flaherty with trends in larger independent film culture. Five other seminars altered the format of the seminar itself by revamping programming structure. Some of the most intense, pitched debates about filmmaking practices erupted, indicating a clash between the older Flaherty participants who wanted to see significant work through the lens of nonpreconception and younger participants schooled in critical theory—a direct opposition to the experiential and to humanism. These seminars put forward programming strategies of crossings and arcs (1983), short experimental work (1984), identity politics and documentary shifts (1986), combustive heterogeneities (1987), and Third Cinemas (1989).

Each spurred the seminar to assume new directions, inflections, and shapes. Their programming model of aggressive montages of heterogeneity often precipitated discursive tumult. These seminars addressed absences and deficiencies in previous seminar programming. They entered into debates and unresolved issues that were being worked out and battled in academia, independent media, and politics. These five seminars disrupted the traditions of the seminar. They veered away from screening artistically validated media toward considering what was at stake aesthetically and politically in contemporary film and media culture. These seminars added a structural tactic missing in earlier seminars: a deliberate mosaic strategy, a designed conceptual interaction between works and makers to instigate dialogue and debates, and a programming arc.

Bruce Jenkins and Melinda Ward proposed a seminar idea to the board for the 1983 seminar. The board had decided to conduct an open call for programming proposals—a direction that deviated from the insider selection process of previous decades. Jenkins was at Media Study/Buffalo and Ward was in Minneapolis at Alive Off Center, a historically significant experiment in programming video art. While attending the 1980 seminar programmed by John Katz, Jenkins discerned the seminar was "not mapped, no arc, no thematics."[26] He had written his Northwestern University dissertation on structural filmmaker Hollis Frampton. He felt the 1980 program was "not all that fresh, not a nice mix of old and new."[27] Although he appreciated seeing the films of Robert Drew, by 1980, direct cinema did not represent the cutting edge of independent media. Commercial and industrial practices had absorbed it.[28]

Jenkins was not only an academic who had researched structural film but was also a very skilled programmer who had run a ciné-club at Northwestern. He had been a film programmer in Buffalo, hosting more than forty visiting filmmakers a year.[29] Ward had been working on the American Independent Features project, a National Endowment for the Arts (NEA)–funded touring program of the "American New Wave," the first generation of independent filmmakers. Jenkins and Ward drafted a proposal to explore the concept of genres crossing over and infiltrating one another, suggesting more fluid borders between experimental, fiction, and nonfiction work. They were not only reacting against the East Coast bloc that controlled the Flaherty, but they also hoped to engender a noncombative dialogue with the institution of the Flaherty in order to expand it.

As Jenkins explained, they wanted to "open the window and let fresh air in" by "introducing the Flaherty to a wider range of work."[30] They proposed a mapping structure where each day would probe one theme—one day on reinventing documentary, putting the work of Jill Godmilow in *Far from Poland* in conversation with Trinh T. Minh-ha's *Reassemblage*, another day on youth, another on the performative.[31] Jenkins and Ward understood the importance of video in both its guerilla TV and video art iterations as a part of contemporary arts culture. They invited Skip Blumberg (*First International Whistling Show* and *JGLNG*), DeeDee Halleck (Paper Tiger Television), and Bill Viola (*Chott el Djerid,* 1979; *Hatsu Yume, Silent Life,* 1979) to their seminar. Invoking the programming strategy of bringing in an established filmmaker as the éminence grise, they featured Filipino filmmaker Kidlat Tahimik, whose *Perfumed Nightmare* (1977) and *Who Invented the Yoyo Who Invented the Moon Buggy* (1979) blurred the boundaries between documentary, experimental, narrative, and personal strategies. Michelle Citron's *What You Take for Granted* (1983) confounded genre borders. This seminar commingled direct cinema with compilation. *Seventeen* (1983) by Joel DeMott and Jeff Kreines, a film following working-class high schoolers in Indiana as part of the Middletown series for public television was juxtaposed with *Seeing Red: Portraits of American Communists* (1983) by Julia Reichert and James Klein. The pitched debates that the seminar became renowned for erupted over the works of Trinh T. Minh-ha: did her experimental style intervene into documentary form, or was it simply poor craft? Skip Blumberg was attacked as a white male photographing communities of color. As DeeDee Halleck recalled, this seminar offered an important amalgamation of communities, genres, and styles. It was here she met Kidlat Tahimik, whose low-tech style echoed the strategies of Paper Tiger. Beyond the films and elegantly considered structures placing works in conversation with one another, Halleck contended the most important aspect of the Jenkins and Ward 1983 seminar was that it produced of a sense of camaraderie and community: "the seminar to me was a way of meeting other filmmakers because the work of media making is so isolating."[32]

In 1984, D. Marie Grieco programmed a seminar historically significant for its focus on short experimental work, never a dominant feature and always a point of contention. Her seminar mobilized an explicit mosaic structure: it assembled short films that would suggest strategies for reading the next film. Grieco had served as a trustee of IFS. She had also programmed the 1968 and 1969 seminars. A Flaherty Seminar veteran, she had attended many seminars where she had observed how audiences looked for confrontations and connections between films as the week unfurled. As Grieco has written, she saw the Flaherty as a space dedicated to two goals: film curation and crafting participants' experience to learn new ways of seeing—a direct influence from her friendship with France Flaherty. According to Grieco, "the seminar's purpose was to learn how to see in new ways through unexpected juxtapositions and illuminating connections across the films, rather than through lectures or master filmmakers' insights. Through carefully assembled programming mosaics, participants would learn to see and think about cinema more deeply."[33]

Her seminar constituted one of the first to focus almost exclusively on aesthetic interventions into form, rather than positioning experimental work as a spicy diversion to compilation film, direct cinema, and humanist portrait documentary. Her interest in experimental work emanated from two vectors. The first was her connection to and influence among film librarians, who purchased independent film and supported the public exhibition of short works. Although film librarians were key figures in the development of an economic infrastructure supporting independent cinema before the rise of media centers, their presence at the seminar was always charged. Barbara Van Dyke worried too many librarians attended the seminar. To compensate, she reached out to art cinema directors and public television producers.[34] Grieco contended these debates disguised a larger gender issue: the major trustees of the seminar were men like Erik Barnouw, Jay Ruby, George Stoney, Willard Van Dyke, and Sol Worth, while the librarians were women. The second vector derived from Grieco's commitment to the ideas of Frances Flaherty, who pushed for the seminars to explore the "creative process." Frances concentrated on the poetic aspects of Robert's practice through an interdisciplinary dialogue between the arts, a trajectory Grieco adopted. This strategy extended her exhibition experiences at Cinema 16, where Amos Vogel programmed according to an heterogeneous, mosaic model of connections and juxtaposition.[35]

Grieco's seminar was held at Cornell University, a venue change facilitated by Richard Herskowitz who was then director of Cornell Cinema. Grieco mixed film and video together. Screening work from video makers Stevenson J. Palfi, Daniel Reeves, and Ilan Ziv unsettled the technological infrastructures of the seminar, which showed 16mm film. Screening video required a different skill set in running lines, mounting monitors, and hooking up decks. Herskowitz recruited Ann Michel and Phil Wilde to help project the video end of the program. They had previously collaborated with the Ithaca Video Project and Daniel Reeves.

Grieco's seminar programmed a staggering eighty titles. The year before, Jenkins and Ward screened thirty-seven titles. This doubling of the number of titles indicates a deliberate shift to exploring the short form rather than the feature. Grieco showed more Flaherty titles than almost any other programmer in the previous ten years, evoking the early days of the seminar when the Flaherty films occupied a prominent position: *Louisiana Story*, *Man of Aran*, and *Nanook of the North*. Grieco's emphasis on avant-garde film and video art revived a part of the Flaherty legacy promoted by Frances Flaherty regarding ways to see the world with nonpreconception through aesthetic exploration. The seminar's programming of compilation and direct cinema films had in some ways repressed this more lyrical and mystical Flaherty legacy. Grieco also presented historical works by experimental filmmaker Maya Deren, including *Study in Choreography for Camera* (1945), *Ritual in Transfigured Time* (1946) and *Haiti Footage-Outtakes* (1950).

The 1984 seminar combined East and West Coast experimental film with animation. A full range of works by San Francisco–based experimental collage filmmaker Bruce Conner were shown: *A Movie* (1958), *Cosmic Ray* (1962), *Ten Second Film* (1965), *Looking for Mushrooms* (1967), *The White Rose* (1967), *Crossroads* (1976), *Valse Triste* (1977), and *Mongoloid* (1978). Conner attended, assuming the established filmmaker role with a body of work screened throughout the week. *Door* (1971) by Stan Brakhage (who lived in

Colorado) was screened. Animation played a large role at the 1983 seminar, with works by Polish animator and visual effects experimenter Zbigniew Rybczyński.[36] Titles included *Kwadrat (Square)* (1972), *Take Five* (1972), *Plamuz (Music Art)* (1973), *Święto* (1975), *Oj! Nie moge sie zatrzymac!* (1976), *Nowa książka (New Book)*(1976), *Weg zum Nachbarn (Way to the Neighbors)* (1976), *Mein Fenster (My Window)* (1979), *Media* (1980), and *Tango* (1981). After the institution of martial law in Poland in the early 1980s, Rybczyński emigrated to the United States in 1983.

The 1984 program rerouted the seminar away from character-centered humanist and political documentary. The 1984 seminar programmed many works by women, spanning documentary to experimental forms across film and video. Women makers included African American documentarian Michelle Parkerson (*Gotta Make This Journey: Sweet Honey in the Rock*), African American feminist animator Ayoka Chenzira (*Hair Piece: A Film for Nappy Headed People,* 1985), and experimental filmmaker Anne Flournoy (*Louise Smells a Rat*). Max Almy (*Perfect Leader,* 1983), Cecelia Condit (*Possibly in Michigan,* 1983), Ed Emshwiller (*Sunstone,* 1979), who was working in experimental computer animation, and Daniel Reeves (*Amida,* 1983), mapped the contours of contemporary video art. Documentary was not the central focus of this seminar. Instead, it was probed as a way to consider formal invention rather than simply humanist topics, with works such as Ilan Ziv's *Hundred Years War: Personal Notes Part II* (1983) and the poetic compilation film on the 1939 World Fair, *World of Tomorrow* (1984) by Tom Johnson and Lance Bird.[37]

The 1986 seminar at Wells College represented a significant turn for the Flaherty: it was the first full-length, annual seminar programmed by a person of color, Tony Gittens. Gittens invited Linda Blackaby to collaborate, with the goal of creating "an inclusive and diverse seminar experience, one that was overly representative in terms of ethnicity, race, genre, class, and sexual orientation in terms of filmmakers, films, and participants." According to Blackaby and Gittens, they intended to push the seminar to "be more open to the world and media arts field around us."[38] Their seminar programming linked discussions of identity politics to independent film and was the first to "embrace video as an equal format to film, and thus we presented works on video in the theater space."[39]

Their wide-ranging program presented important films and video that shifted documentary discourse and practice during the era. Henry Hampton showed his monumental epic public television series on the civil rights movement, *Eyes on the Prize* (1987). Indian-born director Mira Nair shared her film probing female strippers in Bombay, *India Cabaret* (1985). Brazilian Eduardo Coutinho screened his documentary film about the invasion of northeast Brazil and the murder of a political leader, *Twenty Years Later* (1984). Carma Hinton and Richard Gordon's *To Taste a Hundred Herbs* (1986) was a portrait film about an herbal doctor in rural China, where Hinton had grown up. Continuing the seminar's long-standing interest in direct cinema, Ross McElwee's exploration of his own quest for a wife in the southern United States, *Sherman's March* (1985), unspooled for two and one-half hours. Hopi Victor Masayesva mounted one of the most interventionist gestures at the 1986 seminar. He insisted that his poetic video rumination on Hopi mythology and philosophies, *Itam Hakim Hopiit* (1984), be screened "without subtitles to assert the dominance of indigenous language."[40]

One of the landmark seminars of this period was the 1987 seminar, held at Wells College, a small women's college on the shore of Lake Cayuga in upstate New York. Richard Herskowitz's[41] 1987 seminar emulated and expanded the idea of an overall seminar architecture with arcs, a mix of genres and formats, and resonances inaugurated by Jenkins and Ward in 1983.

Herskowitz intensified the strategy of challenging audiences, contradictions, dissonances, and juxtapositions even further than Jenkins and Ward. He produced what was for some participants an upsetting, yet exhilarating, explosive heterogeneity. He reflected attending his first Flaherty was a "life-changing experience," propelled by two factors: conversations with filmmakers and video artists and the Jenkins and Ward programming strategies. "Jenkins and Ward fashioned a coherent program out of a diversity of styles and backgrounds. . . . [T]hey connected a variety and range of material," Herskowitz explained.[42] Attending the seminars throughout the mid-1980s, he observed a "desire by the audience to make connections."[43] As an undergraduate at the State University of New York at Binghamton in the 1970s, Herskowitz had studied with experimental filmmaker Ken Jacobs whose classes explored the whole "range of moving image available for analysis, with no taboos."[44]

Herskowitz was an ardent partisan of the avant-garde. Amos Vogel's democratic and eclectic programming strategies at Cinema 16 deeply influenced him. As a teaching assistant when enrolled in the graduate program at the Annenberg School at the University of Pennsylvania, he had run discussion sections for Vogel's film history class.[45] Researching Vogel's programs, Herskowitz discerned an expansive programming strategy that juxtaposed art films with science films. Under Vogel's supervision, he had edited a volume of Cinema 16 program notes.

As the 1980s advanced, identity politics became a prominent practice and trope in independent media. "Larger cultural pressures [in the 1980s] atomized audiences into experimental, gay, feminist," recalled Herskowitz. "Going to the movies operated as a refuge and an affirmation, going to a protected zone."[46] In the context of these battles to build space for identities to be explored and expressed in independent cinema, Herskowitz saw great untapped potential in the Flaherty Seminar and in the Jenkins/Ward arc and structure model: an opportunity to instigate a political intervention into the separation between identities and subcultures. "Flaherty was more about mixing it up in surprising ways and asking audiences to find connections," he argued. As a professional programmer with graduate education from the University of Pennsylvania and the University of Wisconsin, Herskowitz also operated in the larger independent film world. He discerned the differences between more publicly accessible festivals and the retreat-like Flaherty. As a contained event, the Flaherty Seminar offered closer contact with an audience over time. While audiences at larger festivals could navigate and self-curate their path through screenings, "the Flaherty compels people to go to things they might not—at Flaherty, it forces people to see what they would not choose and then surprises them."[47] Herskowitz noted the Flaherty asked audiences to make connections across discussions and films. He also theorized the political urgency to mix up the programming by intermingling identities and creating surprises. If Jenkins and Ward pushed the seminar into arcs and conceptual structures, and Grieco contributed a mosaic format, Herskowitz conjured elaborate juxtapositions to incite aesthetic, intellectual, and political combustions. Of all the programmers during the 1980s, Herskowitz was the most focused on reception and spectatorship, dedicated to figuring out how to open up and provoke audience dialogue through dazzling provocations and startling surprises.

The 1987 seminar embodied and exemplified these principles of heterogeneity, juxtaposition, and mixing identities for combustion. Herskowitz's strategy—new for the seminar—combined Cinema 16 principles of juxtaposition of forms and genres, evoking a classical avant-garde tactic of shock and surprise, and a daring experiment in political diversity to put separated identities into conversation. Most significantly, as a professional programmer mounting screenings throughout the year at Cornell Cinema, Herskowitz understood reception issues in a deep, on-the ground experiential way. He brought a new innovation to the seminar: a concept of producing a heterogeneous range of screening and emotional registers for an audience— debate, discomfort, fun, pleasure, and rage. The 1987 seminar mixed together black (Darcus Howe and Philip Mallory Jones), experimental (Peer Bode), feminist (Su Friedrich), and queer (John Greyson) makers. It combined activist and advocacy documentary (Pamela Yates and Tami Gold), emerging makers (John Akomfrah and Deanna Kamiel), established directors (Johan van der Keuken and Angela Ricci Lucchi), ethnographic observational films (Alfred Guzzetti's *Beginning Pieces*, 1986), and television producers (Charles Hobson with *The Africans*, 1986). The programming explored a range of animation styles: in film, Emily Breer's *Spiral* (1987) and the Quay Brother's *Street of Crocodiles* (1986); and in video, Robert Ascher's *Festival* (1986), Peer Bode's *Animal Migrations* (1985), and David Daniels's *Buzz Box* (1985). The programming mined a range of documentary styles: activist projects of Pamela Yates (*Who Are the Contras?* 1987) and Tami Gold (*Looking for Love*, 1982, and *Prescription for Change*, 1986); the compilation works of Pennee Bender and DeeDee Halleck (*De Peliculas*, later renamed *The Gringo in Mananaland*); the experimental, feminist, and personal documentaries of Su Friedrich (*The Ties That Bind*, 1984, and *Damned If You Don't*, 1987); ethnographic film; the hybrid styles of John Akomfrah (*Handsworth Songs*, 1987); and video by Stevenson Palfi (*Don't Start Me to Talking*, 1985) from New Orleans. Dutch documentarian Johan van der Keuken occupied the role of éminence grise, with a rare retrospective of his work, for the most part not screened in the United States, which few had ever seen stateside. With their evocative, painterly compositions, his films challenged traditional definitions of documentary and experimental film in works such as *Hermann Slobbe* (1966), *Reading Lesson* (1973), *The White Castle* (1973), and *The Way South* (1981).

Herskowitz's conceptual model of arcs, combustion, daring programming choices, heterogeneity, identities, and an overall program structure galvanized intense debates at the 1987 seminar. These confrontations underscored artistic and intellectual frissons between form, politics, and spectatorship, importing key debates circulating in academic film studies during the 1980s. The first debate centered on the works of queer Toronto-based video activist and artist John Greyson. His humorous works embraced open gay male sexuality. They disturbed some older Flaherty attendees. A decade later,

Greyson wrote a poem about his experience of this debate, parodying "La Habanera" from Bizet's *Carmen*:

> They huffed their way out to the lawn
> Only Pam Yates would walk with me
> Richard rushed over, nervous and drawn
> He'd just had a fight with George Stoney
>
> "George won't chair your Q and A
> He feels the work is problematic."
> I said: "Puh-leeeze! What's he scared of?"
> Richard amended to "pornographic."
>
> The crowd was riled, my back was tense
> The questions were hostile in the extreme
> "exploitation?" and "degradation?"
> Objectivation?" and "Obscene!"[48]

Greyson's videos brought gay film practice to the Flaherty and precipitated pointed debates about identities, politics, and sexualities. The work of British filmmaker Peter Watkins spurred a different kind of debate, unsettling audience expectations about documentary exhibition and temporality. Watkins had produced a demanding fourteen-hour work on the antinuclear movement called *The Journey, Parts 1–19* (1987).[49] As Jared Rapfogel has noted, Watkins advanced a hybrid political cinema combining documentary and fictional strategies. Watkins had produced landmark films challenging documentary veracity which simultaneously pirated its realism: *Culloden* (1964), *The War Game* (1965), and *Punishment Park* (1971). Rapfogel argued, "*The Journey* unveils its multitude of settings and topics relatively quickly, letting each strand develop in tandem with every other. . . . It is a monumental film, yet a carefully constructed and tightly woven one." Produced by the Swedish Peace and Arbitration Society, *The Journey* was epic in length, locations, and topics. The film was shot with local support teams in Australia, Canada, Denmark, France, Japan, Mexico, Mozambique, New Zealand, Norway, Polynesia, Scotland, Soviet Union, Sweden, United States, Norway, and West Germany.[50] The film investigated a wide range of political themes such as class divisions between the rich and the poor, media representations, nuclear proliferation, and peace.[51]

Herskowitz's decision to program *The Journey* was bold and daring. It displaced the idea of screening discrete works that formed the seminar's three-decade legacy. In the history of the seminar, no programmer had ever screened a work of this length over so many days. At the insistence of Watkins, who was a featured guest at the seminar, the film was programmed in its entirety, with all nineteen sections shown. Some sections screened during regular sessions, others in optional late-night sessions. The film demanded the audience's patience as it unwound its issues and locations at a slower pace than public television documentaries with their characters and narrative arcs. Whether stretched beyond their exhibition comfort zones or angered by the increasingly salient durational issues, the Flaherty audience turned on the film. Herskowitz had suggested to Watkins that the film be shown in parts, with careful selection of sections, in order to facilitate a more accessible viewing framework for the Flaherty audience. Herskowitz analyzed the debate on audience expectations and duration that engulfed the film during postscreening discussions. These debates underlined how the Flaherty Seminar's structuring of reception was as important as the films themselves: "I kick myself for not being more insistent on my sense of a programming, as I know more about reception of films with audiences than filmmakers," Herskowitz argued.[52]

Two years later in 1989, Pearl Bowser and Grant Munro mounted a seminar that pulled together these seminar programming strategies of arcs, disrupting audience expectations, heterogeneous films and videos, structures, and themes exemplified in the 1983, 1984, and 1987 seminars. Bowser selected works that exemplified what Teshome Gabriel, a scholar based at UCLA who had been invited to lead seminar discussions, called "Third Cinema" or "nomadic cinema." The seminar featured a tribute to the NFB programmed by Grant Munro, screening works by himself, Donald Brittain, and Caroline Leaf. Several works from the emerging Glasnost documentary movement in the Soviet Union from Ivars Seleckis, Valery Solomin, and Mark Soosaar were also screened, facilitating the seminar's connection with this emerging documentary movement that eventually led to the 1990 Russo-American seminar in Riga, Latvia.

Without the breakthrough seminars of 1983, 1984, 1986, and 1987 that reconfigured programming as a metastrategy to assemble connections, conversations, and ideas, Bowser and Munro's seminar might not have happened. Without the pressures from outside funders insisting the Flaherty move beyond its own historical legacy as a club for East Coast media insiders, the seminar's focus on African, African diaspora, and Russian film might have been more difficult. Significant funding for the seminar came from a generous grant from the Rockefeller Foundation, which supported the attendance of filmmakers from Brazil, England, Ghana, Mali, and Zimbabwe.[53] Films from three continents were screened, with a record numbers of countries represented: Burkina Faso, Brazil, Canada, England, France, Ghana, Guinea, Haiti, Jamaica, Mexico, Mali, Martinique, South Africa, Trinidad, the United States, and Zimbabwe.

With its explicit focus on Third Cinema (African, African American, African diaspora, Asian American, and Latin American work), this seminar signaled an important intervention into the mostly white, male, and East Coast North American Flaherty seminars of decades past. As Bowser explained, "The seminar's theme of third world cultures and histories attracted African and African diaspora filmmakers, programmers, and educators in record numbers (perhaps the largest gathering at a Flaherty Seminar any of us could remember)."[54] This seminar was exceptional and significant in the history of the seminar. Its programming created a platform for producers of color and for discussions about racial identities and politics across Africa, the Caribbean, England, France, Latin America, and the United States. In 1989, it was difficult to see works from Africa, with New Yorker Films one of the few distributors of films from that continent, mostly highlighting the work of Ousmane Sembène from Senegal. Although the Pan African Film Festival in Burkina Faso, which started in 1969, functioned as an important node for the exhibition of films from across the continent, few of these films were ever screened in the United States.[55]

By 1989, only a few books analyzing African cinemas by film studies scholars had been published, including Teshome Gabriel's landmark book, *Third Cinema in the Third*

World: The Aesthetics of Liberation (1982) and Françoise Pfaff's *The Cinema of Ousmane Sembène* (1984). Manthia Diawara, who later emerged as a leading theorist of African cinema with several field-defining books published in the 1990s and 2000s, had written an important essay in the 1988 *Film Quarterly* entitled "Popular Culture and Oral Traditions in African Film."[56] Bowser reinvigorated a Flaherty programming strategy from the 1950s: she brought in scholars to lead the discussions. Over the course of the seminar's history, many scholars had been drafted to moderate discussions, but their role was to facilitate dialogue rather than to present lectures on their research. Bowser invited four notable scholars of African cinema—Dr. Toni Cade Bambara (independent scholar), Manthia Diawara (University of California, Santa Barbara), Abiyi Ford (Howard University), and Teshome Gabriel (UCLA), to serve as "interpreters, translators, and moderators."[57] Bowser's 1989 seminar was seminal as an early and significant contribution to expanding independent film culture to include African and third world works. In Bowser's conceptualization, these scholars provided "theoretical maps," with Gabriel presenting his ideas about "nomadic cinema."[58]

The 1989 seminar was organized around a theme of works from marginalized minority communities, the first seminar of its kind to deliberately insist on the primacy of works from producers of color. Within the larger context of identity politics emerging in film studies, media work, and the larger political field, programmers throughout the 1980s had slowly displaced the maleness and whiteness of the seminar. With pressures from NYSCA to address new media constituencies, the days of the all-white, all-male, and mostly East Coast Flaherty were over.[59] This seminar featured the works of American filmmakers of color who were to become important figures in independent film history: Ayoka Chenzira (*Zajota and the Boogie Spirit*, 1989); Julie Dash (*Hi Life*); Henry Hampton, Louis Massiah, Jacqueline Shearer, and Orlando Bagwell (with episodes of the monumental PBS multipart series on the civil rights movement, *Eyes on the Prize*); Philip Mallory Jones (*Dreamkeeper*, a three-channel installation chronicling his trip to Burkina Faso); and Trinh T. Minh-ha (*Surname Viet Given Name Nam*, 1989). Lynne Sachs, a white feminist filmmaker, showed *Sermons and Sacred Pictures* (1989), a compilation work using the Reverend Taylor collection from Mississippi. For the first time in the seminar's history, the programming featured many works from Africa and Latin America. From Africa, Olley Maruma (Zimbabwe) screened *After the Hunger and the Drought* (1987). Cheick Oumar Sissoko (Mali) showed *Finzan* (1989). Gaston Kaboré (Burkina Faso) showed *Zan Boko* (1988) and Oliver Schmitz (South Africa) screened the narrative *Mapantsula* (1989). British video gay activist and video maker Pratibha Parmar screened two works: *Emergence* (1986) and *Sari Red* (1986).

A bold and necessary intervention into Flaherty Seminar programming history and scope, the 1989 seminar also precipitated two intense debates: one regarding a Flaherty film and the other about a contemporary documentary. Rather than screening one of the Flaherty documentaries such as *Nanook of the North*, Bowser opted for an unusual choice—she selected *Elephant Boy* (1937), a narrative film shot in India by Robert Flaherty and Alexander Korda. The film's star was Sabu, a young Indian boy. The post-screening discussion exploded into an extended, vociferous debate about orientalism, race, and representation of people of color by white filmmakers.

Another debate ensued after the screening of *Omega Rising: Women of the Rastafari* (1988) by West Indian–born member of the British independent film movement, D. Elmina Davis. The documentary followed women devotees of Rastafarianism. It was the first film on the Rastafari done by a member of the movement. Jake Homiak, an anthropologist who had spent years studying the Rastafari and who was affiliated with the Human Studies Film Archive at the Smithsonian Institution, made an intervention. In the postscreening discussion, he charged the film "omitted the frequent association which Rastafari make between women and original sin as well as the fact that women are prohibited from participating in the central rituals of the culture."[60]

Throughout the seminar, Homiak observed polarized discussions between "black and white participants" over political struggles, race, and representation. He also perceived a racial "essentialism," where black and white participants failed to speak across racial lines: "the cine-babel which served to essentialize and partition 'black' from 'white' experience."[61] According to Homiak's account, throughout the seminar, various participants expressed hostility to anthropologists for their colonialist views.[62]

Reading these two debates from the 1989 seminar as examples of the legendary and overblown reputation of the Flaherty as a filmmaker-bashing enterprise is far too reductive and simple. These two debates actually evidenced a more complex historical moment in independent media, where questions of race, which the seminar had somewhat marginalized, burst out into the open. The Bowser/Munro seminar rendered the conflicts and debates about racialization and representation visible.

Louis Massiah worked on *Eyes on the Prize* and founded the Scribe Video Center in Philadelphia. For him, this seminar ushered in a necessary change to the Flaherty. The questions of race had been simmering at the Flaherty Seminar for over a decade. Massiah contended that the two "most positive transformative agents in the recent history of Flaherty have been Pearl Bowser and B. Ruby Rich."[63] He argued that Pearl Bowser organized filmmakers of color to "share in the seminar's critique and expand the discourse" in order to work for diversity in discussions, governance, and programming that would add "creative synergy" to IFS as a media arts organization and the Flaherty as a retreat to refuel those in the independent media sectors. He pointed out that B. Ruby Rich, in her NYSCA leadership role, had advanced that as a publicly funded project, the seminar "had a responsibility to the diversity of the field in regards to genre, ethnicity, class, gender, and sexual orientation." Massiah asserted that Rich gave IFS "the confidence that openness might actually lead to greater excellence."[64] By the end of the 1980s, the Flaherty Seminar had transformed from its auteurist origins in the 1950s and entered debates coursing through international independent media.

1981 ED PINCUS—ON *DIARIES (1971–1976)* (C. 1980)

Flaherty seminarian (F): We're going to go right into the discussion. Ed wants it to be known that the cameras and recording equipment in the room have nothing to do with his autobiographical work. [laughter]

So we're ready for the first question.

F: Richard Peña mentioned to me that your first edit was entirely different from the film we just saw. Could you talk about how *Diaries* has evolved and changed?

Pincus: Well, when I started the film, I had no idea what the format would be. Within the first two months after I started filming, I stopped looking at the rushes and had other people sync them up. One idea I had was that it would be a series of loosely connected portraits of people over a five-year period; you could show one or many in whatever order you wanted.

In 1973, I had a retrospective at the Walker Art Center in Minneapolis, and they wanted me to show some of the diary stuff. I had made a commitment to myself that I wasn't going to edit anything until 1976, until the shooting was over, but I knew if the heat was on and I had to edit something, I'd edit the section called "South by Southwest." It was the least threatening section to work with, and I figured it would make a nice ten-twelve-minute film. Anyway, I edited that section, and it turned out to be an hour-long film that I liked a whole lot (it was very different from the version you see in *Diaries* now). It had a lot of David Neuman's energy in the editing.

The current version of "South by Southwest" in *Diaries* is one of the controversial sections of the film: a lot of people think it's irrelevant. When I came back to edit that section for *Diaries* some seven years later, I was a little more mature and saw it as a film about renewed adolescence or whatever you want to call it. I wasn't capable of editing it with that same energy that the original version had, and also, it had to serve a function in *Diaries*, where it's a twenty-some-odd-minute piece.

What's Richard Peña doing now?

F: He's head of the Film Center at the Art Institute of Chicago. [Peña, who was Pincus's student at MIT, became program director of the New York Film Festival in 1988 and retired in 2012. He teaches at Columbia and Harvard.]

Pincus: He had been a graduate student of mine and came up to Vermont in the early stages of the editing. By that time, I had given up the biography/portraiture idea and was more interested in a chronology of events. I was planning to do a series of films of various lengths: some would be an hour; some would be five minutes. I'd decide where each film began and ended, but you could show them in any order you liked.

It took me better than a year to get what was going to be ten total hours of film together, and then the woman I was editing with at that time and I went down to Cambridge to do an interlock. We started at nine in the morning and got out at midnight. It was clear to us that what was most interesting and unique in the film had to do with time as a formal and causal element and the changes in consciousness. It was not merely that you saw people change over time but that the *camera* as a way of seeing the world changed over time. At the beginning, the camera kind of searches out antagonism or tension or whatever; later, things aren't filmed by virtue of being tense, but by virtue of being what they are.

And it seemed clear that this aspect of the film could be available to people only if they saw it in one sitting. So I said, "What's the longest people could sit down for a screening and see a film without hating me?"—not from a personality point of view but from the point of view of a filmmaker subjecting people to an experience. I decided it had to be well under four hours. It took me basically a year to get it from the series of films to what you saw this morning [the current version is 200 minutes].

By 1979, I had also realized that I didn't have anything near the money I would have needed to finish ten hours of film!

Mitchell Block: Could you talk more about how you were able to accomplish such an ambitious, expensive, long-term, time-consuming project?

Pincus: It wasn't so expensive. *Diaries* was shot by one person. Almost everybody I knew was a filmmaker or at least had a familiarity with film; they were free to pick up the camera when they wanted. The final budget was actually very low: for five years of shooting and two years of editing, fifty thousand dollars. Eighty percent of that came from foundations. An NEA grant made it possible to make the interneg.

There are a lot of personal, political, and aesthetic reasons why this film came together. In the sixties, I had done a series of films that you could call social documentaries—films about other people. Some of the films were about blacks, and a black friend asked why I didn't do films about people from my own social class. In the sixties, the answer seemed obvious: people like me didn't seem worth talking about. By the seventies, the women's movement was under way and occupied a lot of my thought and personal relationships; there was the notion that the personal was political, that in the microcosm you could see lots of big issues. So that was important.

I was also realizing that the vision of people that came out in my earlier films wasn't at all the way I now felt about people. If you look at the period from 1965 to 1970, you can see that at the end of that five-year period, people were *really* in different places. Typically, early cinéma vérité films, partially because of the economic constraints, were shot over a relatively short period of time. The typical approach was to find a crisis situation and film people in relation to that crisis in a way that would reveal who they were. Cinéma vérité filmmakers used to think that people revealed themselves by a particular line or gesture. Basically, that's the format of the Robert Drew films (which Mitch is distributing, and I think that's terrific). In other words, because of the time constraints, that approach didn't deal with people as complicated and changeable.

I had done a film about a bombing in a black community in the South and the struggle between the young Turks and the black bourgeoisie about how to deal with that bombing [*Black Natchez*, 1967, co-made with David Neuman]. And I had done a film about a Northern California hippie commune in the same style of filming, though the editing was more up-front: for example, the film was sequenced anecdotally [*One Step Away*, 1968, co-made with David Neuman]. With these and various other films, I thought I had come to the end of what was possible in cinéma vérité, at least for me. I wasn't sure what to do next.

Then in 1968, I was shooting two films at the same time: one in the afternoon and one at night. For the afternoon film, I was holding my camera in an unusual way and I ended up with bursitis and tendonitis, and I couldn't film anymore for a while. For me, not filming is like a painter not painting. Anyway, just about the time my arm started getting better, a new generation of lightweight cameras came out, and that was the cure to my illness. Then Kudelski—Kudelski makes Nagra tape recorders, standard tape recorders—came out with this tiny little Nagra called an SN that you could slip into your pocket, and I thought, "That's it! That's the answer to all these problems. What I need to do is get somebody to design a radio start/stop for it!"

The guy who tells the denim lady story was the engineer who designed the radio start/stop device (it almost bankrupted him): the idea was that essentially you slip the SN into somebody's pocket; you have a radio connection from the camera and your subject becomes the mic boom. All of a sudden, you have a new kind of filming where you don't need a crew. If your breadwinning was taken care of—and mine *was*, by teaching—you could be free as a filmmaker, just like a writer is. And now it was possible for a film to deal with consciousness, with consciousness over time.

I didn't think I would be *in Diaries*. Part of my training in the sixties was that the filmmaker had no reason to be in the film; who's interested in filmmakers anyway? But I could now make a film about the people I cared about, and my caring about them would be a kind of guarantee that I would be true *to them*, rather than true to the other kinds of concerns, economic or whatever, that filmmakers had had to deal with.

Another thing: I had also done a film called *Panola* [1970]; I don't know if any of you have seen it. It's about a black wino in Mississippi. There's a difficult scene at the end, which is meant to shake the audience in relation to their feelings of sympathy toward Panola. I felt that this shaking-up would be the cost of moral arrogance on the part of film audiences. Rousseau criticized theater on the grounds that bad people would go to the theater, have all these correct moral feelings at the theater, then walk out, and be just as bad as they always were. When I would show *Panola*, which was supposed to upset people, it would just upset them in white liberal guilt ways, which meant nothing to me. I knew that the people in the audience couldn't have stood to be with Panola for more than two minutes, but *in the film*, they feel all the proper feelings of sympathy. I felt that part of that had to do with the fact that in a sense, the audience was hidden behind the camera; essentially, the crew's safety behind the camera was a metaphor for the audience. I saw *Diaries* as a way of undercutting that safety, that distance; and in fact, I think that's what gives audiences of *Diaries* a lot of trouble.

F: I was intrigued, Ed, by the difference between the angle at which subjects talked to you and the angle of the camera. Normally, in a subjective filmmaker's film, the subjects look into the lens.

Pincus: Well, I don't know who you mean by subjective filmmakers, but if you mean something like *The Lady in the Lake* [1947, Robert Montgomery], which was shot from the point of view of the main character, in fact that's a comedy, because when somebody socks or kisses Robert Montgomery, they're doing it to a camera! In *Diaries*, the conditions of filming are part of the film; people might be annoyed by camera references, but that was part of the reality I was trying to deal with.

F: Frequently, when you're talking to your son or to your wife, there seems to be more than just a body-length distance between where they're looking and where the camera is.

Pincus: The wide-angle lens sometimes exaggerates the space.

F: I guess you've seen *An American Family*. During that picture, I was empathetic with the filmmaker, but in *Diaries*, as you were working out your relationships with your wife and the other people, I didn't feel empathy. Didn't you find that by filming the process of trying to find a solution to your problems, you were interfering with that process or creating a different set of problems?

Pincus: Are you asking if the presence of the camera made it more difficult to work out relationships?

F: Yes. In *An American Family*, when the kid is saying he's homosexual, or the parents are deciding to get a divorce, the filmmaker is outside of what's happening. There is a certain amount of questioning, but nonetheless, he's not part of the problem being dealt with.

Pincus: But in *An American Family*, that's a lie. If you talk to members of the crew, you find out that Pat Loud fell in love with the producer and the producer had to leave the shoot. You don't see that in the film. Also, the house is *lit*. And what does it mean to have a crew present? None of this is dealt with in the film.

F: Answer his question about *your* film.

Pincus: In essence, *Diaries* tries to answer that question in a complicated way; I'm not sure I can say anything more. The problem Jane was having with the camera early in the film, which may have led to the question, was just a metaphor for our personal problems...

F: But I don't see what choice Jane has.

Pincus: You mean, to be in the film? That's a really tough question to answer...

F: It's a crucial question.

Pincus: At the beginning, Jane said it was fine; then later, she said it wasn't OK; and still later, it was. At a certain point *in* the film she says it's OK, but I think it still wasn't in some ways. See, that's exactly the point: it's not like you can give simple answers to these questions. By the end, it wasn't any problem; in fact, by the end, she was wondering why I wasn't filming her more.

F: But at the beginning, before you started filming, was there any discussion with Jane?

Pincus: Jane and I have different versions of that. I said I told her about it, and she said, "No, you didn't!" and later she said she hadn't really understood what it meant to be in a film. I discovered that when our other problems disappeared, there wasn't problem about filming. Jane and I were interviewed for an article, and this very question was asked: we took opposite positions. Then after the interview, Jane told me, "You know, you're right; it really wasn't an issue." It's not that she's fickle; it's just that a lot of different things are relevant, and the film tries to deal with that on a complicated level. It's the first film I ever did where I felt that I didn't have to simplify those issues and provide nice little explanations.

F: The most interesting line in the film is near the end, when your daughter is trying to convince your son that he should stop crying, and she says, "Turn the camera off; it makes him worse," or words to that effect. That's the thing that concerns me about this style of filmmaking, that things can be contrived, can be completely changed because of the presence of the camera. And I wonder what it was like for two little kids to grow up with all this going into the public record...

Pincus: That was another reason I wanted to make this film. I knew that Sami was going to grow up and that there would be no way to tell her what her growing up was like, and I thought that if I made a film, she could see it. When *Diaries* was finished, Sami was the person I was most afraid about seeing the film. Jane had seen it on an editing table and didn't want to see it projected with an audience, so I arranged a screening for Sami and Jane and a couple of friends; and when Sami came out, she said, "I thought it was great! I didn't know I had such interesting parents!" [laughter]

F: I have a follow-up question. Videotape is often used in psychotherapy now. When Ben would see himself on film going through some emotional trauma, did he learn from this? Would Ben or Sami change because they didn't like what they saw?

Pincus: No. Ben changed because he grew up. Actually, it's only as of this summer that I think he's ready to see the whole film.

F: How old is he now?

Pincus: He's twelve. When he was eleven, he was still threatened by being a baby; since he's still a baby in the film, I think this would have bothered him.

I didn't think of the film as psychotherapy. One thing I did realize about myself and about everybody I knew, from the process of getting stuff out of that subjective space and into the objective space of film during the editing of "South by Southwest," was that 90 percent of what people say is either self-deception, lies, or posturing.

F: One of the most interesting lines in the film for me was where someone asks you, "Have you changed?"—presumably as a result of your making the film. You said, "Yes, but I don't want to talk about it." Would you care to talk about it now?

Pincus: I'm talking to Christina, and I say something like, "Yeah, I've learned something about light," and she says, "That's bullshit; you give me a technical answer to a philosophical question," and I say, "Yeah, I've changed, but I don't want to talk about it." My first answer is true, as is Christina's response to it (I *am* being evasive), but in fact, light really had become something of incredible importance to me. It has something to do with making an aesthetic of life, which is what the film is about. The film is meant to be beautiful. I don't know if you liked it or didn't like it, but it's meant to be not only difficult or revealing but beautiful as an object.

F: That's not quite what I mean. It is beautiful, and it is about light, but it's also about *you*, and it almost certainly has to be. How did you change?

Pincus: Well, some of this is implicit in the film. One thing is that at the beginning of the film, I have lots of love, but I can't express it. Later that became possible to express.

F: Maybe you just grew up, like your son.

Pincus: Right. I think growing up is what a lot of the film is about. Ben just did it at an earlier age than I did. [laughter]

F: Judging from your responses in the dialogues between you and Jane, it seems like your receptivity was somewhat impaired.

Pincus: That was more true at the beginning than later on.

Cinematographers are like musicians, but musicians who can't practice every day. All of a sudden they're called upon to do a big shoot, and it's very difficult to shoot for three months and then not shoot for a year. When I started *Diaries*, I hadn't shot in almost three years. Not only that, in order to shoot in this new way, I had to relearn to be a person while I was shooting. I'd been making films for five years or so, and I'd never said a word when I was behind the camera, except "Give me a slate."

I also had to relearn what it is to be a *man* with a movie camera. The seventies were a very difficult time to be a male. Women were trying give payback for years of repression. I was being confronted a lot and didn't really know how to deal with that.

Alan Rosenthal: An earlier question was did Jane give you permission to film her. I find that the question is always only half-asked. It may also be important to ask if, after the film is finished, does this same person see the film with an audience and respond to the film, and do you take that response into consideration before you release the film? I'm thinking of Pat Loud, who gave permission to be filmed and then after seeing the reaction of her friends, was totally distraught, because she had had no awareness of how other people would see her. When you finished *Diaries*, did you show it to any of the people in the film; did they make any comments; did you make any alterations because of their comments?

Pincus: I didn't. When I showed *Diaries* to early audiences, Ann Popkin came out very dislikable, and I thought that was incredibly unfair to her. She's a wonderful, complicated woman, and I wanted that to be clear in the film. I think there's a tradition of audiences responding positively to female masochism in film. Jane is more masochistic than Ann, so she came out better for audiences. Ann wants to seize the camera and control it, and I think audiences had a problem with that. I wanted to create a character that was honest and true; I felt *that* was my responsibility, not to satisfy the whims of the moment. Indeed, if there had been surprising revelations, I would have felt a moral responsibility.

Other than as artists or filmmakers, the producers of *An American Family* in no sense put themselves on the line in the way that Pat Loud did. But in *Diaries*, every main character is more sympathetic than me. The only person I feel I was unfair to was the marriage counselor. I did represent him the way I saw him, and I thought there was enough information in the film for people to see that he is helpful, but the comedy seems a little overwhelming there, and I'm not happy about that.

F: I want to know what affairs had been going on! [laughter] The film makes you ask not only about its technique but about *your* technique!

Pincus: Austin wanted to start the discussion off by saying that Jane and I are still together, but I asked him not to because I thought that would be a form of special pleading, something like "Don't get angry folks, it's all OK." I'd rather pass on talking about the rest.

F: But you and Jane *are* still together?

Pincus: Yes.

F: I think Alan's point is one that's critical to today's documentary film. Is the filmmaker responsible and the author of the film or are the subjects responsible for having a say in how they participate? This is a fundamental issue between anthropologists and filmmakers. The anthropology people now feel there is an obligation not only to reveal themselves in the process of the film's creation but to give a say in creating representations of people to the people being represented.

Pincus: I think of my relationship to the people I film as similar to the relationship between a painter and the person whose portrait he paints.

F: I feel very strongly that film, as Flaherty used it, and as it has been developed in contemporary society, is a personally expressive medium. The film is *your* message, not a piece of objective research material to be analyzed and interpreted, the way films are used in ethnography.

Pincus: In fact, I'd say *Diaries is* a form of anthropology, but in no way is it academic anthropology. I don't think academic anthropology tells us about other people in the way that art can.

F: I have some real problems believing that this was actually all there was to your relationship with your wife and the other women. Also, to me it was people *talking* about emotions very statically, but there was no real emotion. Didn't you guys ever fight with each other, scream at each other; don't you ever yell at your children?

Another problem that I'm having is that the only character in the film that came alive was David in the Las Vegas sequences: he joked around; he got angry; he had life to him, whereas all these women just sat around talking but without really saying anything. I'm wondering whether this is just a result of the way that you relate to your women; when they're running around doing all the fun, exciting, lively things, weren't you there? [laughter]

During those five years I didn't see characters changing or growing—just people *talking* about their emotions without really *being* emotional.

Pincus: That's not my perception. I think the people undergo a lot of change in this film, but I think it has to do with how you measure change in people. There are real changes in camera style, for example, which I think are expressions of my changing. And I think the sequence with Ann after a year shows that she's quite different; she's much less involved with trying to control the camera. As she says, she's much more inward. And I think Jane undergoes real, complicated changes.

F: But in five years didn't you and your wife ever have a knock-down-drag-out fight? You never told Ben to stop whining? It's hard for me to believe that.

Pincus: Some of that gets expressed in other ways, generally in ironic comments. I'm sorry if that's not clear for you.

F: It's very hard for me to tell exactly what it was that tied the two of you together in this long, ongoing relationship, other than obviously the children and a shared history, because I never saw anything of Jane's life, other than what you showed as you two struggled with the verbalization of how she felt about your affairs. She did batiks, for example, and there was one shot somewhere in there where she's working on them but pretty much in the abstract. In the background on the clothesline in the kitchen, we see these magnificent fabrics—the only inkling of something that was part of *her* life. So many dimensions of all of the people, germane to the quality of their lives, are missing.

Pincus: I in no way make claims about *Diaries* being an exhaustive portrait of all the people in it. It's part of the film that you never see things I'm not present at: for example, you never see the kids in school.

F: From your point of view, what is the film about, now that you have the perspective of ten years?

Pincus: I think the film is about time and love.

F: Could you elaborate?

Pincus: Well, I'm not sure what kind of answer one can give to the question of why someone loves someone. I do think that if there's any medium where that question is visually answered, it's film. If *Diaries* doesn't say why I loved the different women, then I failed on that level. I mean it to just be there, not in any kind of verbalized way, just *there*. I mean for you to see these women as likable and interesting, even though you only see them from my very skewed point of view. In fact, because both Ann and Jane were politically active feminists, they faced a lot of criticism from women in Boston for the way they appear in the film.

F: You use the people in your life as your subject material with your camera in front of you, but you're not revealing a great deal about yourself. What disturbs me is that without your presence and a discussion of the film, you remain hidden.

Pincus: I don't agree. I think my presence here is both irrelevant and, in fact, hurtful to the film. This was one reason I was happy that at least there was going to be lunch after the screening and before this discussion. I used to say there's something in the film to offend everybody. I think that it's important for people to cope with the difficulties of the film; it's a complicated work and the thing to do is to deal with the *work*, not with *me*.

F: You're exhibiting your whole life here, and we're all voyeurs of your very sophisticated home movie. If you weren't here, you would be an abstraction for the audience. But you are here: what is it like for you to deal with this film in front of real audiences?

Pincus: What's the name of the saint who has all the arrows in him? Saint Sebastian? Something like that.

F: How do you define the word *diary*? And why "Diaries" instead of "Diary"? I think of "diaries" as having multiple perspectives, as opposed to "diary."

Pincus: "Diaries" was a bailout title; I wasn't happy with it. Virtually every reviewer who liked the film made an excuse for the title. You know, "A three-hour-and-twenty-minute film named *Diaries*? Who'd want to see *that*? But in fact, it works." The long version definitely was "Diaries," and I would make no excuses about the title, but the five-and-a-half-hour version was kind of split between narrative line and diary. I've never felt that "Diaries" is the perfect title. I just thought "diaries" would be a little looser than "diary."

F: With the title, there's an assumption that you're going to reveal your life, and what I realized afterward, and it made me very angry, was that I knew a lot about the people in your life—you were exposing them—whereas you were never put in that position; you were safely behind the camera. There was an opportunity for you to reveal yourself in the voice-over, but the only time you narrated was to give a sense that you were here or there. You never exposed *yourself,* and I think that's what provokes a lot of the anger on the part of audiences, and particularly women.

Pincus: Not all women feel that way, though that is a comment that I mostly hear from women. . .

F: I'm not a woman, but I see this film as a massive ego trip. I'd like to hear from whoever chose this for the seminar because they obviously must have seen some worth in it.

F: I would like to go back to the notion of diary. It's very seductive to think we're seeing your life and that you're really exposing your feelings, but when I thought about it, I realized this really hadn't happened. Your whole feeling about multiple relationships is never dealt with; the most that you say is, "Well, I don't believe in monogamy."

Pincus: I don't think that "diary" is a defined term in filmmaking, though some filmmakers have been called "diary filmmakers." I think "diary" gets its primary meaning from the written word. By the way, I think that "diary" is a pretty open term. There are diaries that don't reveal much about the diarists. I used the term to represent my skewed point of view—maybe "skewed" is too strong: "personal"—and to reference the notion of chronology: diaries are presented chronologically, and in fact the film, except for two minor instances, is strictly chronological.

F: There are two kinds of diaries that get published. One is the diary of someone who has been through something exceptional. And you can have a diary of someone who also does something in the arts: a novelist might keep a diary that might become interesting if his work is of interest. Why the hell did *you* present us with *your* diaries? You didn't live anything extraordinary, and this is not the diary of artist who's known for other forms of art that would be of interest to us.

Pincus: There are lots of diaries of ordinary people.

F: That get published?

Pincus: Most diaries don't get published.

F: I like the film very much. I would like to thank you for it; I think it's lovely to see people like us, as the subjects of a film. I thought it was very rich, but I wind up feeling disappointed at your unwillingness to reveal your*self* in the film, and it's kind of paradoxical because sitting here now, you're very open and very revealing. Your willingness to make this film is very courageous, but I'm left with disappointment.

Trinh T. Minh-ha: Comments or questions?

F: I think the soundtrack was a disaster! Right from the beginning. And the visuals! At least half a dozen times, all we were greeted with was a blank wall! Nothing! Several times there were out-of-focus shots! Many times, repeated shots. Some of the camerawork is brilliant, but at other times, it's amateurish. How do you account for the inconsistency?

Trinh: Why do you think the soundtrack was a disaster?

F: The silences, the repetitions, the lack of communication; you say the same thing over and over. Or you say nothing. Or sentences are suddenly cut off in midsentence. . .

F: The soundtrack is beautiful! It's poetic! [applause] She can teach the American documentary movement something. The softness of that narrative voice—what a pleasure! And those silences give you time to think. Most of the cinéma vérité films are reel-to-reel, wall-to-wall verbal information.

F: I'd like to know why you chose women subjects only.

Trinh: For three reasons. First, usually in ethnodocumentary film, the focus is on men and on men's activities. You rarely see women and especially women's daily activities. The second reason is that I was traveling at the time of the year when most of the men go to the city to look for jobs and many of the villages are populated by women and children. Finally, I was dealing with women most of the time.

F: How long did you stay in that village?

Trinh: It's not one village. I traveled through the eastern part of Senegal, starting in the south and moving to the north. At the beginning, I'm in the jungle; near the end, I'm in the north, where the influence of Islam is very strong and all the women are very richly dressed.

F: I found it a little heavy on the dead carcasses. Was that done for some purpose, possibly to suggest the close connection of life and death?

Trinh: Everything in the film is intentional. All the repetitions are intentional, all the "out-of-focus," the "not-brilliant" shots are intentional. With this audience, one can talk about the dead animals as suggestive of the coexistence of life and death. But in Senegal, those dead animals are a result of the drought. I wouldn't want to show just the happy part of Africa. But read it as you like.

F: Can you talk about your decision to use sound, and silence, the way you did?

Trinh: Rhythm was one of the most important things to me when I was editing the film. The rhythm of the film is created by the images, by the music and the voices, and also by the repetitions of image, voice, and music. Sometimes you have an image—say, of the women pounding millet—without the sound, and at other times the sound without the image. The connection is still there; you don't always need to see image and sound in sync. Music that goes on all the time in a film tends to put people to sleep; by including music at some times but not at others, I hope to keep viewers alert.

Also, you hear the language of the people, but nothing is translated. My intent was to bring back the experience I had of these sounds when I first heard them. I was not interested in finding the meaning of the images or of the language. The whole film was shot without sync sound in order to emphasize the fact that conventional anthropological film blooms once sync sound is possible. This film was done with no sync at all, so the silence of the women, for example, is for me a way of *not* trying to "give voice." The idea of "giving voice" is an illusion that I disagree with in many anthropological films. Anthropologists tend to legitimize what they have to say by giving us a fleeting moment where you hear what the indigenous people say, and it's translated without the filmmaker's providing any knowledge of the translator.

Alan Rosenthal: I'm very uneasy with your relationship with the people you portray. You seem to put anthropological film down most of the time, but you're also saying, "Come with me and have a look at this society." Do people not get angry? Do they not teach their children? Are these things you didn't observe? Or are they things you didn't want to show us? Maybe you're right in not wanting to ask questions all the time, and yet at the end of the film, you put one very heavy question, about polygamy. Once you opened up that one question, why didn't you open up others? Or was that one question centrally important to you?

Trinh: It was a choice. The whole film is the choice of the filmmaker. I make no pretension of offering a totality, a so-called "complete" or "objective" look at Senegal. The question I raise at the end of the film concerns women a lot, and it kept coming up during my travels. But to me, your question is like saying, "Why did you film this and not other things?" It was a choice.

F: All through, the soundtrack is successful in invoking phenomenological doubt and doubt about ethnography. If we were to turn the soundtrack off, would we see visual correlatives? Do you break the rules in the visuals, too?

Trinh: The film has its own specific patterns. It's not just a reaction against the conventional rules. But yes, the jump cuts, the hesitation in my framing, and the moments where I tend to chase after the subject—those are visual correlatives to the soundtrack.

One of the things I object to in anthropological films is the orientation toward the object: the way filming always fixes an object and stays on the object. I wanted to alleviate the tyranny of the camera, and the abrupt cuts help me do that. I show my hesitation in framing because usually filmmakers offer you what they judge as the best framing, but "best" is relative. One can also show how one hesitates in trying to frame a person.

F: When the man is carving, you have the standard shots: the medium shot, the wider shot, the chips he makes. . . . But it has no flow to it. You don't let the audience experience what the man is doing.

Trinh: The film is a critical reflection on documentaries in general and especially on ethnodocumentary film. But I'm not situating myself outside of that type of filmmaking. So you still recognize many of the elements that are the norms of documentary film. . .

F: You show us the chips on the ground but never the carving itself.

Trinh: Yes. That's another question: what is important, the finished object or the chips produced during the making of it?

F: But where are *you* placing the value? You show us the chips, but that doesn't communicate to me. If this is a commentary on ethnographic film. . .

Trinh: There are other things in that shot: the dancing of the little boys in the background, for example, which goes with the larger rhythm of the film.

F: That was way in the background; you could barely see them!

Trinh: There are different layers of looking at things. For me, the movement of those boys was more important than a focused image.

F: So the background is as important as the foreground? Very confusing!

Trinh: The different aspects of the image are important in different ways. The activity of the carving is important, but that's the kind of activity anthropologists show all the time: A to Z of how a person would carve something. But you also have in the background the little boys dancing, and the rhythm of their dancing has the same importance in my film as the focused subject in the foreground.

F: For me, what's missing in the foreground *and* the background is a real attempt at communicating with an audience. Frankly, I would have thrown a lot of that footage out.

Trinh: Evidently, not everybody here would agree with you.

F: Well then, please, audience, explain it to me!

F: There's not just one audience here. There are many. One missing element in this discussion is the question of what audience is being addressed by the film? I see *Reassemblage* as a film that is mimetic of consciousness. It has to do with the texture of being in that culture, with the experiences of trying to look at a cultural group that's new to you. And it's very sensual.

Patricia Zimmermann: This film and a lot of the other films we've been seeing today raise the question of a theoretical practice articulating itself in filmmaking and are informed by theoretical thinking about the positioning of spectators in forms of film that are reactions against conventional Hollywood style. I do think it's important to make a distinction between ethnographic film and documentary. They are two very distinct traditions. Ethnographic film is based in a set of positivist, scientific rules for making films that ensure "value-free" filmmaking. Documentary is something different. The question is how do all these critiques of the conventional interface with accessibility? I'm not trying to postulate an answer; I think it's a problematic that all of the films today have raised in different ways. Maybe this film seems more polemical because it's clearly discounting the scientific tradition of making ethnographical films.

F: I want to go back to something raised earlier. Why did you end with the question of polygamy?

Trinh: That's one of the most complex issues in the film (along with the fire), and I left it open: the question is not answered; it is returned to me. The women said, "What about you? Do you have a husband all for yourself?" There are many ways to understand that question, which is why I wanted to end with it.

F: One problem with the history of ethnographic film is that very frequently, the subjects are only looked at by men. In this instance, one was very conscious of the fact that the cameraperson was a woman and the people who were interacting with you were aware of your being a woman. Their asking you about polygamy personalizes the entire film and its poetic structure. You're not objectifying the culture; you have a loving look that allows you to show the culture in a way that defies the very idea of primitivism. The audience doesn't have to have things spelled out letter by letter by letter, even if it is an ethnographic film. And I thank you for that.

F: A statement: You question ethnographic filmmaking and I think there are lots of reasons to question ethnographic filmmaking. But what I think you've done in your film is more dangerous than a lot of what ethnographic filmmaking does. Because while the soundtrack questions ethnographic filmmaking and your position as a filmmaker, the images are much stronger than your narration, and those images are like a series of *National Geographic* shots that objectify the women; you make them the Other, still more exotic creatures to be observed. I feel very angry about looking at these images. And these women have no power, no voice. . .

Trinh: I don't think *National Geographic* would show the hesitation in framing or my chasing after the subject. As I've said, I didn't "give voice" to these people intentionally. Anthropologists perpetuate the idea that by giving the camera to the indigenous people, they will capture the truth of what the people see, but this is just an attempt to legitimize what the anthropologists themselves are doing. . .

F: The question is, how do you legitimize what *you're* doing?

Trinh: There's nothing to legitimize. . .

F: Then we might as well turn the lights out and go home. . .

Trinh: What is your point?

F: My point is that there are good ways of doing films and not good ways. It's easier to criticize something for being bad than to try and do it well.

Trinh: How does that apply to *Reassemblage*? You mean my film doesn't succeed?

F: You don't want my comments about the film!

Trinh: I'm just asking about the answer you've just given me.

F: I feel the same as you—just to give the camera to indigenous people doesn't necessarily legitimize the films that get made. It has to be done *well*: to be true to that culture and communicate something of it to people who don't understand it is very difficult.

Trinh: I agree, but I would add that no matter how difficult what they do is, anthropologists do what they do to legitimize *their* position. The look that *they* offer of the Other is a crucial issue in anthropology, and it comes up in every aspect of the work they are doing, whether it be writing, filming, or recording.

F: I can't quite decide whether you're an objective filmmaker who is deliberately digressing, which I'm all in favor of, or someone reacting very personally. I enjoyed the images that you showed me, though I do think the film is a bit cold.

Trinh: I would not make a division between what is personal and what is objective or impersonal —since I think nothing is purely subjective or purely objective. The person holding the camera is choosing; any moment you are filming, you are choosing—though I am not interested in a purely subjective point of view: *Reassemblage* is not just a series of personal anecdotes, a travel diary.

F: It's an error to think there's only one model of ethnographic filmmaking, and we're making a mistake if we see *Reassemblage* as an ethnographic film. It may be a film about ethnography, but it's not about tribes in Senegal. It's about the ethnographic eye. These images *are* like *National Geographic* images, but I don't think they're offered in a way that's comparable to the way *National Geographic* offers them. The filmmaker is placing herself very squarely between you and the images, and that's absolutely intentional. I assume you're trying to get people to question how they see.

The film uses material that's traditionally the subject of ethnographic film, to get us to see that same material a different way. All these films today are trying to change the way we see. We see out of our own cultural conditioning, and when our expectations are not met, it's disturbing. I'm not complaining: we have to be able to shift, to move.

F: We've had a broad-ranging discussion of this film, but I still want to know what in your mind elevates this film above a piece of exotica. Can you just tell me in a few words the objective of the film, just the thrust of what you wanted to do?

Trinh: I don't want to control how you understand the film...

F: No, no, that won't work. A work stands as a work. And it must, in your eyes; otherwise you wouldn't have made it. So, what is it, exactly, for you?

1984 BRUCE CONNER—ON *TEN SECOND FILM* (1965), *PERMIAN STRATA* (1969), *MONGOLOID* (1978), AND *AMERICA IS WAITING* (1981)

D. Marie Grieco: Bruce, did you want to say something?

Conner: Yes, I wanted to tell you that the first three films that you saw were my first three films. *A Movie* made in 1958; *Cosmic Ray*, in 1961–62. *Looking for Mushrooms* was shot about the same time as *Cosmic Ray*, but the final edit was two years later. The last two films you saw today, *Mongoloid* [1978] and *America Is Waiting* [1981], are the last two I've made.

You may be wondering about the titles on a number of the movies. The first one you saw this evening was *Ten Second Film* from 1965; it was made up of ten strips of film, each of them twenty-four frames in length, that were collected onto one format that could be shown as a logo for the New York Film Festival in 1965. The film wasn't used; the committee rejected it because they felt it went too fast. I offered to let them measure the film so they could prove to themselves that it didn't go any faster than twenty-four frames a second, but they weren't interested. The strips were used on a poster for the film festival.

Grieco: I'm sure you know that Bloomingdales put the framed poster in some of their rooms. I bought the last one Lincoln Center had.

Conner: *Permian Strata* was made in 1969; "Permian strata" refers to the sedimentary rock that is found in Kansas, where I grew up.

Grieco: Do you want to say something about the music in *Mongoloid*? Those in my generation might not know Devo.

Conner: Toni Basel has worked with David Byrne and she's done choreography for Elvis Presley and Bette Midler, and all sorts of Hollywood people; she's had a couple of records out recently, and she's a marvelous video artist. I made a film with her, which you'll see later: *Breakaway* [1966]. Toni called me in San Francisco in 1977 and told me I should go see what she said was currently the greatest rock and roll band in the United States: Devo. I went to see them and loved the band; it seemed like a whole new style of rock and roll. Within two months, I had made a film of their song, "Mongoloid."

The main forces in the group are Jerry Casale and Mark Mothersbaugh (each has a brother named Bob, also in the group). Devo has a sort of industrial sound that reflected their growing up in Akron, Ohio; it was partly robotics and partly mechanics. They do songs about their own experiences, and in fact, the song "Mongoloid" is basically autobiographical. Mark Mothersbaugh, who wrote the song and sings it, was thought to be a mongoloid when he was a small child, so he's singing about himself.

So, is there a question?

F: Do you have to get music rights? Also, how do you get your stock footage?

Conner: Basically, I'm setting black-and-white period pieces to contemporary music.

The footage comes from the 16mm collection I've gathered over the years. People have given me films; I've bought educational films that were taken out of distribution by educational film distributors; in 1963 I pulled stuff out of the reject bin at the Boston University film school.

Initially, there was no arrangement between the musicians and me. The sound I wanted to use for *A Movie* is Respighi's *The Pines of Rome*, and since I didn't know how to get in touch with Respighi, I just went ahead and used the music and made the film.

I didn't have a movie camera, but I did have about four-hundred dollars, and discovered that I could make a movie by collecting Castle Film condensations of feature films and documentaries and working with those. This was much less expensive than going out and shooting my own film. Prior to making *A Movie*, I'd spent a lot of time looking at movies and imagining a collage film made up of the movies I'd seen. Of course, when I got around to actually making the movie, I discovered how difficult it was to get the rights to anything.

My usual process for dealing with sound has been to send a copy of each film to the musicians, asking them to look at the film and telling them that if they did not want me to use their music, I'd withdraw the film from distribution. It was fine with the Beatles [the Beatles song "Tomorrow Never Knows" was the original music in *Looking for Mushrooms* (1965); it was replaced by "Poppy Nogood and the Phantom Band" by Terry Riley]. I sent a copy of *Permian Strata* [1969] to Bob Dylan; I don't know if he received it. I made a contractual arrangement with Devo for "Mongoloid," at a very small fee.

Before I did *America Is Waiting*, David Byrne sent me tapes of some of the music he had done for what would be the album *My Life in the Bush of Ghosts*. He asked me if there was a song that I would like to work with, but it wasn't until David was working with Brian Eno on that album in San Francisco that "America Is Waiting" seemed appropriate, and we worked out an agreement for me to do that film. Then when *America Is Waiting* was completed, it was shown in Los Angeles to a representative with Warner Brothers, who said that they would *love* to use it as a promotional film for the album, but that the only way they could do that was if I signed a piece of paper assuming all legal liability for copyright infringement. They also said that they wouldn't pay me anything, and David was not in a position to pay me anything more. Within a month or so, they went further, saying that they wouldn't even use the film if I signed, because they didn't want to take the trouble of having the lawyers answer the letters and telephone calls that might be involved. However, I understand from some people who watch MTV that they've seen it on MTV.

But that's the way I dealt with the music. If I were to show these films outside of the context that we're in here, and if there were going to be any kind of economic return, I would probably run into problems. Basically, these are still poverty production movies, underground films; and anybody who wants to show them in that context is assuming the responsibility for the copyright issues. Later on, when I thought about trying to get the rights, I concluded that if anybody said no at any point to my using an image or a piece of music, that *no* would essentially destroy the movie. So there are very few films that I really own the rights to; mostly I think of myself as owning the splices.

F: Which comes first, the concept or the footage or the music, or does it vary?

Conner: It changes for every film. Sometimes it starts with the music and the images are put to the music; sometimes the images are assembled and are later put to music, or maybe *part* of the imagery is assembled before I find the music. *America Is Waiting* is full of footage that I edited twelve, fifteen years ago. Doing that film was a very intense and difficult process for me, but it was made easier by the fact that David and Brian's music was being developed as if it were going to be illustrated by film footage.

My films are all comedies but black comedies; they're funny *and* they're not funny. In a way, that was already clear in *A Movie*; there are comic relationships in the ways imagery relates to the soundtrack and in how the shots follow one another. But you also get an inkling that perhaps what you're seeing isn't quite as funny as it looks. The race cars turning over comes across as a comic event, but you know that somebody got badly hurt in those events, so at a certain point the tables are turned and those shots become more tragic than comic. I feel that the same is also true in *Permian Strata*, *Mongoloid*, and *American Is Waiting*.

F: Since you made *A Movie*, have you rethought any of the images of sexuality and violence in that film?

Conner: The original concept wasn't for a movie; until 1957, I had a concept for an environment and a film *loop*, without a soundtrack, though at random intervals you would hear sound from TV sets, radios, and such. Every time you'd see the footage, you'd have an entirely different auditory cue. Basically, the joke of having titles—"A Movie" and "by Bruce Conner" and "The End"—was that the piece never really ended.

About the images of sexuality, I think you're speaking about two sequences. One is at the very beginning where there's countdown leader in the midst of which there's a picture from a girlie film of a woman taking off her stockings; she has nothing else on. I was always aware that there was a hidden aspect of filmmaking that was comparable to the hidden obsessions of people, that what you saw on the screen was a censored or acceptable social image but that something was hidden. I was thinking of what might happen if a movie were run, and as you were watching the numbered countdown leader, all of a sudden you saw something on the screen that you were not expecting to see, not *supposed* to see, an image that existed on a subliminal level in a lot of movies in the 1940s and 1950s, where there were sexual implications of all sorts without your ever seeing a naked woman in an erotic one-to-one relationship with the camera. A movie presupposes a particular society and a set of traditional concepts that allow you to view imagery only in certain ways, a form of censorship. I think my idea at that time, although I couldn't have verbalized it then, was that that image of the naked woman was an image normally kept hidden but is *there*, an implicit part of the movies.

The other sequence you're talking about is the dramatic continuity where the Western, male-oriented tradition of viewing violence as sex is evoked. It's comic in the way I've dealt with it: a U-boat captain is looking through his periscope. He's in this isolated community of men in a submarine, and you know that within that kind of environment during war, the creative relationship that exists between men and women, the urge to procreate, is redirected toward destruction. In back of the weapons that are made to destroy is this *mis*directed creative impulse, basically a sexual impulse. All the weapons are designed practically as phallic emblems. The dominance of that life-destructive force was an obsession with me. The only possible release that this man looking through the periscope could have was to send out a torpedo, which then becomes the atomic bomb.

Nobody could face up to the ramifications of the atomic bomb, and that's still true. At most, the bomb is dealt with as a theatrical device, as a transformation in the characterization of evil in movies in the 1940s and 1950s. After the atomic bomb, the destructive forces that were fantasized in movies were those that came out of atomic radiation, generally in the form of absurd creatures: some kind of monster comes out of the ocean and stomps around destroying cities.

I also noticed that there was a way in which those concepts of a monster or a creature that has been produced by society was emblematically presented in a symbolic way in films like *Frankenstein*; the monster in *Frankenstein* is basically a child that's been created artificially and is malformed and out of control.

By calling my film *A Movie*, I wanted to draw attention to the fact that all the images in the film are something like archetypes and symbols from movies made over the years. I'd like to believe that I'm *using* those archetypes and those symbols, that I'm not entrapped by them myself, but I do find that I *am*, and I'm embarrassed at times by this.

Often, either through the process of making a movie or by the way that other people talk about one of my movies after it's finished, I discover what it is that I am trying to understand through this process. You'll be asking me questions about these films, but I can't really divorce a film from the whole story that happens before and afterward. I usually find that people tell me things about my movie that I couldn't verbalize when I was making it; I made the movie because I *couldn't* verbalize these things.

F: In the films we saw tonight, there was a lot of scientific stuff from educational films. Are you antiscientific or anti-pseudoscientific?

Conner: I can't make a categorical judgment. There are any number of foolish things that people do which are rationalized as science. There's plenty of humbug and medicine-show activity done in the name of science, because science is our religion. Anything that needs to be justified in our society is called science. This doesn't mean that I'm antiscience or against the scientific method, but this category is easily abused and consistently abused.

F: I don't really have a question. I would like to come back to the issue of the sexuality of the imagery. Something that permeates all of Bruce's films is his feeding back to us our media image of ourselves, which is full of absurdity and ridiculousness and contradictions and exploitation. Bruce's films are very open texts, open to a lot of interpretation, but they *can* be considered to be feminist films. . .

Conner: They can also be considered sexist!

F: Yeah, I know, but Freude Bartlett was distributing them as feminist films until Serious Business, her distribution company, closed.

F: The reason why I asked if Bruce had rethought the sexual imagery is that in the years since that imagery was made, what's politically correct has changed.

Conner: There's one movie that Marie has insisted that I show that I don't want to show. I haven't wanted to show it because it has made things so difficult for me. It's called *Marilyn Times Five* [various versions, 1969–73], and you will see it. It's made up of footage from a girlie movie attributed to Marilyn Monroe. Whether it *is* her or not is not important to me, because I did not feel that she owned her own image; her image was out of control and she herself was a victim of that image. The sexuality in the imagery I use and the exploitation it represents are very sad for me, and I've found it extremely difficult to talk to people about the film *if* they take the point of view that I am the enemy, which has happened: I've been told *I've* murdered Marilyn Monroe and that my film is a personal vendetta. I've also had people who have identified themselves as feminists tell me it's the funniest movie they've ever seen; others have said it's tragic; and still others have said it's absurd. I'd stopped showing it, but Freude insisted that she distribute it, and so for the last five or six years she has. But personally, I find it a difficult film to cope with.

Grieco: You're raising a very important question not just about the artist's responsibility toward his audience, but about the audience's responsibility to reach out to understand. For Freude, the question in *Cosmic Ray* and other of your films is what *is* the obscenity: sex or violence? In our society, sex is censored but violence is not.

I would ask, does the artist have the right to withdraw a film from distribution just because a lot of people aren't ready for it? What about those of us who *are* ready? We're constantly learning and in time, more of us will come to understand.

Conner: I don't feel that any of the reactions to *Marilyn* that I've described, including the attacks, are wrong; but it became so difficult for me emotionally to deal with these reactions that I had to stay away from the film.

From my point of view, from my own personal history in these United States, I see that we are almost compelled to view things in a certain way, but that many times what I'm working with are those things that appear to be paradoxical, that seem to be impossible to correlate into the rational structure that we have been trained to use—mainly because I think we ask ourselves the wrong questions and assume that we have come up with answers.

I believe that we have a systematic indoctrination into an almost-unconscious philosophical way of viewing the world and that this has gone on for centuries. You could compare *A Movie* with any news broadcast, supposedly a reality program: you turn on your TV set and you think you're seeing and hearing reality. But what *do* you hear? Ronald Reagan has been presented with a baby elephant and he patted the elephant and said, "What a long nose!" Three-hundred-forty-eight people have died in an air crash in Afghanistan. The risk of atomic annihilation is in a ratio of a certain percentage of such and such. And then there's a commercial. Now, this is the form that we've traditionally used to see reality. But it doesn't look like reality. I think we live in illusion, that we continue to reaffirm illusions, time after time, and by that reaffirmation, we make the world what we say it is going to be. Amen.

My feeling is that if I'm going to take anything seriously, I'm not going to take it secondhand from anybody else. I know that personally I can be enormously deceived in my own firsthand perceptions, so I can't assume that what is presented as a realistic survival structure in the society is actually real.

This is why I'm currently involved in making a film about religion in black society, a documentary about the Soulsters, a black gospel group that started in 1926. This group is an affirmation of life values that I respect, values that relate to those aspects of life that most people ignore. The Soulsters do sing beautiful songs about dying and being sick and having people turn against you—they do a variety of songs—but there's also a life affirmation, where the highest ideals can be a part of your own personal life. That's also what's partly organized in our society as the "national park" we call Art.

I don't have a concept that any value system is supreme in itself or that you should advocate one belief or another as a solution to problems. Probably one of my main defects in trying to deal with my own life and one of the main reasons I've made these movies is that I've been trying to solve problems that maybe can never be solved. I'm suspicious of the ingrained Western heroic concept that we can solve all the problems, but I also feel that there is something that you *can* do.

F: One of the advantages that video has over film is that when the video test pattern comes on, it uses pure color. Film test patterns out of Hollywood, still always show a woman, the China Girl, between numbers 4 and 3, holding a chart. I have yet to see a man.

Conner: Actually, I see her as a traditional emblem of the life force.

F: The films of yours we've seen here use imagery in connection with music; do you ever plan to break with that form?

Conner: Well, I've done work in video, 8mm, 16mm, 35mm, at various speeds; I've done light shows, drawings, paintings, sculpture, performance pieces. What we're dealing with here is what I see as the viable way to show an image in an auditorium. I know and respect people who make silent films, films that use entirely different formats from mine. But for work that is projected in an auditorium, I do see myself very much locked into the format you've been seeing. The style of the recent films that I've just shown you is almost exactly the same as *A Movie*; they're all black and white, use the same concepts, the same editing structure.

I tried to move out of that in the sixties, and I *did* move out of it in certain directions. I worked in light shows, which I felt was an obvious extension of my relationship with music. The light shows involved improvising as a jazz band might improvise, only we were improvising with visual images. We performed in the Avalon Ballroom for months, four nights a week, six or seven hours a day, improvising with Buddy Guy and Muddy Waters and with Big Brother and the Holding Company and The Doors—all of those great energies of 1967 or 1968. After that period of working on a 180-degree screen (it didn't have to be on a screen; we projected on people, on anything), and performing for an audience whose presence would transform the music and the event itself, there was a period when I couldn't conceive of sitting down and locking myself in solitary confinement for months to edit a film that would be shown in a darkened room where everybody had to sit still and look at a little rectangle.

F: Is your sense of an audience important to you as you're making a film?

Conner: I don't think that any artist exists without an audience.

Grieco: Except that sometimes the audience forms fifty years later.

Conner: But the *concept* of the audience has to be there. If you don't have a concept of an audience, why do a painting on a canvas that's going to go into a frame? Why make a film? Why do anything that's going to function within a traditional communicative social structure, unless you are playing on that audience relationship?

I don't feel that I *create* that much; I do choose things, but I don't feel that I am in the position of determining a concept and then revealing it to people, because many times, I'm not aware of what I'm doing enough to say to myself, "This is what I'm doing." Later, I learn what I was doing from what audiences tell me.

F: Marie, you asked that question about the film Bruce didn't want to show: should Bruce have the right to take a film out of distribution so we can't see it. . .

Grieco: He did that to *The White Rose* [1967], for example, which is one of my favorites.

F: Well, it seems to me that if the audience understands what the filmmaker is doing enough to enlighten the filmmaker, if the response to the work is part of the process as Bruce has said, then to keep a film from the audience isn't logical.

F: I want to come back to the question about the naked woman in the film as a comment on the convention that traditional films exploit women. If I wanted to parody that convention today, I would stick a naked man in that frame.

F: That wouldn't make the same comment on media that Bruce was making.

F: Well, whatever, but the point is that the social context of an image changes over time. The confusing thing about that particular film is that it was made in 1958, and the social context of that imagery has changed substantially, and you get yourself into a hopeless boggle if you try and approach the manufacture of that image in 1958 from the social context of 1982.

F: Things haven't changed that much. I think we can still read that image. . .

F: True, but when I saw the film, my reaction was I would like to see naked men in there instead of naked women because *A Movie* is really about little boys who play with guns turning into big boys who play with guns. It seemed to me that if I were a woman, if I were the woman who made *Possibly in Michigan* [1983, Cecelia Condit], I would be offended by that image of the naked woman because it goes to a source of great anger; but then I thought, well that film was made a long time ago, and you don't just go back and change a film.

F: We can't forget that provocation may be part of the aesthetic.

Conner: When I made *A Movie*, I was making an antique movie. In 1958, which is more than twenty-five years ago, I made this movie out of footage from the previous fifty years, and I was dealing with concepts and images that I considered to be antique then. This film could have been made, except for certain later footage, fifteen to twenty years before I made it. One of the things I've discovered over all these years, particularly with *A Movie*, is that it continually comes back to me in new ways. What you're telling me is something I've never heard before, but I've heard so many different relationships with these images and each is unique to the times.

In 1967, I showed *A Movie* in San Francisco at the Canyon Cinematheque, and at the beginning, when the Indians are chasing the cowboys, everybody was applauding the Indians and booing the cowboys. I thought, "Gosh, that's amazing! Is this gonna keep on going?" But it didn't; that didn't happen again. I've seen *A Movie* many, many times, and often it has changed for me. And people who have seen the film once and then see it a second time will say to me that this time it was shorter, or it was longer, or I introduced footage that was not there before, or I reedited it, or I took things out, or I changed the music. *A Movie* is a composite of images which continue to shift meanings and create new emotional/conceptual relationships, and for me this is an essential aspect of communication.

1987 PETER WATKINS AND OTHERS—ON *THE JOURNEY* (1987)

[At the large-group discussion, *The Journey* was represented by Watkins and by several of those who had participated in the production: Manfred Becker (editing and sound editing), Vida Urbonavicius (sound editing), Joan Churchill (graphic design), Don Tracy, Scott MacDonald, and Patricia O'Connor (producers of the Utica/Ilion, New York, shooting), and John Campbell (assistant camera, Portland, Oregon, shooting). Nearly all the questions were directed to Watkins.]

F: Could you share with us your thoughts about the length [*The Journey* runs 14½ hours]? Was it part of your original conceptualization of the film?

John Columbus: And do you think it's appropriate to confine people to chairs? I was trying different ways of staying with the film. One way was to lie on the floor and not look at the image, and if I did not go to sleep (and a few times I did, and I'm certainly not the only one [laughter]), but if I did not—and in fact most of the time I did not—there were times when something that was said intrigued me and I'd pop up and look. Sometimes, I thought, "Why didn't he just make a sound tape and intersperse visual imagery?"

Peter Watkins: The point about sound and visuals is a very strong one, and I thought about it a great deal. I haven't measured this exactly, but 5 to 7 percent of the film is black—there's no image at all—and I have wondered why I didn't do that more. As to the length, we're going to propose that community groups and other groups work with the film in a very stretched-out process, so that people can look at a couple of hours and either talk about what they've seen or leave. Then sometime later, a bit more could be shown and discussed. The film should be only one part of an expanding social process, against which the film's profile is gradually diminishing.

I'll be writing a teaching guide this fall—a bad expression because the "guide" is going to be as open as possible. I'll be exploring places in the film where I feel I've been able to get out of the conventional traps and where I feel I'm still stuck in them. I'm going to try to be as frank as I can. Of course, one can set out to be tough with oneself, but actually it's very difficult: during filming, decisions are made very fast and very intuitively and deep. But I'm going to write about those decisions as openly as I can.

When I started *The Journey*, I'd been thinking about the questions it raises since before *The War Game* [1965] was banned back in 1965. Over the years, I've been part of many discussions in schools and with public audiences. At first, those discussions were often focused on the question, "Why aren't we told information? Why are governments hiding information from us?" This was a common theme in many countries, and for a while, *The War Game* was a good way of getting that discussion going.

By the seventies, discussions were focusing more on, "What about the material we *are* getting? How is that affecting us?" We're all feeling our way in the dark, and many of the public (I would guess) now have an enormous concern, but no easy way of talking about it. Many people feel they can't verbalize effectively about the control of information, because they've had no practice in such verbalizing. In most schools, it's never been the practice to talk in any detail about the ways we get information; and our profession—to put it bluntly—doesn't talk about such issues very much with the public. I don't mean only the forms into which information is structured, but also our relationship as professional media people, or lack of a relationship, with the public.

I've just recently been in Australia and New Zealand, where the film opened with the help of core groups, like the one here with me tonight. Something we discussed a great deal there—in secondary schools and universities and publicly—is that if you look at the whole social matrix (or whatever you want to call all of us when we interrelate), where exactly is the media? Are we inside that matrix? Are we outside it? Most seem to assume the media is apart from the social matrix, and many people vocalize that separation now.

So to come back to your question about the length, I suppose originally I thought the film would be about three hours or so, but you know what happens: we shot a lot of material and then it became possible to film in more countries, and by the time I got back to the National Film Board [of Canada, where *The Journey* was edited], I had about a hundred hours of material. I felt that a lot of it was going in very strong directions, and just did not want to do the usual chop, chop, chop, which I would have had to do, even to reduce what I had to four or five hours.

In any case, the length is really absolutely irrelevant because (I don't have to tell you good people, you *know*) it doesn't really matter these days whether something is six hours, sixteen hundred hours, or six minutes. If they're not going to show it, they're not going to show it. And these days they are not showing most broad challenges to the system.

Michael Grillo: I did not have any trouble with the length (granted I was the projectionist, so I could get up and pace around). I don't think you have to see the whole thing with studied, staring attention—and I'm willing to bet none of us did. I would suggest that *The Journey* reinforces by its duration the fact that one cannot devote even an hour a week to any serious issue, without changing the principle of one's life, the very details of one's day-to-day experience. The film has much redundancy. By the fifth time we've seen the Hiroshima photographs, there's a certain amount of tuning in and tuning out; but this points to the whole necessity of feeling and thinking about such issues in the banal, rather than during special moments apart from everyday life.

Sally Berger: After a while, I began focusing on the body language of the people being interviewed, and more and more, I noticed that there was someone in each group who seemed tense. There seemed to be a lot of tension among many of the families.

Watkins: I suppose it's because we're dealing with people—*people*. I can't really tell you exactly what relationship each person had to the camera; you'd have to go back and ask the families (though we talked a lot about those issues before we started filming). I didn't have the luxury of working as much as I might have liked with all the families. As it was, the film necessitated three trips around the world: to meet the families; to go back and see them a few months later; then, to shoot. But wherever possible, we did try (and without being patronizing) to talk about the equipment and the process. After a while I think most people grew more accustomed to the shooting than they thought they would—even to looking into the camera, which I asked them to do. As you said, in the shots when a person is talking, the camera is often showing more than one person: we were trying to broaden the reference by showing the children fidgeting, for example, and the various dynamics that are occurring between members of each family.

F: A long film, and extended shots, don't necessarily get people to question media. Having taught about media, I felt during a lot of the film that the only action it would encourage people to take is to leave the room where the film is being screened and get some fresh air! There is powerful stuff in the film, but it could be collapsed a lot.

Did you consult peace groups and educational institutions to try and figure out the best way to structure the segments so people could really work with the film?

Watkins: No. I've been with about twenty audiences in five countries, and their responses have been very varied. Sure, some people don't like the length. Roughly speaking, maybe 40 to 50 percent of the audience stay through; the others leave at various points.

Many of the positive reactions have come from teachers.

F: It's just *too long.* [laughter] I sat through most of it, and enjoyed a good bit of it. I tend to agree with your positions in the film so you're preaching to the converted. But I'm assuming you want to make some change, and I question seriously whether those you want to change are going to sit through 14½ hours of film, regardless of the content. Also, I question the simplistic assumption that if the governments of the world don't spend money on arms that money will be available for social welfare. I know of no instance where that's been the case.

Watkins: As far as I know (I may be wrong here), none of us made that assumption. I certainly didn't, and I don't remember any of the families doing so. Of course, many of the families would be aware of the irony you have raised—that, of course, if the money weren't used for arms, it would get absorbed somewhere else—but the purpose of the film, nonetheless, is to raise the point, not as an assumption, but as an enormous tragic irony that we live under now.

Scott MacDonald: A point about the length. I teach American literature as well as film, and I routinely ask my students to read long novels. Any major novel takes many hours to read. I realize that given the conditioning we have, it doesn't seem practical or comfortable to deal with a 14½-hour film, but even in the mass media, there are long works. Virtually every television series is watched an hour a week for a whole season.

David Tafler: I think the film should be even longer than it is, so that it could deal more thoroughly with even more of the relevant issues. My relationship with the families continued to grow throughout the entire film because the information we receive between the family sections continually recontextualizes these people.

Raul Zaritsky: I could learn from the survivors of Hiroshima, and even from the woman who lives near the tracks where the White Train passes, but when the camera arrives in the homes of the families, it takes on this messianic quality. I feel that the families were put in an extremely difficult position of having to respond to these transcendent questions and having to reveal their ignorance about so many things. I agree we should all be aware of these issues and should talk about them. But I also feel an invasion of those homes. And *nobody* knew *anything.* There are millions of people all over the world working on these issues. *Somebody* is aware, *some* people know, some schools deal with these things! Where were *they?*

Watkins: Maybe our perception of people is different. Of course there are peace groups working with these issues, but the problem is that, nonetheless, the arms race has been escalating out of control. Sure you find people who know a good deal about such things, but most don't. The large majority don't.

Juan Mandelbaum: I came to feel that this was just another form of media manipulation, of forcing people into a situation. I know they agreed to participate, but they didn't know what they were agreeing to. . .

Watkins: Excuse me; here, I must interrupt. You've made an assumption there, which to be fair to us, to me, is incorrect. Wherever possible, and it nearly always was, we spent an enormous amount of time with each family that had agreed to be in the film, discussing the questions we would ask and our filming process. Obviously, that's not the same thing as doing it—I agree with that—but we absolutely did not do the more traditional thing of just rushing in with a camera.

F: It just seemed so set up! They're always sitting there, very gloomy [laughter], saying how they never knew anything [laughter]. . .

Watkins: Well, excuse me, everyone. I must say here that I don't think this is funny. Maybe we have a different sense of humor. . .

F: But his point is very well taken. . .

Watkins: Possibly, yes, I just don't find it amusing.

Maria DeLuca: I don't think the laughter was meant as disrespect to anyone who made the film. It's just a breaking of tension. We're all really tense here—at least *I'm* really tense.

Watkins: It is difficult to talk about things you don't know, and most of the families, once the process was over, said they felt glad to have shared what was essentially an educational process.

There was a German family—a well-educated farming couple in their midthirties—who had a hostile reaction to our process. They took what I would call a conservative position on these issues, and I thought it would be good to include them. I thought we might have a different kind of discussion than we had with the other families.

The family was very disturbed by the information, particularly by the Hiroshima pictures, and they said, "You are trying to manipulate us!" I thought, "Well, I hope we'll get through this because it'll be very useful for the film." But they became more and more hostile to the process and did not want their children to participate in the filming, even the sixteen-year-old daughter, because as they said—and this is a quote—"We're already angry about the way teachers manipulate them; we don't want anyone else manipulating them. That's our function." We did what we could to continue, but it just went from bad to worse, and finally everyone was so uncomfortable that we stopped filming.

I didn't know what to do with the material we had. On one hand, I thought it would add something to the film, but on the other hand, they didn't like it. Finally, the man told us, "If you use it, I will put a lawyer onto you." I could have gone ahead but decided not to. The German crew were very shaken by this experience, which was the only such experience *during* the filming; there were several families in Japan and on the West Coast of this country (in the arms-industry strip in the Northwest) where people didn't want to get into trouble by appearing in a "peace film."

Manfred Becker: I know the German family personally, and they changed after this experience. The man raised a stink when the army later used the local school during maneuvers.

DeLuca: They changed because of the film?

Becker: This is what they told me.

John Akomfrah: You need to be congratulated for doing something quite unique. This is a film that appears to me, on a whole number of issues, to be very patient and to have listened to voices that usually aren't heard, some of them from the third world and some from races not usually heard from in the industrialized world. I was here for only a few sections of *The Journey*, but what I saw gave me the impression that your idea was to overturn certain Eurocentric assumptions at work in the European peace movement, where nuclear apocalypse is held up as the ultimate evil which everything else has to kneel in front of. This is the first film I've seen that at least tries to work with a mixed economy within which a whole set of issues are raised, and which allows people to work out of their own priorities and skills with regard to the nuclear arms race.

I would want to add that recently in the United Kingdom a number of television programs have used precisely your strategy for making films that are tied to specific regions and support groups.

And finally a question: What argument did you use, in the third world especially, to persuade people to participate in the film? Having tried to work in Angola, I know it's very difficult.

F: Can I add a related question? I only saw about six hours of the film, but it seemed to me that when you talked with the European families, you discussed the nuclear issue, but when you talked with the third world families, you discussed food. Did you mean to do that?

Watkins: I traveled with a list of all the questions, and I tried—almost ritualistically— to go through *all* of them with each group, so as *not* to make such distinctions. Sometimes, in the editing, certain responses were left out—in the interests of time. And of course, different groups responded to different questions differently. The women's collective in Mozambique had seen the Hiroshima pictures, as had the Mexican family, and the Polynesians. . .

F: So *they* were the ones that took the discussion in the direction it went?

Watkins: Absolutely, and very much with the Mozambique group.

[to Akomfrah] I had a lot of discussions with the various groups and families, to see if they related to the questions I was interested in asking and to see if they wanted to be involved. But I didn't try to persuade them. I tried *not* to lean on them at all— that wouldn't have been productive on any level.

Ruth Bradley: The film has experimental *form*, but it reiterates another, conventional social form: the patriarchal family. With the exception of the women's collective, I see father, mother, children—all over the world. And I kept hearing, "They're just like us! They're just like us!" when the families saw each other on the video. They *are* alike in what the effect would be on them of nuclear war, but they're *not* alike in terms of cultural difference.

Watkins: Well, I thought a lot about the patriarchal question. I know that's a very strong point. Obviously, I don't bring the sensitivity to this issue that a woman would, but I decided, rightly or wrongly, that since the nuclear family (a very ironic expression in these circumstances) is dominantly of this form all over the world, it would be better to deal with that and to confront it and see what would be revealed during the general dynamics of the filming.

F: As a third world person, I come from a different position than many of those here. People all over the third world are already under attack. To focus on the nuclear issue is to ignore what is already going on: in the West *white* people will die in a nuclear war, but *we* are already dying.

F: At the beginning of the film, I was very excited by what you were attempting, but as the hours went by, I came to hate being bludgeoned by it, and I was horrified when I heard you say that because of time, you *didn't* have feedback sessions with community groups and with the teachers you hope will use the film.

Watkins: I can only reply that horrifying though it may be, the film was made with very little money, and because of that, we had tremendous time pressures.

But to be honest, time and money were not the primary considerations. The primary consideration was that in the editing, I wanted to work with the film personally and privately. Having worked collectively as best I could before the shooting and even during the shooting, I then went inside myself—maybe at a time you would have liked me to go out.

F: I've been raising my hand for ages!

I'm a former clinical psychologist, and I've found over and over again that you should never give your own surveys because when you do, you reveal, through your body language and in all sorts of ways, the answers you want. You *continually* led your respondents in that way.

One more statement. I'm not being mean when I say this, just brutally real— please understand that. I liken your film to radical surgery with a rusty knife without anesthesia. And I'll tell you why. I'm a professor at a small, white, conservative university. Last semester, I used a Winnie Mandela documentary about race, only a fifty-five-minute film but very painful to watch. And as a protest, my students got up and removed their seats out of the classroom. They didn't say, "We're not going to look at fifty-five minutes of this nigger bitch in South Africa"; they just moved. That was fifty-five minutes! Do you really think there is any way in the world I could get those students—who really need their consciousness raised—to sit through 14½ hours of *this*?

Watkins: I'm sorry, I can't respond to your question.

1987 SU FRIEDRICH—ON *DAMNED IF YOU DON'T* (1987)

F: I found both your films courageous, but I wonder in the case of the second film [*The Ties That Bind* (1984) had been screened earlier in the seminar], did you start with a fictional concept or a documentary concept?

Su Friedrich: *Damned If You Don't* started when I was living in Berlin and was very depressed and didn't have any friends. I was making all these long-distance calls to America and was really drunk one night, saying to a friend, "My God, I've been sitting here for six months and I don't have one idea!" Jokingly I said, "I should make a film about a schoolgirl who falls in love with a nun, ha, ha, ha." The next morning, I thought, "That might be a good idea!" It seemed to strike a chord in me. So as I traveled with *The Ties That Bind*, I shot a lot of footage of churches and nuns, and at the end of my stay, I went to Israel to get footage of Bethlehem and Nazareth (all of which was ruined). Back in the States, I filmed confirmation services and kids playing at recess at Catholic schools. Most of the footage of the nuns was shot in Italy on a later trip.

So I had all this wild footage. I definitely wanted to deal with a nun coming to terms with her sexual feelings. I didn't want to try and find a nun who had come out of the order and gotten married, so I decided to create a fictional situation, which began to script my cutting of the wild footage. It was a weird balance; the film evolved as part documentary, part fiction.

F: There are a lot of legal issues around *Damned If You Don't*. Did you get permission to use the *Black Narcissus* [1947, Michael Powell and Emeric Pressburger] material? And if you didn't, do you see that as a problem for distribution?

Friedrich: Yes! [laughter] I contacted Volunteer Lawyers for the Arts and had one meeting with them; then I met someone who'd spent a lot of time getting rights for films. I said, "Oh, I have this little problem!" and she said, "Who distributes the film?" I said, "The original production company—Rank Films—owns the rights." She said, "You're kidding me! They're the worst!" The film is showing at the National Film Theater in London in September, so who knows what will happen! [laughter]

I also called Arista Records and Warner Brothers. Arista owns the rights to the version of the Patti Smith song I use, and Warner Brothers owns the rights to the song itself. They *both* want $4,500 for use of the song. So I said, "OK, fine," and hung up—and that was *that*! [laughter]

I've talked to Yvonne Rainer and other people who have used footage from other films, and music, without getting rights, and Yvonne said she's never run into problems. I figured her films have shown a lot more than mine probably will, so maybe I'm OK. At this point, I think the only problem would be television, where you have to clear rights. I'm going to hope no one will notice, and if they do, I'll declare bankruptcy because I *cannot* pay to use these quotations.

Richard Herskowitz: If it's any comfort, in about fifty years, *Black Narcissus* will be in the public domain. [laughter]

F: I was so excited to see a film that allowed me to have pleasure without identifying with a male viewer. Your ability to create a woman's viewpoint seems so effortless. Have you reached a point in your work where it really *is* effortless?

Friedrich: My films are certainly *not* effortless *in any way*. In *The Ties That Bind*, I realized that while my mother was the subject of the film, she was a person in her own right. I had to make a very conscious effort to respect her because I think there's a sense in which we don't respect our mothers. I would have to remind myself of that when I was slipping away, or thinking, "Oh, she doesn't know what she's talking about." I had to hold on to myself. . .

F: I guess what impressed me is that I don't remember any shot where she's objectified, and the few times when she is shot from the front, the shots are short, so there's no time to get back into the male-gaze way of seeing.

Friedrich: I hate being in front of the camera, so I always feel very apologetic when I'm shooting someone else. I expected my mother to be much more self-conscious. But she was great; she was always having conversations with me while I was shooting, and that allowed me to move around her while still being involved with her.

F: A follow-up question about *Damned If You Don't*. The problem with women taking pleasure in most movies is that we're forced into a male-identified point of view. Your method of avoiding the male gaze in *Damned If You Don't* was very different from your method in *The Ties That Bind* because you're striving for a different kind of pleasure. It was nice to be able to take total pleasure in the women's bodies *as a woman* and not have to go through guilt because of a male point of view. Has it been problematic for you to show *Damned If You Don't* to a mixed audience?

Friedrich: I don't have any problem about showing it to a mixed audience.

I, for one, really dislike films that discuss the theory of filmmaking (to be fair, some of them have moments) because to me that's *not* a film, that's something else. And I'm very tired of having a Laura Mulvey essay, written thirteen years ago [Mulvey defines "the male gaze" in "Visual Pleasure and Narrative Cinema," first published in *Screen* in 1975], cited every time someone wants to say something about women's filmmaking or women as audience.

I guess at some point, I thought, "What is all this debate about? If I'm a woman and I'm making a film, then why is everyone assuming that what I'm making is responding to a male audience or to some 'male gaze'"? If I'm true enough to how I see the world, the film I make will be genuine; and since I am a woman, it will have a woman's point of view.

The whole issue of whether you're "allowed" to show women's bodies on screen is loaded, and every film responds to that issue in its own particular way. I just decided I wanted to see these beautiful women, and I wanted to portray these funny moments between them. I wanted to express their anxiety and use very sensual images. Someone might be offended because a naked woman is shown on the screen, but I don't care because that's the image I wanted to make.

Not that I find shooting erotic imagery easy! I found it extraordinarily embarrassing. We all did. It was the end of August, about 110 degrees [laughter] in a tiny room [laughter]. We didn't rehearse or anything. The one woman is gay and the other isn't (her sister is, so it wasn't that big a deal for her), but it turned out she was very modest. Anyway, we got into it, and once they were finally on the bed, I'd say, "Let's try Ela [Troyano] on top," or whatever, and in the middle of shooting, one of the three of us would inevitably burst out laughing. It just went on and on. After we had a certain amount of material, I thought maybe we should have Peggy [Healey] taking Ela's outfit off, and I looked at Ela's face and thought, "No, we *shouldn't* try that." [laughter] So no, I don't have a problem showing the erotic material in the film, but I had some difficulty filming it.

I think if you don't make something *you* want to see, if you're only making something that's trying to be what you think *they* want, something that's (implicitly) apologizing to people, there's no point in making films.

Notes

1. D. Marie Grieco, phone interview by Patricia R. Zimmermann, September 9, 2009.
2. Lucy Kostelanetz, "The Flaherty: Four Decades in the Cause of Independent Cinema," ed. Erik Barnouw and Patricia Zimmermann, *Wide Angle* 17, Special Issue (1995): 37 (hereafter cited as "The Flaherty").
3. Lucy Kostelanetz, phone interview by Patricia R. Zimmermann, September 17, 2009.
4. Juan Mandelbaum, phone interview by Patricia R. Zimmermann, September 23, 2009.
5. Nadine Covert, "International Film Seminars: A Work in Progress," retrieved June 2, 2013 (www.namac.org/node/1219).
6. Covert, "International Film Seminars: A Work in Progress."
7. B. Ruby Rich, phone interview by Patricia R. Zimmermann, October 26, 2009.
8. Ibid.
9. Ibid.
10. Ibid.
11. Ibid.
12. For a list of many of these groups, see the Experimental Television Center's Video History Project timelines for 1977–84, retrieved June 5, 2013 (http://www.experimentaltvcenter.org/history-chronology).
13. Ruby Rich, interview by Patricia R. Zimmermann, October 26, 2009.
14. Ibid.
15. Video History Project, retrieved June 6, 2013 (http://www.experimentaltvcenter.org/history-chronology).
16. The US Army lifted the ban in 1980.

17. A longtime NFB producer, Brittain was also later the first director to work in IMAX.

18. Schreiber later became a major narrative film director of photography who worked with independent feature director Martha Coolidge.

19. Vincent Canby, "Eight Minutes to Midnight: A Portrait of Dr. Helen Caldicott," *New York Times*, June 9, 1982. Retrieved June 17, 2013 (http://www.nytimes.com/movie/review?res=940CEFDB143BF93AA35755C0A964948260).

20. Blacklisted in the 1950s, Grant had won an Academy Award in 1975 for Best Supporting Actress in *Shampoo*.

21. Arthur Unger, "The Network Documentary: Why Is It an Exclusive Club?," retrieved July 1, 2013 (http://www.csmonitor.com/1980/1212/121200.html).

22. Kirchheimer worked in the commercial film industry in New York, taught at the School of Visual Arts, and self-financed his own independent films.

23. "BAM Screen Indie Cult Classic," *Bay Ridge Journal*, May 18, 2014 (http://bayridgejournal.blogspot.com/2014/05/bam-screens-indie-cult-classic-stations.html).

24. For analysis of the rise of community-based video, see Deirdre Boyle, *Subject to Change: Guerrilla Television Revisited* (Oxford: Oxford University Press, 1997). For discussions of video art in the 1970s and 1980s, see Doug Hall and Sally Jo Fifer, *Illuminating Video: An Essential Guide to Video Art* (New York: Aperture, 1990).

25. For a mapping of the rich independent media scene in the State of New York in the 1980s, see Video History Project, retrieved July 8, 2013 (http://www.experimentaltvcenter.org/history-chronology).

26. Bruce Jenkins, phone interview by Patricia R. Zimmermann, July 17, 2012.

27. Ibid.

28. Jenkins's own background evidenced how independent media had changed since the early days of the Flaherty, with experimental film now the subject of doctoral dissertations.

29. Ibid.

30. Ibid.

31. Bruce Jenkins, e-mail to Patricia R. Zimmermann, July 11, 2014.

32. DeeDee Halleck, phone interview by Patricia R. Zimmermann, June 12, 2014.

33. D. Marie Grieco, "Recollection," in "The Flaherty," 24.

34. D. Marie Grieco, phone interview by Patricia R. Zimmermann, November 1, 2009. Grieco contends that the librarians had more power than the producers advanced by Van Dyke because they purchased work and also promoted it through exhibitions.

35. D. Marie Grieco, phone interview by Patricia R. Zimmermann, November 1, 2009.

36. "Zbig Rybczynski—Film and Video Productions," retrieved July 21, 2016 (http://www.zbigvision.com/). Rybczyński had trained at the Łódź Film School.

37. Aljean Harmetz, "Film Looks at '39 World's Fair," *New York Times*, October 1, 1939. Retrieved August 23, 2015 (http://www.nytimes.com/1984/10/01/movies/film-looks-at-the-39-world-s-fair.html).

38. Tony Gittens and Linka Blackaby, e-mail to Patricia R. Zimmermann, May 31, 2016.

39. Ibid.

40. Ibid.

41. Herskowitz initially attended the Flaherty at the urging of a graduate school friend. That graduate school friend was Patricia R. Zimmermann, coauthor of this volume and a professor at Ithaca College. Richard Herskowitz, phone interview by Patricia R. Zimmermann, July 27, 2009.

42. Ibid.

43. Ibid.

44. Ibid.

45. Richard Herskowitz, "Intro to the 2012 Festival Program," retrieved September 13, 2014 (http://cinemartsociety.org/media/intro-to-the-2012-festival-program/).

46. Richard Herskowitz, phone interview by Patricia R. Zimmermann, July 27, 2009.

47. Ibid.

48. John Greyson, "La Flahertia," in "The Flaherty," 22.

49. For a discussion of Watkin's career, films, and significance in the world of documentary, see Jared Rapfogel, "The Cinema of Peter Watkins," *Cineaste,* retrieved October 2, 2014 (http://www.cineaste.com/articles/the-films-of-peter-watkins.htm).

50. For full disclosure, Scott MacDonald, one of the authors of this volume, worked on the Utica section of *The Journey.*

51. For an analysis of *The Journey,* see Scott MacDonald, "Filmmaker as Global Circumnavigator: Peter Watkins, *The Journey* and Media Critique," *Quarterly Review of Film and Video* 14, no. 4 (1993): 31–54.

52. Richard Herskowitz, phone interview by Patricia R. Zimmermann, July 27, 2009.

53. Pearl Bowser, "Testing the Waters: African Diaspora Filmmaking and Identity," in "The Flaherty," 194.

54. Ibid.

55. Ibid.

56. Françoise Pfaff, *Cinema of Ousmane Sembène* (Westport, CT: Greenwood, 1984); Teshome Gabriel, *Third Cinema in the Third World: The Aesthetics of Liberation* (Ann Arbor, MI: UMI Research Press, 1982); Manthia Diawara, "Popular Culture and Oral Traditions in African Film," *Film Quarterly* 4, no. 3 (1988): 6–14.

57. Bowser, "Testing the Waters," 193.

58. Ibid.

59. The program included fifty-five films, spanning documentary and experimental works. See "The Flaherty," 457.

60. Jake Homiak, "Recollections," in "The Flaherty," 30.

61. Ibid., 31.

62. Ibid., 31–32.

63. Louis Massiah, "Recollections," in "The Flaherty," 46.

64. Ibid., 46.

The 2007 Flaherty Seminar at Vassar College, Poughkeepsie, NY. Photo courtesy of International Film Seminars, Inc./The Flaherty, New York.

6

CRISES, 1990–1999

"The Flaherty Seminars have always been a tough sell to funders," explained Tom Johnson, a documentary filmmaker and philanthropist with a six-decade Flaherty engagement.[1] Johnson served as president of the board of trustees from 1990 to 1992, which was a time of organizational crises. The turbulent confluence of arts defunding in the public and private sectors, debates about identity politics, and the emergence of new technologies (e.g., digital media systems and interfaces such as CD-ROM) and performance with technologies generated crises and unravelings during the 1990s.

This period begins after Pearl Bowser's African and African diaspora seminar and ends with Pacific Film Archive programmer Kathy Geritz's wide-ranging, diverse 2000 seminar, entitled "Essays, Experiments, and Excavations." International Film Seminars (IFS), the board, and the seminar programming and discussions confronted complex challenges and crises. The impact of the culture wars and the push for more multicultural programming from both funders and participants prompted debate. The expansion of the independent documentary world in festivals and public television, as well as its legitimation from journalists and scholars shifted the vectors of independent media. Debates about who could represent whom combined with a reduction in grant resources propelled changes in who programmed the seminar, where it was held, what it showed, who attended, and how long it was. Contentious board meetings rocked the organization. Intense debates about the avant-garde, postmodern displacements of authenticity, postcolonial theory critiques of racialization and empire, and race converged at the seminars.

The ideological context framing the arguments erupting during the 1990s were multiple and layered. Although many participants involved in the Flaherty Seminar contended the intimate environment of intense screenings and discussions three times a day pushed participants' endurance, this somewhat essentialist argument ignored the larger structural changes in academic film theory, film culture, international political culture, and the seminar itself. Participants interrogated the racial representations embedded in the films. Flaherty Seminar veterans, many of whom held tightly to the more romanticized, humanist notion of nonpreconception, often butted heads with participants engaged in identity politics and multiculturalism. These younger filmmakers and scholars dismissed the false universalisms of humanism, nonpreconception, and pathos. With more university-based filmmakers and scholars in attendance, a critical language questioning meaning, purpose, political economy, and structure displaced simply reacting to a film on a more intuitive, immediate level.

Johnson had attended his first seminar in 1964. There, he experienced the work of Richard Leacock, an early pioneer of direct cinema who had worked as the cinematographer on Robert Flaherty's Standard Oil–sponsored film *Louisiana Story*. Johnson worked as an assistant seminar projectionist for Bill Alexander, "a hippie with a surfboard" who had projected seminar films for decades. Erik Barnouw programmed the seminar. Johnson describes his experience as "intimidating . . . I had not made any films, I didn't know any film history, and only a half dozen film schools existed in the United States."[2] During the 1960s and 1970s, according to Johnson, "no place showed nonfiction film—experimental, documentary, independent . . . the seminar always focused on exploring the independent spirit."[3]

By the time Johnson assumed the board presidency in 1990, he had attended the seminar for three decades. He had produced three award-winning compilation documentaries that screened at the seminars: *America Lost and Found* (1973), *No Place to Hide* (1979), and *World of Tomorrow* (1984). By 1990, the arts defunding crisis confronted the board, forcing a reevaluation of goals, identity, operations, and purpose within a changing independent media landscape.

By the 1990s, undergraduate and graduate media programs had developed at public and private universities across the United States, many featuring public screening programs with media artists. Supported by public and private grants to expand exhibition, media centers and museums screened a wider range of documentary and experimental work. Degree programs, university libraries, and museums had mutually beneficial relationships with a range of nonprofit film and video distributors such as California Newsreel, Canyon Cinema, Documentary Educational Resources, Electronic Arts Intermix, New Day Films, Third World Newsreel, Video Data Bank, and Women Make Movies to secure access to independent works. The Visible Evidence Conference on Documentary, primarily for scholars, was inaugurated in 1993.

The Flaherty now operated in a different independent film environment. Festivals showcasing a variety of independent film and media, such as the Sundance Film Festival, emerged. The festivals presented more work to larger and more specialized, identity-focused audiences. Many thematic festivals emphasized critical analyses and open debates, rather than jury prizes and markets.[4] As Marijke de Valck argues in *Film Festivals: From European Geopolitics to Global Cinephilia*, the third phase of film festivals occurred in their global spread after 1989. She has argued, "The small and intimate gatherings of like-minded cinephiles in the 1970s were put under pressure by technological advances, the subsequent make-over of the film industry, and the global proliferation of festivals in the 1980s."[5] An international film festival circuit developed combining high art with work oriented to a larger population.[6] Engaging cinephilia, these festivals sought distinction in quality programming to discover new auteurs, film movements, and new waves frequently from the Global South.[7]

IFS's disarray, institutional identity, and organizational crises were linked to larger social and political contexts of the 1990s. The debates about identity and multiculturalism intensified into what was called the "culture wars," where the religious political right questioned the deployment of public funds for art and media as well as the expansion of canons to include African American, Asian Americans, Latinos/Latinas, and women. As Henry Louis Gates has argued, these "culture wars" traced their origins to the civil rights movement of the 1950s, the women's movement in the 1960s and 1970s, and increased organizing around Asian American, Latino/a, and Native American identities throughout the 1980s.[8]

These binaries were comprised of a majoritarian white culture and a more pluralistic, inclusive culture addressing abortion, feminism, homosexuality, multiculturalism, popular culture, school curricula, and school prayer. In his 1992 speech to the Republican National Convention, Pat Buchanan had launched the phrase *culture wars* and identified it as a "struggle for the soul of America."[9] Irene Thomson has argued these binaries were reduced to a war between the fundamentalists versus the progressives, fought out in the pages of the *The Nation, National Review,* and the *New Republic.* On the one side, the religious right expressed hostility toward all forms of multiculturalism. On the other side, progressives redefined culture toward more diverse perspectives and representations, positioning culture as constructed.[10]

The culture wars were often framed as a battle between the religious right and progressive groups to define American culture. In the 1990s, the Flaherty Seminar showed another, more complicated side of how the culture wars were debated within nonprofit organizations. Often considered a progressive organization, the Flaherty's origins resided in cultural elites connected to East Coast museums and universities. Until the 1990s, the majority of Flaherty board members were white and male. The seminar grappled with how to recruit a more diverse board and implement multicultural programming.

The Flaherty Seminar was not the only nonprofit media arts organization needing to diversify its programming with ethnicity, gender, identity, and race orientations. These crises, debates, and instabilities were salient in media exhibition, where public funding met the public. In 1989, a landmark event spurred shifts in programming and exhibition practices. The New York State Council on the Arts (NYSCA), together with the Rockefeller Foundation and Film News Now (headed by Christine Choy and Renee Tajima-Peña), launched a conference called "Show the Right Thing."[11] The conference title alluded to the Spike Lee independent narrative film on race relations *Do the Right Thing* (1989).

Held at New York University and organized with a committee of distributors, media activists, and NYSCA administrators, B. Ruby Rich noted the conference brought together the "biggest players like the Museum of Modern Art and the Whitney Museum" with smaller entities such as community media and the nonprofit film distributors "to force them to talk to each other about what gets shown." For Rich, "Show the Right Thing" was "not a confrontational event, but [was] to create a level playing field that assumed change could happen." The conference probed exhibition, an increasingly polarized debate about cultural equity in New York City. Community-based media organizations questioned why funding was being funneled to major mainstream institutions to program artists of color rather than to community organizations.[12]

Another development tested the role of IFS. After a decade of political organizing to push public television to engage independent producers by organizations such as the Association of Independent Video and Filmmakers (AIVF), in 1988, Congress instituted a separate fund for independent producers to promote diversity by giving voice to minority, underserved, and underrepresented populations.[13] By 1991, the Independent Television and Video Service (ITVS) was formed, funding independent documentaries for public television.[14] ITVS was created to foster diversity, innovation, and plurality.[15] With the emergence of the Association of Independent Film and Video Makers in 1978 and the institution of ITVS in 1991, independent no longer meant artisanal. Independent now represented a movement of filmmakers who worked outside of commercial institutions as a constituency. Independent documentary was linked with public television and its larger funding opportunities. Larry Daressa worked at distributor California Newsreel and had served on the ITVS board. In 1995, he questioned how ITVS would reconcile serving independent producers and dealing with underserved audiences. He identified challenges in community service, emerging technologies, open calls, and production partnerships.[16]

During Tom Johnson's presidency, the expansion of the independent media ecosystem of production, distribution, and exhibition engaging festivals, libraries, media arts organizations, and museums pushed IFS to reconsider its role. It no longer served as a unique venue for independent film and video or the only place for meaningful discussions about documentary and experimental film. The US independent media nonprofit field had developed business models based on grants as well as rental fees from universities. Festivals showcased works produced outside commercial sectors and convened communities, generating recognition and reviews.[17]

The Flaherty Seminar's economic and identity crises surfaced in its administration, board, programming, and in the seminar itself. The number of paying participants declined. The seminar assumed many different shapes: multiple programmers representing different identities; offshore programs in Latvia and Israel; partnerships with universities that could provide funds, space, and infrastructure; and themed programs. The executive directors were mostly women (Sally Berger) and included women of color (Bobbie Tsumagari, 1994–95; Michelle Materre, 1995–97).[18] L. Somi Roy was the first male executive director. The Flaherty Seminar struggled for an institutional identity and a role in a nonprofit, public media landscape it had never participated in as an organization. It had always operated as more of an outlier, retreat, and think tank, despite its significant impact on distributors, filmmakers, and programmers. The 50 percent reduction in grant funds, the changing contours of the independent media sector in the United States, the insistence on more multicultural board development and programming, and the pressures of the culture wars precipitated enormous organizational crises.

Sally Berger assumed the executive director position in 1989, a position she held for six years. She entered an organization rife with historical and institutional contradictions: although it needed to adapt to the recalibrated independent media landscape in order to survive, it clung fervently to its traditions of engaging participants in postscreening discussions, promoting a secluded, shared experience for approximately a hundred participants, and showing works on film. Festivals, media arts organizations, and schools adopted strategies of immersion in film culture and its debates, weakening the claims of the seminar's unique contributions. Its small group of mostly East Coast–based participants convened for fierce and intimate exchanges framed the seminar within an aura of privileged elitism out of step with media funders' goals of public engagement. The cost of attending the seminar was expensive. A cloistered environment, the Flaherty Seminar's small numbers of attendees compared to a film festival raised questions of engagement with underserved audiences.

Berger attended her first seminar at the urging of Deirdre Boyle, a historian of documentary as well as video activism and art teaching at Fordham University. Berger was enrolled in one of Boyle's classes. Berger received what was then called a grant-in-aid, a fellowship awarded to emerging makers, scholars, and curators. For Berger, the seminar's power was a "shared experience where people meet and engage with good content that is well considered and carefully selected."[19]

At the end of his term as president of IFS (1987–89), Jack Churchill recognized a need for the organization to move in new directions. An educational filmmaker whose work had screened at seminars in the 1950s, he had a five-decades-long commitment to the Flaherty Seminar. He asked Sally to take the job as executive director. Berger was working part-time in the video area of the Museum of Modern Art (MoMA). Symptomatic of the institutional crises unsettling the seminar as it transitioned from a family-run organization, first with the Flaherty family and then with the Van Dykes, Berger was the first IFS administrator to be called an executive director, the language of the nonprofit arts sector.[20]

The executive director title operated as a smokescreen for an organization in disarray. Berger was hired as a part-time paid employee, splitting her time between IFS and MoMA. This part-time status underscored the organization's limited financial stability. The Flaherty Seminar's reputation far exceeded its resources. Reflecting on her six-year stint as executive director, Berger noted, "everything was on a shoestring": she had to unpack the office from a New York City apartment where IFS records had been stored in deteriorating cardboard boxes. Tom Johnson offered to house the office in the basement of his brownstone rent-free.[21]

As Berger recalled, during this period the board had "a hard time coming to consensus or agreement."[22] Contentious issues about identity politics and representation continued. Questions about how to diversify the board, the organization, the participants, and the programming that had spawned in the 1980s persisted, infusing board meetings with debates about direction and purpose, exacerbated by reduced grant support.[23] From 1990 to 1994, the board of trustees included a mix of administrators, artists, filmmakers, programmers, and scholars from East Coast institutions. It became more diverse, with more African Americans, Asians, and women—a shift from the club-like, white male boards of the earlier decades.

In the 1990s, the board included Barbara Abrash (New York University), Austin Allen (filmmaker), Pat Aufderheide (American University), Mary Lea Bandy (MoMA), Carroll P. Blue (independent filmmaker), Pearl Bowser (filmmaker), Ruth Bradley (*Wide Angle* and Athens International Film Festival), Jack Churchill (filmmaker), John Columbus (Black Maria Film and Video Festival), Faye Ginsburg (New York University), Henry Hampton (executive producer of *Eyes on the Prize*), Richard Herskowitz (Cornell Cinema), Tom Johnson (independent filmmaker and philanthropist), Scott MacDonald (Utica College), Christine McDonald (librarian), Louis Massiah (Scribe Video Center), William Sloan (MoMA) Edin Velez (video artist), Lise Yasui (filmmaker), and Patricia R. Zimmermann (Ithaca College).

During the 1990s, the number of paid seminar participants declined. Full-pay participants were needed subsidize the airfare and housing costs of national and international filmmakers. No longer the intimate gathering of preceding decades, the seminar now needed at least a hundred participants for economic viability. About 10 percent to 25 percent of the participants received what IFS termed grants-in-aid, a program supporting the attendance of emerging artists, programmers, and scholars. These subsidies covered only 50 percent of the seminar's registration. Since the 1950s, the seminar had operated on a commitment to creating intergenerational dialogues between emerging and established filmmakers, programmers, and scholars. This mission distinguished the seminar from more market-driven film festivals. In the 1980s, the registration fee—which included room, board, and all the films for one full week—averaged about $500. By 2000, the registration fee for the full seminar increased to $700.[24]

In response to declines in full-paying participants and grant reductions, the board adopted a multipronged strategy for organizational viability and visibility. To save money on hosting filmmakers and space rental, the board reduced the length of the seminar from a full Saturday to Saturday week to a shorter week, running from Saturday to Thursday.[25] It initiated a "special weekend package" for a reduced rate of $400 to recruit more Flaherty veterans. Senior-level distributors, festival directors, filmmakers, librarians, and programmers who supplied financial resources and institutional memory could not afford a week away from their jobs. The weekend package was designed to present an attractive alternative to longtime attendees.[26]

The board reached out to two undeveloped constituencies: academics in cinema studies and funders interested in supporting scholarships for emerging makers. Academics had attended the seminar since the 1950s. For some Flaherty veterans, however, the influx of film studies and visual anthropology academics in the 1970s and 1980s with their critical theory–inflected style threatened the tenets of nonpreconception and open dialogue. Some felt the academics yanked the seminar away from filmmakers and their processes, promoting an inaccessible, overly dense, theoretical language.[27]

However, in 1992, the organization desperately needed full registration fees—an income source never fully cultivated. Unlike the rest of the financially strapped independent media field, professors worked at institutions with resources to support their professional development. The seminar ran in the summer months when they were not in classrooms delivering courses. The festival circuit spanned September to May, exactly when professors needed to be on campus in their classrooms. Trustees Scott MacDonald and Patricia Zimmermann—upstate New York college professors—and Tom Johnson sent a letter to academics, urging them to attend the seminar. Their letter pitched the seminar as an antidote to scholarly conferences: "unlike academic conferences where we present papers and hope to find time for film and video screenings during the late post conference hours, the Flaherty Seminar foregrounds screenings and discussions about them."[28]

The tactic to attract more faculty offered an added advantage: it increased the seminar's visibility because this constituency wrote books, journalistic reviews, and scholarly essays. If the seminar seemed invisible in the 1980s and prompted the board to ask where were the writers who could move it out of obscurity, by the 1990s, the seminar's controversies, debates, and filmmaker confrontations were much more public. Articles appeared in *Afterimage, Felix, The Independent, International Documentary, The Village Voice*, and *Wide Angle*.[29]

The board and executive director expanded the grants-in-aid funds by reaching out to new institutional funders. For decades, interest from IFS's small endowments—its Leo Dratfield Endowment and Paul Ronder Endowment—as well as gifts from former Flaherty attendees' contributions subsidized grants-in-aid. In 1992, the Pew Charitable Trusts awarded a special three-year grant to IFS to support six Philadelphia-based video artists and producers to attend the seminar, now billed as "a forum dedicated to innovative and cutting edge film and video."[30]

In 1991, these continually contentious, unresolved issues about defunding, diversity, race, and representation as well as the purpose of the Flaherty reached a climax in IFS board dissensus over a never-materialized seminar to showcase indigenous media makers. Anthropologist Faye Ginsburg proposed a 1992 seminar featuring Amazonian, Australian, and North American Arctic indigenous filmmakers. After the board approved the proposal, Ginsburg invited visual anthropologist Jay Ruby to collaborate. Both were IFS board members at the time. IFS sent out an open call for work. According to Ruby's analysis, "Faye was the most knowledgeable person on this subject. None of the board members shared her knowledge."[31]

The goal was for the Flaherty to intervene into the popular culture colonialist imaginary circulating around the quincentennial of Christopher Columbus's so-called "discovery" of America in 1492. Native communities across the Americas organized to protest this anniversary as an obfuscation of colonialism and genocide. To mount this ambitious program, Ginsburg proposed to collaborate with indigenous media groups. Her proposed collaborators included Vincent Carelli (Amazon/Video nas Aldeias), Zacharias Kunuk (Inuit), Victor Masayesva Jr. (Hopi), Merata Mita (Maori), Alanis Obomsawin (Abenaki), Rachel Perkins (Arrente/Kalkadoon) and Loretta Todd (Metis/Cree).[32] Ginsburg's idea was that these filmmakers could recommend "new work coming out of their worlds."[33] During the 1980s, critical ethnography advocated for collaborative relationships. Their program would extend these concepts to the programming process. She invited anthropologist Jay Ruby to join her. Ginsburg and Ruby were central figures in the scholarly discourse rethinking visual anthropology's racialized power relations.

In a November 1991 press release, IFS described the 1992 seminar as exploring "how cultural identities are being negotiated through film and video." The press release explained the 1992 seminar program goals: "We are particularly interested in works done by and in collaboration with members of disenfranchised groups, and ethnic, religious, and sexual minorities who are using film and video as a powerful means to claim and revive identity and history, and to envision a cultural future. One focus of the program is the recent innovative work being done by indigenous peoples—Native American, Inuit, Amazonian Indians, Australian Aborigines, Papua New Guineans, and other Pacific Islanders—who for so long have been the 'exotic' subjects of the documentary gaze."[34]

In contrast to other programmers who curated works through a referral process and research, Ginsburg and Ruby issued an open call for animation, documentary, experimental, and narrative forms that "carry on the Flaherty tradition of cinematic exploration."[35] The press release evidenced Ginsburg and Ruby's fluency with ethnographic representations, identity politics, multiculturalism, and how indigenous work rerouted them.

This proposal to explore indigenous-produced media spanning cable television, community-based works, and transnational networks came at a pivotal point for the board and for the organization. Since the 1950s, the Flaherty had experienced a somewhat uneven relationship with university-based scholars. It needed their access to resources (their institutions could provide funding for registrations and host seminars) and their expertise in film aesthetics and histories. But it found their analytical, intellectual approach ancillary to its public image focused on films and filmmakers.

The debates about whether two white, North American–based, university-located anthropologists could program a seminar featuring indigenous makers pitched practitioners against scholars within a larger national identity politics debate. After reading this proposal, board members Pearl Bowser[36] (programmer) and Louis Massiah (filmmaker), important figures in African American documentary, sent a fax to the board. Their fax outlined their political concerns about two white scholars presenting the work of indigenous makers. They asked the board to retain an indigenous programmer.[37] Ruby contends he never received a copy of the memo nor was he directly informed of the board's decision to cancel the seminar due to excessive transportation costs.[38] Ruby learned of the board's reversal of its earlier decision to support the program. Feeling resolution was hopeless, Ginsburg and Ruby resigned as programmers.[39] According to Ruby and Ginsburg, "it is crucial to realize that the Bowser/Massiah memo provided no names of qualified people who were members of an indigenous community nor did any board member or the president or the executive secretary offer any suggestions."[40] However, it is historically important to understand that IFS had a history of attempting to address underrepresentation through programming initiatives. In 1978, Barbara Van Dyke and Ruby mounted an Arden House seminar entitled "The Underrepresented in US Television," a collaboration with African American, Latino/Latina, and Native coprogrammers.[41]

After the 1989 program focusing on African and African diaspora filmmaking, the Flaherty Seminar seemed to be gradually figuring out a way to address concerns from both funders and participants about its white, East Coast bias. New board members, such as Pearl Bowser, Henry Hampton, Juan Mandelbaum, and Louis Massiah, indicated a more multicultural board. But this more diverse board could not isolate itself from larger identity politics debates. The quincentenary of Columbus's "discovery" of America and the ensuing postcolonial critique launched by indigenous groups seeped into board debates.

The Ginsburg/Ruby proposal for the 1992 seminar probing fourth world cinemas can be situated within the international political struggles over interpretation and representation of 1492. Despite the claims of racism mounted by some on the board, Ginsburg and Ruby's ideas for the seminar clearly aligned with those of indigenous groups critiquing the US government's celebration plans. Rather than focusing on the conquest of the Americas, their seminar proposed to carve out space for indigenous makers—the conquered, as noted in some circles—to tell their own stories. The larger debates surrounding the quincentennial pitched modernist unities against postmodern multiplicities. After nearly a decade of national debates about identity and multiculturalism, the rancor over the quincentennial moved postcolonial critiques into the public sphere. Many Latino/Latina, Latin American, and Native American indigenous groups objected to the anniversary celebration and launched counteractivities. The debate was larger than the Flaherty board or individuals.

In 1984, during Ronald Reagan's presidency, Congress created the Christopher Columbus Quincentenary Jubilee Commission to celebrate the "New World" turning five hundred. Arriving during a decade where multiculturalist politics pushed for more minority representation in cultural and educational institutions, the commission and quincentenary generated significant public debate about "American identity, nationalism, and 'otherness.'"[42] Native groups across the country protested. The commission "failed to sit an Indian member," prompting major public agencies such as the National Endowment for the Humanities and private foundations such as the MacArthur Foundation to announce special initiatives to support Native American topics and perspectives. [43]

As Alicia Gaspar de Alba has observed, the quincentennial was conceived from the point of view of the conquerors rather than the conquered. She argues that counter-quincentennial groups formed in North, Central, and South America to protest the continuing issues of colonialism and its aftermath with conferences, gatherings, performances, protests, and publications, and symposia.[44] As Robert Rodriguez explained in a 1990 *Los Angeles Times* article, while the US government saw the anniversary in 1992 as cause for celebration of national identity and discovery, indigenous groups throughout the Americas interpreted the anniversary as five hundred years of indigenous resistance to colonialism, "one of the bloodiest chapters in the annals of human history." Rodriguez noted the proposed celebrations erased the colonialism of native peoples, "to deny the genocide, the theft of land, the destruction of civilizations, and the enslavement of indigenous peoples of the Americas."[45]

Indigenous groups throughout the Americas mounted strong opposition to the quincentennial, arguing it was an anniversary of enslavement, genocide, and torture.[46] Peter Ricketson analyzed the quincentennial controversies as a conflict between the master narrative of individualism, opportunity, and progress figured in Christopher Columbus and the emergence of postcolonial countermemories by native peoples regarding long-standing grievances about genocide and environmental destruction. For those protesting the quincentennial, Columbus represented exploitation and cultural hegemony. Indigenous groups campaigned against the anniversary. The National Council of Catholic Bishops and the Protestant National Council of Churches joined them.[47]

The exclusion of indigenous voices in the planned official proceedings of the congressional commission animated what Jeremy Smith has called a "transnational politics of indigenous modernity" in historical revisions and protests. Alliance building between indigenous groups created new continental networks.[48]

Ginsburg and Ruby's proposal must be read within the context of these tumultuous debates about colonialism, multiculturalism, postcolonialism, and white hegemony. As the US government fashioned a cohesive national imaginary, indigenous groups marshaled counter-readings. Ginsburg and Ruby's proposed seminar clearly aligned with multicultural and postcolonialist interventions. Showcasing works by indigenous makers, it rerouted the Flaherty away from its high-art emphasis on auteurs toward exploration of communities excluded from documentary but often the object of its gaze.

Questions about the role of anthropologists had percolated through the seminar since the 1950s. Jean Rouch had attended. Frances had strategized about how to connect with ethnography to legitimate Robert Flaherty's legacy. A seminal film studied at the early seminars and screened frequently in subsequent decades, *Nanook of the North* had been both deified as one of the first independent films and vilified as a colonialist imaginary.[49] Although reenacted, it was sometimes positioned as an ethnographic film of Inuit peoples. In the 1960s, the seminar often screened direct cinema and ethnography side by side. In the 1970s, visual anthropologists such as Jay Ruby and Sol Worth had regularly attended the seminars. Many anthropologists who attended the seminar critiqued the colonialist, racialized gaze of classical ethnography and instead advocated for a countermovement of collaborative, participatory, and sometimes poetic ethnographic field work, film practice, and scholarly writing grounded in a fierce examination of image ethics: Timothy Asch, Sarah Elder, Robert Gardner, Faye Ginsburg, Jake Homiak, John Marshall, Jay Ruby, and Sol Worth. Thus, Ginsburg and Ruby's conceptualization of an indigenous program converged with a decades-old seminar trajectory investigating ethnography.

A lack of context and information was evident in board debates. "There was a whole board discussion on our proposal based on ideas from people who did not know anything about indigenous media," Ruby reflected.[50] The board debate underscored IFS's difficulties in absorbing scholarly debates. However, it is important to situate the Bowser/Massiah questions about the proposed program as a significant driver of IFS organizational change to rethink the films presented and programmers selected through a multicultural framework. Their letter did not suggest dropping the proposed seminar. Instead, they queried whether an indigenous programmer could be added to counteract the perception of two white programmers presenting indigenous makers of color, which appeared to replicate a colonialist, racist modality despite the collaborative practices Ginsburg and Ruby advanced in their own research.[51]

Questions concerning the power relations of ethnography and the ethical solutions offered in indigenous produced work were not new. Influenced by the collaborative work of Jean Rouch, anthropologists and ethnographic filmmakers had engaged in significant critique of the colonialist gaze, the racialized power relations of representing others, and traditional ethnography's imperialist agendas since the 1970s. In their scholarly books and essays published in the late 1980s, critical anthropologists such as James Clifford,

Michael Fisher, David MacDougall, George Marcus, and Jay Ruby questioned traditional ethnographic tropes, arguing for collaborative encounters, complex multiplicities, and the ethics of speaking across differences to replace the one-way power relations of colonialist imaginaries.[52] Faye Ginsburg (Australian aboriginal media), Eric Michaels (Australian aboriginal), and Terry Turner (Kayapo in the Amazon) had published on indigenous-produced media—a major intervention into ethnography and a destabilization of the term *ethnographic film*.[53]

In this larger context, Ginsburg's proposal materialized nearly a decade of conversations and research in critical ethnography and indigenous self-representation in media production now possible with more democratically accessible cable television, portable video technologies, and satellites. Ruby notes that during the early 1990s, "anthropologists were wrestling with what was called the crisis of representation. Both Faye and I had published articles that dealt with the profound problem of who has the right to represent another. I am fairly certain none of the people involved with IFS were aware of how much these issues were being discussed."[54] As Ginsburg noted in her groundbreaking 1991 scholarly essay entitled "Indigenous Media: Faustian Contract or Global Village" published in *Cultural Anthropology*, "indigenous media offers a possible means—social, cultural, and political—for reproducing and transforming cultural identity among people who have experienced massive political, geographic, and economic disruption."[55] For Ginsburg, indigenous media presented a creative solution to the crisis in representation: indigenous people previously figured as exotic others now produced their own representations and new forms of reception.[56]

As Ruby pointed out, Ginsburg was "the leading North American expert on indigenous media." He viewed the vociferous board debate over whether IFS should do the indigenous seminar with two white academics as programmers as an example of the "continuing problems the seminar has had as it has tried, over many decades, to deal with underrepresented minorities."[57] The concept of "programmer," contended Ruby, was an "upper middle-class phenomenon."[58] On the other hand, Massiah and others on the board advanced that programmers needed to emerge from indigenous communities, insisting programming was not based only on academic scholarship but possessed a cultural power relation necessitating open discussion.[59] A daunting logistical problem lurked underneath these debates on indigeneity and the quincentennial: the high expense of international travel costs to bring makers from the Arctic, the Amazon, and Australia to the seminar.

IFS had issued a public announcement about the Ginsburg/Ruby 1992 seminar on indigenous media. After board debates ensued over the Bowser/Massiah fax, Ginsburg and Ruby resigned as programmers and trustees. The seminar was canceled. For Ruby, the class bias and political economies of programmers needed to be addressed, as programmers needed to have jobs that would allow them to program. Writing decades later, Ruby suggested that IFS institute a programmer apprentice initiative where emerging programmers could secure some experience.[60] Sally Berger, the executive director at the time, observed a "politically charged" bifurcation: older trustees saw the seminar as a space where whatever was new in the world of independent media would be screened and discussed while younger trustees thought the seminar should address specific areas emanating from programmer expertise, scholarly debates, and the urgencies of presenting neglected movements or works.[61] Because she had experienced firsthand how the seminar created community and encouraged emerging makers, programmers, and scholars beyond the programming content, these debates prompted her to think through the role of the seminar more carefully.[62]

In early 1992, IFS established a new seminar structure with multiple programmers, comprised of board members. With financial crises and cutbacks threatening the sustainability of the organization, they declined honoraria.[63] The team was multigenerational and multiracial: William Sloan, from MoMA, was seminar éminence grise; Austin Allen, a filmmaker, was African American; Jacqueline Tshaka, assistant director of the National Black Programming Consortium, was African American; and Lise Yasui, a filmmaker, was Asian American. The programmers represented diverse backgrounds: Ruth Bradley was director of the Athens International Film and Video Festival and editor of *Wide Angle*; John Columbus directed the Black Maria Film and Video Festival, and Scott MacDonald was an experimental film historian.[64] This seminar was less global and more North American than the Ginsburg/Ruby indigenous makers proposal. Each programmer described their approach, a weave of ideas about avant-garde film, archival propaganda films, multiculturalism, personal films, power, and representation. Entitled "From These Shores," the 1992 seminar was the first programmed around an explicit theme, perhaps because IFS sought to unify the disparate ideas of six programmers. The press release explained: "Voice and perspective, power and representations, and hybrid forms and expression are issues to be discussed in light of this challenging new work."[65]

News of the change in programmers drifted into independent media sectors. In a 1992 article for *The Squealer* called "Report from Flaherty," Meg Knowles wrote that Ginsburg and Ruby had pulled out after "vociferous objections were raised to the notion that two white American could fairly represent the study of indigenous populations."[66] In *Afterimage*, Jesse Lerner analyzed the 1992 Ginsburg/Ruby seminar cancellation due to "prohibitive costs of bringing representatives of these projects from all over the world, and in part because of the obvious imperialist connotations of first world anthropologists Faye Ginsberg [sic] and Jay Ruby curating third world media."[67] Sally Berger responded with a corrective letter to the editor in the February 1993 issue of *Afterimage*. She pointed out that although the board of trustees felt there was not "adequate funding to bring indigenous makers from more remote locations to the seminar (despite fundraising efforts), the other concern was one that pervades many contemporary efforts at multicultural programming: who is entitled to curate whose work?"[68]

The board debates over the Ginsburg/Ruby indigenous programming proposal amplified many unresolved issues in IFS as a nonprofit organization as well as the seminar's programming. These debates revolved around questions of diversity, funding, organizational structure, process, race, and representation. The board dissensus about the Ginsburg/Ruby program unsettled the Flaherty organization. It raised questions about its function, identity, impact, operations, and role within independent film and media culture.

In 1993, Richard Herskowitz assumed the presidency of IFS, a position he held until 1995. The head of Cornell Cinema, a cinematheque with a long history at Cornell

University, he had programmed the 1987 seminar and served on the 1990 Riga, Latvia, seminar programming team. An adept programmer, Herskowitz brought enormous experience in thinking through how film programming and postscreening sessions facilitated alternative public spheres.

The board assessed discussions, a seminar legacy and one of its distinguishing characteristics. Directed to the filmmaker, the discussions connected works to larger ideas and probed process. However, confined to forty-five minutes, discussions required careful design. To address discussions dominated by instrumental queries regarding a film's production and the maker's background, Herskowitz instituted background sheets with the film's dates, description, director's bio, and running time. The sheets featured quotes from significant reviews. The handouts indicated a necessary professionalization.

Herskowitz helmed an organization unsettled by its own disorientation in the independent media landscape: it had an institutional crisis about identity politics and race issues. What was the purpose of the seminar? What did it provide participants? In 1994, Herskowitz initiated a board discussion to probe the position, purpose, and value of the seminar in order to develop long-range planning. Barbara Abrash (Center for Media, Culture, and History at New York University), Patricia Aufderheide (a communications professor at American University), Carroll Parrott Blue (film director who had worked on *Eyes on the Prize*), John Columbus (director of the Black Maria Film and Video Festival), Kathy High (feminist video artist and a professor at Rensselaer Polytechnic Institute), Cara Mertes (former head of the Sundance Documentary Institute), and Dorothy Thigpen (Women Make Movies and Third World Newsreel) participated.

The scholarly journal *Wide Angle* reprinted the discussion transcript, entitled "Old Model, New World," a pungent title illustrating IFS's intense contradictions between legacy, more insular models, and new challenges from the larger independent media communities. The discussion showed tensions between the Flaherty's own traditions and the need to adjust to historical and social realignments.[69] Board members outlined the seminar's historical legacies: to engage a passionate community to brainstorm the potentials of independent media; to experience its unique immersion, intensity, isolation; to explore; to participate in a retreat; to see humanistic, poetic documentaries. Herskowitz analyzed the crises: "If the economic climate were different, if the arts weren't in a state of crisis, then an organization like this would get the funding it needs."[70] The discussion noted new challenges: class, gender, and race issues needed more room. Was a retreat in an inaccessible location outdated? Was the Flaherty "the independent media community's retreat center"? Was there still the need for intergenerational dialogue?[71] As John Columbus observed, "the time together arouses passions that can be problematic, but it's the kind of cathartic experience that rejuvenates us."[72]

Between 1996 and 2000, IFS board debates about the culture wars, economic disarray, identity, organizational problems, and programmers escalated. Juan Mandelbaum[73] split the presidency for one year with Pearl Bowser. In his role as president, Mandelbaum was concerned films were selected for the seminar based on the politics of representation, rather than aesthetic quality. Mandelbaum believed in the seminar's sustaining power: "The Flaherty had a mystique, an unwritten mission to be a meeting place, a safe environment to meet and explore together around nonfiction film . . . being open to be surprised—this is the essence of the seminar."[74] He understood the organization's unique mission to convene those in nonfiction film. But he saw a larger organization wracked by serious financial, organizational, and planning issues. During his tenure, board membership was extremely diverse in terms of gender and race.

Trustees represented the multiple sectors of independent media: academics, experimental work, film distribution, public television, and work for hire. Board members included Barbara Abrash (independent producer and administrator at the Center for Media, Culture, and History at New York University), Orlando Bagwell (director of episodes of *Eyes on the Prize*), John Butler (audio engineer and faculty at Ohio University), Phred Churchill (cinematographer for public television documentaries and coeditor of *The Gates of Heavenly Peace*), Maria DeLuca (filmmaker, *Green Streets*), Kathy High (feminist filmmaker, *I Need Your Full Cooperation*), Charles Hobson (television producer), Dorothy Thigpen (Women Make Movies, a distributor), L. Somi Roy (independent programmer), Ernesto Sanchez (entertainment industry attorney), Margarita De La Vega Hurtado (Latin American film specialist from the University of Michigan), and Philip Wilde (a professional cinematographer/producer who owned a video production company). Debates about augmenting the number of minority applicants receiving grants-in-aid, dealing with the culture wars and representations, and diversifying the board, filmmakers, and participants rippled through board meetings.

Mandelbaum assessed an organization wracked by administrative deficiencies. The board and executive directors lacked expertise in nonprofit media arts organization business operations, especially financial management of endowments and income.[75] The key issues during Mandelbaum's presidency were "to diversify and be more inclusive."[76] Mandelbaum noted he headed a board where "no one could read a financial statement, had no idea on running finances, had no idea on how to run a nonprofit professionally."[77] For Mandelbaum, the IFS board in the 1980s had functioned "almost like an amateur organization, like a club, with minimal expenses, their only cost in covering the seminar . . . an old white guys' club that had been going on for years."[78]

Mandelbaum recruited Patti Bruck and Tom Johnson to the board. Both had connections to family foundations for possible funding. He worked on organizing IFS's three endowments: the Leo Dratfield Endowment, the Paul Ronder Endowment, and the Sol Worth Endowment. He improved IFS's disorganized, minimal fund-raising profile. He argued seminar alumni, if cultivated more systematically, constituted the largest potential source of gifts. With a part-time executive director and a board unfamiliar with professional fund-raising strategies, IFS's limited resources left these new directions unrealized.

During the 1990s, IFS encountered problems attracting enough full-paying participants to subsidize grants-in-aid and seminar operations. Mandelbaum's solution was to invite funders to experience the seminar firsthand. NYSCA and other funders attacked it for not reaching a wider audience, especially in the context of the burgeoning film festival circuit. With its one hundred participants ensconced in a remote rural setting, the seminar seemed too contained, too elitist, and too precious in comparison, particularly with no written record of its impact on the field, makers, or participants.

In 1997, the board weathered a serious financial crisis: insufficient funds to mount a seminar. Grants from government and private funds had declined. Under Mandelbaum's leadership, IFS suspended the annual full-week seminar. It launched a series of short seminars dubbed "Flaherty on the Road." This dispersed, cost-saving strategy drew on the resources of former featured filmmakers, Flaherty participants, and past programmers at large institutions who could provide financial contributions through partnerships for mini-seminars. This strategy addressed the seminar's lack of visibility by producing six seminars in different locations across the year, more accessible because of a reduced price based on a long weekend and host institution subsidies. These six mini-seminars were presented in collaboration with host institutions around the United States, partnerships leveraging the Flaherty reputation with more resource-rich academic institutions and museums.

The "Flaherty on the Road" flyer explained these smaller seminars were "to develop new audiences in various regions across the country" and to "facilitate connections among a variety of constituencies across the United States, especially emerging filmmakers, students and film professionals." The six 1997 programs included "Gender Dichotomies and Social Spectacle," programmed by Bill Horrigan at the Wexner Center for the Arts in Ohio in April; "Animated Images and Exploration of Multicultural Talents," a two-day seminar programmed by Pearl Bowser at Sony Music in New York City in August; "Exploration in Memory and Modernity," programmed by Michelle Materre and Patricia R. Zimmermann for three days in October at Ithaca College in upstate New York; "Documenting the Community," programmed by Ayoka Chenzira at the City College of New York in October; "Identifying Latin: Contemporary Works from the Caribbean Diaspora," programmed by Pam Sport and Judith Escalona in New York City in October; and "Passin' It On," programmed by Alonzo Speight, Tami Gold, and George Custon at the College of Staten Island in New York City in November.[79]

These seminars explored regional film movements, often overlooked by the larger, more internationally focused seminars in the 1990s. The Wexner Seminar showcased Ohio-based filmmakers Austin Allen, Daniel Friedman, and Julia Reichert. The Bowser animation program focused on Tee Collins, a well-known animator of children's programming. It also showcased African American animators. The "Documenting the Community" program at City College of New York screened works of African American documentary and experimental filmmakers St. Clair Bourne, Ayoka Chenzira, Bill Miles, and Stanley Nelson. The seminar at College of Staten Island drew on the Flaherty tradition of mentoring emerging makers by programming documentary production pedagogues Tami Gold and Alonzo Speight with their students. The seminar at Ithaca College highlighted makers from the upstate New York region. It featured a Cinema 16 revival and Ithaca College alumnus Daniel Reeves with *Obsessive Becoming* and his video installation *Eingang*. This seminar was the first Flaherty Seminar to program works produced in digital interfaces, with presentations by Branda Miller, with her hybrid analog and digital project *Witness to the Future*, a CD-ROM, video, and database of five hundred websites exploring environmental issues, and Reginald Woolery with MMM CD-ROM on the Million Man March. Erik Barnouw spoke with *Nanook of the North*.[80]

These shortened seminars did more than serve as placeholders to wait out a crises. They also opened up the Flaherty to consider the value of a presence throughout the year.

By the end of the decade, the board needed to professionalize as a nonprofit with a scalable, sustainable strategy. Alyce Myatt was a MacArthur Foundation media program officer and a strategic planning consultant. She had attended the 1998 Flaherty to "get educated in independent film." Invited to serve on the board in 2000, she observed IFS challenges to secure funding and to win grants. She encountered an extremely dysfunctional, familial organization, a club of entrenched insiders rather than a board with skills to advance the organization through fiscal responsibility and governance. Blinded by in-fighting, the board, according to Myatt, did not understand the dramatic expansion of the independent film and media environment. A seminar for only one hundred people was a perennially hard sell to funders. Participants were privileged "special campers" attending a week-long closed gathering.

Myatt ascertained four pressing sustainability issues: facilities, fund-raising, location, and questions about the Flaherty Seminar's role in an increasingly developed independent media world of community media centers, festivals, museums, and universities. The Flaherty was no longer the only place to discuss independent film. For Myatt, the seminar operated as an outlier: it served very few people and defied categorization. Expensive, isolated, and small, the Flaherty seemed tangential to the larger environment of public media.[81]

However, Myatt experienced the Flaherty Seminar's contradictions. It was not run like a functioning nonprofit arts organization: it lacked clarity of purpose and professionalism. Yet it provided an intense intellectual engagement with media not available elsewhere. Myatt recognized the Flaherty Seminars as a specialized exhibition site with exceptionally sophisticated curation that required artistry and intellectuality. Myatt understood the Flaherty Seminars offered a unique "place to be conceptual . . . with a rigorous curatorial process that powerfully juxtaposes the old with the new." The seminars possessed extraordinary ability to bring together people from different parts of the independent media ecology for intense and passionate conceptual dialogues. Participation in the seminar spurred immediate immersion in complex ideas, a ripple effect on participants' curating, media making practices, teaching, and writing.[82]

Despite these administrative liabilities, continuing confrontations about identity politics and multiculturalism and financial challenges, the 1990s were an innovative time for the seminar. Significant films were screened from around the globe. Debates unfurled about representation. Postcolonial and postmodern approaches dislodged documentary from its indexical legacies. Programming extended the Herskowitz 1987 heterogeneous model with new forms and different political economies of media spanning the archival, the artisanal, and more industrial modes of production. The days of the lone programmer with command of the entire field were extinguished. The expanded independent media field—spanning genres, modes, nations, and regions, as well as multiple technologies from 16mm, 35mm, installation, and video—was vast. This complex terrain required a team possessing different kinds of expertise to address areas funders felt needed attention, such as different international cinemas and identity politics. The 1990s thus heralded the institution of programming teams.

Multiple programmers combined knowledge with their own connections. The 1989 joint program of Pearl Bowser and Grant Munro dismantled the prevalence of a single programmer. By the 1990s, programming teams ranging from two to six people produced almost every seminar. As the independent film landscape expanded, the seminar's programming required more labor resources to conceptualize the program and to preview films. Potential programmers could not carve out time away from their full-time programming jobs to undertake the preparatory work to plot out a week-long seminar. Collaboration was not only more efficient but also multiplied resources.

Although its club-like, familialist ideology and inadequate nonprofit management skills challenged IFS administrative viability, programmers' credentials suggested the seminar's curatorial orientation was advancing. In the 1990s, the programmers' academic backgrounds, extensive exhibition experience, and institutional affiliations with high-profile festivals and museums indicated the expansion and professionalization of the independent media field in alternative exhibition. These curatorial and research skills were necessary to program an effective seminar in the vastly differentiated independent media ecology spanning activist projects, commercial theatrical documentaries, emerging technologies, experimental work, hybrid forms, installation, investigative projects, public television, and video. If earlier programmers were chosen based on their long-term seminar attendance, programmers in the 1990s were selected based on access to new works, credentials, curatorial track record, and experience. Programmers now needed institutional support—a job where they would get a paycheck, observe audience interactions, and see a range of work.

During this period, most programmers possessed graduate training in film studies, filmmaking, or the humanities. They were full-time professional programmers at major institutions: Linda Blackaby (Philadelphia International Film Festival), Ruth Bradley (Athens International Film and Video Festival), John Columbus (Black Maria Film and Video Festival), Coco Fusco (Third World Newsreel), Stephen Gallagher (The Kitchen, New York), Kathy Geritz (Pacific Film Archive), Richard Herskowitz (Virginia Film Festival), Bruce Jenkins (Walker Art Center), Louis Massiah (Scribe Video, Philadelphia), Richard Peterson (USA Film Festival, Dallas), L. Somi Roy (Asia Society), William Sloan (MoMA), Bo Smith (Museum of Fine Arts, Boston), and Jacqueline Tshaka (National Black Programming Consortium). Several programmers were film academics. They produced specialty programming at their institutions, although not with the frequency or the diverse audiences of the festivals or museums: Austin Allen (Cleveland State University), Erik Barnouw (Columbia University), Tami Gold (Hunter College), Kathy High (Princeton University), Margarita De La Vega Hurtado (University of Michigan), Scott MacDonald (Utica College), Chon Noriega (University of California, Los Angeles [UCLA]), and Patricia R. Zimmermann (Ithaca College).

During this period of crises, IFS produced two offshore seminars, only the second time in its history (the first was the Puerto Rico seminar in 1961), which represented a major accomplishment. These seminars were collaborations and partnerships. Board member Raul Zaritsky had been doing film work in the Soviet Union and saw firsthand the explosion of documentary under Glasnost. He worked with Tom Johnson to establish a partnership with the Latvian Cinematographers Union.[83] The Latvian team programming the Riga Seminar insisted American academics deliver papers on documentary theory, a practice never sanctioned at a stateside seminar.[84] The Riga, Latvia seminar, which explored Glasnost documentary practices and American independent documentary, was held in 1990, and the Israel seminar, entitled "Investigating the Real," in 1998. These two offshore seminars bookend this period.

A large team of Americans and Latvians programmed the Riga Seminar: Erik Barnouw, Richard Herskowitz, Tom Johnson, Amos Vogel, Raul Zaritsky, and Patricia R. Zimmermann on the American team; and Abraham Kalzkins, the documentary director, and Ivars Seleckis, the Latvian cinematographer and director, on the Latvian team.[85] A joint collaboration between IFS and the Latvians, the seminar occurred at an exciting historical juncture where new forms of documentary that were not Soviet state-sponsored and promoted an independent, individual vision were being produced under Glasnost, an opening of culture and society. The seminar took place less than a year after the 1989 fall of the Berlin Wall, before the dissolution of the Union of the Soviet Socialist Republics (USSR).[86] The American films screened mapped diverse documentary practices. Collaborative ethnographic models (Sarah Elder with *The Drums of Winter*, 1988; George Stoney with *How the Myth Was Made*, 1978), compilation (Erik Barnouw with *Hiroshima-Nagasaki 1945*; Tom Johnson with *No Place to Hide*, 1982), direct cinema (Les Blank with *Blues According to Lighnin' Hopkins*, 1968), and guerrilla video (TVTV, *Four More Years*, 1972) were shown. American experimental work was also programmed: feminist film (Su Friedrich, *The Ties That Bind*; Indu Krishnan, *Knowing Her Place*, 1990; and Greta Snyder, *Futility*, 1989), queer work (Marlon Riggs, *Tongues Untied*, 1989), and video (Edin Velez, *Meta Mayan*, 1981). This seminar also screened more realist expository works, including activist exposé (Christine Choy, *Who Killed Vincent Chin?*, 1987; Pamela Yates, *Nicaragua: Report from the Front*, 1983), commercial features (Michael Moore, *Roger and Me*, 1989), investigative film (Errol Morris, *The Thin Blue Line*, 1988), and performative documentary (Steve Roszell, *Writing in Water*, 1984). The Latvian team brought a large range of Glasnost films from different regions of the USSR, with works by Leo Bakradze, Igor Bezrukov, Marina Ivanova, Aron Kanevsky, Artavzad Peleshyan, Alexander Rodnyansky, Henrikas Sablevicius, Alexander Sokurov, Andrei Zagdansky, and Samary Zelikin.[87]

While the American contingent valued the films and writing of Dziga Vertov as inspiration for a formally inventive and socially engaged documentary practice, the Soviet filmmakers embraced Robert Flaherty as a poetic filmmaker possessing an individual vision imagining cinema beyond the state.[88] While the US delegation looked for collectivity and insurgency in Vertov, the Soviet delegation sought individual expression and poetry in Flaherty.[89] With cognac and vodka, the Glasnost filmmakers made toasts at virtually every dinner. This Soviet-style toasting migrated to the stateside seminar. After the Riga seminar, each closing seminar banquet featured multiple toasts to filmmakers, participants, and programmers.

Eight years later, the 1998 Israel seminar developed out of a board member's connections. IFS board member and longtime Flaherty devotee Steve Scheuer wanted a seminar to run in Israel.[90] He financed the entire seminar, a much-needed infusion of capital when IFS battled funding cutbacks. Scheuer was a prominent critic, film and television historian, journalist, and prolific author, who wrote previews previews of television programs in the 1950s. He was the author of *Movies on TV*, published in seventeen editions.[91]

IFS partnered with the new Foundation for Film and Television in Tel Aviv, Israel. The seminar was held on Kfar Blum Kibbutz in Galilee. Mandelbaum made two trips to Israel to iron out the logistics. Barbara Abrash and Linda Blackaby were to program a stateside seminar and then bring the films to Israel, under the theme "Investigating the Real." With the politically charged atmosphere surrounding Israel, IFS insisted on a Palestinian presence. Filmmakers Amos Gitai and Avi Mograbi screened work, as did Ricky Leacock and George Stoney. Israeli participants accused Gitai of being a traitor. The seminar had more impact than anticipated: for the next four years, documentary filmmakers in Israel gathered together for screenings and discussions, emulating the Flaherty model.[92]

As an organization, IFS was recalibrating, redirecting, and rethinking constituencies and content. It experimented with developing models more attractive to funders: partnerships with academic institutions such as the College of Staten Island (1997), Duke University (1999), and Ithaca College (1997), as well as team programming to marshal expertise and represent identity groups. To attract special funding and to edge away from its East Coast, American-centric focus, programming focused on regions such as Russia (1990), the Maghreb (1991), Latin America (1993), and Israel and Palestine (1998). Although a few films had been screened from these areas before, until the late 1980s the seminars primarily concentrated on American, Canadian, and European film.

During this tumultuous period, the seminar changed from promoting the seminar experience and its programmer toward elaborating conceptual and content areas. Paragraphs describing the concepts and film movements to be explored appeared. The 1992 (the year after Ginsburg and Ruby resigned from programming) seminar advertised the theme "From These Shores," featuring a map of Canada and the United States. It was the first seminar to market itself with a theme. If other programmers wove resonances and themes between films, they never revealed their conceptual models: participants discovered these through carefully designed juxtapositions. Three years later, in 1995, Bruce Jenkins and Marlina Gonzalez-Tamrong explicitly organized their curatorial practice with the theme "The Camera Reframed."

The seminar's insistence on actualizing nonpreconception by refusing to announce the films so that participants would be open to new work proved a hard sell to funders and to recruiting new participants. The seminar operated like a secret society for the initiated. The implementation of explicit conceptualizations and themes functioned on three levels. First, the themes demystified the seminar—one could pay one's registration fee and know what would be explored. Second, the themes concretized the mission for funders, clarifying filmmakers, ideas, and underserved constituencies. Third, the themes structured programming choices, rendering programming more dynamic, intellectual, and manageable.

In 1990, Richard Peterson, programmer for the USA Film Festival in Dallas, and Bo Smith, curator at the Museum of Fine Arts in Boston, programmed a themed seminar. The brochure identified special features of the seminar—a shared retreat experience to discuss films. The publicity asserted, "the program will include experimental, narrative, and documentary films and tapes," a phrase of inclusion repeating in most seminar materials across this period. It explicated a terrain: "contemporary cinéma vérité in the context of its thirty year history; the use and manipulation of found footage and archival film in nonfiction work; and a special survey of humor."[93] The brochure contended, "The programmers emphasize that selections will reflect a diversity of cultural perspectives and subject matter."[94]

The 1990 seminar films interwove archival works, cinéma vérité, experimental film, humorous works, and personal documentary—a heterogeneous programming strategy. *I Need Your Full Cooperation* (Kathy High, 1989), *Knowing Her Place* (Indu Krishnan, 1990), *Memories from the Department of Amnesia* (Janice Tanaka, 1989), *Sink or Swim* (Su Friedrich, 1990), and *A Spy in the House That Ruth Built* (Vanalyne Green, 1990) exemplified feminist, personal documentary from significant makers. *DiAna's Hair Ego: AIDS Info Upfront* (Ellen Spiro, 1989), *Green Streets* (Maria DeLuca, 1990), *Paris Is Burning* (Jennie Livingston, 1990), and *Samsara: Death and Rebirth in Cambodia* (Ellen Bruno, 1989) charted the new directions of cinéma vérité as it engaged marginalized communities. Archival films (Rick Prelinger's industrials collected from the Jam Handy Organization such as *Master Hands* 1936, and *Round and Round*, 1939, and from the Calvin Company, *Beware of Metal-itis*, 1936), films mobilizing archival footage to tell different kinds of stories—*Atomic Cafe* (1982) by Pierce Rafferty and Jayne Loader, *No Place to Hide* by Tom Johnson and Lance Bird, and works by experimental filmmaker Joseph Cornell and Hollywood montage editor Chuck Workman—were screened. Patti Bruck's experimental *Slippage* (1989) and Pat O'Neill's *Water and Power* (1989) on environmental issues in the Los Angeles landscape mixed with *Affirmations* (1990) by black queer filmmaker Marlon Riggs and *Cane Toads: An Unnatural History* (1988) by Mark Lewis, a humorous look at the Australian cane toad invasion.

Trained in journalism, Riggs rammed against an entirely different consideration of documentary form at the 1988 seminar, spurring his legendary "conversion experience" toward a more complex aesthetic form he attributed to the Flaherty: "Every idea I'd previously held dear about the media was assaulted and began to crumble. What emerged in the wake of my own ideological rubble was a new vision of what was possible in my work, a new way of articulating and representing both my private and social realities."[95] Inspired, Riggs turned toward a more hybrid experimental documentary practice in works such as *Affirmations* and *Tongues Untied*.

In 1991, this strategy to publicize programming direction continued. This seminar would "reflect the complexity of mediated landscapes," invoking a postcolonial and postmodern turn. It would focus on contemporary Arab cinema, "concentrating on film from the Maghreb area of Morocco, Algeria and Tunisia." This seminar screened fiction film, which—despite Flaherty Seminar mythologies—had always been shown. The 1991 Flaherty was the first seminar to dedicate a major amount of programming to a specific international cinema. Arab cinema resonated with the commencement of the first Gulf War. However, Coco Fusco and Steve Gallagher distanced their programming from references to the war, redirecting participants to engage Maghrebi cinemas. This seminar faced significant constraints on inviting overseas filmmakers: budgetary cutbacks slashed the transportation budget by 40 percent.[96] NYSCA had cut its funding to the Flaherty by 50 percent that year, from $15,000 to $7,500.[97]

Steve Gallagher, a programmer at The Kitchen in New York City, collaborated with Coco Fusco, an independent programmer and development director at Third World Newsreel also in New York City. A prolific writer on postcoloniality and race, she had curated the touring exhibition "Young, British and Black: The Works of Sankofa and Black Audio Film Collective."[98] Probing works with a postmodern deconstruction of "the real" that unsettled the "authentic" with ambiguities between fact and fiction, Fusco and Gallagher continued the tradition of heterogeneity, intensified with international cinemas from Brazil, Canada, England, the Maghreb, the United States, and the former Yugoslavia. As participating filmmaker Jonathan Robinson noted, the 1991 program addressed "exile, displacement, and dispossession of individuals and communities."[99] Works by Merzak Allouache (*Omar Gatlato*, 1977), Férid Boughedir (*Halfaouine*, 1990), Youssef Chahine (*Alexandria Why?* 1979), Mona Hatoum (*Measures of Distance*, 1988), Michel Khleifi (*Canticle of Stones*, 1990), Farida Benlyazid (*A Door to the Sky*, 1989), and Elia Suleiman and Jayce Salloum (*Introduction to the End of an Argument*, 1990), showed the complex range of styles and ideas in Arab and Maghrebi cinemas.

As Laura Marks offered in her 1992 *Afterimage* review, " Fusco and Gallagher endeavored to program films for the North African focus that were unusual in their own countries, and one feature that surprisingly many of these shared was a certain implicit or explicit feminism."[100] Several Arab filmmakers were invited. Only Elia Suleiman, a Canadian of Lebanese origin, came. Férid Boughedir declined. Palestinian exile Michel Khelifi had an expired passport and could not board his plane.[101] To contextualize these films, Fusco and Gallagher assembled three specialists of Maghrebi and Middle Eastern film: Alia Arasoughly, a producer and programmer; Viola Shafik, a programmer from Hamburg, Germany; and Ella Shohat, a film scholar from City College of New York who wrote on multicultural and postcolonial film.

Two programs in the 1991 seminar generated significant debate, questioning documentary as a stable category to engage truth claims or evidence. The first revolved around the rediscovery of a film by prominent African American documentary filmmaker William Greaves, a screening connected with the more contemporary projects exploring race. The second emerged around the works of Ken Feingold, a video artist whose projects rattled the notions of evidence, logocentricism, and the real in documentary practice.

William Greaves's *Symbiopsychotaxiplasm: Take One* (1968), considered an experimental docudrama, was an improvisational film identified with the black new wave. *Variety* called the film "a bizarre, Cassavetes-esque ramble with surprisingly good audience holding power."[102] In 1980, Brooklyn Museum film curator Dara Meyers Kingsley rediscovered this never–theatrically released film screened once in Paris and once in New York. Fusco and Gallagher's programming of it prompted scholars to reconsider black cinema history.[103] Greaves had produced *Black Journal* on PBS, the only black-controlled PBS series.[104]

Made in 1968, *Symbiopsychotaxiplasm: Take One* chronicled a director shooting a couple arguing about abortion and sexuality. The scene was shot from multiple viewpoints, with different pairs of actors undertaking different readings of the script. The film employed handheld camera work and self-reflexivity, where the crew debated the film. It mined the liminal zone between Brechtian dramaturgy, cinéma vérité, and reenactment. Greaves described the film as a way "to see how the camera would change reality in the process of recording it just as the electron microscope changes the structure of the atom."[105] In the postscreening discussion, participants heralded the film and the considered, gracious, thoughtful Greaves.

The second provocation centered on Ken Feingold's *Un chien délicieux* (1991). Feingold was a conceptual artist whose work questioned the veracity of facts, histories, and representations. This eighteen-minute film featured voice-over of a Burmese man telling a story of meeting French surrealists while in Paris on an anthropological mission. In the second half of the film, he stands in front of a thatched-roof hut. Villagers kill and cook a dog. The video plays on slippages between fact, fiction, ethnography, documentary truth claims, and reconstruction. As Laura U. Marks noted in her *Afterimage* essay on this seminar, "When participants discovered that the voice-over account was completely fictional, many were extremely outraged. Feingold defended himself by arguing that with the capacity for manipulation inherent in the media, one should not expect truth."[106] In a *Release Print* article, filmmaker Jonathan Robinson (*Sight Unseen: A Travelogue*, 1990) questioned why seminar discussions resisted interrogating documentary authority and construction. He noted the Feingold discussion opened up more vigorous discussion. However, in Robinson's view, the discussion lacked criticality: "Nobody asked if a decentered approach to filmmaking was a strategy of displacement or simply the result of money-strapped artists creatively winging it."[107]

The Feingold and Greaves discussions had impact beyond the seminar. *Symbiopsychotaxiplasm: Take One* had many screenings the following year, with references to its Flaherty debut. Scholars such as Scott MacDonald who had attended the 1991 Flaherty published scholarly articles on it.[108] Feingold published his own analyses of the negative reactions to *Un Chien Délicieux* in an extended discussion with Coco Fusco and Steve Gallagher in the spring 1992 issue of *Felix*. They articulated their ideas about postmodern destabilizations of documentary from facts, representing others, the so-called real, and universals. Feingold argued, "one can only raise questions about a culture by transgressing the limitation of that culture."

Feingold, Fusco, and Gallagher critiqued the notion of "the other" and "truth." They sought to destabilize white culture and representation. Fusco explained, "because of a Dadaist and kamikaze inclination we were enticed by the idea of subverting what was something of a de facto tradition." Gallagher expanded, "we tried to find films that were self-conscious about their construction." Fusco argued their program critiqued the alignment of documentary with morality, transparency, the truth, and verisimilitude: "It was an interesting reaction that our programming destabilized people's viewing relationship to the film material. To me it seemed like this should be a normal position."[109]

The 1992 seminar adopted diverse tactics. Programmed by the six-person team of Austin Allen, Ruth Bradley, Scott MacDonald, William Sloan, Jacqueline Tshaka, and Lise Yasui, the seminar featured sixty-five titles, an eclectic mix of archival films, experimental shorts, and longer documentary works. Self-consciously multicultural, this seminar included African American filmmakers such as Camille Billips (*Finding Christa*, 1991), Portia Cobb (*Species in Danger Ed*, 1987; *No Justice, No Peace*, 1992), Cheryl Dunye (*Janine*, 1990; *She Don't Fade*, 1991), and Cauleen Smith (*Chronicle of a Lying Spirit by Kelly Gabron*, 1992). Sadie Benning (*It Wasn't Love*, 1992; *Jollies*, 1990) and Holly Fisher (*Bullets for Breakfast*, 1992) showed experimental feminist films. Canadian First Nation and Native American production spanned Victor Masayesva's *Imagining Indians* (1992), David Poisey and William Hansen's *Starting Fire with Gunpowder* (1991) about the Inuit Broadcasting Corporation in Canada, and Randy Redford's *Cowtipping: The Militant Indian Waiter* (1991), a short drama.[110] A mini-retrospective of Willie Varela—"an autodidact, a visionary, and a junior high school teacher from El Paso Texas" according to Jesse Lerner—investigated Chicano experimental art inspired by Stan Brakhage's lyrical cinema.[111]

MacDonald's programming was the most focused, with a thesis on cinematic space, motion studies, and technology. He programmed a retrospective of short works by John Porter, a Toronto bicycle messenger who had produced more than 250 silent short films, including *Mother and Child* (1977), *Animal in Motion* (1980), *Calendar Girl* (1981–88), and *Exams* (1982). He programmed Martin Arnold's *Pièce Touchée* (1989) which reworked midcentury-found footage of a woman sitting in a chair and a man approaching her with flash frames, optical printing, and repetition.

In opposite ways, two filmmakers generated the most discussion and postseminar writing. The first was filmmaker Kazuo Hara, with *Extreme Private Eros: Love Song 1974* (1974) and *The Emperor's Naked Army Marches On* (1987). *The Emperor's Naked Army* focuses on a World War II veteran, Kenzo Okuzaki, obsessed with exposing atrocities from the war, including cannibalism. *Extreme Private Eros* follows Takeda Miyuki on a sexual odyssey to become pregnant. In an 1992 article published in *The Independent*, Laura U. Marks quoted Hara on his relationships with difficult subjects: "He speaks of his subject as his *aite*, or opponent, but the contest is an unusual one . . . he tries to become empty and receive the other."[112] In *The Squealer*, Meg Knowles noted Hara's films provoked the most interesting discussions because they plumbed the filmmaker's responsibility to subjects.[113] In *Afterimage*, Jesse Lerner observed, "Hara's films include extremely emotional or dangerous moments in which the crew chose to continue to shoot rather than to intervene."[114] Even though Hara's films pushed audiences, they addressed ethical issues arising between filmmaker and subject—familiar documentary intellectual territory at the seminar.

However, in Ken Jacobs's Nervous System performance of *XCXHXEXRXRIXEXSX* (1980, in subsequent multiple versions), this same audience reacted to the repetition, reworking, and slowing down of a 1920s pornography film with shock and walkouts. Jacobs performed his dual projection system called the Nervous System, which advanced a film frame by frame. Manipulating the shutter and creating flicker produced an illusion of movement. The Nervous System disrupted the original image. One projector was stationary; the other moved. The system's overlaps and superimpositions rendered, according to Laura U. Marks, a "flicker and a three dimensional effect. The result is that the five minute film fragment is stretched into a two hour performance."[115]

This screening propelled postseminar essays about its provocations into feminist film theory, the gaze, popular culture, and pornography. The postscreening discussion featured Jacobs leaving the room after listening to charges of boredom, gendered power plays, pornography, sexism, and voyeurism. Jesse Lerner observed, "Needless to say, Jacobs's unwillingness to discuss these critical issues (i.e., voyeurism, power, and gender) is distinctly unfashionable, as today even Muybridge's motion studies, ostensibly scientific exercises, are understood as circumscribed by hierarchies of sexuality and power."[116]

As Laura U. Marks analyzed it, the film provoked responses exposing a gender and generation gap in thinking about avant-garde strategies of disruption and discomfort, the gaze, the gendering of experimental film, and sexuality. She observed the Flaherty audience response actually "spanned a historical range of ways of talking about experimental film" and "varieties of feminist approaches . . . (anti-porn, anti-censorship, psychoanalytic, Foucauldian)."[117] She noted the film's "boycotters" who left the screening split between those who objected to the pornographic content of explicit sexuality in the ménage à trois in the original film and those who simply did not connect to experimental films.[118] For her, the performance intersected with feminist issues of pleasure and sexuality. It manipulated formal experimentation, the gaze, and popular culture forms to provoke a spectatorial response.

MacDonald penned a response to Lerner's *Afterimage* essay. He explained the conceptual and political ideas energizing his programming section of the 1992 seminar. He refuted the idea that showing films with progressive content constituted a political act: "My goal as a programmer is always to 'stretch' the audience, the filmmakers, and myself: to use film as a means of instigating an energized social situation we all must work through—and I hope, grow through—together." MacDonald saw himself as a "Trojan horse" programmer: he placed Jacobs's *Nervous System* performance in dialogue with the 1965 Flaherty Seminar when Ken and Flo Jacobs, Jonas Mekas, and others trespassed and attempted to have Jacobs's *Blonde Cobra* (1963) and Jack Smith's *Flaming Creatures* (1963) screened as part of the seminar. Jonas Mekas's *Lost Lost Lost* documented what MacDonald dubbed a "cine-intervention."[119]

MacDonald situated *XCXHXEXRXRXIXEXSX* as a fulcrum looking back to Muybridge's Zoopraxiscope and forward to questions of representation of gender and sexuality. As MacDonald reflected, "I calculated . . . that Jacobs' recycling and analysis of a bit of 1920s French porn would be likely to instigate a more spirited interchange about gender than might otherwise occur."[120] The challenging screening—with clashes between generations, a hand-crafted projection apparatus, politics, and sensibilities igniting volatile discussion—marked a turning point in the seminar. With so many scholars in attendance and with more venues to publish reports, the aesthetic and ideological battles once sequestered within the four walls of the Flaherty Seminar discussion rooms now entered larger, more public spheres of independent media.[121]

The 1993 and 1994 seminars continued the trajectory of programming more international content through regional foci. Latin American and Latino/Latina works were probed in 1993 and Asian and Asian American in 1994. Programming teams with different specialties collaborated, indicating IFS's response to continuing pressure to address diversity struggles. Seminar publicity advertised a range of projects traveling across animation, documentary, experimental, fiction, and hybrid forms. This tactic was added to dislodge perceptions that the Flaherty operated as a secret society for traditional documentary. It emphasized the seminar's unique experience, deploying words such as *debate, dialogue, discussions, exchange, intimate,* and, *an unfolding of ideas.* The word *independent* appeared more frequently in seminar publicity during the 1990s, linking the seminar to the now-established independent media movement.[122]

Four programmers with different locations in the independent media ecology mounted the 1993 seminar, suggesting IFS's attempt to dispel perceptions it was an exclusive organization for elite, white, East Coast media people. These seminars displaced the maleness and whiteness of the seminar with international filmmakers and women and people of color from the United States. Despite the strong reactions the previous year to Jacobs, experimental film was no longer marginalized but now functioned as a necessary critical programming thread. John Columbus was executive director of the Black Maria Film and Video Festival, a traveling festival presenting short films. He was white. Louis Massiah was executive director of Scribe Video Center in Philadelphia, an organization dedicated to resources and training to use video for cultural, political, and social issues and director of two films for *Eyes on the Prize,* the PBS series on the civil rights movement. He was African American. Chon A. Noriega was a UCLA professor specializing in Chicano and Latino culture. Margarita De La Vega Hurtado taught Latino and Latin American cinema at University of Michigan. She was originally from Colombia.

This seminar's programming presented a tapestry of the programmers' various concerns and positions in the international independent media field. It addressed the issues of the avant-garde in the seminar, internationalism, multiculturalism, with white male American filmmakers in the minority. Experimental filmmakers included Vincent Grenier (*Interieur Interiors (To AK),* 1978), Peter Hutton (*In Titan's Goblet,* 1991), and Leighton Pierce (*Deer Isle #5,* 1993; *Red Shovel,* 1992), recognized for their complex compositions of natural environments. Feminist experimental makers Cathy Cook (*June Brides,* 1992; *Match That Started My Fire,* 1992), Barbara Hammer (*Sanctus,* 1990; *Nitrate Kisses,* 1992), and Meena Nanji (*Note to a Stranger,* 1992; *Voices of the Morning,* 1992) answered contentions that the avant-garde was a male domain, debates that had surfaced in the previous seminar. At this seminar, African American and African diaspora makers illustrated a staggering range of genres, locations, and practices problematizing conventional realist documentary with black identities: British John Akomfrah's *Seven Songs for Malcolm X* (1993), an experimental intervention into the biopic; Orlando Bagwell's *Malcolm X: Make It Plain* (1994); the US collective Not Channel Zero with *X ½: The Legacy of Malcolm X* (1993); and American Marlon Riggs's experimental documentary *Black Is . . . Black Ain't* (1994). The Latin American program showcased Colombian feminist Marta Rodriguez with her important documentaries *The Brickmakers* (1972), *Nuestra voz de tierra, memoria y futuro* (1981), and *Love, Women and Flowers* (1989). The program explored Latino film and video, with established documentarians such as Lourdes Portillo (*Columbus on Trial,* 1992) and Juan Mandelbaum (*Builders of Images,* 1992) and emerging makers such as John Valadez with *Passin' It On* (1992) combined with more experimental practitioners such as Juan Downey (*Motherland,* 1986), Harry Gamboa Jr.

(*L.A. Familia*, 1993), Raphael Montañez Ortiz (*Destruction Room*, 1957–67), and Ela Troyano (*Carmelita Tropicana: Your Kunst Is Your Waffen*, 1993), a deliberate intervention to racialize the avant-garde.

Participants writing for the independent media press highlighted the 1993 seminar's aggressive, deliberate approach to diversity in guests, programmers, and programming choices. Writing in *Black Film Bulletin,* Phil Bertelson, a Philadelphia video producer and programmer, commented, "The group dynamic swung from cordial to caustic—making for interesting discussions. Obvious to me was the newness of such a 'multicultural' seminar."[123] Although arguing the group discussion "stayed on the surface level" as a result of poor moderation, O. Funmilayo Makarah, in a 1992 *Afterimage* review, mused, "Even with the missteps I noticed at this year's Seminar, it is clear that Flaherty has moved forward a great deal more than many other organizations and festivals that service the media arts field."[124] The 1993 program had entered into a dialogue not only with critiques of the seminar's white privilege but also with larger international independent media ecologies.

The 1994 seminar focused on Asian and Asian American film, long neglected at the seminar despite its early embrace of the works of Satyajit Ray. It also celebrated the seminar's fortieth anniversary. L. Somi Roy was the former film program coordinator at Asia Society. His program juxtaposed Asian makers with Asian artists working in the "West," a program the seminar brochure claimed reflected the "new internationalism" in "a changing moment in film history resulting from post-war migration and the shifting cultural boundaries, enabling reassessment of Western and Asian film history."[125] A large span of works deploying myriad visual strategies were screened: from Canada (Shani Mootoo, with *Wild Women in the Woods,* 1992; *Her Sweetness Lingers,* 1994), Hong Kong (Yau Ching, with *The Ideal Na(rra)tion, Video Letters 1, 2, 3,* 1993; Ming-Yuen S. Ma, who was born in Buffalo, New York, but raised in Hong Kong, with *Toc Storee,*1992), India (Mani Kaul, with *Uski Roti,* 1969), Japan (Mako Idemitsu, with *Great Mother,* 1983), Korea (Seoungho Cho, with *Opium and Memory,* 1993), Philippines (Nick Deocampo, with *Memories of Old Manila,* 1993; *Revolutions Happen Like Refrains in a Song,* 1987), Taiwan, Vietnam, and the United States (Rea Tajiri, with *History and Memory,* 1991; Janice Tanaka, with *Memories from the Department of Amnesia,* 1989).

Erik Barnouw and Patricia R. Zimmermann programmed the fortieth anniversary retrospective section periodized by decade. Their contribution featured works that expanded independent documentary practice, from *Nanook of the North* to compilations (Newsreels' *Amerika,* 1969 and excerpts from *Eyes on the Prize,* 1987–90) to direct cinema (Robert Drew, with *Primary,* 1960; George Stoney, with *You Are on Indian Land,* 1969, a collaboration with the Mohawk tribe). They showed hybrid feminist, multicultural, and queer works (Kathy High's *I Need Your Full Cooperation* (1989), *Unexposed* (1994); Marlon Riggs's *Tongues Untied,* 1989; Edin Velez's *Meta Mayan,* 1981). They also mounted Philip Mallory Jones's three-channel installation, *Dreamkeeper* (1989).

After the screening of Barnouw's compilation film *Hiroshima-Nagasaki 1945* (1970), the audience read the film as a racist representation of burned, injured Japanese victims without agency—not as a classic antiwar film recovering suppressed bombing documents. The seminar's participants included more Asian and Asian American participants than previous seminars and more participants schooled in multicultural and postcolonial theories. It was the first time this important documentary had screened in a program of works from Asia.[126] Barnouw attested he found the altercation invigorating; the debates were exactly what the seminar needed.

Mani Kaul (India) occupied the established filmmaker role. His works formed the backbone of the seminar. Virtually unknown in the United States, Kaul was linked to the parallel art cinema in India but operated outside of it, a more experimental maker linked to the Indian new wave.[127] Kaul was influenced by both Robert Bresson and Ritwik Ghatak. His work captured unplanned moments to reveal deeper philosophical ideas. Colin Burnett has argued Kaul, who was born Rajasthan, should be analyzed as a transnational filmmaker as well as an Indian experimental filmmaker. His films reworked two aesthetics: on the one hand, the sensuous melodramatic style of his teacher, Ritwak Ghatak, and on the other, the sparse aesthetic of Robert Bresson, whom he studied at the Film and Television Institute of India in Pune. For Burnett, Kaul "launched a narrative avant-garde" and engaged "nonrepresentational" minimalist art practice. Fragmented compositions and layered spatial dimensions challenged illusionist perspectives with local Indian aesthetic traditions.[128]

With film prints unavailable in the United States, Kaul's Flaherty appearance intervened into histories focused on Satyajit Ray and the parallel cinema, the kind of rediscovery the Flaherty Seminar excelled at.[129] The 1994 seminar screened *Uski Roti* (1970), *Dhrupad* (1983), *Siddeshwari* (1989), and *Cloud Door* (1994), some without English subtitles.[130] A filmmaker, teacher, and theorist, Kaul was a forceful presence, conceptually eloquent about his experimental practice invoking documentary, drama, and reenactment. Kaul exemplified how deeply embedded auteurism was at the Flaherty. His films elaborated complex interweavings of European and Indian artistic strategies, demanding thoughtful engagement. His ideas about cinema constituted abstract, metalevel interventions. Screenwriter Ian Iqbal Rashid identified Kaul as the highlight of the program. He noted his work defied categorization in its address of cultural practices, complex narration, and elaborate formalism. "Roy revealed to many of us for the first time, the range and development of a master filmmaker whose work has rarely been screened in the United States," explained Rashid.[131]

After five years of seminars promoting regional, multicultural, and national cinemas, 1995 represented the first seminar to be promoted with its own conceptual title. Programmed by Marlina Gonzalez-Tamrong, an assistant curator of film and video at the Walker Art Center in Minnesota, and Bruce Jenkins, curator of film and video at the same institution, the seminar was entitled "The Camera Reframed: Technology and Interpretation." According to Jenkins, the deployment of a thematic title for the seminar evidenced the influences of professional curators from the museum world, where events and shows were promoted with titles, especially in the visual arts.[132]

IFS publicity identified Gonzalez-Tamrong as "one of the few women of color working as a primary curator within an established institution." Her programming would focus on "the politics of ethnography, the impact of the camera as intrusion, and visual representations and power plays." Gonzalez-Tamrong sought to "examine and do a historical analysis of the camera as subject by curating docus that were self-reflexive."[133] She saw the camera as an "instrument of affirmation for the colonial gaze," especially in the work of Robert Flaherty. She was interested in filmmakers like Shu Lea Cheang, the Asian American experimental media artist, and Nick Deocampo from the Philippines.[134] Jenkins's programs would examine technological advances redefining documentary form.[135] Beyond these analytical programming concerns, IFS confronted continuing financial challenges. As a result, this seminar was the first full-length seminar to offer special reduced-rate weekend packages in order to attract Flaherty veterans.

According to Jenkins, the 1995 seminar was engaging two larger media conjunctures: the centennial of cinema, with its "considerations of the film archive and especially the heterogeneous body of work generated globally by a century of nonfiction filmmaking" and the "impact of the computer."[136] For Gonzalez-Tamrong, their seminar also coincided with the fiftieth anniversary of the bombing of Hiroshima and Nagasaki. She included Rea Tajiri's *History and Memory: For Akiko and Takashige* (1991) as a form of commemoration because "the title itself declared the disparity between what we are taught to remember (as a function of control) and what we are forced to hide in safekeeping though memory, because of what we are taught to forget."[137]

The 1995 seminar unpacked a multiplicity of ways to mobilize new technologies. It presented Jane Gillooly's *Leona's Sister Gerri* (1995), which traced photographic images involved in struggles of reproductive rights; the collaborative projects of Spencer Nakasako and Sokly Don Bonus Ny, *A.k.a. Don Bonus* (1995), about Vietnamese youth in San Francisco; and Brian Springer's *Spin* (1995), composed from videotaped surveillance satellite feeds. DeeDee Halleck screened her compilation film on the US popular culture imaginary of Latin America, *The Gringo in Mañanaland: A Musical* (1995). Daniel Reeves's *Obsessive Becoming* (1995) probed his traumas of abuse and their connections to war in the twentieth century through digital morphing technologies as psychic alchemy. This seminar was among the first to fully engage digital arts practices in new interfaces, with CD-ROMs: Rick Prelinger's *Ephemeral Films* (1995) and *Our Secret Century* (1995), Nino Rodriguez's *Boy* (1994), and Christine Tamblyn's *She Loves It, She Loves It Not* (1993).

At the seminar, the conjunction of the death of Jerry Garcia of the Grateful Dead and the emergence of the World Wide Web underscored how the media landscape had experienced a paradigm shift. Gonzalez-Tamrong had arranged for Shu Lea Cheang to show the collaborative process of one of her installations in real time through the use of golf ball cameras via the internet. Gonzalez-Tamrong observed: "The exercise failed because at the time of our presentation, the Ethernet was ablaze with the news about the death of Jerry Garcia. I thought at the very moment that the technology crashed, its own failure proved its victory. A new form of mass media had emerged. The dominance of multinational broadcast media was dethroned by ordinary people. . . . the masses literally took over the reins of our moment, managing to subvert, albeit accidentally, the very message of our program's theme, deciding for us that Jerry Garcia's death was THE message to which we must pay attention."[138] In *Afterimage*, Yosha Goldstein observed this seminar showed a multiplicity of new technologies, juxtaposing "documentary and experimental film and video with archival collections, home movies, travelogs, advertisements, CD ROMS and the World Wide Web."[139]

The titling of seminars signaled a decisive break from earlier iterations when calling it "the Flaherty" and presenting the works available at the moment was enough to lure devotees. The seminar had entered a new era. No longer a mysterious club, it inaugurated a more professionalized public image. Seminars explicitly identified their conceptual ideas and programming models. However, the films and filmmakers remained a surprise. Prompted by funders who demanded more detail about what they were funding and participants who wanted to know what they were spending their $640 on, titling seminars added clarity and transparency. It also conveyed a unique marketing edge, distinguishing the seminar as a place for exploration of significant ideas distinct from the market pressures of festivals.

The 1996 seminar was entitled "Landscapes and Place." IFS continued to struggle with how to engage multiculturalism, national identities, and race to revise perceptions of the seminar as an elitist, white, East Coast organization. A three-person curatorial team was assembled. Ruth Bradley was a film festival director and journal editor from Ohio University. Kathy High was a video maker who worked on questions of scientific technologies. Loretta Todd was a Cree and Metis who helped to form the Aboriginal Film and Video Arts Alliance promoting First Nations people in film and television in Canada.[140] The seminar featured experimental minimalist filmmaker James Benning (*North on Evers,* 1992). Artist Steina Vasulka built an installation in the woods surrounding Wells College and projected images on a scrim. Participants walked around the image, illuminated by candles in mason glass luminaria. Steina performed *Violin Power* (1978), where an electronic violin connected to a MIDI manipulated images.

Engaging the debate opened up in 1992 about indigenous media, this seminar showcased two of the world's most important feminist indigenous media directors: Merata Mita, a Maori from Aotearoa, New Zealand, and Alanis Obomsawin, a Canadian filmmaker of Abenaki descent. Obomsawin screened her epic documentary on the 1990 Mohawk uprising, *Kanehsatake: 270 Years of Resistance* (1993). Mita showed *Patu* (1983), a documentary about anti-apartheid movement violent clashes after a rugby game played by South Africans touring New Zealand. The seminar's high point arrived when Mita and Obomsawin met. A professional vocalist, Obomsawin welcomed Mita to the seminar by singing a traditional Abenake song from the back of the auditorium. She walked from the back of the auditorium down the aisles to greet Mita.

The 1996 seminar did not unfurl without intense controversy, debate, and the problematic Flaherty filmmaker bashing.[141] George Kuchar was an experimental underground film legend and an astoundingly prolific filmmaker who had shifted to low-cost video. He screened his *Weather Diaries* (1986, 1993, 1996), first-person diary films about his own body, his inner thoughts, and the weather. After the screening, an audience member objected to the "showing of a turd" in a toilet in one scene.[142]

The low-end, lo-fi, handmade quality of Kuchar's video contrasted sharply with the epic feature-length films of Mita and Obomsawin and the rigorous visual formalism of Benning. The Kuchar attack advanced on multiple fronts—amateur form, misguided purpose, and offensive content. The debate congealed divisions between the avant-garde's formal experimentation and social realist documentary. Shy and reclusive, Kuchar felt everything he had viewed in the seminar seemed "disgusting," a comment which agitated the audience even more. His comment was misinterpreted as a reactionary stance to films chronicling political struggles. Kuchar simply wanted to express his passion for cinema.[143] In response to these audience attacks, activist filmmaker Ellen Spiro defended Kuchar as an inspiration for her own low-tech media practice.

The Kuchar discussion exposed the fault lines underneath the Flaherty Seminars cult-like operations and discussion style. Kuchar produced a short film about his alienation at that seminar called *Vermin of the Vortex* (1996). The film served as his revenge on a seminar that assaulted his identity as a white male with a professorship at a film program, his modest diaristic practices, and his unmitigated passion for cinema. Shot at the 1996 Flaherty Seminar and at the Chicago Underground Film Festival, which had given Kuchar an award, the film employs a narrative ruse: aliens abduct Kuchar and deposit him at the Flaherty.

In a 1997 book published with his brother Mike called *Reflections from a Cinematic Cesspool*, Kuchar elaborated on his Flaherty-bashing episode, extending the excrement metaphor as a diary of the entire Flaherty gestalt. He wrote: "Then the silence was broken and the curtain of civility that had previously muffled the malcontents began to rip asunder like an over-loaded diaper . . . one by one, angry heads bared their molars to chew into the video diary itself, claiming that I was an exploiter of Oklahoma settlers. . . . I took my finger, stuck it in my mouth, and verbally threw up all over them—my reaction to the way they were fracturing into splinters the mirror that reflected our true totality."[144] Alongside the films of Appalshop, Benning, Mita, Obomsawin, and Steina, the Kuchar episode illustrated the Flaherty Seminar's strategy of programming for juxtaposition often mobilized destructive contradictions. It sometimes exposed unexamined audience assumptions, unprocessed aesthetics, and unresolved politics in highly volatile ways.

Still struggling with funding problems, IFS partnered with Duke University in 1999. The seminar moved from Wells College in upstate New York to Durham, North Carolina—the first seminar held in the South but not the first to partner with an academic institution. Seminars in the 1950s and 1960s were often collaborations. The move to Durham attracted many PhD students from Duke University, a central node for critical documentary and postcolonial studies. Richard Herskowitz, at the time director of the Virginia Film Festival, partnered with Orlando Bagwell, an award-winning independent filmmaker who had worked on both the *Eyes on the Prize* (1987–90) and *The Great Depression* (1993) series. Entitled "Out-Takes Are History," their seminar emphasized editing rather than shooting, steering the seminar in almost the opposite direction of prior years.[145] A wide range of filmmakers from overseas and the United States spanning experimental to theatrical documentary modes were screened: Elizabeth Barret, John Else, Jacquie Jones, Jeanne Jordan, Richard Leacock, Artavazd Peleshyan (Armenia), Phil Solomon, Caspar Stracke (Austria), Johan van der Keuken (the Netherlands), and David Williams.

One of the most devastating moments of the 1999 seminar erupted around David Williams, a white filmmaker who worked in the African American community. Although Herskowitz wanted to program the films in reverse chronological order to frame their complex racial explorations, Williams insisted the films be screened chronologically. In the postscreening discussion, seminar participants aggressively criticized Williams for his depictions of race. Herskowitz assessed this session as perhaps one of the most brutal filmmaker attacks in the seminar's history. Williams was "mortified," unable to sleep that night. The next morning, when his later work, *Thirteen* (1998) screened, the audience revised their earlier interpretation to applaud its nuanced racialized engagements.[146]

The 2000 seminar ushered in a significant transition from the era of budgetary cutbacks, crises, lack of administrative acumen, and pitched debates about identity politics and multiculturalism. This seminar exhibited deep awareness that exploration of internationalism and racialization were difficult, necessary, and urgent conversations. The 2000 program refashioned the seminar as a zone where different communities would converge, a space of transversal multiplicities rather than one unified position. In addition, the seminar had moved from Wells College to Vassar College, which is much closer to New York City.

Continuing the trend of hiring programming professionals with major institutional affiliations, Kathy Geritz was named programmer. She was the associate curator at Pacific Film Archive at the University of California, Berkeley, with extensive experience programming experimental shorts and international art cinema. Her appointment to helm the 2000 Flaherty issued a strong statement that the seminar was not a closed East Coast enclave but an organization with national reach and impact. This seminar signaled a return to an individual programmer and a singular curatorial vision. It received funding support from the Geraldine R. Dodge Foundation, the French Cultural Service in New York, Goethe House in New York, the IBM Corporation Matching Grants Program, and NYSCA as well as the Leo Dratfield, Paul Ronder, and Sol Worth Endowments. The Geritz seminar offered a broad conceptual theme: "Essays, Experiments, and Excavations."[147]

The 2000 seminar crafted a heterogeneous program of archival materials, gender, genres, modes, nations, race, and styles, emphasizing a polyphonic structure rather than a single exploration of an identity or region. Geritz conceived the seminar as an investigation into the multiple domains of nonfiction, a more complex category than documentary. As Geritz reflected "Early on I decided that my programming for the seminar would not focus just on 'documentary' but explore 'non-fiction' films. This allowed me to consider not only documentaries, but also animation—including documentary animation—and avant-garde work. I wanted to feature artists working within these different realms whose films looked at the world, history, or social and political issues in radical or innovative ways, or explored ideas, even cinema itself, in an experimental or essay form."[148] Social realist, politically activist documentary was elaborated in the work of Big Noise Films Collective (*Black and Gold*, 1997; *Zapatista*, 1999), Vicky Funari (*Live Nude Girls Unite*, 2000), RtMark (*Bringing It to You*, 1999), and Travis Wilkerson (*Accelerated Development*, 1999). Chris Sullivan screened his animated film *Consuming Spirits* (2000).

As an experimental film programmer, Geritz understood how a careful construction of shorts could provoke ideas, insights, and reactions. She explains:

> there is a lot of creativity in curating programs of shorts, but also a lot of pleasure for the audience—they come to understand filmic and intellectual ideas that are embedded in a work through seeing it in relation to other films . . . the vast majority of my seminar programs consisted of short films and videos. One approach that I relished was to mix together works

that had disparate stylistic approaches, yet were linked, sometimes on multiple levels,
whether thematically, by an idea, or even by a mood. Such juxtapositions can create sparks
between works, allowing further readings to arise.[149]

Experimental work underscored that the avant-garde was no longer exclusively white and male: it included significant works by people of color and women, with appearances by Peggy Ahwesh, Brian Frye, Leah Gilliam, Abraham Ravett, Luis Recoder, and Tran T. Kim-Trang. Observational cinema was charted with the films of Sergey Dvortsevoy from Kazakhstan (*Bread Day*, 1998) and John Marshall (*After the Game*, 1973). This seminar featured two established international master filmmakers who operated in different filmmaking styles: the lyrical films of Edgardo Cozarinsky from Argentina (*Sunset Boulevard*, 1992; *Citizen Langlois*, 1999) and the formally rigorous works of Harun Farocki from Germany (*Workers Leaving the Factory*, 1995; *Images of the World and Inscriptions of War*, 1998). Presenting works by Ahwesh, Harun Farocki, Chris Sullivan, Tran, and Travis Wilkerson, the 2000 seminar moved away from the master filmmaker programming motif by showing several works by each filmmaker. As Geritz reflects, "It created a really deep engagement to see more of a person's work but also to hear the artist speak multiple times."[150] Her curatorial strategy of multiplying the voices of invited artists gently dislodged the established auteur model of the earlier seminars, moving the programming and seminar experiences toward engagement with multiple voices that would build and elaborate ideas across the time frame of the seminar.

"Essays, Experiments, and Excavations" demonstrated the Flaherty Seminar and IFS could survive the culture wars, defunding, and institutional challenges around identity politics and race with conceptually sophisticated programming that opened up uncomfortable political debates and rocky aesthetic terrains. Geritz's careful recalibrations of questions of gender, national identities, racialization, and technologies were designed to create an open field of collective exploration. The intellectually complex, nuanced juxtapositions crafted in the Geritz seminar might not have been possible without the previous decade of institutional unravelings and pitched arguments that exposed repressed inequalities and silences.

1990 MARLON RIGGS—ON *TONGUES UNTIED* (1989)

Sally Berger: I'm very pleased to be introducing Marlon Riggs to you today. Marlon has been coming to the Flaherty Seminar for several years, and he's always made wonderful contributions to the discussions. Marlon teaches at the University of California at Berkeley in the School of Journalism; he's been making documentaries there and independently for quite a few years now. Several years ago, his *Ethnic Notions* [1988] was shown at the seminar, and now we have *Tongues Untied*.

This year, Marlon presented *Tongues Untied* at Video Viewpoints at the Museum of Modern Art, and it was an incredible experience for me and for Barbara London—we program Video Viewpoints: over two hundred people showed up for this screening and the energy and the way people reacted *with* the piece as it was happening was a new experience for us.

Marlon, could you talk about the interplay between that audience and *Tongues Untied*?

Marlon Riggs: In making *Tongues Untied*, I was trying to speak very directly to a particular audience, an audience of black gay men, and I never really envisioned showing this work to a group like the one here.

A large part of black culture, African American culture, is signifying: doing the dozens, reading, dissing, dishing. In making the film, I realized that a lot of *Tongues Untied* would be signifying, speaking in tongues, speaking in code in a way that I knew would immediately register with the community because it's a part of our maintaining a distinctive identity through gestures and through particular phrases and sayings. That's rarely represented on film or in video, partly because the tendency whenever it *is* represented is to treat it as caricature and stereotype, so you get "What's *hapnin,*' bro!" as opposed to "What's happening?" Everything gets taken to an extreme.

Partly because I was doing black, gay, male signifying in particular, which hardly ever gets on the screen, I realized that people would really respond, so to make what I thought would be an aesthetically challenging work for a general audience, I decided I would constantly infuse little bits of signifying throughout the piece so that people would be brought back in, if the work was proving a little difficult because of the subject matter or because of the form, which is very nonlinear. So, *Snap* became a large part of the piece. Snapping distinguishes black, as well as Latin, gay culture; anywhere you go in the United States, you will immediately know that somebody is of the fraternity if you see a little snap. So I knew that would get a response.

Because of our sex situation in terms of health these days, I also knew that there would be an immediate response to the Black Chat, the phone sex. It's always interesting for me to see that part of the film within a crowd like this, where, I'm assuming, phone sex is not a large part of your sex lives, and where you have other alternatives. For a number of gay men, phone sex has become *the* safe sex alternative, and the sight of that on the screen creates an immediate recognition.

I'm also trying to infuse a certain political sensibility into the piece, so it's not just Signifying for Fun. When you see the snap, it's snap as cultural defiance: "You won't let me in this bar? Snap you!" "You think that I'm a bitch? Snap you! No, I'm *not*!" It's the snap as a way of asserting one's identity and defying the conventions of what society would regard as being manly.

I was always thinking very specifically of having a dialogue with black gay men and assumed that for that reason I would not need to explain things: I could be highly impressionistic in my editing; I could suggest with a phrase, with a word, the way that people who know each other well can communicate without logically explaining everything they say. I could use images that I knew would resonate in terms of a cultural experience—for me, it was tremendously liberating.

This was different from making *Ethnic Notions*, where I was speaking, very consciously, to everyone, trying to reach whites as well as blacks, bigots as well as progressives. In that film, there was a need for me to address the topic of stereotyping in detail and very logically, as if building a case, a legal case, in terms of understanding the nature of racist stereotypes in America and how they become and stay embedded in our culture. *Here*, I wasn't concerned about what whites thought, what black straight people thought, what Asians or anybody else thought. I wanted to be in direct dialogue with black gay men.

This decision allowed me to be extremely honest. When you're speaking to cultural groups outside of your own, you tend to sanitize your image, and I think all of us who have tried to get access to the mainstream are aware of that dynamic. A safe, palatable, assimilated image is presented for *public* consumption, whereas all kinds of shit is being raised within the family, within the community—but you tone that down when you get outside.

I didn't want to think about the outside, and that allowed me to be very truthful in the experiences that I was exploring, as well as with my own confessional part in the piece—and not fear judgment. I could present images that, when you think about the outside culture, become problematic.

One of the stereotypes of gay men of course is that we're all flaming faggots, imitations, very pale, of women; and I thought about how that sometimes catapults filmmakers into presenting an inverted image of the stereotype (which itself becomes a stereotype): only articulate, college-educated, obviously masculine men. I wanted to show the full range of what is considered, and what *is*, manly within the community.

With that I'll shut up and let you ask questions.

Jay Ruby: I have to assume that Eddie Murphy didn't give you permission to use that material.

Riggs: No, Eddie Murphy didn't give me permission.

Ruby: Was using that material your way of taking him on?

Riggs: I wasn't taking on Eddie Murphy, or Spike Lee. Spike Lee and Eddie Murphy represent a pervasive cultural homophobia in the black community. I used them as examples; they represent something you can hear in the laughter of the people around them in the audience, something that's very poisonous in the community. I wanted to place that kind of very iconic representation of black homophobia within a context where you see from a black gay point of view. When Eddie Murphy, Spike Lee, and others make their movies, and either create their images of black gay men or make reference to black gay men, they do it with the assumption that we're not there, that we don't exist. I wanted to reveal that in fact we do exist and that there's this constant judgment of us.

I wanted to do battle with our own internal silence, which is why the focus during that section of the film is on the face of a man who is reacting, on his complicity with Eddie Murphy and his unwillingness to realize that this silence *is* death, not just in terms of AIDS, but as a cultural death, death in terms of his part in the community, death in terms of his history, death in terms of what he can give to future generations as a black gay man, as a black man, as a man.

Flaherty seminarian (F): On the information sheet about the film [since the late 1980s, seminarians are given a page of information about what they've just seen], you talk about the enormous favorable reaction it's received. Will that reaction influence how you feel about your future work?

Riggs: In some ways, yes, and in some ways, no. I realize now that even when I speak in a direct dialogue with a very particular group, it can actually communicate to others.

But also, I'm always looking for historical antecedents, as you can see in *Tongues Untied* and definitely in *Ethnic Notions*. Almost all of my work reflects a historical continuity, in music or in dance or in images; and with *Tongues Untied*, I wanted to show how we as a people are constantly having to draw from that history for our survival. You're constantly seeing images, references to the past, to show how we withstood various kinds of oppression and how that history informs to some degree what we can do to move beyond where we are now.

Michael Grillo: The piece is highly theatrical. Do you feel that in using this type of theatricality you are instigating a new form that will create an evolution in the established history of documentary?

Riggs: I guess this is where I differ from some of the people who have praised this work. For me it's not bold and groundbreaking in terms of its aesthetic. What I'm doing, quite frankly, is appropriating anything I damn well please in order to make my point. And what for me is liberating about this is that I *didn't* feel confined by documentary tradition. I felt that I could use poetry, that I could use theater, that I could use diaristic confessions, and dance, and songs, that I could use MTV style, that I could use rap, that anything that was part of the community was at my disposal for use in communicating a need for cultural strength and community.

For me in some ways, the form is already there. You see it in works that don't have a political sensibility or a culturally defiant sensibility. I see this form in music videos all the time; I hear it in rap music all the time. I mean the form I used *is* an established form. If you listen to rap, whether it's a political rap or just sort of a singing and dancing rap, there's a constant appropriation of past culture, past black culture, in the music: it's just a beat here, a bit of James Brown, a phrase. So I see myself drawing upon a very established African American form and using it with a different content.

When I talk with postmodernist critics who are white, there's a sense of tradition being in some ways deficient, defective, having little to give us in terms of an understanding of life. But for many African Americans, drawing on tradition is a way of *sustaining* life, and what has sustained us is those cultural forms: music, dance, oratory. Those are the things which we survived through the hard years, so I draw upon them.

F: Can you talk about how you made the leap from *Ethnic Notions* to this piece. I think that process might be helpful to those of us who have a hard time getting inside the less literal work that we've seen at the seminar this week.

Riggs: It wasn't hard. This work started, like most of my work, as a very conventional documentary, about black gay poets. I assumed you would see them writing their poetry and speaking it; you'd hear them in voice-over talking about why they write their poetry, then you'd come back to them performing a little poetry. I remember thinking, "This going to be *easy* to do!" [laughter] So the point of origin for the project was my reading a number of anthologies of black gay poetry and wanting to illustrate the variety of this work to a larger audience.

What I found is that the traditional documentary form didn't live up to the poetry. The form was so staid; in some ways, it sterilized the poetry, distanced it. It distanced *me*, strangely enough, because I was behind the camera. I was trying to say things about *my* experience by having the poets give voice to it—I was putting *them* on the line.

I was getting nowhere with that approach, in part because the poetry is impressionistic and discrete. The discrete poems would have made a very disjunctive work, too disjunctive. I knew that it was going to be very difficult for me to do a work like some of what we've seen this week that has real formal ruptures, for a black gay audience which, whether one likes it or not, is conditioned, like a lot of the African American community, to more traditional television and movie watching. I had to find a way to connect the poems and at the same time to include other kinds of experience.

It took me a good seven or eight months of just letting the project sit in my head, not even thinking about it at times. It wasn't really until, as some of you know, I had my personal health crisis that I started to let my imagination flow. I can't tell you any more than that. It was like the muse was speaking: you hear of artists telling you how they had a dream or saw the words in their head, and this is how it was happening to me.

I saw very clearly the mugging scene that you see after the scene with the white boy. Ordinarily, I would never have made that kind of connection: going from a white boy to a sort of hypothetical, imagined mugging—I've never been mugged— would have never occurred to me beforehand, because it involved such a leap in time and a leap from the literal to metaphor. I was allowing my imagination to flow and confining my sense of audience to those that would be least likely to misinterpret me.

I started to arrange the poems and my life into a structure where I thought there would be a sense of exploration and of discovery, *from* this largely helpless, confused adolescence, in some ways oppressed within as well as by the outside, *to* not only finding self, but community, which again I think is something that is very different for different groups.

I sometimes hear people saying, "Why do you have to deal with the social, cultural, political, ideological aspects of this problem; why don't you sort of do a portrait of the people?" For many of us within the African American community, to consider portraits of people separate from their social, cultural, political sensibility isn't possible *because* so much of what defines us as African Americans *is* cultural and social and political and ideological. Perforce you have to draw upon all of that in your portrait of self; even when it's a very internalized, interior self, it's constantly thrusting outward toward society.

So for me, making *Tongues Untied* was a gradual process, and it was when I decided to put myself into it that everything fell into place. I scripted it essentially in the hospital bed, scripted in my head while watching *Geraldo*. I could see how it would flow, and once I got out of the hospital, I just wrote it all down. My sections came fairly easily, and I knew where the poems would go. I knew that the mood would be constantly changing, would be swinging from high camp humor to tragedy and pathos, but I knew I could get away with that. In any other circumstance I would have thought, "This is too dramatic; the swings are too quick. How can you be laughing fifteen seconds earlier and now be on the edge of tears? And carry an audience with you?"

I see in the response of the audience here a lag time, compared to the black gay audiences I've had. Black gay audiences are *right there* at the moment, getting it immediately. You know, "Three pieces of ID," snap, snap, snap—they *got* it. In a more general audience, it's not until the snap rap that many people get it.

F: Did we see the ending of the film?

Riggs: No, the last line in *Tongues Untied* was actually cut off. I guess that was probably a mistake in the dub: they saw black and figured that's the end.

Berger: Explain how it actually ends.

Riggs: What happens is that you see black and you hear the opening chant again—
"brother to brother, brother to brother"—then, "Black men loving black men, a call
to action, an acknowledgment of responsibility. We take care of our own kind when
the nights are cold and silent. These days the nights are cold-blooded and the silence
echoes with complicity." It's very strong because the voice is this crescendo, and then
you see the credits. And the acknowledgment of NEA funding. [laughter]

F: I'll control myself, Marlon. I've talked to Marlon a lot about this piece, and I saw it in
a crowd in Philadelphia that was one of the most affirming experiences of artist and
community I've ever experienced—just phenomenal. But rather than go on about
how much I love this tape, and how affirming and brilliant I think it is, I want to ask a
really mundane question.

This tape needs to be seen by a wide audience; it speaks to more than just a
black gay male community because it deals with really profoundly human qualities
of identity and honesty and facing the truth within ourselves—it speaks to many
people. You're trying to put this on public television in an era when everything is
against doing that. Could you talk about the places where you *have* been able to get it
shown and any kind of conditions or limits that they might have set, or if there were
none? And why do you think that those particular people are allowing you to show
the film?

Riggs: *Tongues Untied* has been in a number of festivals around the country, and I
anticipated that that would not be a problem. I didn't anticipate television, any
television station, airing it. In fact, it turned out that after the American Film
Institute premiere, a number of public television stations called me up, which
shocked me. WNET in New York called up; WGBH, the New Television Workshop;
KCET and KQED. Three of them decided to air it. KQED has already aired it.

I told everyone no cuts; I mean it's not as if you can sort of bleep a word here
and a scene there. I mean that's the point: the racism, the homophobic epithets, the
language about sex—the film is direct because that's the nature of the experience
that we're dealing with. WGBH didn't like it, or felt in some ways offended by it.
They said, "This should never be aired on public television anywhere in this country."
WNET in New York and KQED and KCET in Los Angeles are showing it in prime
time, uncut and unedited, which again I'm shocked by.

I am going to submit it to POV; I've let Mark Weis know, so we'll see what
happens. He hasn't seen it. I think it has an audience: KQED had the largest number
of calls in their history for any program they have ever shown, and 90 percent of
the calls were enthusiastically positive. They also received the largest number of
unsolicited pledges that they've ever had for one program. [applause]

F: Have they paid to run the show?

Riggs: Well, they didn't pay very much. That's the old broken record: we don't have no
money. But it is getting on television. And it is being distributed educationally, to
community groups, film societies, anybody who wants to show it.

But television is really where people won't feel threatened, particularly people
who think if they go out to anything ostensibly gay, that will label them and therefore
tarnish them. I do recognize the need for people to see this in their homes, in private,
curtains closed, and yet, I hope, feel empowered afterward, so that the next time
something comes along, they'll open up the curtains, they'll go out, they'll march,
they'll sing, they'll snap, they'll dance and do what needs to be done.

Berger: Just one more question, because there is another screening after this.

Linda Lilienfeld: I'd just like to say that that the reaction we've had and that other people have had is interesting in relation to the idea of personal film in the programming of this seminar. For you as a black gay person in our society to be able to be straightforward is such a gift to *everyone*. When you chose to speak to the audience that you saw as your closest group, you thought that being that specific would be leaving everyone else out—that, coupled with the unusual form of the film. But by being *extremely* specific in terms of your audience, by speaking in coded language, and in working in the sort of unconscious way you describe, oddly enough, you are in fact reaching a very large audience. *Tongues Untied* is so honest that it asks everyone to look at their own lives and their own ways of masking themselves to their peers and their families.

One of the problems in Patti's film and I think even in Su's [Patti Bruck had just shown *Slippage* (1989) and Su Friedrich had shown *Sink or Swim* (1990) earlier on this day] is that they're still a little bit caught up in masking their feelings. I think it's a great tribute to you, Marlon, not just as a filmmaker, but as a human being, that you can face the truth of life; and one of the most touching achievements of *Tongues Untied* is that you've had to find a *personal* way of liberating yourself from your own chains, and that's what gives *us* such a gift. [applause]

1991 WILLIAM GREAVES—ON *SYMBIOPSYCHOTAXIPLASM: TAKE ONE* (1972)

Jackie Tshaka: I've seen a lot of your other films, but *Symbiopsychotaxiplasm: Take One* is so different! Where has it been shown?

William Greaves: We showed it at the Brooklyn Museum retrospective [April 1991]; we also showed it at the Federal Theater, and in Paris at the retrospective of black American film in 1980. Those are the only three public showings we've had. The film was never released. We shot it in 1967 and then had difficulty getting money to finish it. We finally got the money for a blowup in 1971, but then we had the problem of trying to get the film launched. I thought maybe I could get it into the Cannes Film Festival and I flew over to France. The problem was that Louis Marcorelles, the influential critic, went to a prescreening of the film and the projectionist got the reels all fouled up. *Symbio* is already chaotic. It's so fragile that if you mix it up even a little you lose the film. Marcorelles and I had dinner after the screening, and he said, "I couldn't understand what the film was about!" I couldn't understand his reaction but later discovered that his projectionist had screened it the wrong way.

I like to think of that incident as a divine intervention: it has kept this film buried for almost twenty-five years. I was so interested to show it tonight because almost no one here has seen it.

Bill Sloan: I've probably known Bill Greaves longer than anyone in this room. In fact, I saw *Symbiopsychotaxiplasm* when it was still in a rough cut back in the sixties. Bill, you had struggled to develop a career as a documentarian, and then, just as you'd gotten things under way, you stopped to make *this* film. What possessed you?

Greaves: There are several different answers. I'd been a member of the Actors Studio since 1949 and knew the Stanislavsky system—The Method, Lee Strasberg, that whole approach to theater and acting. I began teaching actors in Canada, and one of my actors there was extremely adroit at business ventures and became very wealthy.

She wanted me to make a feature and said, "Anything you want to make, just tell me." I began to realize I could put a feature together using some of the actors at the school.

A whole range of other concerns were involved, too. The term *symbiopsychotaxiplasm* is a takeoff on *symbiotaxiplasm*, a concept developed by philosopher/social scientist Arthur Bentley, as part of his study of the processes of social scientific inquiry. The term *symbiotaxiplasm* referred to all those events that transpire in any given environment on which a group of human beings impact in any way. Of course, the most elaborate symbiotaxiplasm would be a city like New York. I had the audacity to put "psycho" into the middle of Bentley's term. I felt the longer term more appropriate to my idea, which was to explore the psychology of a group of creative people who would function as an entity in the process of making a film.

I called it *Symbiopsychotaxiplasm: Take One* because the plan was to make five symbiopsychotaxiplasms. But we couldn't even get the first one off the ground, and never developed the others.

F: It used to be said about a certain generation of experimental films—I guess mostly in the late sixties, early seventies—that a film taught you *how* to watch it *as* you were watching it. In a way *Symbiopsychotaxiplasm: Take One* does that, because you have your surrogates on the screen reacting in the way that the audience is reacting. Their responses confirm ours.

Greaves: Well, the function of that first scene—when all hell breaks loose and you are suddenly seeing three separate images on the split-screen, and, in particular, the ambivalent craziness that surrounds this kind of location shooting—was to push the audience into a state of annoyance. When people in the crew appear on screen and say, "This is not the way you make a movie!" and "What the hell is this all about?" the audience begins to relax and say, "That's right!" They find themselves looking for a clue on the screen that articulates what they have just experienced. The crew says, "This is a piece of shit. He doesn't know what he's doing. I read the script; it doesn't mean anything. It's just bad writing." And the audience thinks, "Yes, it *is* bad writing."

Lazar Stojanovic: In 1970, a Yugoslavian writer came back from the United States and told me about Bill Greaves and this film. He knew that I was very interested in what I call self-analytical movies, movies that consider the medium. I couldn't really get a clear picture of Bill's film—only that it was related to some of Godard's work. Now that I have finally seen *Symbiopsychotaxiplasm*, I think it's a milestone in the history of the sixties.

Michelle Materre: You must have had your ego in a great place to be able to allow the crew to think about you the way they did.

Greaves: It was a calculated risk. In general, my livelihood turns on people's perceiving me as a director, and yet, for this particular film to work, a flawed, vulnerable persona was essential. I must say I feel very good about my relationship with the crew. Even when they spoke about me at their meeting, they didn't speak in anger. They were six characters in search of an author, or like the characters in *Outward Bound* (a play I had a role in when I first started acting) [*Outward Bound* was written by Sutton Vane and premiered in London in 1923], who are on a ship but don't know why, or where they're going.

Maria DeLuca: I have a mundane question about the sequence of the crew at their private meeting. Did I miss something? It's one thing for them to say, "Let's get together and have a conference," but film is expensive. How did it happen that they were shooting film?

Greaves: We were well endowed with raw stock. They saw I was burning it up with these three cameras rolling at once, and I guess they figured I wouldn't miss two or three thousand feet! [laughter]

MacDonald: Certain ways of critiquing conventional film happen in many places simultaneously. In the sixties, for example, there were a number of different attempts to critique cinéma vérité: Shirley Clarke's *The Connection* [1961], Jonas Mekas's *The Brig* [1964], and Peter Watkins's *Punishment Park* [1970] are distinguished instances. The one that strikes me as closest to this film is Jim McBride's *David Holzman's Diary* [1967], which itself was inspired by the work of Andrew Noren. I'm curious as to whether you had any contact with McBride or Noren.

Greaves: I've heard of *David Holzman's Diary,* but I've not seen it. I've been involved in *making* films, and, you know, you stay in an editing room until you're exhausted, then you go home and collapse, and get up and do it again. There was a period in my life when I used to go to the theater a great deal and to the movies. But that stopped after I left Canada in 1960.

Richard Herskowitz: Did you think of *Symbiopsychotaxiplasm* as a satire of cinéma vérité in particular?

Greaves: At the National Film Board of Canada, I was in the unit that pioneered cinéma vérité on the North American continent. Terry Filgate (the English cameraman in *Symbiopsychotaxiplasm*) and I were together at the National Film Board at what was called Unit B. We worked on films like *Lonely Boy* [1961, Wolf Koenig, Roman Kroitor] and *Emergency Ward* [1958, Greaves]. The process of learning to do that kind of shooting made me very attuned to the spontaneous capturing of reality and certainly laid the groundwork for *Symbio*.

But I should tell you some of the other thinking that I had in mind while making *Symbiopsychotaxiplasm*. I went to a science high school in New York City and was in general pointed in the direction of science. I broke that off in college, but I continued to be interested in various scientific theories. The Heisenberg Principle of Uncertainty, in particular, fascinated me. Heisenberg asserts that we'll never really know the basis of the cosmos because the means of perception alters the reality it observes. The electron microscope sends out a beam of electrons that knocks the electrons of the atoms being observed out of their orbits.

I began to think of the movie camera as an analog to the electron microscope. In this case, the reality to be observed is the human soul, the psyche. Of course, as the camera investigates that part of the cosmos, the individual psyches being observed recoil. Behavior becomes structured in a way other than it would have been had it been unperceived—a psychological version of the Heisenberg Principle. In this sense, my film was an environment in which movie cameras were set up to catch the process of human response.

Another scientific law that interested me was the Second Law of Thermodynamics, which describes the distribution of energy in a system. In *Symbiopsychotaxiplasm*, the cameras were to track the flow of energy in the system I had devised. If the cameras looked at one person and the level of spontaneous reality began to recede as a result of their being observed, that energy would show up somewhere else—behind the cameras in the crew, for example. The cameras were set up to track the flow of energy from in front of the cameras to behind them and back to the front. . .

Alan Rosenthal: Did you look at the rushes in between the filming, or did you just continue shooting?

Greaves: Well, we had to look at the rushes to see whether we were getting things on film, but I didn't see the rushes of the crew at their secret meeting until after the shooting was over. Bob Rosen came to me and said, "Bill, we have a little present for you." [laughter]

Patricia Zimmermann: In documentary and in certain narrative forms, there's a long history of self-reflexive filmmaking as a political intervention to disengage the traditional power of the director. It's evident at least as early as Vertov. In the sixties, self-reflexivity became an international movement: Godard, Makavejev, Stojanovic, many American and European avant-garde filmmakers, you. . . . In all these instances, self-reflexivity functioned as a way of disengaging from certain authoritarian power relations to make way for more utopian ways of working in the world. One scene in your film seems to encapsulate this: the scene where you're sitting with your multiracial, mixed-gender crew. And you're an African American director. Could you situate your method within the politics of the time?

Greaves: Well, clearly we were working in a context of the urban disorders of the sixties and the rage of the African American community against the tyranny and racism of the American body politic. There was that general response, plus the more specific struggles: the civil rights marches and the other strategies that were being employed by the African American community. And there was the whole Vietnam problem and the growing dissent over it. There was the emerging feminist movement. And Woodstock. There was an unhappiness of massive dimensions over the way in which society had been run and about the covert authoritarianism that was evident everywhere. True, America was no dictatorship, but there certainly were mores, local and federal laws, social structures in place that inhibited the flowering of the human spirit.

This film was an attempt to look at the impulses and inspirations of a group of creative people who, during the making of the film, were being "pushed to the wall" by the process I as director had instigated. The scene that I had written was fixed, and I was in charge. I was insisting that this scene be done by the cast and crew, even though it was making them very unhappy. The question was, "When will they revolt?" When would they question the validity, the wisdom, of doing the scene in the first place? In this sense, it really *was* a reflection of the politics of the time.

F: The issue this film raises for me is individual power versus collective power. At one point in the film, you say, "I represent the establishment." I find that when I'm directing a mixed crew, particularly a gender-mixed crew, I have power relationship problems because of my gender and race. When you as an African American director said, "I represent the establishment," how did your crew respond?

Greaves: I had an excellent relationship with the crew. You have to think in terms of the sixties, when there was a breaking out of a whole lot of ossified thinking. The people who worked on *Symbiopsychotaxiplasm* were Age-of-Aquarius-type people, who were in many respects shorn of the encumbrances that many white Americans are burdened with. If you investigated the psychology of these people, you wouldn't discover elements of racism or prejudice. They had a very collaborationist approach.

F: Did you expect a counterculture audience for the film? Or did you hope for distribution through commercial theaters?

Greaves: When we first had a blowup, we did show it to a couple of distributors, and their eyeballs went around in their sockets. They just couldn't figure out how to categorize and package it. One of the critics from *Time* had come by my studio in the sixties and said, "Gee, this thing is not going to be acceptable for twenty years." Right now, I have the film with some of the so-called leading lights in innovative distribution, so we'll see.

    The audience here at the seminar represents a high level of appreciation. You're all cinema people: filmmakers, cinema scholars, and so on, and that's always an unusual situation. I think that the film will make its way into art theaters and onto the college circuit and to whatever film societies are out there. But it will probably get wider consumption in the twenty-first century because of its increasing archival value: there were few films made in the sixties that so effectively tracked the psychological and emotional mechanisms of young people. From a sociological or anthropological perspective, it will have more and more utility.

Steve Gallagher: What was the reaction of the cast and crew when they saw the film?

Greaves: Only three or four of them have seen it. Bob Rosen saw it, and he reacted the same way Muhammad Ali did to the film I made about him [*Ali, the Fighter*, 1971]. That film was shot cinéma vérité, too, and while we were filming, Ali wouldn't cooperate, for legal and other reasons, I suppose. So we used a telephoto lens, hidden mics, and so on. About a year later, after the fight was over and the film was finished, I got a call from Ali saying, "Listen, I want to see that film you did." So we set up a screening for him, and he sat in the theater saying, "How did you get this shot? How did you do *that*?" He was amazed. Rosen's reaction was similar; I don't think he anticipated the film that he saw. I think (I hope) he was surprised in a pleasant way.

Jack Churchill: Did you always know what you were doing while you were shooting?

Greaves: There were certain constants that I tried to predetermine as much as possible, and then I released the human consciousness into this field of determinants. It was similar to the way we come into this room. We have all agreed to be here to talk about the film, but what happens takes its own direction.

1992 KEN JACOBS — ON *XCXHXEXRXRXIXEXSX* (MANY PERFORMANCES AFTER 1980)

Richard Herskowitz: A little background on Ken. Many of you know him as one of the central figures in the underground film movement of the sixties, with films like *Blonde Cobra* [1963] and *Little Stabs at Happiness* [1963]. He was involved in some of the key formative events in avant-garde film during that period: the trial about showing Jack Smith's *Flaming Creatures* [1963], the founding of the Filmmakers' Cooperative, and of the Millennium Film Workshop. He went on to make one of the key "structural" films, *Tom, Tom, the Piper's Son* [1971]. Also, since 1970 Ken has been a film professor at SUNY-Binghamton [now Binghamton University], where he's had an enormous influence on many people, including me.

    What Ken taught was not so much how to watch experimental films but how to watch *all* films experimentally. He showed us how we could play with and "reedit" the wide variety of films he showed us, *as we watched them*. That's informed all my work as a programmer.

In the past couple of decades, Ken has been much involved with the Nervous System technology you saw tonight.

Ken Jacobs: Thank you for the kind words. To create the film you saw just now, I use identical rolls of the same film, and two stop-motion projectors. While one projector advances the film one frame at a time, the other is capable of many different kinds of movement during the performance: it can tilt up and down and left and right. The effects on the screen depend on which two frames are superimposed at any given moment and on the particular differences between those frames. A propeller is mounted in front of the projectors; it moves as I'm working and is essential for the effects I create.

John Columbus: I know a lot of things beyond the technology are on people's minds, so I may as well start the ball rolling. Maybe technically, *Cherries* is wonderful. But what about your source material? What went into the choice? Is it a *statement*?

Jacobs: A statement? Well, I wish it *wasn't*. I guess according to the society we live in, it would have to be a statement. Any imagery of sex presented to the public is a statement in a society that is more secretive about its sexual activities than its bathroom habits. For some of us here, there was a short period of time in the late sixties and early seventies where sex ceased to be shocking.

You *are* asking about the use of pornography, right?

Columbus: Well, of course. We could also talk about the perceptual visceralness of the whole performance. But why necessarily pornography? Does it matter what your source material is?

Jacobs: It matters very much in terms of what can happen on screen. The kinds of effects I can get depend on the character of the material. . .

Columbus: The graphic character or the content character?

Jacobs: The graphic character. Where things are in space and what kind of movement takes place.

Herskowitz: Some of your earlier films have strong political thematic content as well. I think John wants to know how you settle on the political nature of the pieces of film that enter your system at any given time.

Jacobs: It depends on my needs and what I'm concerned with. *Camera Thrills of the War* [1981] was done upon the approach of the Reagan presidency. I had tremendous fears at that time: I was afraid that with Reagan in power, apocalyptic forces in the country might actually *have* an opportunity to achieve their goal of destroying life on earth so it could be replaced with a New "Christian" World. I began doing works in response to my fear. They were cries in the dark. They reached very few people.

Herskowitz: Could you bring us back to your use of this particular pornographic footage?

Jacobs: I was working with a lot of very unhappy material—there was also a work called *The Philippines Adventure*, which had to do with the history of American imperialism in the Philippines—and I just needed a break from all this negativity, so I chose the porn film. [laughter, much of it ironic]

I also wanted to get into the potential of the Nervous System to work with rounded objects, curved volumes, up-close; and I wanted to see if I could create a motor action in the imagery that was appropriate to the motor action of the Nervous System itself. The Nervous System projectors "copulate." It seemed natural to think about sex.

I wanted something as explicit as possible because I find coyness disgusting. I find beating around the bush reprehensible. So I wanted the body, and I wanted what bodies do with each other. A friend, a woman who was editing pornographic film for the mafia, said they were throwing out some old black-and-white porn films, and I said, "Ideal." I got two little films and loved them both. I like the people in the piece I used tonight. I think they're very nice to each other. They seem to know what they're doing.

F: One of the effects you make with the two projectors made me nauseous—especially when you sprayed the cherry scent.

Jacobs: I didn't do that!

F: You didn't? [laughter]

Do other people complain about the strobe-like effect? I could only watch *Cherries* in bits, though in some parts you created effects that didn't bother me—for example, where the imagery was like sculpture.

Jacobs: Of course it's easier on the eye not to have the strobe effect, but I'm always trying to create effects that are appropriate to the specific frames and to their position within the overall work. In *Cherries*, I need the strobing.

F: But you're not going *for* a visceral effect, right?

Jacobs: I'm not going for the flicker for the sake of flicker. I have to use the flicker to get all the other effects, which I hope we can mention. Like the continuous rolling effect. And the 3-D, which is sometimes very apparent. Some of these effects are very beautiful for me—purely aesthetic satisfactions that drive me on. When I hit something that's satisfying, I stay with it and try to build on it. Martin Arnold's *Pièce Touchée* [1989], which we saw last night, doesn't introduce flicker, so it's easier to stand—I understand that—and he does some beautiful things. *Pièce Touchée* is a joy to see. But he doesn't get quite the kinds of effects I get. He creates more surface information about a space; I create more of an illusion of space in depth.

Herskowitz: You also create new imagery: you create spaces where we see things that we know can't possibly be there.

Jacobs: Yes, I really give you a workout with some very uncanny spaces that are not trying to create the verisimilitude of the original scene. Positive and negative spaces change location. Things you *know* are forward—once you've learned to read a photograph—seem further back, and vice versa. Crazy illusions take place.

Alan Rosenthal: The first twenty minutes of this film, as we come to grips with perceiving the images, are absolutely fascinating. But after an hour, a third of the audience was outside, and I think this is a relatively sophisticated and open audience. They weren't just outside; there were a number of people saying, "Let's kill the programmer!" [laughter]

Now I know there are different perceptions of experimental film and where it's at and some of us like it, some of us don't. Those of us who don't are trying to find out what we're missing if we're not getting it and if we're driven out by boredom. For some of us, there was a feeling that staying in the theater another hour would not have enlarged the experience.

Now, can *anybody* tell us what we're missing? I mean this as an open question, not as an accusation.

F: I can tell you why *I* left, if that will start things off. I'm really disturbed that we've spent at least twenty minutes talking about technique—and ignoring *content*! I left because I found the experience offensive and disturbing, and very violent. I'm not against violence. I think violence can be useful in movies, if it's a critique . . . but *you* think it's *fun* or something. For me to watch this is like watching a rape. Pornographic imagery has to do with women and power. I don't know if you're interested in that, but for me it was just this male gaze thing for two hours. And that's something *we* have to live with *every day*!

Jacobs: Well, it disturbs *me* that you don't want to talk about *art*! It's a very important subject that you bring up, but I think that you're stapling it onto this film. You're unable to see that in *Cherries* nobody hurts anybody else. People are engaging each other, both giving and taking pleasure. This "violence" you're reacting to is just the excitement of the scene—nature *is* energetic!—but no one gets punched in the jaw, or shot. . .

F: That's not the only kind of violence!

Jacobs: No one in the film is forced to do anything!

Herskowitz: The voyeuristic gaze is a fascinating issue in connection with *Cherries*. When I first saw it ten years ago, it expanded my thinking about pornography and voyeurism. Pornography is more *how* we look at things than what we look at. When one's look is distanced, mastering, controlling, voyeuristic—that to me is a pornographic *look*. The images themselves can be changed, transformed into something else. The original film was probably directed totally at a voyeuristic gaze, but in the expansion of this material, something independent of, transcendent of the original takes place. You go beyond the original intent, and something repressed in the original is liberated.

When I look at pornographic images, I look at myself looking. I see the film looking at me looking, and at my ways of looking. *Cherries* gives me time to think about these issues. I didn't program this film [laughter], but I've recommended it to many programmers [the 1992 Flaherty was programmed by several Flaherty board members; *Cherries* was programmed by Scott MacDonald as part of the week focusing on cinema as motion study].

Jacobs: There's a problem in dealing with hot social material of any sort: this kind of material makes it very difficult for people to see the art . . . I hear a kind of *sneering* from some of you, as if *art* is some dumb, trivial thing to bring up! Art! Maybe it's worth a conversation about what art is about; to me it's about whether we even come into existence. . .

Columbus: Oh, we know, artists are gods! And we all have to listen to God. . .

Jacobs: I despise the far-righteous!

Herskowitz: Please, please, let's go on.

Laura U. Marks: I think there are some really interesting ways to talk about the use of pornography in this film. But I think the opposition Ken is setting up between hot social material and art is not it. And to say this is an interesting film because of the rounded objects isn't it. The reason why pornography in particular is interesting as a subject for motion study—which your film is, and which is the theme of the curating these past two days—has to do with stopping motion to investigate the body and attain a kind of mastery. Pornography is, among many other things, about a gaze that possesses.

But another interesting thing is that your film is about engaging desire and prolonging it at the same time. You took a short film and stretched it out to more than two hours. The original film's purpose was to be watched and jacked off to, but how do we deal with the *prolongation* of the original film? Do we jack off several times over the two hours or what? I'm not opposed to pornography, and I think your choice of porn was pretty good—the women do take pleasure, not just the man—and I think it was open to a pretty wide variety of readings. But what's also interesting is that your means have a very fundamental connection to pornography, and there's no point pussy-footing around that issue.

Jacobs: I don't understand what you're saying. If you're hopped up on the male gaze, and patriarchy, and power, I guess that's the way you'll see my film. But *Cherries* and my other work is also about becoming conscious of what exists, of *seeing* what exists.

I *don't* think I stretched a minute and a half into a two-hour masturbation festival...

Marks: That was a cheap shot on my part.

Jacobs: It was disgusting! *Disgusting!* Oh, you're all such fools!

Columbus: Well, *that* opens the dialogue! ¹

Jacobs: I took something that was meant to be used as an abuse of the body, an abuse of even what the camera can do, and I transmuted it into something glorious. I took it back to life!

Columbus: That's what...

Jacobs: SHUT UP! Don't interrupt me.

Columbus: You're such an elitist, fascist...

Jacobs: FUCK YOU! You disgusting creeps!

[Jacobs walks out. After a short break, those still in the discussion space continue the discussion.]

Austin Allen: There's a consensus that the discussion is ending too quickly. Why leave it at this point? [laughter] Willie, do you want to start?

Willie Varela: I'm sure a lot of you don't know me. I'm from El Paso, Texas. I've been making films for about twenty years. I'm going to give you a little background to position what's happened here because I think some of it has to do with a change between the generation of Ken, and Stan Brakhage and Jonas Mekas, and the generations that have come after them, for whom the social and political aspects of art—whatever form a film takes, whether it's an experimental film, a social documentary, whatever—are very important, and many times so important that they cancel out the formal aspects.

I've never met Ken Jacobs before. I'm not an apologist. But I have to say that film artists like Ken had to make work in a climate that was extremely hostile. They were vilified for their work a great deal of the time, sometimes even persecuted legally for work like we saw here today.

This is the first time I've seen *Cherries*. I stayed through the whole thing, and as I watched I was trying to figure out my position on looking at this very loaded sexual material. Years ago, I also went through a period when I was interested in pornography, and at the same time, I was reading "Visual Pleasure and Narrative Cinema" by Laura Mulvey and a lot of film theory—trying to figure out what was happening in my interface with pornography, and what it would mean to a woman to be looked at in this way.

I think the response of the young woman back there was very valid. The male gaze, the exploitation of the female body, all these issues *are* important and central for the generations that have come after Ken, to their consciousness of *what is seen*. I myself have had to *learn* that.

However, I also see Ken's side and recognize that he was truly interested in establishing a formal relationship to the material. What happened here is unfortunate because I think Ken is a great artist, and I think he had a lot to say.

F: We have to be careful not to let ideology put blinders in our brains and our sensitivities. I found it a very sexy, funny film.

William Rowley: I had the experience of thinking I was looking at a zoom-in, a continuous enlargement of the frame, and then I'd look at the edge of the frame and see that in fact it wasn't changing size. Also, at certain points, those were no longer people we were watching: they were shadows. Some of us forget that and think we're watching people.

Varela: We're watching representations of people. I don't think we can forget *that* either. I want a *frisson* where you're balancing the formal aspects with the content: that creates a unique, exquisite tension.

Rowley: There's also the tension of holding on to the imagery, recognizing it *as* a representation, *and* letting it become just an abstract shape for a while when the whole business of content falls away.

F: About this generational split. It's not being characterized to my satisfaction. I don't think the younger generation separates formal concerns/Art and social issues/Ideology: we see those things as woven together and quite inseparable. All of us, always, speak through the ideologies that shape us.

Rowley: Of course, even "Art" is a set of blinders. . .

Scott MacDonald: But the idea that ideology and art can't be separated is not new. I'd guess that what upsets Ken is the assumption that after all these years of working with these issues, *he* doesn't know what he's doing. *His* assumption at a certain point in his career, and still to some degree I'd guess, is that one of the oppressive systems one has to liberate oneself from is certain attitudes toward sexuality. Ironically, at one point not so long ago, pornography seemed to embody a *healthier* attitude about sexuality than had existed in most of the culture before porn was so widely available. Ken is coming out of a period when it was ideological and courageous to *represent* sexuality.

F: Our generation is reclaiming porn, too. There's all this great, funky porn coming out right now, and there's lots of discourse about porn made by women for women, and by men for men.

Alan Rosenthal: The question that continues to bother me, because no one's addressed it, is how we are to evaluate experimental art. It intellectually engages you while you're looking to see what the artists are playing around with. If I'm looking at a piece by Picasso or any modernist painter, I might take five or ten minutes to absorb what he's trying to do, and then I've had my pleasure. I'm not growing any more by giving it *another* five minutes. In a film like this, twenty minutes is fascinating. Then for me, there's no further growth. But a lot of people were obviously enjoying it immensely. Maybe it's just a kind of pleasure that's beyond me.

Varela: I can address that. When you see a piece like this, duration *is* important, because it provides the opportunity to go beyond your normal barriers, the normal defenses we all have, into a space where the artist wants you to be. And I think especially in this particular gathering we should be able to meet the artist more than halfway.

Rosenthal: There were people outside, at least thirty, who stayed fifty minutes to an hour. I would have thought that was enough time to find that "exquisite tension" you talked about.

Ruth Bradley: I think it's a terrific two-hour film! So after twenty minutes, you've learned how to watch the film. The next hour and a half, I tested what I knew. I got bored at times; I got turned on at times; I fell asleep once, came back. I enjoyed the whole thing. And the last few minutes were amazing!

F: About the duration: after a while you have time to ruminate. That's why I think pornography was a shrewd choice because if there's an issue we need to spend time thinking about, it's pornography. I had time to enjoy the imagery as a typical male *and* to think about how the women in the original film might have been feeling *and* to wonder if, when the lights came on, Jacobs was going to get kicked in the nuts [laughter], and how he was going to take it. I had time to think all kinds of things.

MacDonald: There are films I go to for information, knowledge, a reconfirmation that I'm intelligent, or ideologically legitimate, or whatever. But there are other films I go to in order to have an *unusual experience*. I don't always say to the filmmaker, the experience has to be of a certain duration or I won't consider it. Sometimes I say (implicitly), I want to have the experience *you* have in mind: *you* decide the duration, and I will access it as best I can.

I don't see why the fact that a third of the people in the room are bored after an hour, which is predictable and understandable, is the crucial issue. The fact that two-thirds of the people stay, and many of those people are finding it fascinating, makes the experience worth offering. In my view, everybody's justified in choosing how long they engage the performance. If it were a matter of just *getting it*, well, I guess I can go into any commercial film, no matter how wonderful, or to any documentary, no matter how well informed; and in fifteen minutes, *I know where it's going*. I could say, "I know where it's going!" and walk out. But usually, I stay for the whole experience.

1992 KAZUO HARA—ON *EXTREME PRIVATE EROS* (1974)

[I am indebted to Stephen Schible for his translation of Kazuo Hara's comments at the 1992 seminar and during my work on the Hara discussion.]

Jesse Lerner: Many of us have this image of Japan, a stereotypical image maybe, as a place where the pressure to conform is very strong. The woman in *Extreme Private Eros*, and Mr. Okuzaki in *God's Army Marches On* [known in the US as *The Emperor's Naked Army Marches On*, 1987], really break that stereotype.

Kazuo Hara [as translated by Stephen Schible]: *Extreme Private Eros* was made twenty years ago, so you're looking at Japan in the seventies. That was a very active time, a very liberal time. It was not just Miyuki Takeda who acted as she did. Of course, Mr. Okuzaki is a person who goes beyond generations and time and everything else.

As a filmmaker it is not interesting for me to portray subjects who are "normal." It is easier for me to follow somebody who is aggressive, who is living an interesting life. As an independent filmmaker, I don't have much money, and I don't have all the time I would like for making films. Therefore, I need a subject that makes me really want to jump into a project and work.

I have become interested in the difference between Japanese and American documentary. I've spoken to some filmmakers and critics in Japan, and those people and I agree that there *is* a difference. I'm not talking about all American documentaries but very generally. American documentaries often criticize something, whereas the films of Ogawa Shinsuke and Tsuchimoto Noriaki [for example, *Minamata: Kanji-sans to sono sekai (Minamata: The Victims and Their World*, 1972), a well-known exposé about a village whose inhabitants got mercury poisoning from factory waste] do not criticize but move along with the subjects. I'm not saying one approach is better than the other, but I always feel that difference.

F: When you say, "move along with the subject," do you mean they literally live with the subject for a while, or that they create a kind of synergic relationship with the subject?

Hara: In Japanese there is a phrase, "eating rice from the same bowl." There's a sense of community that is born from a close relationship, and conflicts develop from that closeness as well. A working relationship involves a kind of kinship. Of course, American filmmakers become very deeply involved with their films, but they tend to leave space between themselves and their subjects.

Also, there is a tendency in recent American documentary filmmaking to rely too heavily on interviews and also to feel that you can just edit bits and pieces together to make a documentary. Many recent works use interviews in a very superficial way, and they put too much trust in the words spoken by the subjects. In Japanese there is a phrase: "peeling pickled garlic." You peel a pickled garlic one layer at a time, and you peel another layer and there is still another layer beneath it . . . there is no core in a pickled garlic. When we have a relationship with reality and explore it, we peel one layer of reality, and we think we can see another layer of reality. But the trouble with *that* level of reality is that if we peel *it*, we see still *another* layer of reality. And the third or fourth layer is not exactly the real truth either.

What is interesting about making documentary films is peeling those layers, and it is difficult to do that simply by relying on the words you record, on the interview process, where you only face the first level of reality. There is a difference between what a person is saying and what a person is feeling. I try to peel the expression on a person's face and go to other levels of truth.

Margarita De La Vega Hurtado: I have a question about the relationship between the subject and the director. How much control did your subject have over the final film? There are a couple places where I see Miyuki Takeda objecting to being filmed and yet you continue to film.

Hara: Extreme Private Eros began at the point when Miyuki Takeda decided to go to Okinawa and asked me to come to Okinawa and film her. I think she still had feelings toward me. She was not pregnant yet, but she had told me that she would like to become pregnant and deliver a baby on her own, to prove her existence as a woman, and that this should be part of the film. I asked her if she was serious, and she answered, "Yes." I decided to do the project. She did not have a final say about the content of the film. I saw it as my film, and I believe she saw it as my film.

Lise Yasui: I have complex feelings about Miyuki Takeda: I liked her sometimes and I hated her sometimes. The attitudes about the black GIs she expresses in the pamphlet she passes out in Okinawa are disturbing. She accuses the black GIs of using the women in Okinawa, and yet she, as an independent woman, seems to be using you *and* the black man *and* her baby.

Hara: What I wanted to do in this film was to express my feelings as I lived through and filmed the events, and that is a very difficult thing to do. When Miyuki Takeda was going out with the black guy, Paul, I went to film them; and while I was filming, I became very jealous. When you operate the camera, you have to worry about the aperture, the focus, the distance between the subjects and yourself—you have to be very logical. But I was very emotional. For some reason, during that time a friend was present, and I asked my friend to film for me because I could not continue. I was crying.

Later, I wondered about what to do next. I thought, "I cannot shoot like this anymore." And so instead of filming alone, in a one-on-one situation, I begged my current wife to come into the project.

F: Were you jealous because the man was black? What were your feelings about the interracial situation in Okinawa?

Hara: I would have been equally jealous if the man were Japanese. At the time, there were ideas about Black Power in Okinawa, as well as in America. Miyuki Takeda intentionally spent time in the black area because she was interested in the Black Power movement in the States.

Laura U. Marks: What was in the pamphlets the woman was passing out in Okinawa and who were the gangsters? You got beaten up by the gangsters; was the woman also beaten?

Hara: Only I was beaten. It was a local Okinawan gang, and Miyuki Takeda was from the mainland. In the seventies, within Japan, Okinawa was considered a third world area, and many people who were challenging the emperor's Japan went to Okinawa, including Miyuki Takeda. Since she was not a person from Okinawa, most likely the gang misunderstood her act of distributing the pamphlets. It may be very hard to understand the content of the pamphlets in the English subtitles. For most of their stay in Okinawa, Miyuki Takeda and the other woman were staying in the black section of Okinawa. In that area, there were many couples, Japanese women and black men. In the pamphlet, she wrote about those relationships. In my film, it may seem like she was looking down on Okinawa, but that wasn't the case. Really, she respected Okinawa very much. She loved Okinawa.

Yasui: Feeling about Miyuki Takeda as you did, was it difficult to portray her bad side, as well as her good side?

Hara: Well, I don't think she has a "bad side."

Toward the end of the film, Miyuki Takeda was part of a commune, and when that commune ended three or four years later, she raised her two children on her own. Two or three years ago, Yu, the half-American/half-Japanese girl, was adopted and moved to America. It is difficult in Japan for black/Japanese children.

Generally, our lives have gone separate ways.

Marks: In *Extreme Private Eros* and *The Emperor's Naked Army Marches On*, you raise the issue of Japan being a racially pure country. Both films explore some sort of racial mixing. There's the interest of the Japanese women in black American soldiers in *Extreme Private Eros*. And in *The Emperor's Naked Army Marches On*, we learn that when there was cannibalism at the end of the war, there were racial taboos about who could be eaten. Are you interested in attacking the idea of racial purity in your films?

Hara: A politician has said that Japan is a homogeneous country. Our generation laughs at that. There are differences even among Japanese. Okinawa has been returned to Japan, but the people living in Okinawa feel they are Okinawan. They believe they are a separate race.

F: Sometimes filmmakers have a hard time figuring out when a story is over. How did you decide that *Extreme Private Eros* was finished?

Hara: When I am filming, I will suddenly get a feeling that I can end this project now. I obey that feeling. Sometimes it takes me three or five years to make one film, because I will continue until that feeling comes.

F: Can you talk about your editing decisions?

Hara: I shot the events one by one, chronologically, and during the editing process, I compressed all the information I had gathered. I didn't change very much. I feel that when you edit this kind of film, it's most natural to just connect everything the way it was shot.

Phred Churchill: How do you see your own presence as a character in your films? How do others in Japan see you?

Hara: One Japanese film critic said that I must be a very masochistic person, since I like to film strong subjects and am often dragged around by them. But I consider myself normal. I *am* drawn to strong characters and it's interesting that when you confront a strong character and work face-to-face with this person on a film, you become confused within yourself. In that state of confusion, the world starts to look different, and you have the opportunity to show your audience something special.

What's important is that the subject and the filmmaker get together, energize each other, and develop a process. I never intend to step out of that process and film objectively. I'm not only following what is happening, I try to set up a situation where the tension between filmmaker and subject is energetic. Miyuki Takeda did what she did and Mr. Okuzaki did what he did, but I do things *with* the subjects. We become parts of each other's living and developing.

F: What's it like to make personal films in your society? There's a saying, "It's the nail that sticks up that is beaten down." How is it as the nail that sticks up, *you* have not been beaten down?

Hara: In Japan you need the power to bounce back at the hammer that is pounding on you. That's what Mr. Okuzaki did and what Miyuki Takeda did. They acted their way no matter who was hammering or how much they hammered.

Portia Cobb: I have a question about the birthing scene. How come no one was there in the room with Miyuki Takeda, other than you shooting? And how come you and the person with the mic [Sachiko Kobayashi] did not put the equipment down and help?

Hara: Miyuki Takeda had told us not to help at all. We did plan to call an ambulance if we figured there was a threat to the baby's life. In Okinawa, Miyuki Takeda had worked for a midwife, so she had had experience and was confident that she would be able to do it on her own.

Alan Rosenthal: But at what point do you stop being a filmmaker and become a human being? Several times in the film we hear the words, "Is the baby choking? Is the baby choking? Is it swallowing some blood?" As far as I can understand, there is no reaction from the person with the mic or from you. Was there in fact no problem at all or were you simply avoiding the problem in the interest of your work?

Hara: While I like to become involved in a relationship with my subject and see how I myself am changed by the relationship, I don't want to become physically involved, except by holding a camera. It's not that I didn't feel any emotions during the birth scene. I felt many things. But I also felt it wouldn't be appropriate for me to say something, or to express my emotions in a voice-over later. During that scene, I did mention that I was very worried about the baby. I was sweating so much that my glasses became foggy and I couldn't see. I was using two cameras, one with a wide-angle lens. With that camera it's sometimes hard to tell if you're in focus. Being nervous is no excuse for my shooting the footage out of focus, but I feel that my emotions are reflected in that out-of-focus imagery.

When Miyuki Takeda was asking me if the baby was moving or not, I was responding. My voice is in the film.

Rosenthal: How come it's not in the subtitles?

Hara: I was whispering and decided not to have the whispers translated.

One more thing. I promised her I would show the film to her and the child, Yu, after ten years. And after ten years I did get a call from Miyuki Takeda and I set up the screening. During the film, Yu watched very attentively. Afterward we went to a restaurant, and I asked her, "What did you think?" Yu answered, "It was very good." When I heard those words, I felt the film was worth the work.

Yasui: There's a Japanese tradition of women choosing to give birth like this, isn't there?

Hara: Yes, but in our time, birth has become an industry. Miyuki Takeda wanted to express herself through the act of giving birth to a baby, and she felt she wouldn't be able to do that if she gave birth in a hospital. In modern Japan, she is a very rare case.

Maria DeLuca: So often, I feel repelled by films that seem voyeuristic, especially when the camera seems silent, remote, and very fixed on an intense emotional scene. I did not feel that way about your film. The sex scene—which no one has mentioned—was very disturbing at first, but almost immediately I felt very involved, in an unusual way.

Hara: I wanted to do something that could be called voyeuristic but would not repel the audience. In Japan there are many social systems: the system of the imperial family, other cultural systems. And there are many restrictions: you cannot do this or that. But the biggest restriction is privacy. What I want to do is not to intrude on *other* people's privacy but to reveal my own and to see how far I can go in that revelation. I want to aggressively drag my audience into my life, and I want to create a mood of confusion. I am very frightened by this and by the things I film—but it's *because* I am frightened that I feel I must do these films.

1994 NICK DEOCAMPO — ON *REVOLUTIONS HAPPEN LIKE REFRAINS IN A SONG* (1987), *MEMORIES OF OLD MANILA* (1993), AND *ISAAK* (1993)

Nick Deocampo: I come here to represent the independent cinema of the Philippines, which is really an eighties phenomenon. Those were the dying years of the dictatorship, as well as the birth of some democratic reforms in my country. The eighties were a very tough period for a lot of us young filmmakers because even the movie industry was co-opted by the regime. It was state controlled. Everything that was publicly articulated in that society was state controlled, so we had to find our own space.

At that time, I was a theater arts student, but slowly I went toward cinema. I arrived in Manila thinking I would be able to *study* film; I ended up *teaching* film. My students and I made Super-8mm films as a political move. It was the age of alternatives: alternative economies, alternative press, alternative media, alternative lifestyles. For us, it was alternative cinema. We created a space within our university and then started moving on to other universities—like little monks going from one village to another, and from one island to another, preaching the Gospel of the True Cinema.

Our Philippines movie industry produced 120 films a year, and we're one of the few countries in the world where a local industry film can outgross American movies, even Stallone. We make a lot of money at the box office.

In any case, during the eighties, we young filmmakers had to remain underground. We did documentaries and experimental films—without having seen the works of Warhol or Brakhage or George Stoney. When I met my first class, I had only the *Film Culture* book [P. Adams Sitney, ed., *Film Culture Reader* (New York, Washington: Praeger, 1970)] with Annette Michelson's essay ("Film and the Radical Aspiration").

It is now ten years since we started that movement and it's bearing fruit. Since I returned from New York University, I've been running a film school. We have been producing twenty-five to thirty short films a year. The biggest development is that from the little Super-8s we made ten years ago, we went on to 16mm, and finally, to 35mm.

Now a few words about the three films you're going to see. They represent different periods in my "filmmaking career." The first, *Revolutions Happen Like Refrains in a Song*, is the third film in my Super-8 trilogy. I made the first part of that in 1983, at the time Aquino was killed and repression became really intense [On August 21, 1983, Benigno Aquino Jr., husband of Corazon Aquino, was assassinated in the international airport in Pasay, Philippines]. It was about a transvestite who supports his family by doing sex shows in the red light district of Manila.

Then, two years after that, I made the second part of the *Trilogy*, a film about child prostitution (long before anyone would talk about child prostitution). Many times, I was invited to go to a precinct station jail to spend some nights, because we were not allowed to talk about such things. It was a good experience seeing things from the inside. Working with the children was difficult because they were always on the run. It was one of my most difficult films. It took five years to shoot because I, too, was always on the run. Also, I had been able to document a military man who was giving protection to a gay bar and I was getting threatening phone calls. I had to ship that film out of the country just three months before the fall of the Marcos dictatorship.

The third part of the Super-8 *Trilogy* is *really* an exercise in low-budget filmmaking. I only had ten rolls of Super-8 film, three minutes each, and went out into the streets to document the revolution—without knowing how long the revolution was going to last! Thank God I was able to cover at least four of the crucial days. Later, I thought, "Once I edit the thirty minutes, I'll have just a ten-minute film," so I dug up all the outtakes from my other films and strung them together with my home movies and *voilà*!, a film—and a *Trilogy*.

Five or six years later, I got a grant from Channel 4 in London and was able to make a film on five centuries of art history in twenty-two minutes. You'll see that film, *Memories of Old Manila*, second. And the third film, *Isaak*, was made just last December. It's 35mm, and the shortest film I've made. It was done overnight, in between trips promoting Philippines cinema. A one-night shoot—a ten-minute film. I worked for twenty-four hours and slept on the plane on the way to Paris!

They're diverse works, in various gauges, with various social functions. But for those perceptive enough, there are recurring themes.

[The films are shown and the group meets for discussion.]

F: What sorts of censorship problems have you had? Your films are politically challenging and sexually politically challenging.

Deocampo: During the time of Marcos, there was heavy censorship, so we had to go underground. That term appealed to us, more than "experimental," more than "independent," more than "abstract." We identified with "underground" because we really were running from authority, and only because we ran were we successful at avoiding censorship. Ironically, my first censorship came during the time of Cory Aquino. We were all under the illusion that we were now in a democracy. I immediately fed my film to the TV station, and *that's* where I got censored, right on screen: Oliver's ass was covered by a black dot!

That kind of deception was true in a lot of ways during the Cory Aquino years, and that's when I left for NYU. I knew I was the master of Super-8 in all of Asia [laughter]—nobody could steal *that* crown from me. At NYU I got my introduction to Eisenstein and became an avid reader of Eisenstein.

F: I'd like to hear more about the relationship between the independent movement you spearheaded and the Filipino commercial cinema.

Deocampo: It's seldom that I make a film, because much of my time is spent in administration work and on social action. As director of a film school, my sphere is cultural production. I've studied the careers of the seventies generation—Lino Brocka, Ishmael Bernal, Kidlat Tahimik—trying to see what exactly their solutions were to the problems of the movie industry. I think I'm posing different solutions to those problems.

The Filipino industry is very commercial. We are introducing the whole idea of independent cinema and education to them, and they've been responding. I used to run the film school on $500 a year from the industry. Five hundred dollars! Now, after five years, I have a million pesos, around $25,000. Still, running a film school on $25,000 doesn't sound like NYU!

George Stoney: That's what it costs to *go* to NYU!

Deocampo: Advocacy is very much a part of the creative process. At the moment, the industry is questioning the whole validity of independent cinema, and whether it's going to be productive for the movie industry, which is currently in a state of crisis. The good thing is that I can outtalk any bureaucrat and any producer. I confront them in meetings and at conferences and tell them we need to train young filmmakers if we want this industry to survive.

At the same time, I always caution everyone that we should not immediately try to become part of the industry because I have studied the case of Brazil, where they made it a requirement for every feature to be shown with a domestically produced short film. Ultimately, all the commercial values filtered into those short "independent" films. We want to have more options than that! We want to pluralize the modes of articulation.

I am happy that at least the industry no longer accuses us of elitism and assumes our films will only survive in academe. Not everybody likes our independent films, but we show them regularly, and an audience is growing. During December, we show *only* Filipino films, for ten days. *Isaak* and films by five of my students were presented as a package during last December and were seen by millions of people. A lot of Asian countries are now beginning to look at our model.

So my position toward the movie industry is constructive. Before I left most recently, they delegated my institute to be the training school for the whole movie industry. Wow! That's a big burden, but I said, "So long as you give me the right budget, we'll start training the people." Right now, they're constructing a building for us, which we hope will be the training center for Asia. I'm going to festivals to talk to donors. In Berlin, a studio closed down, and I was able to convince them to donate three Arriflex cameras and a Steenbeck! Wow! And everything was free! We're asking UNESCO to have training programs with us. It's my dream to bring George Stoney to Manila.

Patricia Zimmermann: I wonder what kinds of "equipment" you ransack for your students from theoretical or historical paradigms around the world?

Deocampo: I throw myself into actual filmmaking, into teaching, so that these theoretical, Western questions and constructions are always deflected into praxis. I can tell a student the history of mise-en-scène, or I can grab a wicker chair and *show* the student what it is. But I *don't* want us to intellectually ghettoize ourselves. I met some of the teachers in the Beijing Film School and, my God, they're teaching psychoanalysis! So why should *we* be afraid of all these theoretical models? We're beginning to introduce theory in our classes, but easy does it!

The first generation of independent filmmakers were all *personal* filmmakers (even Lino Brocka, who did try to make a lot of institutional changes, and we respect him for that; he was a role model for lots of us), and we remember the wonderful films that they did. But did that change the structures of the movie industry? Not at all.

I thought we needed another strategy, that we needed to come in *as a generation* with institutional *structures*. And the first structure needed to be a film school. Our generation is beginning to affect the movie industry. They are now producing short films. They are now open to experimental films. They are open to animation. Filipino animation on the big screen! Can you imagine? It's just Disney that shows there!

What we asked for during the revolution was a democratic plurality. I'm trying to translate that into cinematic plurality.

1994 MANI KAUL—ON *USKI ROTI (A DAY'S BREAD, 1969)* AND *DHRUPAD* (1982)

L. Somi Roy: Welcome to this evening's program. We're going to be showing a film by the Indian director Mani Kaul, called *Uski Roti* (the English title is *A Day's Bread*). It's a film Mani Kaul made twenty-six years ago, when he was a young man of twenty-five. He had just completed his student film at the Film Institute of India.

India, as you know, has the largest film industry in the world; its films are seen from Morocco to Indonesia (and sometimes in New York!), but the majority of the films tend to be formulaic. You all know the Indian musicals, the melodramas, and so on. The new Indian cinema started in the late sixties and early seventies, and

Uski Roti was one of two or three films that can be seen as the beginning of this new development (another was *Bhuvan Shome* [1969] by Mrinal Sen, who had been working with political films and was influenced by the French new wave; and a third was *Ankur* ["The Seedling," 1974] by director Shyam Benegal). In comparison to what had been going on in the Indian film industry, most of these new Indian films were trying to be socially conscious while still appealing to a large audience.

The artistic integrity of this new Indian cinema was expressed in a couple of different ways. First, this cinema was rooted in particular regions. You have the Bengali cinema (Satyajit Ray, a precursor of the new Indian cinema, is the most famous instance), and you have cinemas from the many other regions (and languages). Shyam Benegal and other new Indian filmmakers made films with Hindu language, which is the language of the Indian commercial cinema, but tried to deal with new themes and reach a new audience. Another precursor of the new cinema was Ritwik Ghatak, an unsung master of Indian cinema, at least in the West (and especially here in America). Ghatak was also a political filmmaker who derived his film technique from the theatrical tradition of Benegal. He became the vice principal of the Film Institute and was tremendously influential on a group of young Indian filmmakers, including Mani Kaul.

Uski Roti caused quite a bit of controversy when it was first seen in India. It is a nonlinear, non-narrative film. In many ways, it represents a real departure from what had been considered Indian film up to that point. *Uski Roti* is based on a very short story by Mohan Rakish, who wrote in Hindi. The film does not have English subtitles, though there is very little dialogue. It's about a woman in a village in the Punjab who every day walks from the village to the highway with her husband's lunch, his daily bread. He's a bus driver who drives by twice a day. He spends little time at home and doesn't seem to care much about his wife (he has a mistress in another town and does a lot of drinking with his buddies). One day, the wife misses the bus and is distraught—after all, he provides her livelihood and she's a traditional good Indian wife. This is when a lot of things begin to happen in her head, and the film is very much about the interior of her mind. The filmmaker starts commenting on her past in flashbacks, and she starts having fantasies.

Mani Kaul told me several things about the style of the film that I'd like to share. *Uski Roti* is a film about time, and Mani Kaul deliberately plays with extended shots. The film is about waiting; it is deliberately slow. Also, he used only two lenses in shooting this film: a 28mm lens and a 135mm lens—basically, a wide-angle lens and a long lens. He did not employ the normal, 50mm lens. At the beginning of the film, he employs the two lenses in the traditional way: that is, when you want a universal focus to bring all the action into play, you use a wide-angle lens with great depth of field; and when you want to get into more introspective material, you use the long lens and shorten the depth of field. But later on, when the flashbacks and the woman's fantasies come into play, he switches the lenses, so you're no longer sure what is fantasy and what is the filmmaker commenting on the past.

[*Uski Roti* is shown, and Kaul takes questions afterward.]

Mani Kaul: I don't want to talk about this film. [laughter] It's so many years ago!

George Stoney: What was the *plot*? We had no idea what was going on!

Kaul: When I made *Uski Roti*, I wanted to completely destroy any semblance of a realistic development, so that I could construct the film almost in the manner of a painter. In fact, I've been a painter and a musician. You could make a painting where the brush stroke is completely subservient to the effect of the painting, to the figure, which is what the narrative is, in a film. But you can also make a painting stroke by stroke so that both the figure and the strokes are equal. I constructed *Uski Roti* shot by shot, in this second way, so that the "figure" of the narrative is almost not taking shape in realistic terms. All the cuts are delayed, though there is sometimes a preempting of the generally even rhythm, when the film is a projection of the woman's fantasies.

My way of looking at women has changed over the years, as you will see in my later films. But it's not as if I saw this woman as pathetic. Indian women are very close to the idea of tradition, and this woman's actions implied much more than her just being subservient to *him*. In any case, it's pointless for me to explain what the problem with her is because there's nothing I can explain. Really, there is no plot at all in the film, except what Somi already explained.

I was living with a family at the time I made *Uski Roti*. At a dinner with a group of people, the man in the family was explaining, "Mani Kaul has made this film where there is a woman who goes to the bus stop and waits," when his wife interrupted to say, "William, don't tell them the whole plot!" [laughter]

I must say, the idea of non-narrative film has stayed with me all these years, and the closest to a conventional story I've made is a three-hour adaptation of Dostoevsky's *The Idiot*, which itself has a narrative that goes haywire.

F: The film is stunning to look at. Could you talk about the process of composing the images?

Kaul: I believe the camera is not so much something you're *seeing* through; it's the way your body extends into life. This is what I teach my students (I should tell you that they make very different films than I make; I never encourage them to make my kind of films). I want them to understand that when I move, I move differently; and when I sit, I sit differently. You have to learn to hold the camera with *your* rhythm, and not just have an idea in your head and try to illustrate that idea. You have to physically understand this, even when a cameraman is shooting the film. We all create differently, precisely because everyone's body extends differently. Your movements are like a dance.

I sincerely believe now that I can make a film without looking through the camera. In fact, I have a project in mind where I won't allow my *cameraman* to look through the camera. Looking through the camera obviously was important to me when I made *Uski Roti* because at that time I *thought* about organizing space. Since the European Renaissance, we have been trained that organizing space, and especially a sacred space—a church or a temple—is what creates a sense of attention and time. But now I believe that I should in fact place myself *in time* and in a certain quality of attention, and let the space become whatever it becomes. It doesn't interest me anymore to compose my shots. I wish to place myself in a particular sense of *time* and let *space* be. Nothing can go wrong—I know that—nothing can go wrong. When I shoot now, I have only a brief script. The film unfolds on the spot as I shoot.

Even when I am editing, my shots have mobility. In a film I will show you later, there was one shot that traveled through all the reels. It was in the first reel; then it went to the second, to the seventh, to the fifth—finally, it found a place! And I know that when the shot finds a place, it has a quality of holding you.

F: When you were shooting *Uski Roti*, did you mentally picture the shots and then teach the actors and the crew how to go about each shot? Or did you see the specific shots come along as you rehearsed?

Kaul: With *Uski Roti*, it was very strange: I had a dream. In the dream, I saw a filmstrip lying on the floor, and on it I saw *all* the shots. So I had a very strong sense of what I was going to do.

But even at that time, locations were very important for me, as important as the actors. When I go to a certain place, like when I came here [Wells College in central New York State], immediately the location itself automatically suggests certain images and movements.

At that time, I used to *think*, *then* go on location. But now I don't want to *think*. I don't want to say to myself, "Now *this* is the scene; therefore she should be in the foreground and somebody should be in the background." Actually I've never done *that* kind of thing, not even in *Uski Roti*.

F: Despite your unstructured, intuitive approach, you're still making feature films, which usually require a lot of organization. What kind of relationship do you have with your crew and with funders. I'm imagining you on location with everyone going crazy...

Kaul: No, no, no. I have a wonderful relationship with my crew; they love working with me—really! Funders, I don't know. [laughter]

This question has been repeated for the last twenty-five years: how have I continued to raise money to make films like this—it's a big mystery. But each time, I am able to raise the money, and every year I've made this kind of film. I've had no problem in finding funds. I can't explain this to you. I tell you because I know of no other similar situation, at least in my country. I have many colleagues who have great trouble raising money.

[The discussion continues after screening of *Dhrupad*.]

Kaul: In *Dhrupad* I tried to give a straightforward introduction to the music of the two musicians you see in the film. Theirs is a music without notation. In a sense, it is not even possible to notate this music—it is too complex. There are continuously ascending and descending tones, and it is impossible to say that these tones are this or that note. The tones are always traveling within the dissonant areas between notes.

I was especially interested in how the musicians transmit the tradition of their music orally. A student can study this music for years and never write a sentence in a notebook. You can only learn the music by continuously listening and practicing until you begin to elaborate it in your own way. The secret of the survival of the traditions of Indian music is that teaching it is very deeply linked with opening up the disposition of the disciple, the pupil.

I'm very closely associated with the family in the film, and one day I was sitting with the younger musician and four students, who were singing a phrase that he had sung and had asked them to repeat. The four sang the phrase, and then he asked me, "What do you think?" I told him they all made mistakes: in some sense they changed the phrase that he had given them. He asked me very gently, "Did you notice that they made *different* mistakes?" I said, "Yes, they made different mistakes." He said, "Well, the only crack through which you can look into the nature and disposition of the pupil is how he insists upon making a certain kind of mistake. Far from getting impatient with him, you should try and understand why he repeatedly insists on making *that* mistake. When he is *not* making that mistake, he is imitating me, and he's nobody. When he's making the mistake, he's himself, and you must build on *that*.

In this music, individual musicians must express their own individual selves *as they are*. That's the secret of this tradition: if you wrote down phrases and forced people to learn only a certain way of playing, the tradition would die.

Another anecdote: an American disciple of the elder musician lived in the village for five years. She was very devoted. Every day she wanted a lesson, but he would say, "No, I've spoken to you today, I'm not going to speak again for fifteen days—you keep on practicing." It takes time to adapt a lesson into yourself.

This student had a habit, as many new students do, of plucking a sound you make when you complete a musical phrase—much too often. When the young students play, their playing does not yet have that continuous ringing that you get when the great masters play, and there's a void. The student tends to play this other sound excessively to fill the void. For some, it's very difficult to get out of this habit.

So he sits there, hearing her making this sound all the time. But he remains silent about it, waiting for *her* to realize what she's doing. After two months, she says, "I have this bad habit." He realized that if he said, "Yes, you're doing it too much," her whole attention would go to controlling this problem, and her main music would suffer. So he says, "No, no, it's fine! There's no problem." The next time, she says, "I do this *too much*." And he says, "No, no!" Every day that month she says, "I have this habit; I must get out of it!" And he says, "There's *no* problem. You don't have to get out of anything!"

Then, after a month, she stopped asking. For fifteen days she said nothing. Finally, she asked, "Do you think I do it too much?" And he said, "Yes, I think you do." And it was corrected forever—and her main music was never disturbed.

F: Would you talk a little about the importance of meditation—in preparing to play the music or perhaps to shoot?

Kaul: I'll tell you something—if you don't mind. This word *meditation*, which is mystified in the West, has no meaning in India. There is simply a question of attention, of a quality of attention. There is a dichotomy between Being and this quality of attention. Being cannot free itself from certain sorrows; it cannot free itself from its past, from its problems and unhappiness, because Being is full of them. The idea of transcending them and reaching a state where there's no sorrow is all a dream. You can talk about it, but until the end of your life, your sorrows will pursue you.

But *attention* can be free. The *quality of attention* can be free. I can improve that quality of attention—of listening, of talking, of seeing, of feeling, of touching until there is no sorrow, no fear, no anger, no desire. In this music, and perhaps in some of my films, one has this quality of attention.

F: I wonder if you would like to comment on the more political vision that we've been seeing in other films this week, a vision that is angry at times and that is desirous of shaking up or disbanding an established order.

Kaul: I'm very proud of the fact that I made *this* kind of film. But my great friends in India make political films, including films in which people are very angry. I sometimes help with those films. It would be horrible if we had to make only one kind of film. *All* that is happening is truthful, and there is nothing wrong because *all* wants to see expression. All kinds of engagements are valid and legitimate as long as they keep within a certain discipline and reach certain truths of perception. They're perfect. No problem. I enjoy films that are *completely* different from mine.

Michael Grillo: I'd like to ask about the innate cultural implications of basically a Western technology: cinema. I don't mean simply the traditional history of cinema but rather its language: the optical system inherited from the Italian Renaissance and the narrative system based on nineteenth-century English and French novels. Given your cultural background and the nature of what you are making, where do you run up against the limitations of these culturally loaded technologies? And how do you resist them? Somi described one instance—your use of lenses in the opposite-of-conventional way—but are there other instances where you turn this Western cultural language into your own vernacular?

Kaul: I speak English, but it's not my language and so I am liable to make mistakes while using this language. While I'm speaking, I'm not consciously following my grammar, but there *is* a very strict grammar to English and my slightest mistake will be detected, and you'll know I don't know English completely. It is my opinion that cinema is *not* a language, whereas Indian classical music *is* a language. Why do I say that? There are strict grammatical rules concerning Indian music and if a musician goes off, his deviation will immediately be evident. But while he sings, he's not at all concerned with that grammar, even though it is so strict that the slightest mistake can be detected. He goes into a completely intuitive singing, which is absolutely correct grammatically *and* perfectly subjective. *This* I would call a language. Cinema is nothing like that. Cinema is merely information, and in particular films, information is saturated or, as is sometimes true in my films, rarefied.

It's true that the camera is a producer of the European principle of perspective, of convergence—which is basically an optical illusion because in reality, parallel lines *don't* converge: you can shut your eyes and walk and you won't come to a convergence point. During the Renaissance, the idea of convergence produced great work. The same is true of Western symphonic music, which is very beautiful (and in a sense, convergent), and of narrative film, which creates climactic "convergences." Earlier chronicles and epics didn't have the convergences that modern narratives do. And it is perfectly legitimate if young filmmakers would rather explore non-narrative ideas. In fact, it's a tragedy that we don't yet have an instrument that can deal with the non-narrative forms we have in our hearts.

1995 CRAIG BALDWIN—ON *SONIC OUTLAWS* (1995)

Richard Herskowitz: It seems to me that some experimental films need experimental movie theaters. During *Sonic Outlaws*, I felt self-conscious just sitting still, quietly facing the screen, not talking back; and I'm just wondering if you've found screening venues that meet this film halfway?

Craig Baldwin: Well, I encourage people to stand up and change seats during the film, to do whatever they want. I cut my teeth in college showing films in clubs, so I'm used to showing films in spaces where there are bodies in motion. But I don't think you need to meet the expectations of the place you go into. Just take it over. The surrealists used to do "exquisite corpse" films in Paris by going from one theater to another, creating their own montages based on chance.

F: Tell us about your archive [one of the "themes" of the 1995 Flaherty seminar was archiving film *within* film].

Baldwin: We started this seminar with some formal discussion about film archives in the traditional sense, and I do acknowledge them, but my project is to liquidate distinctions between official and unofficial history. I think a lot of material from pop culture *is* archival material: it represents a certain sensibility characteristic of the middle part of the century. I do collect stuff, but my "archive" comes mostly from dumpsters. Refuse is the archive of our times and the resource for what I call "*cinema povera*"—those people who are impoverished but still intent on making films. I think we live in a post-Hollywood, postindustrial society. There's so much material already *there*, in the trash (on LP records, for example, and on eight-track tapes), that it's a test of our ingenuity to take that material and redeem it, so to speak: to project new meanings into it. Even my own films become a kind of refuse. Sometimes I cut up my earlier films and rearrange them even *after* they've come to the answer-print stage. I think that's perfectly OK, though it cuts against the whole tradition of the inviolability of the art object and the sanctity of the finished work.

John Columbus: You're an exquisite anarchist, but there is some organization in *Sonic Outlaws*, if only because of your use of *The Wizard of Oz* [1939, several directors].

Baldwin: My use of "Don't mind the person behind the curtain," which is the vocal you hear from *The Wizard of Oz*, was just a formal device to suggest that I want to expose the powers that be behind the media machine. It's one metaphor in *Sonic Outlaws* out of five quadrillion.

F: I've heard the phrase "culture jamming" bounced around this week, but I don't know what it means and what its ramifications are, though it seems to relate to *Sonic Outlaws*.

Baldwin: Mark Hosler of Negativland claims to have invented culture jamming, but I think that's ridiculous, just more egotism. And he's already declared the end of culture jamming because it's been co-opted: there are already *classes* in culture jamming.

The term refers to the idea that in a media-saturated environment, people are going to be taking bits and pieces from what has been done, changing them, and reinserting them back into the cultural process. Culture jamming is different from classical resistance in that it doesn't present an oppositional argument; rather, it's artwork that speaks in the language of the dominant culture but contains a subversive message, so that when it's reinserted into the mainstream cultural process, it becomes a kind of media virus. People see or hear the results and think, "Hold it, something's wrong here!" Hopefully, the process provokes people to question *all* received media.

Patti Bruck: When I think of assemblage films, I think of a filmmaker taking found footage and editing it together, so I was puzzled when I saw in the credits that Bill Daniel edited *Sonic Outlaws*. You're listed as a director. Could you explain how you direct him to edit?

Baldwin: Bill was sitting at the flatbed, but we did it together. He has good instincts, and I wanted to give him a lot of credit, so I called him "editor." I didn't know how to give myself credit, so I called myself "director."

F: Could you say that the ability to *know* history combined with the inability to *make* history leads to appropriation?

Baldwin: In a lot of ways, I think the language of history, the mediated version of history, is internalized. Appropriation is just a way of talking back to what we've internalized. Of course, since we do internalize so much, you can call *Sonic Outlaws* a personal film. Here, it is shown at this documentary seminar, but it's a personal expression of a culturally saturated, obsessive individual who's into talking back. I think it's healthy to be able to work with all the materials cluttering up our brains: *The Flintstones'* tune; the Shell sign; "Snap, Crackle, Pop."

F: How many of the connections that you make between your various sources are serendipity?

Baldwin: To a degree, there is a design, especially when you're making a feature. But there is also serendipity. There's *so much* inside us that there are going to be times when things come out perfectly. I remember Negativland saying, "We can control serendipity and exploit chance." There *is* this tension between randomness/chaos and design. We can't *totally* control what we use, like Hollywood does; we open ourselves out to the social field, the world of media. But when we *do* find something, some kind of definite correspondence, it's a magical moment. And that's what Negativland makes their art out of—and what this film tries to do. There's a certain kind of surrender in my film to social forces. Media is penetrating our bodies right now, so just *take* it, and instead of being a victim, go with the flow long enough to help redirect the flow.

F: There's a history of collaborative work in San Francisco. Have you been part of that history?

Baldwin: I know there was a group called Radio Refusés, but I wouldn't want to localize the approach I'm describing: it's an idea whose time has come. Art as a category with a capital *A* has to be liquidated. I'm part of a generation that recognizes that art has become a commodity and that the art world is just a big industry, just a way for a lot of people to establish careers and get rich by selling objects to rich people.

Motion pictures *are* collaborative certainly. And when you're taking advantage of clips made by hundreds of other people before you, you have to admit to that collaboration. I think *Sonic Outlaws* and my work in general falls into the tradition of anti-art: the Dada tradition, or the Fluxus tradition, or the Situationist tradition, the Punk tradition—all of which try to attack the egoism and the careerism of people who claim to be romantic geniuses receiving inspiration from God. That's a very stupid idea, and of course, we must wipe these people off the face of the earth. [laughter]

F: Who were the Situationists?

Baldwin: The Situationists were very inspirational to me as I was coming up in college, especially their idea of the dissolution of the category "Art" and the diffusion of art into everyday life, and their profound skepticism about the idea of originality and their commitment to attack the academy, to provocation. Hopefully, *Sonic Outlaws* partakes of that spirit of provocation. Of course, "Situationism" is a noun that shouldn't exist. It's an activity, a process, a general way of looking at art making and of trying to reintegrate it into everyday life—of trying to reuse the dead culture as a means of making our lives more meaningful.

R. Bruce Jenkins: Though *Sonic Outlaws* is cut on film, there's an electric feel to it: in your conceptualizing the film and in your editing, have you been influenced by electronic tools: nonlinear editors or time spent on the Internet?

Baldwin: I certainly have and I couldn't help but be. But I want to remind everyone that editing film *is* nonlinear. I can't afford to work on an Avid, but even if I could, I wouldn't. I like film because of its plastic quality. *Sonic Outlaws* is very much a handmade film; it wears its artlessness on its sleeve; it's part of that aesthetic tradition of *not* looking for the quality image but for the *debased* image.

   To go back to your question: a lot of the material in *Sonic Outlaws* was acquired on video, and from audiotape, and radio broadcast—so, yes, there is an electronic dimension to the film.

F: Did you have earlier cuts and how long were they?

Baldwin: Originally, it was going to be a thirty-five-minute film, a twelve-hundred-foot reel; and then I got the AFI grant and one thing led to another. I didn't want to turn the film into a fanzine for Negativland (which it is to an extent); I wanted to stretch it out and talk in a metacultural way, not just about one group that's doing something exemplary but about this kind of practice exploding across the culture. I just started adding on and the film grew. There was a very coarse outline on my wall, but I worked, as someone here said the other day, "from the material up."

   In Hollywood, everything is predetermined: you need to get *this* shot, put the people in *these* clothes under *these* lights, saying *these* lines. It might take twenty takes, or two hundred, but we'll *get* it. My process is totally the opposite: I take what I have and then try to make something *of* it, to find something *in* it. The material suggests its own form; the form grows organically from the material.

F: There's a lot of noise in *Sonic Outlaws*.

Baldwin: It *is* a noisy film and is meant to be. In art making, some people want to refine and purify, to find a beautiful, sublime, precious moment, and I acknowledge that tradition. But it's not *my* aesthetic. What I want to do is to grate against the nervous system. Noise *is* the contemporary environment, and I think true art is a headlong embrace of this reality and an attempt to redeem it, to create an aesthetic of noise—rather than some kind of escapist, elitist, privileged retreat from our real environment.

F: At one point I started not to be able to relate to *Sonic Outlaws* because I was thinking, "Where are the women? Where are the women?"

Baldwin: The field of culture jamming is currently dominated by males—as is rock and roll, as is experimental film. I didn't make a decision to include women in order to give a "balance"; I just gave a survey of what was happening. The Barbie Liberation Organization [a group instigated by Melinda Stone and Igor Vamos who bought Barbie dolls and GI Joe dolls, exchanged their sound components so that Barbie said GI Joe's lines and vice versa, and returned them to the shelves of the stores] includes women. But generally, the field happens to be dominated by men—straight, white males.

F: But even the imagery you use seems male dominated.

Baldwin: It *is* an important question whether a group like the Emergency Broadcast Network [a group that modifies imagery of political figures so that they say the opposite of what they presumably mean to say], which wants to satirize the language of power, actually transcends that language. In my view, the Emergency Broadcast Network doesn't; but Negativland does. You need to talk about each case separately. But of course part and parcel of appropriating and reediting imagery of white, straight political leaders is that you end up with a lot of imagery of white, straight political leaders. You remain in that same circulation of imagery. I hope the film opens up that issue.

Riyad Wadia: I know this is the land of free speech, but I come from a society [Wadia is Indian] that does not have such high standards of freedom, a more bureaucratic society. We're presently in a very interesting stage where America is forcing us to get into the copyright laws, into GATT [General Agreement on Tariffs and Trade], so it's interesting for me to see that America itself seems to be opening up to this new concept that actually there *is* no such thing as copyright. Also, as a person running an archive, I find it very dangerous to think that my material can actually be remade and used commercially. I don't mind if it's used aesthetically, but if the artistic endeavor becomes commercial, there is a worry. Where's it all going?

Baldwin: When you say *America* wants to impose copyright laws on India, of course, you're talking about the *corporations*. The people who are represented in *this* film, and they are Americans, are anticopyright.

Where's it all going? Despite GATT and despite the clampdown on copyrights and the commercialization of the Internet, there's no stopping the subcultural phenomenon I've described. The paradox is that *because* these technologies exist, *because* media is available, there is both *more* cultural democracy in actual practice, and at the same time, an attempt by the corporations to limit this democracy. This film finds itself at the intersection of these forces.

In any event, I don't care what's happening legally. Some people might, but I'm interested in leaving that question behind and doing my own work. As far as I'm concerned, the situation calls for more ingenuity and more crime.

Notes

1. Tom Johnson, interview by Patricia R. Zimmermann, Hamilton, New York, June 16, 2014.
2. Ibid.
3. Ibid.
4. Marijke de Valck, *Film Festivals: From European Geopolitics to Global Cinephilia* (Amsterdam: Amsterdam University Press, 2007), 179–200.
5. Ibid., 191.
6. Ibid., 19–20, 39.
7. Ibid., 179–83.
8. Henry Louis Gates, *Loose Canons: Notes on the Culture Wars* (Oxford: Oxford University Press, 1993), xv.
9. Irene Thomson, *Culture Wars and Enduring American Dilemmas* (Ann Arbor: University of Michigan Press, 2010), 3.
10. Thomson, *Culture Wars*, 3–25, 100–19.
11. "Video History Project Time Line for 1989," Experimental Television Center, retrieved May 20, 2011 (http://www.experimentaltvcenter.org/search/node/1989).
12. B. Ruby Rich, phone interview by Patricia R. Zimmermann, June 29, 2014.
13. John Caldwell, "Independent Television Service," Museum of Broadcast Communications, retrieved May 3, 2011 (http://www.museum.tv/eotv/independent.htm).
14. Betsy McLane, *A New History of Documentary*, 2nd ed. (New York: Bloomsbury Academic, 2012), 307.
15. "About ITVS," Independent Television Service, retrieved April 4, 2011 (http:// www.itvs. org/about).
16. Lawrence Daressa, "Reflections on ITVS," October 12, 1995, California Newsreel. Retrieved June 13, 2011 (http://newsreel.org/articles/goodbye.htm).

17. Johnson, interview, June 15, 2014.

18. "International Film Seminars Organization," in "The Flaherty: Four Decades in the Cause of Independent Cinema," ed. Erik Barnouw and Patricia Zimmermann, *Wide Angle* 17, nos. 1–4 (1995): 414 (hereafter cited as "The Flaherty).

19. Sally Berger, interview by Patricia R. Zimmermann, Hamilton, New York, June 17, 2014.

20. Ibid.

21. Johnson, interview, June 15, 2014; Berger, interview, June 17, 2014.

22. Berger, interview, June 17, 2014; Johnson, interview, June 15, 2014; Richard Herskowitz, phone interview by Patricia R. Zimmermann, September 20, 2009.

23. Juan Mandelbaum, phone interview by Patricia R. Zimmermann, June 30, 2014.

24. Publicity brochures, 1990–2000, International Film Seminars Private Collection, International Film Seminars/The Flaherty, New York (hereafter cited as IFS Collection). Publicity brochure, Thirty-Seventh Annual Robert Flaherty Seminar, August 3–10, 1991, Wells College, IFS Collection, notes a fee of $650 and grants-in-aid up to $500; Publicity brochure, Thirty-Ninth Annual Robert Flaherty Seminar, August 7–13, 1993, IFS Collection, notes a fee of $650, and financial aid scholarships granted between $200 and $500; Publicity brochure, Forty-Second Annual Robert Flaherty Seminar for Independent Video and Cinema, Wells College, August 3–8, 1996, IFS Collection, lists fees of $650 and grants-in-aid of $200 to $400, IFS Collection.

25. Publicity brochure, Forty-Second Annual Robert Flaherty Seminar for Independent Video and Cinema, Wells College, August 3–8, 1996, IFS Collection.

26. Publicity brochure, Forty-First Annual Robert Flaherty Seminar for Independent Video and Cinema, Wells College, August 5–10, 1995, IFS Collection.

27. William Sloan, phone interview by Patricia R. Zimmermann, July 29, 2009; Nadine Covert, phone interview by Patricia R. Zimmermann, July 28, 2009.

28. Tom Johnson, Scott MacDonald, and Patricia Zimmermann to Colleagues in Academia, May 12, 1992, IFS Collection.

29. Unidentified board member to Esme Dick, October 2, 1986, Juan Mandelbaum Private Collection (hereafter cited as Mandelbaum Collection).The letter asked that films and the entire Flaherty Seminar experience be reviewed by film critics.

30. Press Release, "Flaherty Film Seminar Residencies Supported by the Pew Charitable Trusts," July 13, 1992, International Film Seminars, IFS Collection.

31. Jay Ruby and Faye Ginsburg, "The Aborted Indigenous Seminar" (unpublished manuscript, July 24, 2014), Word file.

32. Faye Ginsburg, e-mail message to Patricia R. Zimmermann, May 24, 2014.

33. Ibid.

34. Press Release, International Film Seminars, "38th Robert Flaherty Seminar, August 8–14, 1992," November 1991, IFS Collection.

35. Ibid.

36. Bowser was a prominent black nationalist in the independent film world, advocating for African American programming. She had worked to recover the lost history of early cinema African American director Oscar Micheaux.

37. Jay Ruby, phone interview by Patricia R. Zimmermann, November 24, 2009.

38. Ruby and Ginsburg, "The Aborted Indigenous Seminar."

39. Ibid.

40. Ibid.

41. Ibid.

42. Alicia Gaspar de Alba, *Chicano Arts Inside/Outside the Master's House: Cultural Politics and the CARA* (Austin: University of Texas Press, 2010), 32.

43. Frederick E. Hoxie, "Goodbye, Columbus Day 1992," *Chicago Tribune*, November 21, 1992. Retrieved August 3, 2009 (http://articles.chicagotribune.com/1992–11–21/news

/9204160440_1_columbus-day-quincentennial-columbus-voyage). See also Roger
Petterson, "Quincentennial: Christopher in a Bullet Proof Vest?" AP News Archive,
October 9, 1992. Retrieved August 4, 2009 (http://www.apnewsarchive.com
/1992/Quincentennial-Christopher-Christopher-in-a-Bullet-proof-Vest-/id
-a9fc2116f01a03ab97e72c746a1980cc).

44. de Alba, *Chicano Arts Inside/Outside the Master's House*, 45.

45. Robert Rodriguez, "Perspective on the Quincentennial: 1492 Brought Genocide; Why
Celebrate? Columbus "Discovery" Launched a Terrible Chapter in Human History, and
Millions Still Suffer the Effects," *Los Angeles Times*, July 23, 1990. Retrieved September 6,
2009 (http://articles.latimes.com/1990–07–23/local/me-341_1_human-history).

46. Zachary Carter, "October 1992: How Did the Public React?" Reel American History,
Lehigh University, retrieved June 2, 2009 (http://digital.lib.lehigh.edu/trial/reel_new
/films/list/1_1_9_76). See also David E. Larson, "Some Native Thoughts on the
Quincentennial," *Minnesota History* 53, no. 1 (1992): 25–31.

47. Peter Ricketson, "Political Myth: The Political Uses of History, Tradition and Memory,"
(PhD diss., University of Wollongong, 2001), 529–39 (http://ro.uow.edu.au/theses/1438).

48. Jeremy Smith, "Outside and against the Quincentenary: Modern Indigenous
Representations at the Time of the Columbian Celebrations," *Atlantic Studies* 10, no. 1
(2009): 63–80.

49. For an example of how *Nanook of the North* was viewed as a seminal documentary, see Erik
Barnouw, *Documentary: A History of Non Fiction Film* (Oxford: Oxford University Press,
1993), 33–48. For an example of its critique as an example of the colonialist white gaze, see
Fatimah Tobing Rony, *The Third Eye: Race, Cinema and Ethnographic Spectacle* (Durham,
NC: Duke University Press, 1996), 99–121.

50. Ruby, phone interview, November 24, 2009.

51. Louis Massiah, phone interview by Patricia R. Zimmermann, July 10, 2014.

52. See George Marcus and Michael Fischer, *Anthropology as Cultural Critique: An
Experimental Moment in the Human Sciences* (Chicago: University of Chicago Press, 1986);
David MacDougall, "Beyond Observational Cinema," in *Principles of Visual Anthropology*,
ed. Paul Hockings (Chicago: Aldine, 1975), 109–24; David MacDougall, "Media Friend or
Media Foe," *Visual Anthropology* 1 (1987): 54–58; Jay Ruby, *Crack in the Mirror: Reflexive
Perspectives in Anthropology* (Philadelphia: University of Pennsylvania Press, 1982); James
Clifford and George Marcus, *Writing Culture: The Poetics and Politics of Ethnography*
(Berkeley: University of California Press, 1986).

53. Eric Michaels, "Aboriginal Content: Who's Got It—Who Needs It?" *Art and Text* 23–24
(1987): 58–79; Faye Ginsburg, "Indigenous Media: Faustian Contract or Global Village?"
Cultural Anthropology 6 (1991): 92–112; Terence Turner, "Visual Media, Cultural Politics,
and Anthropological Practice: Some Implications of Recent Uses of Film and Video
among the Kayapo of Brazil," *Visual Anthropology Review* Spring (1990): 8–13.

54. Ruby and Ginsburg, "The Aborted Indigenous Seminar."

55. Ginsburg, "Indigenous Media," 94.

56. Ibid., 96.

57. Ruby, phone interview, November 24, 2009.

58. Ibid.

59. Massiah, phone interview, July 10, 2012.

60. The seminar was canceled.

61. Sally Berger, interview by Patricia R. Zimmermann, Hamilton, New York, June 16, 2014.

62. Ibid.

63. Ibid.

64. Ruby, phone interview, November 24, 2009.

65. Press Release, "38th Annual Robert Flaherty Seminar, August 8–14, 1992," March 1992, IFS Collection.

66. Meg Knowles, "Report from Flaherty," *The Squealer*, Fall 1992, 12–15.

67. Jesse Lerner, "Flaherty in Motion," *Afterimage*, December 1992, 3.

68. Sally Berger, "Letter to the Editor," *Afterimage*, February 1993, 3.

69. Ruth Bradley, "Old Model, New World (1994)," in "The Flaherty," 405–7.

70. Ibid., 406

71. Ibid., 407

72. Ibid.

73. Mandelbaum had attended his first seminar in 1980, prompted by Sol Worth, his professor at the Annenberg School at the University of Pennsylvania. There, Mandelbaum attended the Documentary Film Series, which screened many Flaherty Seminar films. Programmer Erik Barnouw had featured Mandelbaum's documentaries in his 1982 seminar. For Mandelbaum, the seminar during the 1980s showcased works with a very high level of craft at a time when filmmaking was difficult and costly. Each shot and cut required thinking.

74. Juan Mandelbaum, phone interview by Patricia R. Zimmermann, June 20, 2014.

75. Ibid., September 23, 2009.

76. Mandelbaum, interview, June 20, 2014.

77. Ibid.

78. Ibid.

79. "Past Seminars," International Film Seminars/The Flaherty, retrieved July 6, 2011 (http://flahertyseminar.org/the-flaherty-seminar/past-seminars/). See also Brochure, "Flaherty on the Road, April 5–November 7, 1997," IFS Collection.

80. Brochure, "Flaherty on the Road, April 5–November 7, 1997."

81. Alyce Myatt, phone interview by Patricia R. Zimmermann, November 9, 2009.

82. Ibid.

83. The Baltics—Estonia, Latvia, and Lithuania—enjoyed a higher standard of living than the rest of the USSR. They strongly defended their national identities and had resisted Moscow. Latvia had a rich documentary tradition.

84. Patricia R. Zimmermann, "Strange Bedfellows: The Legacy of Vertov and Flaherty," *Journal of Film and Video* 44, nos. 1/2, (1992): 4–8.

85. "Biography of Ivars Seleckis," retrieved July 24, 2009 (http://www.sergei-eisenstein.com/page25.html); "1990—Riga Seminar, Latvia," in "The Flaherty," 235.

86. Patricia R. Zimmermann, "Reconstructing Vertov: Soviet Film and American Radical Documentary," *Journal of Film and Video* 44, nos. 1/2 (1992): 80–90.

87. An important Glasnost film, *Is It Easy to Be Young?* (1986) by Juris Podnieks, who was a central figure in Latvian documentary, had been screened at the 1989 stateside seminar, with Podnieks present. Rigafilm, the national studio, had produced the film. Brenda Bollag, "Is It Easy to Be Young? The Burglar, No Future in Riga or Leningrad," *Jump Cut* 34 (1989): 32–33.

88. Zimmermann, "Strange Bedfellows," 8.

89. Ibid.

90. Mandelbaum, phone interview, September 23, 2009.

91. "Steven H. Scheuer, TV Listing Pioneer, Dies at 88," *Hollywood Reporter*, May 2014. Retrieved July 23, 2009 (http://www.hollywoodreporter.com/news/steven-h-scheuer-tv-listings-709521); William Yardley, "Steven H. Scheuer Is Dead at 88; He Put the TV Review before the Show," *New York Times*, June 5, 2014. Retrieved July 23, 2009 (http://www.nytimes.com/2014/06/06/arts/television/steven-h-scheuer-is-dead-at-88-he-put-the-tv-review-before-the-show.html?_r=0).

92. Juan Mandelbaum, phone interview by Patricia R. Zimmermann, June 30, 2014.

93. Publicity Brochure, "36th Annual Robert Flaherty Seminar, Wells College, Aurora, New York June 9–16, 1990," 2, IFS Collection.

94. Ibid.

95. Marlon Riggs "Recollections," in "The Flaherty," 75.

96. Coco Fusco and Steve Gallagher, "Letter to the Editor," *Afterimage*, December 1991, 2.

97. Jonathan Robinson, "Veneration of the Exiles: Report from the 1991 Robert Flaherty Seminar," *Release Print*, November 1991, 22.

98. Publicity Brochure, "37th Annual Robert Flaherty Seminar, Wells College, Aurora, New York, August 3–10, 1991," IFS Collection..

99. Robinson, "Veneration of the Exiles," 11.

100. Laura U. Marks, "Suspicious Truths: Flaherty 1991," *Afterimage*, December 1991, 16.

101. Robinson, "Veneration of the Exiles," 21.

102. Steve Sklar, "Fledgling Filmmakers Become Hawkers at Indie Gathering," *Variety*, October 7, 1991, 1.

103. Press Release, "Classic Film *'Symbiopsychotaxiplasm: Take One'* Attracting International Attention," Tri-Ad Communications Group, January 7, 1992, IFS Collection.

104. Phil Anderson, "Soul Survivor: *Symbiospsychotaxiplasm: Take One*," *City Pages*, December 4, 1991, 16.

105. Ibid.

106. Laura U. Marks, "Suspicious Truths." See also Laura U. Marks, *Touch: Sensuous Theory and Multisensory Media* (Minneapolis: University of Minnesota Press, 2002), 28–29.

107. Robinson, "Veneration of the Exiles."

108. Scott MacDonald, "The Country in the City: Central Park in Jonas Mekas's *'Walden'* and William Greaves's *'Symbiopsychotaxiplasm: Take One,'*" *Journal of American Studies* 31, no. 3 (1997): 337–60.

109. "Trouble in Truthsville: A Conversation among Ken Feingold, Coco Fusco, and Steve Gallagher," *Felix* Spring (1992): 48–52, 128–31.

110. For a discussion of the significance of *Starting Fire with Gunpowder* in debates on First Nations and media, see Timothy J. Pasch, "*Starting Fire with Gunpowder* Revisited: Inuktitut New Media Content Creation in the Canadian Arctic," *Études/Inuit/Studies* 34, no. 2 (2010): 61–80.

111. Jesse Lerner, "Flaherty in Motion," *Afterimage*, December 1992, 4; see also Willie Varela, "Chicano Personal Cinema," *Jump Cut* 39 (1994): 96–99.

112. Laura U. Marks, "Naked Truths: Hara Kazuo's Iconoclastic Obsessions," *The Independent*, December 1992, 26.

113. Knowles, "Report from Flaherty."

114. Jesse Lerner, "Flaherty in Motion," 4.

115. Laura U. Marks, "Here's Gazing at You: A New Spin on Old Porn Exposes Gender and Generation Gaps," *The Independent*, March 1993, 27.

116. Lerner, "Flaherty in Motion."

117. Marks, "Here's Gazing at You," 31.

118. Ibid., 27.

119. Scott MacDonald, "Lost Lost Lost over *Lost Lost Lost*," *Cinema Journal* 25, no. 2 (1986): 20–34.

120. Scott MacDonald, "Letter to the Editor" *Afterimage*, handmarked as Thirty-Eighth Annual Seminar, IFS Collection.

121. For a more extended and scholarly retrospective discussion of this explosive discussion, see Scott MacDonald, "Ken Jacobs and the Flaherty Film Seminar," in *Optic Antics: The Cinema of Ken Jacobs*, ed. Michelle Pierson, David James, and Paul Arthur (Oxford: Oxford University Press, 2011), 175–95.

122. Publicity Brochure, "The 39th Annual Robert Flaherty Seminar for Independent Film and Video, Wells College, August 7–13, 1993," IFS Collection.

123. Phil Bertelsen, "Flaherty Experiences: The Intangible Experience," *Black Film Bulletin* 1, nos. 3/4 (1993–94): 6.

124. O. Funmilayo Makarah, "Failed Experiment," *Afterimage*, December 1993, 4 and 13.

125. Publicity Brochure, "40th Annual Robert Flaherty Seminar, August 6–12, 2004," IFS Collection, 2.

126. This information is based on my own memory (Patricia R. Zimmermann). I moderated that session with Erik Barnouw. I recall it was a very pitched and intense argument, which Barnouw handled with his usual grace and generosity. He later confided to me he found the debate invigorating and just what the seminar needed!

127. Avijit Ghosh, "Mani Kaul Was, by Far, Our Most Original Filmmaker," *The Times of India*, July 6, 2011. Retrieved September 13, 2013 (http://timesofindia.indiatimes.com/entertainment/hindi/bollywood/news-interviews/Mani-Kaul-was-by-far-our-most-original-filmmaker/articleshow/9127838.cms).

128. Colin Burnett, "Transnational Auteurism and the Cultural Dynamics of Influence: Mani Kaul's Non-Representational Cinema," *Transnational Cinemas* 4, no. 1 (2013): 3–24.

129. Devdutt Trivedi, "Understanding Mani Kaul and His Films," *Indian Independent Films*, July 2011. Retrieved November 2014 (http://dearcinema.com/article/understanding-the-films-of-mani-kaul/4332).

130. Christine McDonald, "Report on the 40th Annual Robert Flaherty Film Seminar," *Multicultural Review* 4, no. 1 (1994): 54–56.

131. Ian Igbal Rashid, "Asian and Asian Diaspora Programme: Flaherty Film Seminars," *Rungh: South Asian Quarterly of Culture, Comment and Criticism* 3, no. 2 (1995): 4.

132. Bruce Jenkins, e-mail message to Patricia R. Zimmermann, July 25, 2014.

133. Marlina Gonzalez-Tamrong, e-mail message to Patricia R. Zimmermann, May 20, 2016.

134. Ibid.

135. Publicity Brochure, "The 41st Annual Robert Flaherty Seminar for Independent Video and Cinema, August 5–10, 1995," IFS Collection.

136. Bruce Jenkins, e-mail message to Patricia R. Zimmermann, July 11, 2014.

137. Gonzalez-Tamrong, e-mail, May 20, 2016.

138. Ibid.

139. Yosha Goldstein, "Here's Looking at You: 41st Annual Robert Flaherty Film Seminar," *Afterimage*, September/October 1995, 7; see also DeSoto Brown, "The Robert Flaherty Film Seminar," *Pacific Islanders in Communications*, February 1992, 5.

140. Publicity Brochure, "Landscapes and Place, the 42nd Annual Robert Flaherty Seminar for Independent Video and Cinema, August 3–8, 1996," IFS Collection.

141. Brian Darr, "Wild Night in El Reno," *Senses of Cinema*, March 2008. Retrieved October 2013 (http://sensesofcinema.com/2008/cteq/wild-night-el-reno/). See also "George Kuchar, Filmmaker," *Film Quarterly* 52, no. 1 (1998): 63–64.

142. "Interview with Ellen Spiro," in *A Critical Cinema 4: Interview with Independent Filmmakers*, ed. Scott MacDonald (Berkeley: University of California Press, 2005), 361–62.

143. J. Cuasay, "42nd Annual Robert Flaherty Film Seminar," retrieved October 12, 2013 (http://www.reocities.com/athens/ithaca/3753/jaystuff/flaherty.html).

144. George Kuchar and Mike Kuchar, *Reflections from a Cinematic Cesspool* (Berkeley, CA: Zanja Press, 1997), 114–18.

145. Publicity Brochure, "Out-Takes Are History, the 45rd Robert Flaherty Film Seminar, June 4–10, 1999," IFS Collection.

146. Richard Herskowitz, phone interview by Patricia R. Zimmermann, July 27, 2009.

147. Publicity Brochure, "The 46th Annual Robert Flaherty Film Seminar June 16–22, 2000, 'Essays, Experiments, and Excavations,'" IFS Collection.

148. Kathy Geritz, e-mail message to Patricia R. Zimmermann, May 21, 2016.

149. Ibid.

150. Ibid.

The 2011 Flaherty Seminar at Colgate University, Hamilton, NY. Photo courtesy of International Film Seminars, Inc./The Flaherty, New York.

7

THE BRAND, 2000–2015

By 2000, the silhouetted image of Nanook poised with bent knees, arms up, his spear thrust forward, became the new logo of International Film Seminars (IFS). Nanook's image branded the Flaherty. It condensed ideologies and practices that defined the seminar in the previous five decades. Adopted by the board in the early 2000s to harken back to its origins in independent cinema and the Flaherty family, this iconic image symbolized a founding film of American independent cinema and of the Flaherty Seminar itself—*Nanook of the North*. It connoted IFS was transitioning from a one-off annual event into a professionalized nonprofit media arts organization with more visibility throughout the year. In the context of serious fund-raising challenges, the organization needed to revamp and recalibrate.

The silhouette of Nanook with his spear removed all background. It transcended history, geography, space, and time. It suggested the porous borders between documentary, experimental, and narrative. Considered a documentary, *Nanook of the North* was a film generating contradictory interpretations: chastised for its reenactments, critiqued for its masculinist and orientalist fantasies, heralded by experimental filmmakers, questioned as a racialized action narrative, and saluted for its collaborative practices.

The critical debates surrounding *Nanook*'s economics, form, function, politics, representations, and significance doubled in the seminar discussions themselves. Newer works also evoked multiple readings. The spear in the image, denoting hunting for survival, transposed into the seminar's mission and vision: a hunt for knowledge and deep connections with like-minded people to inspire those isolated in the independent media worlds. This logo of the lone hunter stood as a metaphor for the continuing auteurist orientation of seminar programming, with its focus on artisanal makers of high artistic merit rather than emerging practices in film collectives, film movements, or new technologies.

With the background removed, the image evoked the seminar's isolation, a week-long retreat from daily life with the outside shut out. As Nanook hunted fox, seal, and walrus, seminar participants hunted documentary, experimental, fiction, and hybrid forms, spearing works that inspired or broke new ground. If Nanook's spear was a hunting weapon to sustain his family, the seminar during this period from 2000 to 2015 worked toward its own survival by expanding its fund-raising efforts and professionalizing its operations.

As executive director from 1998 to 2001, L. Somi Roy had worked to brand and modernize the seminar as it faced the threat of the expanding number of film festivals dedicated to documentary. Hot Docs International Documentary Festival in Toronto was inaugurated in 1993. Full Frame Documentary Film Festival in Durham, North Carolina, had launched in 1998. Rencontres: Internationale du Documentaire de Montréal began in 1998. The American Film Institute Silver Docs festival would start five years later in 2003. Internationally, the Thessaloniki Documentary Festival in Greece was initiated in 1999 and the Doc Point Helsinki Documentary Film Festival in 2001. The Flaherty Seminar was no longer the only place to consider documentary. It was now one among many, with perhaps the least national and international visibility due to its retreat-like status and small numbers of participants compared to a festival.

Phred Churchill served as a board member from the late 1990s to the mid-2000s, a time when IFS was undergoing many transformations from a less familial, less East Coast insider coterie into a more professional media arts organization. He volunteered to work on developing a logo for IFS. Churchill selected the image of Nanook with the spear after sifting through dozens of images, some from *Nanook of the North* and some from Flaherty's still photographs of the Inuit. He worked with Ann Michel and Phil Wilde on the floor of their New York City apartment. Wilde was a trustee. He spent two decades helping the seminar figure out how to screen video. Emily Scott, Churchill's girlfriend at the time, worked to render the photographic image as a graphic by reducing the detail and removing the background.[1]

Phred Churchill represented two competing strands embedded in Flaherty history: on the one hand, its deep roots in a familial way of operating; and on the other hand, its need to operate as a national organization with international impact. Phred was the son of Jack Churchill, a longtime Flaherty filmmaker, participant, and trustee. The elder Churchill's films had screened at the seminars in the 1950s. He had also helped organize the first seminar, going on to a long distinguished career in documentary, educational, and scientific films about mental health issues. Jack Churchill had served as president from 1987 to 1989, a contentious period dealing with multicultural politics. The elder Churchill had a fifty-year commitment to the seminar, passed down to his son as a family obligation.[2] For five decades, the elder Churchill envisioned the seminar as a place where a community gathered for close contact with films of significance. Churchill wrote, "We want to bring participants into close contact with specific films that have reached out to touch the human spirit, and then to put them into down-to-earth communication with the people who made these films, to illuminate how the films came into being."[3]

The Nanook logo condensed into one image the idea of close contact and reaching out, as Nanook extends his arms and leans forward, suggesting movement toward the future. This logo propelled IFS into a long overdue, necessary branding in an increasingly crowded independent media landscape. It appeared on IFS hats, temporary tattoos, tote bags, and T-shirts.

As IFS and the seminar itself entered the period 2000–15, it had recovered from the chasms wrought by many intense debates: between practitioners and academics; around the issue of how to decenter the white privilege of the seminars; about how to engage the difficult questions of multiculturalism and representation; and about how to survive as an organization when grant funding was drying up. Compared to previous decades, this period produced much less volatile discussions. It prompted some longtime seminarians to wonder if the seminar had lost its bearings. They speculated whether the invasion of professors had completely obliterated nonpreconception with theory. Abstraction seemed to replace emotion.

IFS found itself professionalizing as an organization out of necessity in the context of a growing public media sector. It expanded its partnerships to survive. It codified its board policies and procedures, refined selection of programmers, and clarified moderation of discussion. Although IFS and the Flaherty, as it was officially called later in the period, always looked like a much larger, more well-endowed organization given its longevity and impact on faculty, filmmakers, librarians, and programmers, it was managed with one executive director and operated on a very small budget, mostly generated from seminar registrations.

The professionalization of both IFS and the seminar manifested itself on many internal and external levels. This period saw IFS shift away from its familial orientation toward more professional board practices. It refocused on structure, sharpening its mission. Working through debates about diversity, multiculturalism, and the precipitous challenges of limited financial resources, it stabilized. It refocused on its institutional goals and mission to create an energized environment for meaningful encounters between cinema and audiences.

The organization changed its public image from IFS to "The Flaherty," the nickname many participants used. During this period, the organization renewed its focus on participants, a shift away from concentrating on auteurs, filmmakers, and films. It hired professional arts administrators with academic and festival backgrounds as executive directors. It professionalized board practices and policies. It instituted an organizational retreat with a consultant to consider strategic planning and board development. It established more codified systems for selection of programmers. It launched an annual publication as a way to capture the ephemerality of the seminar experience for funders. It facilitated more partnerships. It augmented its development efforts with a more coherent fund-raising strategy. It established a more effective way to organize discussions by implementing a larger variety of forms and structures. Perhaps most significantly, the board dedicated significant time to transforming the grants-in-aid program, critiqued as a welfare program by some Flaherty insiders, into a fellowship program which would attract funding and serve as professional development for the independent media field.[4]

The contradictions between an ideology of familialism filled with pathos and nonprofit organizational professionalism identified with ethos and logos travels through the entire history of the seminar. In previous decades, the familialism, passion, and pathos operated as central seminar affective modalities. The seminar had provided engaged community and intensive immersion at a time when places to convene in real time in the emerging independent media sector were rare. In contrast, the board and organization worked throughout this period to install a more professional, rational, and transparent model for board manuals, fellows, fiscal responsibility, office management, policies, and programmer selection.

During the 2000s, this gradual movement toward a more professionalized operation was epitomized in the three executive directors who led the seminar forward to recovery and stabilization: Margarita De La Vega Hurtado (2002–6), Mary Kerr (2006–12), and Anita Reher (2012–) All three came to their positions with experience working in large nonprofit institutions. With a PhD in Latin American film, Hurtado had taught at the University of Michigan. She had a long and varied involvement with the seminar, as a participant in the 1980s, as a programmer in the early 1990s, and finally as a board member. She moved from her position on the board to an interim role as executive director in 2002 after L. Somi Roy resigned. Hurtado represented a continuation of Flaherty practices, where the executive director emerged from the ranks of Flaherty devotees. However, she came from teaching at a large institution in the Midwest rather than from the inner circles of independent film in New York City.[5]

Mary Kerr was the first Flaherty executive director from the now highly professionalized film festival milieu. She had worked at the Sundance Film Festival from 1993 to 1999 as an assistant to the director of programming and later as an associate programmer. From 2002 to 2005, she served as programming director at the newly established Silver Docs Documentary Film Festival, launched by the American Film Institute. Compared to her festival experience, "the Flaherty had commerce taken out, it was programming for a deep cause, for art or politics," she reflected.[6] Originally from Denmark, Anita Reher had experience as an arts administrator. She cofounded the European Documentary Network (EDN) in 1996, where she coordinated international workshops on documentary distribution, pitching, and storytelling. She was the first European to be named executive director of the Flaherty.

Each woman motored institutional change in distinct ways.[7] The Flaherty had survived nearly a decade of battles over board diversity, decrease in seminar attendance, multiculturalism, organizational challenges, and reduced grant support in the 1990s. Hurtado entered a leadership position requiring hospitality skills to restore a sense of community to the always-contentious seminar itself and organizational skills to straighten out its disorganized administration and financing. She found an organization whose files "were a mess," with no existing digital record of any board minutes or reports on any computer.[8] She located documents, reconstructed a filing system, and worked with board members Nadine Covert and Juan Mandelbaum to create a more transparent and logical financial accounting system to address funders' queries regarding IFS professionalism.[9]

For Hurtado, the seminar was important because "it is not a festival; it is a way to look at work in depth and to think in depth about it, to have space for thinking and to find new ways to see cinema and talk about it."[10] She determined the seminar's unique strength was sustaining a space where different generations could mingle, a social practice hardwired in the seminars from the days of Frances Flaherty. Both highly curated and market-oriented festivals lacked intergenerational exchanges. Hurtado's gracious hospitality to create a welcoming environment distinguished her tenure. After nearly fifteen years of debates and struggles on the board and acidic interactions at the seminar, the Flaherty had garnered a problematic reputation in the media arts field. She saw nurturing participants as central to the seminar's success. Hospitality for filmmakers and participants held strategic importance to repair the perception the seminar engineered "filmmaker bashing" and "nervous breakdowns." Her interest in promoting intergenerational dialogue contributed to development of the fellows program.[11]

With a decade of experience in the festival world, Mary Kerr brought an outsider's insight to the Flaherty. She was one of the first executive directors whose involvement with the seminar was not as a devotee but as a professional arts administrator in the increasingly commercial festival world. She entered her position as what she termed "an outsider," someone not part of the "Flaherty family." She arrived with a track record in arts administration for high-profile organizations. She addressed the isolation of the seminar from the larger world of independent film. She hoped "to make the seminar more visible in the broader documentary world." She established concrete goals to professionalize operations by creating a more developed seminar fellows program, an employee manual, an organized program for interns, and a more rigorous registration system. She insisted programs and discussion start on time, instituting stricter adherence to a schedule. To dispense with the Flaherty habit of operating under an amorphous, elitist familialism, she systematized operations to render them more transparent. She reflected, "it is easier to professionalize if you take emotions, politics, and favoritism out."[12]

The members of the board during this period evidenced this movement from a familialist to a more professional operational mode. Although still comprised of seminar participants with passionate commitments to the community of Flaherty partisans, the board represented not only more gender and racial diversity but also more diversity in skills. If boards from earlier decades replicated the Flaherty Seminar experience with like-minded people arguing about films and filmmakers and operating in an ad hoc way, the board in the 2000s marshaled more organizational expertise in the nonprofit media arts worlds, especially experience at film festivals and museums.

Longtime Flaherty board members and attendees, such as Nadine Covert, Tom Johnson, and Lucy Kostelanetz, brought institutional history as well as experience from the funding and independent media worlds. Attorneys joined the board: Brian Frye, a former microcinema operator who had gone to law school; Lorna Lowe, a producer and attorney; Ricki Roer, from Wilson, Elser, Moskowitz, Edelman, and Dicker in New York City; and Ernesto Sanchez, a Washington, DC–based entertainment attorney. Christine McDonald, who served as treasurer, was a librarian and programmer at the Crandall Public Library in upstate New York, continuing the long tradition of librarians involved with the seminar. Several board members during this period were well-known administrators and curators from major arts organizations who had programmed previous Flaherty seminars: Daniela Alatorre (Morelia International Film Festival), Ariella Ben-Dov (Margaret Mead Film Festival and Mad Cat Women's Film Festival), Sally Berger (Museum of Modern Art), Elaine Charnov (Margaret Mead Film Festival), Kathy Geritz (Pacific Film Archive), Ed Halter (New York Underground Film Festival), Alvin Larkins (Black Maria Film Festival), Julie Levinson (Babson College), Adrienne Mancia (Brooklyn Academy of Music), Lucilla Moctezuma (Rockefeller Foundation and Women Make Movies), and Chi-hui Yang (San Francisco Asian American Film Festival).

Several board members had worked in development: Jennifer David, from the Institute of Philanthropy; Steven Montgomery, a development officer for the New York Philharmonic; Alyce Myatt, from the MacArthur Foundation; and Kathryn Pyle, an officer at the Samuel S. Fels Fund[13] John Bruce was a strategy consultant.[14] The filmmakers on the board during this period also had business experience running their own small entrepreneurial film companies: Ann Michel and Phil Wilde, engineering, environmental, and science multimedia producers; and John Valadez, a producer/director who had worked on his own works as well as contract works for CNN. Filmmakers (Ilisa Barbash, Elizabeth Delude-Dix) and scholars (Pooja Ranjan, The New School and Patricia R. Zimmermann, Ithaca College) held seats on the board but as a minority presence. By the 2000s, in order to function within the more variegated landscape of independent media arts, the Flaherty board depended on expertise from the academic, festival, and foundation sectors—three areas it had traditionally distanced itself from.

By 2000, IFS and the Flaherty Seminar stood at a precarious crossroad: either resolve its administrative, diversity/multicultural, financial and organizational problems in order to survive, or operate at a more reduced, even less visible level, perhaps shutting down. Despite its image of financial stability and the prestige of the Flaherty name, IFS and the seminar operated on an annual budget hovering around $250,000. Throughout its crises in securing nonprofit status in the early 1960s, dealing with the politics of the 1970s, or confronting the multicultural and gender issues of the 1980s and 1990s, the passion of its veterans fueled this perennially financially challenged and understaffed institution. Seminar devotees had volunteered their time and vigorously promoted the seminar as a unique, intense experience.

The idea to brand and professionalize the Flaherty emanated from board leadership. Patti Bruck served the longest continuous presidency in the Flaherty's history, from 2002 to 2009. She first shared the presidency with Tom Johnson. Bruck had joined the board in 2000. Like Nadine Covert, Johnson, Lucy Kostelanetz, and Juan Mandelbaum, Bruck was passionate about the seminar. Her first experience of the Flaherty was Richard Herskowitz's 1987 seminar.

Unlike Covert, Johnson, and Mandelbaum, she did not live in the East Coast corridor of New York/Boston/Montreal that had so defined the Flaherty as an organization. She lived in Boulder, Colorado, where she taught filmmaking at the University of Colorado. Bruck functioned in a very unique dual position as both an insider loyal to the seminar experience and an outsider with organizational acumen sharpened on much more professionally run boards. The informality of board meetings in New York troubled her. "The meetings were trustees sitting around discussing things at someone's house, sitting in a living room like a book club," she observed. Bruck discovered there was no record-keeping system of minutes or committees. Executive Director L. Somi Roy argued he "had everything in his head," a holdover from the more informal decades of familialism. She was concerned about transparency: how to function effectively in decision making during these points of institutional financial and identity crisis with so little information on budgets, discussions, initiatives, and policies?[15]

Bruck was worried so few board members could read a budget. She brought in an outside financial adviser to review investments and the small endowments of IFS. For

Bruck, the key issue revolved around a polarity built into the organization almost from the beginning: did it operate as a family with commitment and passion, or did it operate as an organization with policies and procedures? As Bruck analyzed it, "people involved in the Flaherty want to attract high-powered board members and trustees, but people like this don't like sitting around like a family."[16]

As Bruck assessed the situation, she determined the board, IFS, and the seminar needed to professionalize, excising their cozy familialism and intense emotions to install a more rational structure with oversight, policies, and procedures. Throughout her tenure as president, she worked to create a board policy and procedure manual. She also developed an organizational binder to specify board members' and executive director's roles, clearly delineating borders in a murky, confusing environment with mixed signals on who was responsible for what.

Bruck's impact can be traced in the board of trustees meeting minutes from this period. From 2000 to 2002, the minutes were often obtuse, filled with large, often unrealized and somewhat unscalable plans. International residencies for US filmmakers in other parts of the globe were imagined. Flaherty seminars in Canada and Sweden were proposed. Corporate underwriting from technology industries was floated. An idea for IFS to provide hosting services to tour international filmmakers was proffered. Development of a media arts center was fantasized.[17] These years featured almost-continuous brainstorming to identify the distinct role of the Flaherty. Should it form partnerships with academic organizations? Should it work toward more public visibility beyond the one week of the seminar? Should it become "the premiere think tank of serious media inquiry"? Should it return to its humanist and interdisciplinary roots established in the 1950s?[18]

By mid-decade, topics of the board of trustees meetings transformed, which now focused on discussions to clarify board policies, procedures, and roles. A working board whose members did not separate their own seminar experiences from running the organization constituted a significant and strong IFS legacy. The documentation of these board meetings changed from stream of consciousness paragraphs recounting trustees' musings about cinema and the seminar to meetings organized around specific reports from the executive director and treasurer, as well as development, nominating, programming, publication, and strategic planning working committees.[19]

Throughout the 1990s, the board had launched discussions about their own gender and racial diversity, bringing in more African Americans (Pearl Bowser, Louis Massiah) and Asian Americans (Lise Yasui). It had also grappled with the need to consider representation of a diversity of skills to ensure everyone on the board was not a filmmaker/artist or a professor. Trustees with business skills were necessary. By 2001, board discussions affirmed a diverse board would denote not only ethnic, gender, national, or racial identities but also skills ranging from development specialists, filmmakers, lawyers, and scholars. Board members emerging from the business side of film and media were also sought.[20]

By 2005, Bruck spearheaded board discussions focused on spelling out the role of the board and revising the by-laws.[21] A year later, the board developed a more transparent, committee-organized vetted process for nominating future trustees by establishing their credentials. This process analyzed whether potential trustees contributed to expanding the diversity of skills the board and IFS required. It abandoned the previous process of nominating former seminar participants board members had befriended. Bruck underscored, "future board members should have time to spare and should not have conflicts over requesting funding for the Flaherty as well as their own organizations."[22]

The organization also professionalized by revising its mission statement and fashioning a vision statement. Steve Montgomery joined the board in 2003, serving until 2009. With Bruck, Montgomery motored this professionalization of IFS. He developed logical and reasonable development strategies and crafted mission and vision statements to communicate the Flaherty's unique experience clearly to funders. He contended the mystique of a secret club shrouded its impact. A former filmmaker (*Hobie's Heroes* [1980] and *Morocco: The Past and Present of Djemma el Fna* [1995]), Montgomery served as manager of corporate, foundation, and government development at the New York Philharmonic. In the early 2000s, he had "transitioned from being a casual artist-type to becoming a more disciplined arts administration professional, so perhaps I was urging the Flaherty to make a similar transition."[23]

Bruck, Hurtado, and Montgomery learned external funders had problems comprehending the function and impact of the Flaherty Seminar. It served only a hundred people once a year in a private setting. It not only appeared to be esoteric but had no measurable results. From his experience as a development officer, Montgomery understood the need for a clear, compelling, easy-to-understand mission statement to stimulate fund-raising. "If people cannot describe a program succinctly," he observed, "then a danger arises that the organization and its goals are only a fantasy. It's important to say what the value of the Flaherty Seminar is to the field."[24] The board approved the revision of the mission and vision statement in 2003. These documents returned to the core values of Frances Flaherty in the 1950s, emphasizing immersion in seeing the moving image in a new and deeper way.[25]

A significant turning point in professionalization came at a facilitated strategic planning retreat held at Vassar College in fall 2004, the year of the fiftieth anniversary of the seminar. In 2003 and 2004, board member Alyce Myatt urged more strategic planning. She was concerned the Flaherty Seminar did not "filter out into the outside world." However, she clearly understood its unique value as "an extraordinary opportunity to bring together intellectuals and practitioners" to undertake "an unusual, unique experience to spend a week viewing interesting content within an historical and global framework." For Myatt, the takeaway from a Flaherty seminar was "intellectual enrichment," not easily available at festivals, and "intergenerational engagement."[26]

Bruck and Myatt assessed the board and the organization as exceedingly club-like, dysfunctional, and familial. With allies Hurtado and Johnson, they pushed for an outside facilitator who could lead discussions about external forces in the media arts sector to move the organization forward so it was not stuck in the 1950s. With the help of the Johnson Foundation, IFS/the Flaherty hired James Wiegel, senior associate with the Institute of Cultural Affairs, to facilitate two days of discussion in October 2004.[27] This intensive retreat inaugurated strategic planning and refocused the Flaherty. The board began the process of reconstructing the Flaherty as a media arts organization with goals to serve the international independent media field, rather than as an insiders' group mounting one annual event.

The retreat renewed focus on developing a coherent, systematic fund-raising strategy. Tom Johnson noted that because the seminar was small and in a remote place, it "was a tough sell to funders."[28] As the organization recovered from the economic challenges of the 1990s, fund-raising clarified as a key goal. Bruck, Johnson, and Montgomery emphasized the role of the board was to fund raise.[29] At a 2007 board meeting, Montgomery outlined a more pointed development strategy. He explained the Flaherty was more than a week-long gathering in June. He emphasized that the seminar "was really pioneering [to open] the door to new opportunities."[30] Montgomery worked for months on a subcommittee with Nadine Covert and Lucy Kostelanetz to determine possible external funding sources.[31]

The strategic planning and refocusing on organized fund-raising efforts paid off. Earlier, in 1999–2000, two small family foundations—the William F. Donner Foundation and the Johnson Family Fund—each with long-standing personal connections to the seminar—underwrote the seminar with grants, helping it to recover from its financial challenges. After the retreat, board members with development, institutional management, and legal backgrounds assisted the implementation of more considered grant writing outlining the impact of the seminar. Combined with the determined energy of both Hurtado and Kerr, the Flaherty was awarded more grants during this period than in almost any other time in its history. Hurtado secured $70,000 from the Warhol Foundation. The Academy of Motion Picture Arts and Sciences (AMPAS), CEC ArtsLink, the Geraldine R. Dodge Foundation, the Experimental Television Center, LEF Foundation, the National Endowment for the Arts, the New York State Council on the Arts, the William Penn Foundation, the Pew Charitable Trust, the Scheuer Foundation, and various consulates and embassies supported the appearance of international media artists. The larger number of funders evidenced professionalization and strategic planning had generated results that would sustain the seminar.[32] At a 2008 board retreat, Bruck pushed for 100-percent board contribution to the seminar to show external funders organizational commitment. She urged trustees to work their networks.[33]

During this period, another less grandiose, much more labor-intensive strategy to produce financial stability also emerged: increasing the numbers of full-pay participants. In the late 1990s and early 2000s, the seminar experienced difficulty in attracting sufficient numbers of full pay attendees to support its grants-in-aid scholarships and to underwrite the cost of the seminar. Despite protests from board members arguing the seminar should remain small, to raise funds for programming, the seminar expanded to 160–190 participants during the 2000s. In 2002, facing a precipitous drop in registrations, Hurtado personally called friends and past Flaherty participants, "begging them to come."[34]

By 2003, the board understood more seminar registrations meant more income. They agreed the seminar would run with 165 participants. In many ways, the focus on paid registrations to generate an income stream returned the seminar to its origins. Paid registrations supported legacy operations such as the grants-in-aid/fellowships and increased travel costs for international guests. Hurtado urged each board member to invite three to five of his or her friends to attend to "ensure the full-paying participants quota is reached."[35] This accelerated outreach to paying participants paid off. By 2009, the seminar sold out months before its June launch.[36]

As the Flaherty branded itself and professionalized, it shed its outlier status in the media arts field to establish partnerships with other institutions. These partnerships increased the seminar's national visibility. In the late 1990s, through the efforts of Executive Director L. Somi Roy and Museum of Modern Art (MoMA) assistant curator Sally Berger, MoMA started showcasing select Flaherty seminar filmmakers the week following the seminar to leverage the transportation costs in order to secure national visibility and press attention in a prestigious New York venue.[37] By 2003, Hurtado and the board had secured postseminar screenings at the Smithsonian Institution's National Gallery of Art, with support from the Johnson Foundation.[38] A significant partnership was established with the Black Maria Film and Video Festival, programmed by longtime Flaherty participant and former board member John Columbus. A touring festival, the Black Maria screened across the United States, helping to dispel the Flaherty's exclusive East Coast club aura. When the seminar celebrated its fiftieth anniversary in 2004, Black Maria further deepened its collaboration with a catalog essay on the history of the seminar and an extended tour of Flaherty films.[39]

By the end of the period, the Flaherty New York City (NYC) program—initially brainstormed in the facilitated 2004 retreat—expanded the Flaherty model of meaningful discussion and engagement to a more public setting. At a 2008 retreat, the board discussed inaugurating "Flaherty nights" in New York City. These events would "help us improve our visibility and build our community . . . combining the social as well as substance . . . to give new people a 'taste' and [to help] old friends [find] a way to stay connected."[40] The first Flaherty NYC unrolled in 2008–2009. It featured works by Dominic De Joseph, Alison Kobayashi, Alex Rivera, and Laura Waddington. Programmers for NYC included established figures such as Penny Lane (2010–11), Kathy High and Jim Supanick (2012), and emerging curators such as Jerónimo Rodríguez (2013) and Jason Fox (2014).[41] By 2014, UnionDocs, a Brooklyn alternative programming space for documentary, assumed an important role as a postseminar screening site. The Flaherty transformed from an event into a professional organization with increased visibility. The brand was honed: the Flaherty opened space for difficult works, discussed in a community of like-minded explorers.

In its quest to brand and capture impact for funders, Hurtado instituted two important initiatives. She encouraged journalists and scholars to attend the seminar. And she published a small catalog to commemorate each year's seminar. The first initiative grew out of the 1990s, where scholars such as Erik Barnouw, Ruth Bradley, Jesse Lerner, Scott MacDonald, Laura U. Marks, and Patricia R. Zimmerman published essays about the seminar in *Afterimage*, *Film Quarterly*, *The Independent*, and *Wide Angle*. By the 2000s, more writers published their seminar analyses in print and online. The October 2002 *Independent Film and Video Monthly* published a multipage insert with drawings, essays, and musings called "Documenting Flaherty." This special section chronicled participants' experiences as they encountered Ed Halter's aggressive experimental film programming.[42]

The second initiative—the publication of the annual catalog—addressed fundraising challenges. It enhanced the seminar's national visibility by documenting the program. It evidenced the seminar provided more than a summer camp for independent film aficionados: its curatorial statements, scholarly essays, and testimonials demonstrated critical inquiry and impact. An academic with a PhD, Hurtado recognized the importance of capturing the seminar in writing for contributors, funders, participants, and sponsors. She recruited Nadine Covert, a professional copyeditor, and hired a graphic designer. At the October 2003 meeting, the board argued, "our goal is to make this an annual publication." They hoped to sell ads to be self-sustaining. The first publication was supported by a gift from board member Tom Johnson.[43]

In addition to these external efforts, the Flaherty reorganized seminar operations. The board dedicated committees, meetings, and retreats to the infrastructure of the seminar itself, instituting a more analytical, critical, and reflective approach to improving its own structures. The focus shifted from concerns about film selection to infrastructure: the programmers and the audience. Assessing it needed more "customer service" to cultivate the "Flaherty community," the board established task forces. These committees and task forces were to create more effective structures and policies for the discussions, the fellowship program, and programmer selection. The Flaherty brand now revolved around offering an intense yet welcoming community.

The solidification of fellowships for emerging makers, programmers, and writers formed a central pillar of the Flaherty's stabilization. Frances herself had insisted on recruiting young people to attend the seminar in order to engage in conversations with established filmmakers when no film schools existed. In the twenty-first century, with festivals and film schools in abundance, the function of these grants-in-aid morphed into postcollegiate professional development, a way to interact in intergenerational dialogue on equal footing with midcareer and established makers and scholars. Beyond networking, the fellowships would provide a democratic, level playing field. They offered an introduction to the independent media field where aesthetic sophistication and complex thinking mattered. Board member Alyce Myatt criticized the grants-in-aid, funded by the Paul Ronder and Sol Worth endowments, as a classed and racialized "welfare system."[44] Inspired by the fellowship model of the Telluride Film Festival in Colorado (itself inspired by the Flaherty Seminar), the board renamed the program the Flaherty Fellowships, a more prestigious title in alignment with the public media sector.[45]

Throughout the 2000s, the board assessed deficiencies in the fellowship model, especially in selection of fellows and their interface with the seminar. By 2005, a fellowship committee mapped out better procedures to create an income-generating, self-sustaining program. The committee included Ilisa Barbash, Patti Bruck, Kathy Geritz, Margarita De La Vega Hurtado, and Alvin Larkins. This committee transformed the grants-in-aid into a vibrant fellowship program. It created emerging and midcareer fellows, with a more systematic application and review process double vetting all applicants. It sent fellows background readings on seminar history and program concepts. Fellows arrived at the seminar a day in advance for meetings with board members, special master classes, and a welcome dinner. Daily sessions exclusively for fellows with seminar curators and guests were instituted. Fellows would handle mics during discussion and bar tend at the infamous Bill's Bar, named after longtime Flaherty participant William Sloan. Most significantly, the board affirmed the need for a fellowship coordinator position to run the program, drawn from the expanding pool of media professors now attending the seminar. Margarita De La Vega Hurtado, Irina Leimbacher, Jason Livingston, and Scott Nyerges held this position. No longer an honorific title, board members were now required to welcome fellows to the Flaherty community and to engage them.[46]

The metamorphoses of the grants-in-aid into fellowships proved a major success. It refocused IFS on its historic core values of bringing new people into the field and nurturing intergenerational dialogue. It provided a transitional space for emerging media practitioners and scholars as they moved from school to the more public international media arts world. Fellows needed to secure additional funds to meet the full cost of registration. With written reports on their seminar experience, the fellows program presented a concrete initiative attractive to funders. As Steve Montgomery pointed out, the reconfigured fellowship program provided the seminar with its first new group of funders in almost two decades.[47] CEC ArtsLink, the Fledging Fund, the Ford Foundation, LEF New England, the Philadelphia Foundation, and the Wyncote Foundation funded the fellows program.

Another refinement to this customer service orientation as a form of professionalization was found in the board's attention to addressing the continuing problematic of seminar discussions. If earlier decades of IFS had focused almost exclusively on filmmakers and programming, this period from 2006 to 2010 witnessed a more nuanced board analysis of major institutional assets. The board determined two issues troubling the discussions: the format and the ideas developed.[48] A distinguishing feature of the seminar resided in its lengthy and substantive discussions. In the Flaherty model, the screening and discussion received nearly equal time. The participants were as critical as the filmmakers.

Extended discussions constituted a hallmark of the Flaherty Seminar. Yet their design concerned the board. Antagonisms against featured filmmakers not only propelled bad publicity but also generated participant anxiety and discomfort. With renewed clarity about its market position and goal of hospitality, the board researched discussion structure. Throughout the decades, board members and participants viewed seminar discussions as an incomplete, unfinished experience—the unsatisfactory weak link in the seminar. With the influx of more academics, the discourse changed: it was less antagonistic, somewhat distanced, and more theoretical. The board did not want to lose the spontaneity of engaging works for the first time, a continuing commitment to Frances Flaherty's ideas about "nonpreconception."

Between 2007 and 2009, the board developed a less mystical and more rational discussion structure. They walked a fine line between creating more effective group discussion strategies and more control over design, framing, and goals. They opted for structural rather than content change.[49] This impulse to address the nagging dissatisfaction with large-group discussions was generated by a board composed of academics and professional film programmers. By the 2000s, festival and museum programmers in the nonprofit media world paid as much attention to the audience as to the films. Academics had experience running conceptually directed classroom discussions. Board member Ed

Halter explained there was "no distinction between the audience and the programmer" in the experimental film festival world.[50]

The board established a working group on discussions, underscoring adherence to the seminar traditions of a democratic milieu of equality among participants and non-preconception.[51] Discussions emerged as a significant challenge, as increasing numbers of participants were what the board called "first timers." This working group established clear principles to remedy problems of disorganized discussions, lack of depth, and a repetitive format which deadened participants' enthusiasm.

In 2006, this group advocated that moderators—usually selected from seminar veterans and content area experts—be briefed on programmers' goals. In 2007, the board asked if discussions were necessary after every single program. They instituted smaller groups for a few discussions during the week of the seminar, breaking the 175 participants into discussion pods of twenty or thirty to encourage dialogue. The board suggested the heterogeneity embedded in the programming models also be applied to discussions: some would focus on the films, some would run as a moderated question and answer with the filmmaker, some would open to the audience first.

With numbers of university faculty increasing, the board observed dispassionate academic discussions. Academics were skilled at summarizing histories, ideas, and trends, but not comfortable engaging the films on a more direct, immediate, intuitive level. As identified by the working group, "careerist correctness" toned down the seminar discussions. Within an increasingly competitive environment for exhibitions and grants, emerging makers and scholars often opted for measured contributions. The board instituted a new role of discussion coordinator, a board member who collaborated with the programmer to monitor the discussions and to make decisions on format changes to respond to emerging issues.[52] The first discussion coordinators were Ed Halter and Patricia R. Zimmermann for the Chi-hui Yang 2008 program, "The Age of Migration." Board member's roles at the seminar had clarified. As brand ambassadors, their job was hospitality so that participants would feel part of a community and contribute to post-screening discussions.

The third wing of this structural reorganization revolved around the selection of the programmer, creating more transparent procedures for recruitment and selection. For several decades, the selection of the programmer was shrouded in mystery. Sometimes the board would simply assign someone at the seminar to program the next year. Sometimes the board president would select someone. Sometimes board members would volunteer. These all indicated vestiges of problematic familialist practices.

The Flaherty increasingly transitioned into a training ground for emerging programmers affiliated with regional and more specialized festivals or developing arenas of scholarly research. If programmers from earlier decades emerged from major high-profile institutions such as Cornell Cinema, MoMA, the Walker Art Center or from New York City libraries, programmers from this later period came from new identity-based festivals, microcinemas, niche distributors, and universities—a different media ecology. In 2003, the board and the organization shifted from using the term *programmer* to the title *curator*. This linguistic shift distinguished film programming from computer programming. It invoked the art and museum worlds, where ability, knowledge, sensibility, and taste to ascertain new trends were privileged over audience engagement. As the Flaherty internationalized, the currency of the word *curator* represented more congruence with global art worlds, distinguishing the seminar from festivals with their various collaborative teams of programmers. The term *curator* implied a more elite, rarefied practice more associated with museum culture and its focus on objects, rather than the term *programmer*, which connoted an idea of creating interactions between audiences, films, and ideas.

By 2008, the programming committee, charged with selecting the next year's programmer, established transparent programmer/curator selection protocols. These protocols eliminated ambiguities about the roles of the board, the executive director, and the programmer. The programming committee included four people with long-term professional experience as programmers: Elaine Charnov (Margaret Mead Film Festival), Kathy Geritz (Pacific Film Archive), Ed Halter (New York Underground Film Festival), and Lucila Moctezuma (Rockefeller Foundation). Economics precipitated this change. As programs became more complex with emerging technological interfaces and international guests, a longer grant development and planning period with funders and consulates was necessary. At the January 2008 board meeting, the programming committee proposed longer time lines, policies, and procedures. The programmer was required to have attended a seminar and to possess "a demonstrated body of experience putting together complex programs."[53] These policies diversified programmers beyond the East Coast corridor and the imaginary construct of the "Flaherty family."

By 2003, IFS was known officially by the name most participants used: the Flaherty— a transition from veterans' private shorthand for the seminar to a more recognizable public brand. As it moved from a passion project mounting a single event to a year-round media arts organization, the Flaherty recalibrated, rationalizing its policies to parallel other nonprofits. As one board member remarked in 2008, "hospitality is essential to professionalizing." Despite these improvements, questions of fund-raising and sustainability continued to threaten the organization. A board retreat discussion in 2008 summed up how the organization had survived for six decades by reaffirming values promoted by France Flaherty in the 1950s: community, a diverse audience, emerging programmers, intense immersion in a retreat-like environment, nonpreconception, and a professional board.[54]

The Flaherty brand subtly inflected the programming. From 2001 to 2015, seminar programming increasingly dismantled the binaries of commercial versus independent and documentary versus avant-garde. It shifted toward more polyversal, transnational media practices. Programming adopted an artisanal, rather than industrial, approach, blurred borders between modes, and refuted easy definitions of national cinemas.

This branding resided in format and orientation. For sixty years, although the length of the seminar and who attended it changed, the format did not: morning, afternoon, and evening screenings. Extended discussions followed. Titles were not revealed until participants entered the theater. Ample time for socializing was built in to how the seminar structured participants' experience of the temporalities of the week. Intergenerational dialogue was encouraged. A fellows cohort ensured emerging voices would join the mix. Isolation in a retreat-like setting away from urban areas intensified all interactions. These customs survived over six decades as a quasi-religious ritual participants expected.

The orientation of the seminar did not change course. Despite decades of amateur, activist, and scientific films, collaborative projects, film and media collectives, locative media, distributed participatory projects, and new media networks, the Flaherty brand heralded auteurs. The seminar was a place to explore how complex visual languages and sophisticated concepts generated new vision in artisanal rather than collective, industrial, or televisual modes. This focus on significant auteurs of unique vision privileged the text rather than the context. Cinematic discoveries and retrospectives dominated. Seminar programming often sidelined the more labyrinthine questions of context, distribution, exhibition, funding, history, larger intellectual influences, political economies, new technologies, reception, and spectatorship to center on the text.

Privileging the cinematic text continued a sixty-year tradition. It underscored the seminar's brand as engagement with films and filmmakers. This focus should not, however, be read negatively. Although academic screen studies had moved away from an exclusive focus on the text toward more contextual, historical, and theoretical analyses, the Flaherty Seminar had devised a scalable, sustainable approach. It now served the field by insisting on a return to conceptual, formal, and textual issues, a critical engagement missing in academic conferences and festivals. For example, board minutes and seminar publicity identified filmmakers rather than film and media culture concepts, histories, or movements. This auteurist discourse indicated continuities with seminar legacies, which positioned filmmaking as an artisanal process of individual vision and total control. The antagonisms between avant-garde and documentary positions abated. By this period, every seminar featured experimental work: it reflected the artisanal, auteurist model more than feature-length documentary.

During this fourteen-year period, seminar themes presented conceptual areas of inquiry rather than a specific topic. The themes broadened the seminar's scope beyond the specificities of genres, identity politics, marginalized voices, or national cinemas. Seminar themes reaffirmed the model of heterogeneity in modes solidified by Nadine Covert and William Sloan in the 1970s; Richard Herskowitz, Bruce Jenkins, and Melinda Ward in the 1980s; and Kathy Geritz in 2000 with a twenty-first-century updating from postcolonial and postmodernist schools of thought. Collisions, flows, hybridities, and intersections mattered more than a fixed cinematic topography.

The first two seminars of this period eschewed titles completely, signaling a break with the 1990s: the 2001 seminar, programmed by Elaine Charnov and Jytte Jensen, was simply entitled the Forty-Seventh Annual Seminar; the 2002 seminar programmed by Ed Halter was named the Forty-Eighth Annual Seminar. Every programming theme to follow exemplified a broader conceptual design to accommodate a transnational, transversal, heterogeneity of approaches, countries, forms, and moods. Rather than themes or topics, these seminar titles presented organizing strategies for theoretical inquiry: "Fifty Years of Flaherty: Inspired Filmmaking" (2004), "Cinema and History: Piling Wreckage upon Wreckage" (2005), "Creative Demolition" (2006), "South of the Other "(2007), "The Age of Migration" (2008), "Witnesses, Monuments, Ruins" (2009), "Work" (2010), "Sonic Truth" (2011), "Open Wounds" (2012), "History Is What's Happening" (2013), "Turning the Inside Out" (2014), and "The Scent of Places" (2015).

Although these seminar names read like titles for a scholarly anthology, they underlined a return to the original brand proffered by Frances Flaherty—a commitment to exploration through nonpreconception, here, spelled out in abstract conceptual titles. These titles mark how dramatically the field of independent media had transformed through the decades. Almost all the Flaherty curators possessed graduate educations, which helped to diffuse binary oppositions between theory and practice at seminars. With its economic sustainability dependent on full-pay participants, these titles identified the seminar as a valuable site for professional development unavailable at academic conferences or film festivals.

The programmers from this period suggested a sharpening of brand, function, and purpose. Their backgrounds underscored the professionalization of the seminar: not one of the programmers was on the board or a Flaherty insider. According to Patti Bruck, as more high-profile festival and museum programmers joined the board, it transformed from a conglomeration of East Coast media institution friends, insiders, and seminar devotees into a more professional group. As a result of concerted efforts to standardize and systematize programmer selection, the seminar emerged as "a place for incubating young programmers."[55]

As the term *curator* replaced *programmer*, the influence of the museum world edged out the prior context of independent film and public media. If the 1990s witnessed programming teams, this period heralded the return of the single programmer: out of fourteen seminars, only five were curated by teams. Although the Flaherty Seminar had always positioned itself as distinct from film festivals, by this later period, it increasingly intersected with that world. Most Flaherty curators were midcareer at the time they programmed the seminar. Although the majority of the programmers were Americans from different ethnic or racial groups, their programs were resolutely international. These curators moved between programming, teaching, and writing. They were not affiliated with major, high profile arts and media institutions but with more ancillary sectors such as the archival and orphaned film sectors, Asian American film, mircocinemas, socially engaged cinema, and even universities.

Out of the eighteen curators from 2001 to 2014, the majority worked full time in the festival and museum worlds. Elaine Charnov (2001) was artistic director of the Margaret Mead Film Festival; Jytte Jensen was a curator at MoMA. Other midcareer programmers from specialty festivals included Ed Halter (2002) from the New York Underground Film Festival; Susan Oxtoby (2004) from Cinematheque Ontario;[56] Steve Seid (2006) from Pacific Film Archive; Ariella Ben-Dov (2006) from Mad Cat Women's Film Festival; Mahen Bonetti (2007) from the African Film Festival in New York City; Carlos Gutiérrez (2007) from Latin American film distributor Cinema Tropical; Chi-hui Yang (2008) from the Asian American Film Festival; Josetxo Cerdán (2012) from Punto de Vista International Documentary Film Festival of Navarra (Spain); Pablo de Ocampo from the Images Festival in Toronto; and Laura U. Marks (2015) from Simon Fraser University (Burnby, British Columbia, Canada).

The curators represented diverse sectors of media culture. Several worked as professors or were graduate students at the time, either in critical studies, production or both—evoking the legacy of Flaherty programmers like Erik Barnouw and Jay Ruby.

For example, John Gianvito, a prominent experimental documentary filmmaker and programmer, was a professor at Emerson College in Boston. In 2005, Jesse Lerner, a filmmaker and theorist who taught at the Pitzer College and Michael Renov, a documentary scholar (author of *The Subject of Documentary* and coeditor of *Collecting Visible Evidence*) and associate dean at University of Southern California, mounted a seminar entitled "Cinema and History," at the Pomona Colleges in Southern California, one of few seminars held in the West. As the organizer of the annual Orphans Film Symposium on archival film, Dan Streible (coeditor of *Emile de Antonio: A Reader* and *Learning with the Lights Off: A Reader in Educational Film*) programmed the 2011 Sonic Truths seminar. He was a film studies professor at New York University. In 2014, one of the coprogrammers, Caspar Stracke, an Austrian film and new media artist and curator of Video_Dumbo, held a faculty appointment as professor of contemporary art and the moving image KUVA Art Academy in Helsinki, Finland. Several curators worked as film critics: Ed Halter (*Village Voice*), Irina Leimbacher (scholar and critic), Jesse Lerner (scholar), and Dennis Lim (a contributor to the *New York Times* as a film critic).

In aggregate, the programming during this period underlined how the Flaherty adopted an art world/art cinema turn, absorbing larger arts practices beyond cinema critiquing globalization. This art world/art cinema turn easily absorbed subcultural programming such as microcinema movements and specialized African, Asian American, and Latin American programming. It aligned with global arts practices and postcolonial theories. This turn toward the art world must be read within the context of the increasing commercialization of independent documentary with theatrical, feature-length films.[57] As one writer observed, this twenty-first-century expansion of documentary from television and the art world into theatrical screenings demonstrated documentary had "reclaimed its space on the big screen."[58] In a list of the top hundred grossing theatrical documentaries since 1982 on Box Office Mojo, eighty-three had screened after 2000.[59] The Flaherty Seminars operated in direct opposition to this shift of documentary toward reality television and theatrical film. The seminars preferred films of ethos and pathos rather than logocentrism and linearity. The carefully calibrated formal inflections, oblique angles, and structural ambiguities of art cinema, experimental works, installation, and slow cinema elaborated more complex practices.

The 2001 Digital Flaherty mini-seminar held at Rensselaer Polytechnic Institute (RPI) in Troy, New York, denoted the seminar's decisive break with more accessible, televisual, and theatrical documentary forms. Opening only two months after the September 11, 2001 World Trade Center and Pentagon attacks, the seminar's structure paralleled the 1990s weekend mini-seminars. It imported digital media into an institution heralding analog film and video. Initiated by board member Sally Berger and Executive Director L. Somi Roy, the seminar investigated emerging new media forms. This seminar marshaled a program committee model with Berger, Kathy Brew, Kathy Rae Huffman, Branda Miller, Neil Rolnick, Carol Stakenas, Mary Ellen Strom, and Igor Vamos. Since the 1990s, digital media artists such as Zoe Beloff, Shu Lea Cheang, Philip Mallory Jones, and Kevin and Jennifer McCoy had been featured seminar guests but never central foci. With ninety participants, the RPI Digital Flaherty mobilized a dynamic heterogeneity: Toni Dove, Tirtza Even, Amy Goodman from Democracy Now, DeeDee

Halleck from Deep Dish and Paper Tiger Television, Jennifer and Kevin McCoy, Alex Rivera, Demetri Terzopoulos and Igor Vamos from the Yes Men. New media scholar Sandy Stone delivered a keynote address, evoking the 1950s seminars featuring lectures. This seminar showcased many live performances with digital technologies from Graham Harwood, Art Jones, Sissyfight, Paul Vanouse, and Grahame Weinbren.[60] Live media performances were a Flaherty Seminar historical subcurrent, starting with Frances's music recitals in the 1950s, Shirley Clarke's live video performances in the 1960s and 1970s, Steina Vasulka's MIDI and violin performances in 1996, and the *Arctic Requiem* (2004) performance of live electronic music with *Nanook of the North*.

In 2002, Ed Halter programmed the seminar. With its exclusive focus on experimental film, it signaled the end of the Flaherty documentary versus experimental film civil wars. It represented the only seminar where film movements formed a programming strategy: the microcinema movement and the growing underground film festival scene. Executive Director Somi Roy had contacted Halter about programming, determining the need to recruit younger programmers from outside the "Flaherty family." Halter had been connected with the microcinema movement, which broke with an earlier generation of independent film. Operating in a do-it-yourself (DIY) ethos with no budget, the microcinema movement solved the problem of declining grant support. Perceiving the existing independent film and media arts sector as what Halter dubbed a "top-heavy, bureaucratic, and grant-chasing model," the microcinema movement worked fast and loose, responding quickly to audiences and to larger aesthetic, political, and social debates and developments.[61] After graduating from college, Halter worked for the Frameline Festival, where he learned programming was an "intellectual endeavor." He then attended graduate school at New York University but felt it was disconnected from the energized new film movements. By 1994, he started programming the New York Underground Film Festival.[62]

Unspooling less than a year after 9/11, Halter's 2002 program operated as a twenty-first-century update of the D. Marie Grieco 1984 program of shorts. With eighty-three films, the 2002 seminar screened more titles than most seminars, facilitated by short running times. Featured makers ranged from Jem Cohen (*Benjamin Smoke,* 2000), Kevin Everson (*Daily Number,* 2001; *Imported,* 1999; *Merger,* 1999; *Eleven Eighty,* 1997), Sam Green (*Weather Underground,* 2002), Jeff Kulik (*Harry Potter Parking Lot,* 1999; *Heavy Metal Parking Lot,* 1986; *Neil Diamond Parking Lot,* 1996), Kenji Onishi (*A Burning Star,* 1995), Elizabeth Subrin (*Swallow,* 1995), Ela Troyano (*Carmelita Tropicana: Your Kunst Is Your Waffen,* 1994), and Naomi Uman (*Leche,* 1998 and *Removed,* 1999). The seminar concentrated on a younger generation of filmmakers who circulated their work in short-film festivals such as Cinematexas, microcinemas, the Oberhausen Film Festival, and various underground film festivals. Most seminars featured a mix of emerging, midcareer, and established makers; this seminar zeroed in on a younger generation in their twenties and thirties.

The seminar pivoted on the tensions between amateur and professional, popular culture and underground practices. Kenneth Anger presented a retrospective of his work in the role of master filmmaker, one of the first openly gay filmmakers to occupy this key seminar role. He screened a mini-retrospective: *Puce Moment* (1949); *Eaux d'artifice*

(1953); *Kustom Kar Kommandos* (1965); *Invocation of My Demon Brother* (1969); *Lucifer Rising* (1972); and some new works in progress. With his experimental film focus, Halter shifted the definition of heterogeneity from form, genre, mode, and style to audience. Aware of spectator reactions to films, Halter crafted his program in terms of varying the moods an audience would experience.[63]

By 2003, themes and concepts returned to the seminar. The Flaherty postseminar catalog began in 2003. John Gianvito programmed with the theme "Witnessing the World," a seminar pivoting on socially engaged documentary that countered the experimental, microcinema/underground film festival ethos of the Halter seminar. Gianvito was the former curator at the Harvard Film Archive. At the time of his preparation to mount the 2003 seminar, he was between jobs. In the middle of this process, he learned that the board had reduced the length of the seminar by one day, which pushed constraints onto his program. In early 2003, one of the largest protest events in US history unfolded in response to the US war on Iraq and subsequent invasion. Responding to this surround of political intensity, Gianvito wanted to "bring together a broad swathe of some of the most politically committed and accomplished filmmakers I could find and see what such a dialogue might inspire. Conceptually, I envisioned the program as a mosaic."[64]

The professionalization and transparency the board had determined was necessary to transition the seminar from a "family" into an organization exhibited itself in this conceptual programming to problematize ideas. This professionalization included publishing "curator's statements" in the postseminar booklet. As Gianvito wrote, his seminar "examines a variety of ways contemporary filmmakers have grappled with cinema's abilities and frailties in relation to the concept of social responsibility and political struggle."[65] Gianvito categorized these films as "committed cinema," a cinema to "arouse the conscience, cinema sensitized to injustice and inequality."[66]

The 2003 "Witnessing the World" seminar screened international documentary and experimental documentary makers working in diverse modalities, including Franny Armstrong (*McLibel: Two Worlds Collide*, 1998), Paul Chan (*Let Us Praise American Leftists*, 2000), Katerina Cizek, Mary Filippo (*The Trickle Down Theory of Sorrow*, 2002), Holly Fisher (*Kalama Sutta: Seeing Is Believing*, 2001), Eric Galatas (Independent Media Center), Sam Gregory (WITNESS, the nongovernmental organization using video for social change), Alfred Guzzetti (*Calcutta Intersection*, 2003), Matthew McDaniel (*Birth of a Nation 4*29*1992*, 1993), Avi Mograbi (*August: A Moment before the Eruption*, 2002; *Happy Birthday, Mr. Mograbi*, 1999), Verna Molina and Ernesto Ardito (*Raymundo*, 2003), Marlo Poras (*Mai's America*, 2002), James Rutenbeck (*Company Town*, 1984), Trân Văn Thuy (*The Sound of the Violin of My Lai*, 1999), Travis Wilkerson (*An Injury to One*, 2002), Peter Wintonick (*Seeing Is Believing: Handicams, Human Rights and the News*, 2002), and two collectives, B Room and the Guerilla News Network. Questions about the role "that form and aesthetics play in engendering political efficacy" ran through seminar discussions, according to Gianvito.[67] Since the 1970s Willard era, debates about the relationships between form and politics had constituted a major concern in postscreening discussions. The 2003 seminar brought these debates front and center in the programming itself.

Gianvito saw his program as decidedly global and explicitly political: "From Argentina, Brazil, Canada, Israel, Japan, the Philippines, the United States, the United

Kingdom, and Vietnam, each of that week's guests possessed a core commitment to confronting social and political injustice in all sort of arenas and all sorts of forms."[68] Tran Van Thuy's films had been banned in Vietnam; he provided an example of heroic committed filmmaking against many political obstacles.

Seventy-four-year-old Noriaki Tsuchimoto, dealing with diabetes, occupied the master filmmaker role. According to Gianvito, he was considered one of the most important documentary filmmakers in Japan, with eighteen-plus films over a thirty-five-year period. He screened *Minamata: The Victims and Their World* (1971) and *Shiranui Sea* (1975) at the seminar. According to Gianvito's recounting, Tsuchimoto, whose adage "Remembrance is strength" galvanized seminarians, described an alternative distribution process for his films: "he circumvented the traditional avenues of art house and television exhibition and traveled widely around Japan and elsewhere screening his films in nontraditional venues in small villages and community centers, periodically stopping the films and discussing them with audiences much like Gettino and Solanas with *Hours of the Furnaces*."[69]

Gianvito's program returned to a programming arc to generate dialectics between screenings. Many participants' testimonials elaborated on how this heterogeneous program shifted their conceptual thinking to consider documentary form and politics across different registers. Jenn Guitart, a grants-in-aid recipient, wrote: "John's openness to different filmic languages—new media forms like Paul Chan's, more traditional documentaries like Franny Armstrong's or untrained grassroots media like Matt McDaniel's—and his willingness to include young filmmakers along with older masters . . . inspired us to question the categories of 'conventional' and 'experimental.'"[70] Elizabeth Coll, another grants-in-aid recipient, commented, "I experienced further expansion of my visual vocabulary and my understanding of the possibilities of cinema in the building of resistance."[71] The testimonials in the 2003 seminar booklet evidenced the clarity of the seminar's brand: a focus on changing how one produces and thinks about documentary. The gender, national, and racial mix of the filmmakers answered the 1990s debates by promoting a polyphony of approaches and styles within transnational flows rather than national identities.

The year 2007 marked a turning point in the Flaherty's branding, programming, and public image. It shifted toward an explicit internationalism in its programmers/curators and themes. The name of the organization, International Film Seminars, always suggested a focus beyond the United States, but budgeting frequently inhibited its capacities to program large numbers of international guests. This international focus infused virtually all programming from the 1980s onward. After six programs by nine white North American and European curators from 2001 to 2006, the public image of the Flaherty—despite the international programming foci—appeared to have disengaged from the multicultural critiques launched against it in 1990s.

Of the ten curators hired between 2007 and 2014, only two were white Americans, Dan Streible and Irina Leimbacher, who had a binational identity between the United States and Europe. Mahen Bonetti (2007) was from Sierra Leone, Carlos Gutiérrez (2007) was from Mexico, Chi-hui Yang (2008) was Asian American, and Dennis Lim (2010) was of Chinese Malaysian origin. Josetxo Cerdán (2012) was from Spain and the first programmer of a Flaherty who resided outside the United States. Pablo de Ocampo (2013) toggled between the United States and Canada. Caspar Stracke (2014) was from Germany, and Gabriella Monroy (2014) was from Mexico.

The 2007 seminar, *South of the Other*, signaled this deliberate redirection toward a more international and multicultural brand. This seminar indicated the international turn of the Flaherty Film Seminar, where artists, fellows, filmmakers, and participants were not exclusively from the East Coast/Montreal/Toronto corridor that so defined the Flaherty milieu. Programmed by Mahen Bonetti, artistic director of the African Film Festival in New York, and Carlos Gutiérrez, codirector of Cinema Tropical, a distributor of Latin American cinema, the 2007 seminar exemplified an explicit "international turn."

Mahen Bonetti identified their programming strategy as an "attempt to transcend clichés about otherness, approach cinema without preconceptions." According to Bonetti, their strategy was designed to place subjectivities up against globalization:

> The program did not pretend to be a regional survey of world cinema, or an assessment about geopolitical issues; it was about challenging, subverting, and redefining ideas of subjectivity. It struck me that in the ever-growing context of globalization, time had come to bring in new voices from elsewhere who have a strong personal approach, encourage a more inclusive dialogue, foster a common exploration that could serve as a platform for the flourishing of comparative studies in cinema. . . . Time had come for the Global South to gain a foothold in universal cinema discourse, and our seminar helped shift the focus in that direction (the Flaherty Seminar is still the incubator/indicator that signals new discussions."[72]

In her 2007 catalog statement, Executive Director Mary Kerr described "South of the Other" as "one of the most international Flaherty Seminars in years—guests from Brazil, China, Cameroon, Indonesia, Mexico, Russia, Senegal, South Africa," as well as "Canada, Colombia, Germany, South Africa, Spain, Zimbabwe, the US."[73] By 2007, the construct of "curator" had erased the decades-long moniker of "programmer." Bonetti and Gutiérrez structured their seminar as a "journey" that reoriented the field toward considering "the south, east, west, north, outside of the other." Their seminar programming inverted the idea of the "other" and redefined it as Eurocentrism. Their seminar engaged different movements and vectors. As they explained, "our field, as unfortunately many other aspects of contemporary life, remains unbearably Eurocentric."[74] Their program junked ideas about national cinemas. Instead, it opted to place global cinemas in conversation with one another through form, politics, and provocations. The Flaherty film they selected epitomized this strategy: *Elephant Boy* (1937), a commercial narrative docudrama shot in India.

The program mixed approaches, countries, and styles. For example, experimental Mexican video artist Ximena Cuevas (*Cinépolis, la capital del cine*, 2002, and *Ensayo de un crimen*, 2005) and experimental African American performance artist Kalup Linzy (*Lollypop*, 2006, and a live video performance with *Da Young and Da Mess #3*) screened work alongside documentarians from Africa, Latin America, and Southeast Asia. Works problematized and unsettled the borders between documentary and experimental visual syntax: Natalia Almada (*Al otro lado*, 2005; *El general*, 2007, Mexico), Mahamet Saleh

Haroun (*Bye Bye Africa*, 1999, Chad), Leonard Retel Helmrich (*Eye of the Day*, 2001; *Shape of the Moon*, 2004, Indonesia/the Netherlands), João Moreira Salles (*Santiago*, 2007, Brazil), and Juan Carlos Zaldivar (*90 Miles*, 2001, United States). Osvalde Lewat-Hallade (*Un amour pendant la guerre*, 2005, Cameroon) and Khalo Matabane (*Story of a Beautiful Country*, 2004; *Conversations on a Sunday Afternoon*, 2005, South Africa) addressed rapes in the Congo and significant ongoing political issues in South Africa. Their realist documentaries demonstrated the continuing urgency of documentation and witnessing. Resonating with Pearl Bowser's landmark 1989 seminar, and one of the few times a filmmaker from Africa occupied the position of senior established film-maker, Senegalese filmmaker, musician, painter, and poet Moussa Sene Absa served the role of master filmmaker. His highly stylized mise-en-scène–centric narrative/docu-drama films *Tableau Ferraile* (1998) and *Madame Brouette* (2002) evoked the Flaherty visual tradition of lyrical reenactments.

As Gutiérrez later reflected, their seminar intervened into "gringo-centric" Flaherty Seminar history. He and Bonetti positioned themselves as more than political insurgents or provocateurs. They were committed to "exorcising the seminar" and "cleansing the organization," by changing the subjectivities engaged (only Kalup Linzy was US born). In their inversion, North American whites were the other. Their gracious affect, engagement, and openness eschewed a doctrinaire line, offering a way into "building community in a communal way" by putting aside one's privilege. Gutiérrez pointed out the 2007 seminar disposed of screen studies binaries between commercial and independent, and between different national cinemas. It programmed works that resolutely refused these classifications. For Gutiérrez, programming was not about selecting auteurs or exquisite films as much as creating contexts for meaning production around the films. He was extremely aware of audience and creating dialogues.[75]

This international turn continued in the 2008 seminar "The Age of Migration," programmed by Chi-hui Yang. One of the few West Coast programmers in the semi-nar's history, Yang was the director and programmer of the San Francisco International Asian American Film Festival, one of the largest national showcases for Asian and Asian American cinemas. Yang's program continued to refine the heterogeneous programming model with questions of globalization and its impact on bodies: "I was interested in creating a space where films from radically different traditions and econo-mies could be seen alongside each other, to test the capacity of documentary form to express the complexities of diaspora and globalization. This included works made for public media, the gallery, the Internet, and of course the cinema—a combination which makes sense to me, but which is difficult to find in an increasingly siloed curatorial world."[76]

After several years at Vassar College, where inadequate professional projection and uncomfortable screening rooms posed a continual challenge, the seminar moved fur-ther upstate to Colgate University in central New York. A new building with state-of-the-art projection facilities promised to resolve problems encountered in Vassar's older exhibition facilities. John Knecht, an art and media professor at Colgate, facilitated the connection between the seminar and the university. Yang's seminar attracted increased funding for fellows from the Asian Pacific American Film Group, CEC ArtsLink, the

Experimental Television Center, the Fledgling Fund, the Philadelphia Foundation, and the Southwest Alternate Media Project.[77]

Yang positioned his theme of migration as a "framework which could illuminate much of what is unseen about our globalized world," highlighting issues of movement (exiles, laborers, refugees, soldiers, tourists) and transmissions. He considered the seminar a way to "provoke and disrupt, to stir up ideas."[78] He saw the seminar as a "social petri dish, bringing together a group of disparate individuals, films, and ideas." Yang self-consciously implemented a deliberate programming arc: this seminar was "carefully planned to unfold in an arc that balanced rigor with joy, theoretical with lived experience, local with global."[79] As Yang reflects: "'The Age of Migration' was built to consider how the global circulation of bodies—refugees, artists, soldiers—is linked to the increasing mobility of images, from screen to gallery, to device, and so on. The question here was to understand the relationship between the sheer materiality of bodies that are compelled to move by forces economic and political, and the immateriality of their digital representations."[80] The films, new media, and videos redefined heterogeneity as different countries, genres, and modes disturbed by bodies and human movement.

This seminar concentrated on what Scott MacDonald has called the "avant-doc," a liminal zone that functions as a new genus, complex enough to generate a conceptual discussion and distinct from more realist broadcast fare.[81] Experimental works by James T. Hong (*The Form of the Good*, 2004, United States), Alison Kobayashi (*From Alex to Alex*, 2006), Sylvia Schedelbauer (*Memories*, 2004, Germany), and Laura Waddington (*Cargo*, 2001) were screened. The program was wide ranging, with more analytical political documentaries, ranging from the essay films of Ursula Biemann (*Black Sea Files*, 2005; *Sahara Chronicle*, 2006; *Contained Mobility*, 2006, Switzerland) to public television broadcast work such as Renee Tajima-Peña (*My America Honk If You Love Buddha*, 1997; *Calavera Highway*, 2008) to the lyrical documentary style of Thavisouk Phrasavath (*The Betrayal*, 2007, United States/Laos).

"The Age of Migration" seminar deconstructed the single master filmmaker model. Yang positioned four established master makers, two men and two women, each from a different country: Ursula Bieman (Switzerland), Pedro Costa (*Colossal Youth*, 2006; *Casa de lava*, 1994; *In Vanda's Room*, 2000, Portugal), Bahman Ghobadi (*Half Moon*, 2006; *A Time for Drunken Horses*, 2000, Iran; Skyped into his discussion sessions), and Renee Tajima-Peña (United States). Each represented a different cinematic style and exhibition vector: Beiman, the essay film and the gallery installation; Costa, long-form slow art cinema; Ghobadi, international art cinema and genre cinema; and Tajima-Peña, American independent documentary and public television.

Seminar programs throughout this period battled against simplistic notions of national cinemas, preferring the hybrid, the migratory, and the polyphonic. However, most programs held on to the artisanal and the auteur, which now defined the Flaherty brand. With the expansion of screen studies and master of fine arts (MFA) programs, the explosion of film festivals with their commercial impulses, and the retreat to privatized online spaces, this auteurism should not be interpreted as conservative, revisionist or a throwback to the seminars of the 1950s and 1960s. If filmmakers at festivals needed to present themselves as charming raconteurs and enticing commodities, at the Flaherty, they could reveal how they thought about their practice in the luxury of forty-five- to sixty-minute discussions unavailable elsewhere in the independent film landscape.

The increasing numbers of both production and screen studies faculty attending the seminar offered access to an important political economy to sustain independent cinema. University faculty had no other place to go to see a panoply of carefully curated, hard-to-access films contextualized by lengthy discussions and skillful moderation. By 2007, over 30 percent of the 150 participants were affiliated with colleges or universities. By 2008, this number increased to 40 percent, with 70 participants out of 173. By 2009, nearly 50 percent of the participants—82 out of 170—were academics. With their bibliographies and reading lists, the program booklets evidenced not so much a rigorous scholarly approach as a way to communicate the brand to its largest market sector. Amid the virtualization of labor and social life, the seminar's traditional emphasis on embodied interactions now seemed radical.

This brand of international artisanal cinema reached an apex in three noteworthy seminars: "Witness, Monuments, Ruins," 2009; "Work," 2012; and "Turning the Inside Out," 2014. These three seminars shifted away from accessible character-driven documentary, the popular, the realist, and the televisual toward the complex ambiguities of international art cinema. The year 2009 served as a conceptually sophisticated reprocessing of works from international film festivals and galleries. The 2012 seminar elaborated into a flow merging powerful film movements from Asia and Latin America garnering international film festival praise. Two years later, the seminar embraced the art world and its "documentary turn," focusing on works designed for galleries and other venues beyond movie theaters. All four curators traversed academia, the art world, curating, and journalism: Irina Leimbacher, a programmer, scholar, and writer; Dennis Lim, a critic, journalist, and programmer; and Caspar Stracke and Gabriella Monroy, artists and programmers.

Curator of the 2009 seminar, Irina Leimbacher worked as a film programmer, scholar, and university lecturer. At the time of her seminar, she was completing her PhD at University of California, Berkeley. The former artistic director of the San Francisco Cinematheque, her programming and scholarly work examined both experimental and nonfiction modes. Her 2009 seminar imported two innovations to the Flaherty. It was the first seminar to bring numerous filmmakers from the Arab Middle East and the first seminar to showcase installations extensively rather than as a singular example. She brought filmmakers from Iraq, Palestine, and Syria. In 2009, the United States was engaging in wars in Afghanistan and Iraq.[82] Arguing her program identified what she called the "spatial turn" in documentary as it migrated to installation and museums, Leimbacher echoed strategies of other Flaherty curators by creating arcs and resonances across heterogeneous works. Her programming structure focused on "arranging and rearranging them [the films] into as dynamic a composition as possible."[83] Her seminar catalog essay emphasized a "suggestive, fluid, open to inquiry" approach.[84]

This seminar featured experimental filmmakers such as Juan Manuel Echavarría (*Guerra y pá*, 2001, Colombia) and Paweł Wojtasik (*Dark Sun Squeeze*, 2003; *The Aquarium*, 2006; *Nascentes Morimur*, 2009, United States), as well as artists working in hybrid avant-doc forms such as Ilisa Barbash and Lucien Castaing-Taylor (*Sweetgrass*, 2009) and

Amar Kanwar (*The Lightning Testimonies*, 2007, India). The Arab Middle Eastern film-makers included Kasim Abid (*Life after the Fall*, 2008, Iraq), Kamal Aljafari (*The Roof*, 2006, Palestine), and Omar Amiralay (*The Chickens*, 1977; *A Flood in Ba-Ath Country*, 2003; *A Plate of Sardines*, 1997, Syria). From St. Petersburg, Russia, Pavel Medvedev, director of *On the Third Planet from the Sun* (2006), was an audience favorite.[85] In a radical move, the seminar's Tuesday afternoon session focused on the installation, photographic, and site-specific work of Juan Manuel Echavarría, Jeanne C. Finley, Amar Kanwar, Beryl Korot, and John Muse, all of which spread over two floors in the media building at Colgate University. Amar Kanwar's eight-screen installation, *The Lightning Testimonies* (2007, India), probing accounts of the entwining of narratives of political traumas and sexual violence in India, ran for four days—a significant shift at the seminar which had typically focused on projected films/videos in a conventional theatrical setting. The established filmmaker role was virtualized, with Abderrahmane Sissako from Mauritania and Mali Skyped in for discussions. His films *Waiting for Happiness* (2002) and *Bamako* (2006) were screened.

By 2010, conceptual themes, extended discussions, formalist heterogeneity, internationalism, and programming arcs to shape participants' experience of the seminar constituted key components of the Flaherty brand of considered, demanding, and intellectually rigorous programming that was unavailable elsewhere. A highly refined structural sensibility deploying programming to probe a theoretical question camouflaged the recurring essentialist ideology of nonpreconception. "Nonpreconception" had transitioned from its Buddhist origins into a component of the brand.

The 2010 theme was "Work." Curator Dennis Lim explained work "is by and large an underrepresented cinematic subject, something that happens offscreen or in the margins." An editor and journalist, Lim wrote film criticism for publications such as the *Los Angeles Times*, the *New York Times*, and the *Village Voice*. He had served as film editor of the *Village Voice* from 2000 to 2006. Lim created his programming to answer a series of research questions about the economics, implications, invisibilities, meaning, and observations of labor and work.[86] The theme emerged just two years after the 2008 economic collapse. Like most Flaherty curators from this period, he exhumed what was invisible through "geographic and formal diversity."[87]

Lim saw the seminar as a unique node in the media ecology where creating space for conversations was paramount. He wrote: "Flaherty has a well-deserved reputation as a testing ground for filmmakers and a battle zone for ideas about their work—the sheer intensity of the experience and the combustible mix of participants ensure that the fault lines rapidly emerge."[88] Lim understood the impact of a Flaherty program resided as much in the curator's choices as in the conversations the films conjured among participants.

His program featured filmmakers from two regions with exploding new film movements: Asia and Latin America. From Latin America, he brought Lisandro Alonso (*Los Muertos*, 2004, Argentina), Eugenio Polgovsky (*Tropic of Cancer*, 2004, Mexico), and Pedro González-Rubio (*Alamar*, 2009, Mexico), and complicating even this regionalism, Latino American Alex Rivera (*Sleep Dealer*, 2008). Zhao Dayong (*Street Life*, 2010, China) and Uruphong Raksasad (*Agrarian Utopia*, 2009, Thailand) represented two important emerging independent cinemas. Experimental makers included Benj Gerdes, Jennifer Hayashida, and Naomi Uman, all from the United States. This seminar returned to the single master filmmaker model in Austrian Michael Glawogger (*Megacities*, 1998; *Workingman's Death,* 2005). His films exemplified the new coordinates of the Flaherty: carefully conceived, global in structure, and rigorously photographed with attention to composition. Most of this seminar's filmmakers had garnered recognition at international film festivals. The seminar screened Robert Flaherty's collaboration with John Grierson, *Industrial Britain* (1931), a work rarely seen outside of university documentary film history classes.

By 2012, this trend toward abstract themes as both containers for intellectual inquiry and interventions into Flaherty programming history reached its apex in the curatorial work of Josetxo Cerdán, artistic director of the Punto de Vista International Documentary Film Festival Navarra in Spain and a film professor. Cerdán was the first overseas curator in the history of the Flaherty. Two-thirds of the 2012 featured artists lived outside the United States, which can be attributed to the increasing abilities of the Flaherty as an organization to attract funding to underwrite ambitious internationally focused programming.

Cerdán's theme was abstract and conceptual: "Open Wounds." In describing his programming, he wrote that "Open wounds are those unresolved questions that pursue us, in so many diverse ways, over the course of our lives." He was interested in a "period of crisis rather than stability."[89] "Open Wounds" screened the works of Susana De Sousa Diaz (Portugal), Andrés Duque (Spain/Venezuela), Su Friedrich (United States), Sylvain George (France), Isaki Lacuesta (Spain), Sebastian Lingiardi (Argentina), Minda Martin (United States), Laila Pakalnina (Russia), Ben Rivers (United Kingdom), Ben Russell (United States), Dustin Guy Defa (United States), Sami van Ingen (Finland), and Sun Xun (China). In one of the rare times a woman occupied the role of éminence grise and established filmmaker, Lourdes Portillo, the Mexican American documentarian who had developed a more performative documentary style, screened *La Ofrenda: The Days of the Dead* (1988) and *The Devil Never Sleeps* (1999).

Cerdán twisted the seminar model. He programmed musical selections before each screening, setting the mood. Previously, the Flaherty had most frequently opted for the more reverential tactic of participants simply waiting for the film. Second, Cerdán attenuated his thematic programming by creating subthemes for each session, such as Anti-Anthropologist, Clash, Family Affairs, Ghosts, and Sutures. These subthemes functioned as chapters, focusing discussions. Despite these more intellectual programming goals, the notion of the "Flaherty family" persisted. In the catalog for the 2010 seminar, fellows coordinator Jason Livingston entitled his essay "It's a Family Affair."[90]

By the sixtieth anniversary in 2014, the branding of the seminar with conceptual themes and its increasing product differentiation from the festival and television worlds was complete. Large, one-sheet white posters of the Nanook logo in blue, green, and pink adorned Bill's Bar and the discussion room. Beyond commerce and popular culture, the Flaherty Seminar provided sanctuary for deep, theoretical considerations of cinema. In the context of festivals operating in more economically driven and public worlds of film marketing or city tourism, the Flaherty Seminar offered an antidote of total immersion in ideas. In the context of the explosion of film and media programs at universities, the seminar provided professional development and a refueling in challenging works, complex ideas, and international dialogues often absent from academia, which more and more adopted a neoliberal industrialist rather than critical orientation. It now functioned as an alternative universe for the artisanal, the complex, and the dialogic.

The Flaherty brand was secure. Seminar packets included a short mission statement: "The Robert Flaherty Film Seminar's mission is to nurture exploration, dialogue, and introspection about the art and craft of the moving image and its potential to illuminate the human spirit."[91] Programmers were curators; practitioners were artists. The fierce divides between the avant-garde and documentary camps from the 1950s, 1960s, 1970s, 1980s, and 1990s dissolved. In the art gallery, biennial-driven, hybridized, transnational landscape, these modes functioned not as political positions but as an arsenal of tactics to problematize and unsettle representations. The sometimes mean-spirited, unsettling debates between practitioners and theorists from previous eras melted: the artists had read as much theory as the academics, and the academics were more artist friendly. Artists and participants came from twenty-one countries and twenty-one different states for the 2014 seminar, evidencing its expansion beyond the East Coast corridor and the internationalism of the Flaherty. Out of the 160 participants, 32 were fellows, constituting 20 percent of attendees. Funding for fellowships had increased from fifteen years earlier, with fourteen different funders, including California College of the Arts, Duke University, Harvard University, and University of Rochester. Media groups such as the Center for Asian American Media and Pacific Islanders in Communications also underwrote fellowships.[92]

Programmed by artist/curators Gabrielle Monroy (Mexico/United States) and Caspar Stracke (Germany/United States), "Turning the Inside Out" probed the "documentary turn" in the international art and gallery world, the first time an entire seminar had been dedicated to how other arts sectors utilized documentary as a strategy, syntax, and tactic. The postcard announcing this seminar explained the sixtieth Flaherty seminar would probe "the state of documentary as it travels between the art gallery, the cinema, and the interactive screen. . . . [W]hich genre (essay film, autobiography, docufiction) and exhibition form (gallery installation, web-based platform) best supports the expression of an idea?"[93]

Monroy and Stracke saw documentary form migrating beyond the screen as a significant shift. They probed this movement in their seminar, arguing that the fine arts field had been underrepresented at the Flaherty, despite its engagement with the American avant-garde: "what distinguished the works shown in these exhibitions from conventional documentary was their openness to interdisciplinary practices. Beyond the film itself, many conceptual art projects included sculpture, installation, performance, or public interventions. This concept caught our interest."[94] In his *Artforum* article called "Flaherty Will Get You Everywhere," Leo Goldsmith argued this seminar was in dialogue with developments in the art world related to the "documentary turn" in fine art and installation, particularly Documenta X in 1997 and later in Manifesta 5 in 2004. Goldsmith observed the program focused on "hybrid, essayistic, collectively made work." Most artists presenting work considered the image as an "object to be shaped, collected, and curated by the archivist/artist" rather than a seamless representation of the world.[95]

. Extending the conception of the spatialized turn in documentary advanced by Leimbacher in 2009, the 2014 seminar featured a record seven installations on two floors of the Colgate University media arts building. Brad Butler and Karen Mirza's (United Kingdom) *The Autonomous Object?* (2008) and *Speech Act 00157* (2011) interrogated political speech and actions as global dissonances. The CAMP Collective's (India) *The Radio Tap(e)s, Act 11, Hum Logos* (2011) featured a black screen with translations of collected cell phone conversations in the surveillance state. The RAQS Media Collective's (India) *Strikes at Time* (2011) used a worker's diary juxtaposed with quotes from Jacques Rancière to theorize urban labor. This seminar featured collaborative, collective, and participatory projects in greater numbers than any preceding seminar, exemplified in the CAMP Collective (*From Gulf to Gulf to Gulf*, 2013) and RAQS Media Collectives (*The Capital of Accumulation*, 2010) from India as well as the transmedia performance, writing, and video relational aesthetics projects (*Letters to Max*, 2014) of Eric Baudelaire from France.

By their own assessment, Monroy and Stracke argued they intended to explore, "the given potential for the self-reflexive, which enables a continuously shifting relationship between author and subject" and "radical accounts of political commitment echoed in uncompromising forms."[96] Featured artists Duncan Campbell (Scotland), Cao Guimarães (Brazil), Jesse McLean (United States), and Lois Patiño (Spain), as well as Butler and Mirza, reconfigured documentary practice as an inflection rather than as an intervention. Their work unhinged the image from its facticity and referentiality, a discourse and a performance rather than a rhetorical argument as it migrated between gallery, online, and screen spaces. Johan Grimonprez's (Belgium) landmark *dial H-I-S-T-O-R-Y* (1997) had been featured in the Documenta X show. Many participants anointed him the master filmmaker of the seminar, in part because his groundbreaking political films exemplified this documentary turn in the galleries, and in part because he displayed verbal virtuosity with politics and theory. Others saw Jill Godmilow (*What Farocki Taught*, 1998, United States) and Hito Steyerl (Germany), an installation/gallery artist whose works were shown single channel, as sharing this role, especially with their explicit feminist politics. They represented different historical periods of the "documentary turn."

By the 2014 Flaherty Seminar, the image performed as an object and not only as representation. The programmers understood that the seminar needed to move beyond the films as consummate texts to remake the audience as active participants in dynamic, unfolding dialogues. From 2000 to 2015, the Flaherty not only professionalized and rebranded itself but also rebalanced the seminar, asserting that the audience as a participant was as critical as what was projected on the screen. This position embodied a reconnection with—and a revitalization of—ideas Frances Flaherty advanced at the first seminars in the 1950s.

Across many decades, the Flaherty has evolved from a family operation to a viable nonprofit media arts organization. It has also moved from its East Coast corridor milieu toward a more national and international organization. It has transformed from an almost private club or secret society run by bickering, like-minded aficionados who saw themselves as the "Flaherty family" into a nonprofit organization with policies, procedures, and rules, and with a focus on the ambassadorial role of the Flaherty board for hospitality, another indication of a participant-centered ethos. The Flaherty possessed a potent history of contributing to the development of international independent film in its myriad forms; and it had become a destination for those in these marginalized sectors—a place to convene and refuel.

Although programmers transmuted into curators in the last period, the audience remained participants—the core of the seminar. The Flaherty was unusual for an independent media arts event and organization because it valued the filmmakers and participants equally. The Flaherty Seminar was first and foremost an experience. It removed participants from daily life. It immersed them emotionally, intellectually, physically, and socially into engagements with cinematic ideas, makers, and texts, as well as with those in other sectors of the international independent media ecologies.

These participants have always represented the most important element of the Flaherty seminars: the creation of a community where debate and engagement with others truly matters. The Flaherty has continued to offer a dynamic collage not only of different kinds of filmic practices, but also of people. It offers something few institutions can: time to be conceptual, to build conceptual and practical alliances, to experience nurturing intergenerational dialogues, and to think about connections between heterogeneous forms, people, and practices.

If, in the rest of their work lives, the participants were isolated in classrooms and editing rooms and libraries, at the Flaherty Seminar, they experienced an imagined community of collectivity, purpose, and social engagement beyond the self. Beyond the auteurs, the board, the filmmakers, the programmers, and the veterans, the Flaherty has survived because it offers a place for community. In the end, its lifeblood and sustainability has always depended on nurturing and supporting participants, especially those emerging in the field.

Most everyone seems to disagree about what "the Flaherty" was, is, or should be. And these debates, for which there are no easy resolutions, are, in the end, most likely what keeps "the Flaherty" pulsing with life, thriving. As Erik Barnouw used to say in his closing benedictions at many seminars, the seminar and its participants have always needed to move in one uncharted direction—onward.

2000 SERGEY DVORTSEVOY—ON *PARADISE* (1995); VICKY FUNARI—ON *PAULINA* (1998)

[Usually, postscreening discussions last around an hour, but sometimes, for one reason or another, shorter discussions are scheduled, as was the case in this instance.]

> *Flaherty seminarian (F):* About twenty-five years ago, there was a debate between Colin Young and David MacDougall about observational cinema and its virtues, MacDougall talking about what might go beyond that. When you talk about the kind of films you're making and the need for a trust in the image, how does that compare with other kinds of trust that might have been evident in the observational ethnographic films of the last fifty years? Do you see trusting the image as something we really don't understand yet?

Dvortsevoy: It doesn't matter what kind of film we're talking about, ethnographic film or feature narrative film, and for me, it doesn't matter whether someone is working in video or film. Whenever we work with imagery, we are working with time. What is a photograph? For me, a photo is the shortest film, a one-second film, even less. And what is the difference between a photograph and a film? The one difference is time. When we start to analyze our tools, we realize that it's not easy to start to make a film because time is money. And so, when you try to do something on film that takes time, you feel this barrier, the barrier of money. All producers want to do film faster.

When filmmakers understand what time is in film, they will realize that with more time, films can be more emotional, stronger, more precise. *Bread Day*, which you will see tomorrow, is a step in the direction of taking more time and taking time more seriously.

F: I think it's so appropriate that we're seeing your film at a Flaherty Seminar. *Paradise* is a Flaherty kind of film. I wonder whether you saw his films during your education at film school.

Dvortsevoy: Yes, I did. I wondered why are his shots so short? Just one year ago, I understood why. When I talked to Richard Leacock, he told me that he was a cameraman for Flaherty, and that Flaherty had used a camera with a very small magazine. I realized that the length of Flaherty's shots was just a matter of equipment.

I'm sure that Flaherty understood time very well. In Flaherty's films, which I think are close to mine, I see in front of me a life, and I don't feel the pressure of the director. Most directors in Russia and everywhere else try to prove something. In the Soviet Union, it was propaganda mostly, but everywhere, filmmakers are trying to prove something. When I see a film and in five minutes understand what the director wants to prove to me, the film is not interesting. If I don't feel some kind of mystery inside the film—and I don't mean confusion—I am not interested. In my opinion, film has to be simple but very deep; for me, depth is beauty. Even if you have good composition and good sound and scenes of beauty, your film is beautiful only if it is deep. Flaherty made beautiful films because they are deep. I can imagine how unusual it was to do his kind of films at the beginning of the century.

Amie Siegel: My question is about *Paradise*. The sound seemed extremely close-miked, to the point where even the cows seem to be wearing microphones. Was the sound done postproduction?

Dvortsevoy: *Paradise* was my diploma film, and we had two problems with the sound. One problem was that it was a diploma film, and we were not working with good equipment. The second problem was that the wind was very strong in Kazakhstan, all the time very strong, and we had problems with the shotgun microphone. Sometimes it was possible to catch sound well and sometimes it was not. Eighty percent of the sound in *Paradise* is the original sound, but in some parts, we needed to replace the sound during the editing. It's very difficult to record sound in the steppe.

F: This is a question for Vicki, kind of a personal question but one that comes from my own assessment of the kind of work that I do; I think we have similar motivations. You introduced your film by saying that you were very concerned with class, race, struggle, and that you were interested in using film as a way of addressing the things that you feel very deeply about. Do you feel pleased with the medium of film and what *Paulina* has been able to do in terms of its distribution; do you feel satisfied with the work that you're doing?

Vicki Funari: Film and video, any of the mass media that affect the way we see things, are limited tools; they can only do so much. In a certain sense, what they can do is never enough. On the other hand, if I hadn't done the work I do, it wouldn't have been there at all. I guess all I can say is that I think this work is worth doing. I don't see filmmaking as a particularly great way to make social change, but it is a great way to create dialogue, and that's what I hope for with any film.

   You brought up the issue of distribution, a key issue because you can knock yourself out making a film that's motivated by a desire for change of some kind, but if there's no distribution system that can help it do what it's meant to do, then it's not going to have any effect. That's been a frustration with *Paulina*; even though the film has a distributor and is getting out there, for it to fulfill its entire potential I would need another couple of years of fund-raising for special distribution financing, and I don't think I have it in me; and of course, as we all find out, nobody else is going to do it for us. In the meantime, there's other work I want to do.

F: *Paulina* took ten years of your life; do you feel it was worth that in the end?

Funari: It would be too depressing to say it wasn't worth it! [laughter] When I'm feeling particularly positive, I remember the first time I saw someone come up to Paulina and say, "This happened to me," and thank her for having done the film. That was already enough. Basically, my hope was to create some tenuous threads of communication that would actually make something happen, and I think that the film is doing that work in the world right now. If I didn't have the personal evidence of having conversations with people and having translated conversations for Paulina, where I watched somebody go through a particular emotional process from having seen the film, then maybe I would feel differently.

F: Both of you used the word *paradise* specifically. Sergey has a film entitled "Paradise" and Vicki, you talked about the fact that Paulina called the village where she grew up "paradise." Where do we find paradise? Is it a geographic place or is it something that we arrive at once we acquire the right technology, or is paradise—as is suggested in Sergey's film—a world without all that clutter?

Funari: I think part of my fascination with Paulina's story (or initially *stories*, because when I started the film, she had told me a lot of pieces but didn't tell me the whole thing until the first day when we started recording) had a lot to do with a sense that she and I shared a particular approach to the natural world. She would talk about the way she spent her childhood and how she had a very strong connection with the plants and animals around her, and I would feel that she was telling my own childhood back to me but in different locations. I grew up in big cities in different parts of the world, but my basic relationships were initially with plants and animals, rather than with people. I think a lot of why the film looks the way it does is because I was reacting to or responding to that element of Paulina's personality. I think a different filmmaker, one who didn't have that same identification with her, would have done different things, but that's certainly why I focus on the tactile, on children's hands and women's hands touching things, just trying hard to put you inside the senses of a child as she's learning what's around her. But I don't really know how to address the idea of paradise; I have a completely uncool, unintellectual approach, which is why I like nature.

F: It also seems that over the course of ten years, you allowed Paulina to develop her understanding of herself and her past. Her ideas of paradise must have changed.

Funari: Paulina would still say that where she comes from is paradise. Something that didn't end up in the film is that many years ago, she traveled with a family that she was working with—the American family that's in the film; they took her to Cape Cod for a couple of summers to take care of the kids, and she said Cape Cod is paradise. One of her dreams is to end up in a cottage there. I don't think that the person she is now believes any less in paradise; it's just hard to find it and be there. I think you have to be rich to live in paradise.

Dvortsevoy: It's a very difficult question, this matter of paradise. It's a philosophical question and you must be careful when you ask a Russian a philosophic question about paradise! [laughter] We can talk all day! Chekhov said that behind every door of every house there should be a man with a very small hammer, to knock us on our heads to remind us that we are happy.

Elaine Charnov: Well, what a note to end on! Thank you, Vicki and Sergey. Everyone head over to the dorm; at 5:30 there's open bar.

2008 BAHMAN GHOBADI—ON *LIFE IN FOG* (1997), *A TIME FOR DRUNKEN HORSES* (2000), AND *HALF MOON* (2006)

[The Flaherty discussion with Ghobadi was conducted on Skype, with the help of an interpreter. The original hope was that Ghobadi would attend the seminar, but he was not able to obtain a visa in time. His interpreter was Roxana Saberi, who in 2009 was jailed by the Iranian authorities and charged with spying. Museum of Modern Art video curator Sally Berger arranged for and guided the conversation.]

Ghobadi: Can you hear me?

Seminar: Yes!

Ghobadi: My English is not good, so Roxana Saberi will help me; she is from the US and speaks perfect English.

Sally Berger: Thank you, Bahman. I wanted to start with a couple of the questions that we sent to you, to help begin our conversation. We are interested in the interplay between fiction and nonfiction in your work. We have seen *Life in Fog* and *A Time for Drunken Horses*, which seem related, though one is a documentary and the other a fiction film. Could you talk a little bit about the development from *Life in Fog* to *A Time for Drunken Horses*?

Ghobadi [through Roxana]: I shot the documentary *Life in Fog* in five days and then realized that there was a possibility to make more of a film. Both the short and the feature were in many ways totally amateur productions. When I started making short films, I didn't have money to pay actors. I used the people around me: the children of my landlord, my mother, and other relatives.

I'm thirty-eight years old now and so far I've made thirty-six short films. I learned how to work with amateurs during those films, and I was and still am more comfortable with them than I am with professional actors. And these neighbors and relatives are not only my actors; they contribute to the stories that my films tell. Fifty percent of the stories in my films are mine and 50 percent are the stories of the "amateurs" who are in the films.

When I shoot, I often return to the locations where I grew up, and as I've become older, those locations refresh my childhood memories. My memories and the lives of the Kurds I work with and live with are very close, and all these stories become mixed into a sort of fiction-documentary. I feel that the actors who work in my films are not actors in the usual sense; they're living their own lives for the film.

About the next question: how did *Life in Fog* develop into *A Time for Drunken Horses*. At the time of the internal domestic war between the new Islamic regime of Iran and the Kurds of Iran, I was displaced for about three years. My family and I lived in Baneh and Sanandaj and also in Beji, Buyin, Sardab, and Surab.

After that, I took courses at the University of Tehran. I didn't feel that I was learning much, so I left the university and decided to make *Life in Fog*.

First of all, I went to photograph those areas where I had lived and I discovered that many things had changed. Based on what I saw, I made this documentary, which became the most successful short film in Iran's history. It won many awards, but for all the attention it got, it didn't get the kind of visibility feature films get. A short film has a limited audience.

I felt that I had many more stories to tell that could be made into a feature-length film, and so with a one-page script and a group of amateurs—everybody in *A Time for Drunken Horses* was an amateur—I began filming a feature. My brothers and sisters worked as my assistants. My uncle helped me. My mother made food for us. My whole budget was fifty thousand dollars, which came from the rentals of my short films—and also my mother sold some of her belongings. From the beginning to the end, this film was very much a family film.

When we were shooting, I needed a scene that had snow in it, but there was no more snow that season, so we had to wait one year—it was difficult to wait—but after that, we were able to finish the film. *A Time for Drunken Horses* was made with a lot of love. And it *was* much more widely seen than *Life in Fog*.

Berger: We've just seen *Half Moon* and with that film, you seem to have changed your approach. *Half Moon* is more like magic realism or like a surrealist film. For example, there's this landscape with a small town built into it, where thirteen hundred women live and sing.

Ghobadi: *Half Moon* was made at the request of the Austrian Culture Ministry, as part of a celebration of the 250th birthday of Mozart. Four filmmakers were to make films for this celebration. I was in Toronto when the Austrians suggested the project to me, and I didn't really have a lot of interest or belief in it at that time. I came back to Tehran, and they called and convinced me to do the film, and they gave me three months to finish it.

We looked for actors in the streets, talking with ordinary people. At night, I was working on the script. We shot for forty-five days and did the editing at the same time. The entire film took, from the very beginning to the very end, about three months. I tried to bring Mozart's life and existence into the story of the film, into the individual sequences, and into the personality of the main character, Mamo, who has a childish mischievousness and a certain view of death that I saw in Mozart.

Through the whole process, I kept saying to myself, "This isn't *my* film; it's just a film that I'm doing upon request." But when it was finished, I felt that I did have a place in the film. I would say 50 percent of the film is what *I* wanted and 50 percent is what I felt the people who commissioned the film wanted me to do.

About magic realism and surrealism: Iranian Kurdistan is full of magic—all of Kurdistan really. The sequences that may seem surreal in my film are actually reality: for example, the sequence of the thirteen hundred women singing in the village represents a reality that is alive in my mind. There may be two thousand women musicians in Iran who don't have the legal right to sing solos or distribute their own CDs or have public concerts. It's as if all these women are quarantined; it's not that they're all in one village—they're spread out across Iran—but basically, it's the same thing. So this scene is real for me.

Every night while I was working on the film, especially when I was shooting, I would listen to Mozart's work, mainly his *Requiem*. I feel that there is a shadow of death in Iran for filmmakers like me. Because of the difficulties of making films here and the negative attitude that I have on life as a result, *Half Moon* became a kind of requiem. I did try to bring some energy to the film and some satire and comedy, to mix it all together. If you see *Half Moon* in the United States, in the West, you might think it seems surreal, but here, it's reality. From what I've read of Márquez, I feel that his magical realism is not far from my own sense of things.

Mamo's attempt to get into Iraq is based on an experience that I had myself when I was going to Iraq to make *Turtles Can Fly* [2004]. We wanted to take women with us as part of the team to make the film, but the Iranian authorities didn't let women cross the border between Iran and Iraq. We had to smuggle our women team members in. The role of Mamo is based on Mr. Hassan Kamkar, a Kurdish singer who wanted to perform in Iraq. He and his family of musicians followed the same path that Mamo and his musicians do in *Half Moon* and they had the same kinds of problems.

Berger: Here at the Flaherty this year, the theme is "The Age of Migration." Borders are a really critical element in your films.

Ghobadi: I was born in Baneh, in western Iran. It's a border town. Baneh is thirty or forty kilometers from Iraq, and when I was younger, there was always fighting in that area. We were all very conscious of the border; five of the girls who lived on my street were named Sinour, which means "border." I remember asking myself, why do they make us afraid of this border? For twenty-seven years I wanted to go to Iraq; it was so close to me, yet I couldn't go.

When I went to Europe, I found that I could go everywhere very easily, and I thought again, why can't I, a Kurd who has family in Iraq, go there to see my family and Kurdistan Iraq? When I was finally able to go there and crossed the border, I began to cry; my hands and my legs shook. It wasn't that I was afraid of crossing the border; I was relieved to finally have the opportunity.

I feel that Kurdistan is like a person who has stepped on a mine and has been blown into four parts. Saddam Hussein oppressed the Kurds, and Turkey has been even more fascist and dirtier than Saddam Hussein. When we had the Iran-Iraq war, it was the Kurds who were hurt most whenever Iran or Iraq would attack: the Kurds along the border would always be in harm's way. Fifty percent of the landmines in the world are in the Kurdish areas of these countries. I think if I have children one day, I might name one of them "Border" and another "Mine," and another, "Refugee," and another, "Homeless."

Berger: Just one last comment from me, and then we're going to turn this over to questions from the audience. Your films have made a huge impact on international audiences and you've really brought the Kurdish plight to light. Do you foresee new Kurdish filmmakers coming to our attention?

Ghobadi: First of all, I'm very proud to be Kurdish and to have made feature films, and I feel that I have established a good platform from which other Kurds can reach out to the world through filmmaking. After *A Time for Drunken Horses* was released and had some success, many Kurdish filmmakers began to make films. In the alley where I live, thirteen or fourteen of my neighbors thought to themselves, "Hey, we used to play with Bahman in the street. If Bahman can become a filmmaker, we can, too"; they've begun making films. I would say that in Baneh, there are now a hundred Kurdish filmmakers. In five or six years, I think seven or eight top Kurdish filmmakers will be introduced to the world.

Most young Kurds are either unemployed or have very difficult living conditions, and now many of their parents want them to be filmmakers. They've lived with pain and they've had many experiences—they have many stories to tell.

Chi-hui Yang: Earlier today, we saw two short films that you produced. Do you see yourself as a mentor for young Kurdish filmmakers, and what is your role in the films you produce?

Ghobadi: Through the office that I have established here, I try to help young people produce short films. The office is called Mij Film; it's in Tehran. Our website: www.mijfilm.com. We have editing equipment that we use to help young filmmakers. This year, I'm helping a couple of them produce features. Independent production is very difficult here because there are no government programs or foundations to help filmmakers. Doing this work takes much time and energy. I hope that in two to three years I'll have a better financial situation so we can better equip ourselves and help more filmmakers. I've written about 90 percent of the scenarios for the films I've produced, and I've assisted in other ways as well.

Dorothea Braemer: In *A Time for Drunken Horses*, how was it to work with the mules and what kind of alcohol were they drinking? [laughter]

Ghobadi: I love animals, especially monkeys and horses and donkeys. The most defenseless animals are the donkeys: they get beaten very much. I was raised at the border, so I always saw donkeys and horses carrying goods back and forth between Iran and Iraq; there were lovely horses and not many cars.

At one point when I was shooting *A Time for Drunken Horses* I needed clouds, but it was all sunny. I went into a coffee shop and sat there, and one of my colleagues pointed out somebody who was there drinking tea who had four mules. I talked with him and found out that he was a smuggler who gave alcohol to his mules when they took goods back and forth across the border so that they could tolerate the heavy loads. I came out of the coffee shop and put a scene of giving alcohol to the horses in the movie, and this eventually became the title of my film. I get some of my best ideas from talking with people, ideas I couldn't have found in any book.

The title "A Time for Drunken Horses" has symbolic meaning for me. It suggests that even in their most difficult situations, when you might assume people would be thinking mostly about death, Kurds often find ways to keep going. In this movie, you see children willing to work desperately to lengthen the life of their little brother for even a few months. The Kurdish people are really like this: life is very important to them, and despite all the troubles and dark times that they have, they always have hope. You can hear this in their music and see it in their dancing which is very energetic.

Let me get back to the question about animals. Humans, not animals, cause harm to the world. There is a border between the US and Iran, and between me and you. I couldn't attend the Flaherty Seminar because your government, which talks about democracy, didn't allow me to come to you. But such borders don't exist between animals. I think this is why we care so much about them, and it's why I sometimes include animal names in the titles of my films.

As to what kind of alcohol I served the animals, I can't tell you, and it's better you don't think about it. [laughter]

F: When I was watching *Half Moon*, I was very struck by the fact that you were able to show the cruelty of the Iranian border guards; and I was wondering whether, as a result of this, you ran into problems with showing the film in Iran? Are things getting worse for filmmakers in Iran?

Also, one of the things that's really surprising and delightful about your work is how open ended it is. Often you end films without a sense of classical closure, and yet your endings work beautifully.

Ghobadi: Every time I talk about politics, they say, "You're a filmmaker, what do you have to do with politics?" But the truth is that we live with politics from the day we are born. From the day that a Kurd is born, the political atmosphere surrounds him. And in the Middle East in general, politics is everywhere. So we have to speak about it in our lives and in our films.

Unfortunately, after Ahmadinejad became president, the atmosphere became ten times worse for filmmakers in Iran. Nothing can be done now, and these are some of the most depressing days of my life. I have been waiting two years to get permission to make my upcoming film, and until I get that permission, I can't work. I'm like a mother who wants to give birth to her child but can't. Last night, I was up all night thinking about what I should do. Should I leave Iran? I don't *want* to leave Iran; I love my country.

I am developing three or four projects at a time, and I'm not sure yet which will be the next one I'll produce, but if I can find a way to make another film here, it may be my last in Iran. I want to make it with or without permission, and then leave maybe to come back every two to three years if they give me permission to make a film. So the situation is very bleak. Just thinking about it, I start to choke up.

About the unclear endings of my films: when the ending of a film or a novel is ambiguous, viewers or readers can make up their own endings. In this way, the work of art remains in the mind. Also, in my films the stories don't end; the *films* end but the stories continue. For example, in *A Time for Drunken Horses*, I could have made ten more episodes, pursuing what happened to the little boy and to the other children as they grew up.

We filmmakers don't understand what danger we pose for our government. We don't put sex in our movies; we don't have anti-Islamic themes. I don't know when I'll be able to make a film about other, less painful issues, the way a filmmaker like Woody Allen can. Unfortunately, in Iran we've been kept behind because of the polluted atmosphere that exists here.

Berger: Bahman and Roxana, we want to thank you very much; this has been very moving, and we look forward to talking with you again very soon.

Yang: On behalf of the Flaherty Film Seminar and everyone here, we wish you the best; we thank you so much for your time, and we are looking forward to interacting and hopefully meeting you one day.

Ghobadi: Thank you. [Standing ovation]

2013 EYAL SIVAN—ON *THE SPECIALIST* (1999)

Paige Sarlin: My name is Paige Sarlin, and we have a fantastic film to discuss. I'm certain that I don't need to say very much to prime the pump in terms of thoughts or questions, but Eyal has graciously submitted to my request, and in fact it's partly his request, that we collect your thoughts and comments on the film for 15–20 minutes. Over the years, Eyal has talked about this film at length—we all know he's very talkative! [laughter]—so he's interested in what *we* have to say.

"History Is What's Happening" is the title of this seminar, and in today's *New York Times* there's a report from Hungary that a ninety-eight-year-old man has been charged with Nazi-era war crimes; he is accused of regularly beating the Jewish men, women, and children under his supervision and helping to send almost twelve thousand Hungarian Jews to Nazi death camps during World War II.

With that, I open up the discussion to you.

F: *The Specialist* is about spectatorship, but—the way I'm receiving it—it seems to be highlighting the spectacle, the nature of performance.

F: I'm just thinking out loud. There's nothing absurd about the archival material itself, of course, but it felt a little absurd to watch Eichmann evade all the questions about details. Throughout the film, we're given great access to the banality of evil, Eichmann chalking it all up to his position in this hierarchy; but at the end when he's finally articulating something that he *felt*—at that moment the editing distances us from his words. We keep talking about the polarization of perpetrator and victims, but these aren't two entirely polar positions.

F: My question for Eyal, and I asked him this outside, is whether he felt restrained in making this film, because I very much felt like I was stepping into an opera, and yet the film is very restrained. In some ways, the companion piece is Mel Brooks's *The Producers* [1968].

F: I was thinking throughout the film of Melville's *Bartleby, the Scrivener*, where the clerk serves Capital in an office on Wall Street; here, the clerk serves the state.

F: I have a question about the relationship between empathy and the intelligence of the accused and the role of language in creating bonds or notions of empathy both in the judges serving at the hearing and in the audience.

F: I was wondering if, when you started editing, you had a goal in mind or if you were just watching all of the footage and making your way through it intuitively.

Sarlin: Did anyone have a violently negative reaction to the film, or not necessarily *violently* negative, but a reaction on the other side of neutral?

Pablo de Ocampo: No violent reaction and no question—just a ramble. This is really a wonderful film and the cacophonous, deafening prologue of the film was spectacular. I had no idea that the film would have such power.

But there are a couple of things that I have questions about. One is about the framing of the archive within the archive: there is 16mm film evidence shown in the court, but the projection is framed so that we can't really see the imagery. Another thing: in the glorious, massive image of 35mm, we see the face of Eichmann: his eyelids, his lips, his nose, his fingers, all these tiny details. Little ticks are amplified. I'm wondering about the ethics of representing some of those things. We're working with archival material and a cameraman did not make those choices; they were made in the editing.

F: I want to follow up on that. There were moments where I wondered if there was any manipulation or editing intervention. At times, the repetition in these moments felt almost like a Martin Arnold film. The repetition of Eichmann's glance emphasized something very sneaky about him. And also, the exaggeration with the foley sound: there were moments that felt almost like Jacques Tati, that were a bit comical, so I'm wondering about your play with sound and editing.

Sarlin: Let me try again for someone who wants to say, "I didn't like that!" or "Eyal just played with history and made too many editorial choices!"

F: A really interesting moment was when Eichmann steps out of the booth to point at the map. I was braced for him to make a run for it. I found it interesting that I was able to get to that point emotionally by watching archival footage and sound. I don't know how much of this reaction is a result of conditioning from watching too much Hollywood film, but I felt palpable tension.

F: I know that it was a foregone conclusion what the finding of the trial would be. But near the end of the film, I was wondering where Eichmann's lawyer was. I missed the defense of Eichmann—the film doesn't seem balanced there. Maybe there was a lawyer and I didn't recognize him.

F: I wonder where the film fits within the categories of experimental and documentary. You took history, but then you experimented with it. We pretty much know the outcome and the storyline of the event, but I wonder, was there any manipulation of the material?

Those last three shots of Eichmann really troubled me. Was that to show, or to ask us to show, some empathy toward him?

F: I found myself hung up on Eichmann's saying that in German bureaucratic language "I" is not "I." He is able to separate himself from his criminal acts until what we're watching is not a man on trial but actions on trial. It seems insane that one can separate oneself so drastically from one's actions, and throughout the film I kept thinking about *Route 181* [2003, Sivan and Michel Khleifi] and *Aqabat-Jaber, Passing Through* [1987, Sivan]. There's a feeling in all these films that you're collecting information for a trial. The people that you're talking to in those two films are not representing a state, but they are speaking for groups of people. The same thing happens in this film, although there's a big difference in the archival nature of what you were working with. I would be happy to hear you speak about that.

Ilisa Barbash: I think when you're dealing with a historical event in a film, you have to tread very lightly in terms of how much context you add, and I disagree with Pablo about needing to see the film that is projected at the trial, because that is imagery that most of us are familiar with. I was very happy *not* to have those images shown, because I think that reseeing them perpetuates the violence within the images.

However, there was another choice that Eyal made in not showing something, that did disturb me: you cut short the testimony of many of the victims so that what we hear is just a litany of victimization. I don't know if you needed to show *any* of the victims, other than those whose testimony was given a bit more room—but I was deeply offended by the truncated presentations of people who have unbelievably tragic stories.

E. E. Miller: I want to talk about Hannah Arendt. I had never seen any of this footage and it was incredible to see it because all my impressions of the trial were based on her book, *Eichmann in Jerusalem: A Report on the Banality of Evil*, which was important to me. And I remember reading about the impact that the series of articles that she wrote for the *New Yorker* (and that became the book) had on her career.

It seems like some of what you did with sound and the way that you created moments of intense drama worked against some of what Arendt says in *Eichmann in Jerusalem*. I was confused by the difference between her interpretation of the trial and the way that you worked with what you found inspiring in her work.

John Gianvito: There's a critical discourse going through my head, that's coming off the comments that Pablo made about the fetishization of the Nazi war criminal that happens when you're so focused on this person and are looking at every gesture, hoping that these gestures will reveal the mystery of how these things happened.

For me, one of the most interesting, maybe the most interesting, moment is where Eichmann speaks about the split in his consciousness between his conscience and his activity. I chose to feel that at that moment he was being authentic, that he wasn't just trying to get himself off the hook but trying to describe how this operates.

In thinking about that and trying to put the film in a wider context, I'm trying to be mindful about just how much we all shoulder a degree of responsibility for the horrible things that are happening around us. Here in the United States, we're in the longest war in our history, and every day, horrible things are happening that barely register—unless they're so extreme that they suddenly rise to our attention. We can have our president and Congress talking about "a red line" in Syria when chemical weapons are used on people, but not when bombs are dropped on their heads. And this passes for normal discourse.

When I was watching *Route 181*, I was making notes on how many times people made the comment, "Well, there's nothing to be done about it" or "I can't do anything about it." This idea of impotence has come up at various times this week, and Eichmann feels it himself. This is important in terms of how the film can help us start thinking about our feeling impotent, which I assume Eyal wants us to do. I welcome that. I would be unhappy if the film were just trying to understand the mystery of a particular kind of criminal who killed many people.

Jean-Paul Kelly: Something that I think we're skipping over in a lot of these discussions is the actual materiality of the medium we're dealing with. That's especially true here with the two-inch open-reel taping that was done in 1961. There's the feel almost of a television control room. Does this control-room feeling happen forty years later than when the raw tapes were recorded, in the editing? I'm thinking of Woody and Steina Vasulka and of how Vito Acconci and others used unedited performance tapes, so that the length of their pieces is linked to the specifics of that medium. Often, a complete sense of history is lost within the limitations of the medium that records events. We need to talk about these material dimensions of the media used, as well as about the content—and of how these material dimensions are integrated into our readings of the content, or vice versa.

Sarlin: I'm going to cut this off. Eyal is overloaded with questions and we've set up an interesting tension between talking about *The Specialist* in terms of content and as a representation. So I'm just going to throw it to you, Eyal.

Eyal Sivan: I would like to start not from the questions but from the way Paige framed this discussion at the beginning. While Paige was reading about the arrest of a Nazi criminal from Hungary, I was looking for the interview with the people from Google and Facebook where they justify allowing the current American government to access people's personal Google and Facebook accounts. *This* is what *I* understand by the idea that history is what's happening *now*, which is not so much the finding of new evidence of a past event but the persistence of what I would call "a regime of justification": the regime of justification that a person acting within a system uses. This regime of justification does not function just a posteriori but also a priori. I would argue that the regime of justification is not just what allows a person to justify what he has done after the fact, but what allows him to act in the first place.

Earlier, someone wondered whether at the end of the film I meant to create empathy for Eichmann as a human being, and I would like, in a good Jewish tradition, to ask a question of that question, why is he not "human" from the beginning? At the trial, the introductory discourse of the attorney general, Gideon Hausner, expressed the idea that Eichmann is an animal, a beast in the jungle, that by his acts he has extracted himself from the family of men and so doesn't deserve to live, et cetera. If Hausner is correct, we can say that this was the first animal trial in the world since the Middle Ages.

But, in fact, if we are interested in the Eichmann trial, it's because it's the trial of a *human*. We can argue about his ethics and his morality, but he *is* human—though it is annoying to consider him part of the family of man, part of *our* family. But in *our family* there *are* perverts, criminals, psychopaths—though I don't think that Eichmann is a psychopath. I think that Eichmann is a *normopath* and that normopathy is one of the extreme psychoses of modernity.

My goal in *The Specialist* was not to document the trial of a beast: that is, my goal was *not* to do what was done in the earlier films about the Eichmann trial—there are many of them. If you will look at those films, you will see that Eichmann is not speaking in them. Until *The Specialist*, we knew only a few sentences from Eichmann: "I'm not guilty"; "I obeyed orders"—that's about all. For thirty years until the beginning of the project that resulted in *The Specialist*, there were available to public use only sixty-eight hours of the trial. This was an extraction by Alan Rosenthal from the original 360 hours of two-inch video material (recorded at the trial by Leo Hurwitz and his assistants) that was done in 1974; Rosenthal reduced the record of the trial to sixty-eight hours, and his cut was what the Spielberg Jewish Film Archive in Jerusalem has been selling to people who want to make a film about the trial.

The sixty-eight hours of that material that was all that had been available for thirty-seven years was entirely survivors' testimony, along with the opening discourse of Hausner—a three-day opening discourse that my Israeli generation learned by heart in school: "Here I stand before you, the judges of Israel. I am not alone. Six million died and I would speak for them," et cetera. This sixty-eight hours was the only representation of the Eichmann trial for thirty-seven years—until I was insistent about seeing *all* the original video material.

The 1961 videotape recording of the Eichmann trial was the first time that video was recorded outside of a television studio. At the time, Israel didn't yet have TV, so Capital Cities brought the cameras, the two-inch machines, and so forth to Jerusalem.

(I apologize for this lecture, but I will be trying to answer everybody's questions.)

In making *The Specialist*, one of the things I became committed to was breaking what I will call the canonical image of the Nazi perpetrator—in order to shift to an essay on responsibility for political evil. What I mean by "the canonical image of the Nazi perpetrator" is, first, the question of putting forward the survivors of the European genocide *as* the witnesses. There are huge collections of victim testimony: the Yale collection, the Spielberg archive . . .

But there is no archive for other kinds of witnessing. Apparently no one said, "It's important to collect the testimony of the drivers of all the trains that took Jews to the camps"—because perpetrators were not considered witnesses. As we thought about the archive available to us, we were influenced by a very important text: Primo Levi's introduction to *Commandant of Auschwitz: The Autobiography of Rudolf Höss*. When the diary of Rudolf Höss was published, Primo Levi, himself a survivor from Auschwitz, prefaced it with an introduction in which he says that Höss was, in Italian, "il testimonio primo": the primary witness. So for us making *The Specialist*, this was one point: to shift away from seeing the survivors as the *only* witnesses.

The other point in focusing on Eichmann was to break with the conventional way Nazis are portrayed. The paradoxical thing is that the Hollywood image of the Nazi may be the biggest success of Leni Riefenstahl and the Nazis themselves. If we take *Schindler's List* as our example, the Nazis in that film look just as the Nazis would like to be represented. And this is even true in the Holocaust Museum: Nazis are always represented as big, tall, blue-eyed, and blond (and I'm always doing this joke: even in *black-and-white* films, they're blond and blue-eyed!). This image of the Nazi is the big success of Nazism.

But to look at Eichmann is to break that image. Here we have a *real* Nazi, who doesn't fit that image at all. *Not* showing Eichmann in films about the trial allows the mythological imaginary of the monster, the Absolute Evil, to continue, which is, in fact, comforting: if the Nazi is *a monster*, he is basically different from me. If I cannot see him and, as a result, have an imaginary image of Absolute Evil, then *I'm* OK. This is also the answer to Pablo's earlier question about my focusing on the close-ups of Eichmann's face.

It's important to remember that the Eichmann trial didn't take place in a courtroom; it took place in the House of the People, which was built in Jerusalem especially for the Eichmann trial; at that time, it was the biggest auditorium in the country. The Court of Jerusalem came and sat in what was basically a public theater, and there was a very clear idea about what public should be present: journalists; soldiers, young soldiers; school students; and survivors. This public was selected, and it changed every day. So from the very beginning this was a *public* trial, a spectacle, which is what Israel wanted it to be. The public is visible in *The Specialist* all the time, "reflected" in the glass of Eichmann's glass booth—"reflected" artificially: we were able to add all those reflections digitally.

Also, we have to remember that nobody wanted to judge Eichmann, *except* for Israel.

The close-ups of Eichmann's face create in some people a desire to try to understand, through tiny gestures, the *psychology* of Eichmann. But in fact, I don't give a shit about Eichmann's psychology. If his mother touched his penis when he was a little boy and this is the reason that he joined the Nazi Party—that's *his* problem. If Eichmann went home from work every day and cried to his wife, "Oh, it's so horrible what I'm obliged to do"—so what? I'm dealing with politics, and what I learned from Arendt and her book is that in politics we judge *acts*, not *intentions*.

This interest in psychology reflects on the spectator: why are we interested in the psychology of Eichmann? If he was suffering over what he did, was he less criminal? I will be hard on Eitan [Efrat] about what you said about perpetrator and victim yesterday [*Complex* (2008) by Sirah Foighel Brutmann and Eitan Efrat was shown the previous day]. The group of former Israeli soldiers you filmed for that piece committed criminal acts; they are free criminals who come to a space where you film and then they go back home. Whether they are traumatized or not by what they have done, and whether their bodies carry the trauma, is none of my business. It's their *crimes* that are important.

If there is no possibility of judgment, there is no possibility of justice. To decide who is guilty or who is not guilty is a primary need in order to create justice, and here I am coming to John Gianvito's comments about the nature of responsibility. In *The Specialist*, I'm not simply trying to portray a *Nazi* criminal—because I'm among those who don't think that Nazi criminals have any kind of absolute specificity and uniqueness. We just have to listen to the American senators' questioning of the bankers who were responsible for what you call the crash. We heard the same regime of justification: "If it wouldn't have been *our* bank, it would have been another bank"; "I obeyed orders"; "If it wouldn't have been me, it would have been somebody else"; "What could *I* do?"

It is important to *listen* and to not use the image of the monster to distance us from hearing. But at the same time, the question of responsibility can be a big problem. If we say, "America is committing crimes and we are all responsible"— maybe; but if *all of us* are *guilty*, the notion of guilt disappears completely. We are *all* destroying the planet; *all* countries are committing crimes in the name of their people. If we are all guilty of everything, there is no guilt anymore, and we live in depression because of our impotence.

This is exactly Eichmann's position: if it's not me, it's somebody else. Arendt's response to Eichmann—and here I am coming back to the question of the relation of my film to her book—is "You're right, Mr. Eichmann; it's true: if it wouldn't have been you, it would have been somebody else. But it happened *to be you*, and this is why *you* are on trial."

I would also like to respond to the comment about the material image . . .

Sarlin: Let's just have one more comment, then we'll throw it back to the group for a few more questions.

Sivan: I was very happy to hear Jean-Paul raise the issue of what happens in the moment when what was recorded on videotape is shifted onto the movie screen and becomes a spectacle of cinema. This transformation is implied at the very beginning of *The Specialist*, by the empty chairs in the auditorium. A student of mine once asked me if I was quoting *The Man with the Movie Camera*. Now I can say, "Yes!"—because it's a great idea! But at the time, this had not occurred to me.

You can now find all the Eichmann trial footage on YouTube; but the people who put it onto YouTube did not do the work that we did with the original video recordings. It took me a year just to organize the material. I created a cut of the original videotapes, which I found in an unused toilet in the Department of Law at

Hebrew University. Nobody had taken care of them. Our production paid for the transfer to DigiBeta in order to save the material, and we paid for the rights to use it (we had to give them back the DigiBetas that we made; the Law School sold them to the Holocaust Museum in Washington). But now you can find all the material on YouTube—in *very* bad condition. Those interested can see the difference between the original material and what is in the film.

When *The Specialist* came out, I read in many places that the original material looked very good, and I wanted to answer, do you *know* the *original* material? What you're seeing in *The Specialist* is a digital attack on the idea of the veracity of the original document. For example, *all* the camera movements in the film are artificial; *all* the reflections on the glass booth were put there digitally; the lighting in the courtroom was redone, and the sound that you hear, the voices, is in fact sometimes not the sound on the original videotapes. During the trial, audiotape was recorded, microphone by microphone; this allowed my assistants to resynchronize the sound minute by minute, and also to spatialize the trial. In *The Specialist*, the only unaltered moments from the original material are the survivor witnesses; in that section of the film, the frame becomes smaller and there we are in the video material framed as it originally was (the originals were in even worse shape than what you see).

In *The Specialist*, I was interested in questioning what I was actually looking at. In the film, I'm looking at the past; I'm looking at the present; maybe I'm looking at the future. How does the nature of the medium, the original videotapes or my 35mm film, affect what we understand? There is even a problem with looking at the film on a modern DVD, rather than as a 35mm projection, because something disappears.

The images at the end of the film are recorded from TV screens; these are the six images we found where Eichmann is, unknowingly, staring directly at the camera. He knows that there are cameras, but he (and you) cannot see them because they were hidden in the courtroom behind the walls and were shooting through small windows.

Sarlin: I'm going to take three more questions.

F: You've said if there is no possibility of judgment, there is no possibility of justice. I've been watching a lot of trial footage recently, from the Pussy Riot trial and in the film, *The Redemption of General Butt Naked* [2011, Daniele Anastasion and Eric Strauss], about a Liberian warlord. What I keep coming back to, especially if we're talking about history (and I assume that one of the underlying questions is how do we prevent history from repeating itself, if that is even possible), is the difference between judgment and punishment.

At first, I was mesmerized by the absurdity of the decorum in the courtroom and how decorum functions, even at the Flaherty—the ways in which decorum dictates how knowledge is produced and what's at stake in this knowledge. Later, I thought that one of Eichmann's comments was disturbingly prophetic: his point about remorse being pointless, that what we need to do is prevent what happened in Germany from happening in the future. Basically, he was advocating for himself to be rehabilitated, which is one of the tenets of our justice system that is often ignored. We love punishment.

Watching *The Specialist*, I kept coming back to the purpose of the trial as part of a criminal justice system, and there were moments when I felt that much of what was revealed by the trial was impotence.

F: From the beginning when I saw Eichmann sit down in the glass booth and the door close, I had a sneaking suspicion I was hearing foley sound, that the sound was added later. It's amazing to hear you say that all the camera movements were fake and the reflections, too. There's this stupid but widespread idea about objectivity. I'm sure people ask, "Why didn't you do something more objective," and I think it's good that you obviously weren't concerned with being "objective." Anyone who works in archives knows that archives themselves are subjective because of what's seen as important enough to be included, and how things are ordered, and who is given access to this material. The question of selection and exclusion is central not only to making documentaries but to understanding history itself. The point isn't objectivity.

   And for you to say that the camera movements were created, the reflections were added, is brave.

Sivan: I've heard that word a few times from people here, and while I take it as a compliment, I would like to call attention to the use of "brave": "You were so brave." "Brave" works only if you are facing real danger. There is nothing brave about what I do; it's hard work, that's all. The word *brave* shouldn't be banalized; not everything is brave.

Sarlin: Scott's will be the last question.

Scott MacDonald: For me, Eyal's films have been a revelation, partly because I can't imagine a place on the planet where these films are more immediately relevant. We *need* these films and what they're teaching. I'm wondering why we haven't seen them. Where have your films been seen? Have they been shown in the United States—am I just oblivious to what's going on?

Sivan: My films were and are shown all over the world—though not a lot in the United States. I think that one of the biggest sources of distribution in this country for films on the subjects that I'm dealing with are the many Jewish film festivals—and I still wonder why *they* haven't taken my films.

Sarlin: Unless someone is burning to say something . . .

F: I am!

Sarlin: Say it, then we'll wrap up.

F: I watched the Eichmann trial on television when it was originally broadcast. I'm still trying to process it. My father worked for RCA and was involved in designing the engineering for television. For a while he refused to buy a television set, but he bought one to be able to watch the Eichmann trial, and seeing it remains among the first memories I have of watching television. Seeing the trial in this new context has felt revelatory.

Sivan: There was a boom of buying TVs for the broadcast of the Eichmann trial, but the Eichmann trial broadcast stopped when Eichmann started to speak. The trial was in two parts. First, 122 survivors spoke, then Eichmann spoke; but by that time, nobody was interested in what Eichmann might say.

   I should say that Leo Hurwitz did the most amazing job recording the trial. I could do what I did because of what *he* did. I read the last interview with Hurwitz, where he says, "When I went to Jerusalem, I was interested in the mechanics of fascism" (like Arendt, he hadn't had the chance to see the Nazis at Nuremburg). He realized, he said, that the Israelis were not interested in the mechanics of fascism; they were not ready to think beyond what had happened to the Jews.

I want to go back to the question about how Arendt's book inspired *The Specialist*, how I went *with* her book. At the trial, there were 380 journalists in the hall, the 380 that were accredited (almost 2,000 journalists were in town). You can see in the tapes that during the trial, *everybody* looked to the right, to the survivors; only Arendt looked to the *left*—this was her cinematic genius. She performed a documentary *act*: that is, when everybody looked to one point, Arendt looked to another. (Arendt didn't attend the whole trial; she left after five sessions. She wrote her book from the minutes of the trial and from the broadcast on TV.)

In *The Specialist*, I only used imagery recorded by three cameras, not all four cameras that were recording the trial, one of which filmed the spectators; I wanted the spectator of the film to be in the same position in terms of the action as the public attending the trial, including Arendt—so my only use of the footage of the audience filmed by the fourth camera is in the reflections on the glass.

And to finish, I want to return to the notion of objectivity and manipulation. I'm accused all the time of not being objective, not allowing both sides to speak—and of manipulation. And when I am charged with manipulation, I always respond the same way. "Manipulation" often has a negative connotation, but *as a filmmaker*, I *must* manipulate images—filmmaking *is* the manipulation of images. Yes, I'm manipulating images in *The Specialist*, and from there we can start to speak about the film and about the events presented in the film.

Ironically, there is one "manipulation" that nobody has ever attacked me for: my throwing away 358 hours of the trial and using only two hours of it in *The Specialist*!

But now I'm coming to what was for me maybe the most important question, which is that the trial itself could have taken 128 minutes, like the film. If the Eichmann trial had started with the question, "Mr. Adolf Eichmann, son of Karl Eichmann, what were you doing between 1939 and 1945?" he could have told the court what he did, and they could have said, "OK, we're charging you with that."

As he says in his defense (somebody asked where Eichmann's lawyer was— he's there, and if you watch the 360 hours of the trial on YouTube, you'll see that percentage-wise, the lawyer is more present in *The Specialist* than during the trial), Eichmann was far from the act of killing itself, and this is why there was a gap between 1956, when the Israelis first knew where Eichmann was living (they got information that Eichmann was in Argentina, raising rabbits in Buenos Aires), and when they first looked for him four years later. Israel wanted Josef Mengele for the trial because Mengele was the doctor of Auschwitz, who did *with his own hands* brutal experiments on people, killing many.

The feeling of a lot of us, including me—the first spectator of the entire trial after thirty-seven years—was that Eichmann, this huge criminal, wasn't good enough for the purposes of that trial. Arendt said that what the court couldn't deal with was the gap between the monstrosity of the crime and the size of the criminal who was on trial, a terrifyingly ordinary person.

In *The Specialist*, there is no ending to the trial: no ending and no judgment. There is this very annoying nonending, and a sudden departure from the decorum of the rest of the film: the use of color. Color seems contemporary, and this allows us to remember that the young Eichmann was a member of the "jeune cadre dynamique," as we say in French: Eichmann and the other Nazis were all young careerists. Heinrich Himmler, the head of the SS, was thirty-two years old. In their early careers and then as Nazi officials, only one thing was asked of them: efficiency—be efficient. And indeed they *were*.

So the basic question is not how we judge Eichmann in particular, but how we judge this kind of crime, the crime of normopathy, how we break with the regime of justification.

What we wanted to show in our edit of the trial was that what Eichmann was saying over and over (and what he would have said in his book) is what Arendt called "clichés": statements like "This was the biggest crime in the history of humanity!" "Never again!" "Such monsters cannot be allowed to live!" Those are clichés that, in fact, allow such things to continue—aphoristic clichés.

When there is a horde of people going to one side, as a filmmaker I'm automatically going to the other side—even if the horde seems to be going to the best place possible. This is what I understand as "historical conscience." Eichmann was not somebody who came from the extremes. Our idea that the radicals, the extremes, are dangerous is a delusion. No, it's the *mainstream* that is dangerous and what characterizes the mainstream is the aphoristic cliché: "Never again!"—but we continue as before . . .

2015 MOUNIRA AL SOLH—ON *RAWANE'S SONG* (2006); MARIE-HÉLÈNE COUSINEAU—ON *BEFORE TOMORROW* (2008, COMADE WITH MADELINE IVALU); HASSAN KHAN—ON *FUCK THIS FILM* (1998)

[*Rawane's Song* and *Fuck This Film* are shorts (seven minutes and ten minutes, respectively); *Before Tomorrow* is a ninety-three-minute feature.]

Margarita De La Vega Hurtado: I want you to remember that at the Flaherty all films are equal, no matter what length, subject, or style, so during this session we're going to discuss the three films as equally as we can, and we're going to address general things that they might have in common. I'll suggest some and you can argue with me. It's perfectly wonderful to disagree as long as you explain why. I'd like us to avoid asking for information about the filmmakers, because the material you've been given to read supplies that.

Also, we're going to talk about these films *as they are*, not as we'd like them to be and not as the filmmaker wanted them to be, but as the objects we have in front of us. Here at the Flaherty, we have the advantage of coming to these films without any preexisting knowledge.

My first suggestion about these three films that have been so magnificently programmed to be seen together by Laura Marks is that they play with the problem of representation: how are you going to transmit your idea, the concept that you have of reality or of something from the imagination, in your new film? I worked on a film from conception to exhibition last year for the first time. I was not the director but was involved throughout the process and realized for the first time the huge distance between the idea you have for a film and the finished work.

One of the three films (*Before Tomorrow*) dramatizes something that happened in the nineteenth century, so obviously it's not a documentary. There was no film when the events happened, and even the films that were made early in the twentieth century about that same people by the man whose name is on this seminar were a little fake, as we know. The other two films (*Rawane's Song* and *Fuck This Film*) are personal expressions, but I think all three films deal with the problem of representing ideas, of expressing and communicating a feeling.

[To Hassan Khan] I really love how in *Fuck This Film* you ask, "How can I ever do a film?" You put this challenge of yourself at the center, because the film you want to make is about you. Am I right?

Hassan Khan: No. [laughter]

De La Vega Hurtado: No? OK, let's start with that. In *Fuck This Film* you are the maker and the protagonist . . .

Khan: Actually, there's an actor who plays the protagonist . . .

De La Vega Hurtado: But the actor represents you, no?

Khan: Not necessarily. I see this piece just as a little joke. Back in 1998, I wanted to list all of the "possibilities" for a film that would have been exciting to make, from a gritty documentary of kids dropping cough syrup to a fake French *nouvelle vague* film about a man obsessed about a woman—all those clichéd ideas that filmmakers sit around talking about. *Fuck This Film* is a little take on that, but it's also invested with real concerns—though it's a bit hard for me to remember what my real concerns were in 1998. I was interested in what exactly I was doing and why was I doing it, in the thin line between what seduces you and what you resist and why.

De La Vega Hurtado: That takes me to Mounira. What led you to make *Rawane's Song*?

Mounira Al Solh: I also have to go back, to 2005–6/7. When I was around twenty-three, I left Beirut for the first time to study in a university in Holland, and by chance, it was a time where in almost every museum I visited, I would see works from the Arab world—while when I was in Beirut, I wasn't exposed to so much work or to the kinds of work I was seeing. I thought, Ah, so all these people know about Cornish Beirut, which was one of the places in Beirut I would visit every day.

Rawane's Song was a result of my suddenly being in Holland and being seen as *Lebanese*. At the university, one teacher always wanted me to talk about the war, which I didn't want to do. My generation was born during the war, so the *last* thing we wanted to talk about was the war. We wanted to dream; we wanted to be allowed to live in our imaginations.

By coincidence, two of my classmates were from Israel. This was strong for me because I was raised by parents who are very leftist pro-Palestinian, and it was also a time in the seventies when if you were politically engaged, you were engaged in that direction. The first year, I tried to convince my Dutch friends that these Israelis were criminals; and *they* tried to convince the Dutch that I was going to blow myself up, that at any second I could explode. But in the long run, this was quite therapeutic for all of us: when we first started to talk, it was a clash, then we started to realize that actually we shared things.

It took about a year, but I started to have Israeli friends. Early on, I would be in a market and think, "Oh, these avocados are from Israel—shall I buy them or not? What would it mean if I buy them?" But later, I bought them on purpose because I wanted to get rid of my prejudice. It took me some time to tell my father, and after I told him, each time we had a fight, he would blame "your friends from Israel."

De La Vega Hurtado: Thank you. So, again, we have the problem of identification and how to express yourself. Now I'm going to speak with Marie-Hélène Cousineau who is codirector of *Before Tomorrow* with Madeline Ivalu, who is also the lead actress in the film.

[To Cousineau] It must be difficult to depict a world for which there are no images, to speak of people and a way of life that are only a memory.

Marie-Hélène Cousineau: That's exactly how we felt on the set. For example, since the Inuit did not shake hands 150 years ago, how would they greet each other? Even the Inuit themselves don't necessarily know. Susan [Avingaq] and Madeline [Ivalu] remember how their parents and their grandparents did things, and there's probably not a big difference between what their grandparents were doing in 1850 and what the Inuit were doing in 1500. Of course, even then, the culture was changing but at a different rate, so I think they do have a memory. But there are a lot of things you have to invent because you *don't* know.

Most of the actors in the film were from Igloolik, but we shot the film in another Inuit community maybe a thousand kilometers south of Igloolik, in Puvirnituq in northern Quebec. The Inuit there didn't remember how to make the costumes or how to use the tools on the kayak, so the people from Igloolik had to tell them—and the Igloolik women told the Puvirnituk men what to do, which was interesting for the women; they felt a little awkward about this.

So, OK, yes, we used invention to remake history, but also not invention in the normal sense. The Inuit can go back and be inspired by their ancestors. Oral tradition is very strong; the fact that it's not written doesn't mean that people don't remember. They remember songs and stories from a thousand years ago, and the story Ninioq tells about ptarmigan in the film is a very old story that has been told over and over and over.

De La Vega Hurtado: OK, now, I'd like to open the discussion. Try and think of the three films together. But if you're not ready to do that, go for a particular film—maybe eventually we'll come to the point where you can relate them.

F: Something that I'm thinking about in all three of the films is the idea of aspiration and failure, which was represented very differently in these films. There is the angst of failure and the comedy of failure.

De La Vega Hurtado: OK, that's a good contribution.

F: I was interested in why you [Al Solh] chose to tell your story using text and what you think the role of text is. Also, a general question for Marie-Hélène: my impression is that in Canada native peoples are legally divided into several categories and that there is a difference between the Inuit and the other native groups.

Cousineau: Well, there is a treaty relating to First Nation indigenous peoples, but the Inuit people are not under the same treaty. They never went onto reservations. They made other deals with the government of Canada.

Igloolik, the village where I worked for ten years and lived, was created in 1960, so that's very recent. The Igloolik people accepted television in 1982, also very recent. In southern Inuit communities, television arrived much earlier.

De La Vega Hurtado: I've read that maybe because of the late arrival, the Igloolik people started using television to tell their own stories in a more organized fashion . . .

Cousineau: The community of Igloolik is very active in filmmaking, yes; but there are now active filmmakers across Nunavut. For sure, the community of Igloolik has been very outspoken; they've created scripts and made both documentaries and fiction films. They're proud of this and still enjoy it.

Al Solh: About my use of text: I just didn't want to impose my voice or my accent. I thought that when you *read* something, you hear your own voice or imagine someone's voice. Also it's more immediate.

And I treat text in relation to time: how long do words stay on-screen; what you see is not only text; it's text and image become one.

Bob Nessan: Both *Rawane's Song* and *Fuck This Film* were very personal, coming from your own deep experiences, but I'm wondering whether *Before Tomorrow* came from personal experiences, and what Marie-Hélène's personal motivation was in engaging this huge, beautiful film.

Cousineau: I was living up north for many years. One summer, I was there to make a documentary and was reading Jørn Riel's book, *Før morgandangen*. The book was so touching; I was able to get into the emotions of the women, and I really liked that because I find that often when there are films about indigenous people, you never feel their *emotions*. It's like, AH, look at those people; they do this like that; isn't that interesting?

This book had already been translated into Greenlandic, so Madeline and Susan read the book and we discussed it. They said, "Oh, we love this story; this is the story of our grandmothers and great-grandmothers; we know people to whom this happened—this is how we used to live. We would love to do the film! And Madeline was, "Oh, I want to be the actress!" By this time, we'd been working together for maybe fifteen years, on smaller projects. We saw this project as a challenge, as our chance to try to tell a big story, and to make it like a dream—and to see how we could work together with a big budget and within a community.

For me personally, the challenge was not just making the film but making the film well: that is, so that the *process* of making the film would be a great experience for *all* of us. And in fact, it was: we had *so* much fun making this film; it was a life-changing experience for everyone involved. We had a good team, and going to Puvirnituk was a great cultural exchange. We had meetings in the morning and in the evening. We had day care on set. Not all films are like this: sometimes you make a film and there are problems, and you just try to get through the process—it took about four years to make *Before Tomorrow*, but we enjoyed every minute.

Irina Leimbacher: Something I felt across the three films that was *not* similar has to do with safety and commitment. I watched the first film, then the second film, and I thought this is very ironic, this is very clever, this is very ironic, this is very clever— and wondered, "What's the third film going to be?" The third film felt extremely sincere, and I want to talk about that in a couple of ways or ask you to talk about it.

Hassan, in your film there's a fabulous line to the effect that narrative and drama are just ways of manipulating images to allow the audience to feel safe. I felt both in your film and in Mounira's film that in a way *you* two were finding safety (and I realize that these were early films) in *not* committing to an idea, or to narrative and drama. Both of you could throw out interesting ideas: "I could do this, I could do that, I could do the other, but the problem with doing this would be that and the problem with doing that would be this; therefore, I'm *not* going to do more than present you with the problem."

Because you, Hassan, are Egyptian and Mounira is Lebanese, you bear a burden of representation, and that's what I felt in both those films: "I'm not taking on that burden."

Marie-Hélène's film felt quite the opposite. The two filmmakers had decided, yes, we have a big problem with representation, but we're going to fully commit to a process that involves an entire community. I thought the result was quite provocative and that the storytelling scenes in the dark were absolutely beautiful; they were long, they were slow, you really had to engage *that* mode of storytelling, which I thought was very powerful. In the two short films, there was a somewhat safe ironic position; in *Before Tomorrow*, there was a committed, less safe position.

F: I wonder how much of Irina's distinction might come from the fact that in *Before Tomorrow* we have a cinematically conventional Hollywood structure, a three-act structure, with shot-reverse-shots and so on, whereas the two short films are experimenting with form. I think all three films are committed to what they're saying but that the formal choices that were made are very different. Audiences who have grown up with Hollywood studio-system production can understand the formal choices in *Before Tomorrow*. The short films require a different lens.

De La Vega Hurtado: Could you clarify, do you think that Marie-Hélène's film is like traditional Hollywood storytelling?

F: Yes, there's a central protagonist . . .

Cousineau: I think *Before Tomorrow* is *not at all* a Hollywood film. If someone from Hollywood were to watch this film, the response would be, "This is no Hollywood film! We couldn't put this film in theaters! We couldn't use those extended shots of a woman elder speaking Inuktitut. Impossible. And those scenes in the dark! No! No! No!" You *can't* call *Before Tomorrow* "Hollywood"—impossible.

Arthur Jafa: When I looked at *Before Tomorrow*, I was thinking, wow, how are we going to discuss *this* film? It raised a lot of important issues for me, but first of all, I wondered, is the filmmaker here? How frank can I be?

OK, for me, *Before Tomorrow* was *grueling* to sit through. This is not inherently connected to the value of the film at all: it may be the most masterful film ever made. I'm just saying that for me to sit through it was a grueling experience.

When she said the film is like Hollywood, I don't think she really means *Hollywood*; I think she means *narrative*. It was a narrative film with actors acting out parts. The two short films felt to me more personally sincere, though there's nothing really new about their form.

I think Marie-Hélène took on a much more complicated problem, which is how do you cinematically render experiences for which we have no pictures. This has come up for me recently. I worked on *Selma* [2014, Ava DuVernay] last summer, which is about the civil rights movement—maybe some of you have seen it. There was a film the year before, produced by some of the same people: *12 Years a Slave* [2013, Steve McQueen]. For me *12 Years a Slave* was an abomination.

Nobody knows what slavery looked like; there were the oral accountings of slaves; there are written accounts of slavery, which are themselves totally problematic.

And the book that *12 Years a Slave* is based on is also totally problematic.

So now *you've* got the question of how do you render the experience of indigenous or oppressed people when there are no pictures of them? No one person can do it. Rendering that kind of experience happens over the course of one person trying to do it and failing, somebody else trying, failing, failing, failing, failing. I thought your film failed; for me, it failed. You had a great experience making it. It was a great experience for the town. I love all that. But good intentions don't make good movies. To me, *Before Tomorrow* felt like a film that's early in the process of translating Inuit experience into a cinematic form that can carry actuality.

This film is like looking at the side of my grandmother's head for two hours. Who I *love*! And who tells incredible stories! As a podcast, *Before Tomorrow* would be phenomenal.

Cousineau: I think *you* may have Hollywood in mind because exactly what you've just described is why it's *not* a Hollywood film.

Jafa: Right, it's not a Hollywood film.

Cousineau: You have a right to feel that the film fails. But a lot of people like the film. We've not talked about audience and the audience is superimportant. So who is this film *for*? The Inuit actually love *Before Tomorrow*. They *love* it.

Jafa: That's a big generalization . . .

Cousineau: No, no, no. Some people don't like it. I know, I've lived with this film for five-six years—it was finished in 2008. So I know what the reactions to the film have been. You were not there. I mean you can talk, but you were not in Igloolik, you were not in Puvirnituq. You were not there when people watched the film!

Jafa: I started off by saying that the film could be a masterpiece. The issue I'm trying to raise is not specifically about this film, about the quality of this film; I'm trying to raise the issue of rendering people's experiences during a time when there are no representations of them.

Cousineau: But you cannot say there is one way to render reality or history. Cinema is not like that, which is why we're here to talk—there's no one way of making films or of representing people.

De La Vega Hurtado: There are others wanting to say something.

F: One of the things I noticed is an affective schism between the three films. Hassan's film and Mounira's film have a kind of flippant irony, while in Marie-Hélène's film, there's a kind of intense earnestness. In *Before Tomorrow*, what's been addressed here as "Hollywood" is not so much Hollywood as it is a familiar structure of cinematic identification: we're supposed to identify with the grandma, with the grandson. In terms of the editing and the structure of the film, there are really long parts where people are crying, and when the grandma dies, she dies for a really long time— things that are actually anti-Hollywood, since the temporality of Hollywood films tends to be really fast.

So I was wondering if that approach was mapped onto actual affective structures or narrative structures within the Inuit community. Do people really function this way; is this a kind of realism—or is it a flourish by the scriptwriters?

De La Vega Hurtado: I'll take two more.

F: It seems that the difference between the films is that two are very early works and one is a mature work. The early works seem to be about process and getting somewhere, and I'd be interested in comments from those two filmmakers as to how making the films freed them to go somewhere new.

In relation to *Before Tomorrow*, I have to say that I'm offended by people who presume to judge it on the basis of their reading of a Western film canon and to argue against the assertions of indigenous self-performativity and attachment to the project.

F: I want to say something to Marie-Hélène about memory. As filmmakers, we want to address the crucial questions of the time: are we *using* people? *Why* are we telling stories? There were several moments in your film that I found very difficult, but many other moments touched me deeply and I could see that you had a very intimate relationship with all the people involved. Everything you shared with us about how you enjoyed the process was moving, and although I found it a difficult movie to watch, I thank you for letting me see it.

De La Vega Hurtado: Someone who hasn't talked yet?

F: All three movies are adventures, personal adventures, big adventures . . . they're a wonderful trilogy. I think *Before Tomorrow* is a big adventure about the grandmother and the grandson. I loved all three movies, but I didn't like the song that was used in *Before Tomorrow* ["Why Must We Die" by the McGarrigle sisters is heard over the opening and closing credits]. Why did you choose *that* song for the credits?

De La Vega Hurtado: We are over our time.

Kahn: I want to say something. Just a quick comment. People have described *Fuck This Film* as ironic. I don't think so; I've actually written extensively against irony and have a very committed position against irony. Also, I did not feel a "burden of representation" because at the time, I was completely unknown and was just doing things that I felt like doing.

De La Vega Hurtado: You all know that this is not a final conversation; there are no conclusions. Our conversation is just beginning, so let's continue to talk individually, over dinner tables, then later over drinks.

2015 TARIQ TEGUIA—ON *La clôture* (THE FENCE, 2002), *GABBLA* (INLAND, 2008), AND *THWARA ZANJ* (RÉVOLUTION ZANJ, 2012)

[Here, one complete discussion on *La clôture* and *Inland* is combined with that portion of a second discussion that focused on *Révolution Zanj*.]

Peter Limbrick: We're going to be using Skype because Tariq Teguia is in Paris. Nicholas Elliott will be translating Tariq's French into English and, when necessary, English into French. Also, we're going to go one-question-one-response because I think that's going to work more efficiently for everybody.

[To Tariq Teguia] Thank you so much for making time for us at such a late hour. As we discussed, I'll start with a couple of questions and then we'll open it up to the audience.

I think what's uppermost in many of our minds is how stunningly beautiful *Inland* is. Could you talk a little bit about how you worked with light, and with desert light in particular?

Tariq Teguia: Good evening, and thank you for your question. I'm going to talk in French because my English is not quite good enough to speak to you.

As far as the question of light and light in the desert, as you can probably tell, I work with very small, primitive instruments. I think that kind of tool, that level of economy, has a direct influence on the production of images. I don't work with a director of photography; I work with a friend who is a photojournalist. We work as simply as possible, and what I don't hesitate to do, perhaps because we are working with very primitive tools, is to go against technology. My work does not consist in making broadcast images.

Inland is the story of a quest, and a disappearance. I think you can film the desert in many ways. Most of the time when you photograph or film the desert, you're going to try to show blue skies; you're going to photograph dunes, camels.... In the case of *Inland*, if we're talking about desert light, we're talking about the whiteness of the light at the end of the film. I wanted to film a pure vibration in the air. That vibration was the symptom of a disappearance, a disintegration. You just need to reread D. H. Lawrence to understand where I'm coming from.

Limbrick: Could you talk a little bit about making *Inland* as an independent production?

Teguia: Happily. *Inland* was made, if we speak in dollars, for about $500,000—not really a lot for this kind of film, at least in Europe. Where did we find the money? We found it in Algeria, at the Algerian Ministry of Culture; in France, at the French Ministry of Culture; and at the Hubert Bals Fund, which is part of the Rotterdam Film Festival.

We spent a very small percentage of the budget shooting in Algeria—most of the money was spent in Europe to pay for the editing, the subtitling, color correction, et cetera. Most of the technicians on the set were Algerians, with the exception of the sound engineer who is French.

In Europe an independent film generally costs $800,000 to a million dollars—so $500,000 is not a lot. But I know a few American independent filmmakers—I don't mean those who go to Sundance; I mean *really* independent filmmakers—and understand that in the US, $500,000 can seem like a *lot* of money.

Limbrick: Let's open it up for questions.

Arthur Jafa: You said that you use primitive equipment; could you be specific? What format did you shoot in? Did you use any artificial lighting or just available light?

Teguia: When I say I was shooting with a primitive instrument, I'm speaking of a video camera that cost less than $4,000 in 2008. I'm not going to name the camera because I'm not here to advertise a product, but I will tell you that it's a tiny camera whose lenses aren't even interchangeable—we were shooting with the lenses that came with the camera.

We didn't use a lot of artificial lighting, particularly on this shoot—we did use some neon bulbs. We shoot with available light and to return to the final sequence of *Inland*, the overexposure at that moment is not due to color correction, but to a decision made on the shoot.

Afterward, the video imagery was transferred to 35mm in a Swiss lab.

Chi-hui Yang: I was very interested in the route of the journey and the idea of escape. Could you talk a bit about the politics of the route, the possibilities for escape, and how, as political subjects, *we* are shaped by the geographic paths we choose and the possibilities for liberation within that geography?

Teguia: Thank you for the question, which is one of the fundamental questions of the film. But I need to resituate this question, using films that I did before *Inland*, including a film that you won't see, my first feature, *Rome Rather Than You* [2006].

In this first feature, we tried to create a cartography of Algiers and its suburbs during the civil war—it's a kind of road movie in slow motion. Four years later, my brother Yacine and I (I cowrite my films with Yacine) started thinking about the next film. We had done a cartography of Algiers; so now that we were getting past the civil war, which I will remind you was between Muslim fundamentalists and Algerian society, we wanted to go "into the heart of the country," to quote William H. Gass.

The question we asked ourselves is how can we account for Algeria after the war? Our answer was the character of the surveyor, a man whose work is to draw lines, delineations across the land—in this case, lines that prepare for the arrival of electricity in the Algerian countryside.

In *Inland*, various kinds of lines intersect, layer over each other. In addition to the surveyor's lines, there is also the "line" of clandestine immigrants who are trying to go from the south of Algeria to the north in order to get to Europe, and there is the "line of escape" of the young rioters who the surveyor, Malek, meets at one point. There is also a line of words, of discourse, including the lines of the activists who initially we see enclosed in a cell, trying to figure out how to reinvent Algeria, and later, walking in the desert, saying that it's walking that will free them, that will rid us of tribes, family, fathers—authorities. And then, of course, there is the personal "line" of the surveyor who's trying to escape a world that he's not able to grasp.

I hope I've partially answered your question.

Tiona McClodden: I'd like to know something about your musical choices for *Inland*.

Teguia: Inland, and my later feature *Révolution Zanj*, were films that took a long time to make. First of all, I really have to *see*, meaning that before I shoot, before I write even one line of a script, I have to go and see. It takes a long time to go from one place to another in a car, in a train, to do what's called location scouting; and so, during these trips (which I took with friends, with my brother), we listened to music. So that's the music that inhabited the making of *Inland* and that you hear when you see the film.

Perhaps you'll have noticed that I try to avoid going for local color. I don't like to use the music that corresponds with the spaces that are being filmed. Obviously, there *is* Algerian music in the film, but you also hear John McLaughlin; you hear Terry Riley, you hear an Indian musician whose music is in Satyajit Ray's movies.

You may also have noticed that there's very little music in *Inland*. The film lasts two hours and eighteen minutes and there are thirteen minutes of music. In my films, music is not there to fill the gaps; it's not there to hold things together. If you want things to be *heard*, you have to make room, to empty things out. You have to remove a lot in order for the music you do use to be really heard.

Jeffrey Skoller: Last night, we got to see your film, *The Fence* [*La clôture*], which is a very powerful testimony about the hopelessness of escape and the hopelessness of transformation—political, personal, professional, and otherwise—for young men.

In *Inland*, escape becomes represented as a form of the sublime: it's hallucinatory, directionless; it dissolves into light, into weightlessness, into absolute time. I'm wondering how to think about the idea of the sublime in relation to the state.

Teguia: Thank you for that strong question; it's a fundamental question, one that always consumes me—because it's the question of form. How do you articulate the formal with the political? That's always the challenge because you don't want simply to make a militant film, a film that would just be about discourse and would forget everything else.

In *The Fence*, the issue was how do we account for enclosure, for being shut in, and at the same time, allow for breaking out of the thing that suffocates us? We made *The Fence* at a time when Algeria was still experiencing, in a very harsh way, the civil war. We made the film without shooting authorizations, using an even more worthless camera than the one we used in *Inland*. And yet I think that our tool was the one that corresponded to our subject. I didn't want what the young men say in *The Fence* to turn into mere complaints. Despite the harshness of this country, despite the difficulty of living there, of finding work, these young men still express vitality. We were able to use our primitive camera with dignity, and *The Fence* became what I describe, in the plural, as video *stones*, like the stones you throw in a riot.

To return to the question of the sublime: of course you know there are filmmakers besides myself who challenge themselves to articulate the most extreme poverty with great beauty—Pedro Costa is one.

Irina Leimbacher: I have a question about the distribution of *Inland*. I know that in the seventies, there was an important film industry in Algeria and that film was a popular art form. Now that there seem to be quite a few young Algerian filmmakers who, like you, are grappling with the current cultural situation, what is the possibility for distribution of your films in Algeria? How do you reach an audience? Do you think of Algerians—for example, the young men and not-so-young men in *La clôture*—as an audience that you try to speak with?

Teguia: Distribution in Algeria is simply not possible—for a simple reason: there are no cinemas. When Algeria became independent in 1962, there were four hundred movie theaters. Today, in all of Algeria, there may be ten that are open from time to time. So I have absolutely no hope of showing my films in movie theaters in Algeria. And these films were never bought by Algerian television.

We do have a special premiere in Algiers for each feature, then try to do some supplementary screenings in other big cities, like Oran, Constantine, and in what remains of the network of the Algerian Cinematheque. But that's it.

However, the films are bootlegged and *are* seen in pirated editions. So, while I don't have a lot of audience, I know that *The Fence* and *Inland* are circulating, and I know that filmmakers younger than I see these films. I don't care if they say, "Oh, these are great films!" That's not what I'm interested in. I want them to see that it's possible to make thoughtful films with very little money.

I *don't* think that one should give up on making films. I hope that one day these films will be rediscovered and understood as a cinematic archive of a certain moment in Algeria.

Limbrick: I think we can take one more question. Marie-Hélène's been waiting.

Marie-Hélène Cousineau: Who are the actors? Where are they from? *Are* they actors or are they people who live in the villages? Who is the policeman? Who is the girl? How and for how long did you work with them? Do you work with precise dialogue?

And what are you working on now?

Teguia: I do want to make clear that *The Fence* is *not* a documentary. Everything that you saw was prepared, acted, repeated several times.

Most of the people in *Inland* are not actors. The state of Algerian cinema means that there are very few professional actors. Abdelkader Affak, the man who plays Malek, is a theater actor. He made his first films with me. He doesn't work a lot because he doesn't have a lot of opportunities. I think that most of Kader's activity is focused on political activism.

The most professional actor in *Inland* is the one who plays Malek's friend, the man who follows him and tries to find him. His name is Ahmed Benaïssa; he's quite well known in Algeria: he's done fiction features, a lot of television—mostly stuff that's very different from what I do.

The rest are all nonprofessionals: farmers, shepherds that I met in the Algerian steppe. As for the lead actress in *Inland*, Ines Rose Djakou, she was a student from Cameroon living in Algiers. She had never done a film.

Regarding the text and how I work with the actors. The script is written; the dialogue is written. My brother and I write in French, then it's translated into Algerian Arabic. I just offer people the opportunity to be in a movie and try to convince them to become involved in my project. There are no rehearsals; there's no work with the actors.

I give the actors, even the main actors, their lines the night before we're going to shoot. During the shoot, my job as director is simply to have the actors remove superfluous things: I ask them to remove what *they* think is acting, what they think is cinema. My work consists in decertifying them; I want them to resemble lizards.

With my early short films, I did do rehearsals—maybe because I was scared. Maybe now I'm less scared. The important thing is not to make a mistake about who you choose to be in a film. And I have made mistakes in the past. I *thought* I had made a mistake in *Inland*. Early on, a guy comes on a moped to give the surveyor the news that he's received a telegram. While they're having a coffee, Malek and this young man have a discussion about a riot that took place in the village. I filmed this scene as if it were the beginnings of Greek philosophy—they are two men on a hill, talking.

So I thought I'd made a mistake with Mohamed Agoun, who plays the young man. Mohamed was a student in communications. At the start, he couldn't remember his lines. He wasn't *inside*; he was somewhere off to the side. I thought he'd never be able to do the scene and nearly gave up on him. Also you need to know that while we were shooting his scene, there were policemen maybe ten meters away, there to protect the French sound engineer. And yet, despite the pressure, Mohamed worked at it and ultimately managed to do the scene well, and I think that it's one of the most correct, successful scenes in the film. He impressed me.

Limbrick: Well, Tariq, we have to stop, but we want to thank you for your generosity in being here for your two films.

Teguia: Thank you very much. I wish I could be with you. Au revoir!

Second Discussion:

[Several small-group discussion points are summarized by Paige Sarlin, and Laila Sheeren Sakr speaks about her short film *Liberalism, Egypt, and Zizek Remixed* (2015), which was shown with *Révolution Zanj*; a seminarian argues that *Révolution Zanj* is "ahistorical."]

Teguia: You've asked me about history, but if you don't mind, I'm not going to talk about history; I'm going to talk about geography. I don't mean this as a joke or as a way of avoiding the question. It's just that my fundamental challenge in *Révolution Zanj* was cartographic.

Révolution Zanj was my third feature film. The first was *Rome Rather Than You*; the second was *Inland*. In *Rome Rather Than You*, we made a map of Algiers. True, it was a map drawn in the dark, during a time of martial law when you weren't supposed to go out at night—but we made a cinematic map. So *Rome Rather Than You* was related to the history of Algeria at that time—but that history is the background, not the foreground. The foreground is geography, the spaces that need to be crossed. In *Inland*, we extended the map, to cover not just Algiers and its suburbs but the depths of the country.

When we came around to making the third film, the question was, how do we continue to expand the map? What other regions, what other zones does Algeria share? We decided on Africa and the Arab world (or as Fernand Braudel would say, the Arab subcontinent), and perhaps even more fundamentally, the Mediterranean world—which is perhaps the oldest in terms of civilization.

So the project that I was constructing with my brother when I was making what became *Révolution Zanj* is a map—and history came into this map in terms of samples. We wanted to ask ourselves about questions of struggle, political struggle; and my primary interest is the present—so what did I do? I traveled: I went to Beirut; I went to Cairo; I went to Alexandria. And what did I find? I found history in the present.

Jim Supanick: I'm interested in your use of Michel Butor's *Mobile*, which we hear some students talk about during the film. *Mobile* is a very beautiful book, and an act of creative cartography. Could you expand on how it was important for the performers in the film, how it was important for you, and how it's important in the broader context of the film?

Teguia: Thank you for this vast question. *Mobile* is a book I've been reading and studying for fifteen years at least. I came to it through a work on Robert Frank, who creates cartographic fictions. The Butor book, which formally resembles a Calder mobile, provided the principle for organizing *Révolution Zanj*. The film is organized around elements that orbit each other, that sometimes intersect, sometimes bang into each other.

Yacine and I spent time with certain texts—for instance, Ginsberg's *Howl* in *Inland*, which shows a shattered America.

F: The audiovisual texture of the film is extremely striking.

I was also struck by the theme of absence, especially since the film refers to the Zanj revolution, a revolt of black slaves. One of the most striking absences for me in the film was the status of migrant workers.

Teguia: I'm happy that you noticed the question of texture.

Yes, there are absences in the film, that's true—because the question of this film was how do you give a body, a thickness, to ghosts? *Révolution Zanj* is first and foremost about persistence, the persistence of struggle. But what I was most interested in was to film the light in the eye of the black Arab man by the Tigris. To do that takes a lot of time.

But to really answer your question about the absence of migrant workers in Beirut: you can't put everything into a film. However, if you speak Arabic and you're able to tell accents apart, you'll be able to see that the people working on the construction site in the film are Syrian workers—and they are the exploited.

Hassan Khan: This is not specifically about *Révolution Zanj*. I would like to take Tariq up on his stated intention in this film of tackling current political struggles, by looking at what he did in *Inland* with his portrayal of the intellectuals in that film. In *Inland* we have a complex relationship to the intellectuals. There is some empathy and interest in what they're saying, but the film is not purely a celebration of their position. As *Inland* goes on, they become a bit absurd as they walk through the desert making statements.

Révolution Zanj, it seems to me, revolves around people who are identified as representing specific positions, and their positions become part of their self-presentation: part of how they dress, part of how they speak, part of how they act. My question is, is the film a celebration of these poses? Does the film equate the depiction of these types with political struggle?

And to wrap this up, I would like to say that in all societies and locations that are full of turmoil, the turmoil is a structural thing. Yes, there are activists, but this turmoil is happening not because of activists, but because there are deep forces within society that need to be articulated. How is that evident in *Révolution Zanj*?

Teguia: As to the question of struggles and what causes them—I'm not sure what you're asking. In *Inland*, I didn't show people who are just talking the talk between four walls. I showed people whose work, I believe, transforms societies. They know failure; sometimes they've been ridiculous. But despite it all, they're working on transformation. They're not the only ones who will make it come, but I profoundly respect their commitment.

Your very analytical way of apprehending *Révolution Zanj* is very distant to me. Of course, our discussion is particularly difficult because of our issues with Skype—I can't see you, so I'm sitting here, looking at a Colgate University logo, trying to answer very complex questions.

Linda Lilienfeld [in French, which she then translates herself]: Tariq, we wish you were here with us, being able to have the conversations that we have been having over dinner, over breakfast—because the subjects are so deep. We love your films; and they are so stimulating that we are drowning in words. But the spirit of your work has touched us deeply. It's a frustration that you're only here on Skype and not with us in person, and we send you our love.

Teguia: I do want to finish my response to the last question that was asked.

It's not that the intensity of that question invalidates it for me. It's just that I approach things differently. I approach things through sensation. I do things by feel, by touch. I never distinguish a body by what it does or how it looks. Nothing is typified. I deal with what individual people *are*. Janis Avril, the actress who plays the Palestinian woman, is a young dancer; and my work with her was to show a grace, a smile, a form of irony. The same is true of everyone else: the Palestinian, the black bodies in the Château Arabe, even the Anglo-American people. I dealt with their bodies and how they *were*. They're not in the film to illustrate particular ideas that I had.

I want to go back to the beginning question about the film's relation to history: my film *traverses* history. *Révolution Zanj* was written at the end of 2009, the beginning of 2010. And the shooting began in Athens a few weeks before the riots that started in Tunisia that would eventually [in January 2011] put Ben Ali out—which tells you that this film was not developed as an illustration of those riots—since the writing and shooting started before the events. The shoot was very long; it lasted over three years. We started shooting the riots in Athens, which you see at the end of the film, in November of 2010, and we continued until the period of January–March 2013.

So this film, which someone referred to as "ahistorical," became traversed by history. The film may have begun outside history, but history caught up with it.

2016 LUKE FOWLER—ON *TO THE EDITOR OF AMATEUR PHOTOGRAPHER* (2014, COMADE WITH MARK FELL) AND LUIS OSPINA—ON *Aggarabdo pueblo* (*VAMPIRES OF POVERTY*, 1978, COMADE WITH CARLOS MAYOLO)

[After the screening, the seminarians divided into small groups for half an hour, then convened to discuss the films.]

Jason Livingston: Thank you again, David [Pendleton], for some very strong programming. The coupling of films in this program reveals some similarities: both films deploy very powerful, affective, controversial (historically and perhaps even in the present moment) self-reflexive techniques; and questions around collaborative roles seem foregrounded in both films—though they have different tonal ranges and different intentions. There are many things I could prattle on about, but now is the time to hear from the small groups. In our group conversation, we talked about who speaks for whom, and about forms of satire: Jamie [Henschel] suggested that satire only works when you empower those who are oppressed.

Chike Nwabukwu: One thing that came up in our group was the laughter that occurred during Luis's film; we wondered what the laughter meant—even when we saw that the joke was on the audience. I was disturbed by the amount of [it]. I thought that certain things should have made people uncomfortable rather than making them laugh. This could be about cultural differences.

Livingston: Thank you, and over there.

F: Group 5's findings and thoughts are hard to simplify. We were interested in the nature of the collaboration in Luke's film between you and your women subjects. Secondly, the experimental nature of *To the Editor* raised a question: if you're trying to disseminate this information to as many people as possible and have them empowered by this knowledge, how effective is your experimental lens for people who don't attend the Flaherty Seminar or don't go to university?

Livingston: Thank you. Yes, in the back.

F: Group 9 agreed that the pairing of these two films was very positive. But we were struck by the rawness of these documents from the 1970s–1980s, from that moment of feminism and the critique of representation. But maybe rawness is a virtue. Some members of the group, too young to have had firsthand experience with that era, felt almost a nostalgia for what they missed.

Livingston: Thank you. We'll take one more report.

F: Some in Group 8 thought that the women in *To the Editor* didn't have enough space to develop as individuals; the fact that archival photographs and living persons were accorded the same amount of time felt problematic. In Luis Ospina's film, we wondered if the filmmaker wasn't doing a little bit of what we condemn the characters on screen for doing.

Livingston: Thank you. Let's turn to the filmmakers for some responses.

Luis Ospina: I like to provoke. I think provocation is a way of generating thought, reflection. Sometimes you have to use the means of the enemy to communicate what you want. When you want to avoid a disease, you have to inoculate the disease into your body in order to stay healthy. Buñuel did this many years ago with *Las Hurdas* [1933]. This approach is also evident in Barbet Schroeder's *Idi Amin Dada* [1974] and in Jorge Furtado's Ilha das Flores [*Isle of Flowers*, 1989]. Like us, they all work with dark humor and an aggressive way of addressing the audience.

I've always been interested in the relationship between the person filming and the person being filmed. The camera has an inherent power to vampirize. I understand why people sometimes don't let themselves be photographed and why certain Indian tribes don't let themselves be filmed. On the other hand, one of the great gestures of generosity is allowing the subjects *to be filmed*, and many photojournalists are not aware of this; they think that their time is more valuable than their subjects' time.

You have to make a pact with your subject in order for the subject not to become an object.

Since we're here in the House of Flaherty, I would like to refer to the first definition of documentary that John Grierson proposed after he saw *Moana* in 1926, a definition I like very much: he said that documentary is the creative treatment of actuality. In his definition, manipulation is implicit. I don't believe in objectivity in documentary; the camera changes things when it films. The camera is an instrument of death; we documentary filmmakers are always filming something that is dying or changing. That's why documentary can be very powerful.

With regards to the laughing, my films tend to change tone very abruptly. I like making the audience uncomfortable. Today the audience laughed at first, then the laughter waned, then it became embarrassment; people felt guilty that they had laughed in the first scenes. I like that. I'm not a Don Juan trying to conquer the audience; I like to create discomfort in order to make you think. I'm not politically correct; I don't believe in any causes, and I don't believe in documentaries that are in the service of causes. My only cause is cinema itself.

Luke Fowler: I'm kind of an antithesis of that—I think the first order of the camera is the same as the first order of a physician in treating a patient: do no harm. It was very important for us as filmmakers to be sensitive and to show consideration and care and most importantly respect for the people involved with Pavilion. *Of course* we felt uneasy making this film, and we were made to feel uneasy—with good reason.

Pavilion still exists, but as a different entity from what you see in the film. Now, it's a commissioning body; it commissions new works by mostly younger artists. The current Pavilion people liked both Mark Fell's and my work and saw an affinity between us; they brought us together and presented us with this project. Mark is an electronic musician. He comes from Sheffield, close to Leeds where the film was made.

Mark and I did a lot of wrangling about whether it was appropriate for us, two men, to do the project. Wouldn't it be more appropriate for female artists to make this film? At several junctures, we pressed the committee about that, and they kept saying, "No, we're commissioning *you* to make a film. But we're *not* forcing you to make a Pavilion film; you can make a film about whatever you want."

So the ball was in our court: do you shy away from making a film about a feminist organization *because* you're men? Or do you embrace it because you feel solidarity with the cause? We decided that we shouldn't be chicken, that we should take on the project with all its contentions.

For sure I can understand the question about the accessibility of our film for a general audience, but I can only respond by asking, are radical politics and experimental forms mutually exclusive? I don't think they are, and I think there's a history of films—for example, *Nightcleaners* [1975] by the Berwick Street Collective—that have radical politics and also take a radical position towards form.

Ultimately, neither Mark nor I wanted to reproduce the dominant ideological forms of filmmaking. It would be completely disingenuous for us to make some sloganeering, pamphleteering film. I apologize if that's a simplification of the argument you were presenting, but I think ultimately we needed to be true to ourselves and our interests in filmmaking. I have no interest in making a conventional documentary.

Livingston: At what point in the process did the women from the Pavilion collective begin to push back around the format or around how we see them in the interviews? How much pushback did you build in from the beginning?

Fowler: There was kickback against the project from its inception, before the women had even met us: there was resentment about the fact that it was two male artists, period. So there was a process of discussion, of reassurance that we were going to be sensitive, that we were in solidarity, that we were not going to speak *on behalf of* them.

Livingston: What formal arrangements did you work out?

Fowler: We sent an invitation to women who had been involved with Pavilion during its first decade, making quite clear that ours was a project about the politics of representation and that it was important to us that they'd choose their own images and have agency in how they'd be filmed. Some of the women engaged in discussions with us, and some deferred to Margaret Salmon who had agreed to film the women's responses to our questions.

All the women were given the same five questions about a photograph of their choice that they had either taken or were in. We asked that they talk about what happened before the photograph was taken or afterward. One of our questions was about the problematics of making *any* film about Pavilion (we didn't mention ourselves in that question).

F: To what extent were you trying to evoke the formal elements of late seventies, early eighties feminist cinema—or other formal approaches of the time?

Fowler: Both Mark and I were aware of the work of Peter Gidal (Mark is a huge Gidal fan) and we were conscious of the canon of cinema critique.

Livingston: Something I admire about the film is that its materialism is not an evacuated abstract ethereal materialism, but the materialism of everyday life and struggle and conflict in the community.

F: Luke, you said do no harm. I think sometimes we can't have it both ways. If you're making work, you have to risk pissing people off and letting the history you're portraying seem contradictory.

Fowler: It's evident in the film that there were ruptures and contradictions within the history we're depicting: the environment of that time wasn't a rose garden.

Toby Lee: One might ask how two young men coming from a different generation can make a film about an earlier generation of women. But you make that gap very clear in the film, and I thought that was brave. The film is messy and uncomfortable—and I really liked that productive discomfort.

David Pendleton: Let me bring the conversation back to Luis's film, because it's interesting, Luis, that you talk about wanting to be provocative; yet after the provocation of the film, the conversation with your actor at the end of the film feels healing. *Vampires of Poverty* is all about dramatizing an antagonism, but at the end you sit down and have a conversation that's about bridging this gap between you and your subject, and I think it really enriches the film.

Ospina: Yes. I don't know if everybody noticed, but in the first film that I showed [*Olga Vea* (*Listen, See*), 1971, comade with Carlos Mayolo] Luis Alfonso Londoño appears in a couple of scenes.

I always worry about what happens with my subjects after I film them. So, seven years later, when we thought of making the *Aggarabdo pueblo*, we went back to that neighborhood and found Luis—living in the same conditions as in 1971.

But I think I should speak about the broader context of *Vampires of Poverty*. During the late sixties, from, let's say, 1966 to the midseventies, there was a proliferation of political films made in the third world, especially in Latin America; and there were various theories about filmmaking. There was "For an Imperfect Cinema" [Julio Garcia Espinosa], which came from Cuba; the idea of "Third Cinema," which also had Cuban influence, and many films with a mostly Marxist political agenda. I think that our sense of that period has to be revised and those theories have to be revised, because they don't stand up anymore. At that time European film festivals and European TV channels with a Marxist agenda had an avid hunger for films about poverty.

In Columbia there was an additional context: a law that before the showing of every feature length film, a locally produced short had to be shown. The easiest way to make short films was to make films about poverty: you'd just go out with a camera to capture images of poor people, add a little classical music and a politically correct narration—and you'd make a lot of money.

In *Vampires of Poverty* we were reacting to these two phenomena. When we premiered this film in Paris (I finished the editing in Paris), we put out a manifesto called "Que es la porno-miseria"/"What Is Poverty Porn?" It's a very brief text; you can find it on the Internet.

Vampires of Poverty had quite an impact. We were treated as lepers for making it, especially by the leftist clique that existed at that time, which operated from Cuba, from Oberhausen, from their own niches of power. We wanted to react against that clique. They considered our film anarchistic, and I'm glad they did: it *is* an anarchistic film.

I'm not interested in promoting ideology, especially Marxist ideas. For example, an iconic film of the time, *La hora de los hornos* [*The Hour of the Furnaces*, 1968, Fernando Solanas and Octavio Getino] seen today is just a propaganda film for Peron. And what became of Peron when he returned to Argentina? He was the person who started the persecution of leftists and Marxists and the disappearances; and he and Minister of Social Welfare, José López Rega, were responsible for the Triple A [Alianza Anticomunista Argentina] movement. He was and remains to this day a terrible influence in Argentina. What happened with the Cuban Revolution? It became a dictatorship.

I'm very interested in expressing my disenchantment about those outdated ideas—though I am glad that I lived through that period because at that time we young people thought we *could* make change. Young people now only think about saving the planet. [laughter]

Not long ago, *Vampires of Poverty*, which was made thirty-nine years ago, made a comeback, and it's still being shown everywhere—because the question of the ethics of filmmaking, of the relationship you establish with your subject, will always be important. I think that *anything* can be filmed; I don't think that certain subjects are taboo—but it all depends on your point of view. There's a cliché that says film is a window to the world, but I think that's not enough. I think that film should be a window to the soul, a window into the filmmaker who tries to express himself with all his virtues, prejudices, faults, and doubts.

In my group, we were talking about the proliferation of images in the modern world, which is overpowering. I myself film fewer and fewer images and tend to rely on archival material. It's very difficult to be original with images. In the middle ages, people saw images in only two places: in the Bible and in church. Now we see images all the time. So I look inward, more and more. I think that the soul, the inner soul, is very important and it hasn't been treated very well, especially by Hollywood, at least in recent years.

I grew up in the fifties, when the films of the great European and American directors—Buñuel, John Ford, Howard Hawks, Billy Wilder, Bergman, Dreyer—would come to popular movie theaters, which were temples—you always associated a movie with the movie house where you saw it. Now you see a film in a multiplex in Columbia or Singapore or even here at the Flaherty, and the feeling is the same: films have lost their sacredness . . .

Am I talking too much?

Livingston: No, no, but we do have to wrap things up and move on.

Notes

1. Charles Phred Churchill, e-mail message to Patricia R. Zimmermann, July 25, 2014.
2. Phred Churchill, "A Tribute: Jack Churchill, 1925–2006," International Film Seminars/The Flaherty, retrieved July 3, 2015 (http://flahertyseminar.org/archives /writings-on-the-flaherty/).
3. Jack Churchill, "The Evolution of the Seminar," International Film Seminars/The Flaherty, retrieved July 1, 2015 (http://flahertyseminar.org/archives/writings-on-the-flaherty/the -evolution-of-the-seminar/).
4. Alyce Myatt, phone interview by Patricia R. Zimmermann, November 9, 2009.
5. Margarita De La Vega Hurtado, phone interview by Patricia R. Zimmermann, July 18, 2012.
6. Margarita De La Vega Hurtado, phone interview by Patricia R. Zimmermann, September 16, 2009.
7. "Anita Reher Biography," International Film Seminars/The Flaherty, retrieved July 2, 2015 (http://flahertyseminar.org/about-us/staff/).
8. De La Vega Hurtado, phone interview, July 18, 2012.
9. Ibid., September 16, 2009.
10. Ibid.
11. Patti Bruck, phone interview by Patricia R. Zimmermann, July 8, 2014; De La Vega Hurtado, phone interview, September 16, 2009.
12. De La Vega Hurtado, phone interview, September 16, 2009.
13. "Board Members of International Film Seminars 2001," 1–2; "International Film Seminars, Inc., Board of Trustees 2003," 1–2; Minutes of the Board of Trustees Meeting, January 11, 2008; All documents from Patti Bruck Private Collection (hereafter cited as Bruck Collection). See also "Board of Directors," International Film Seminars/The Flaherty, retrieved July 14, 2014 (http://flahertyseminar.org/about-us/board-of-directors/).
14. "International Film Seminars, Boards of Trustees 2003," Bruck Collection.
15. Bruck, phone interview, July 8, 2014.
16. Ibid., October 14, 2009.
17. L. Somi Roy to Patti Bruck Internal Memo, November 18, 1999; Minutes of the Board Meeting of International Film Seminars, June 16, 2000; Lucy Kostelanetz to Patti Bruck and Tom Johnson Internal Memo, October 1, 2000; Minutes of the International Film Seminars Board of Trustees Meeting, October 6, 2000, 1–2; Minutes of the International Film Seminars Retreat, October 7, 2000, 1–2. All documents from Bruck Collection.

18. "Suppose there were no IFS: What kind of media organization could we, in this room, form today from scratch; one that fills a need in the field and utilizes our individual resources," Board Retreat Document, October 7, 2000, Bruck Collection.

19. Minutes of the Board of Trustees Meeting, International Film Seminars, January 11, 2003; Minutes of the Board of Trustees Meeting, International Film Seminars, April 5, 2003; Minutes of Executive Committee Conference Call, International Film Seminars, July 1, 2003; Minutes of the Board of Trustees Meeting, International Film Seminars, January 17, 2004; Minutes of the Board of Trustees Meeting, June 11, 2005; Minutes of the Board of Trustees Meeting, International Film Seminars, December 15, 2005; all documents from Bruck Collection.

20. Minutes of the Board of Trustees Meeting, International Film Seminars, January 6, 2001, 3, Bruck Collection.

21. Minutes of the Board of Trustees Meeting, International Film Seminars, October 15, 2005, 4, Bruck Collection.

22. Minutes of the Board of Trustees, International Film Seminars/The Flaherty, April 9, 2006, 3, Bruck Collection.

23. Steve Montgomery, e-mail message to Patricia R. Zimmermann, July 28, 2014.

24. Ibid.

25. Minutes of the Board of Trustees, International Film Seminars, April 5, 2003, 2, Bruck Collection; and Montgomery, e-mail, July 28, 2014.

26. Alyce Myatt, phone interview by Patricia R. Zimmermann, September 11, 2009.

27. Minutes of the Board of Trustees Meeting, International Film Seminars, August 7, 2004, 3, Bruck Collection.

28. Tom Johnson, interview by Patricia R. Zimmermann, Hamilton, New York, June 16, 2014.

29. Bruck, phone interview, July 8, 2014; Montgomery, e-mail, July 28, 2014; Minutes of the Board of Trustees, International Film Seminars, October 15, 2005, 3, Bruck Collection.

30. Minutes of the Board of Trustees, January 12, 2007, International Film Seminars, 2, Bruck Collection.

31. Montgomery, e-mail, July 28, 2014.

32. Margarita De La Vega Hurtado, ed., *Flaherty 2003: Witnessing the World* (New York: International Film Seminars, 2003), 1.

33. Montgomery, e-mail, July 28, 2014; De La Vega Hurtado, phone interview, September 16, 2009; see also Minutes of the Board of Trustee Meeting and Retreat, The Flaherty/International Film Seminars, January 11–13, 2008, Bruck Collection.

34. De La Vega Hurtado, phone interview, September 16, 2009.

35. Minutes of the Board of Trustees Meeting, International Film Seminars, April 9, 2006, 1, Bruck Collection.

36. Mary Kerr, phone interview by Patricia R. Zimmermann, July 23, 2012. For an example of De La Vega Hurtado's efforts to increase outreach to participants to meet the budget, see Minutes of the Board of Trustees Meeting, International Film Seminars, April 5, 2003, 1, Bruck Collection.

37. Sally Berger, interview by Patricia R. Zimmermann, Hamilton, New York, June 16, 2014.

38. De La Vega Hurtado, phone interview, September 16, 2009.

39. Minutes of the Board of Trustees Meeting, International Film Seminars, January 11, 2003, 4, Bruck Collection. John Columbus, interview by Patricia R. Zimmermann, Hamilton, New York, June 16, 2014.

40. Strategic Planning Committee Report, International Film Seminars/The Flaherty, January 12, 2008, Bruck Collection.

41. "Flaherty NYC," International Film Seminars/The Flaherty, retrieved July 28, 2014 (http://flahertyseminar.org/flaherty-nyc/flaherty-nyc-past/).

42. "Documenting Flaherty," *Independent Film and Video Monthly*, October 2002, 20–36.

43. De La Vega Hurtado, phone interview, September 16, 2009; Minutes of the Board of Trustees, International Film Seminars, October 17, 2003, 1–2, Bruck Collection. Examples of annual catalogs include Nadine Covert, ed., *50 Years of Flaherty: Inspired Filmmaking* (New York: The Flaherty/International Film Seminars, 2004); Mahen Bonetti, Carlos A. Gutiérrez, and Mary Kerr, eds., *South of the Other: The 53rd Robert Flaherty Film Seminar* (New York: The Flaherty/International Film Seminars, 2007); Mary Kerr, ed., *The Age of Migration: The 56th Annual Robert Flaherty Film Seminar* (New York: The Flaherty/International Film Seminars, 2008); Mary Kerr, ed., *Open Wounds: The 58th Robert Flaherty Film Seminar* (New York: The Flaherty/International Film Seminars, 2012).

44. Alyce Myatt, phone interview by Patricia R. Zimmermann, September 11, 2009.

45. Bruck, phone interview, July 8, 2014.

46. The elaboration and refinement of the fellows program was a point of extended, in-depth discussion at board meetings throughout the 2000s. For an example of the level of detail discussed in restructuring this program, see Notes from the Fellowship Committee, International Film Seminars, October 13, 2005, Bruck Collection, and Minutes of the Board of Trustees Meeting, June 11, 2005, Bruck Collection, which outlined specifics for implementing the new fellows program.

47. Montgomery, e-mail, July 28, 2014; Mary Kerr, phone interview, July 23, 2012; for documentation of these grants, see Mary Kerr, ed., *Witnesses, Monuments, Ruins: The 55th Robert Flaherty Film Seminar* (New York: The Flaherty/International Film Seminars, 2009), 7; Bonetti, Gutiérrez, and Kerr, eds., *South of the Other*, 7; Kerry, *The Age of Migration*, 7; Mary Kerr, ed., *Work: The 56th Robert Flaherty Film Seminar* (New York: The Flaherty/International Film Seminars, 2010), 7; Mary Kerr, ed., *Sonic Truth: The 57th Robert Flaherty Film Seminar* (New York: The Flaherty/International Film Seminars, 2011), 7.

48. Minutes of the Board of Trustees Meeting, International Film Seminars, April 9, 2006, 3, Bruck Collection.

49. Minutes of the Board of Trustees Meeting, International Film Seminars, January 12, 2007, 2, Bruck Collection.

50. Ed Halter, phone interview by Patricia R. Zimmermann, July 28, 2014.

51. Minutes of Board of Trustees Meeting, April 9, 2006, 3–4.

52. Minutes of the Board of Trustees Meeting, International Film Seminars, April 15, 2007, 3–4, Bruck Collection.

53. Programming Committee Meeting Notes, International Film Seminars/The Flaherty, January 12, 2008, 1 and 5, Bruck Collection.

54. Patti Bruck, Notes from the Board Retreat, January 12–13, 2008, 1, Bruck Collection.

55. Bruck, phone interview, July 8, 2014.

56. "Susan Oxtoby Named New Senior Film Curator at the Berkeley Art Museum and Pacific Film Archive, Pacific Film Archive," retrieved August 1, 2014 (http://www.bampfa .berkeley.edu/press/release/TXT0114).

57. "The Shocking Truth: The Rise of Documentary," *The Economist*, August 27, 2013. Retrieved August 11, 2014 (http://www.economist.com/blogs/prospero/2013/08 /rise-documentary-film).

58. Ipswich Film Theatre Trust, "Rise of the Documentary," June 16, 2010. Retrieved August 2, 2014 (http://www.iftt.co.uk/rise-of-the-documentary/).

59. "Documentary 1992–Present," retrieved August 11, 2014 (http://www.boxofficemojo.com /genres/chart/?id=documentary.htm).

60. Kathy Brew, "The Dialectic of Digital Dialogues: Flaherty Does Digital," *The Independent*, March 2, 2002, 9–10.

61. Ed Halter, "Notes on the Recent History of a Self-Sustained Exhibition Scene for Experimental Forms of Cinema in North America" (unpublished manuscript, 2004), PDF.

62. Halter, phone interview, July 28, 2014.

63. Ibid.

64. John Gianvito, e-mail message to Patricia R. Zimmermann, May 22, 2016.

65. John Gianvito, "Curator's Statement," in Nadine Covert, ed., *Flaherty 2003: Witnessing the World* (New York: The Flaherty/International Film Seminars, 2003), 9.

66. Ibid.

67. Gianvito, e-mail, May 22, 2016.

68. Ibid.

69. Ibid.

70. Jenn Guitart, "Testimonial," in *Flaherty 2003*, 42.

71. Elizabeth Coll, "Testimonial," in *Flaherty 2003*, 36.

72. Mahen Bonetti, e-mail message to author, May 28, 2016.

73. Mary Kerr, "What Is the Flaherty?" in *South of the Other*, 9.

74. Mahen Bonetti and Carlos A. Gutiérrez, "Curators' Opening Remarks," in *South of the Other*, 11.

75. Carlos Gutiérrez, interview with Patricia R. Zimmermann, Hamilton, New York, June 15, 2014.

76. Chi-hui Yang, e-mail message to author, June 2, 2016.

77. Kerr, *The Age of Migration*, 7.

78. Chi-hui Yang, "The Age of Migration," in *The Age of Migration*, 14.

79. Ibid.

80. Yang, e-mail, June 2, 2016.

81. Scott MacDonald, *Avant-Doc: Intersections of Documentary and Avant-Garde Cinema* (Oxford: Oxford University Press, 2014).

82. Irina Leimbacher, e-mail message to Patricia R. Zimmermann, August 2, 2014.

83. Irina Leimbacher, "Witnesses Monuments Ruins," in Mary Kerr, ed., *Witnesses Monuments Ruins: The 55th Robert Flaherty Film Seminar* (New York: The Flaherty/International Film Seminars, 2009), 12.

84. Ibid.

85. Irina Leimbacher, e-mail message to Patricia R. Zimmermann, August 3, 2014.

86. Dennis Lim, "Work," in Mary Kerr, ed., *Work: The 56th Annual Robert Flaherty Film Seminar* (New York: The Flaherty/International Film Seminars, 2010), 12.

87. Lim, "Work," 13.

88. Ibid., 15.

89. Josetxo Cerdán, "Open Wounds," in *Open Wounds: The 58th Annual Robert Flaherty Film Seminar* (New York: International Film Seminars, 2012), 13.

90. Jason Livingston, "It's a Family Affair," in *Open Wounds*, 50.

91. About the Robert Flaherty Film Seminar Information Sheet in Participants Seminar, International Film Seminars, 2014, Patricia R. Zimmermann Private Collection (hereafter cited as Zimmermann Collection).

92. "Major Funding for the 60th Annual Robert Flaherty Film Seminar Is Provided By," Handout in 60th anniversary participants folder, International Film Seminars, 2014, Zimmermann Collection.

93. "Turning the Inside Out," postcard announcing the 60th Robert Flaherty Film Seminar, International Film Seminars/The Flaherty, 2014, Zimmermann Collection.

94. Caspar Stracke and Gabriela Monroy, e-mail to Patricia R. Zimmermann, June 1, 2016.

95. Leo Goldsmith, "Flaherty Will Get You Everywhere," *Artforum*, July 4, 2014. Retrieved November 13, 2015 (http://www.artforum.com/film/id=47404).

96. Stracke and Monroy, e-mail, June 1, 2016.

INDEX

Note: Pages numbers in italics refer to photographs.

PATRICIA R. ZIMMERMANN is Professor of Screen Studies at Ithaca College. She is the author of *Reel Families: A Social History of Amateur Film* (Indiana University Press, 1995), *States of Emergency: Documentaries, Wars, Democracies, Mining the Home Movies: Excavations in Histories and Memories, Thinking through Digital Media: Transnational Environments and Locative Places,* and *Open Spaces: Openings, Closings, and Thresholds of International Public Media.* She also serves as codirector of the Finger Lakes Environmental Film Festival at Ithaca College.

SCOTT MACDONALD is Professor of Art History at Hamilton College where he teaches film history. He is author of the series *A Critical Cinema: Interviews with Independent Filmmakers,* and eleven other books, including *Avant-Garde Film/Motion Studies, The Garden in the Machine: A Field Guide to Independent Films about Place, American Ethnographic Film and Personal Documentary: The Cambridge Turn, Avant-Doc: Intersections of Documentary and Avant-Garde Cinema,* and *Binghamton Babylon: Voices from the Cinema Department (a nonfiction novel).* In 2012 he was named an Academy Scholar by the Academy of Motion Picture Arts and Sciences.